4. Use a workshop approach. Just as students  they profit from varied approaches to a skill. One way to cover a skill is to work through a chapter page by page, alternating between putting some of the material on the board and explaining or reading some of it aloud. When you get to a practice in a chapter, give students a couple of minutes to do the practice. When a majority of the class has finished the practice, call on someone to read the first question and answer it. If the answer is right, say "Good job," and call on someone else to read the next question. If the answer is wrong, say something like "Does anyone have a different answer?" This can lead to a discussion where you can see if students are catching on, and you can find a way to move them in the right direction.

You should feel confident about having students read a sentence or so out loud. Even if they have limited reading skills, a sentence or two will not cause them undue anxiety or embarrassment. On the other hand, reading an entire paragraph may be too much for some students. It is best to call on volunteers for paragraphs or to read them aloud yourself. Or, if there are time constraints, have students read the paragraph silently and then ask them to read aloud the questions that follow the paragraph.

5. Use a small-group approach at times. When you get to a review test, you may want to divide the class into groups of four and ask them to work together to do the answers for the test. Tell them that when they are done and everyone in the group agrees on the answers, a representative from the group should go to the board and write down the group's answers. Say, "Let's see which group is first to answer all the questions correctly."

Put a grid such as this one on the board:

	1	2	3	4	5
Kim's Group					
Robert's Group					
Nelson's Group					
Nina's Group					

Students will enjoy the competition, and peer pressure will keep everyone attentive and involved. When all of the groups have finished, you and the class can look at the board together to see just where the groups agree and disagree. You can then focus discussion on answers where there is disagreement.

6. Use a pairs approach at times. Having two students work together on questions is another way to energize students and help them teach one another. When an exercise has been completed by the majority of the class, one way to go over the material is to have one student in each pair read a question and the other student read the answer.

7. Use a one-on-one approach at times. If your class is small, have students work on their own on a given chapter, reading the explanations and doing the activities. Call students up to your desk individually to check their answers and to confer on the skill. Make the conference short—five minutes per student is enough time. Students really benefit from the individualized, personal contact.

8. Evaluate frequently. Students have been conditioned to work hard on tests. Take advantage of this conditioning by giving a lot of tests. The mastery tests in Part I and the combined-skills tests in Part III will give students a chance to see that they are learning the material and will show them that they are capable of success. The tests are also clear signals to students who are not learning the skills. Note that there are over seventy tear-out mastery tests in the book as well as thirty more tests available online.

When you grade a test, try to include some praise or encouragement for each student. A personal comment such as "Good job, Elena" or "Well done, Hakim" can do wonders for a student's self-esteem.

9. For variety, make some tests count and some not. When it is time to do a test, have students put their names on it and tell them that you may or may not count the test. The fact that you may count the test will ensure that students give their full effort. At times, don't collect the test, but simply go over it in class. Doing so will help to provide immediate feedback to students. Afterward, you can give another mastery test that will count as a grade.

When tests do count, have students exchange papers. The best way to do this is to collect the papers and distribute them to students in other parts of the room. (Some students resist marking an answer as wrong on a paper that belongs to the person sitting right next to them.) Have class members read and answer the questions as well as grade the papers.

10. Require some writing at the end of each class. To help students integrate what they have learned in a given class, have them do a writing assignment in the last part of the class. One good summarizing activity is to have students write a "Dear _____" letter to a missing classmate, telling him or her what was learned in the class that day. Have students give you the letters before they leave, and explain you will read the letters and then pass them on to the missing student.

Another exercise is to have students write about a reading selection discussed in class. The Appendix provides three writing assignments for each of the twenty readings in the book. Ask students to choose one of the three and to turn in a paper to you before they leave. In some cases, you may want to make the paper an overnight assignment instead.

These activities will help make your classroom alive and will turn learning into an active process. I think you will find them rewarding, and I encourage you to try them out. I wish you luck!

John Langan

TEN STEPS
to
ADVANCED
READING

John Langan

ATLANTIC CAPE COMMUNITY COLLEGE

INSTRUCTOR'S EDITION

Books in the Townsend Press Reading Series:

Groundwork for College Reading
Ten Steps to Building College Reading Skills
Ten Steps to Improving College Reading Skills
Ten Steps to Advancing College Reading Skills
Ten Steps to Advanced Reading

Books in the Townsend Press Vocabulary Series:

Vocabulary Basics
Groundwork for a Better Vocabulary
Building Vocabulary Skills
Building Vocabulary Skills, Short Version
Improving Vocabulary Skills
Improving Vocabulary Skills, Short Version
Advancing Vocabulary Skills
Advancing Vocabulary Skills, Short Version
Advanced Word Power

Supplements Available for Most Books:

Instructor's Edition
Instructor's Manual and Test Bank
Online Exercises

Copyright © 2007 by Townsend Press, Inc.
Printed in the United States of America
9 8 7 6 5 4 3 2 1

ISBN-13 (Student Edition): 978-1-59194-079-1
ISBN-10 (Student Edition): 1-59194-079-6
ISBN-13 (Instructor's Edition): 978-1-59194-081-4
ISBN-10 (Instructor's Edition): 1-59194-081-8

**For book orders and requests for desk copies or supplements,
contact us in any of the following ways:**
By telephone: 1-800-772-6410
By fax: 1-800-225-8894
By e-mail: cs@townsendpress.com
Through our website: www.townsendpress.com

To my competitors, for inspiring me to try harder.
May I do the same for you, and may all our students benefit.

Contents

Preface:
To the Instructor

We all know that many students entering college today do not have the reading skills needed to do effective work in their courses. A related problem, apparent even in class discussions, is that students often lack the skills required to think in a clear and logical way.

The purpose of *Ten Steps to Advanced Reading* is to develop effective reading and clear thinking. To do so, **Part I** presents a sequence of ten reading skills that are widely recognized as essential for basic and advanced comprehension. The first five skills concern the more literal levels of comprehension:

- Recognizing main ideas
- Identifying supporting details
- Recognizing implied main ideas and the central point
- Understanding relationships that involve addition and time
- Understanding relationships that involve illustration, comparison and/or contrast, and cause and effect

The remaining skills cover the more advanced, critical levels of comprehension:

- Making inferences
- Identifying an author's purpose and tone
- Evaluating arguments
- Separating fact from opinion, detecting propaganda, and recognizing errors in reasoning
- Using a study and notetaking system

In every chapter in Part I, the key aspects of a skill are explained and illustrated clearly and simply. Explanations are accompanied by a series of practices, and each chapter ends with two review tests. The second review test consists of a reading selection so that students can apply the skill just learned to real-world reading materials, including magazine articles and textbook selections.

Together, the ten chapters provide students with the skills needed for both basic and advanced reading comprehension.

Following each chapter in Part I are **six mastery tests for the skill in question.** The tests progress in difficulty, giving students the additional practice and challenge they may need for the solid learning of each skill. While designed for quick grading, the tests also require students to think carefully before answering each question.

Part II is made up of ten additional readings that will improve both reading and thinking skills. Each reading is followed by questions that will help students practice all ten skills presented in Part I. Each reading also includes "Discussion Questions" that engage students in a variety of thinking skills and deepen their understanding of a selection. In addition, for the first five readings, an activity titled "Active Reading and Study of a Textbook Selection" improves students' skill in learning and taking notes on textbook material. For the final five readings, an activity in "Outlining" or "Summarizing" helps students think carefully about the content and organization of a selection.

Part III consists of a series of twenty combined-skills tests that review the skills in Part I and help students prepare for the standardized reading test that is often a requirement at the end of a semester. An appendix then includes a limited answer key as well as writing assignments for all twenty readings in the text. When time permits, asking students to write about a selection will help reinforce the reading and thinking skills they have practiced in the book.

Important Features of the Book

- **Focus on the basics.** The book is designed to explain, in a clear, step-by-step way, the essential elements of each skill. Many examples are provided to ensure that students understand each point. In general, the focus is on teaching the skills—not just on explaining or testing them.

- **Frequent practice and feedback.** Because abundant practice and careful feedback are essential to learning, this book includes numerous activities. Students can get immediate feedback on the practice exercises in Part I by turning to the limited answer key at the back of the book.

    The limited answer key increases the active role that students take in their own learning. They are likely to use the answer key in an honest and positive way if they know they will be tested on the many activities and selections for which answers are not provided. (Answers not in the book can be copied from the *Instructor's Edition* and passed out at the teacher's discretion.)

- **High interest level.** Dull and unvaried readings and exercises work against learning. Students need to experience genuine interest and enjoyment in what they read. Teachers as well should be able to take pleasure in the selections, for their own good feeling can carry over favorably into class work. The readings in the book, then, have been chosen not only for the appropriateness of their reading level but also for their compelling content. They should engage teachers and students alike.

- **Ease of use.** The logical sequence in each chapter—from explanation to example to practice to review test to mastery test—helps make the skills easy to teach. The book's organization into distinct parts also makes for ease of use. Within a single class, for instance, teachers can work on a new skill in Part I, review other skills with one or more mastery tests, and provide variety by having students read one of the selections in Part II. The limited answer key at the back of the text also makes for versatility: the teacher can assign some chapters for self-teaching. Finally, the mastery tests—each on its own tear-out page—and the combined-skills tests make it a simple matter for teachers to test and evaluate student progress.

- **Integration of skills.** Students do more than learn the skills individually in Part I. They also learn to apply the skills together through the reading selections in Parts I and II as well as the combined-skills tests in Part III. They become effective readers and thinkers through repeated practice in applying a combination of skills.

- **Online exercises.** As they complete each of the ten chapters, students are invited to go online to the Townsend Press website to work on three additional practice exercises for each skill—exercises that reinforce the skill taught in the chapter.

- **Thinking activities.** Thinking activities—in the form of outlining, mapping, summarizing, and taking study notes—are a distinctive feature of the book. While educators agree that such organizational abilities are important, these skills are all too seldom taught. From a practical standpoint, it is almost impossible for a teacher to respond in detail to entire collections of class outlines or summaries. This book then, presents activities that truly involve students in outlining, mapping, summarizing, and taking study notes—in other words, that truly make students *think*—and yet enable a teacher to give immediate feedback. Again, it is through continued practice *and* feedback on challenging material that a student becomes a more effective reader and thinker.

- **Supplementary materials.** The two helpful supplements listed below are available at no charge to instructors who have adopted the text. Any or all can be obtained quickly by calling Townsend Press (1-800-772-6410), by sending a fax to 1-800-225-8894, or by e-mailing Customer Service at **cs@townsendpress.com**.

  1 An *Instructor's Edition*—chances are that you are holding it in your hand—is identical to the student book except that it also provides hints for teachers (see the inside front cover of the book), answers to all the practices and tests, and comments on most items. *No other book on the market has such detailed and helpful annotations.*

  2 *Online exercises* provide three additional mastery tests for each of the ten skill chapters in the book. The exercises contain a number of user- and instructor-friendly features: brief explanations of answers, a sound option, frequent mention of the user's first name, a running score, and a record-keeping score file.

- **One of a sequence of books.** This is the most advanced text in a series that includes four other books. The first book in the series, *Groundwork for College Reading,* is suited for ESL students and basic adult learners. The second book, *Ten Steps to Building College Reading Skills,* is often the choice for a first college reading course. The third book, *Ten Steps to Improving College Reading Skills,* is an intermediate text appropriate for the core developmental reading course offered at most colleges. The fourth book, *Ten Steps to Advancing College Reading Skills,* is a higher developmental text than the *Ten Steps to Improving* book. It can be used as the core book for a more advanced class, as a sequel to the intermediate book, or as a second-semester alternative to it. *Ten Steps to Advanced Reading* can be used as a sequel or alternative to *Ten Steps to Advancing College Reading Skills.*

  A companion set of vocabulary books, listed on the copyright page, has been designed to go with the TP reading series. Recommended to accompany this book is *Advancing Vocabulary Skills* (300 words and word parts) or *Advanced Word Power* (300 words).

  Together, the books and all their supplements form a sequence that should be ideal for any college reading program.

To summarize, *Ten Steps to Advanced Reading* teaches and reinforces ten essential reading skills. Through an appealing collection of readings and a carefully designed series of activities and tests, students receive extensive guided practice in the skills. The result is an integrated approach to learning that will, by the end of the course, produce better readers and stronger thinkers.

Acknowledgments

A number of teachers have urged me over the years to write a higher-level reading book—one they could use for advanced reading courses or as an alternative to the books in the Ten Steps series. Their encouragement, and the many generous words I have received about the helpfulness of the Ten Steps books, inspired me to spend the time needed to create *Ten Steps to Advanced Reading*. In particular, I am grateful for the input provided by Joanne Ernst of Manatee Community College.

At Townsend Press, I thank Bill Blauvelt, Beth Johnson, and Ruth A. Rouff for the help they provided along the way. And I owe special thanks to my long-time colleague Janet Goldstein for her superb design, editing, and organizational skills. She is an editor extraordinaire, and her talents have also made possible the creation of the *Instructor's Edition*, complete with answers and marginal comments, that accompanies the book. It is always a special pleasure to work with people who aspire toward excellence. With help from my colleagues in the teaching profession and at Townsend Press, I have been able to create a much better book than I could have managed on my own.

John Langan

INTRODUCTION

1

How to Become
a Better Reader
and Thinker

The chances are that you are not as good a reader as you should be to do well in college. If so, it's not surprising. You live in a culture where people watch an average of *over seven hours of television every day!!!* All that passive viewing does not allow much time for reading. Reading is a skill that must be actively practiced. The simple fact is that people who do not read very often are not likely to be strong readers. *Answers will vary.*

• How much TV do you guess you watch on an average day? _____

Another reason besides TV for not reading much is that you may have a lot of responsibilities. You may be going to school and working at the same time, and you may have a lot of family duties as well. Given a hectic schedule, you're not going to have much time to read. When you do have free time, you're exhausted, and it's easier to turn on the TV than to open up a book.

• Do you do any regular reading (for example, a daily newspaper, weekly

magazines, occasional novels)? _____

• When are you most likely to do your reading? _____

A third reason for not reading is that school may have caused you to associate reading with worksheets and drills and book reports and test scores. Experts agree that many schools have not done a good job of helping students discover the pleasures and rewards of reading. If reading was an unpleasant experience in school, you may have concluded that reading in general is not for you.

- Do you think that school made you dislike reading, rather than enjoy it?

_____

Here are three final questions to ask yourself:

- Do you feel that perhaps you don't need a reading course, since you "already

  know how to read"? _____

- If you had a choice, would you be taking a reading course? (It's okay to be

  honest.) _____

- Do you think that a bit of speed reading may be all you need? _____

Chances are that you don't need to read *faster* as much as you need to read *smarter.* And it's a safe bet that if you don't read much, you can benefit enormously from the reading course in which you are using this book.

One goal of the book is to help you become a better reader. You will learn and practice ten key reading comprehension skills. As a result, you'll be better able to read and understand the many materials in your other college courses. The skills in this book have direct and practical value: they can help you perform better and more quickly—giving you an edge for success—in all of your college work.

The book is also concerned with helping you become a stronger thinker, a person able not just to *understand* what is read but to *analyze* and *evaluate* it as well. In fact, reading and thinking are closely related skills, and practice in thoughtful reading will also strengthen your ability to think clearly and logically. To find out just how the book will help you achieve these goals, read the next several pages and do the brief activities as well. The activities are easily completed and will give you a quick, helpful overview of the book.

HOW THE BOOK IS ORGANIZED

The book is organized into four main parts:

Introduction (pages 1–19)

In addition to this chapter, which will give you a good sense of the book, there are three other parts to the introduction. "Some Quick Study Tips" presents four hints that can make you a better student. If I had time to say just four things to incoming college students based on my thirty years of teaching experience, these are the things I would say. Turn to page 10 and then write, in the space on the next page, the second of these tips:

Learn how to understand what your instructors want from you in a course.

There is also a section titled "Notes on Vocabulary in Context," which will review the importance of using context clues to figure out the meanings of unfamiliar words. And there is a section titled "A Reading Challenge," which will give you a chance to earn some free books.

Part I: Ten Steps to Advanced Reading Power (pages 21–390)

To help you become a more effective reader and thinker, this book presents a series of ten key reading skills. They are listed in the table of contents on pages vii and viii. Turn to those pages to fill in the skills missing below:

1 Main Ideas
2 *Supporting Details*
3 Implied Main Ideas
4 Relationships I
5 *Relationships II*
6 Inferences
7 Purpose and Tone
8 *Argument*
9 Critical Reading
10 Active Reading and Study

Each chapter is developed in the same way:

First of all, clear explanations and examples help you *understand* each skill. Practices then give you the "hands-on" experience needed to *learn* the skill.

- How many practices are there for the first chapter, "Main Ideas" (pages 23–62)? ___*Three*___

Closing each chapter are two review tests. The first review test provides a check of the information presented in the chapter.

- On which page is the first review test for "Main Ideas"? ___*44*___

The second review test consists of a story, essay, or textbook selection that both gets you reading and gives you practice in the skill learned in the chapter as well as skills learned in previous chapters.

- What is the title of the reading selection in the "Main Ideas" chapter?
  "Getting a Good Night's Sleep"

Following each chapter are six mastery tests which gradually increase in difficulty.

- On what pages are the mastery tests for the "Main Ideas" chapter? _____*51–62*_____

The tests are on tear-out pages and so can be easily removed and handed in to your instructor. So that you can track your progress, there is a score box at the top of each test. Your score can also be entered into the "Reading Performance Chart" on the inside back cover of the book.

Part II: Ten Reading Selections (pages 391–504)

The ten reading selections that make up Part II are followed by activities that give you practice in all the skills studied in Part I. Each reading begins in the same way. Look, for example, at "Personal Conflict Styles," which starts on page 393. What are the headings of the two sections that come before the reading itself?

- _____*Preview*_____
- _____*Words to Watch*_____

Note that the vocabulary words in "Words to Watch" are followed by the numbers of the paragraphs in which the words appear. Look at the first page of "Personal Conflict Styles" and explain how each vocabulary word is marked in the reading itself.

- _____*It has a small circle after it.*_____

Activities Following Each Reading Selection

After each selection, there are three kinds of activities to improve the reading and thinking skills you learned in Part I of the book.

1 The first activity consists of **reading comprehension questions**—questions involving vocabulary in context, main ideas (including implied main ideas and the central point), supporting details, relationships, inferences, purpose and tone, argument, fact and opinion, propaganda devices, and logical thinking.

   - Look at the reading comprehension questions for "Personal Conflict Styles" on pages 398–402. Note that the questions are labeled so you know which skill you are practicing in each case. How many questions deal with understanding vocabulary in context? _____*Two*_____

   - How many questions deal with critical reading? _____*Three*_____

2 The second activity involves **outlining**, **summarizing**, or **taking study notes**. Each of these activities will sharpen your ability to get to the heart of a piece and to think logically and clearly about what you read.

• What kind of activity is provided for "Personal Conflict Styles" on page 402? _____*Taking study notes*_____

• What kind of activity is provided for the reading titled "In My Day" on page 491?_____*Summarizing*_____

3 The third activity consists of **discussion questions**. These questions provide a chance for you to deepen your understanding of each selection.

• How many discussion questions are there for "Personal Conflict Styles" (page 403)—and indeed for every other reading? _____*Four*_____

Part III: Combined-Skills Tests (pages 505–547)

This part of the book is made up of short passages that give you practice in all the reading skills taught in the book.

• How many such tests are there in all? _____*Twenty*_____

Appendixes (pages 549–570)

Following Part III are appendixes that include a pronunciation guide, a limited answer key, and writing assignments for all twenty of the reading selections in the book. Reading and writing are closely connected skills, and writing practice will improve your ability to read closely and to think carefully.

HELPFUL FEATURES OF THE BOOK

1 The book centers on *what you really need to know* to become a better reader and thinker. It presents ten key comprehension skills and explains the most important points about each one.

2 The book gives you *lots of practice*. We seldom learn a skill only by hearing or reading about it; we make it part of us by repeated practice. There are, then, numerous activities in the text. They are not "busywork" but carefully designed materials that should help you truly learn each skill.

Notice that after you learn each skill in Part I, you progress to review tests and mastery tests that enable you to apply the skill. And as you move from one skill to the next, the reading selections help you practice and reinforce the skills already learned.

3 The selections throughout the book are *lively and appealing.* Dull and unvaried readings work against learning, so subjects have been carefully chosen for their high interest level. Almost all of the selections here are good examples of how what we read can capture our attention. For instance, if you, like many Americans, have some sleep problems, you will probably read with great interest the article from *Time* magazine on "Getting a Good Night's Sleep" (page 45). Or look at the textbook selection on page 393; its title, "Personal Conflict Styles," may seem unpromising, but you will be intrigued to compare the way you react to conflict with how other people react. Or read "A Civil War Soldier's Letter to His Wife" on page 453 and try not to shake your head and shed a tear at the heartbreak of war.

4 The readings include *ten selections from college textbooks.* Therefore, you will be practicing on materials very much like those in your other courses. Doing so will increase your chances of transferring what you learn in your reading class to your other college courses.

HOW TO USE THE BOOK

1 A good way to proceed is to read and review the explanations and examples in a given chapter in Part I until you feel you understand the ideas presented. Then carefully work through the practices. As you finish each one, check your answers with the "Limited Answer Key" that starts on page 553.

For your own sake, *don't just copy in the answers without trying to do the practices!* The only way to learn a skill is to practice it first and then use the answer key to give yourself feedback. Also, take whatever time is needed to figure out just why you got some answers wrong. By using the answer key to help teach yourself the skills, you will prepare yourself for the review and mastery tests at the end of each chapter as well as the other reading tests in the book. Your instructor can supply you with answers to those tests.

If you have trouble catching on to a particular skill, stick with it. In time, you will learn each of the ten skills.

2 Read the selections first with the intent of simply enjoying them. There will be time afterward for rereading each selection and using it to develop your comprehension skills.

3 Keep track of your progress. Fill in the charts at the end of each chapter in Part I and each reading in Part II. And in the "Reading Performance Chart" on the inside back cover, enter your scores for all of the review and mastery tests as well as the reading selections. These scores can give you a good view of your overall performance as you work through the book.

In summary, *Ten Steps to Advanced Reading* has been designed to interest and benefit you as much as possible. Its format is straightforward, its explanations are clear, its readings are appealing, and its many practices will help you learn through doing. *It is a book that has been created to reward effort*, and if you provide that effort, you will make yourself a better reader and a stronger thinker. I wish you success.

John Langan

2
Some Quick Study Tips

While it's not my purpose in this book to teach study skills, I do want to give you four quick hints that can make you a better student. The hints are based on my thirty years of experience working with first-year college students and teaching reading and study skills.

TIP *Tip 1* The most important steps you can take to succeed in school are to *go to every class* and *take a lot of notes*. If you don't go to class, or you go but just sit there without taking notes, chances are you're heading for a heap of trouble.

TIP *Tip 2* Let me ask you a question: Which is more important—learning how to read a textbook or learning how to read your professor? Write your answer here:

Learning how to read your professor.

You may be surprised at the answer: What is far more important is learning how to read your professor—to understand what he or she expects you to learn in the course and to know for tests.

I remember becoming a good student in college only after I learned the truth of this statement. And I have interviewed hundreds of today's students who have said the same thing. Let me quote just one of them:

> *You absolutely have to be in class. Then you learn how to read the teacher and to know what he or she is going to want on tests. You could read an entire textbook, but that wouldn't be as good as being in class and writing down a teacher's understanding of ideas.*

TIP *Tip 3* Many teachers base their tests mainly on the ideas they present in class. But when you have to learn a textbook chapter, do the following:

First, read the first and last few paragraphs of the chapter; they may give you a good overview of what the chapter is about.

Second, as you read the chapter, look for and mark off definitions of key terms and examples of those definitions.

Third, as you read the chapter, number any lists of items; if there are series of points and you number them *1, 2, 3,* and so on, it will be easier to understand and remember them.

Fourth, after you've read the chapter, take notes on the most important material and test yourself on those notes until you can say them to yourself without looking at them.

TIP *Tip 4* Here's another question: Are you an organized person? Do you get out of bed on time, do you get to places on time, do you keep up with school work, do you allow time to study for tests and write papers?

If you are *not* an organized person, you're going to have trouble in school. Here are three steps to take to control your time:

First, pay close attention to the course outline, or *syllabus,* your instructors will probably pass out at the start of a semester. Chances are that syllabus will give you the dates of exams and tell you when papers or reports are due.

Second, move all those dates onto a *large monthly calendar*—a calendar that has a good-sized block of white space for each date. Hang the calendar in a place where you'll be sure to see it every day—perhaps above your desk or on a bedroom wall.

Third, buy a small notebook and write down every day a *"to do" list* of things that need to get done that day. Decide which items are most important, and focus on them first. (If you have classes that day, going to those classes will be "A" priority items.) Carry your list with you during the day, referring to it every so often and checking off items as you complete them.

Questions

1. Of the four hints listed above, which is the most important one for you? Why?

2. Which hint is the second most important for you, and why?

3. You may not realize just how quickly new information can be forgotten. For example, how much class material do you think most people forget in just two weeks? Check (✓) the answer you think is correct.

   _____ 20 percent is forgotten within two weeks

   _____ 40 percent is forgotten within two weeks

   _____ 60 percent is forgotten within two weeks

   __✓__ 80 percent is forgotten within two weeks

   The truth is that within two weeks most people forget almost 80 percent of what they have heard! Given that fact, what should you be sure to do in all your classes?

   Take lots of notes.

3

Notes to the Instructor:

1. All answers and comments (in this smaller red type) appear only in the *Instructor's Edition.*
2. Pronunciations are provided for the words in this chapter and for vocabulary questions that follow the readings in Parts I and II. You may want to review with students the brief guide to pronunciation on pages 551–552.

Notes on Vocabulary in Context

In this advanced reading skills book, there is no separate chapter on the skill of understanding vocabulary in context. Instead, this section will review the skill, and many of the readings in the book will include vocabulary-in-context questions.

Understanding vocabulary in context is an inference skill that most of us learn in the course of reading. For example, if you were asked to define the words *hyperbole*, *querulous*, and *surreptitious*, you might have some difficulty. On the other hand, if you saw these words in sentences, you might be able to infer their meanings by looking at the other words in the sentence.

See if you can define the words in *italics* in the three sentences below. In the space provided, write the letter of the meaning you think is correct in each case.

____A____ Marcella uses a lot of *hyperbole* to express herself: a restaurant is never just "good"—it's "the most fabulous food in the universe"; her boyfriend isn't just "good-looking"—he's "divine beyond belief."

Hyperbole (hī-pûr′bə-lē) means
A. overstatement.   B. compliment.   C. accuracy.

____C____ People who work in the complaint department of a store must get used to dealing with lots of *querulous* customers.

Querulous (kwĕr′ə-ləs) means
A. shaky.   B. dishonest.   C. dissatisfied.

____C____ Students naturally want to know what will be covered on a test. Instead of trying to find out by *surreptitious* means, it is often better to simply ask the instructor a direct question.

Surreptitious (sûr′əp-tĭsh′əs) means
A. straightforward.   B. useless.   C. secret.

In each sentence above, the *context*—the words surrounding the unfamiliar word—provides clues to the word's meaning. You may have guessed from the context that *hyperbole* means "overstatement," that *querulous* means "discontented," and that *surreptitious* means "secret."

Using context clues to understand the meaning of unfamiliar words will help you save time when reading. You will not have to stop to look up words in the dictionary. (Of course, you won't always be able to understand a word from its context, so you should always have a dictionary nearby as you read.)

TYPES OF CONTEXT CLUES

There are four common types of context clues:

1 Examples

2 Synonyms

3 Antonyms

4 General Sense of the Sentence or Passage

Following are brief practices that will give you a sense of each type of clue.

1 Examples

If you are given **examples** that relate to an unknown word, you can often figure out its meaning. For instance, note the examples in the sentence "Marcella uses a lot of *hyperbole* to express herself: a restaurant is never just 'good'—it's 'the most fabulous food in the universe'; her boyfriend isn't just 'good-looking'—he's 'divine beyond belief.'" The examples help you figure out that the word *hyperbole* means "overstatement."

Now read the items that follow. An *italicized* word in each sentence is followed by examples that serve as context clues for that word. These examples, which are in **boldface** type, will help you figure out the meaning of each word. On the answer line, write the letter of each meaning you think is correct.

Note that examples are often introduced with signal words and phrases like *for example, for instance, including,* and *such as.*

   C   1. Jean is a difficult roommate because her moods are so *volatile*. **One day she's on top of the world; the next day she's in the depths of despair.**

        Volatile (vŏl′ə-tl) means
        A. insensitive.   B. indirect.   C. changeable.

___B___ 2. The boss, a *parsimonious* man, **keeps the office lights dimmed, frowns upon coffee breaks, and seldom turns on the heating or air conditioning**.

Parsimonious (pär′sĭ-mō′nē-əs) means

A. mischievous.   B. stingy.   C. moody.

___A___ 3. My father has a *voracious* appetite for news. **He gets two morning papers, listens to an "all news" program in the car, and watches CNN every night**.

Voracious (vô-rā′shəs) means

A. all-consuming.   B. small.   C. unconcerned.

In the first sentence, the examples show that *volatile* means "changeable." In the second sentence, the examples show that *parsimonious* means "stingy." Finally, the examples in the third sentence indicate that a *voracious* appetite is an "all-consuming" one.

2 Synonyms

Context clues are often found in the form of **synonyms**: one or more words that mean the same or almost the same as the unknown word. In the sentence "People who work in the complaint department of a store must get used to dealing with lots of querulous customers," the word *complaint* suggests that *querulous* must mean "complaining" or "dissatisfied." A synonym may appear anywhere in a sentence as a restatement of the meaning of the unknown word.

Each of the following items includes a word or phrase that is a synonym of the italicized word. Underline the synonym for each italicized word. Then, on the answer line, write the letter of each meaning you think is correct.

___B___ 1. The heat wave *enervated* the kids. They were too tired to play outside.

Enervated (ĕn′ər-vā′tĭd) means

A. frightened.   B. exhausted.   C. awakened.

___C___ 2. Children may believe they are the only ones who are happy to see summer vacation arrive, but their teachers feel *exuberant* also.

Exuberant (ĭg-zōō′bər-ənt) means

A. fearful.   B. bored.   C. overjoyed.

___C___ 3. Larry always becomes *morose* when he drinks. Since alcohol makes him so dreary and blue, you'd think he'd give it up.

Morose (mə′rōs) means

A. confused.   B. frantic.   C. gloomy.

You should have underlined "tired" as a synonym for *enervated*, "happy" as a synonym for *exuberant*, and "dreary and blue" as synonyms for *morose*. These synonym clues tell you that *enervated* means "exhausted," *exuberant* means "overjoyed," and *morose* means "gloomy."

3 Antonyms

Antonyms—words and phrases that mean the opposite of a word—are also useful as context clues. Antonyms are sometimes signaled by words and phrases such as *however, but, yet, on the other hand,* and *in contrast.* In the sentences "Students naturally want to know what will be covered on a test. Instead of trying to find out by *surreptitious* means, it is often better to simply ask the instructor a direct question," the antonym *direct* helps you figure out the meaning of *surreptitious.*

In each of the following sentences, underline the word or phrase that means the *opposite* of the italicized word. Then, on the answer line, write the letter of the meaning of the italicized word.

_B_ 1. Who says that cats and dogs are <u>enemies</u>? Our dog and two cats live together in the most *amicable* way.

    Amicable (ăm′ĭ-kə-bəl) means
    A. hostile.   B. peaceable.   C. cute.

_C_ 2. I enjoyed the speaker's easygoing, *colloquial* style. She made the topic more interesting than a <u>stiff, formal</u> speaker could have done.

    Colloquial (kə-lō′kwē-əl) means
    A. deceptive.   B. unclear.   C. informal.

_B_ 3. The two women who were waiting to hear the results of their mammograms were quite different. One was a <u>bundle of nerves</u> while the other seemed quite *placid.*

    Placid (plăs′ĭd) means
    A. tense.   B. untroubled.   C. sad.

In the first sentence, the opposite of *amicable* creatures is *enemies;* thus *amicable* means "peaceable." In the second sentence, *colloquial* is the opposite of *stiff* and *formal,* so *colloquial* means "informal." Last, someone who is "a bundle of nerves" is the opposite of someone who is placid, so *placid* means "untroubled."

4   General Sense of the Sentence or Passage

Sometimes it takes a bit more detective work to puzzle out the meaning of an unfamiliar word. In such cases, you must draw conclusions based on the information given.

By considering carefully the general sense of each of the following sentences, see if you can decide what the italicized word means in each case.

___A___ 1. The students asked if they could use their notes during the test. They were pleased when the teacher *acquiesced.*

   Acquiesced (ăk'wē-ĕst') means
   A. consented.   B. refused.   C. was puzzled.

___A___ 2. A person suspected of a crime has the *prerogative* of refusing to answer questions unless his or her lawyer is present.

   Prerogative (prĭ-rŏg'ə-tĭv) means
   A. choice.   B. duty.   C. belief.

___C___ 3. An introductory music course in college can *engender* a lifelong love of music.

   Engender (ĕn-jĕn'dər) means
   A. endanger.   B. complete.   C. begin.

The first sentence provides enough evidence for you to guess that *acquiesced* means "consented." *Prerogative* in the second sentence means "choice." And *engender* means "begin." (You may not hit on the exact dictionary definition of a word by using context clues, but you will often be accurate enough to make good sense of what you are reading.)

An Important Point about Textbook Definitions

You don't always have to use context clues or the dictionary to find definitions. Very often, textbook authors provide definitions of important terms. They usually follow a definition with one or more examples to ensure that you understand the word being defined. Moreover, they may set off their definitions in *italic* or **boldface** type. When an author takes the time to define and illustrate a word, you can generally assume that the material is important enough to learn.

More about textbook definitions and examples appears on pages 174–175 in the "Relationships II" chapter.

4

A Reading Challenge

It's no secret. Reading researchers, teachers, and people with common sense everywhere know that the best way to become a better reader is to do a lot of reading. Here's why:

1 **Reading provides language power.** Research has shown *beyond any question* that frequent reading improves vocabulary, spelling, and reading speed and comprehension, as well as grammar and writing style. If you become a regular reader, all of these language and thinking abilities develop almost automatically!

2 **Reading increases the chances for job success.** In today's world, more than ever before, jobs involve the processing of information, with words being the tools of the trade. Studies have found that the better your command of words is, the more success you are likely to have. *Nothing will give you a command of words like regular reading.*

3 **Reading creates human power.** Reading enlarges the mind and the heart. It frees us from the narrow confines of our own experience. Knowing how other people view important matters helps us decide what we ourselves think and feel. Reading also helps us connect with others and recognize our shared humanity. Someone once wrote, "We read in order to know that we are not alone." We become less isolated as we share the common experiences, emotions, and thoughts that make us human. We grow more sympathetic and understanding because we realize that others are like us.

With all the above in mind, Townsend Press is going to offer you a reading challenge. Send us $50. We will then send you the 40 paperback books pictured on page 19. Read all 40 books and then e-mail us at **cs@townsendpress.com**. We'll send you a toll-free phone number you can use to speak to a person on our staff, who will ask you questions to confirm that you've really read the books. If you've read all 40, we'll return your $50 and award you an Advanced Reading Achievement Certificate.

What happens if you read just five or ten or so of the 40 books? You will have the benefit of having read those books, and you will also have a lot of good paperbacks in your house to eventually read yourself or to give to others. One of the best ways to clutter up your living space is with a lot of books.

To get the 40 books, you must currently be taking a college reading course. You must tear out **this original page** (a copy will not do), fill in the order form, and send the page to us along with your payment. You must then call us no later than three months after the course ends.

ORDER FORM

YES! Please send me the 40 books pictured. Enclosed is $50.00 to cover the cost of shipping and handling and to partly offset the cost of the books.

Please PRINT the following very clearly. It will be your shipping label.

Name _____

Address _____

City _____ *State* _____ *Zip* _____

Please provide the following information as well:

My school _____

Title of the reading course I am currently taking _____

Name of my instructor _____

MAIL TO:

Townsend Press Book Center, 1038 Industrial Drive, West Berlin, NJ 08091.

READING CHANGED MY LIFE! THREE TRUE STORIES
Beth Johnson

Letters My Mother Never Read: AN ABANDONED CHILD'S JOURNEY
By JERRI DIANE SUECK

Great STORIES of SUSPENSE & ADVENTURE

Surviving Abuse: Four True Stories
Beth Johnson

It Couldn't Happen to Me: Three True Stories of Teenage Moms
Beth Johnson

CHARLOTTE BRONTË
JANE EYRE

Dracula
BRAM STOKER

ANNA SEWELL
BLACK BEAUTY
The Autobiography of a Horse

MARY WOLLSTONECRAFT SHELLEY
FRANKENSTEIN
The Strange Case of DR. JEKYLL and MR. HYDE
ROBERT LOUIS STEVENSON

EDITH WHARTON
ETHAN FROME

LAUGHTER AND CHILLS
SEVEN GREAT STORIES
THE STORYTELLER
THE RANSOM OF RED CHIEF
THE OPEN WINDOW
THE CASK OF AMONTILLADO
THE TELL-TALE HEART
THE LEGEND OF SLEEPY HOLLOW
A CHRISTMAS CAROL

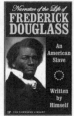
Narrative of the Life of FREDERICK DOUGLASS
An American Slave
Written by Himself

Harriet Jacobs
Incidents in the Life of a Slave Girl
Written by Herself

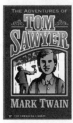
THE ADVENTURES OF TOM SAWYER
MARK TWAIN

MARK TWAIN
The Adventures of HUCKLEBERRY FINN

SHIRLEY RUSSAK WACHTEL
THE STORY OF BLIMA
A Holocaust Survivor

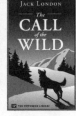
Booker T. Washington
UP FROM SLAVERY: An Autobiography

JACK LONDON
The CALL of the WILD

JACK LONDON
White Fang

THE Merry Adventures OF ROBIN HOOD
HOWARD PYLE

TARZAN OF THE APES
EDGAR RICE BURROUGHS

SISTER Carrie
Theodore Dreiser

MARK TWAIN
The Prince and The Pauper

Bully
Paul Langan

PAUL LANGAN & BEN ALIREZ
Brothers in Arms

Search for Safety
John Langan

Charles Dickens
A TALE OF TWO CITIES

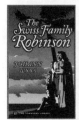
The Swiss Family Robinson
JOHANN WYSS

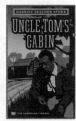
L. FRANK BAUM
THE WIZARD OF OZ

HARRIET BEECHER STOWE
UNCLE TOM'S CABIN

EDGAR RICE BURROUGHS
A PRINCESS OF MARS

THE HOUND OF THE BASKERVILLES
ARTHUR CONAN DOYLE

NATHANIEL HAWTHORNE
The Scarlet Letter

H. G. WELLS
WAR OF THE WORLDS

ROBINSON CRUSOE
DANIEL DEFOE

HORATIO ALGER, JR
RAGGED DICK or STREET LIFE IN NEW YORK

THE VIRGINIAN
OWEN WISTER

Johnston McCulley
The Mark of ZORRO

TEN REAL-LIFE STORIES
THE YELLOW RIBBON
SHAME
RIDING THE BUS
THE SCHOLARSHIP JACKET
A DRUNKEN BRIDE, A TRAGIC AFTERMATH
THE PROFESSOR IS A DROPOUT
DO IT BETTER
LIFE OVER DEATH
BECOMING A READER
LEARNING SURVIVAL SKILLS

JONATHAN SWIFT
GULLIVER'S TRAVELS

Part I

TEN STEPS TO ADVANCED READING POWER

(How)
Does it
talk/refer to every
point in the ? ?
passage? ?
the author ?
...es

1

Main Ideas

WHAT IS THE MAIN IDEA?

© 2005, Mike Tw...

"What's your point?" What is the point the author is trying to make?

"You've dialed a super wrong number!"

"What's the point?" You've probably heard these words before. It's a question people ask when they want to know the main idea that someone is trying to express. The same question can guide you as you read. Recognizing the **main idea**, or point, is the most important key to good comprehension. Sometimes a main idea is immediately clear, as in the above cartoon. The point—that the caller has dialed the worst possible number—is vividly supported by the figure of the Grim Reaper, Death, answering the phone. To find a point in a reading selection, ask yourself, "What's the main point the author is trying to make?"

For instance, read the paragraph on the following page, asking yourself as you do, "What is the author's point?"

¹Social psychologists have found that almost everyone gossips. ²Male or female, young or old, blue-collar or professional, humans love to talk about one another. ³All too often, such gossip is viewed as a frivolous waste of time. ⁴However, it actually serves several important functions in the human community. ⁵For one thing, gossip is a form of networking. ⁶Talking with our friends and coworkers about each other is our most effective means of keeping track of the ever-changing social dynamic. ⁷It tells us who is in, who is out, and who can help us climb the social or professional ladder. ⁸A second function of gossip is the building of influence. ⁹When we engage in gossip, we are able to shape people's opinions of ourselves. ¹⁰We tell stories that show ourselves in a good light—wise, compassionate, insightful, clever. ¹¹And when we listen sympathetically to the gossip of other people, they perceive us as warm and likable. ¹²A final and very powerful function of gossip is the creating of social alliances. ¹³There are few quicker ways to form a bond with another person than to share private information with him or her. ¹⁴The words "I wouldn't tell most people this, but . . ." instantly interest and flatter the listener. ¹⁵To talk about a third party, especially in a critical way, creates a bond with our listener and gives a feeling of shared superiority.

A good way to find an author's point, or main idea, is to look for a general statement. Then decide if that statement is supported by most of the other material in the paragraph. If it is, you have found the main idea.

Following are four statements from the passage. Pick out the general statement that is supported by the other material in the passage. Write the letter of that statement in the space provided. Then read the explanation that follows.

Four statements from the passage:

A. Social psychologists have found that almost everyone gossips.

B. However, it [gossip] actually serves several important functions in the human community.

C. For one thing, gossip is a form of networking.

D. There are few quicker ways to form a bond with another person than to share private information with him or her.

The general statement that expresses the main idea of the passage is ___B___.

Explanation:

Sentence A: Only the second sentence supports the idea that everyone gossips—not the entire paragraph. While sentence A cannot be the main idea, it does introduce the topic of the paragraph: gossip.

Sentence B: The statement "However, it [gossip] actually serves several important functions in the human community," is a general one. And the rest of the passage goes on to describe three important functions of gossip. Sentence B, then, is the sentence that expresses the main idea of the passage.

Sentence C: This sentence refers only to the first function of gossip. It is not general enough to include the other two functions that are cited in the paragraph.

Sentence D: This sentence simply provides a detail that supports the third function of gossip. It does not cover the other material in the paragraph.

The Main Idea as an "Umbrella" Idea

Think of the main idea as an "umbrella" idea. The main idea is the author's general point; under it fits all the other material of the paragraph. That other material is made up of supporting details—specific evidence such as examples, causes, reasons, or facts. The diagram below shows the relationship.

The explanations and activities on the following pages will deepen your understanding of the main idea.

HOW DO YOU RECOGNIZE A MAIN IDEA?

As you read through a passage, you must **think as you read**. If you merely take in words, you will come to the end of the passage without understanding much of what you have read. Reading is an active process, as opposed to watching television, which is passive. You must actively engage your mind, and, as you read, keep asking yourself, "What's the point?"

Here are three strategies that will help you find the main idea.

1 Look for general versus specific ideas.
2 Use the topic to lead you to the main idea.
3 Use key words to lead you to the main idea.

Each strategy is explained on the following pages.

1   Look for General versus Specific Ideas

You saw in the paragraph on gossip that the main idea is a *general* idea supported by *specific* ideas. The following practices will improve your skill at separating general from specific ideas. Learning how to tell the difference between general and specific ideas will help you locate the main idea.

➤ Practice 1

In each of the following groups—many based on textbook selections—one statement is the general point, and the other statements are specific support for the point. Identify each point with a P and each statement of support with an S.

Example

 _S_ Women are less likely than men to become full professors.

 _S_ Women who become professors are generally paid less than their male counterparts.

 _P_ Women often face discrimination in the field of education.

 _S_ Female professors are not given an equal number of important committee assignments.

(The third statement is the general idea. It is supported by three examples of discrimination against women.)

1. _S_ A. Lottery winners have been known to use their winnings to feed their addictions to gambling and/or drugs.

   _S_ B. Other lottery winners report squandering their money to help out a never-ending stream of "hard luck" relatives and friends.

   _S_ C. Some lottery winners invest large sums on business ventures they know nothing about and wind up losing all they have invested.

   _P_ D. Winning the lottery can create as many problems as it solves.

   Answers A, B, and C describe three problems of winning the lottery.

2. _S_ A. People like to interact with other people as they shop.

   _S_ B. People like to see, touch, try on, and sometimes even smell the items they intend to buy.

   _S_ C. Many people still use shopping as simply an excuse to get out of the house.

   _P_ D. Despite its growing popularity, Internet shopping will never entirely replace shopping in stores.   Answers A, B, and C give specific reasons why Internet shopping is not enough.

3. _S_ A. For much of the twentieth century, people regarded cancer as a death sentence.

   _P_ B. Attitudes toward cancer used to be very different from those of today.

   _S_ C. Few people with cancer were willing to speak openly about battling the disease.

   _S_ D. Many people thought that having cancer was contagious.   Answers A, C, and D give examples of old attitudes toward cancer.

4. _S_ A. Instead of simply offering printed material on loan, modern libraries now allow patrons to borrow CDs, videos, and DVDs.

   _S_ B. Even very small libraries now feature access to computers, where patrons may "surf" the Internet.

   _P_ C. Libraries have changed drastically in the past decade to keep up with the demands of an ever-changing society.

   _S_ D. Some libraries even feature refreshment stands that sell beverages and snacks.   Answers A, B, and D describe three specific ways libraries have changed.

5. _S_ A. By age 14, 81 percent of young people have tried drinking.

   _S_ B. By the time they graduate from high school, more than 43 percent of teenagers have experimented with illegal drugs.

   _P_ C. In the United States, teenage drug and alcohol use is especially common.

   _S_ D. About one-third of teenagers who have tried illegal drugs have also tried at least one highly addictive and toxic substance, such as cocaine or heroin.   Answers A, B, and D give three statistics on drug and alcohol use by American teenagers.

6. _S_ A. Franklin's discoveries relating to electricity and lightning led him to invent lightning rods, which could safely conduct strokes of lightning into the ground.

   _P_ B. Benjamin Franklin regularly used scientific principles in inventing useful items.

   _S_ C. Franklin employed contemporary scientific principles to develop his "Pennsylvania Fireplace"—a design for a more efficient stove.

   _S_ D. Franklin's study of optics led him to invent bifocals.   Answers A, C, and D give examples of Franklin's use of scientific principles to invent useful items.

7. _S_ A. Many infant girls are given up to Westerners for adoption.

   _P_ B. The traditional Chinese preference for boys, coupled with that country's "one child" policy, has led to some disturbing consequences.

   _S_ C. Other infant girls are not given adequate medical care.

   _S_ D. The development of ultrasound technology to determine a child's gender prior to birth has led to the death by abortion of hundreds of thousands of unborn Chinese girls.   Answers A, C, and D describe specific consequences of China's "one child" policy.

8. _S_ A. A butcher by the name of Phillip Armour opened a meat market in California gold rush territory and then channeled his profits into creating one of the nation's largest meat processing plants in Chicago.

   _S_ B. Henry Wells and William Fargo offered many miners secure, honest banking, which led their company, Wells Fargo, to become a giant in the banking industry.

   _P_ C. Many people used their wits, not their shovels, to find a fortune during the California gold rush of 1848–1849.

   _S_ D. A merchant by the name of Levi Strauss made large profits by selling clothing and other necessities to miners.   Answers A, B, and D give examples of people who used their wits to make fortunes during the gold rush.

9. _S_ A. The number of Category 4 and Category 5 hurricanes has nearly doubled in the past three decades, fulfilling some scientists' predictions that global warming will lead to more severe weather.

   _P_ B. There is growing evidence that global warming is real.

   _S_ C. In the past 100-plus years of record-keeping, eight of the ten hottest years have occurred since 1996.

   _S_ D. According to scientists who study the movement of fields of ice, the ice surrounding the North Pole has entered a state of accelerating, long-term decline.   Answers A, C, and D give evidence indicating that global warming is real.

10.   _S_ A. The separation stage involves the removal of the individual from his or her former status.

   _S_ B. The third stage is the rite of aggregation, which is the readmission of the individual into society in the newly acquired status.

   _P_ C. Rites of passage, which mark the transition of an individual from one stage of life to another, involve three crucial stages.

   _S_ D. The rite of marginality is a period of transition involving specific rituals and often suspension from normal social contact.   Answers A, B, and D describe three crucial stages in rites of passage.

2   Use the Topic to Lead You to the Main Idea

You already know that to find the main idea of a selection, you look first for a general statement. You then check to see if that statement is supported by most of the other material in the paragraph. If it is, you've found the main idea. Another approach that can help you find the main idea of a selection is to find its topic.

The **topic** is the general subject of a selection. It can often be expressed in one or more words. Knowing the topic can help you find a writer's main point about that topic.

Textbook authors use the title of each chapter to state the overall topic of that chapter. They also provide many topics and subtopics in boldface headings within the chapter. For example, here is the title of a chapter in a sociology textbook, followed by a topic within the chapter and subtopics under that topic:

> Socialization (29 pages)
> >Agents of Socialization
> >>The Family
> >>The Neighborhood
> >>Religion
> >>Day Care
> >>The School
> >>Peer Groups

If you were studying the above chapter, you could use the headings to help find the main ideas—one of which is that there are six different agents of socialization.

But there are many times when you are not given topics—with standardized reading tests, for example, or with individual paragraphs in articles or textbooks. To find the topic of a selection when the topic is not given, ask this simple question:

Who or what is the selection about?

For example, look again at the beginning of the paragraph that started this chapter:

> [1]Social psychologists have found that almost everyone gossips. [2]Male or female, young or old, blue-collar or professional, humans love to talk about one another. [3]All too often, such gossip is viewed as a frivolous waste of time.

What, in a phrase, is the above paragraph about? On the line below, write what you think is the topic.

Topic: _____ *Gossip* _____

You probably answered that the topic is "gossip." As you reread the paragraph, you saw that, in fact, every sentence in it is about gossip.

The next step after finding the topic is to decide what main point the author is making about the topic. Authors often present their main idea in a single sentence. (This sentence is also known as the **main idea sentence** or the **topic sentence**.) As we have already seen, the main point about gossip is "it actually serves several important functions in the human community."

☑ Check Your Understanding

Let's look now at another paragraph. Read it and then see if you can answer the questions that follow.

> [1]Since 1883, most American schools have used the A–F grading system. [2]But many experts believe that the current letter grading system is bad for students. [3]One problem is that letter grades are too simplistic. [4]A student who gets feedback in the form of a letter may not understand how to improve. [5]An "A" doesn't tell a student what she did right, nor does an "F" tell a student what she did wrong. [6]Another flaw is that schools and teachers are inconsistent in their use of letter grades. [7]An "A" might be easy to get at one school and very difficult to get at another school. [8]It is not fair to give students the same grade for different amounts of work. [9]Finally, grades may be inaccurate, with some teachers giving good marks because they don't want to hurt their students' feelings or because they want to help students improve their self-esteem. [10]This sends a confusing message to students who don't do their work. [11]It is also unfair to the students who actually try hard to earn good grades.

1. What is the *topic* of the paragraph? In other words, what is the paragraph about? (It often helps as you read to look for and even circle a word, term, or idea that is repeated in the paragraph.)

   The A–F grading system
   _____

2. What is the *main idea* of the paragraph? In other words, what point is the author making about the topic? (Remember that the main idea will be supported by the other material in the paragraph.)

The current letter grading system is bad for students.

Explanation:

As the first sentence of the paragraph suggests, the topic is "the A–F grading system." Continuing to read the paragraph, you see that, in fact, everything in it is about this grading system. And the main idea is clearly that "the current letter grading system is bad for students." This idea is a general one that sums up what the entire paragraph is about. It is an "umbrella" statement under which all the other material in the paragraph fits. The parts of the paragraph could be shown as follows:

Topic: A–F grading system

Main idea: The current letter grading system is bad for students.

Supporting details:
1. Too simplistic.
2. Used inconsistently.
3. Inaccurate.

➤ **Practice 2**   *Wording of answers to the topic questions may vary.*

The following practice will sharpen your sense of the difference between a topic, the point about the topic (the main idea), and supporting details.

Read each paragraph below and do the following:

1 Ask yourself, "What seems to be the topic of the paragraph?" (It often helps to look for and even circle a word or idea that is repeated in the paragraph.)

2 Next, ask yourself, "What point is the writer making about this topic?" This will be the main idea. It is stated in one of the sentences in the paragraph.

3 Then test what you think is the main idea by asking, "Is this statement supported by most of the other material in the paragraph?"

> **Hint:** When looking for the topic, make sure you do not pick one that is either **too broad** (covering a great deal more than is in the selection) or **too narrow** (covering only part of the selection). The topic and the main idea of a selection must include everything in that selection—no more and no less.

Paragraph 1

[1]Halloween is often associated with ancient, pagan festivals or with the Catholic observance of All Saint's Day. [2]But the truth is that Halloween as we celebrate it today is mostly an American invention. [3]The Irish and Scottish, who may have first observed the holiday, didn't even carve pumpkins before coming to the United States. [4]Because the pumpkin is an American fruit, they carved their jack-o'-lanterns only out of turnips and potatoes. [5]So it wasn't until immigrants brought the holiday to the United States around 1840 that scary, glowing orange faces became a regular sight on Halloween. [6]Observers of Halloween didn't dress up in scary costumes, either, until the holiday had been American for over sixty years. [7]That practice originated around 1900, when communities started organizing costume parties to prevent children from taking part in the vandalism that was then the tradition. [8]Before 1900, people were more likely to see children tipping over outhouses than walking around in costumes on Halloween. [9]Finally, even "trick-or-treating" was an American invention. [10]It was the Boy Scouts of America who popularized the practice in the 1930s, as an even more appealing alternative to getting into mischief. [11]Many Americans might be surprised to learn that their own grandparents were some of the first people in history to go door-to-door asking for candy on Halloween.

1. What is the *topic* of the paragraph? In other words, what (in one or more words) is the paragraph about? _____ *Halloween* _____

__2__ 2. What *point* is the writer making about the topic? In other words, which sentence states the *main idea* of the paragraph? In the space provided, write the number of the sentence containing the main idea.

> The word *Halloween* is mentioned six times in the paragraph. Sentence 1 introduces the topic. The details in sentences 3–11 give examples of how Americans altered the traditional observance of Halloween.

Paragraph 2

[1]The American criminal justice system is often unjust. [2]Many of the poor spend months awaiting trial, while those with money are able to use bonds to secure their release. [3]Defense attorneys encourage plea bargaining or pleading guilty (whether or not one committed the crime) in return for being charged with a lesser offense. [4]Judges dislike "unnecessary trials," and they impose harsher sentences on those who insist on going to trial. [5]Judges also have biases which influence their sentencing. [6]Factors that have nothing to do with the offense, but which affect sentencing, include age, employment, and the number of previous arrests. [7]Even when the offense is the same, older defendants receive more lenient sentences, as do those with higher-status jobs and those with a better employment history.

1. What is the *topic* of the paragraph? _____
   _____ *The American criminal justice system* _____

_____1_____   2. What *point* is the writer making about the topic? In the space provided, write the number of the sentence containing the main idea.

> Sentences 2–7 provide details supporting the point that American criminal justice is often unjust.

Paragraph 3

¹The ability to empathize seems to exist in a rudimentary form in even the youngest children. ²Research sponsored by the National Institute of Mental Health revealed what many parents know from experience: Virtually from birth, infants become visibly upset when they hear another baby crying, and children who are a few months old cry when they observe another child in tears. ³Young children have trouble distinguishing others' distress from their own. ⁴If, for example, one child hurts his finger, another baby might put her own finger into her mouth as if she were feeling pain. ⁵Researchers report cases in which children who see their parents in tears wipe their own eyes, even though they might not be crying.

1. What is the *topic* of the paragraph? _The ability to empathize [in children]_

_____1_____   2. What *point* is the writer making about the topic? In the space provided, write the number of the sentence containing the main idea.

> Sentences 2–5 list evidence which supports the idea that very young children are empathetic.

Paragraph 4

¹Popular during the 1950s, the drive-in movie disappeared for a number of reasons. ²The most important was land value. ³Drive-ins were built on undeveloped edges of cities and towns. ⁴When these areas expanded in the 1960s and 1970s, it didn't make sense for a business used only after dark and mostly in warm weather to take up valuable space. ⁵Drive-ins were replaced by industrial parks, tract housing, and shopping malls with indoor theaters. ⁶Another reason was daylight savings time, which became standardized in most areas by the late 1960s. ⁷Theaters had to synchronize their first show with the setting sun. ⁸In the summer, they couldn't get started until nine o'clock, too late for families that had to get up early. ⁹Also, moviegoers began to expect more sophisticated projection and sound than those offered by drive-ins. ¹⁰Furthermore, people lost interest in drive-ins for family entertainment as movies became more violent and sexually explicit. ¹¹The last of the drive-ins vanished when cable television and VCRs came on the scene. ¹²People could now see recent movies without leaving their homes.

1. What is the *topic* of the paragraph? _____ _Drive-in movies_ _____

_____1_____   2. What *point* is the writer making about the topic? In the space provided, write the number of the sentence containing the main idea.

> The word *drive-in(s)* appears six times in the passage. Sentence 1 contains the key words *a number of reasons*. Sentences 2–12 list reasons why drive-ins have disappeared.

3 Find and Use Key Words to Lead You to the Main Idea

Sometimes authors make it fairly easy to find their main idea. They announce it by using **key words** that are easy to recognize. First to note are **list words**, which tell you a list of items is to follow. For example, the main idea in the paragraph about gossip was stated like this: "However, it actually serves several important functions in the human community." The expression *several important functions* helps you zero in on your target: the main idea. You realize that the paragraph will be about specific functions of gossip.

Here are some common word groups that often announce a main idea. Note that each of them contains a word that ends in *s*—a plural that suggests the supporting details will be a list of items.

List Words

several kinds (or ways) of	several causes of	some factors in
three advantages of	five steps	among the results
various reasons for	a number of effects	a series of

When expressions like these appear in a sentence, look carefully to see if that sentence might be the main idea. Chances are a sentence with such list words will be followed by a list of major supporting details.

☑ *Check Your Understanding*

Underline the **list words** in the following sentences.

> *Hint:* Remember that list words usually contain a word that ends in **s**.

Example   Children become unpopular for <u>several common reasons</u>.

1. Researchers have identified <u>two factors</u> that play a significant role in our dreams.

2. <u>Several steps</u> can help you overcome the fear of speaking and become an effective speaker.

3. <u>Three key differences</u> exist between the House and the Senate.

4. Money is a strong priority for people—even for those with plenty of it—for <u>a number of reasons</u>.

5. There are <u>four ways</u> that we often express our thoughts by body language rather than by speaking.

Explanation:

You should have underlined the following groups of words: *two factors, several steps, three key differences, a number of reasons,* and *four ways.*

In addition to list words, addition words can alert you to the main idea. **Addition words** are generally used right before a supporting detail. When you see this type of clue, you can assume that the detail it introduces fits under the umbrella of a main idea.

Here are some of the addition words that often introduce major supporting details and help you discover the main idea.

Addition Words

one	to begin with	also	further
first (of all)	for one thing	in addition	furthermore
second (ly)	other	next	last (of all)
third (ly)	another	moreover	final (ly)

☑ Check Your Understanding

Reread the paragraph about gossip and underline the **addition words** that alert you to supporting details.

¹Social psychologists have found that almost everyone gossips. ²Male or female, young or old, blue-collar or professional, humans love to talk about one another. ³All too often, such gossip is viewed as a frivolous waste of time. ⁴However, it actually serves several important functions in the human community. ⁵For one thing, gossip is a form of networking. ⁶Talking with our friends and coworkers about each other is our most effective means of keeping track of the ever-changing social dynamic. ⁷It tells us who is in, who is out, and who can help us climb the social or professional ladder. ⁸A second function of gossip is the building of influence. ⁹When we engage in gossip, we are able to shape people's opinions of ourselves. ¹⁰We tell stories that show ourselves in a good light—wise, compassionate, insightful, clever. ¹¹And when we listen sympathetically to the gossip of other people, they perceive us as warm and likable. ¹²A final and very powerful function of gossip is the creating of social alliances. ¹³There are few quicker ways to form a bond with another person than to share private information with him or her. ¹⁴The words "I wouldn't tell most people this, but . . ." instantly interest and flatter the listener. ¹⁵To talk about a third party, especially in a critical way, creates a bond with our listener and gives a feeling of shared superiority.

Explanation:

The words that introduce each new supporting detail for the main idea are *For one thing, second,* and *final.* These addition words introduce each of the three functions of gossip.

Note also that the main idea includes the list words *several important functions,* which signal that the supporting details will be a list of the functions of gossip. In this and many paragraphs, list words and addition words often work hand in hand.

The following chapter, "Supporting Details," includes further information about words that alert you to the main idea and the details that support it. But what you have already learned here will help you find main ideas.

LOCATIONS OF THE MAIN IDEA

Now you know how to recognize a main idea by 1) distinguishing between the general and the specific, 2) identifying the topic of a passage, and 3) using verbal clues. You are ready to find the main idea no matter where it is located in a paragraph.

A main idea may appear at any point within a paragraph. Very commonly, it shows up at the beginning, as either the first or the second sentence. However, main ideas may also appear further within a paragraph or even at the very end.

Main Idea at the Beginning

Main Idea
Supporting Detail
Supporting Detail
Supporting Detail
Supporting Detail

or

Introductory Detail
Main Idea
Supporting Detail
Supporting Detail
Supporting Detail

In textbooks, it is very common for the main idea to be either the first or the second sentence. See if you can underline the main idea in the following paragraph.

[1]As a result of more than sixty years of election surveys, we now know a great deal about American voters. [2]The wealthier and more educated they are, the more likely people are to support Republican candidates. [3]Men are a bit more likely to vote for Republicans, while women slightly favor Democrats. [4]African Americans vote for Democrats by a margin of more than four to one. [5]For generations, Catholics voted for Democrats, and Protestants (outside the South) favored Republicans; but today, Catholics and

Protestants have similar party preferences, and Southern voters have swung from the Democrats to the Republicans. [6]But perhaps the most significant fact has to do with the general lack of interest in politics. [7]Most Americans say politics is not an important part of their lives. [8]Only 42 percent of Americans bothered to vote in the 2004 presidential election.

In this paragraph, the main idea is in the first sentence. All the following sentences in the paragraph provide details about American voters.

☑ Check Your Understanding

Now read the following paragraph and see if you can underline its main idea:

[1]Today, most people in the Western world use a fork to eat. [2]<u>But before the eighteenth century, using a fork was highly discouraged.</u> [3]Most people in Europe ate with their hands. [4]People from the upper class used three fingers, while the commoners ate with five. [5]When an inventor from Tuscany created a miniature pitchfork for eating, Europeans thought that it was a strange utensil. [6]Men who used a fork were often ridiculed and considered feminine. [7]Priests called out against the fork, claiming that only human hands were worthy to touch the food God had blessed them with. [8]One wealthy noblewoman shocked clergymen by eating with a fork she designed herself. [9]Over dinner, they accused her of being too excessive. [10]When the woman died from the plague a few days later, the priests claimed her death was a punishment from the heavens. [11]They warned others that using a fork could bring them the same fate.

Explanation:

In the above paragraph, the main idea is stated in the second sentence. The first sentence introduces the topic, using a fork, but it is the idea in the second sentence—that before the eighteenth century, using a fork was highly discouraged—that is supported in the rest of the paragraph. So keep in mind that the first sentence may simply introduce or lead into the main idea of a paragraph.

Hint: Very often, a contrast word like *however, but, yet,* or *though* signals the main idea, as in the paragraph you have just read.

Main Idea in the Middle

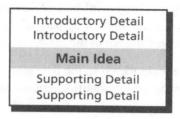

The main idea at times appears in the middle of a paragraph.

☑ *Check Your Understanding*

Here is an example of a paragraph in which the main idea is somewhere in the middle. Try to find it and underline it. Then read the explanation that follows.

> [1]Each year, as days grow shorter and nights grow colder, animals take action to survive the winter. [2]Many animals fly, swim, or walk hundreds or thousands of miles to the south in search of a warm winter home. [3]Earthworms travel too slowly to make a long journey to warmer regions. [4]But they will die if they get trapped in the frozen ground. [5]<u>To survive a brutal winter, earthworms practice vertical migration.</u> [6]They move from dirt that's close to the surface to dirt that's deeper down. [7]Each fall, the same instinct that sends geese flying south causes earthworms to start moving downward. [8]As little barbs that stick out of their bodies poke into the dirt, the earthworms contract their muscles. [9]This moves them downward to a point where they're below the soil that will freeze in the winter. [10]Only after winter passes and soil overhead warms up to 36 degrees or more do the earthworms tunnel back upward.

Explanation:

If you thought the fifth sentence gives the main idea, you were correct. The first four sentences introduce the topic of migrating for the winter and the challenge faced by earthworms. The fifth sentence then presents the writer's main idea, which is that they practice vertical migration. The rest of the paragraph develops that idea.

Main Idea at the End

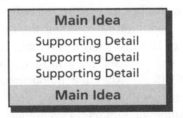

Sometimes all the sentences in a paragraph will lead up to the main idea, which is presented at the end. Here is an example of such a paragraph.

[1]Throughout history, a pinch of arsenic has been known as the weapon of choice for murderers who wished to discreetly do away with their victims. [2]Yet, in 1910, scientists created a compound containing a microscopic amount of arsenic that became the first effective remedy for the treatment of syphilis. [3]Today it remains an effective chemotherapy agent for acute forms of leukemia. [4]Botulinum toxin is another potent poison. [5]But in extremely diluted form, delivered as the drug Botox, it has proven effective in softening wrinkles, relieving migraine headaches, and lessening the spastic contractions caused by multiple sclerosis and cerebral palsy. [6]These are but two examples of the medical maxim that the difference between a substance being a poison or a medicine lies in the dosage.

Main Idea at the Beginning and End

At times an author may choose to state the main idea near the beginning of the paragraph and then emphasize it by restating it in other words later in the paragraph. In such cases, the main idea is both at the beginning and the end. Such is the case in the following paragraph.

[1]Most birds may be small, cute, and comical, but the more closely one looks at them, the more they come to look like little dinosaurs. [2]The most obvious similarity between birds and dinosaurs is the way they raise their young. [3]Specifically, dinosaurs are known to have laid eggs, just as birds do. [4]Paleontologists have discovered dinosaur eggs in over two hundred sites just

within the United States, and in Montana they have even found such eggs arranged in nests, suggesting that some dinosaurs cared for their young as they grew up, just as birds do. [5]Another, less obvious clue that birds are related to dinosaurs is that birds have scales and feathers. [6]Many birds have scales like a dinosaur's on their feet and ankles, and feathers themselves grow out of the same kinds of tissues that generate reptilian scales. [7]In fact, some dinosaurs are known to have had feathers themselves. [8]The most important similarity between birds and dinosaurs can be seen in the shape of their bones. [9]Scientists have discovered that the skeletons of many dinosaurs, even of the ferocious Tyrannosaurus Rex, contain wishbones, porous neck-bones, and disks of cartilage called "growth plates" at the ends of their long bones—features that are common in the skeletons of birds. [10]It may be difficult to accept, but swallows, sparrows, and even chickens are all distant relatives of the fearsome dinosaurs of ages past.

Note that the main idea—that birds may be related to dinosaurs—is expressed in different words in the first and last sentences.

➤ Practice 3

The main ideas of the following paragraphs appear at different locations—at the beginning, somewhere in the middle, or at the end. Identify each main idea by filling in its sentence number in the space provided.

_____3___ 1. [1]Everyone knows what it's like to have the "jitters" after one cup of coffee too many. [2]Those shaking hands and sleepless nights have convinced many that coffee is as unhealthy as alcohol or cigarettes. [3]However, the health benefits of coffee greatly outweigh its negative effects. [4]In addition to reducing the risk of diseases like diabetes and cirrhosis of the liver, those morning cups of joe have been shown to ward off two of America's most common killers: heart disease and cancer. [5]Coffee flushes the bloodstream of the excess fat that clogs arteries and also supplies a large dose of antioxidants, which prevent the formation of tumors. [6]Psychologically, the stimulant effects of a daily cup have proven to reduce suicide rates. [7]And as for the fear of a troublesome addiction to caffeine, that risk is often overstated. [8]Physical dependence on coffee becomes a possibility only after drinking five or more cups daily, significantly more than the two or three cups a day that Americans drink on average.

Sentences 1 and 2 are introductory details. Sentence 3 (the main idea) makes an assertion that sentences 4–8 support.

_____1___ 2. [1]Offering on-site child care for employees' children provides many physical and financial benefits to companies. [2]Such child-care facilities ease the strain on parents. [3]While they are at work, they can keep in touch with a baby or toddler and observe the care their child is receiving. [4]They are able to spend time with their children during breaks and lunch hours, and mothers can even nurse their babies at the center. [5]These benefits attract and keep capable workers with the company. [6]Surprisingly, providing child care can even reduce labor costs. [7]When the United Bank of Monterey, California, decided to measure the cost of its daycare center, officials found that the annual turnover of employees who used the center was just one-fourth that of employees who did not use it. [8]Users of the centers were also absent from work less often, and they took shorter maternity leaves. [9]After subtracting the center's costs from these savings, the bank saved more than $200,000.

Sentences 2–9 provide specific details showing the many benefits of on-site child care.

_____8_____

3. [1]In 1957, a team of archaeologists from the University of Pennsylvania uncovered a fabulous burial site just west of Ankara in Turkey. [2]From the richness of its trappings and the remains of an ancient palace nearby, the researchers concluded that it was the tomb of the legendary King Mita, or Midas. [3]Most remarkable of all was the fact that the dry climate had preserved the remains of a funeral meal that had been prepared some 2,700 years ago. [4]The remains of this elaborate feast were packed up and preserved for another forty-some years, until techniques for analyzing food residues had advanced enough to permit the re-creation of the funeral feast. [5]Using these archaeological findings, a chef at the University Museum created the "Midas Touch Banquet." [6]The most golden thing about the feast was the re-creation of the liquor that had been found in crystallized form in the goblets used at Midas's funeral. [7]It was an alcoholic beverage made from honey, barley and golden Muscat grapes. [8]Sometimes ancient fables, like the legend of King Midas, the man who could turn everything to gold, have a basis in fact.

Sentences 1–7 provide specific details which illustrate that ancient fables sometimes have a basis in fact.

_____7_____

4. [1]What do you think of as "cute"? [2]Kittens? [3]Paintings of children with big sad eyes? [4]Little dolls? [5]Golden retriever puppies? [6]If none of these examples triggers a fond "awwwwww" response in you, you are truly a rare individual. [7]Scientists who study human behavior say that we are hard-wired not only to identify certain characteristics as "cute," but to respond to them with affection and protectiveness. [8]Simply put, *cute* (as opposed to *beautiful*) means "baby-like, vulnerable, young, helpless." [9]And what we identify as "cute" are characteristics borrowed from our own human babies. [10]Those include big round faces, forward-facing eyes set low on the face, awkward floppy arms and legs, and a clumsy, side-to-side walk. [11]Because human babies are so helpless for so long, it is essential for our species' survival that adults respond strongly to such "cute" signals. [12]And indeed, nature has been so successful in this regard that we respond to collections of "cute" characteristics that are

Sentences 1–6 are introductory details. Sentences 8–15 support the assertion, contained in sentence 7, that we are hard-wired to identify and respond in a positive manner to characteristics termed "cute."

outside our own species—just witness our reaction to pandas, penguins, and puppies. [13]We have such a deeply-rooted response to cuteness that we respond even to cute non-animals. [14]It's no mystery why designers of cars like the Beetle and the Mini Cooper made their vehicles look round-headed and smiling. [15]They know that as absurd as it may be, people want to take "cute" things home and care for them.

A Note on the Central Point

Just as a paragraph may have a main idea, a longer selection may have a **central point**, also known as a **central idea** or **thesis**. The longer selection might be an essay, an article, or a section of a textbook chapter. You can find a central point in the same way that you find a main idea—by identifying the topic (which is often suggested by the title of the selection) and then looking at the supporting material. The paragraphs within the longer reading will provide supporting details for the central point. You will see, for example, that the essay that ends this chapter has a central idea.

A Final Thought

Whether we are readers, writers, listeners, or speakers, the "heart" of clear communication is the main idea, or point, and the support for the main idea. Look at the following diagram:

THE HEART OF CLEAR COMMUNICATION

Good writers and speakers:
1. Make a point
2. Support the point

Good readers and listeners:
1. Recognize the point
2. Recognize the support for the point

The diagram underscores the importance of the most important of all reading skills: the ability to identify main ideas. The diagram also shows that the ability to identify supporting details for the main idea is an almost equally important skill.

CHAPTER REVIEW

In this chapter, you learned the following:

- Recognizing the main idea is the most important key to good comprehension. The main idea is a general "umbrella" idea under which fits all the specific supporting material of the passage.

- Three strategies that will help you find the main idea are to 1) look for general versus specific ideas; 2) use the topic (the general subject of a selection) to lead you to the main idea; and 3) use verbal clues to lead you to the main idea.

- The main idea often appears at the beginning of a paragraph, though it may appear elsewhere in a paragraph.

The next chapter—Chapter 2—will sharpen your understanding of the specific details that authors use to support and develop their main ideas.

On the Web: If you are using this book in class, you can visit our website for additional practice in recognizing main ideas. Go to **www.townsendpress.com** and click on "Online Exercises."

➤ *Review Test 1*

To review what you've learned in this chapter, answer each of the following questions by filling in the blank.

1. To become an active reader, you need to think as you read a paragraph or selection by constantly asking yourself the question, "What is the _____*point*_____?"   See page 23.

2. To help decide if a certain sentence is the main idea, ask yourself, "Is this statement _____*supported*_____ by most or all of the other sentences in the paragraph?"   See page 31.

3. One strategy that will help you find the main idea is to look for the _____*topic*_____—the general subject of a selection.   See page 29.

4. Addition words such as *first, second, also,* and *finally* often introduce key supporting _____*detail*_____s for a main idea.   See page 35.

5. While a main idea may appear at any place within a paragraph, in textbooks it most often appears at the _____*beginning*_____.   See page 36.

➤ *Review Test 2*

Here is a chance to apply your understanding of main ideas to a full-length selection. Read the article from *Time* magazine below, and then answer the questions that follow on main ideas. There are also vocabulary questions to help you practice the skill of understanding vocabulary in context.

Preview

Are you starving? Not for food; for sleep. If you're like many Americans, you've been sleep-deprived so long you no longer know how tired you are. Maybe you even take pride in being able to "get by" on little sleep. But as this article explains, sleep is not a luxury you can afford to be without.

Words to Watch

plummet (2): fall
mimic (5): imitate
circadian rhythm (6): recurring naturally on a twenty-four-hour cycle

GETTING A GOOD NIGHT'S SLEEP

Sora Song

1   Americans are not renowned for their powers of self-deprivation; doing without is not something we do particularly well. But experts say there is one necessity of life most of us consistently fail to get: a good night's sleep. The recommended daily requirements should sound familiar: eight hours of sleep a night for adults and at least an hour more for adolescents. Yet 71 percent of American adults and 85 percent of teens do not get the suggested amount, to the detriment of body and mind. "Sleep is sort of like food," says Robert Stickgold, a cognitive neuroscientist at Harvard Medical School. But, he adds, there's one important difference: "You can be quite starved and still alive, and I think we appreciate how horrible that must be. But many of us live on the edge of sleep starvation and just accept it."

2   Part of the problem is we are so used to being chronically sleep-deprived—and have become so adept at coping with that condition—that we no longer notice how exhausted we really are. In 2003, sleep expert David Dinges and colleagues at the University of Pennsylvania School of Medicine tested the effects of restricting slumber to eight, six, or four hours a night for two weeks. During the first few days, subjects sleeping less than eight hours admitted to being fatigued and lacking alertness. But by Day 4, most people had adapted to their new baseline drowsiness and reported feeling fine—even as their cognitive performance continued to plummet°.

3   Over time, the experiment's sleep-restricted subjects became so impaired that they had difficulty concentrating on even the simplest tasks, like pushing a button in response to a light. "The human brain is only capable of about 16 hours of wakefulness [a day]," says Dinges. "When you get beyond that, it can't function as efficiently, as accurately or as well."

4   In the real world, people overcome their somnolence—at least temporarily—by drinking coffee, taking a walk around the block or chatting with office mates. But then they find themselves nodding off in meetings or, worse, behind the wheel. Those short snatches of unconsciousness are what researchers call microsleep, a sure sign of sleep deprivation. "If people are falling asleep because 'the room was hot' or 'the meeting was boring,' that's not coping with sleep loss. I would argue that they're eroding their productive capability," says Dinges.

5   What most people don't realize is that the purpose of sleep may be more to rest the mind than to rest the body. Indeed, most of the benefits of eight hours' sleep seem to accrue to the brain: sleep helps consolidate memory, improve judgment, promote learning and concentration, boost mood, speed reaction time and sharpen problem solving and accuracy. According to Sonia Ancoli-Israel, a psychologist at the University of California at San Diego who has done extensive studies in the aging population,

lack of sleep may even mimic° the symptoms of dementia. In recent preliminary findings, she was able to improve cognitive function in patients with mild to moderate Alzheimer's simply by treating their underlying sleep disorder. "The need for sleep does not change a lot with age," says Ancoli-Israel, but often because of disruptive illnesses and the medications used to treat them, "the ability to sleep does."

6   If you're one of the otherwise healthy yet perpetually under-rested, there's plenty you can do to pay back your sleep debt. For starters, you can catch up on lost time. Take your mom's advice, and get to bed early. Turn off the TV half an hour sooner than usual. If you can't manage to snooze longer at night, try to squeeze in a midday nap. The best time for a siesta is between noon and 3 p.m., for about 30 to 60 minutes, according to Timothy Roehrs, director of research at the Sleep Disorders and Research Center at Henry Ford Hospital in Detroit. He advises against oversleeping on weekend mornings to make up for a workweek of deprivation; later rising can disrupt your circadian rhythm°, making it even harder later to get a full night's rest.

7   According to Dinge's analysis of data from the 2003 American Time Use Survey, the most common reason we shortchange ourselves on sleep is work. (The second biggest reason, surprisingly, is that we spend too much time driving around in our cars.) But consider that in giving up two hours of bedtime to do more work, you're losing a quarter of your recommended nightly dose and gaining just 12 percent more time during the day. What if you could be 12 percent more productive instead? "You have to realize that if you get a good night's sleep, you will actually be more efficient and get more done the next day. The more you give up on sleep, the harder it is to be productive," says Ancoli-Israel. "What is it going to be?"

8   If mental sharpness is your goal, the answer is clear: stop depriving yourself, and get a good night's sleep.

Reading Comprehension Questions

Vocabulary in Context

_B_   1. In the sentence below, the word *detriment* (dĕt′rə-mənt) means
    A. consideration.
    B. harm.   Ask, "How does failure to get enough sleep
    C. influence.   affect the body and mind?"
    D. benefit.

    "Yet 71 percent of American adults and 85 percent of teens do not get the suggested amount, to the detriment of body and mind." (Paragraph 1)

_C_   2. In the sentence below, the word *baseline* (bās′līn) means
    A. a baseball term which refers to the area within which a runner must stay when running between bases.
    B. a line bounding each back end in a tennis court.
    C. a line serving as a base, as for purposes of measurement.
    D. caused by extreme boredom.   Ask, "How do researchers measure
                                 the effects of drowsiness on cognitive performance?"
    "But by Day 4, most people had adapted to their new baseline drowsiness and reported feeling fine—even as their cognitive performance continued to plummet." (Paragraph 2)

_D_   3. In the sentence below, the word *somnolence* (sŏm′nə-ləns) means
    A. lack of sensitivity.
    B. laziness.   The activities mentioned in the sentence suggest that
    C. boredom.   people are trying to overcome sleepiness.
    D. sleepiness.

    "In the real world, people overcome their somnolence—at least temporarily—by drinking coffee, taking a walk around the block or chatting with office mates." (Paragraph 4)

_A_   4. In the sentence below, the words *accrue to* (ə-krōō′ tōō) mean
    A. improve.
    B. put pressure on.   The words *helps, improve, promote, boost, speed,*
    C. wear away.   and *sharpen* all suggest gains or benefits.
    D. communicate to.

    "Indeed, most of the benefits of eight hours' sleep seem to accrue to the brain: sleep helps consolidate memory, improve judgment, promote learning and concentration, boost mood, speed reaction time and sharpen problem solving and accuracy." (Paragraph 5)

Main Ideas

___C___ 5. The central idea of this selection is that
      A. Americans are willing to deprive themselves of sleep in order to complete more work.
      B. Americans use unsuccessful strategies in order to compensate for lack of sleep.
      C. Americans may not realize it, but chronic sleep deprivation is actually harming them and lowering their productivity.   Answer A
      D. the need for sleep does not change a lot with age.   is stated only in paragraph 7; answer B only in paragraph 4; and answer D only in paragraph 5.

___B___ 6. The main idea of paragraph 1 is stated in the
      A. first sentence.   The first sentence introduces the general topic
      B. second sentence.   of deprivation. Sentences 3–7 support the
      C. third sentence.   main idea by telling what research indicates
      D. fourth sentence.   about Americans' sleep deprivation.

___A___ 7. The main idea of paragraph 2 is stated in the
      A. first sentence.   The rest of the paragraph
      B. second sentence.   explains the effects of
      C. third sentence.   chronic sleep deprivation.
      D. fourth sentence.

___A___ 8. The main idea of paragraph 5 is stated in the
      A. first sentence.   The rest of the paragraph
      B. second sentence.   provides examples of how
      C. third sentence.   sleep benefits the mind.
      D. fourth sentence.

___C___ 9. The topic of paragraph 6 is
      A. sleep-deprived people.   All the sentences in the
      B. oversleeping on weekends.   paragraph focus on how to
      C. paying back your sleep debt.   pay back the sleep debt.
      D. midday naps.

___A___ 10. The main idea of paragraph 6 is stated in the
      A. first sentence.   The rest of the paragraph lists
      B. second sentence.   ways in which people can pay
      C. sixth sentence.   back their sleep debt.
      D. seventh sentence.

Discussion Questions

1. How much sleep do you typically get in a night? Do you feel that you sleep enough? If not, what do you think are the major reasons you aren't sleeping more? What are some ways in which you could restructure your life in order to get a full eight hours of sleep a night?

2. A scientist quoted in paragraph 1 compares sleep with food, but notes that while we would not accept being deprived of food, we accept being sleep-deprived. Why do you think so many people simply accept the fact that they don't get enough sleep?

3. The selection mentions nodding off at meetings and falling asleep at the wheel as two potential consequences of sleep deprivation. What are some other negative consequences that you can think of? Conversely, what might some positive consequences be if people got more sleep?

4. In your view, are there any factors which contribute to Americans' sleep deprivation other than those mentioned in the selection? If so, what are they, and what—if anything—could be done to counteract them?

Note: Writing assignments for this selection appear on page 561.

Check Your Performance   **MAIN IDEAS**

Activity	Number Right	Points	Score
Review Test 1 (5 items)	_____	× 6 =	_____
Review Test 2 (10 items)	_____	× 7 =	_____
		TOTAL SCORE =	_____%

Enter your total score into the **Reading Performance Chart: Review Tests** on the inside back cover.

MAIN IDEAS: Mastery Test 1

A. In each of the following groups, one statement is the general point, and the other statements are specific support for the point. Write the letter of each point in the space provided.

_D_ 1. A. German immigrants added such words as *kindergarten*, *hoodlum*, and *delicatessen* to the American vocabulary.

B. We owe common phrases like *to bad-mouth*, *a high five*, and *jam session* to African speech patterns.

C. If you've eaten spaghetti, pizza, or lasagna, you've eaten a dish named by Italians.

D. Various ethnic groups and races have contributed to the English language as Americans speak it.   What have *various ethnic groups and races* (list words in answer D) contributed to American English? Answers A, B, and C list examples.

_C_ 2. A. Most tall buildings in the United States are struck, on average, 100 times per year.

B. In one recorded incident, the Empire State Building was struck 15 times in 15 minutes.

C. The old saying that lightning never strikes twice is far from true.

D. The exceptions don't just apply to buildings: Roy Sullivan, a U.S. forest ranger, was struck by lightning seven times over the course of 40 years.   Answers A, B, and D are examples which disprove the saying that lightning never strikes twice.

_B_ 3. A. While many people fear a piranha will bite off their finger, in fact the majority of a piranha's diet is vegetable matter.

B. Although piranhas are most notorious as fearsome killers, they actually make good pets.

C. Although piranhas will attack other types of fish in an aquarium, they don't attack one another and can coexist peacefully.

D. Piranhas are very hardy and adaptable to different types of water, so they require a minimum of tank maintenance.

Answers A, C, and D are examples which support the main idea that piranhas make good pets: they eat mostly vegetable matter, don't attack one another, and are hardy and adaptable.

(Continues on next page)

B. The main idea may appear at any place within each of the two paragraphs that follow. Write the number of each main idea sentence in the space provided.

_____3_____ 4. [1]Thoughts are forever coming into and going out of our minds. [2]They are a lot like an ongoing movie. [3]There are a number of types or categories of thoughts that are commonly featured in the movies of our minds. [4]Planning thoughts are those in which we try to decide exactly what to do, specifically ("I'll go to Burger King for lunch today") or generally ("I really should quit this job"). [5]Desire thoughts include wishes for anything, from sex to world peace. [6]Fear thoughts include any type of worry: unhealthy eating, money, work, you name it. [7]Happy or appreciative thoughts are often noting pleasurable sensations such as the sun on one's face or the smell of freshly brewed coffee. [8]Judging thoughts are those in which we approve of, or, more likely, criticize anything or anyone. [9]Righteous thoughts are those in which we are right and other people are wrong. [10]Angry thoughts can be self-hating thoughts or feelings of hatred for the behavior of others.

Sentences 1 and 2 introduce the topic of thoughts. Sentence 3 contains the list words *a number of types*. Sentences 4–10 list types of thoughts.

_____2_____ 5. [1]One of the contradictions of humanity is that people long for peace while at the same time they glorify war. [2]War is so common that a cynic might say it is the normal state of society. [3]Sociologist Pitirim Sorokin counted the wars in Europe from 500 B.C. to A.D. 1925. [4]He documented 967 wars, an average of one war every two or three years. [5]Counting years or parts of a year in which a country was at war, at 28 percent Germany had the lowest record of warfare. [6]Spain's 67 percent gave it the dubious distinction of being the most war-prone. [7]Sorokin found that Russia, the land of his birth, had experienced only one peaceful quarter-century during the entire previous thousand years. [8]Since the time of William the Conqueror, who took power in 1066, England was at war an average of 56 out of each 100 years. [9]Spain fought even more often. [10]It is worth noting the history of the United States in this regard: Since 1850, it has intervened militarily around the world about 160 times, an average of once a year.

Sentence 1 introduces the topic of war. Sentences 3–10 support the main idea in sentence 2: "War is . . . common."

MAIN IDEAS: Mastery Test 2

A. In each of the following groups—all based on textbook selections—one statement is the general point, and the other statements are specific support for the point. Write the letter of each point in the space provided.

___D___ 1.

Answers A, B, and C are examples from around the globe of parent and infant bed sharing: in Appalachia, Japan, and rural Guatemala.

A. Appalachian children of eastern Kentucky typically fall asleep with their parents for the first two years of their life.

B. Japanese children usually lie next to their mothers throughout infancy and early childhood and continue to sleep with a parent or other family member until adolescence.

C. Among the Maya of rural Guatemala, mother-infant co-sleeping is interrupted only by the birth of a new baby, at which time the older child is moved beside the father or to another bed in the same room.

D. Parent and infant bed sharing is common around the globe, in industrialized and unindustrialized countries alike.

___C___ 2.

Answer C contains the list words Some mountain ranges. *Answers A, B, and D list mountain ranges which have been formed by collisions between continents: the Himalayas, the Alps, and the Urals.*

A. About 45 million years ago, the subcontinent of India collided with the continent of Asia to form the spectacular Himalaya Mountains.

B. The Alps are thought to have formed as a result of a collision between Africa and Europe many millions of years ago.

C. Some mountain ranges have formed as the result of collisions between continents.

D. The European continent collided with the Asian continent to produce the Ural Mountains, which extend in a north-south direction through present-day Russia.

___A___ 3.

Answer A contains list words (fewer social divisions). Answers B, C, and D list reasons why people in hunting and gathering societies are not divided socially.

A. Hunting and gathering societies tend to have fewer social divisions than other societies.

B. Because what they hunt and gather is perishable, hunters and gatherers accumulate few personal possessions.

C. There is no money and no way to become wealthier than anyone else in hunting and gathering societies.

D. Hunters and gatherers place a high value on sharing their food resources, which are essential to their survival.

(Continues on next page)

B. The main idea may appear at any place within each of the two paragraphs that follow. Write the number of each main idea sentence in the space provided.

_____1_____ 4. [1]Data across time, cultures, and methodologies strongly support the notion that people lose their cool and behave more aggressively in hot temperatures. [2]More violent crimes occur in the summer than in the winter, during hot years than in cooler years, and in hot cities than in cooler cities at any given time of year. [3]The numbers of political uprisings, riots, homicides, assaults, rapes, and reports of violence all peak in the summer months. [4]Indirect acts of aggression also increase in excessive heat. [5]As temperatures rise to uncomfortable levels, laboratory participants become more likely to interpret ambiguous events in hostile terms, and drivers in cars without air conditioning become more likely to honk their horns at motorists whose cars are stalled in front of them. [6]Researchers have also found that as the temperature rises, major-league baseball pitchers are significantly more likely to hit batters with a pitch.

Sentences 2–6 support the main idea, stated in sentence 1, that people "behave more aggressively in hot temperatures."

_____8_____ 5. [1]Is it really possible to convince people that they are guilty of a crime they did not commit? [2]To search for an answer, researchers recruited pairs of college students to work on a fast- or slow-paced computer task. [3]At one point, the computer crashed, and students were accused of having caused the damage by pressing a key that they had been specifically instructed to avoid. [4]All students were actually innocent and denied the charge. [5]In half the sessions, however, the second student (who was really an actor, posing as a participant) said that she had seen the student hit the forbidden key. [6]Demonstrating the process of compliance, many students confronted by this false witness agreed to sign a confession handwritten by the experimenter. [7]Next, demonstrating the process of internalization, some students later "admitted" their guilt to a stranger (also an actor) after the experiment was supposedly over and the two were alone. [8]In short, innocent people who are vulnerable to suggestion can be induced to confess and to internalize guilt by the presentation of false evidence.

Sentence 1 introduces the topic. Sentences 2–7 give details that support the main idea (sentence 8) that "innocent people . . . can be induced to confess and to internalize guilt by the presentation of false evidence."

MAIN IDEAS: Mastery Test 3

A. In each of the following groups—all based on textbook selections—one statement is the general point, and the other statements are specific support for the point. Write the letter of each point in the space provided.

___C___ 1.

Answer C contains list words *(things they used to do)*. Answers A, B, and D list examples of things that American women are now too busy to do.

    A. In the 1950s, more than 75 percent of American households owned sewing machines, but now that figure is under 5 percent.

    B. As more women began working outside the home, fewer and fewer undertook unpaid volunteer work.

    C. Women who work outside the home are too busy to do the things they used to do.

    D. Women used to clip manufacturer's coupons—today less than 3 percent of manufacturers' coupons are ever redeemed.

___D___ 2.

Answers A, B, and C are examples of differing conditions under which marriages may be dissolved in different societies: preindustrial, traditional Islamic, and American.

    A. In many preindustrial societies in which children are of particular importance, sterility or impotence are primary grounds for divorce.

    B. In some traditional patriarchal Islamic societies, husbands needed only to proclaim "I divorce thee" three times in front of two witnesses for marriages to end.

    C. Throughout most of American history, cruelty, desertion, or adultery were the most common legal grounds for divorce.

    D. Just as norms regulate marriage and family relationships, they also specify conditions under which marriages may be dissolved.

___A___ 3.

Answers B, C, and D are examples that support the main idea contained in answer A, that "the natural world is not particularly moral."

    A. Contrary to what some animal lovers believe, the natural world is not particularly moral.

    B. Infanticide, siblicide (killing of siblings), and rape can be observed in many kinds of animals.

    C. Infidelity is common in so-called pair-bonded species.

    D. Cannibalism can be expected in all species that are not strictly vegetarians.

(Continues on next page)

B. The main idea may appear at any place within each of the two paragraphs that follow. Write the number of each main idea sentence in the space provided.

___5___ 4. [1]Married people are more likely than those who are single, divorced, or widowed to survive cancer for five years, gay men infected with HIV are less likely to contemplate suicide if they have close ties than if they do not, and people who have a heart attack are less likely to have a second one if they live with someone than if they live alone. [2]Among students stressed by schoolwork, and among the spouses of cancer patients, more social support is also associated with a stronger immune response. [3]Based on a review of eighty-one studies, researchers have concluded that in times of stress, having social support lowers blood pressure, lessons the secretion of stress hormones, and strengthens the immune system. [4]On the flip side of the coin, people who are lonely exhibit greater age-related increases in blood pressure and have more difficulty sleeping at night. [5]There's no doubt about it: Being isolated from other people can be hazardous to your health.

Sentences 1–4 illustrate the main idea expressed in sentence 5—that being isolated from others can be a health hazard.

___2___ 5. [1]Individuals vary widely in what they dream about, the feelings associated with their dreams, and how often they remember dreams. [2]Nevertheless, there are some patterns that seem to apply to all dreams. [3]One pattern found in dream content relates to gender. [4]For example, although the dreams of men and women have become more similar over the last several decades, men more often dream about weapons, unfamiliar characters, male characters, aggressive interactions, and failure outcomes, whereas women are more likely to dream about being the victims of aggression. [5]Dream content also varies by age. [6]Very young children (ages 2 to 5) tend to have brief dreams, many of which involve animals; but the images are usually unrelated to each other, and there is seldom any emotional narrative or story line. [7]It is not until the child is 7 to 9 years old that dreams take on a narrative, sequential form. [8]Feelings and emotions also make their appearance in dreams in the years between 7 and 9, and children more often appear as characters in their own dreams at that age. [9]Between ages 9 and 15, dreams become more adult-like: Narratives follow well-developed story lines, other people play important roles, and there are many verbal exchanges in addition to motor activity. [10]Finally, cross-cultural studies have shown that people from different cultures report dream content consistent with the unique cultural patterns inherent in their respective cultures.

Sentence 1 introduces the topic of dreams. Sentence 2 contains the list words some patterns. Sentences 3–10 list examples of patterns related to gender, age, and culture. Note the addition words also (sentence 5) and Finally (sentence 10).

MAIN IDEAS: Mastery Test 4

The main ideas of the following paragraphs appear at different locations—the beginning, somewhere in the middle, or at the end. Identify each main idea by filling in its sentence number in the space provided.

_____3_____ 1. [1]Less than a hundred years ago, many people saw adolescence as a time of great instability and strong emotions. [2]For example, G. Stanley Hall, one of the first developmental psychologists, portrayed adolescence as a period of "storm and stress," fraught with suffering, passion, and rebelliousness. [3]Recent research, however, suggests that the "storm and stress" view greatly exaggerates the experience of most teenagers. [4]The great majority of adolescents do not describe their lives as filled with turmoil and chaos. [5]Most adolescents manage to keep stress in check, experience very little disruption in their everyday lives, and generally develop more positively than is commonly believed. [6]For instance, a cross-cultural study that sampled adolescents from ten countries, including the United States, found that over 75 percent of them had healthy self-images, were generally happy, and valued the time they spent at school and work.

Sentences 1–2 introduce the topic of how people view adolescence. The word *however* in sentence 3 introduces the main idea—that the experience of most teenagers is not one of "storm and stress." Sentences 4–6 support the idea that teenagers are generally better adjusted than was once thought.

_____3_____ 2. [1]Scientists have calculated that in the year 2029, there is a 1 in 38 chance that an asteroid will smash into our planet. [2]That may not be a high probability, but when that probability represents a hole the size of several European countries, 1 in 38 is still cause for concern. [3]Luckily, scientists have developed an effective strategy for avoiding an asteroid collision. [4]Rather than blow up the asteroid and risk its fragments chaotically raining down on the Earth, the best strategy is to slowly deflect the asteroid's path. [5]Using a nuclear-powered engine that consumes very little fuel, a spacecraft would hover beside the asteroid for as many as twenty years. [6]Since the force of gravity is such that any object exerts a pull on the objects around it, the spacecraft's mass would slowly pull the asteroid off course. [7]Although the pull would be very weak, space would offer no resistance, and the asteroid could be safely pulled away from its collision course over a period of many years.

Sentences 1–2 introduce the topic of an asteroid hitting Earth. Sentence 3 is the main idea. Sentences 4–7 demonstrate how a spacecraft could prevent a collision between an asteroid and Earth.

_____1_____ 3. [1]AIDS is an excellent example of the relationship between behavior, environment, and disease. [2]This disease was first noted in male homosexuals. [3]One person, Gaetan Dugas, an airline steward from Canada, played a key role in its rapid transmission, for he or one of his sex partners had sex with 40 of the first 248 AIDS cases reported in the

(Continues on next page)

United States. [4]The disease then hit another group whose lifestyle also encouraged its transmission—intravenous drug users who shared needles. [5]The third of the groups that were the hardest hit represents an environmental risk: Hemophiliacs, who need regular blood transfusions, were exposed to the disease through contaminated blood. [6]Lifestyle was also central to how the disease entered the general population; the bridge was prostitutes who had sex with intravenous drug users and with bisexual and heterosexual men. [7]Lifestyle and environment continue to be significant: AIDS is more common among drug users who share needles and among people who have multiple sexual partners.

Sentences 2–7 show how the spread of AIDS illustrates "the relationship between behavior, environment, and disease."

___2___ 4. [1]Today, people who find themselves with too much debt can get help from the government. [2]But before the mid-19th century, Americans who couldn't pay their debts were often given harsh punishments. [3]Some people were put in a jail called "debtors' prison." [4]They were forced to sit in their cells until they had the money to pay back their debts. [5]However, since they couldn't go to work, there was no way for them to get the money unless someone gave it to them. [6]Many people died in debtor's prison because they could not afford to leave. [7]Some people were required to give away everything they had, except for their bedding, in order to pay back a debt. [8]Other people were forced to become indentured servants. [9]Indentured servants were forced to do work without a salary until their debt was paid. [10]Sometimes even the children of people who owed money were required to work in order to pay off their parents' debt.

Sentence 1 introduces the topic of debt. The word *But* in sentence 2 introduces the main idea. Note the list words *harsh punishments.* Sentences 3–10 detail the harsh punishments inflicted on those who couldn't pay their debts.

___1___ 5. [1]Religion sometimes teaches that the existing social arrangements of a society represent what God desires. [2]For example, during the Middle Ages, Christian theologians decreed the "divine right of kings." [3]That doctrine meant that God determined who would become a king, and set him on the throne. [4]The king ruled in God's place, and it was the duty of a king's subjects to be loyal to him (and pay their taxes). [5]To disobey the king would be to disobey God. [6]The religion of ancient Egypt claimed that the Pharaoh himself was a god. [7]The Emperor of Japan was similarly declared divine. [8]In India, Hinduism supports the caste system by teaching that an individual who tries to change caste will come back in the next life as a member of a lower caste—or even as an animal. [9]In the decades before the Civil War, Southern ministers used Scripture to defend slavery, saying that it was God's will—while Northern ministers legitimated their religion's social structure by using Scripture to denounce slavery as evil.

Sentences 2–9 give examples showing that religion sometimes teaches that existing social arrangements reflect God's will.

MAIN IDEAS: Mastery Test 5

The main ideas of the following paragraphs appear at different locations—the beginning, somewhere in the middle, or at the end. Identify each main idea by filling in its sentence number in the space provided.

_____1_____ 1. ¹The spread of an invention or idea from one area to another can have extensive effects on people's lives. ²Consider a simple object such as the axe. ³When missionaries introduced steel axes to the Aborigines of Australia, it upset their whole society. ⁴Before this, the men controlled axe-making. ⁵They used a special stone, available only in a remote region, and they passed axe-making skills from father to son. ⁶Women had to request permission to use the axe. ⁷When steel axes became common, women also possessed them, and the men lost both status and power. ⁸The idea of citizenship, the belief that people have certain rights based on their birth and residence, changed political structure around the world. ⁹It removed monarchs as an unquestioned source of authority. ¹⁰Similarly, the concept of gender equality is now circling the globe. ¹¹Although taken for granted in a few parts of the world, the idea that it is wrong to withhold certain rights on the basis of someone's sex is revolutionary. ¹²Like citizenship, this idea is destined to transform basic human relationships and entire societies.

Sentence 1 contains the list words *extensive effects.* Sentences 2–12 detail the extensive effects caused by the spread of inventions and ideas.

_____4_____ 2. ¹Humans breathe automatically every few seconds. ²Dolphins, by contrast, breathe only voluntarily and can hold their breath for longer than thirty minutes. ³So how do they go to sleep without risking oversleeping and drowning? ⁴To maintain control of their breathing during sleep, dolphins sleep with only half of their brain at a time. ⁵Electroencephalograms, measuring the electric levels in dolphins' brains, show that the left side of a dolphin's mind shuts down while the right side powers its basic life functions. ⁶Later, the right side sleeps while the left side takes over. ⁷In this way, the dolphin achieves a full eight hours of sleep while still maintaining the ability to swim to the surface and take a breath of air. ⁸The strange sleep habits of dolphins might explain a behavior known as "logging" that sailors commonly observe, in which dolphins swim very slowly near the surface of the ocean.

Sentences 1–3 introduce the topic of dolphins and sleep. Sentence 4 is the main idea. Sentences 5–8 detail how dolphins manage to sleep and breathe voluntarily at the same time.

_____3_____ 3. ¹We've all heard stories about people whose spectacular abilities are apparent at an early age. ²Mozart started composing music at the age of five, Picasso turned out masterly paintings by the time he was ten, and some mathematicians have enrolled in college before entering their teens. ³Yet a significant number of famous people were thought to be "slow" rather than gifted when they were children. ⁴Thomas Alva Edison was a prime example of this. ⁵Little Tom Edison did not learn to talk until he was almost four years of age. ⁶When Tom was seven, his teacher lost patience with the boy's

Sentences 1 and 2 discuss famous child prodigies. The word *Yet* in sentence 3 introduces the contrasting main idea—that a significant number of famous people were thought to

(Continues on next page)

be slow learners as children. Sentences 4–11 give examples of highly accomplished people who started off slowly. Note the addition word *another* (sentences 7 and 9).

persistent questioning and lack of interest in the rote lessons he was supposed to be learning, and expressed his belief that the boy's brains were "addled" or scrambled. [7]Albert Einstein was another example of a genius who started off slowly. [8]In the primary grades, he was considered to be a slow learner, possibly due to dyslexia, shyness, or simply a lack of interest in formal schooling. [9]Another future scientist who made great contributions to the atomic age, Ernest Rutherford, could read by the age of eleven, but not write. [10]Pierre Curie, who with his wife, Marie, discovered the element radium and won the Nobel Prize, had at an early age demonstrated a remarkable lack of ability in reading and writing. [11]Indeed, throughout his life, his handwriting remained that of a child, and his spelling was awful.

_____1_____

Sentences 2–6 give examples proving that people failed to immediately realize that radium could be deadly.

4. [1]When a specimen of pure radium was first isolated in 1902, people failed to realize that the glowing radioactive substance could be deadly. [2]Radium in extremely diluted form was added to face creams, health tonics, cosmetics, bath salts, and so on. [3]One drink, Radithor, which contained one part radium salts to 60,000 parts zinc sulfide, was said to cure cancer and mental illness, as well as restore sexual vigor and vitality. [4]Upper-class men and women carried small vials of radium bromide around with them as the latest "status symbol." [5]Watches with glowing, radium-painted numbers and dials were also extremely popular. [6]Eventually, radium became linked with an alarming rise in incidences of cancer.

_____3_____

Sentences 1–2 introduce the topic of presidential health. Sentence 3 is the main idea. Sentences 4–13 detail instances where presidents kept their health problems a secret. Note the addition words *first* (sentence 4) and *also* (sentence 6).

5. [1]Aside from admitting to a bad back, young, dynamic President John F. Kennedy appeared the picture of health. [2]Yet several years after his assassination, the truth came out that he had suffered from Addison's disease, a debilitating disorder involving the adrenal glands. [3]Kennedy was not the only president to keep his health problems a secret. [4]The first president to lie about his health was Chester A. Arthur, our 21st president, who was diagnosed with Bright's disease, a fatal kidney disorder, shortly after he took office. [5]Unwilling to jeopardize what he wanted to accomplish, Arthur kept his disease a secret, struggled on for four years, then died shortly after he left office. [6]President Grover Cleveland also kept the true state of his health a secret. [7]In 1893, when the country was experiencing an economic depression, doctors secretly operated on Cleveland to cut out a large cancerous growth on the roof of his mouth. [8]A cover story about the removal of two bad teeth kept the suspicious press from learning the rather alarming truth. [9]In October 1919, President Woodrow Wilson suffered a serious stroke which incapacitated him until the end of his term in 1921. [10]The public was never informed of this situation, and Wilson's wife, Edith, virtually ran the government for more than a year. [11]Our 32nd president, Franklin D. Roosevelt, failed to reveal the fact that he had been diagnosed with life-threatening hypertension before he ran for and was elected to a fourth term. [12]The American people were shocked when he died in office less than a year later. [13]Today the media would be far more likely to expose the truth about a sitting president's health.

MAIN IDEAS: Mastery Test 6

The main ideas of the following paragraphs appear at different locations—the beginning, somewhere in the middle, or at the end. Identify each main idea by filling in its sentence number in the space provided.

_____5_____ 1. ¹The media sprinkle their reports of school shootings with such sensationalist phrases as "new outbreak of violence" and "out of control." ²They create the impression that schools all over the nation are set to break out in gunfire. ³Parents used to consider schools safe havens, but no longer. ⁴And the public views school shootings as convincing evidence that something is seriously wrong. ⁵But research has shown that the media's reporting has created a myth, and there is no trend toward greater school violence. ⁶In fact, shooting deaths at schools are decreasing. ⁷In 1992–1993 there were 45 shooting deaths; ten years later, in 2002–2003, there were only five. ⁸This is not to say that school shootings are not a serious problem. ⁹Even one student being wounded or killed is too many. ¹⁰But the clear trend is less school violence.

Sentences 1–4 introduce the topic of school violence. The word *But* in sentence 5 introduces the main idea—that contrary to media reports, school violence is *not* on the rise. Sentences 6–10 support the idea that school violence has declined.

_____12_____ 2. ¹While the telephone is associated with Alexander Graham Bell, Elisha Grey of Chicago filed for a patent for the same invention within hours of Bell on the same day in 1876. ²After extensive litigation, Bell was awarded the patent. ³In fact, neither of them may have been first. ⁴Italian Antonio Meucci had a successful working model years earlier. ⁵Orville and Wilbur Wright are forever associated with the invention of the airplane in 1903. ⁶However, there is evidence that in New Zealand, a farmer named Richard Pearse made a successful flight some months ahead of the Wright brothers. ⁷Others claim that Gustave Whitehead flew a homemade plane two years earlier in Bridgeport, Connecticut. ⁸The invention of the television is usually credited to Philo Farnsworth of San Francisco in 1926. ⁹However, that same year a Russian immigrant in New York, Vladimir Zworykin, was working on a similar invention. ¹⁰In Scotland, also in 1926, John Logie Baird demonstrated a machine he called the "televisor." ¹¹When Baird and Farnsworth met and compared inventions some months later, Baird admitted Farnsworth had the better design. ¹²Clearly, while famous inventions usually come to be associated with one person, there are often competing claims for the same invention.

Sentences 1–11 contain details which show that there are often competing claims for the same invention (the main idea in sentence 12).

_____3_____ 3. ¹Most of us, when we are in a depressed mood, are able to relieve it through our own thoughts and actions. ²After a certain period of gloom, we grab our bootstraps and pull ourselves up, using such means as positive thinking, problem solving, talking with friends, or engaging in

Sentences 1–2 are introductory details. The word *However* in sentence 3 introduces the main idea—

(Continues on next page)

that severely depressed people think and act in ways that work against their recovery. Sentences 4–6 detail how a severely depressed person's mood, thought, and action interact negatively.

activities that we especially enjoy. ³However, severely depressed people have patterns of thought and action that work against their recovery, rather than for it. ⁴Imagine severe depression as a vicious triangle in which a person's mood, thought, and action interact in such a way as to keep him or her in a depressed state. ⁵Depressed mood promotes negative thinking and withdrawal from enjoyable activities; negative thinking promotes depressed mood and withdrawal from enjoyable activities; and withdrawal from enjoyable activities promotes depressed mood and negative thinking. ⁶Each corner of the triangle supports the others.

_____ 2 _____

4. ¹Most of us assume that color is "out there," in the environment; our eyes simply take it in. ²While many animals—including some reptiles, fish, and insects—have color vision, what colors they see vary. ³Humans and most other primates perceive a wide range of colors. ⁴Most other mammals experience the world only in reds and greens or blues and yellows. ⁵Hamsters, rats, squirrels, and other rodents are completely colorblind. ⁶So are owls, nocturnal birds of prey that have only rods in their eyes. ⁷At the same time, however, other animals can see colors that we can't. ⁸Bees, for example, see ultraviolet light. ⁹To a bee's eyes, flowers with white petals that look drab to us flash like neon signs pointing the way to nectar. ¹⁰Birds, bats, and moths find red flowers irresistible, but bees pass them by. ¹¹Tradition notwithstanding, bulls can't see red either; they are red-green colorblind. ¹²The matador's cape is bright red to excite the humans in the audience, who find red arousing, perhaps especially when they expect to see blood.

Sentence 1 introduces the topic of color. Sentence 2 contains the main idea: that color vision varies among animals. Sentences 3–12 give examples of how color vision varies.

_____ 2 _____

5. ¹Have you ever wondered what on earth some of those strange nursery rhymes you learned as a child were supposed to mean? ²Rhymes such as "Jack and Jill" and "Three Blind Mice" have fairly gruesome explanations, but the seemingly innocent "Ring Around the Rosy" takes the prize for its ghastly meaning. ³Written around 1348, this brief song refers to the bubonic plague—a horrifying epidemic that killed 25 million people in Europe in the mid-1300s. ⁴Because contracting the illness meant almost certain death, those who fell ill were simply sent home to die and were instructed to pray continuously with their rosary beads ("Ring around the rosy"). ⁵And because people were dying faster than they could be buried, a little bundle of flowers known as a "posy" was carried in one's pocket and held up to the nose in order to mask the smell of rotting bodies ("A pocket full of posies"). ⁶In time, churches resorted to burning the dead instead of burying them when the corpses began piling up too high in the streets ("Ashes, ashes. We all fall down"). ⁷Ultimately, the plague killed one-third of Europe's inhabitants, leading Europeans at that time to understandably imagine that, in the end, everyone would be killed.

Sentence 1 introduces the topic of the meanings of children's rhymes. Sentence 2 states the main idea: the innocent-sounding "Ring Around the Rosy" has the most ghastly meaning— it refers to a horrific 14th century epidemic. Sentences 3–7 provide details supporting this gruesome meaning.

2

Supporting Details

In Chapter 1 you worked on the most important reading skill—finding the main idea. A closely related reading skill is locating supporting details. Supporting details provide the added information that is needed for you to make sense of a main idea.

This chapter describes supporting details and presents three techniques that will help you take study notes on main ideas and their supporting details: outlining, mapping, and summarizing.

WHAT ARE SUPPORTING DETAILS?

It was not going well.

Supporting details are reasons, examples, facts, steps, or other kinds of evidence that explain a main idea. In the cartoon shown above, the main idea is that "It was not going well," a statement with strong support. A man who has died and is being evaluated at heaven's gate admits that "I never prayed a day in my life." The details clearly support the idea presented!

Supporting Reasons

In the paragraph below, three major details in the form of *reasons* support the main idea that women are underrepresented in U.S. politics. As you read the paragraph, try to identify and check (✓) these three major reasons.

[1]Eight million more women than men are of voting age, and more women than men vote in U.S. national elections. [2]However, men greatly outnumber women in political office. [3]Since 1789, over 1,800 men have served in the U.S. Senate, but only 13 women have served. [4]Women are underrepresented in U.S. politics for a number of reasons. [5]First,✓women are still underrepresented in law and business, the careers from which most politicians emerge. [6]In addition,✓most women find that the irregular hours kept by those who run for office are incompatible with their role as mother. [7]Fathers, in contrast, whose ordinary roles are more likely to take them away from home, are less likely to feel this conflict. [8]Last, preferring to hold on to their positions of power,✓men have been reluctant to incorporate women into centers of decision-making or to present them as viable candidates.

☑ *Check Your Understanding*

Now see if you can complete the basic outline below that shows the three major reasons supporting the main idea.

Main idea: Women are underrepresented in U.S. politics.

Supporting detail 1: *Women are still underrepresented in law and business, the usual starting place for politicians.*

Supporting detail 2: *A politician's hours are incompatible with the role of a mother.*

Supporting detail 3: *Men have been reluctant to give women power.*

Explanation:

You should have added 1) women are still underrepresented in law and business, the usual starting place for politicians; 2) a politician's irregular hours are incompatible with the role of a mother; and 3) men are reluctant to give women power. These major supporting reasons help you fully understand the main idea.

Supporting Facts

In the paragraph above, the supporting details are *reasons*. Now look at the paragraph on the next page, in which the main idea is explained by a series of *facts*.

[1]Several factors contribute to our pickiness about eating certain foods. [2]One factor which influences what foods we find tasty is how old we are. [3]In young people, taste buds die and are replaced about every seven days. [4]As we age, the buds are replaced more slowly, so taste declines as we grow older. [5]Thus children, who have abundant taste buds, often dislike foods with strong or unusual tastes (such as liver and spinach), but as they grow older and lose taste buds, they may come to like these foods. [6]Pickiness is also related to our upbringing. [7]Many food and taste preferences result from childhood experiences and cultural influences. [8]For example, Japanese children eat raw fish and Chinese children eat chicken feet as part of their normal diet, whereas American children consider these foods "yucky." [9]A third factor relating to pickiness over food is our built-in sense of taste, which enables us to discriminate between foods that are safe to eat and foods that are poisonous. [10]Because most plants that taste bitter contain toxic chemicals, we are more likely to survive if we avoid bitter-tasting plants. [11]We have a preference, then, for sweet foods because they are generally nonpoisonous.

☑ Check Your Understanding

Put a check (✓) by the number of separate factors that contribute to our pickiness about eating certain foods.

___ One fact   ___ Two facts   _✓_ Three facts

Explanation:

There are three supporting facts for why we are picky about eating certain foods: 1) our age and how it affects our taste buds; 2) our upbringing; and 3) our built-in sense of taste. The supporting details give the added information we need to fully understand the main idea.

Supporting Example(s)

Now look at the paragraph below, where the supporting details are in the form of an extended *example*.

[1]An old Chinese story illustrates the emotional healing power of touch. [2]A woman went to a traditional herbal healer, asking for a potion to kill her cruel mother-in-law. [3]The herbalist gave her some tea, telling her to make some for her mother-in-law every day for three months. [4]In addition, he told her to massage the older woman every day, claiming that the poison would enter the woman's system more effectively that way. [5]At the end of the three months, the mother-in-law would die, apparently of natural causes. [6]The

daughter-in-law did as she was told. [7]But at the end of two and a half months, she had come to know and understand her mother-in-law through giving her massage. [8]In turn, her mother-in-law had started to love her. [9]The young woman ran back to the wise old doctor to ask for an antidote to the poison. [10]He told her the tea was not poison at all, only flower water.

☑ *Check Your Understanding*

Which sentence contains the main idea? ___1___

Which sentence starts the extended example? ___2___

Explanation:

The first sentence presents the main idea, and the second sentence starts the extended example.

OUTLINING

Preparing an outline of a passage often helps you understand and see clearly the relationship between a main idea and its supporting details. Outlines start with a main idea (or a heading that summarizes the main idea) followed by supporting details. There are often two levels of supporting details—major and minor. The **major details** explain and develop the main idea. In turn, the **minor details** help fill out and make clear the major details.

Below is the paragraph on gossip that appeared in Chapter 1. Reread the paragraph, and put a check (✓) next to each of the three major supporting details.

[1]Social psychologists have found that almost everyone gossips. [2]Male or female, young or old, blue-collar or professional, humans love to talk about one another. [3]All too often, such gossip is viewed as a frivolous waste of time. [4]However, it actually serves several important functions in the human community. [5]For one thing, gossip is a form of networking. [6]Talking with our friends and coworkers about each other is our most effective means of keeping track of the ever-changing social dynamic. [7]It tells us who is in, who is out, and who can help us climb the social or professional ladder. [8]A second function of gossip is the building of influence. [9]When we engage in gossip, we are able to shape people's opinions of ourselves. [10]We tell stories that show ourselves in a good light—wise, compassionate, insightful, clever. [11]And when we listen sympathetically to the gossip of other people, they perceive us as warm and likable. [12]A final and very powerful function of gossip is the creating of social alliances. [13]There are few quicker ways to form a bond with another person than to share private information with him or her.

[14]The words "I wouldn't tell most people this, but . . ." instantly interest and flatter the listener. [15]To talk about a third party, especially in a critical way, creates a bond with our listener and gives a feeling of shared superiority.

☑ Check Your Understanding

Now see if you can fill in the missing items in the following outline of the paragraph, which shows both major and minor details.

Main idea: Gossip serves several important functions in the human community.

Major detail: **1.** Form of networking
   Minor details: Networking is the best way to know who's out, who's in, and who can help us socially or professionally.

Major detail: **2.** _Building of influence_

   Minor details: By gossiping we can impress others as clever and compassionate, warm and likable.

Major detail: **3.** _Creating of social alliances_

   Minor details: _Sharing private information creates bonds by flattering the listener and giving a feeling of shared superiority._

Explanation:

You should have added two major supporting details: (2) Building of influence; (3) Creating of social alliances. And to the third major supporting detail, you should have added the minor detail that sharing private information flatters our listener and gives a feeling of shared superiority.

Notice that just as the main idea is more general than its supporting details, major details are more general than minor ones. For instance, the major detail "Form of networking" is more general than the minor details about talking with friends or coworkers to keep track of what's going on and to climb the social or professional ladder.

Outlining Tips

The following tips will help you prepare outlines:

TIP *Tip 1* **Look for words that tell you a list of details is coming.** Here are some common list words:

List Words

several kinds of	various causes	a few reasons
a number of	a series of	three factors
four steps	among the results	several advantages

For example, look again at the main ideas in two paragraphs already discussed and underline the list words:

- However, it [gossip] actually serves <u>several important functions</u> in the human community.
- Women are underrepresented in U.S. politics for <u>a number of reasons</u>.

Here the words *several important functions* and *a number of reasons* each tell us that a list of major details is coming. But you will not always be given such helpful signals that a list of details will follow. For example, there are no list words in the paragraph on the reasons people are "picky" about eating certain foods. Simply remember to note list words when they are present, as they help you to understand quickly the basic organization of a passage.

TIP *Tip 2* **Look for words that signal major details.** Such words are called **addition words**, and they will be explained further on page 134. Here are some common addition words:

Addition Words

one	to begin with	also	further
first (of all)	for one thing	in addition	furthermore
second (ly)	other	next	last (of all)
third (ly)	another	moreover	final (ly)

☑ *Check Your Understanding*

Now look again at the selection on gossip on page 66:

1. The word *one* (in *For one thing*) signals the first major supporting detail.

2. What addition word introduces the second major supporting detail?

   second

3. What addition word introduces the third major supporting detail?

   final

And look again at the selection on the underrepresentation of women on page 64:

1. What word introduces the first major detail? _____*First*_____
2. What words introduce the second major detail? ___*In addition*___
3. What word introduces the third major detail? _____*Last*_____

Also look again at the selection on page 65 about pickiness in eating.

1. What word introduces the first major detail? _____*One*_____
2. What word introduces the second major detail? _____*also*_____
3. What word introduces the third major detail? _____*third*_____

Explanation:

In the selection on gossip, the second major detail is introduced by the word *second*, and the third major detail by the word *final*. In the selection on the underrepresentation of women, the first major detail is introduced by the word *First*, the second major detail by the words *in addition*, and the third major detail by the word *Last*. In the selection on pickiness about eating certain foods, the first major detail is introduced by the word *One*, the second major detail by the word *also*, and the third major detail by the word *third*.

TIP *Tip 3* **When making an outline, put all supporting details of equal importance at the same distance from the margin.** In the outline of the paragraph on the functions of gossip, on page 67, the three major supporting details all begin at the margin. Likewise, the minor supporting details are all indented at the same distance from the margin. You can therefore see at a glance the main idea, the major details, and the minor details.

☑ Check Your Understanding

Put appropriate numbers *(1, 2, 3)* and letters *(a, b)* in front of the items in the following outline.

Main idea

_1_ **Major detail**

  _a_ Minor detail

  _b_ Minor detail

_2_ **Major detail**

  _a_ Minor detail

  _b_ Minor detail

_3_ **Major detail**

Explanation:

You should have put a *1, 2,* and *3* in front of the major details and an *a* and *b* in front of the minor details. Note that an outline proceeds from the most general to the most specific, from main idea to major details to minor details.

The practice that follows will give you experience in finding major details, in separating major details from minor details, and in preparing outlines.

➤ **Practice 1**

Read and then outline each passage. Begin by writing in the main idea, and then fill in the supporting details. The first outline requires only major details; the second calls for you to add minor details as well.

A.   ¹Although only human beings communicate through words, other animals also communicate in their own ways. ²First, animals can communicate by means of nonverbal sounds, such as chirps and birdsong, mews, barks, howls, and roars. ³Next, animals communicate through chemical signals: male dogs, for instance, use urine to mark their own turf. ⁴A third means of animal communication is touch, such as nuzzling and licking—as well as grooming among, for example, monkeys. ⁵Last of all, animals communicate by visual signals. ⁶Dogs, of course, wag their tails; also, they and some other furry animals raise their hackles (the hairs between the shoulders) when threatened, in order to appear larger. ⁷Baring the teeth is another visual signal. ⁸And honeybees perform a famous "wiggle dance" to inform each other about sources of food.

Passage A:
The main idea is stated in sentence 1. (Note the list words *their own ways*.) The major details in sentences 2–5 are signaled by addition words: *First, Next, third, Last of all.*

Main idea: _[Non-human] animals communicate in their own ways._

_____

Major detail: 1. _Nonverbal sounds_

Major detail: 2. _Chemical signals_

Major detail: 3. _Touch_

Major detail: 4. _Visual signals_

Wording of answers to the outlines in this chapter may vary slightly.

B.   ¹The diseases that afflict humans can be classified into a number of basic types. ²Infectious diseases are probably what most of us have in mind when we think of "getting sick." ³These are the illnesses that are caused by bacteria, viruses, and other tiny organisms and that we can "catch" from another person, or from an infected animal. ⁴Examples include colds, flu, and tuberculosis. ⁵Another category is hereditary diseases, such as sickle-cell anemia, which are passed on from parent to child in the genes. ⁶A third category, degenerative diseases, includes disorders that result from aging and wear and tear on the body; one example is arthritis. ⁷Still another category, hormonal disorders, are caused by having too much or too little of certain body chemicals. ⁸Diabetes is one hormonal disease. ⁹The category of environmental diseases is becoming a matter of increasing concern. ¹⁰Environmental diseases—which include some allergies and lead poisoning—are caused by chemical and physical substances in air, water, and food. ¹¹Finally, deficiency diseases are the type caused by a lack of certain nutrients, such as vitamins. ¹²Scurvy and pellagra are vitamin-deficiency disorders.

Passage B:
The main idea is stated in sentence 1. (Note the list words *a number of basic types*.) Four of the major details in sentences 5, 6, 7, 10, and 11 are signaled by addition words: *Another, third, Still another, Finally*.

Main idea: _Human diseases can be classified into a number of basic types._

Major detail: 1. Infectious

　　Minor detail: Examples—colds and flu

Major detail: 2. _Hereditary_

　　Minor detail: Example— _Sickle-cell anemia_

Major detail: 3. _Degenerative_

　　Minor detail: Example— _Arthritis_

Major detail: 4. _Hormonal_

　　Minor detail: Example— _Diabetes_

Major detail: 5. _Environmental_

　　Minor detail: Examples— _Allergies and lead poisoning_

Major detail: 6. _Deficiency_

　　Minor detail: Examples— _Scurvy and pellagra_

Study Hint: At times you will want to include minor details in your study notes; at other times, it may not be necessary to do so. If you are taking notes on one or more textbook chapters, use your judgment. It is often best to be aware of minor details but to concentrate on writing down the main ideas and major details.

MAPPING

Students sometimes find it helpful to use maps rather than outlines. **Maps**, or diagrams, are highly visual outlines in which circles, boxes, or other shapes show the relationships between main ideas and supporting details. Each major detail is connected to the main idea, often presented in title form. If minor details are included, each is connected to the major detail it explains.

☑ *Check Your Understanding*

Read the following passage and then see if you can complete the map and the questions that follow.

¹With the possible exception of very small, isolated, primitive groups, every human society has had some sort of class system. ²In ancient Rome, there were four major social classes. ³To begin with, at the top of the heap were the aristocrats, called "patricians." ⁴This term derived from the word for father—*pater*—and is still sometimes used today; it also survives in the name Patricia. ⁵Second, as a practical matter if not in principle, were the soldiers, an enormously powerful group. ⁶One Roman emperor, on his deathbed, advised his son: "Enrich the soldiers; nothing else matters." ⁷Next came the common people, called the plebeians. ⁸(This term too survives today: a freshman at a military academy is called a plebe.) ⁹The plebeians were artisans, shopkeepers, and laborers. ¹⁰Fourth, at the bottom, were slaves. ¹¹They could work as domestic servants, manual laborers, and so on; but some slaves were educated and served as teachers.

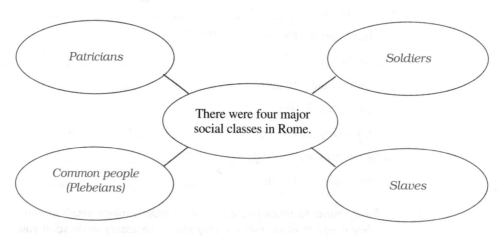

Which word or words introduce:

1. The first major detail? _____ *To begin with* _____

2. The second major detail? _____ *Second* _____

3. The third major detail? _____*Next*_____

4. The last major detail? _____*Fourth*_____

Explanation:

The map sets off the major details in a very visual way. You see at a glance that the four major social groups were aristocrats, soldiers, common people, and slaves. The words that introduce the major details are *To begin with, Second, Next,* and *Fourth.*

➤ Practice 2

Read each passage, and then complete the maps that follow. The main ideas are given so that you can focus on finding the supporting details. The first passage requires only major details. The second passage calls for you to add both major and minor details.

A. ¹Today, most people smile when someone takes a picture of them. ²Look at a few of the earliest American photographs, however, and you'll see a batch of frowning grumps staring back at you. ³But that doesn't mean our ancestors were angry all the time. ⁴There are several reasons why early photographic subjects never smiled in pictures. ⁵For one thing, photography was a serious business back then. ⁶Not everyone was lucky enough to be in a picture, and those who were wanted to do it right. ⁷People expected their photos to be passed on from generation to generation. ⁸They wanted their posterity to remember them as being serious and dignified. ⁹Second, smiling would have taken too long. ¹⁰People had to stay perfectly still for ten or twenty minutes while the camera took the photo. ¹¹If they moved at all during that time, the picture would come out blurry. ¹²Holding a smile that long would be quite difficult, not to mention uncomfortable. ¹³Third, most people did not want to show their teeth. ¹⁴Since no one had toothpaste and few brushed their teeth at all, dental problems were commonplace. ¹⁵No one wanted to be remembered for a mouth full of cavities and rot.

Addition words introduce the major details: *For one thing* (sentence 5), *Second* (sentence 9), and *Third* (sentence 13).

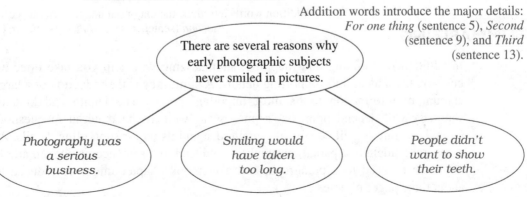

B. ¹Contrary to popular assumption, ancient slavery was not usually based on racism, but on one of three other factors. ²The first was debt. ³In some societies, creditors could enslave people who could not pay their debts. ⁴The second was crime. ⁵Instead of being killed, a murderer or thief might be enslaved by the family of the victim as a compensation for their loss. ⁶The third was war and conquest. ⁷When one group of people conquered another, they often enslaved some of the vanquished. ⁸Historian Gerda Lerner notes that the first people enslaved through warfare were women. ⁹When tribal men raided a village or camp, they killed the men, raped the women, and then brought the women back as slaves. ¹⁰The women were valued for sexual purposes, for reproduction, and for their labor. ¹¹Roughly twenty-five hundred years ago, when Greece was but a collection of city-states, slavery was common. ¹²A city that became powerful and vanquished another city would enslave some of the vanquished. ¹³Both slaves and slaveholders were Greek. ¹⁴Similarly, when Rome became the supreme power about two thousand years ago, following the custom of that time, the Romans enslaved some of the Greeks they had conquered. ¹⁵More educated than their conquerors, some of these slaves served as tutors in Roman homes.

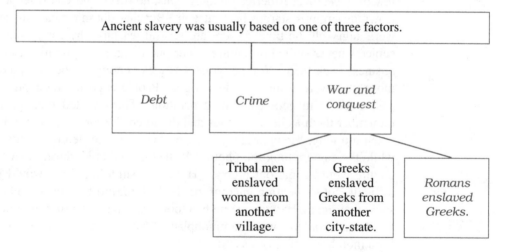

Addition words introduce the major details: *first* (sentence 2), *second* (sentence 4), *and third* (sentence 6).

SUMMARIZING

In addition to outlining and mapping, summarizing will help you take effective notes on main ideas and supporting details. A **summary** is the reduction of a large amount of information to its most important points. The length and kind of summary will depend upon one's purpose as well as the material in question. Often, a summary will consist of a main idea and its major supporting details. As a general guideline, a paragraph might be reduced to a sentence or two, an article might be reduced to a paragraph, and a textbook chapter might be reduced to about three pages of notes.

One of the most common types of summarizing occurs when you are taking study notes on textbook material. Very often you will find it helpful to summarize examples of key terms. For instance, look at the following textbook passage and the summary that follows.

[1]**Habituation** is the tendency to ignore environmental factors that remain constant. [2]The brain seems "prewired" to pay more attention to changes in the environment than to stimuli that remain constant. [3]Have you ever gotten a new clock and thought it had a very loud tick, but in a short time you realized you weren't aware of its ticking at all? [4]This happens because you become habituated to the regularity of the sound. [5]If the sound changed every few minutes, you would notice every change because you would not have enough time to become habituated each time. [6]High-end car security systems take advantage of this. [7]When activated, the security system begins with a siren, which then changes to honking, then back to a siren, and so forth, so that it is impossible to habituate to the noise and ignore the alarm. [8]These types of alarms are annoying, but effective.

Summary:

Habituation—the tendency to ignore environmental factors that remain constant. For example, you will lose awareness of the ticking of a new clock.

Note that a textbook definition of a key term (such as *habituation*) should generally not be summarized, but should be worded in the language chosen by the author. On the other hand, it usually makes sense to summarize the supporting information. Summarizing often involves two steps:

1 *Select* one example from several that might be given. Which example you select is up to you, as long as it makes the term clear for you. In the summary above, the example about becoming used to the tick of a new clock was chosen to illustrate habituation. The other example, about car security systems, could have been chosen as well.

2 *Condense* the example if it's not already very brief. Notice that the example about the new clock has been condensed from a long sentence to a short one.

A definition of a key term followed by one condensed example is a very useful way to take notes—especially in introductory college courses, where many terms are defined and illustrated.

> *Study Hint:* If you have a textbook chapter to learn, very often you can get what you need by doing two things: 1) writing down the definitions in the chapter and summarized examples of the definitions, and 2) writing down lists of major supporting details and any minor details that you think are important.

Summarizing a Passage

Read the selection below, taken from an introductory textbook for a college social science course. As is often the case in such introductory texts, a new term is presented and then followed by an extended example. Complete the study notes by circling the answer choice that best summarizes that example.

[1]Soon after birth, some animals will follow and become attached to the first thing they see or hear that happens to move, a behavior known as **imprinting**. [2]Ordinarily, the "thing" on which the animal imprints is its mother, but experience can dictate otherwise. [3]When animal behaviorist Konrad Lorenz hatched young geese in an incubator, they imprinted on him, following him around and responding to his calls as if he were their mother. [4]In the laboratory, ducklings have imprinted on decoys, rubber balls, and wooden blocks. [5]Once imprinting has occurred, it is usually hard to reverse, even when the "mother" is an inanimate object that can offer neither food nor affection. [6]These facts suggest that imprinting is a special type of perceptual learning that occurs because at a particular stage in development, the animal's nervous system is geared to respond to a conspicuous moving object in a certain way.

Study notes:

Imprinting—some animals soon after birth follow and become attached to the first moving thing they see or hear.

Example—

A. Imprinting is hard to reverse even if the "mother" is an inanimate object.
B. An animal's nervous system is geared to respond to a conspicuous moving object in a certain way.
C. Young geese hatched in an incubator followed around and responded to an animal behaviorist as if he were their mother.

Explanation:

Useful study notes should include a clear example of a new term. In the case of the paragraph above, answer C summarizes a specific example that helps us clearly understand the term. Neither of the other two answers provides an example of the term.

> *Practice 3*

Read each textbook selection on the next page. Then complete the study notes by circling the letter of the answer that best summarizes an example of the term being defined.

A. [1]Displacement involves the redirection of repressed motives and emotions from their original objects to substitute objects. [2]The woman who has always wanted to be a mother may feel inadequate when she learns that she cannot have children. [3]As a result, she may become extremely attached to a pet or to a niece or nephew. [4]Perhaps the most familiar example of displacement is the person who must smile and agree with a difficult boss, then comes home and "blows up" at family members for no reason.

Study notes:

Displacement—the redirection of repressed motives and emotions from their original objects to substitute objects.

Example— *Answers A and B are not specific examples of redirection; they describe causes of redirection.*

A. A woman who has always wanted to be a mother feels inadequate when she learns that she cannot have children.

B. A man must smile and agree with a difficult boss.

C. A man comes home and "blows up" at family members for no reason.

B. [1]How do we explain cultural differences in emotional expressions? [2]Each culture has its own **display rules**—rules that govern how, when, and where to express emotions. [3]Parents teach their children display rules by responding angrily to some outbursts, by being sympathetic to others, and on occasion by simply ignoring them. [4]In this way, children learn which emotions they may express in certain situations and which emotions they are expected to control. [5]There are almost as many variations in display rules as there are cultures in the world. [6]In Japanese culture, for instance, children learn to conceal negative emotions with a stoic expression or polite smile. [7]Young males in the Masai culture are similarly expected to conceal their emotions in public by appearing stern and stony-faced. [8]Public physical contact is also governed by display rules. [9]North Americans and Asians are generally not touch-oriented, and only the closest family and friends might hug in greeting or farewell. [10]In contrast, Latin Americans and Middle Easterners often embrace and hold hands as a sign of casual friendship.

Study notes:

Display rules—rules which govern how, when, and where to express emotions.

Example— *Answer A discusses variations in display rules. Answer C describes how parents teach children display rules.*

A. There are many variations in display rules in cultures all over the world.

B. In Japan, children are taught to conceal negative emotions with a stoic expression or polite smile.

C. Parents teach their children display rules by varying their response to the child's behavior.

A Final Note

This chapter has centered on supporting details as they appear in well-organized paragraphs. But keep in mind that supporting details are part of readings of any length, including selections that may not have an easy-to-follow list of one major detail after another. Starting with the reading at the end of this chapter (page 80), you will be given practice in answering all kinds of questions about key supporting details. These questions will develop your ability to pay close, careful attention to what you are reading.

CHAPTER REVIEW

In this chapter, you learned the following:

- Major and minor details provide the added information you need to make sense of a main idea.
- List phrases and addition words can help you to find major and minor supporting details.
- Outlining, mapping, and summarizing are useful note-taking strategies.
- Outlines show the relationship between the main idea, major details, and minor details of a passage.
- Maps are very visual outlines.
- Writing a definition and summarizing an example is a good way to take notes on a new term.

The next chapter—Chapter 3—will show you how to find implied main ideas and central points.

On the Web: If you are using this book in class, you can visit our website for additional practice in identifying supporting details. Go to **www.townsendpress.com** and click on "Online Exercises."

➤ Review Test 1

To review what you've learned in this chapter, answer each of the following questions by filling in the blank.

1. Two key reading skills that go hand in hand are finding the main idea and identifying the major and minor _____*details*_____ that support the main idea.

    See page 63.

2. List words—phrases such as *several types of, three steps,* and *four reasons*—are important to note because they alert you that a list of _____*details*_____ is coming.

    See page 68.

3. Outlining is a way to show at a glance the relationship between a main idea and its _____*supporting details*_____. It is a helpful way to take study notes on what you have read.

    See page 66.

4. Another good way to take study notes is to use a _____*map*_____—a highly visual outline that uses circles, boxes, and other shapes to set off main ideas and supporting details.

    See page 72.

5. When taking notes on textbook material, you will often find it useful to write out each definition in full and then select and _____*summarize*_____ one example of that definition.

    See page 75.

➤ Review Test 2

Here is a chance to apply your understanding of supporting details to a selection from a college textbook, *Understanding Psychology* (Pearson Prentice-Hall), by Charles G. Morris and Albert A. Maisto. Read the selection and then answer the supporting-detail questions that follow. There are also questions on understanding vocabulary in context and finding main ideas.

Preview

Is "getting high" a modern phenomenon? How long have mood-altering substances been around? Do modern people use psychoactive substances in ways different from those of their ancestors? The answers to these and other provocative questions appear in this reading.

Words to Watch

lozenges (2): small medicated candies intended to be dissolved in the mouth
imbibe (4): to drink
toxicity (6): the quality of being poisonous

DRUG-ALTERED CONSCIOUSNESS

Charles G. Morris and Albert A. Maisto

1   The use of psychoactive drugs—substances that change people's moods, perceptions, mental functioning, or behavior—is almost universal. In nearly every known culture throughout history, people have sought ways to alter waking consciousness. Many of the drugs available today, legally or illegally, have been used for thousands of years. For example, marijuana is mentioned in the herbal recipe book of a Chinese emperor, dating from 2737 B.C. Natives of the Andes Mountains in South America chew leaves of the coca plant (which contain cocaine) as a stimulant—a custom dating back at least to the Inca Empire of the fifteenth century.

2   In the nineteenth century, Europeans began adding coca to wine, tea, and lozenges°. Following this trend, in 1886, an Atlanta pharmacist combined crushed coca leaves from the Andes, caffeine-rich cola nuts from West Africa, cane sugar syrup, and carbonated water in a patent medicine he called "Coca-Cola." Laudanum—opium dissolved in alcohol—was popular in the United States at that time and was used as a main ingredient in numerous over-the-counter (or patent) medicines.

3   Of all psychoactive substances, alcohol has the longest history of widespread use. Archaeological evidence suggests that Late-Stone-Age groups began producing mead (fermented honey flavored with sap or fruit) about 10,000 years ago. The Egyptians, Babylonians, Greeks, and Romans viewed wine as a "gift from the gods." Wine is frequently praised in the Bible, and drinking water is hardly mentioned. In the Middle Ages, alcohol earned the title *aqua vitae*, the "water of life," with good reason. Wherever people settled down, water supplies quickly became contaminated with waste products. As recently as the nineteenth century, most people in Western civilizations drank alcohol with every meal (including breakfast) and between meals, as a "pick-me-up," as well as on social and religious occasions.

4   Is today's drug problem different from the drug use in other societies and times? In many ways, the answer is yes. First, motives for using psychoactive drugs have changed. In most cultures, psychoactive substances have been used as part of religious rituals, as medicines and tonics, as nutrient beverages, or as culturally approved stimulants (much as we drink coffee). The use of alcohol and other drugs in our society today is primarily recreational. For the most part, people do not raise their glasses in praise of God or inhale hallucinogens to get in touch with the spirit world, but to relax, have fun with friends (and strangers), and get high. Moreover, Americans most often imbibe° and inhale in settings specifically designed for recreation and inebriation: bars, clubs, beer parties, cocktail parties, "raves" (large, all-night dance parties), and so-called crack houses. In addition, people use and abuse drugs privately and secretly in their homes, sometimes without the

knowledge of their family and friends—leading to hidden addiction. Whether social or solitary, the use of psychoactive substances today is largely divorced from religious and family traditions.

5   Second, the drugs themselves have changed. Today's psychoactive substances often are stronger than those used in other cultures and times. For most of Western history, wine (12% alcohol) was often diluted with water. Hard liquor (40 to 75% alcohol) appeared only in the tenth century A.D. And the heroin on the streets today is stronger and more addictive than that available in the 1930s and 1940s.

6   In addition, new, synthetic drugs appear regularly, with unpredictable consequences. In the 1990s, the National Institute for Drug Abuse created a new category called "Club Drugs," for increasingly popular psychoactive substances manufactured in small laboratories or even home kitchens (from recipes available on the Internet). Because the source, the psychoactive ingredients, and any possible contaminants are unknown, the symptoms, toxicity°, and short- or long-term consequences are also unknown—making these drugs especially dangerous. The fact that they are often consumed with alcohol multiplies the risks.

Examples include "Ecstasy" (methylenedioxymethamphetamine [MDMA]), a combination of the stimulant amphetamine and a hallucinogen; "Grievous Bodily Harm" (gamma hydroxybutyrate [GHB]), a combination of sedatives and growth hormone stimulant; "Special K" (ketamine), an anesthetic approved for veterinary use that induces dreamlike states and hallucinations in humans; and "Roofies" (flunitrazepam), a tasteless, odorless sedative/anesthesia that can cause temporary amnesia, which is why it is also known as the "Forget-Me Pill" and is associated with sexual assault.

7   Finally, scientists and the public know more about the effects of psychoactive drugs than in the past. Cigarettes are an obvious example. The Surgeon General's Report, issued in 1964, confirmed a direct link between smoking and heart disease, as well as lung cancer. Subsequent research, establishing that cigarettes are harmful not only to smokers, but also to people around them (secondhand smoke) and to their newborn babies, transformed a personal health decision into a moral issue. Nonetheless, tens of millions of Americans still smoke, and millions of others use drugs they know to be harmful.

Reading Comprehension Questions

Vocabulary in Context

__A__ 1. In the excerpt below, the word *subsequent* (sŭb′sĭ-kwĕnt′) means
A. later.
B. serious.
C. earlier.
D. thorough.

> Context clue: The excerpt first mentions the Surgeon General's Report of 1964. This indicates that what follows is later research.

> "The Surgeon General's Report, issued in 1964, confirmed a direct link between smoking and heart disease, as well as lung cancer. Subsequent research, establishing that cigarettes are harmful not only to smokers, but also to people around them . . . transformed a personal health decision into a moral issue." (Paragraph 7)

Main Ideas

__A__ 2. The main idea of paragraph 3 is stated in the
A. first sentence.
B. second sentence.
C. third sentence.
D. fourth sentence.

> The rest of the paragraph is a brief history of the use of alcohol.

__D__ 3. The main idea of paragraph 4 is stated in the
A. first and second sentences.
B. third sentence.
C. fourth sentence.
D. final sentence.

> Sentences 1 and 2 introduce the topic. Sentence 3 is a major detail. Sentence 4 is a minor detail.

__A__ 4. The main idea of paragraph 6 is stated in the
A. first sentence.
B. second sentence.
C. third sentence.
D. fourth sentence.

> The rest of the paragraph gives examples of new synthetic drugs and explains why such drugs have unpredictable consequences.

__C__ 5. The central idea in this selection is that
A. most Americans use new synthetic drugs.
B. the use of psychoactive drugs has been relatively constant throughout various cultures and times.
C. today's drug situation is different from the drug use in other cultures and times.
D. most Americans prefer to keep their use of drugs a secret.

> Answers A and D are not supported. Answer B covers only paragraphs 1–3.

Supporting Details

_C_ 6. In contrast to other cultures and times, Americans use drugs primarily as

    A. a matter of custom and tradition.

    B. a way to get in touch with the spirit world.   See paragraph 4,

    C. a means of recreation.   fifth sentence.

    D. culturally approved stimulants.

_D_ 7. A key difference between drugs today and those used in other cultures and times is that today's drugs are often

    A. weaker.

    B. diluted with water.   See the second sentence of paragraph 5.

    C. more readily obtainable.

    D. stronger.

_B_ 8. The authors point to cigarette smoking as an example of

    A. a drug that has the longest history of widespread use.

    B. a drug whose harmful effects we know a great deal about.

    C. a synthetic drug.   See paragraph 7.

    D. a drug with comparatively mild side effects.

9–10. Add the details missing in the following partial outline of the reading. Do so by filling in each blank with the letter of one of the sentences in the box below.

Details Missing from the Outline

    A. New, synthetic drugs have unpredictable consequences.

    B. Americans take drugs primarily for recreation, not as the result of religious or family traditions.

Central point: Today's drug problem is different from the drug use in other cultures and times in three key ways.

A. Motives for using psychoactive drugs have changed.

    1. _B_   See paragraph 4.

    2 Many Americans take drugs in settings specifically designed for recreation and inebriation (bars, clubs, etc.).

    3. Some Americans use and abuse drugs in secret.

B. The drugs themselves have changed.

    1. Today's psychoactive substances, such as alcohol and heroin, are often stronger than those used in other cultures and times.

    2. _A_   See paragraph 6.

Discussion Questions

1. Were you surprised by some of the facts mentioned in this reading? If so, what surprised you?

2. Why do you think people are drawn to the use of mood-altering substances? Are drug- and alcohol-users necessarily unhappy with the reality of their lives? Why might they want to change their mood?

3. From this reading, we can infer that for centuries, the use of mood-altering substances was regarded as morally neutral, sometimes even positive. The reading suggests that it is only in relatively recent times that such substance use has been looked at with disapproval. Why do you think these attitudes have changed?

4. In contrast to other times and cultures, Americans tend to use drugs that they know to be harmful. In your opinion, what are some of the major causes of drug and alcohol abuse in our country?

Note: Writing assignments for this selection appear on page 561.

Check Your Performance			SUPPORTING DETAILS
Activity	*Number Right*	*Points*	*Score*
Review Test 1 (5 items)	_____	× 6 =	_____
Review Test 2 (10 items)	_____	× 7 =	_____
		TOTAL SCORE =	_____%

Enter your total score into the **Reading Performance Chart: Review Tests** on the inside back cover.

SUPPORTING DETAILS: Mastery Test 1

A. Answer the supporting-detail questions that follow the passage below.

¹The other day I heard someone say, "I wish I'd known then what I know now." ²The statement made me ask myself what I *do* know now that I didn't know when I was a teenager, still in high school, living at home with my parents. ³I eventually decided that I have learned several important lessons. ⁴The first is that almost any decision is better than no decision. ⁵Gather the best information you can, make a decision, and then show up and do your best. ⁶No matter what happens next, you will learn and grow from the experience. ⁷Another lesson I've learned is that life is not fair. ⁸Good people sometimes suffer unimaginable hardships; bad people sometimes live seemingly charmed lives. ⁹You can protest, "But that's not fair!" until you're blue in the face, but it won't change a thing. ¹⁰All you can do is to try to be fair and just in your own life and not be embittered by the reality around you. ¹¹A final lesson I've learned is that people are very complex. ¹²The worst of us are capable of moments of generosity and compassion; the best of us can be petty, small-minded, and hurtful. ¹³To decide that you know everything about someone is to set yourself up for a shock. ¹⁴We are all full of surprises; we are wonderfully and maddeningly complicated.

___A___   1. Sentence 3 provides
     A. the main idea.
     B. a major detail.
     C. a minor detail.

List words in sentence 3: several important lessons. Sentences 1–2 introduce the topic. The rest of the paragraph provides details of the lessons.

___B___   2. Sentence 7 provides
     A. the main idea.
     B. a major detail.
     C. a minor detail.

The addition word Another announces this second major detail.

___C___   3. Sentences 12–14 provide
     A. the main idea.
     B. a major detail.
     C. minor details.

Sentences 12–14 support the major detail contained in sentence 11—that people are very complex.

___B___   4. How many major supporting details does the paragraph include?
     A. Two
     B. Three
     C. Four

The addition words first (sentence 4), Another (sentence 7) and final (sentence 11) announce the three major supporting details.

     5. *Fill in the blank:* One addition word that introduces a major supporting detail is __*first* **or** *Another* **or** *final*__.

See sentences 4, 7, and 11.

(Continues on next page)

B. (6–10.) Complete the outline of the following textbook passage by adding the main idea and the missing major details.

> [1]Advertising fulfills four basic functions in society. [2]First, it serves a marketing purpose by helping companies that provide products or services sell their products. [3]Personal selling, sales promotions, and advertising work together to help market the product. [4]Second, advertising is educational. [5]People learn about new products and services, or improvements in existing ones, through advertising. [6]Third, advertising plays an economic role. [7]The ability to advertise allows new competitors to enter the business arena. [8]Competition, in turn, encourages product improvements and can lead to lower prices. [9]Finally, advertising performs a definite social function. [10]By vividly displaying the material and cultural opportunities available in a free-enterprise system, advertising helps increase productivity and raises the standard of living.

Main idea: *Advertising fulfills four basic functions in society.*

1. *Marketing*

2. *Educational*

3. *Economic*

4. *Social*

The main idea is stated in sentence 1. Note the list words: *four basic functions.*
Addition words that announce major details are *First* (sentence 2),
Second (sentence 4), *Third* (sentence 6), and *Finally* (sentence 9).

Name _____

Section _____ Date _____

SCORE: (Number correct) _____ × 10 = _____%

SUPPORTING DETAILS: Mastery Test 2

A. (1–5.) Answer the supporting-detail questions that follow the passage below.

¹Although hunger is clearly a motive that is tied to biological needs, psychological factors are also involved in the regulation of food intake. ²Learning plays a powerful role in determining *what* we eat, *when* we eat (we are often ready to eat at our customary times for eating, even if we have just had a snack), and even *how much* we eat (many families encourage and model overeating). ³Studies of nonhuman animals show that even rats and chimpanzees learn what to eat by watching older animals. ⁴Emotions also play a role in eating. ⁵People who are anxious often eat more than usual, and people who are depressed may lose their appetite for long periods of time. ⁶Perhaps the most troublesome psychological factor to those who are trying to control their eating, however, is incentives—external clues that activate motives. ⁷The smell of freshly baked bread makes you hungry; passing a fast-food joint on your way home from school creates a craving for french fries; and the sight of the dessert creates a desire to eat even when you are way past the point of biological hunger. ⁸Laboratory research with animals has shown that incentives can be powerful enough under some circumstances to push weight above the natural set point. ⁹All rats will overeat to the point of obesity if they have easy access to large quantities of a variety of tasty high-calorie foods.

___A___ 1. Sentence 1 provides
   A. the main idea.
   B. a major detail.
   C. a minor detail.

The paragraph presents psychological factors involved in the regulation of food intake—an idea stated in sentence 1.

___B___ 2. Sentence 2 provides
   A. the main idea.
   B. a major detail.
   C. a minor detail.

Sentence 2 introduces learning as a psychological factor influencing food intake.

___C___ 3. Sentences 7–9 provide
   A. the main idea.
   B. a major detail.
   C. minor details.

Sentences 7–9 contain examples which illustrate the major detail presented in sentence 6—that incentives are another psychological factor influencing food intake.

___B___ 4. How many major supporting details does the paragraph include?
   A. Two
   B. Three
   C. Four

See sentences 2, 4, and 6. The only major detail introduced with an addition word is emotions, in sentence 4 (*also*). The other details, learning and incentives, do not have addition words listed in Chapter 2.

5. *Fill in the blank:* The addition word that introduces a major supporting

detail is _____*also*_____.

See sentence 4.

(Continues on next page)

87

B. (6–10.) Complete the outline of the following textbook passage by adding the main idea and the missing major details.   *Wording of answers may vary.*

> ¹For many adolescents, finding an identity requires a period of intense self-exploration called an identity crisis. ²Psychologists have identified four possible outcomes of this process. ³One is *identity achievement.* ⁴Adolescents who have reached this status have passed through the identity crisis and succeeded in making personal choices about their beliefs and goals. ⁵They are comfortable with those choices because the choices are their own. ⁶In contrast are adolescents who have taken the path of *identity foreclosure.* ⁷They have prematurely settled on an identity that others provided for them. ⁸They have become what those others want them to be without ever going through an identity crisis. ⁹Other adolescents are in *moratorium* regarding the choice of an identity. ¹⁰They are in the process of actively exploring various role options, but they have not yet committed to any of them. ¹¹Finally, there are teens who are experiencing *identity diffusion.* ¹²They avoid considering role options in any conscious way. ¹³Many are dissatisfied with this condition, but are unable to start a search to "find themselves." ¹⁴Some resort to escapist activities such as drug or alcohol abuse.

Main idea: _Psychologists have identified four possible outcomes of an_

adolescent's identity crisis.

1. _Identity achievement: making successful personal choices about beliefs_

and goals

2. _Identity foreclosure: settling for an identity provided by others_

3. _Moratorium: exploring options without yet committing to any_

4. _Identity diffusion: avoiding considering the options in any conscious way_

The main idea is stated in sentences 1–2. List words: *four possible outcomes.*
Note that the four outcomes are printed in *italics.*
Item 7—In sentence 3, the addition word *one* signals the first major detail.
Item 8—See sentence 6.
Item 9—See sentence 9 (addition word: *Other*).
Item 10—See sentence 11. *Finally* introduces the last major detail.

SUPPORTING DETAILS: Mastery Test 3

A. Answer the supporting-detail questions that follow the passage below.

Item 1:
Sentence 1 introduces the topic of family violence as well as the main idea—that there are myths surrounding family violence.

Item 2:
The paragraph presents myths about family violence, but does not attempt to explain their causes or results.

¹Because family violence is a difficult and even taboo subject, the reality surrounding it has become shrouded in myths and misperceptions. ²A first widespread myth is that family violence occurs only among the poor. ³It is true that among families living at or below the poverty level, domestic violence occurs five times as frequently as in more affluent families. ⁴While this does mean that poor people are more likely to experience family violence, it does not mean that most, let alone all, poor families are violent. ⁵Another myth is that violence cannot happen in families where genuine affection exists. ⁶Unfortunately, people who have not learned constructive ways of dealing with anger or frustration may well lash out violently at people that they love. ⁷Parents can become violent while disciplining their beloved children, and a spouse can resort to violence against a spouse that he or she loves. ⁸While such violence is always unacceptable, it does not prove that love does not exist in the relationship. ⁹An additional common myth is that abused children grow up to be abusive parents. ¹⁰Again, this myth represents a misrepresentation of data. ¹¹While it is true that abused children are more likely to become abusive parents, the majority of child-abuse victims do not grow up to abuse their own children. ¹²A last myth is that alcohol and drug use cause family violence. ¹³It is true that people who drink heavily or use drugs are more likely to abuse their spouses and children. ¹⁴It does not follow, however, that the drug or alcohol use is the cause of the violence. ¹⁵While abusers often use their drinking or drug use as the excuse for their loss of control, personal problems and choices are at the root of their violent actions.

_____A_____ 1. The main idea is expressed in sentence
    A. 1.   B. 2.   C. 3.

_____B_____ 2. The major supporting details of this paragraph are
    A. causes of myths.   B. types of myths.   C. results of myths.

_____B_____ 3. The second major detail of the paragraph is introduced in sentence
    A. 4.   B. 5.   C. 7.   The second
        major detail is introduced with the addition word *Another*.

_____A_____ 4. The third major detail of the paragraph is introduced in sentence
    A. 9.   B. 10.   C. 12.   The word
        additional introduces the third major detail.

_____C_____ 5. The fourth major detail is signaled with the addition word
    A. *also.*   B. *while.*   C. *last.*
        See sentence 12.

(Continues on next page)

B. (6–10.) Complete the map of the following textbook passage by filling in the main idea and the missing major supporting details.   *Wording of answers may vary.*

> ¹It's a rare person who hasn't at one point worked for a "difficult" boss. ²Difficult bosses have their own personal quirks, but many of them fall into the following categories. ³One common "bad boss" is the bully. ⁴Like a schoolyard bully, this boss thrives on domination. ⁵He will attempt to intimidate everyone around him by shouting and blustering. ⁶Attempting to mollify a bully boss by being super-nice and cooperative rarely works; he perceives the behavior as weakness, and will be more abusive than ever. ⁷On the other end of the bad boss spectrum is the jellyfish. ⁸Unlike the bully, who loves to tell people what they've done wrong, the jellyfish hates conflict so much that he won't correct anyone. ⁹Tasks are done badly or not at all, damaging the workflow and the morale of other employees, while he looks the other way. ¹⁰He refuses to accept responsibility for being the boss. ¹¹Another common difficult boss is the workaholic. ¹²He lives for his job, and he expects his employees to do so as well. ¹³He feels no qualms about calling workers at home in the evenings or on weekends, assuming that they, too, will consider the job more important than their personal lives. ¹⁴Still another difficult boss is the aloof boss. ¹⁵No one knows what he is thinking except him. ¹⁶He makes what appears to be sudden, arbitrary decisions without consulting anyone. ¹⁷Workers have no idea from day to day whether he is satisfied with their performance or planning to fire them.

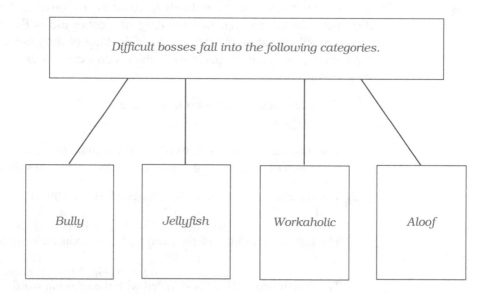

Difficult bosses fall into the following categories.

Bully   Jellyfish   Workaholic   Aloof

Sentence 2 contains the list word *categories*. The four major details are introduced with the addition words *One* (sentence 3), *other* (sentence 7), *Another* (sentence 11), and *another* (sentence 14).

SUPPORTING DETAILS: Mastery Test 4

A. Answer the supporting-detail questions that follow the passage below.

Item 1:
The paragraph presents characteristics of robberies— an idea stated in sentence 2. The list words *several... characteristics* are a clue.

[1]While criminal acts may seem random and unpredictable, in fact they, like almost everything, follow their own patterns. [2]Robbery, for instance, has several very distinctive characteristics. [3]To begin with, the majority of robberies occur in the cold winter months. [4]There are several reasons for this. [5]Around the holiday season, stores are taking in more money and shoppers are likely to be carrying more cash than usual, making both tempting targets. [6]The cold weather makes it look natural for the robber to wear a heavy coat, which makes it easier to conceal a weapon. [7]And the cold weather keeps most people off the street, thereby making it less likely that anyone will witness a holdup. [8]Another distinctive characteristic of robberies is that most take place outdoors, on or near a highway. [9]Such easy access to a highway enables the robber to make a quick escape from the scene of the crime. [10]Yet another characteristic of robberies is that most are committed by people carrying weapons. [11]While purse-snatchings and the like may be committed unarmed, the great majority of robberies are planned ahead of time and involve a weapon, usually a gun. [12]A final characteristic of robbery is that it usually occurs between strangers. [13]Unlike other violent crimes such as murder and rape, which usually involve people who know each other, a robber and his victim or victims are rarely acquainted.

_B_ 1. The main idea is expressed in sentence
    A. 1.   B. 2.   C. 3.

_B_ 2. The major supporting details of this paragraph are
    A. results.   B. characteristics.   C. reasons.   See sentences 2, 8, 10, and 12.

Item 5:
Sentences 4–7 support the major detail, contained in sentence 3, that most robberies occur in the cold winter months.

_A_ 3. The first major detail of the paragraph is introduced in sentence
    A. 3.   B. 4.   C. 8.   The addition words *To begin with* signal the first major detail.

_A_ 4. The second major detail of the paragraph is introduced in sentence
    A. 8.   B. 10.   C. 12.   The second major detail is introduced with the addition word *Another*.

_B_ 5. Sentences 4–7 contain
    A. major supporting details.   B. minor supporting details.

6. *Fill in the blank:* One addition word that introduces a major supporting detail is __*To begin with* **or** *Another* **or** *final*__.   See sentences 3, 8, 10, and 12.

(Continues on next page)

B. (7–10.) Complete the outline of the following textbook passage by adding the main idea, the missing major details (definitions), and one summarized example of a definition.   *Wording of answers may vary.*

¹David Elkind used Piaget's notion of adolescent egocentrism to account for two fallacies of thought he noticed in this age group. ²The first is the imaginary audience—the tendency of teenagers to feel they are constantly being observed by others, that people are always judging them on their appearance and behavior. ³This feeling of being perpetually "onstage" may be the source of much self-consciousness, concern about personal appearance, and showing off in adolescence.

⁴The other fallacy of adolescent thinking is the personal fable— adolescents' unrealistic sense of their own uniqueness. ⁵For instance, a teenager might feel that others couldn't possibly understand the love he or she feels toward a boyfriend or girlfriend because that love is so unique and special. ⁶This view is related to the feeling of invulnerability we mentioned earlier. ⁷Many teenagers believe they are so different from other people that they won't be touched by the negative things that happen to others. ⁸This feeling of invulnerability is consistent with the reckless risk-taking among people in this age group.

Main idea: *Egocentrism accounts for two fallacies of thought in adolescents.*

Major detail: 1. *Imaginary audience—the tendency of teenagers to feel they are constantly being observed and judged by others*

Major detail: 2. *Personal fable—adolescents' unrealistic sense of their own uniqueness*

    Example: *A teenager feels that others couldn't possibly understand the love he or she feels toward a boyfriend or girlfriend.*

Or: *A teenager believes he or she is different from other people and won't be touched by the negative things that happen to others.*

In sentence 1, the list words *two fallacies* signal the main idea.
The first major detail (sentence 2) is signaled by the addition word *first*.
The second major detail (sentence 4) is signaled by the word *other*.
Sentences 5–8 provide examples of the personal fable.

SUPPORTING DETAILS: Mastery Test 5

A. Answer the supporting-detail questions that follow the passage below.

¹Managers don't always do a good job of evaluating their employees. ²The halo effect, the Hawthorne effect, and uniformity are three common problems in employee performance reviews. ³The halo effect is one of the most well-known threats to the accuracy of performance reviews. ⁴In the classic situation, a person is given a good rating solely because all previous evaluations have been good. ⁵A good evaluation is given on faith in previous reviews and without paying attention to the current work habits of the worker. ⁶Another threat to reviews is the Hawthorne effect, which says that the act of measuring something changes that thing, so one can never exactly predict anything by relying on observation alone. ⁷In other words, if you observe people to evaluate them, they will change their behavior. ⁸Because people change their behavior when they are observed, we don't really know what their typical performance is; and not knowing that, we can't really predict if it will continue in the future. ⁹Uniformity, or giving everyone in a team or department the same evaluation, is yet another problem in performance reviews. ¹⁰When everyone is rated the same despite differing achievements, there is a serious de-motivating effect. ¹¹In addition to being unfair, if managers rate everyone high or average, they will have a much more difficult time trying to fire someone who deserves to be released.

___B___ 1. The main idea is expressed in sentence
    A. 1.   B. 2.   C. 3. List words in the main idea are *three common problems*.

___C___ 2. The paragraph is made up of a series of
    A. types.   B. reviews.   C. definitions. The rest of the paragraph defines and illustrates the terms in sentence 2.

___A___ 3. The first major detail of the paragraph is introduced in sentence
    A. 3.   B. 4.   C. 5. The first major detail is introduced with the addition word *one*.

___A___ 4. The second major detail of the paragraph is introduced in sentence
    A. 6.   B. 7.   C. 9. The addition word *Another* signals the second major detail.

___B___ 5. The third major detail of the paragraph is introduced in sentence
    A. 8.   B. 9.   C. 11.

The third major detail is signaled with the addition word *another*.

(Continues on next page)

B. (6–10.) Complete the map of the following textbook passage by filling in the main idea and the missing major supporting details. *Wording of answers may vary.*

¹America has always been a nation of immigrants. ²Unlike old countries with a homogenous population, America has defined what it is to be an American in terms of a political tradition. ³Ideally, American political culture is thought to include the following beliefs. ⁴First is the American principle of liberty. ⁵This holds that people should be free to act as they choose, providing that they do not interfere unreasonably with the well-being of others. ⁶A second component of the political culture is the principle of self-government. ⁷It proclaims that the people are the ultimate source of authority, and that their general welfare is the only legitimate purpose of government. ⁸A third component is equality—the belief that all individuals have moral worth, are entitled to fair treatment under the law, and should have equal opportunity for material gain and political influence. ⁹Finally there is unity: the principle that despite our individual differences, Americans are one people that form an indivisible union.

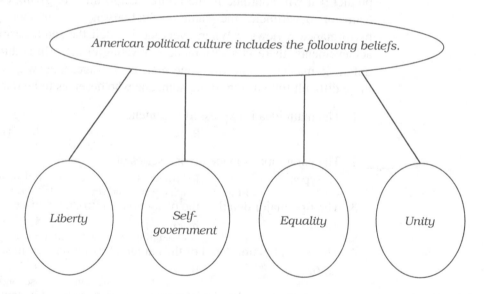

American political culture includes the following beliefs.

Liberty

Self-government

Equality

Unity

Sentence 3 contains the list words *the following beliefs*. The four major details are introduced with the addition words *First* (sentence 4), *second* (sentence 6), *third* (sentence 8), and *Finally* (sentence 9).

SUPPORTING DETAILS: Mastery Test 6

A. (1–7.) Outline the following textbook passage, which includes two main ideas and supporting details for each of those main ideas.

Items 1–7:
In sentence 1, the *s* word *reasons* signals a main idea.

Sentences 2 and 3 contain the two major reasons that people use birth control.

In sentence 4, the list words *choice of birth control methods* introduce the second main idea. The word *one* signals that this sentence also contains a major detail.

In sentence 8, the addition word *Another* signals a second major detail.

Sentence 11 contains no addition word but is still a major detail.

[1]People use birth control for different reasons. [2]Many career-minded individuals carefully plan the timing and spacing of children to best provide for their children's financial support without sacrificing their job status. [3]Others choose methods of birth control to ensure that they will never have children.

[4]In the choice of birth control methods, financial and legal considerations are one significant factor. [5]Many people must of necessity take the cost of a method into account when selecting appropriate birth control. [6]The cost of sterilization and abortion can prohibit some low-income people from choosing these alternatives, especially because federal funds do not support such procedures. [7]A number of states have established statues and policies that make contraceptive information and medical services relatively difficult to obtain.

[8]Another important consideration in the use of birth control methods is the availability of professional services. [9]For instance, some colleges and universities provide contraceptive services through their student health centers. [10]Students in colleges that do not provide such services may find that access to accurate information and clinical services is difficult to obtain and that private professional services are expensive.

[11]For many people, religious doctrine will be a factor in their selection of a birth control method. [12]One example is the opposition of the Roman Catholic Church and other religious groups to the use of contraception other than natural family planning.

Main idea: *People use birth control for different reasons.*

_____

1. *To provide financial support for children without sacrificing job status*

2. *To ensure they will never have children*

Main idea: *The choice of birth control method is based on various considerations.*

1. *Financial and legal reasons*

2. *Availability of professional services*

3. *Religious doctrine*

(Continues on next page)

B. (8–10.) Complete the map of the following textbook passage by filling in the missing major supporting details.   *Wording of answers may vary.*

¹In the late nineteenth century, millions of Americans moved from the country to the city. ²Big cities had the allure of jobs, entertainment, and socialization. ³However, city life also had its drawbacks. ⁴Sanitation was a serious problem in big cities. ⁵Whereas free-roaming scavengers—chickens, hogs, dogs, and birds—handily cleaned up the garbage in small towns, and backyard latrines were adequate in disposing of human wastes, neither worked when a hundred people lived in a building and shared a single toilet. ⁶City governments provided for waste collection, but even when honestly administered (which was the exception), sanitation departments simply could not keep up. ⁷Health was another major problem in the city. ⁸Crowding led to epidemic outbreaks of serious diseases like smallpox, cholera, measles, typhus, and scarlet fever. ⁹Even less-dangerous illnesses like chicken pox, mumps, whooping cough, and influenza were killers in crowded cities. ¹⁰Another problem was the increase of crime in the city. ¹¹With 14,000 homeless people in New York in 1890, and work difficult to get and unsteady in the best of times, many found the temptation of sneak thievery, pocket picking, purse snatching, and even violent robbery too much to resist. ¹²Whereas the rate of homicide and other serious crimes declined in German and British cities as they grew larger, it tripled in American cities during the 1880s.

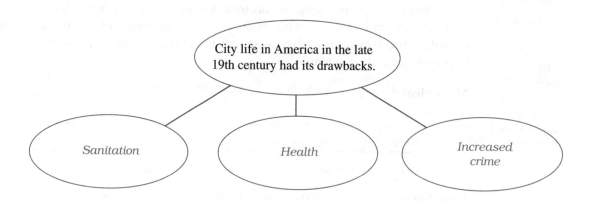

Sentence 4 presents the first of three serious problems in city life.
The addition word *another* in sentence 7 signals the second major problem.
The addition word *Another* in sentence 10 introduces the third problem.

3

Implied Main Ideas

In Chapters 1 and 2, you learned the two basic parts of anything you read: a main idea and the supporting details that explain and develop that idea. As you have seen, the main idea may be clearly stated in one sentence of a selection.

However, the main idea may be **implied**—only suggested by the supporting details and not clearly stated in one sentence. The reader must figure out such an implied main idea by considering the supporting details. In the above cartoon, you can figure out the main idea by noting the details: the newlyweds' car has broken down; and since they are hitchhiking in opposite directions, the implied point is that their marriage has broken down as well. This chapter offers practice in finding implied main ideas, whether in paragraphs or in longer selections.

IMPLIED MAIN IDEAS

Sometimes a selection lacks a sentence that directly states the main idea. In such cases, the author has simply decided to let the details of the selection suggest the main idea. You must figure out what that implied idea is by deciding upon the point all the details support. For example, read the following paragraph.

[1]Researchers who study the "science" of shopping note that men always move faster than women through a store's aisle. [2]Men spend less time looking, too. [3]They usually don't like asking where things are, or any other questions. [4]When a man takes clothing into a dressing room, the only thing that stops him from buying it is if it doesn't fit. [5]Women, on the other hand, try things on as only part of the consideration process, and garments that fit just fine may still be rejected on other grounds. [6]Here's another contrast: 86 percent of women look at price tags when they shop. [7]Only 72 percent of men do. [8]For a man, ignoring the price tag is almost a measure of his masculinity. [9]As a result, men are far more easily encouraged to buy more expensive versions of the same product than are women shoppers. [10]They are also far more suggestible than women—men seem so anxious to get out of the store that they'll say yes to almost anything.

You can see that no sentence in the paragraph is a good "umbrella" statement that covers all of the other sentences. To decide on the main idea, we must ask the same three questions we've already used to find main ideas:

- "Who or what is this paragraph about?" That will be the topic.
- "What is the main point the author is trying to make about that topic?"
- And when we think we know the main point, we can test it by asking, "Does *all or most* of the material in the paragraph support this idea?"

In the paragraph above, all of the details are about men and women shoppers, so that must be the topic. Which of the following statements expresses the general point that the author is trying to make about the topic? Check (✓) the answer you think is correct.

____ A. Men always move faster than women when shopping.

____ B. Women look at price tags more than men.

_✓_ C. Men and women behave differently when shopping.

____ D. Men make more expensive choices when shopping.

The details reveal the author's general point to be answer C: men and women behave differently when shopping. All the other statements above are supporting details for this main idea—each tells of a way in which men and women shoppers behave differently. Although the main idea is not directly stated, it is clearly implied by all the material in the paragraph.

Figuring Out Implied Main Ideas in Paragraphs

Remember, to find implied main ideas, it often helps to decide on the topic first. Do so by asking yourself, "Who or what is the selection about?" After you find the topic, then ask yourself, "What is the author's main point about the topic?"

☑ *Check Your Understanding*

Read the following selection and try to answer the questions that follow.

¹Fifty years ago, Americans were sleeping an average of eight to twelve hours a night, but by 1990 they were down to only seven hours a night. ²Now many Americans average only about six hours of sleep a night. ³Extensive research shows that losing an hour or two of sleep every night, week after week, month after month, makes it more difficult for people to pay attention (especially to monotonous tasks) and to remember things. ⁴Reaction time slows down, behavior becomes unpredictable, logical reasoning is impaired, and accidents and errors in judgment increase, while productivity and the ability to make decisions decline. ⁵Students fall asleep in class and fail to learn all that they should. ⁶Marriages become more stressful as sleep-exhausted parents try to cope with their children and each other. ⁷Truck and auto drivers fall asleep at the wheel, and experts estimate that accidents result in over 1,500 deaths in this country a year. ⁸Workers perform less efficiently, and those in high-risk positions can endanger us all. ⁹For example, sleep deprivation led to the accident at the nuclear power plant at Three Mile Island, Pennsylvania.

_B_ 1. What is the topic of the above paragraph?
  A. Sleep
  B. Loss of sleep in America
  C. Sleep loss for students and parents
  D. Sleep loss for drivers and workers

_A_ 2. Which statement best expresses the unstated main idea of the paragraph?
  A. The loss of sleep in America has led to serious problems.
  B. Americans have lost sleep steadily over the last fifty years.
  C. Sleep loss affects the performance of students and parents.
  D. Sleep loss affects the performance of drivers and workers.

Explanation:

The topic, referred to directly or indirectly in several sentences, is "Loss of sleep in America." The implied main idea is Statement A, that the loss of sleep in America has led to serious problems. Statement B, "Americans have lost sleep steadily over the last fifty years," does not include the serious problems that result from a loss of sleep and that are developed in the paragraph. Statements C and D are too narrow—each referring to only two groups that are affected by sleep loss.

When you think you have determined an implied main idea, be sure to test yourself by asking, *"Does all or most of the material in the paragraph support this idea?"* Only statement A covers all of the content of the above paragraph.

➤ Practice 1

Read each paragraph and then answer the questions that follow. Remember to find a topic by asking "Who or what is the selection about?" and to find an implied main idea by asking "What is the author's point about the topic?"

> **Hint:** Noticing addition words (such as *first, another, also, moreover,* and *finally*) will help you identify the major supporting details that can suggest the main idea.

Paragraph 1

[1]Pet owners like to assume that the cat's purr is an expression of pleasure, but this assumption is only partly true. [2]Originally, the purr probably evolved as a homing device. [3]Because newly born kittens cannot see, hear, or smell, they need some signal to help them feed. [4]Since they can feel vibratory movement, they can locate their mother through her purring. [5]Cats may also use the purr as self-comfort. [6]Felines that are anxious, injured, or ill often issue the same low, continuous, rattling hum. [7]Like submissive posturing among dogs, purring may be a signal of appeasement to other cats or to people. [8]In this case, it communicates that the purring cat is not a threat. [9]Recently, scientists have discovered that cats may purr to help themselves get better when they're injured. [10]In this theory, purring is actually a low-energy mechanism that stimulates muscle and bones. [11]The healing power of their purring may even explain their "nine lives." [12]Then again, the purring cat may simply be reminding its owner to keep stroking.

___B___ 1. What is the topic of the above paragraph?
- A. Pet owners
- B. A cat's purr
- C. The purr as a homing device
- D. Science and a cat's purr

> Answer A is not developed in the passage.
> Answer C covers only sentences 2–4.
> Answer D covers only sentence 9.

___A___ 2. Which statement best expresses the unstated main idea?
- A. There are actually a number of theories about why cats purr.
- B. A cat's purr is both homing signal and signal of appeasement.
- C. There are many false assumptions about why cats purr.
- D. When cats purr, they comfort themselves as well as their owners.

> Answer B covers only sentences 2 and 7. Answer D covers only sentences 1 and 5.
> Answer C is not supported in the passage.

Paragraph 2

[1]The family introduces children to the physical world through the opportunities it provides for play and exploration of objects. [2]It also creates bonds between people that are unique. [3]The attachments children form with parents and siblings usually last a lifetime, and they serve as models for relationships in the wider world of neighborhood and school. [4]Within the family, children also experience their first social conflicts. [5]Discipline by parents and arguments with siblings provide children with important lessons in compliance and cooperation as well as opportunities to learn how to influence the behavior of others. [6]Finally, within the family, children learn the language, skills, and social and moral values of their culture.

_B_   1. What is the topic of the above paragraph?   The topic is not the general
                                                      subject of family histories (A) or children
    A. Family histories   (C). The topic of children's attachments
    B. The family and children   (D) is too narrow because it covers only
    C. Children   sentences 2 and 3.
    D. Children's attachments

_B_   2. Which statement best expresses the unstated main idea?
    A. The family teaches children compliance and cooperation.
    B. The family has a profound effect on child development.
    C. The bonds that children form with their parents last a lifetime.
    D. Through the family, children first learn about the world.   Answer A
covers only sentence 5. Answer C covers only sentence 3. Answer D does not include
developing models for relationships (sentence 3), acquiring social skills (sentence 5), or
learning cultural skills and values (sentence 6).

Paragraph 3

[1]Today, a football team in possession of the ball has four plays to make a ten-yard first down, but during the late nineteenth and early twentieth centuries, the offensive team had three plays to make a five-yard first down, and passing was severely restricted, both by the rules and by tradition. [2]As a result, coaches emphasized "mass plays" that directed the maximum amount of force against one isolated player or point on the field. [3]The flying wedge was the most notorious mass play. [4]It entailed players grouping themselves into a V formation and starting to run before the ball was put into play. [5]At the last moment, the ball was snapped and passed to a player within the wall of the wedge. [6]The wedge of runners then crashed into their stationary opponents. [7]Given that their equipment was crude—players often played without helmets, and no helmet had a facemask—this use of a massed brute force injured hundreds of players a year. [8]If such plays were not bad enough, referees rarely enforced rules against slugging, kicking, and piling on. [9]During the 1909 season, such allowances resulted in 30 deaths and 216 serious injuries. [10]Victory was the supreme object, and any method seemed justified in pursuit of that goal.

_____C_____ 1. What is the topic of the above paragraph?

    A. Football

    B. Violence in football

    C. Football a hundred years ago

    D. The flying wedge

Answers A and B are too broad. Answer D is too narrow because it does not cover sentences 1–2 and 8–10.

_____A_____ 2. Which statement best expresses the unstated main idea?

    A. Football was a dangerous sport during the late nineteenth and early twentieth centuries.

    B. Schools should enforce strict safety measures with their football teams.

    C. The flying wedge is a brutal and dangerous football play that often leads to injury.

    D. During the late nineteenth and early twentieth centuries, no one was concerned about the safety of football players.

Answers B and D are too narrow, although they are inferences that some may draw from the passage. Answer C covers only sentences 3–7.

➤ Practice 2

The main idea of each of the following paragraphs is unstated, and each paragraph is followed by four sentences. In the space provided, write the letter of the sentence that best expresses each unstated main idea.

Remember to ask yourself, "What is the implied main idea?" Then test your answer by asking, *"Does all or most of the material in the paragraph support this idea?*

Paragraph 1

¹Although many schools have increased funding for girls' sports (volleyball, softball, and basketball) and some have created coeducational teams (usually in volleyball or swimming), few have opened up the "rough sports" to girls. ²Football, hockey, and wrestling continue to be male-dominated activities. ³Generally, the lion's share of spending goes to these exclusively male sports. ⁴When female athletes participate in sports as aggressive and fierce competitors, they face social stigma for demonstrating the same attributes that bring male athletes praise. ⁵There is a widespread myth that competing in sports masculinizes females and may even cause them physical harm. ⁶Consequently, many female athletes attempt to emphasize their "femininity" while competing by wearing hair ribbons, jewelry, or makeup.

_____D_____ Which statement best expresses the unstated main idea of the paragraph?

    A. Schools need to provide equal funding for male and female sports.

    B. Participating in sports does not make women more masculine.

    C. Women must deal with gender stereotypes on a daily basis.

    D. In sports, women still have not achieved equal status with men.

Answer A covers only sentences 1–3. Answer B covers only sentences 5–6. Answer C is too broad because the passage does not discuss gender stereotypes in daily life.

Paragraph 2

¹A hungry wasp flies over to investigate an enormous burgundy flower. ²It has one stalk that stretches up to two feet tall and has a giant flower at the tip. ³The wasp discovers the smell of nectar coming from the large, curled green leaves that surround the stem at ground level. ⁴The sides of each leaf wrap together and stick closed, forming a container shaped like a water pitcher, giving the pitcher plant its name. ⁵These hollow leaves hold rainwater, dew, and something else—an enzyme that helps digest food. ⁶The wasp lands on a leaf edge and begins to drink nectar from the red vein of the leaf. ⁷As it drinks, it follows the vein downward to get more nectar. ⁸Soon the wasp has gone too far; it lands in the water in the bottom of the leaf, and it can't crawl back up. ⁹That's because the thick hairs on the leaf point downward, making the leaf easy to climb down but almost impossible to climb up. ¹⁰The wasp has fallen prey to the pitcher plant's deadly design. ¹¹It struggles in the water, but the enzyme soon kills and dissolves the wasp. ¹²The plant then absorbs phosphorus, nitrogen, and other vitamins and minerals from the waspy water. ¹³Wasps are not the only victims. ¹⁴Pitcher plants trap and dissolve ants, bees, butterflies, spiders, and even small frogs.

___C___ Which statement best expresses the unstated main idea of the paragraph?
A. Insects can become victims of a deadly design.
B. The pitcher plant gets its name from the way its leaves curl together.
C. The pitcher plant is a deadly trap for insects and other small prey.
D. The design of the pitcher plant's leaves makes it impossible for insects to escape.   Answer A fails to mention the pitcher plant. Answer B covers only sentence 4. Answer D covers only sentence 9.

Paragraph 3

¹By the late 1920s, Americans' food preparation became easier because a variety of foods were now available in cans. ²This meant that the typical housewife no longer had to shop daily for fresh food. ³Instead, she could store everything from tuna to pineapple. ⁴Soon, ready-made foods like drink mixes, gelatin desserts, cheese, and peanut butter were staples in the kitchen. ⁵Even men and children could now prepare meals if they used these foods. ⁶Then, in 1949, Clarence Birdseye, a biologist, made a startling discovery. ⁷He noticed that meat exposed to the Arctic air tasted as good cooked as fresh meat, even when it was cooked several months later. ⁸He noticed that the speed at which something was frozen made the difference. ⁹The faster the freeze, the less chance that ice crystals would tear apart cell walls and release natural juices. ¹⁰Birdseye soon applied his methods to poultry, fruits, and vegetables. ¹¹People could now eat a wide variety of seasonal foods any time during the year. ¹²Eating became even easier when Carl Swanson, owner of a food-processing plant, thought of a way to package complete meals. ¹³In 1954, he introduced the first frozen TV dinner in a three-compartment

aluminum tray. [14]People who didn't own freezers could buy TV dinners and eat them the same day.

___C___ Which statement best expresses the unstated main idea of the paragraph?
- A. The development of convenience foods freed women from daily shopping.
- B. Frozen foods allowed people to eat a wide variety of seasonal foods all year long.
- C. Convenience foods changed cooking and eating habits in America.
- D. Americans are indebted to Clarence Birdseye and Carl Swanson.

Answer A covers only sentences 2–3. Answer B covers only sentence 11. Answer D is incorrect because the passage emphasizes the effects of the development of convenience foods, not the two men's contributions.

Putting Implied Main Ideas into Your Own Words

When you read, you often have to **infer**—figure out on your own—an author's unstated main idea. The implied main idea that you come up with should cover all or most of the details in the paragraph.

See if you can find and write the topic of the paragraph below. Then write the implied main idea in your own words. Finally, read the explanation that follows.

> *Hints:* Remember that you can help yourself identify the topic and main idea if you 1) look for repeated words as you read and 2) try to mark major supporting details. Major details are often signaled by such common addition words as the following:

Addition Words

one	to begin with	also	further
first (of all)	for one thing	in addition	furthermore
second (ly)	other	next	last (of all)
third (ly)	another	moreover	final (ly)

[1]All people have a strong need to belong to groups, stemming from evolutionary pressures that increased people's chance of survival and reproduction when in groups rather than in isolation. [2]This need may also be driven by the desire to feel protected against threat and uncertainty in everyday life or to gain a greater sense of personal and social identity. [3]Moreover, people join specific groups in order to accomplish things that they cannot accomplish as individuals. [4]Neither symphonies nor football games can be played by one person alone, and many types of work require team effort. [5]Further, people join groups because of the social status and identity that they offer. [6]An important part of people's feelings of self-worth comes from their identification with particular groups. [7]Even a relatively low-status group can be a source of pride for individuals who are held in

high esteem within the group; being big fish in small ponds can make people feel good about themselves, particularly people from individualist cultures. [8]Finally, people may join groups simply because they like the members and want to have the opportunity to interact with them.

What is the topic of this paragraph? _____ *Joining groups* _____

What is the implied main idea of this paragraph? _____

_____ *People join groups for a number of reasons.* _____

Explanation:

One key to the topic here is the words *join groups*, which are repeated through the paragraph. The other key to the topic is the major details in the paragraph. Many of the details are signaled by addition words *(also, Moreover, Further, and Finally)*. Each major detail is one of the reasons why people join groups. The author's main point about the topic can simply be stated like this: *People join groups for a number of reasons.*

➤ Practice 3

In the spaces provided, fill in the topic of each paragraph. Then, using your own words, write the implied main ideas of the paragraphs.

Hints: *Wording of answers may vary.*

1. To find the topic, it often helps to look for repeated words in a paragraph.

2. To identify the topic and main idea, mark major supporting details as you read. These major details are often signaled by such common addition words as the ones shown in the box on the previous page.

A. [1]Because most students are unmarried, high schools and colleges serve as matchmaking institutions. [2]It is at school that many young people find their future spouses. [3]Schools also establish social networks. [4]Some adults maintain friendships from high school and college; others develop networks that benefit their careers. [5]Another function of schools is to provide employment. [6]With 53 million students in grade and high schools, and another 15 million enrolled in colleges, U.S. education is big business. [7]Primary and secondary schools provide jobs for 2.9 million teachers, while another million work in colleges and universities. [8]Schools also help stabilize employment. [9]To keep millions of young people in school is to keep them out of the labor market, protecting the positions of older workers. [10]Last of all, schools help stabilize society by keeping these millions off the streets,

Passage A:
The word *schools* is used ten times in the passage; *colleges* is used four times. All the details show the various functions of schools. The addition words *Another function* help suggest the implied main idea.

Passage B:
The words *body temperature* are used five times in the passage. Sentence 3 suggests the unstated main idea: "… one of many biological factors …" The word *factor* is repeated in the remainder of the passage, reinforcing that notion.

Passage C:
The word *ethanol* appears five times in the passage. All the details show advantages of ethanol use. The words *Another plus* (sentence 7) indicate that the passage lists advantages of ethanol.

where they might be marching and protesting in search of unskilled jobs long lost to other nations.

Topic: _____ Schools and colleges _____

Implied main idea: _____

_____ Schools and colleges serve a number of functions in our society. _____

B. [1]Do you sometimes feel cold, or hot, while others around you seem comfortable? [2]Don't worry—you are not alone. [3]Weight is one of many biological factors that affect how warm or cold you feel: the more body fat you have, the greater the amount of insulation, so you tend not to be as cold. [4]Muscle mass is another factor affecting our body temperature. [5]The more muscular you are, the better your body will be at regulating temperature. [6]Moreover, diet affects body temperature. [7]People who don't get enough essential nutrients may find themselves feeling cold and tired because their body is not getting the "fuel" it needs to work efficiently. [8]In addition, gender plays a part in one's body temperature. [9]Women generally have less muscle mass than men do, which reduces their average body temperature. [10]Age is yet one more biological factor to consider. [11]As people age, their hormonal systems don't produce as many hormones as when they were younger. [12]As a result, the elderly often feel colder. [13]Finally, stress is a factor affecting people's body temperature: tension could reduce your circulation, making you feel colder.

Topic: _____ Body temperature _____

Implied main idea: _____

_____ Several factors affect body temperatures in humans. _____

C. [1]Ethanol, an alternative energy source for our automobiles, is derived primarily from the starch of corn kernels, so it's biodegradable. [2]Its emissions are cleaner than gasoline, thus reducing harmful levels of carbon monoxide, particulate matter, greenhouse emissions, and other toxic pollutants. [3]Ethanol also "fuels" the economy. [4]It's cheaper than gasoline, thus providing an immediate savings to consumers. [5]But, since it pollutes less than gasoline, it provides an indirect savings, too. [6]Namely, costly pollution control measures across many industries may be able to be reduced from having a cleaner environment. [7]Another plus for ethanol is that it provides jobs for American workers. [8]It's estimated that 200,000 people currently work in this industry, many in rural areas that are desperate for jobs. [9]Some estimates project that figure could grow to 500,000 in the next decade. [10]Lastly, ethanol permits our country to be less dependent on foreign oil and all of its potential pitfalls. [11]As long as there is farm land, there will be a supply of ethanol.

Topic: _____ *Ethanol* **or** *Ethanol's advantages*

Implied main idea: _There are several advantages to using ethanol as an_

alternative fuel.

Figuring Out Implied Main Ideas in Longer Passages

When you read, you may have to infer an author's unstated central idea (also called a **thesis**) in a longer passage. The implied central idea that you come up with should cover all or most of the details in the passage. For example, read the following passage.

[1]Commonsense views about abortion include the ideas that abortion is a last resort, that women who get abortions do not know how to use contraceptives, and certainly, that women who get abortions did not want to get pregnant. [2]Consider, however, that abortion is not always a last resort. [3]In Russia, abortion is a major means of birth control, and the average Russian woman has six abortions during her lifetime. [4]Abortion is so common in Russia that there are twice as many abortions as births.

[5]Nor is it true that women who have abortions don't know how to use contraceptives. [6]Sociologist Kristen Luker, who studied an abortion clinic in California, found that many women did not use contraceptives, even though they knew how to use them and did not want to get pregnant. [7]They avoided contraceptives, Luker discovered, because they interfered with intimacy, were expensive, were disapproved of by their boyfriends, or caused adverse side effects. [8]Some even avoided contraceptives to protect their self-concept. [9]If they used contraceptives, they would think of themselves as "available" or sexually promiscuous, but without them they looked at sex as something that "just happened." [10]Luker's study shows that some women take chances—and then get pregnant and have abortions.

[11]Sociologist Leon Dash, who studied pregnancy among teenagers in Washington, D.C., found that the third commonsense idea is not necessarily true. [12]Some girls get pregnant deliberately. [13]Some want children so that, as they said, "I can have something to hold onto that I can call my own." [14]Some boyfriends also urge their girlfriends to get pregnant. [15]They say that this will make them "feel like a man." [16]And, as Luker discovered, some women get pregnant to test their boyfriends' commitment. [17]Often the relationship sours, and the young women decide not to bear the child. [18]In short, contrary to a middle-class perspective, many poor, young, unmarried women get pregnant because they want to.

You can see that no sentence in the passage is a good "umbrella" statement that covers all of the other sentences. To decide on the implied central idea, we must ask the same three questions we've already used to find main ideas:

- "Who or what is this passage about?" That will be the topic.

- "What is the central point the author is trying to make about that topic?"

- And when we think we know the central idea, we can test it by asking, "Does all or most of the material in the passage support this idea?"

☑ Check Your Understanding

In the passage above, all of the details concern commonsense views about abortion, so that must be the topic. Which of the following statements expresses the central point that the author is trying to make about the topic? Check (✓) the answer you think is correct.

_____ A. Abortion is not always a last resort.

_____ B. Abortion is not always the result of a lack of knowledge about contraceptives.

_____ C. Abortion is not always the result of accidental pregnancy.

__✓__ D. Commonsense views about abortion are not necessarily true.

The details reveal the author's central idea to be answer D: Commonsense views about abortion are not necessarily true. All the other statements above are supporting details for this central idea—each tells of a view about abortion that is not necessarily true. Although the central idea is not directly stated, it is clearly implied by all the material in the passage.

➤ Practice 4

The central idea of each of the following passages is unstated, and each passage is followed by four sentences. In the space provided, write the letter of the sentence that best expresses each unstated central idea.

Remember to first ask yourself, "What is the implied central idea?" Then test your answer by asking, "Does all or most of the material in the passage support this idea?"

Passage 1

[1]Education programs used to be widely available in prisons in the United States, especially after the notorious Attica rebellion in 1971, which left 43 dead. [2]Among the demands of the inmates, who were pressing for improved prison conditions, was a better education program. [3]This demand

was met, not only at Attica but also in prisons around the country. [4]Over the next decades, prison education flourished.

[5]Then, in 1994, Congress effectively abolished all federally financed college education for prison inmates when it voted to eliminate Pell Grants for federal and state prisons, despite strong resistance from the Department of Education. [6]Critics pointed out that education greatly reduces recidivism; only one-tenth of 1 percent of the Pell Grant budget went to the education of prisoners anyway. [7]But Senator Kay Bailey Hutchison, a Republican of Texas, argued that it was unfair for felons to benefit from Pell Grants when as many as 100,000 low-income students were denied them each year. [8]Why should prisoners be educated for nothing when so many honest folks failed to get a break? [9]And besides, she said, the federal government already spent far too much money on prison education and training programs. [10]Today, what federal money is still spent on prison education goes largely toward vocational training.

[11]Hutchison's arguments arose from a more generalized desire—not just among Republicans—to get tough on crime, or more precisely on criminals. [12]Even though crime rates were actually dropping in the 1990s, many argued that judges were letting felons off too lightly and that the "rights" of victims needed to be taken into account. [13]Thus, beginning in the early 1990s, prison regimens were tightened, even as mandatory minimum sentences and three-strikes laws meant more and more people came into the system and stayed. [14]In this climate, few politicians were ready to stand up for higher-education programs for prisoners. [15]Before 1995 there were some 350 college-degree programs for prisoners in the United States. [16]Today there are about a dozen, four of them in New York State.

___A___ Which sentence best expresses the implied central idea of the entire selection?

    A. Higher-education programs for prisoners in the United States, while once flourishing, have drastically declined in recent years due to a generalized desire to get tough on crime.

    B. In 1994 Congress voted to eliminate Pell Grants for federal and state prisons, because it wanted to get tough on crime.

    C. Although crime rates dropped in the 1990s, there was increasing demand to get tough on crime in the United States.

    D. In the 1990s, few politicians were courageous enough to stand up for higher education for prisoners in the United States.

Answer B covers only sentences 7–11. Answer C covers only sentence 12.
Answer D covers only sentence 14.

Passage 2

[1]In New England, chicken farmers realized that chickens born in the spring fetched better prices than the older, tougher birds that had lived through a winter. [2]Sometimes they tried to pass the older chickens off as young, tender birds. [3]But smart buyers learned to reject these birds, complaining that they were "no spring chickens." [4]The phrase has come to mean anyone who is past his youth.

[5]Today, a "white elephant" means an unwanted item you have lying around the house. [6]White elephants are often the subject of gag gift exchanges. [7]But the original "white elephant" was no gag at all. [8]In Burma, albino elephants were considered sacred. [9]They could not be used for work, and they had to be lavished with the best food and great attention. [10]Eventually a "white elephant" meant something that was costly to maintain and provided few benefits.

[11]Did you ever wonder where the phrase "to bite the bullet" came from? [12]In the days before anesthesia, amputations and other surgeries were agonizing affairs. [13]The surgeon could offer a patient little pain relief other than to give him an object, often a bullet, to clench between his teeth. [14]Today "to bite the bullet" means to pay a painful price in order to get an ordeal over with.

[15]When we suspect we know what's going to happen next, we sometimes say we "see the writing on the wall." [16]This phrase is Biblical in its origin. [17]In the book of Daniel in the Old Testament, the wrongdoing of a corrupt king was revealed by a mysterious hand which appeared and wrote a message on the wall, warning that the king's days were numbered.

___C___ Which sentence best expresses the implied central idea of the entire selection?
  A. Long ago, life was much simpler than it is today.
  B. Some common phrases have come down to us as the result of old-time customs.
  C. Some of today's common phrases have surprising origins.
  D. Long ago, people entertained each other by making up humorous expressions.   Answers A and D are not supported by the passage.
        Answer B is too narrow because it covers only sentences 5–10.

Passage 3

[1]As American colonists became consumers, they developed a taste not only for tea (from China) but also for coffee (from Arabia), hot chocolate (from Central America), and rum (distilled from sugar, which also sweetened the bitter taste of the other three). [2]These four exotic beverages moved swiftly from luxury to necessity.

³Each beverage had its own pattern of consumption. ⁴Chocolate, brought to Spain from Mexico and enjoyed there for a century before spreading more widely throughout Europe, became the preferred drink of aristocrats, consumed hot at intimate gatherings in palaces and mansions. ⁵Coffee, by contrast, became the preeminent morning beverage of English and colonial businessmen, who praised its caffeine for keeping drinkers sober and focused. ⁶Coffee was served in new public coffeehouses, patronized only by men, where politics and business were the topics of conversation. ⁷The first coffeehouse opened in London in the late 1660s; Boston had several by the 1690s. ⁸By the mid-eighteenth century, though, tea had supplanted coffee as the preferred hot, caffeinated beverage in England and America. ⁹It was consumed in the afternoons, in private homes at tea tables presided over by women. ¹⁰Tea embodied genteel status and polite conversation. ¹¹In contrast, rum was the drink of the masses. ¹²This inexpensive, potent distilled spirit, made possible by new technology and the increasing production of sugar, was devoured by free working people everywhere in the Atlantic world.

¹³The American colonies played a vital role in the production, distribution, and consumption of each of these beverages. ¹⁴Chocolate, most obviously, originated in America, and cacao plantations in the South American tropics multiplied in size and number to meet the rising demand. ¹⁵Coffee and tea (particularly the latter) were as avidly consumed in the colonies as in England. ¹⁶And rum involved Americans in every phase of its production and consumption. ¹⁷The sugar grown on French and English Caribbean plantations was transported to the mainland in barrels and ships made from North American wood. ¹⁸There the syrup was turned into rum at 140 distilleries. ¹⁹The Americans themselves drank a substantial share of the distilleries' output—an estimated four gallons per person annually—but exported much of it to Africa. ²⁰There the rum purchased more slaves to produce more sugar to make still more rum, and the cycle began again.

___D___ Which sentence best expresses the implied central idea of the entire selection?

    A. At one time, tea, coffee, chocolate, and rum were considered exotic, but they became increasingly common after the mid-seventeenth century.

    B. Rum was the drink most in demand in American and English society.

    C. Chocolate, coffee, tea, and rum were each consumed by different segments of society in colonial America.

    D. The demand for chocolate, coffee, tea, and rum among different segments of American and English society contributed to the colonies' economic and social development.

Answers A, B and C are too narrow. A does not include social and economic aspects. B covers only sentence 12. C covers only sentences 3–12.

CHAPTER REVIEW

In this chapter, you learned the following:

- At times authors imply, or suggest, a main idea without stating it clearly in one sentence. In such cases, you must figure out that main idea by considering the supporting details. When you think you know the main idea, test it by asking, "Does *all or most* of the material support this idea?"

- To find implied central ideas in longer reading selections, you must again look closely at the supporting material.

The next two chapters—Chapters 4 and 5—will explain common ways that authors organize their material.

On the Web: If you are using this book in class, you can visit our website for additional practice in recognizing implied main ideas. Go to **www.townsendpress.com** and click on "Online Exercises."

➤ **Review Test 1**

To review what you've learned in this chapter, answer each of the following questions by filling in the blank.

1. When a paragraph has no sentence that states the main idea, we say the main idea is suggested, or _____*implied*_____.   See page 97.

2. To figure out an implied idea, it often helps to first determine the _____*topic*_____ of the paragraph by asking, "Who or what is this paragraph about?"   See page 98.

3. After you figure out what you think is the implied main idea of a paragraph, test yourself by asking, "Does all or most of the material in the paragraph _____*support*_____ this idea?"   See page 98.

4. Just as a paragraph has a main idea, a longer selection has a central _____*idea* (**or** *point)*_____, or thesis, that is supported by all or most of the material in the selection.   See page 107.

5. The central point of a long selection may be stated directly, or it may be _____*implied*_____.   See page 107.

➤ **Review Test 2**

The essay below is followed by questions on implied ideas and also on vocabulary in context, stated main ideas, and supporting details.

Preview

Americans are getting fatter. The statistics keep coming out, and they are steadily worse. As a people, our weight keeps climbing, while our physical fitness is declining. What is going on? In this essay, the author encourages us to look at the point where most obesity begins: childhood.

Words to Watch

diabetes (4): a chronic health condition in which the body is unable to break down sugar in the blood

coma (12): a state of prolonged unconsciousness

staple (13): a basic item or feature

"EXTRA LARGE," PLEASE

Alice M. Davies

1 School lunches have always come in for criticism. When I was a kid, we complained about "mystery meat" and "leftover surprise casserole." Half a canned pear in a shaky nest of Jell-O didn't do much to excite our taste buds. I hid my share of limp green beans under my napkin, the better to escape the eagle eye of lunchroom monitors who encouraged us to eat our soggy, overcooked vegetables.

2 But the cafeteria lunches were there, and so we ate them. (Most of them. OK, I hid the gooey tapioca pudding, too.) I think we accepted the idea that being delicious was not the point. The meals were reasonably nutritious, and they fueled our young bodies for the mental and physical demands of the day. In my case, that demand included walking a quarter mile to and from school, enjoying three recesses a day, and taking part in gym class a couple of times a week. After-school hours, at least when the weather was good, were spent outdoors playing kickball or tag with neighbor kids.

3 I can imagine you wondering, "Who cares?" I don't blame you. My memories of school days in northern Indiana thirty-some years ago aren't all that fascinating even to me. And yet I think you should care, because of one fact I haven't mentioned yet. When I was a kid and looked around at other kids my age, I saw all kinds of differences. There were tall ones and short ones and black and white and brown ones, rude ones and polite ones, popular ones and geeky ones, athletic ones and uncoordinated ones. But you know what? There weren't many heavy ones. The few there were stood out because they were unusual. I think that if you had asked me at the time, I would have told you that kids are just naturally skinny.

4 Flash forward to the present. Walk down any city street in America. Sit in a mall and watch the people stream by. You don't need to be a rocket scientist to notice something's changed. Whether you call them big-boned, chubby, husky, or plus-sized, kids are heavy, lots of them. If your own eyes don't convince you, here are the statistics: Since 1980, the number of American kids who are dangerously overweight has tripled. More than 16 percent of our children—that's 1 in 6—qualify as "obese." Hordes of them are developing diet-related diabetes°, a disease that used to be seen almost always in adults. When

California's students in grades 5 through 12 were given a basic fitness test, almost 8 out of 10 failed.

5   Part of the problem is that many kids don't have good opportunities to exercise. They live in neighborhoods without sidewalks or paths where they can walk, bike, or skate safely. Drug activity and violent crime may make playing outside dangerous. They can reach their schools only by car or bus. Many of those schools are so short of money they've scrapped their physical-fitness classes. Too few communities have athletic programs in place.

6   Electronic entertainment also plays a role in the current state of affairs. Kids used to go outside to play with other kids because it was more fun than sitting around the house. Today, kids who sit around the house have access to dozens of cable TV channels, the Internet, DVD players, and a dizzying assortment of video games.

7   Still another cause is the lack of parental supervision. When I was a kid, most of us had a mom or an older sibling at home telling us to get off our butts and go outside. (The alternative was often to stay inside and do chores. We chose to go out and play.) Now, most American families have two working parents. For most of the daylight hours, those parents just aren't around to encourage their kids to get some exercise. A related problem is that parents who can't be home much may feel guilty about it. One way of relieving that guilt is to buy Junior the game system of his dreams and a nice wide-screen TV to play it on.

8   These are all complicated problems whose solutions are equally complicated. But there is one cause of the fattening of America's kids that can be dealt with more easily. And that cause is the enormous influence that fast-food restaurants and other sources of calorie-laden junk have gained over America's kids.

9   I'm no health nut. I like an occasional Quarter Pounder as well as the next mom. There is no quicker way to my kids' hearts that to bring home a newly-released DVD, a large pepperoni pie, and a bag of Chicken McNuggets. But in our home, an evening featuring extra mozzarella and bottles of 7-Up is a once-in-a-while treat—sort of a guilty pleasure.

10   To many of today's kids, fast food is not a treat—it's their daily diet. Their normal dinnertime equals McDonalds, Pizza Hut, Domino's, Burger King, Taco Bell, or Kentucky Fried Chicken, all washed down with Pepsi. And increasingly, lunchtime at school means those foods too. About 20 percent of our nation's schools have sold chain restaurants the right to put their food items on the lunch line. Many schools also allow candy and soft-drink vending machines on their campuses. The National Soft Drink Association reports that 60 percent of public and private middle schools and high schools make sodas available for purchase.

11   Believe me, when I was a kid, if the lunch line had offered me a couple of slices of double-crust stuffed pepperoni-sausage pizza instead of a Turkey Submarine, I would have said yes before you could say the words "clogged arteries." And when I needed a mid-afternoon pick-me-up, I would have gladly traded a handful of change for a Coke and a Snickers bar.

12   And then I would have gone back into algebra class and spent the hour bouncing between a sugar high and a fat-induced coma°.

13   Stopping off at Taco Bell for an occasional Seven-Layer Burrito is one thing. But when fast food becomes the staple° of young people's diets, it's the kids who become Whoppers. And it has become the staple for many. According to researchers at Children's Hospital in Boston, during any given week, three out of four children eat a fast-food meal one or more times a day. The beverages they chug down are a problem, too. The U.S. Department of Agriculture says that every day, the average adolescent drinks enough soda and fruit beverages to equal the sugar content of 50 chocolate-chip cookies.

14   The problem isn't only that burgers, fries, and sodas aren't nutritious to begin with—although they aren't. What has made the situation much worse is the increasingly huge portions sold by fast-food restaurants. Back when McDonald's began business, its standard meal consisted of a hamburger, two ounces of French fries, and a 12-ounce Coke. That meal provided 590 calories. But today's customers don't have to be satisfied with such modest portions. For very little more money, diners can end up with a quarter-pound burger, extra-large fries, and an extra-large cup of Coke that add up to 1,550 calories. A whole generation of kids is growing up believing that this massive shot of fat, sugar, and sodium equals a "normal portion." As a result, they're becoming extra large themselves.

15   As kids sit down to watch the after-school and Saturday-morning shows designed for them, they aren't just taking in the programs themselves. They're seeing at least an hour of commercials for every five hours of programming. On Saturday mornings, nine out of ten of those commercials are for sugary cereals, fast foods, and other non-nutritious junk. Many of the commercials are tied in with popular toys or beloved cartoon characters or movies aimed at children. Watching those commercials makes the kids hungry—or at least they think they're hungry. (Thanks to all the factors mentioned here, many children can no longer tell if they're genuinely hungry or not. They've been programmed to eat for many reasons other than hunger.) So they snack as they sit in front of the TV set. Then at mealtime, they beg to go out for more junk food. And they get bigger, and bigger, and bigger.

16   There is no overnight solution to the problem of American children's increasing weight and decreasing level of physical fitness. But can anything be done? To begin with, fast-food meals and junk-food vending machines should be banned from schools. Our education system should be helping children acquire good nutritional habits, not assisting them in committing slow nutritional suicide.

17   In addition, commercials for junk food should be banned from TV during children's viewing time, specifically Saturday mornings.

18   And finally, fast-food restaurants should be required to do what tobacco companies—another manufacturer of products known to harm people's health—have to do. They should display in their restaurants, and in their TV and print ads as well, clear nutritional information about their products. For instance, a young woman at Burger King who was considering ordering a Double Whopper with Cheese, a king-size order of fries and a king-size Dr. Pepper could read something like this:

— *Your meal will provide 2030 calories, 860 of those calories from fat.*
— *Your recommended daily intake is 2000 calories, with no more than 600 of those calories coming from fat.*

19   At a glance, then, the customer could see that in one fast-food meal, she was taking in more calories and fat than she should consume in an entire day.

20   Overweight kids today become overweight adults tomorrow. Overweight adults are at increased risk for heart disease, diabetes, stroke, and cancer. Schools, fast-food restaurants, and the media are contributing to a public-health disaster in the making. Anything that can be done to decrease the role junk food plays in kids' lives needs to be done, and done quickly.

Reading Comprehension Questions

Vocabulary in Context

_____B_____   1. In the excerpt below, the word *hordes* (hôrdz) means
   A. small groups.
   B. large groups.
   C. selected groups.
   D. concerned groups.

> If the number of American kids who are dangerously overweight has tripled, large groups of them must be developing diet-related diabetes.

"Since 1980, the number of American kids who are dangerously overweight has tripled. . . . Hordes of them are developing diet-related diabetes, a disease that used to be seen almost always in adults." (Paragraph 4)

Main Ideas

_____A_____   2. The main idea of paragraph 10 is stated in the
   A. first sentence.
   B. second sentence.
   C. third sentence.
   D. last sentence.

> The remainder of the paragraph supports the idea that fast food is many kids' daily diet.

_____B_____   3. The main idea of paragraph 14 is stated in the
   A. first sentence.
   B. second sentence.
   C. third sentence.
   D. last sentence.

> The first sentence tells what the main idea *isn't*, but not what it is. The third and last sentences are too narrow.

Supporting Details

_____C_____   4. Which of the following is **not** presented as a reason that kids are growing heavier?
   A. Lack of exercise
   B. Overly large portions of food
   C. Genetics
   D. Overconsumption of soda

> Answer A is mentioned in paragraphs 5–7; answer B is mentioned in paragraph 14; and answer D in paragraph 13.

___D___   5. According to the author, what should fast-food restaurants be required to do?
   A. Not be allowed to advertise on TV.
   B. Not be allowed to build restaurants near schools.
   C. Serve more fruits, vegetables, and other nutritious foods.
   D. Provide nutritional information for every meal they serve.

   See paragraph 18.

Implied Main Ideas

___C___   6. Which sentence best expresses the implied main idea of paragraph 4?
   A. Kids today spend too much time in malls.   Answers A, B, and D
   B. Diabetes is the most serious health threat today.   are not supported.
   C. Kids today are heavier and less physically fit than ever before.
   D. Kids in California are heavier and less fit than children elsewhere.

___D___   7. Which sentence best expresses the implied main idea of paragraphs 5–7?
   A. Moms should stay home and supervise their kids rather than join the work force.
   B. Electronic entertainment influences kids to stay inside and get less physical exercise than they need.
   C. Kids are only going to get heavier and less fit as the years go on.
   D. There are at least three major reasons for young people's increased obesity.   Answers A and C are not supported by paragraphs 5–7.
                                          Answer B covers only paragraph 6.

___A___   8. The implied main idea of paragraph 15 is that
   A. kids are pushed to overeat by the commercials that they see.
   B. children's television has one hour of commercials for every five hours of programs.
   C. many commercials aimed at children feature tie-ins with toys and movies.
   D. children do not always realize when they are genuinely hungry.
   Answers B, C, and D are too narrow. Each covers only one detail of the paragraph.

___B___   9. The implied main idea of paragraphs 16–18 is that
   A. it will be nearly impossible to counteract the forces that are making America's kids fatter.
   B. there are steps that can be taken to counteract the damaging effects of fast food and junk food.
   C. fast food has no place in schools.
   D. if people realized how unhealthy a fast-food meal is, they might think twice about eating it.   Answer A is not supported.
                    Answers C covers only paragraph 16; D covers only paragraph 18.

___B___ 10. Which sentence best expresses the implied central point of the selection?

  A. This generation of children is heavier than previous generations.

  B. Our kids' growing obesity is a serious public health problem that has several causes.

  C. The fast-food industry should be more closely regulated.

  D. Nothing is more important for today's generation of children than getting more exercise.   Answers A covers only paragraph 4; answer C covers only paragraph 18. Answer D is not supported.

Discussion Questions

1. When you were a child, how much—and what kinds of—exercise did you typically get? Did you grow up in a place where kids could and did play outside? If not, were you able—or encouraged—to find opportunities to exercise?

2. The author of the selection proposes that fast-food restaurants should be required to display clear nutritional information about their products. Do you think that the presentation of this information would result in a significant reduction in the amount of fast food that people consume? Would it change *your* eating habits? Why or why not?

3. Recently, some people have attempted to sue fast-food companies, claiming that consuming their food has led to a host of serious health problems. What is your opinion of these lawsuits? Should fast-food manufacturers and advertisers be held liable for our society's obesity problem? Or are individuals the only ones responsible for their weight? Explain your reasoning.

4. The author admits that when she was a kid, she probably would have preferred pizza to something more nutritious. She also mentions that eight out of ten California students failed a basic fitness test. Given the fact that most kids prefer fast foods and passive entertainment, what can be done to promote healthier lifestyles to young people?

Note: Writing assignments for this selection appear on page 562.

Check Your Performance		IMPLIED MAIN IDEAS	
Activity	*Number Right*	*Points*	*Score*
Review Test 1 (5 items)	_____	× 6 =	_____
Review Test 2 (10 items)	_____	× 7 =	_____
		TOTAL SCORE =	_____%

Enter your total score into the **Reading Performance Chart: Review Tests** on the inside back cover.

IMPLIED MAIN IDEAS: Mastery Test 1

In the space provided, write the letter of the sentence that best expresses the implied main idea of each of the following paragraphs.

___D___ 1. [1]Teen girls are often told, "If you just say 'no,' you'll never have to worry about an unwanted pregnancy." [2]But if you're in love—or at least think you are—you don't want to say "no" to your boyfriend, about sex or anything else. [3]You want to please him, make him happy, and above all, not lose him. [4]Furthermore, you may be as interested in sex as he is. [5]Even if you don't have a steady boyfriend, it's not always easy to say "no" to sex. [6]You hear rumors about other girls who are popular because they are sexually available. [7]You reason that boys might like you better, too, if you would sleep with them. [8]If you make out with a boy, he may make you feel guilty about not going further. [9]He may blame you for "leading him on" and making him feel frustrated, or even grow angry with you. [10]What do you do?

A. Teen girls who are in love with their boyfriends often run the risk of unwanted pregnancy.

B. Those who encourage teen girls to just say 'no' to sex usually have the best interests of the girls in mind.

C. Teenage girls who refuse to have sex with their boyfriends may lose them to girls who are sexually available.

D. While "just saying no" sounds like the perfect solution, sometimes it may not be as simple as it seems.   Answers A and B are not supported. Answer C covers only sentences 3 and 6–7.

___A___ 2. [1]Most healthy people are able to tell if something is sweet or salty within .1 second of its touching their tongue. [2]They are able to taste .04 ounces of salt dissolved in 550 quarts of water. [3]Normal people can distinguish among anywhere from 4,000 to 10,000 different odors. [4]They can even smell a single drop of perfume let loose anywhere in a three-bedroom apartment. [5]They can see millions of colors. [6]They can even spot a small candle flame from up to thirty miles away on a dark night. [7]They can feel a tiny bee's wing fall on a cheek. [8]They can decide if something is hot or cold almost immediately after it touches their skin. [9]Most people can hear a pin drop across the room or hear a baby cry on another floor of a house.

A. Human senses are remarkably sensitive.

B. Some people have a better sense of smell, hearing, and sight than others.

C. Most people use their senses to detect slight variations in their environment.   Answers B, C, and D are not supported.

D. Human senses are as sensitive as those of animals.

(Continues on next page)

121

_C_ 3. [1]Consider a pesticide aimed at insects that are attacking a crop. [2]The pesticide may kill almost 100 percent of them, but thanks to the genetic variability of large populations, some insects are likely to survive exposure. [3]The resistant insects can then multiply free of competition and produce many offspring that are resistant to the pesticide and can attack the crop with new vigor. [4]To control these resistant insects, a new and more powerful pesticide must be applied, and this leads to the appearance of a population of still more resistant insects. [5]Consequently, still more pesticides and herbicides must be used.

A. No pesticide can kill 100 percent of insects that are attacking a crop.

B. The genetic variability of large populations of insects ensures their survival.

C. Because of genetic resistance in insects, more powerful pesticides must be used over time.

D. Harmful insects will continue to vigorously attack crops in the future.   Answers A and B each cover only part of sentence 2.
Answer D is not supported.

_C_ 4. [1]If your roommate is washing the dishes and says acidly, "I hope you're enjoying your novel," the literal meaning of his words is quite clear, but you probably know very well that he is not expressing a concern about your reading pleasure. [2]He is really saying, "I am furious that you are not helping to clean up after dinner." [3]Other emotions can be expressed through voice quality as well. [4]When Mae West, a once famous film star and master of sexual innuendo, asked, "Why don't you come up and see me sometime?" her voice oozed sensuality. [5]Similarly, if you receive a phone call from someone who has very good or very bad news, you will probably know how she feels before she has told you what happened. [6]In the same way, we can literally hear the fear in a person's voice, as we do when we listen to a nervous student give an oral report.

A. People don't always mean what they say.

B. Human beings are able to sense each other's fear.

C. Information may be contained not in the words people use, but in the way they express those words.

D. In order to truly communicate with those around them, people must practice interpreting subtle linguistic cues.

Answer A is supported by the example in sentences 1–2, but not by the rest of the passage. Answer B covers only sentence 6. Answer D is not supported.

IMPLIED MAIN IDEAS: Mastery Test 2

In the space provided, write the letter of the sentence that best expresses the implied main idea of each of the following paragraphs.

___A___ 1. [1]As a general rule, if it tastes good, it must be bad for you. [2]So when the artificial sweetener saccharin—the chemical in Sweet 'n Low—first appeared on the market, it's no wonder that many healthy eaters thought it too good to be true. [3]In fact, saccharin is indigestible, so it passes through our bodies without providing any of the energy that is often converted into fat. [4]Likewise, the bacteria that form together to become plaque don't receive any nutritional benefit from saccharin, so the sweet substitute doesn't attract tooth-decaying microbes the way that sugar does. [5]Some have claimed that saccharin causes cancer, leading to the warnings you see on Sweet 'n Low products. [6]But the study that led to these warnings has been debunked: it's been revealed that the rats in this study that developed bladder cancer were receiving ridiculously high doses of the chemical. [7]To ingest an equivalent amount, a human would have to drink hundreds of cans of diet soda every day for his or her entire life.

Answer B covers only sentences 3–4; answer C covers only sentence 6; and answer D covers only sentence 7.

   A. Despite initial doubts, saccharin is a good substitute for sugar.
   B. Unlike sugar, saccharin won't make you put on weight or rot your teeth.
   C. The scientific study that linked saccharin consumption to bladder cancer was later debunked.
   D. A human being would have to consume ridiculously high doses of saccharin to develop bladder cancer.

___D___ 2. [1]During World War II, more adolescents worked than ever before. [2]Over a million students dropped out of school to contribute to the war effort. [3]By 1943 almost three million boys and girls were working on farms and in factories. [4]In the new prosperity following the war, their jobs gave them freedom and spending money. [5]They soon became an important new segment of the consumer economy as they snapped up records and clothing. [6]Before long, advertisers aimed marketing campaigns at them, magazines were dedicated to their interests, and even newspapers ran columns about teen news and views. [7]The result was an emergence of a distinct youth subculture that helped shape the nation. [8]Their dances, their rigidly conforming clothing, and their choice of recreation set them apart from adults. [9]The word *teenager* was added to the vocabulary, confirming the importance of those thirteen through nineteen years of age.

Answer A covers only sentence 4; answer B covers only sentence 6; and answer C covers only sentence 3.

   A. As a result of World War II, teenagers worked at jobs which gave them freedom and spending money.
   B. Because of World War II, advertisers, magazines, and newspapers began catering to a distinct youth subculture.
   C. In World War II, adolescents made a major contribution to the war effort by working on farms and in factories.
   D. World War II led to a change in the status and lifestyle of young people.

(Continues on next page)

_____ B _____ 3. [1]Parents tend to discipline their firstborns more than their later children and to give them more attention. [2]When the second child arrives, the firstborn competes to remain the focus of attention. [3]Researchers suggest that this situation instills in firstborns a greater drive for success, which is why they are more likely than their siblings to earn higher grades in school, to attend college, and to go further in college. [4]Firstborns are even more likely to become astronauts, to appear on the cover of *Time* magazine, and to become president of the United States. [5]Although subsequent children may not go as far, most are less anxious about being successful and are more relaxed in their relationships. [6]Firstborns are also more likely to defend the status quo and to support conservative causes, with later-borns tending to upset the apple cart and support liberal causes.

Answers A and D are not supported. Answer C covers only sentence 6.

A. Because parents give them more attention, firstborns are able to develop more fully than later children.
B. Birth order plays an important role in determining a person's traits and accomplishments.
C. Firstborns tend to be conservatives, while later-borns tend to be liberals.
D. Giving a child more discipline is likely to make him or her more successful later in life.

_____ C _____ 4. [1]Thomas Jefferson's inaugural on March 4, 1801, was the first to take place in the nation's new capital on the Potomac. [2]If Washington, D.C., was a symbol of the nation's future, or even the future of the federal government, the prospects looked grim indeed. [3]There was no sign there of the prosperity that touched the government's previous homes in New York and Philadelphia: Washington was a backwater, a "city" with unpaved streets that turned to dust in the dry days of summer and into mud streams when it rained. [4]The executive residence, first occupied by the Adamses, remained, like the Capitol, unfinished. [5]What was built had been constructed so poorly that chunks of ceiling fell and pillars split within a few years of their installation. [6]There were no streetlights, no street signs; grand avenues became cow paths. [7]The city was home to flies and mosquitoes, frogs, and also hogs, which happily gobbled up garbage in the roadways. [8]An uninformed visitor witnessing the scene could only wonder whether some disaster had occurred. [9]Was Washington half built—or half destroyed?

Answer A is not supported. Answer B covers only sentence 7. Answer D covers only sentences 5 and 9.

A. The major problem with Washington, D.C., back in 1801 was that its streets had not yet been paved.
B. In 1801, Washington, D.C., was an unimpressive place because no one made any effort to control the insects and animals which lived there.
C. Washington, D.C., at the time of Jefferson's inaugural, was a very unimpressive place.
D. Due to the poor construction of its buildings, in 1801 Washington, D.C., appeared to be either half built or half destroyed.

IMPLIED MAIN IDEAS: Mastery Test 3

In the space provided, write the letter of the sentence that best expresses the implied main idea of each of the following paragraphs.

___D___ 1. [1]If you are an avid reader of self-help books, you know that this advice-filled genre urges people to actively envision the state they hope to achieve in the future. [2]Yet research suggests that this idea is badly misleading. [3]In a study that tested this point, researchers asked college students who were studying for an exam a few days away either to envision their satisfaction and celebration in achieving a good grade on the exam or to envision themselves studying so as to produce a good grade on the exam. [4]That is, one group focused on the outcome to be achieved, whereas the other group focused on the process for achieving it. [5]Those students who had focused on the process improved their grades substantially over a control group that practiced neither mental simulation; but those students who focused on the outcome they wanted to achieve had lower scores on the exam than the control group.

Answer A is too broad.
Answer B covers only sentence 5.
Answer C is not supported.

   A. Researchers have studied the effects of mental simulation on groups of college students.
   B. Students who envision studying so as to produce a good grade do better than students who don't.
   C. Mental simulation doesn't help students who don't work to achieve their goals.
   D. Mental simulation helps achieve goals if it is focused clearly on what you must do to reach them.

___B___ 2. [1]It has been demonstrated that moviegoers will eat 50 percent more popcorn if given an extra-large tub of popcorn instead of a container one size smaller, even if the popcorn is stale. [2]If a tabletop in the office is stocked with cookies and candy, coworkers tend to nibble their way through the workday, even if they are not hungry. [3]One study showed that if the candy was in plain sight on workers' desks, they ate an average of nine pieces each. [4]Storing candy in a desk drawer reduced consumption to six pieces, as compared to putting the candy a couple of yards from the desk, cutting the number to three pieces per person. [5]In response to these and other findings, many public schools have begun offering only healthy foods in their cafeterias, replacing soft drinks, candy, and chips with juice, milk, fruit, and granola bars.

Answers A and D are not supported.
Answer C covers only sentences 2–3.

   A. The average person loves to snack while working.
   B. Reducing people's consumption of snacks depends in large part on making the snacks harder to obtain.
   C. People will eat whatever is readily available, even if they're not hungry.
   D. Students in public schools will consume whatever food is readily available.

(Continues on next page)

125

_A_   3. ¹If you buy a house and borrow the money to pay for it, all of the interest you pay to the bank or mortgage company can be deducted from your income before you pay taxes. ²For most consumers, this represents a sizable savings. ³For example, suppose you buy a $120,000 house and borrow $100,000 to help pay for it. ⁴Let's say that the interest you pay every year on that $100,000 comes to $7,000. ⁵You can deduct that $7,000 from your income before you pay taxes on it. ⁶If you are in the 28 percent tax bracket, you get a tax saving of almost $2,000; the interest on your loan is, in effect, costing you about $5,000. ⁷Then imagine that you and your family live in the house for ten years. ⁸When your employer transfers you to another city, you must sell your house. ⁹Because real estate values have increased, you earn a capital gain of $80,000 when you sell your house for $200,000. ¹⁰This $80,000 is tax-free, a pure profit that you can use to help buy a new house.

Answer B covers only sentences 1 and 4–6; answer C covers only sentence 10; and answer D covers only sentences 9–10.

A. The tax benefits of home-ownership are significant.
B. Homeowners can deduct the interest they pay on their mortgage from their income.
C. Some people use the profit they make when they sell their home to buy a new home.
D. The increase in real estate values means that many people can earn large tax-free capital gains when they sell their house.

_B_   4. ¹Due to the increasing concern about contaminated meat and meat products, the first irradiated meat, ground beef, arrived in American supermarkets in early 2000. ²Irradiated frozen chicken was introduced more recently. ³Irradiation is a process that causes damage to the DNA of disease-causing bacteria such as salmonella and E. coli as well as insects, parasites, and other organisms so that they can't reproduce. ⁴While irradiated meat has much lower bacteria levels than regular meat, irradiation doesn't destroy all bacteria in meat. ⁵In fact, irradiation actually destroys fewer bacteria than does proper cooking. ⁶There is also some concern that irradiation will lull consumers into a false sense of security so that they erroneously believe that they don't have to take the usual precautions in food handling. ⁷For example, under-cooking, unclean work surfaces or cooking utensils, or improper storage can still cause contamination in the meat. ⁸Some also claim that irradiated meat has a distinct off-taste and smell likening it to "singed hair."

Answer A covers only sentences 4–5; answer C covers only sentences 6–7; and answer D covers only sentence 8.

A. Despite the introduction of irradiated food in early 2000, bacterial contamination of meat has not been eliminated in the United States.
B. The irradiation of food has both advantages and disadvantages.
C. Even though food has been irradiated, consumers should still take the usual precautions in food handling.
D. Some people prefer the smell and taste of meat that has not been irradiated to the smell and taste of meat that has.

IMPLIED MAIN IDEAS: Mastery Test 4

In the space provided, write the letter of the sentence that best expresses the implied main idea of each of the following paragraphs.

___D___ 1. [1]Most young girls are more likely to see their fathers reading magazines and watching TV programs about sports than they are to see their mothers doing the same. [2]Additionally, most participants in public sports are men. [3]Although girls may be encouraged to participate in sports, parents are likely to believe that their sons are better at athletics and to feel that sports are more critical for the development of boys. [4]A recent study of over 800 elementary school pupils found that parents hold higher expectations for boys' athletic performance, and children absorb these social messages at an early age. [5]Kindergartners through third-graders of both sexes viewed sports in a gender-stereotyped fashion—as much more important for boys. [6]Boys were also more likely to indicate that it was important to their parents that they participate in athletics. [7]These attitudes affected children's physical self-images as well as their behavior. [8]Girls saw themselves as having less talent at sports, and by the sixth grade they devoted less time to athletics than did their male classmates.

Answer A covers only sentence 3; answer B covers only sentence 8. Answer C is not supported.

  A. Parents tend to believe that their sons are better athletes than their daughters.
  B. Females spend less time participating in sports than do males.
  C. Schools and parents should work together to encourage girls to participate in sports.
  D. Social expectations and stereotypes often influence girls' participation in athletics.

___A___ 2. [1]The higher that people are on the social class ladder, the more likely they are to vote for Republicans. [2]In contrast, most members of the working class believe that the government should intervene in the economy to make citizens financially secure. [3]The majority of these working-class citizens are Democrats. [4]Although the working class is more liberal on economic issues (policies that increase government spending), it is more conservative on social issues (and is likely to oppose, for example, abortion, gay marriage, and the banning of prayer in schools). [5]People toward the bottom of the class structure are also less likely to be politically active—to campaign for candidates, or even to vote.

Answer B covers only sentence 1; answer C covers only sentence 5. Answer D is not supported.

  A. Social class tends to influence political beliefs.
  B. Rich people are usually Republicans.
  C. The less money someone has, the less likely he or she is to participate in politics.
  D. Money is the sole determiner of a person's political attitudes.

(Continues on next page)

_B_   3. [1]At the beginning of the twentieth century, families often hired older women to keep watch over their daughters. [2]When a young man asked a girl on a date, he automatically invited her chaperone as well. [3]If a young lady entertained her boyfriend in the parlor, the chaperone did not budge from the room. [4]Because of her responsibilities, the chaperone had the power to make courtship pleasurable or miserable. [5]Some chaperones had soft hearts and gave young lovers some privacy. [6]Others were such sticklers for appearances that they prevented the young couple even from exchanging personal remarks. [7]In addition to being guardians, chaperones sometimes functioned as private eyes. [8]They investigated the backgrounds of gentlemen who called on their charges to see which one would make the best match. [9]The chaperone could be a nuisance, but she could also be a good excuse for avoiding unwanted courtships.

Answers A and C are too narrow— they fail to mention that chaperones sometimes functioned as private eyes. Answer D is also too narrow—it fails to mention that chaperones kept watch over daughters.

A. The role of chaperones was to keep a close watch over their charges.
B. At one time, chaperones played an important role in courtship.
C. In the past, families hired older women to keep watch over their daughters.
D. Some chaperones actually helped their charges by investigating the backgrounds of gentlemen and providing excuses for avoiding unwanted courtships.

B. (4.) Write out, in your own words, the implied main idea of the following paragraph.

Sentences 3–5 list inaccurate predictions about the future. Sentence 6 lists aspects of life today that forecasters in 1893 failed to predict.

[1]When the World's Columbia Exposition opened in Chicago in 1893, 74 prominent Americans tried their hands at forecasting the future. [2]What would the world be like one hundred years later? [3]One expressed the prevailing view that in 1993 the railroad would still be the fastest means of travel. [4]Another was convinced that mail in a hundred years' time would still travel by stagecoach and horseback rider. [5]A few forecasters enthused about air travel—or more precisely, "balloon travel." [6]None of the 1893 forecasters apparently anticipated the automobile, let alone the cell phone, the Internet, a world of six billion people, the publication of a map of the human genome, or the globalization of both our economy and our environmental problems.

Wording of answer may vary.

Implied main idea: _____

_____ *Accurately predicting the future is extremely difficult.* _____

IMPLIED MAIN IDEAS: Mastery Test 5

In the space provided, write the letter of the sentence that best expresses the implied main idea of each of the following paragraphs.

___C___ 1. [1]In virtually all rich nations, schooling is mandatory through high school, and illiteracy rates of 5 percent or less of the population are common. [2]By contrast, in most low-income nations, less than half of eligible school-age children are enrolled in school. [3]Further, most schools in low-income nations are poorly funded. [4]A recent study showed that high-income nations spent an average of $769 per child on education. [5]By contrast, low-income countries spent about $33 per pupil. [6]With poor school facilities, and farm and other work to perform, most children in low-income countries drop out of school before the fourth grade. [7]Consequently, in many poor countries, illiteracy rates are often as high as 80 percent or more.

Answer A covers only sentences 4–5; answer D covers only sentences 6–7. Answer B is not supported.

   A. Poor nations spend less on students.
   B. Rich nations should help fund educational programs for poor nations.
   C. A country's wealth has a significant effect on its educational programs and literacy rates.
   D. Poor school facilities in poor nations are a common cause of high illiteracy rates.

___A___ 2. [1]Low-income parents often feel a sense of powerlessness and lack of influence in their relationships beyond the home. [2]For example, at work they must obey the rules of others in positions of power and authority. [3]When they get home, their parent-child interaction seems to mirror these experiences, only with them in the authority roles. [4]In contrast, middle-class parents have a greater sense of control over their own lives. [5]At work, they are used to making independent decisions and convincing others of their point of view. [6]At home, they teach these same skills to their children.

Answer B covers only sentences 2–3. Answers C and D are not supported.

   A. Parents often duplicate within their own families the class-related social experiences they encounter beyond the home.
   B. Because low-income parents must obey their supervisors at work, they demand that their children obey them at home.
   C. Parents learn all their child-rearing skills from their work.
   D. People from the middle class make the best parents.

___B___ 3. [1]Should marketers tell their audiences only the good points about their products, or should they also tell them the bad (or the commonplace)? [2]Should they pretend that their products are the only ones of their kind, or should they acknowledge competing products? [3]These are very real strategy questions that marketers face every day. [4]If the audience is friendly (for example, if it uses the advertiser's products), if it initially favors the

(Continues on next page)

communicator's position, or if it is not likely to hear an opposing argument, then a *one-sided (supportive) message* that stresses only favorable information is most effective. [5]However, if the audience is critical or unfriendly (for example, if it uses competitive products), if it is well-educated, or if it is likely to hear opposing claims, then a *two-sided (refutational) message* is likely to be more effective. [6]Two-sided advertising messages tend to be more credible than one-sided advertising messages because they acknowledge that the advertised brand has shortcomings. [7]Two-sided messages can also be very effective when consumers are likely to see competitors' negative counterclaims or when consumer attitudes toward the brand are already negative.

> Answer A covers only part of sentence 5; answer C covers only sentence 7. Answer D is too narrow because it does not include information about the audiences most receptive to each type of message.

A. In promoting their products, marketers must keep in mind the educational level of the audience and whether or not it is friendly.

B. Marketing decisions depend on the nature of the audience and the nature of the competition.

C. When consumers are likely to see competitors' negative counterclaims or when consumers' attitudes toward the brand are already negative, marketers should use two-sided messages.

D. There are two types of advertising messages—supportive and refutational.

B. (4.) Write out, in your own words, the implied central idea of the following textbook passage.

[1]Some just shake their heads and say that if we can't stop the drugs from coming in, we at least can lock up the dealers and users. [2]But there are so many dealers and users that we don't have enough jails and prisons to lock them up. [3]Consider these statistics: Several million Americans use cocaine each year, while other millions use heroin, hallucinogens, barbiturates, and inhalants. [4]During just the past month, about 13 million Americans smoked marijuana. [5]How could we possibly lock all of these people up? [6]How many dealers does it take to supply just the marijuana smokers? [7]If each dealer has 25 customers, there are a half million dealers.

[8]And consider this: To build one prison cell costs about $100,000. [9]To keep one inmate locked up for one year costs a minimum of $25,000. [10]If we were going to lock up just the drug dealers, where would we get the money? [11]If we put two drug dealers in a cell, a half million new cells would run $50 billion. [12]It would then cost another $25 billion a year to keep those million people in prison.

[13]Not yet mentioned is the fact that there are people waiting in line to take the places of dealers who are arrested. [14]Get rid of one dealer, and two fight to take his or her place.

> The passage lists reasons why locking up all drug dealers and users would be virtually impossible.

Wording of answer may vary.

Implied central idea: ___*Jailing drug dealers and users is not a realistic*___

solution to America's drug problem.

IMPLIED MAIN IDEAS: Mastery Test 6

In the space provided, write the letter of the sentence that best expresses the implied main idea of each of the following paragraphs.

___C___ 1. [1]Scientists once believed that large meat-eating dinosaurs lived and hunted alone. [2]Recent discoveries of the buried remains of a dozen large carnivores in the same riverbed in western Canada, however, tell researchers that the dinosaurs may have hunted in packs. [3]For a long time, scientists thought dinosaurs were slow-moving, cold-blooded creatures like crocodiles and lizards. [4]Some scientists changed their thinking when, in 2000, CT scans of a dinosaur's petrified heart showed that it was remarkably similar to that of mammals. [5]The scientists then decided that dinosaurs, too, may have been warm-blooded. [6]Up until recently, scientists thought that all dinosaurs had scaly skin resembling modern-day lizards and snakes. [7]Recent discoveries of numerous feathered dinosaur remains make them look more like weird birds than giant lizards.

Answer A is not supported. Answer B covers only sentences 2 and 6; answer D covers only sentences 6 and 7.

A. People hold a number of mistaken beliefs about dinosaurs.
B. Scientists now know that some dinosaurs may have hunted in packs and had scaly skin.
C. Scientists' thinking about dinosaurs has undergone major change in recent years.
D. Scientists now know that not all dinosaurs resembled lizards, crocodiles, or other cold-blooded animals.

___A___ 2. [1]In the early 1900s, most inmates in state poorhouses were older people, and almost one-third of Americans age 65 and older depended financially on someone else. [2]Few employers, including the federal government, provided for retired employees. [3]Noting that the government fed retired horses until they died, one postal worker complained, "For the purpose of drawing a pension, it would have been better had I been a horse than a human being." [4]Resistance to pension plans finally broke at the state level in the 1920s. [5]Led by Isaac Max Rubinow and Abraham Epstein, reformers persuaded voluntary associations, labor unions, and legislators to endorse old-age assistance through pensions, insurance, and retirement homes. [6]By 1933 almost every state provided at least minimal support to needy elderly people, and a path had been opened for a national program of old-age insurance.

Answer B covers only sentences 1 and 2; answer C covers only sentence 3; and answer D covers only sentences 5–6.

A. Between the early 1900s and 1933, America made progress in providing for its elderly.
B. In the early 1900s, America failed to provide for the financial welfare of its elderly citizens.
C. In the early 1900s, the U.S. government treated its retired horses better than it treated its retired human beings.
D. By 1933, a national program of old-age insurance appeared likely to happen, due to the efforts of reformers.

(Continues on next page)

___D___ 3. [1]In preindustrial societies that rely on hunting and gathering, physical strength and good health are important. [2]Consequently, the elderly (who in those societies may be people as young as in their late 30s or 40s) may be viewed as burdens to the family and society. [3]In desperate circumstances, where the survival of the group is at stake, the elderly may be literally abandoned, as in the case of the North American Eskimo. [4]Conversely, in preindustrial societies that rely on growing food or raising animals, physical possessions are regarded as more important than health and strength. [5]In such societies, the elderly, who are the most likely to own land, may be held in higher esteem than younger members of society. [6]For example, among the Berbers of Morocco, elderly tribesman are accorded the highest status because they generally own more land, larger herds, and more material possessions than younger society members.

Answer A covers only sentence 3; answer B covers only sentences 4–6. Answer C is not supported.

A. In some preindustrial societies, abandoning the elderly is common.
B. In many societies, the elderly are given respect only if they have material possessions.
C. Elderly people deal with death and aging in different ways.
D. Preindustrial societies tend to value the elderly according to their contributions to the community.

B. (4.) Write out, in your own words, the implied central idea of the following passage.

[1]Defenders of professional boxing like to point out that serious injury is more common in such sports as horse racing, skydiving, mountaineering, and college football than in the sport they love. [2]Yet even boxing fans must admit that boxing is the only sport where the goal of the participants is to inflict bodily injury on one another. [3]If you've ever, even briefly, watched a boxing match on TV, you've probably seen boxers give and receive blows to the head. [4]What you might not realize is that when a boxer's gloved hand slams with brute force against his opponent's head, the brain is literally pushed against the skull bone. [5]This action, over time, results in the neurological impairment known as being "punch drunk."

The passage presents graphic evidence which supports the point that boxing can result in injury and death.

[6]Such boxing greats as Muhammad Ali, Sugar Ray Robinson, and Wilfred Benitez all suffered permanent neurological damage due to their years in the ring. [7]Symptoms include slurred speech, loss of memory, and loss of coordination. [8]In worst-case scenarios, fighters have been hit so hard that they died in the ring, or soon after. [9]A particularly chilling outcome: on March 24, 1962, at Madison Square Garden, Emile Griffith beat Benny "Kid" Paret so brutally that Paret crumbled to the canvas and never regained consciousness. [10]He died ten days later.

[11]From 1920 until the present day, there have been 592 fatalities due to professional boxing. [12]Recently 34-year-old Becky Zerlentes was knocked out during a bout at a Colorado boxing event. [13]She died shortly afterward when blood pooled on the surface of her brain. *Wording of answer may vary.*

Implied central idea: Professional boxing is more dangerous than most

people realize.

4

Relationships I

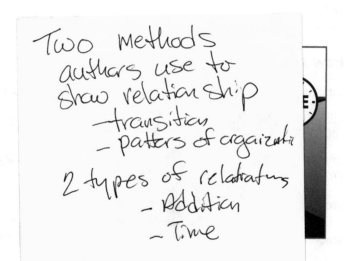

Two methods
authors use to
show relationship
— transition
— patterns of organization

2 types of relationships
— Addition
— Time

Autho_____ips and make their ideas
clear. T_____anization—are explained
in turn in this chapter. The chapter also explains two common types of relationships:

- Relationships that involve **addition**
- Relationships that involve **time**

TRANSITIONS

Look at the following items and put a check (✓) by the one that is easier to read and understand:

____ Most people choose a partner who is about as attractive as themselves. Personality and intelligence affect their choice.

✓ Most people choose a partner who is about as attractive as themselves. Moreover, personality and intelligence affect their choice.

You probably f ... The word *Moreover* makes it cle ... choosing a romantic partner. **Tr** ...) that show relationships between ... le travelers. Or they can be seen a ... one idea to the next:

Most people choose ... nd intelligence about as attractive as th ... hoice.

Two major type ... d words that show time.

Words That Show Addi

Once again, put a check (✔) beside the item that is easier to ... understand:

___ There are several reasons not to fill babies' bottles with sugary juice. It can rot their teeth.

✓ There are several reasons not to fill babies' bottles with sugary juice. First of all, it can rot their teeth.

As you probably noted, the second item is easier to understand. The words *first of all* make it clear that the writer plans on giving a series of reasons why babies should not be fed sugary juice. *First of all* and words like it are known as addition words.

Addition words signal added ideas. These words tell you a writer is presenting one or more ideas that continue along the same line of thought as a previous idea. Like all transitions, addition words help writers organize their information and present it clearly to readers. Here are some common words that show addition:

Addition Words

one	to begin with	also	further
first (of all)	for one thing	in addition	furthermore
second (ly)	other	next	last (of all)
third (ly)	another	moreover	final (ly)

Examples:

 The following examples contain addition words. Notice how these words introduce ideas that *add to* what has already been said.

- Depression can be eased through therapy and medication. Physical exercise has *also* been shown to help.

- Bananas are the most frequently purchased fruit in the U.S. Why are bananas so popular? *To begin with*, they are convenient to carry around and to eat.

- It is annoying to have to sort through a pile of junk mail every day. *Moreover*, junk mail represents a waste of trees and other natural resources.

➤ **Practice 1**   *Answers may vary.*

Complete each sentence with a suitable addition word from the box on the previous page. Try to use a variety of transitions.

> **Hint:** Make sure that each addition word or phrase that you choose fits smoothly into the flow of the sentence. Test each choice by reading the sentence aloud.

1. Computers have affected the lives of people in positive ways, providing all kinds of information and making it easy to keep in touch with loved ones. But computers have _____*also*_____ touched people's lives in hurtful ways, such as by contributing to identity theft and sex crimes.

2. Scolding children too often is actually counterproductive. The kids get used to being scolded and stop taking it seriously. Frequent scoldings, _____*moreover*_____, can encourage a child to act aggressive and bully-like.

3. There are various reasons homeless people resist moving to a shelter. For one thing, they may dislike being compelled to follow a shelter's rules. A _____*second*_____ reason is fear of being robbed while they sleep with people around them.

4. Antarctica is a place of extremes. _____*In addition*_____ to being the coldest place on earth, it is also both the wettest and the driest place. How can this be? It is wettest because it contains 70 percent of the world's fresh water, in the form of ice. It is driest because it receives only about two inches of precipitation per year.

5. Typically, men and women have different styles of communication. Women frequently talk about people, while men are more likely to talk about things. _____*Another*_____ difference in styles is that men tend to lecture, while women are more likely to listen and ask questions.

Words That Show Time

Put a check (✓) beside the item that is easier to read and understand:

___ The dog begins to tremble and hide under the couch. A thunderstorm approaches.

_✓_ The dog begins to tremble and hide under the couch when a thunderstorm approaches.

The word *when* in the second item makes clear the relationship between the sentences. It is when a thunderstorm approaches that the dog's behavior changes. *When* and words like it are time words.

Time words tell us *at what point* something happened in relation to when something else happened. They help writers organize and make clear the order of events, stages, and steps in a process. Here are some common words that show time:

Time Words

before	immediately	when	until
previously	next	whenever	often
first (of all)	then	while	frequently
second (ly)	following	during	eventually
third (ly)	later	as (soon as)	final (ly)
now	after	by	last (of all)

Note: Some additional ways of showing time are dates ("In 1890 . . . ," "Throughout the 20th century . . . ," "By 2012 . . .") and other time references ("Within a week . . . ," "by the end of the month . . . ," "in two years . . .").

Examples:

The following examples contain time words. Notice how these words show us *when* something takes place.

- The old woman on the park bench opened a paper bag, and a flock of pigeons *immediately* landed all around her.

- *After* completing medical school, a future doctor continues her training as a "resident" in a hospital.

- *In August 2005,* Hurricane Katrina caused tremendous devastation in New Orleans.

H

Highlight these two tips

ıt transitions:

ıme meaning. For example, *also, moreover,* ın." Authors typically use a variety of

ıfferent types of transitions, depending on d *first* may be used as an addition word to ı series of ideas, as in the following:

ıs not to share personal information on the sure of the identity of the person you're

ıme sequence, as in this sentence:

daily use of the nasal spray. *First*, shake the bottle gently for a few seconds and remove the protective tip.

➤ Practice 2

Answers may vary.

Complete each sentence with a suitable time word from the box on the previous page. Try to use a variety of transitions.

> **Hint:** Make sure that each time word or phrase that you choose fits smoothly into the flow of the sentence. Test each choice by reading the sentence aloud.

1. Three years _____*after*_____ signing the Emancipation Proclamation, President Abraham Lincoln was assassinated by an angry Southern sympathizer.

2. _____*When*_____ the school announced that several students had lice, many parents nervously inspected their own children.

3. The first human heart transplant occurred in 1967. _____*By*_____ 2006, approximately 2,300 were being performed every year.

4. _____*Before*_____ going to a job interview, it's a wise idea to anticipate questions the interviewer might ask and prepare answers for them.

5. American women were not allowed to vote _____*until*_____ 1920, when the 19th Amendment to the Constitution was passed.

PATTERNS OF ORGANIZATION

You have learned that transitions show the relationships between ideas in sentences. In the same way, **patterns of organization** show the relationships between supporting details in paragraphs, essays, and chapters. It helps to recognize the common patterns in which authors arrange information. You will then be better able to understand and remember what you read.

The rest of this chapter discusses two major patterns of organization:

- The **list of items pattern**
  (Addition words are often used in this pattern of organization.)

- The **time order pattern**
  (Time words are often used in this pattern of organization.)

Noticing the transitions in a passage can often help you become aware of its pattern of organization. Transitions can also help you locate the major supporting details.

1   The List of Items Pattern

List of Items
Item 1
Item 2
Item 3

To get a sense of the list of items pattern, try to arrange the following sentences in a logical order. Put a *1* in front of the sentence that should come first, a *2* in front of the sentence that comes next, a *3* in front of the third sentence, and a *4* in front of the sentence that should come last. The result will be a short paragraph. Use the addition words as a guide.

_3_   Next is moderate poverty, defined as living on $1 to $2 a day, which refers to conditions in which basic needs are met, but just barely.

_1_   Nearly half of the six billion people in the world experience one of three degrees of poverty.

_4_   Last, relative poverty, defined by a household income level below a given proportion of the national average, means lacking things that the middle class now takes for granted.

_2_   First is extreme poverty, defined by the World Bank as getting by on an income of less than $1 a day, which means that households cannot meet such basic needs for survival as food, clothing, and shelter.

This paragraph begins with the main idea: "Nearly half of the six billion people in the world experience one of three degrees of poverty." The next three sentences go on to describe the three degrees of poverty. The transitions *First, Next,* and *Last* each introduce one of the kinds of poverty. Here is the whole paragraph in its correct order:

> [1]Nearly half of the six billion people in the world experience one of three degrees of poverty. [2]First is extreme poverty, defined by the World Bank as getting by on an income of less than $1 a day, which means that households cannot meet such basic needs for survival as food, clothing, and shelter. [3]Next is moderate poverty, defined as living on $1 to $2 a day, which refers to conditions in which basic needs are met, but just barely. [4]Last, relative poverty, defined by a household income level below a given proportion of the national average, means lacking things that the middle class now takes for granted.

A **list of items** refers to a series of reasons, examples, facts, or other supporting details that support an idea. The items have no time order, but are listed in whatever order the author prefers. Addition words are often used in a list of items to tell us that other supporting points are being added to a point already mentioned. Textbook authors frequently organize material into lists of items, such as a list of the sources of knowledge, types of diseases, or the kinds of families that exist today.

Addition Words Used in the List of Items Pattern

one	to begin with	also	further
first (of all)	for one thing	in addition	furthermore
second (ly)	other	next	last (of all)
third (ly)	another	moreover	final (ly)

☑ *Check Your Understanding*

The paragraph below is organized as a list of items. Complete the outline of the list by first filling in the missing part of the main idea. Then add to the outline the three major details listed in the paragraph.

To help you find the major details, do two things:

- Underline the addition words that introduce the major details in the list.

- Number (*1, 2, . . .*) each item in the list.

> [1]Because women were not allowed to act in English plays during Shakespeare's time, young male actors pretended to be women. [2]Acting companies had to work hard to make boys sound and look like women. [3]To begin with,[1] they chose teenage boys who had not reached puberty. [4]They

found boy actors who had high-pitched voices and didn't need to shave. [5]Next,[2] they dressed the boys in women's clothing. [6]An upper cloth called a bodice was tightened with string so that the boys looked as if they had feminine waists. [7]The boys wore dresses and high-heeled shoes that matched their characters. [8]A long-haired wig completed the costumes. [9]Finally,[3] they added makeup. [10]A white paste made the boys look pale, and red blush gave them rosy lips and cheeks. [11]The boy actors would step on stage looking like ladies.

Main idea: Shakespearian acting companies had to work hard to _____

make boys look and sound like women.

1. _Chose boys who had not yet reached puberty_

2. _Dressed boys in women's clothing_

3. _Added makeup_

Explanation:

The main idea is that Shakespearian acting companies had to work hard to make boys sound and look like women. Following are the three items you should have added to the outline:

1. Chose boys who had not reached puberty. (This item is signaled with the addition phrase *To begin with*).

2. Dressed boys in women's clothing. (This element is signaled by the addition word *Next*).

3. Added makeup. (This element is signaled by the addition word *Finally*.)

To the Instructor:
In this *Instructor's Edition*, throughout this chapter and the tests that follow, transitions relevant to the patterns of organization are underlined.

➤ *Practice 3*   *Wording of answers may vary.*

A. The following passage uses a listing pattern. Outline the passage by filling in the main idea and the major details.

> *Hint:* Underline the addition words that introduce the items in the list, and number the items.

[1]Most people visit a doctor's office when they are concerned about one health issue or another. [2]They are often too distracted to prepare for their visit. [3]However, there are three important lists that people should make before visiting a doctor's office. [4]<u>For one thing</u>, they should make a list of[1] all the medications that they are taking. [5]Many drugs, even over-the-counter remedies, can have dangerous side effects when combined with new prescriptions, so it is important to let the doctor know what pills are being taken on a regular basis. [6]<u>In addition</u>, people visiting a doctor's office should make a list of[2] their symptoms. [7]The list should start with whatever symptoms—nausea, fever, joint pain, etc.—have been most troubling, but should include everything that's been bothering them since their last visit to the doctor. [8]Such lists can aid the doctor in making a diagnosis, and they will also ensure that patients don't forget any important complaints. [9]<u>Last of all</u>, people visiting their doctor should bring along a short list of[3] questions. [10]A typical doctor sees at least twenty patients every day and can't devote a lot of time to explaining every detail involved in a diagnosis or a treatment. [11]So patients who bring specific questions are more likely to have all of their major concerns addressed. [12]It may seem tiresome to sit down and prepare such lists, but the proactive patients who do so will get the most out of their visits.

Main idea: _____

There are three important lists people should make before going to the doctor.

1. *All the medications they are taking*

2. *The symptoms they are experiencing*

3. *Any specific questions they have*

> Sentence 3 contains the main idea (note the list words *three important lists*). The three major supporting details are signaled by the words *For one thing* (sentence 4), *In addition* (sentence 6), and *Last of all* (sentence 9)

B. The following passage uses a listing pattern. Complete the map of the passage by completing the main idea and filling in the missing major details.

[1]While getting a tattoo hurts, the sting of a tattoo needle is nothing compared to the sting of regret felt later in life by nearly half of those who have tattoos. [2]Luckily, modern medicine has developed a variety of techniques for tattoo removal. [3]In the most basic method, dermabrasion, a high-speed buffing tool is used to literally "sand" off several layers of skin. [4]Another technique, and a less painful one, is cryosurgery, in which skin is frozen to render it numb before removal. [5]If the tattoo is small enough, surgeons simply snip off the skin and sew the area closed or even graft a "patch" of skin borrowed from elsewhere on the body. [6]While these methods may all leave scars, the most advanced method, laser removal, leaves virtually no trace. [7]Lasers are calibrated to pass harmlessly through the surface layers of the skin, breaking apart the tattoo's pigments so that they can be naturally removed by the body's immune system. [8]While the process feels similar to being snapped with a small rubber band or spattered with tiny drops of hot oil, the pain is considerably less than the discomfort of seeing a tattoo that features, say, the name of a person who is no longer in one's life.

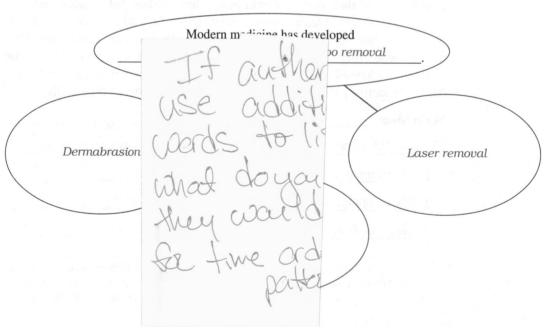

Modern m~~edicine has~~ developed
~~tattoo~~ removal.

Dermabrasion

Laser removal

The list words *a variety of techniques* (sentence 2) are a clue. The major details are in sentences 3, 4, and 6. Note that while *most basic* and *most advanced* are not listed in the transitions box, they, like other words at times, help indicate a list of details. The minor details are in sentences 5, 7, and 8.

2 The Time Order Pattern

To get a sense of the time order pattern, try to arrange the following sentences in a logical order. Put a *1* in front of the sentence that should come first, a *2* in front of the sentence that comes next, a *3* in front of the third sentence, and a *4* in front of the sentence that should come last. The result will be a short paragraph. Use the time words as a guide.

_2_ Then, in 1638, a press in Cambridge, Massachusetts printed a book of psalms that became an instant bestseller.

_1_ The first books in the United States were imports, brought by the new settlers.

_4_ Eventually, in 1731, Benjamin Franklin asked fifty subscribers to help him start America's first circulating library.

_3_ During the years that followed, booksellers emerged in the Boston area, and by 1685 the leading bookseller offered over three thousand books.

Authors usually present events and processes in the order in which they happen, resulting in a pattern of organization known as **time order**. Clues to the pattern of the above sentences are the transitions *(Then, Eventually, During,* and *by)* that show time. The sentences should read as follows:

[1]The first books in the United States were imports, brought by the new settlers. [2]Then, in 1638, a press in Cambridge, Massachusetts printed a book of psalms that became an instant bestseller. [3]During the years that followed, booksellers emerged in the Boston area, and by 1685 the leading bookseller offered over three thousand books. [4]Eventually, in 1731, Benjamin Franklin asked fifty subscribers to help him start America's first circulating library.

As a student, you will see time order used frequently. Textbooks in all fields describe events and processes, such as the events leading to the start of the Civil War, the important incidents in the life of Franklin Roosevelt, the steps in looking for a job, the process involved in financial planning, or the stages in biological aging.

In addition, most fiction and biography—and virtually any communication that tells a story—uses time order. (For example, look at the opening lines from a famous story that starts on page 471 of this book.)

The two most common kinds of time order are 1) a series of events or stages and 2) a series of steps (directions in how to do something). Both kinds of time order are discussed on the following pages.

Series of Events or Stages

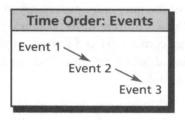

☑ Check Your Understanding

Here is a paragraph that is organized according to time order. Complete the outline of the paragraph by listing the missing stages in the order in which they happen.

To help you find the stages, do two things:

• Underline the time words that introduce each stage in the process;

• Number (*1, 2, . . .*) each stage.

> [1]People who move into affordable city neighborhoods may not realize it, but they are often part of a process that ends in the change of a community. [2]The <u>first</u> stage of this "gentrification" process begins when *1* young artists move into a low-income working-class neighborhood. [3]These artists, who generally have little income themselves, are often attracted by the low rents, the availability of studio space, and the proximity to the urban centers where they can't afford to live. [4]In the <u>next</u> stage, *2* young professionals follow the artists into the neighborhood. [5]These city-dwellers tend to be between the ages of 25 and 35, are single or at least childless, and are often attracted to the trendy restaurants, galleries, and nightclubs that open in neighborhoods popular with artists. [6]The <u>final</u> stage of the gentrification process occurs when *3* upper-class families take over the neighborhood. [7]The fancy restaurants and stores that have grown up around the young professionals draw wealthier people and businesses into the community. [8]The end result is a neighborhood where the rising rents are too costly for both the original working-class inhabitants and for the artists who started the process of gentrification to begin with. [9]The artists, therefore, are forced to move on to another working-class neighborhood, where they will start this transformative process all over again.

Main idea: The process of gentrification can transform a community.

Stage 1   *Young artists move into a low-income working-class neighborhood.*

Stage 2   *Young professionals follow the artists into the neighborhood.*

Stage 3   *Upper-class families take over the neighborhood.*

Stage 4—The artists are forced to move on to another working-class neighborhood, and the process begins all over again.

Explanation:

You should have added these points to the outline:

1. Stage 1—Young artists move into a low-income working-class neighborhood.

2. Stage 2—Young professionals follow the artists into the neighborhood.

3. Stage 3—Upper-class families take over the neighborhood.

As signaled by the transitions *The first stage, In the next stage,* and *The final stage,* the relationship between the points is one of time, with one stage in the process of change leading to the next. A series of stages or events is a common kind of time order.

➤ Practice 4

Wording of answers may vary.

The following passage describes a sequence of events. Outline the paragraph by filling in the major details.

> *Hint:* Underline the time word or words that introduce each major detail, and number each major detail.

[1]In World War II, Sir Winston Churchill refused to bargain with Hitler. [2]Defiantly, he told his people that he would resist any German assault: "We shall fight on the beaches . . . we shall fight in the fields and in the streets . . . we shall never surrender." [3]A furious Hitler quickly went on the attack against Britain. [4]First, he unleashed German submarines against British shipping. [5]A short while later, he sent his air force, the Luftwaffe, to destroy Britain's military defenses from the air. [6]At the time the assault began, the Royal Air Force (RAF) had just 704 serviceable planes, while Germany had 2,682 bombers and fighters ready for action. [7]Throughout July and August, the Luftwaffe attacked airfields and radar stations on Britain's southern and

eastern coasts. [8]Then, in September, Hitler shifted strategy and[3] began to bomb civilian targets in London. [9]These air raids, known collectively as the blitz, continued through the fall and winter. [10]In May 1941, the blitz ended. [11]The RAF, while outnumbered, had won the Battle of Britain. [12]Churchill expressed his nation's gratitude with these famous words: "Never in the field of human conflict was so much owed by so many to so few."

Main idea: A furious Hitler quickly went on the attack against Britain.

1. _Used submarines against British shipping_

2. _Sent air force to destroy Britain's military defenses_

3. _Bombed civilian targets in London_

> The major details are signaled by the transitions *First* (sentence 4),
> *A short while later* (sentence 5), and *Then, in September* (sentence 8).

Series of Steps (Directions)

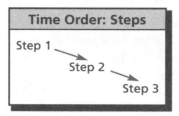

When authors give directions, they use time order. They explain step 1, then step 2, and so on through the entire series of steps that must be taken toward a specific goal.

☑ Check Your Understanding

Below is a paragraph that gives directions. Complete the outline of the paragraph that follows by filling in the main idea and listing the missing steps in the correct sequence. To help yourself identify each step, do two things:

- Underline the time words that introduce each item in the sequence.
- Number (*1, 2, . . .*) each step in the sequence.

> [1]It's important to take time to reflect upon your goals in life. [2]To begin with,[1] take out a sheet of paper and label it "My Lifetime Goals." [3]Imagine that you are very old, looking back at your life. [4]What did you want to accomplish? [5]What do you feel best about? [6]Write down anything that pops into your mind. [7]Next,[2] take a second sheet of paper and write "My Three-Year Goals." [8]On this, write what you would like to accomplish within the

next three years. [9]Third,[3] take a sheet of paper and title it "What I Would Do If I Knew I Had Six Months to Live." [10]Assume that you would be in good health and have the necessary resources, and list everything you might like to squeeze into those six months. [11]Now[4] go back over all three lists, and rate each item as A (very important), B (somewhat important), or C (least important.) [12]Finally,[5] evaluate the "A" items on your lists and select the goals that are most important to you.

Main idea: It's important to take time to reflect upon your goals in life.

1. _Take out a sheet of paper and write down "My Lifetime Goals."_

2. _Take out a second sheet and write down "My Three-Year Goals."_

3. _Take a third sheet and list "What I Would Do If I Knew I Had Six Months to Live."_

4. _On the three lists, rate each item as A, B, or C._

5. _Evaluate the "A" items and select the goals that are most important to you._

Explanation:

You should have added the following steps to the outline:

1. Take out a sheet of paper and write down "My Lifetime Goals." (The author signals this step with the time phrase _To begin with_.)

2. Take a second sheet and list "My Three-Year Goals." (The author signals this step with the time word _Next_.)

3. Take a third sheet and list "What I Would Do If I Knew I Had Six Months to Live." (This step is signaled with the time word _Third_.)

4. On the three lists, rate each item as A, B, or C. (This step is marked by the time word _Now_.)

5. Evaluate the "A" items and select the goals that are most important to you. (_Finally_ signals this last step.)

➤ *Practice 5*   *Wording of answers may vary.*

The following passage gives directions involving several steps that must be done in order. Complete the map below by filling in the main idea in the top box and the four missing steps.

¹To write effectively, practice four rules of thumb. ²<u>First of all,</u> decide what point you want to make in your paper. ³Your main idea is often best expressed at the beginning of your paper. ⁴It is a guide for both you and your reader as to what your paper is about. ⁵<u>Next,</u> be sure to provide sufficient support for your point. ⁶To do so, you need to provide specific reasons, examples, and other details that explain and develop the point. ⁷The more precise and particular your supporting details are, the better your readers can "see," "hear," and "feel" them. ⁸The <u>third</u> rule of thumb is to organize your support. ⁹You can often use a listing order in which you present and explain your first supporting detail and then your second and perhaps finally a third or fourth. ¹⁰The <u>last</u> rule of thumb is to write clear, error-free sentences. ¹¹If you spell correctly and follow grammar, punctuation, and usage rules, your sentences will be clear and well written. ¹²To find errors, read your sentences aloud and make whatever changes are needed so they read smoothly and clearly. ¹³If you have questions, refer to a dictionary or a grammar handbook as needed.

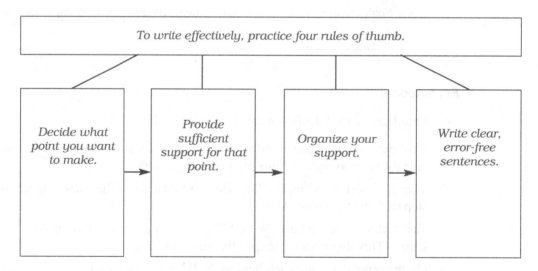

To write effectively, practice four rules of thumb.

| *Decide what point you want to make.* | *Provide sufficient support for that point.* | *Organize your support.* | *Write clear, error-free sentences.* |

The four steps are introduced with the time words *First* (sentence 2), *Next* (sentence 5), *third* (sentence 8), and *last* (sentence 10).

A Note on Main Ideas and Patterns of Organization

A paragraph's main idea may indicate its pattern of organization. For example, here is a sentence from this chapter that suggests a list of items will follow:

> Luckily, modern medicine has developed a variety of techniques for tattoo removal.

And here is a sentence from the chapter that suggests the paragraph will have a time order:

> People who move into affordable city neighborhoods may not realize it, but they are often part of a process that ends in the change of a community.

Paying close attention to the main idea, then, can often give you a quick sense of a paragraph's pattern of organization. Try, for instance, to guess the pattern of the paragraph with this main idea:

> Research has uncovered a number of possible explanations for the link between hostility and heart disease.

The phrase "a number of possible explanations" is a strong indication that the paragraph will list those explanations. The main idea helps us guess that the paragraph will be a list of explanations.

➤ *Practice 6*

Most of the main ideas below have been taken from college textbooks. In the space provided, write the letter of the pattern of organization that each main idea suggests.

_____B_____ 1. A woman's pregnancy is usually divided into trimesters, each with its own developmental milestones.
    A. List of items   B. Time order

_____A_____ 2. Various tests have been developed specifically to measure the intelligence of infants and children.
    A. List of items   B. Time order

_____A_____ 3. Almost any food item you find in a supermarket will be dated in one of several ways.
    A. List of items   B. Time order

_____B_____ 4. Widowed adults often go through a series of stages as they adjust to their loss.
    A. List of items   B. Time order

Note: List words and transitions that indicate each pattern of organization are underlined in red in this *Instructor's Edition.*

_____A_____ 5. Scientists have <u>a number of methods</u> for using current data to make estimates about the total number of species on Earth.
    A. List of items   B. Time order

_____B_____ 6. The development of a drug or alcohol addiction typically unfolds in <u>four stages.</u>
    A. List of items   B. Time order

_____B_____ 7. <u>When</u> the first rains began to fall on the first igneous rocks, the <u>process</u> of weathering began.
    A. List of items   B. Time order

_____A_____ 8. <u>A number of studies</u> have demonstrated that high-quality daycare has beneficial effects on many children's development.
    A. List of items   B. Time order

_____A_____ 9. People often respond to conflict with one of <u>three distinct kinds of behavior.</u>
    A. List of items   B. Time order

_____B_____ 10. A nuclear reactor works like this. <u>First,</u> a neutron strikes a uranium-235 nucleus in one fuel rod, causing that nucleus to split apart.
    A. List of items   B. Time order

Two Final Points

1 While many passages have just one pattern of organization, often the patterns are mixed. For example, you may find that part of a passage uses a list of items pattern, and another part of the same passage uses a time pattern. In the passage below, sentences 8 and 9 list ways to complete the third step in the series:

> [1]Do you know what to do if you lose a tooth in an accident, fall, or fight? [2]Doctors can replace a knocked-out tooth, but only if you act quickly. [3]First, find the loose tooth. [4]Pick it up by the top part, and don't touch the roots. [5]Second, rinse the tooth with milk. [6]Don't use tap water, soap, or chemicals because they could cause harm. [7]Third, keep the tooth from getting dry. [8]If possible, put the tooth back in its socket. [9]If you cannot do this, store it in milk or keep it between your tongue and cheek, taking care not to swallow it. [10]Finally, go as quickly as possible to a dentist's office or an emergency room. [11]If more than an hour or so passes, your tooth will become unusable.

2 Remember that not all relationships between ideas are signaled by transitions. An author may present a list of items, for example, without using addition words. So as you read, watch for the relationships themselves, not just the transitions.

CHAPTER REVIEW

In this chapter, you learned how authors use transitions and patterns of organization to make their ideas clear. Just as transitions show relationships between ideas in sentences, patterns of organization show relationships between supporting details in paragraphs and longer pieces of writing.

You also learned two common kinds of relationships that authors use to make their ideas clear:

- **Addition relationships**

  ✳ Authors often present a list or series of reasons, examples, or other details that support an idea. The items have no time order, but are listed in whatever order the author prefers.

  — Transition words and phrases that signal such addition relationships include *for one thing, second, also, in addition,* and *finally.*

- **Time relationships**

  ✳ Authors usually discuss a series of events or steps in the order in which they happen, resulting in a time order.

  — Transition words that signal such time relationships include *first, next, then, after,* and *last.*

The next chapter—Chapter 5—will help you learn three other important kinds of relationships: definition-example, comparison and/or contrast, and cause-effect.

On the Web: If you are using this book in class, you can visit our website for additional practice in understanding relationships that involve addition and time. Go to **www.townsendpress.com** and click on "Online Exercises."

➤ **Review Test 1**

To review what you've learned in this chapter, answer each of the following questions by filling in the blank.

1. Transitions are words or phrases (like *first of all* or *another* or *then* or *finally*) that show the _____relationships_____ between ideas. They are like signs on the road that guide travelers. See page 134.

2. Words such as *for one thing, also,* and *furthermore* are known as addition words. They tell us the writer is presenting one or more _____ideas_____ that add to the same line of thought as a previous idea. See page 134.

3. Words such as *then, next,* and *after* are known as time words. They tell us _____when **or** at what point_____ something happened in relation to when something else happened. See page 136.

4. Just as transitions show the relationships between ideas in sentences, patterns of _____organization_____ show the relationships between supporting details in a paragraph or longer passage. See page 138.

5. Sometimes the _____main idea_____ of a paragraph may suggest the paragraph's pattern of organization. See page 149.

➤ **Review Test 2**

The selection that follows is from the college textbook *Communicate!* (Wadsworth) by Rudolph F. Verderber and Kathleen S. Verderber. Read it and then answer the relationships questions that follow. There are also questions on understanding vocabulary in context, finding main ideas, identifying supporting details, and recognizing implied main ideas.

Preview

Good conversationalists are not born; they are made. If you cringe at the thought of having to make "small talk," this excerpt from a communications textbook will give you some very concrete tips about how to keep the conversational ball rolling smoothly.

Words to Watch

initiator (before paragraph 3): the person who begins
filibuster (13): prolonged speechmaking
paraphrases (18): rewordings

SKILLS OF EFFECTIVE FACE-TO-FACE CONVERSATIONALISTS

Rudolph F. Verderber and Kathleen S. Verderber

1 Regardless of how well we think we converse, almost all of us can learn to be more effective. In this section, we discuss several skills that are basic to effective conversationalists.

Have Quality Information to Present

2 The more you know about a range of subjects, the greater the chance that you will be an interesting conversationalist. Here are some suggestions for building a high-quality information base:

- Read a newspaper every day (not just the comics or the sports).
- Read at least one weekly news or special-interest magazine.
- Watch television documentaries and news specials as well as entertainment and sports programs. (Of course, sports and entertainment are favorite topics of conversation too—but not with everyone.)
- Attend the theater and concerts as well as going to movies.
- Visit museums and historical sites.

Following these suggestions will provide you with a foundation of quality information you can share in social conversations.

As an Initiator°, Ask Meaningful Questions

3 What happens in the first few minutes of a conversation will have a profound effect on how well a social conversation develops. Although asking questions comes easy to some, many people seem at a loss for what to do to get a conversation started. These four question lines will usually help to get a conversation started. Notice that none of them is a yes or no question—each calls for the person to share some specific information.

- *Refer to family:* How is Susan getting along this year at college? How is your dad feeling?
- *Refer to the person's work:* What projects have you been working on lately?
- *Refer to a sporting activity:* How was the fishing trip you went on last week? What is it about Tiger Woods that enables him to be near his best at major tournaments?
- *Refer to a current event:* What do you think is driving people back to more conservative stocks? What do you think we can do to get kids more interested in reading?

Perhaps just looking at these four suggestions will bring other ideas to mind that you can use to start conversations with various acquaintances.

As a Responder, Provide Free Information

4 Effective conversationalists provide a means of enabling others to continue a conversation by providing free information with their responses. Free information is extra information offered during a message that can be used by the responder to continue the conversation.

5   Many people have difficulty building conversations because of a tendency to reply to questions with one-word responses. If, for instance, Paul asks Jack, "Do you like tennis?" and Jack answers "Yes" and then just looks at Paul, Paul has nowhere to go. To keep the conversation going (or to get it started), Paul has to think of a new line to pursue.

6   Suppose, however, that after Jack answers "Yes," he goes on to say "I've only been playing for about a year, but I really enjoy it." Now, Paul has a direction to follow. He might turn the conversation to his own experience: "I haven't been playing long myself, but I'm starting to get more confidence, especially with my forehand." Or he might use the information to ask another question: "Are you able to play very often?"

7   As a respondent, it is important to give free information. As the initiator, it is important to listen for free information. The better the quality of the free information, the more likely it is that the conversation will grow and prove rewarding to both participants.

Credit Sources

8   Crediting sources means verbally footnoting the source from which you have drawn your information and ideas. In a term paper, you give credit to authors you have quoted or paraphrased by footnoting the sources. Similarly, when you use other people's words or ideas in your oral communication, you can credit the source verbally.

9   By crediting you enable the participants to evaluate the quality of the information you are sharing. Moreover, by crediting ideas from people who are acquaintances, you make people feel better about themselves and avoid hard feelings. For instance, if a friend presents a creative idea and verbally acknowledges you as the source, you probably feel flattered. If, however, the person acts as though the idea were his own, you are probably hurt or angry. So, when you repeat ideas that you have gotten from others, make sure you give proper credit.

10   Crediting is easy enough. To give credit where it is due and avoid possible hard feelings, just include the name of the person you got the idea from. For example, in a discussion about course offerings, you might say, "I like the list of courses we have to choose from, but, you know, we should really have a course in attitude change. Laura was the one who put me on to the idea, and I can see why it's a good idea."

Balance Speaking and Listening

11   Conversations are most satisfying when all participants feel that they have had their fair share of speaking time. We balance speaking and listening in a conversation by practicing turn-taking techniques.

12   **1. Effective conversationalists take the appropriate number of turns.** In any conversation, the idea is for all to have approximately the same number of turns. If you discover that you are speaking more than your fair share, try to restrain yourself by mentally checking whether everyone else has had a chance to talk once before you talk a second time. Similarly, if you find yourself being inactive in a conversation, try to increase your participation level. Remember, if you have information to contribute, you are cheating yourself and the group when you do not share it.

13   **2. Effective conversationalists speak an appropriate length of time on each turn.** People are likely to tune out or become annoyed with those conversational partners who make speeches, filibuster°, or perform monologues rather than engaging in the ordinary give-and-take of conversation. Similarly, it is difficult to carry on a conversation with someone who gives one- or two-word replies to questions that are designed to elicit meaningful information. Turns do, of course, vary in length depending on what is being said. If your average statements are much longer or shorter than those of your conversational partners, however, you need to adjust.

14   **3. Effective conversationalists recognize and heed turn-exchanging cues.** Patterns of vocal tone, such as a decrease of loudness or a lowering of pitch, and use of gestures that seem to show obvious completion of a point are the most obvious turn-taking cues. When you are trying to get into a conversation, look for them.

15   By the same token, be careful of giving inadvertent turn-exchanging cues. For instance, if you tend to lower your voice when you are not really done speaking, or take long pauses for emphasis when you expect to continue, you are likely to be interrupted, because these are cues that others are likely to act on. If you find yourself getting interrupted frequently, you might ask people whether you tend to give false cues. Moreover, if you come to recognize that another person has a habit of giving these kinds of cues inadvertently, try not to interrupt when speaking with that person.

16   **4. Effective conversationalists use conversation-directing behavior and comply with the conversation-directing behavior of others.** In general, a person who ends his or her turn may define who speaks next. For instance, when Paul concludes his turn by saying, "Susan, did you understand what he meant?" Susan has the right to the floor. Skillful turn takers use conversation-directing behavior to balance turns between those who freely speak and those who may be more reluctant to speak. Similarly, effective turn takers remain silent and listen politely when the conversation is directed to someone else.

17   Of course, if the person who has just finished speaking does not verbally or nonverbally direct the conversation to a preferred next speaker, then the turn is up for grabs and goes to the first person to speak.

18   **5. Effective conversationalists rarely interrupt.** Although interruptions are generally considered inappropriate, interrupting for "clarification" and "agreement" (confirming) are interpersonally acceptable. For instance, interruptions that are likely to include relevant questions or paraphrases° intended to clarify, such as "What do you mean by 'presumptuous'" or "I get the sense that you think presumptuous behavior is especially bad," and reinforcing statements such as "Good point, Max" or "I see what you mean, Suzie." The interruptions that are likely to be viewed as disruptive or incomplete include those that change the subject or that seem to minimize the contribution of the interrupted person.

Reading Comprehension Questions

Vocabulary in Context

_____A_____ 1. In the sentence below, the word *elicit* (ĭ-lĭs′ĭt) means

A. bring out.

B. describe.

C. do away with.

D. challenge.

> The sentence suggests that it is difficult to hold a conversation when questions do not bring out meaningful information.

"Similarly, it is difficult to carry on a conversation with someone who gives one or two-word replies to questions that are designed to elicit meaningful information." (Paragraph 13)

_____D_____ 2. In the excerpt below, the word *inadvertent* (ĭn′əd-vûr′tnt) means

A. intentional.

B. obvious.

C. rude.

D. accidental.

> The cues mentioned are things people normally do without thinking. Therefore, they are accidental.

"By the same token, be careful of giving inadvertent turn-exchanging cues. For instance, if you tend to lower your voice when you are not really done speaking or take long pauses for emphasis when you expect to continue, you are likely to be interrupted because these are cues that others are likely to act on." (Paragraph 15)

Central Point and Main Ideas

_____C_____ 3. Which sentence best expresses the implied central point of the selection?

Answer A covers only paragraphs 4–7; answer D covers only paragraphs 14–17. Answer B ignores the four other ways (in paragraphs 3–18) of being an interesting conversationalist.

A. Many people fail to provide enough free information and therefore cannot be considered skilled conversationalists.

B. The key to becoming a skilled conversationalist is to have something interesting to say and to know how to say it.

C. By following some simple suggestions, people can improve their skills as conversationalists.

D. To become an effective conversationalist, one must heed turn-exchanging cues and comply with the conversation-directing behavior of others.

_____B_____ 4. The implied main idea of paragraphs 4–7 is that

Answer A covers only paragraph 5. Answer C ignores the idea of the respondent's role in giving free information. Answer D is suggested only in the last sentence of paragraph 7.

A. if responders don't provide enough free information, the conversation may end.

B. all conversationalists need to be aware of the need to provide and listen for free information.

C. initiators need to listen for free information in order to keep a conversation going.

D. some conversations can reward both initiators and responders.

___A___ 5. The main idea of paragraphs 16–17 is stated in
  A. the first sentence of paragraph 16.
  B. the second sentence of paragraph 16.
  C. the last sentence of paragraph 16.
  D. paragraph 17.

Answers B, C, and D each focus on only a single aspect: B on defining the next speaker; C on behaviors of effective turn takers; and D on non-directional behavior.

Supporting Details

___C___ 6. According to the authors, free information is
  A. information available in any newspaper or magazine.
  B. information that doesn't require an oral response.
  C. extra information offered during a message that can be used by the responder to continue the conversation.   See paragraph 4.
  D. information about carefree topics such as tennis and other sports.

___B___ 7. According to the article, two appropriate reasons to interrupt a speaker are
  A. to express disapproval and disgust.   See paragraph 18.
  B. for clarification and agreement.
  C. to dispute the speaker's facts and to ask for elaboration.
  D. to change the subject and to minimize the contribution of the interrupted person.

Transitions

___B___ 8. The relationship of the second sentence below to the first sentence is one of
  A. addition.   The word *Now* signals a time relationship.
  B. time.

   "Suppose, however, that after Jack answers 'Yes,' he goes on to say 'I've only been playing for about a year, but I really enjoy it.' Now, Paul has a direction to follow." (Paragraph 6)

___A___ 9. The relationship of the second sentence below to the first sentence is one of
  A. addition.   The word *Moreover* signals an addition relationship.
  B. time.

   "By crediting you enable the participants to evaluate the quality of the information you are sharing. Moreover, by crediting ideas from people who are acquaintances, you make people feel better about themselves and avoid hard feelings." (Paragraph 9)

Patterns of Organization

_____*A*_____ 10. The pattern of organization in this selection is mainly

    A. a list of items.

    B. time order.

                       The selection lists skills that are basic to effective conversationalists.

Discussion Questions

1. Do you consider yourself a talkative person—or a quiet person? Which of the specific skills mentioned in this essay would be valuable for you to work on? Which of them do you think would work less well for you? Explain.

2. Think of the last time you had an extremely interesting conversation with someone. What was it about the conversation, or the conversationalist, that made it so interesting?

3. Have you ever been in a conversation with someone who dominated the conversation? Conversely, have you ever tried to carry on a conversation with a person who failed to provide any "free information," or who demonstrated other inappropriate conversational behaviors? If so, how did you react in each situation?

4. In your opinion, what advantages do people who are skilled conversationalists have over people who are not?

Note: Writing assignments for this selection appear on page 562.

Check Your Performance			**RELATIONSHIPS I**
Activity	*Number Right*	*Points*	*Score*
Review Test 1 (5 items)	_____	× 6 =	_____
Review Test 2 (10 items)	_____	× 7 =	_____
		TOTAL SCORE =	_____ %

Enter your total score into the **Reading Performance Chart: Review Tests** on the inside back cover.

RELATIONSHIPS I: Mastery Test 1

A. Fill in each blank with an appropriate transition from the box. Use each transition once. Then, in the space provided, write the letter of the transition you have chosen.

A. also	B. finally	C. in addition
D. next	E. then	

___B___ 1. ¹A butterfly goes through four stages of life. ²First, it is an egg; next, it becomes a caterpillar; after that, a pupa inside a cocoon; and _____*finally*_____, an adult butterfly.   Time order pattern—a series of steps.

___A___ 2. ¹Identifying a true food allergy requires a thorough health history, physical examination, and diagnostic tests to eliminate other diseases. ²Skin pricks with food extracts are a common test for food allergies, even though the high incidence of false positive results can complicate diagnosis. ³Physicians _____*also*_____ conduct dietary trials in which they eliminate the offending food and reintroduce it in small quantities to substantiate that reactions occur only when that particular food is eaten.   List of ways to identify a food allergy.

___E___ 3. ¹When administering a lie-detector test, the tester begins by asking general, non-threatening questions. ²He _____*then*_____ moves on to questions that may cause the subject to feel anxious or guilty.   Time order pattern—steps in a process.

___C___ 4. ¹People today communicate in ways that earlier generations could have never dreamed of. ²They can now speak to each other almost anywhere using cell phones. ³_____*In addition*_____, they communicate via e-mail, text and instant messaging, webcams, fax machines, and overnight letters.   List of ways people can communicate.

___D___ 5. ¹On the sunny Tuesday morning of September 11, 2001, nineteen hijackers seized control of commercial jets that had taken off from East Coast airports. ²At 8:46 a.m., one plane crashed into the 110-story North Tower of the World Trade Center in New York City, causing a huge explosion and a fire. ³_____*Next*_____, at 9:03 a.m., a second plane flew into the South Tower. ⁴In less than two hours, both buildings collapsed, killing thousands of office workers, firefighters, and police officers.   Time order pattern—a series of events.

(Continues on next page)

B. (6–9.) Fill in each blank with an appropriate transition from the box. Use each transition once.

A. during	B. finally	C. first
D. then		

¹There has been an overwhelming interest in the story of King Kong from its first appearance in a 1933 movie to the popular remake of that film in 2005. ²The basic story is pretty simple. ³The _____*first*_____ thing that happens is that filmmakers go to a mysterious island to make a movie about an enormous ape. ⁴The ape _____*then*_____ snatches the leading lady, with whom he falls in love. ⁵After the ape is captured, he is taken back to the United States and put on display in New York. ⁶The next turn in the plot is that he escapes, grabs the girl again, rampages through the city, and climbs to the top of the Empire State Building. ⁷_____*During*_____ all of this action, he manages to tenderly protect the girl. ⁸_____*Finally*_____, he is mortally wounded by fighter planes, and the massive creature falls to his death. ⁹The story will probably be around forever, having a grip for whatever mysterious reasons on our collective imagination.

_B_ 10. The pattern of organization of the above selection is
   A. list of items.
   B. time order.   The paragraph tells a story by describing the sequence of events leading to the death of King Kong.

RELATIONSHIPS I: Mastery Test 2

A. Fill in each blank with an appropriate transition from the box. Use each transition once. Then, in the space provided, write the letter of the transition you have chosen.

A. before	B. for one thing	C. in addition
D. later	E. second	

___C___ 1. [1]"Functional literacy" does not refer only to a person's ability to read words. [2]_____*In addition*_____, it has to do with a person's ability to understand a map and do simple arithmetic.   List of abilities
                                                                    included in functional literacy.

___A___ 2. [1]Right _____*before*_____ the pain of a migraine headache begins, many people experience a visual "aura" consisting of flashing or wavy lights.
                                        Time order pattern—a sequence of events.

___D___ 3. [1]Some peace movements include no more than a dozen dedicated pacifists. [2]Others have widespread popular appeal and the ability to mobilize thousands or even millions of citizens. [3]In 1828, Quakers, evangelical preachers, and intellectuals joined to form the American Peace Society, a national organization that promoted world peace as well as abolitionism and women's rights. [4]_____*Later*_____ in the century, they were joined by feminists, suffragettes, and social reformers.

Time order pattern describing the evolution of the society. The words In 1828 are a clue.

___B___ 4. [1]Forget the spanking clean, neat, freshly painted houses in "colonial villages" constructed for modern tourists. [2]Most 17th- and 18th-century colonial homes looked nothing like them. [3]_____*For one thing*_____, few were painted on the outside. [4]Most were made of split or sawed boards that, like modern wooden garden benches, faded into a gray that blended into the landscape. [5]Secondly, they were small affairs, often consisting of a single room measuring perhaps eighteen by twenty feet on the inside with a chimney at the end. [6]And some, but by no means all, had white-washed interior walls; otherwise, the interiors went unfinished.
                                        List of characteristics of colonial houses.

___E___ 5. [1]An early method of writing was sign writing, in which each symbol was based on a picture that resembled what it stood for. [2]Thus, a circle with wavy lines radiating from it might stand for the sun, while a horizontal series of wavy lines might stand for water. [3]One early form of this style of writing developed in Sumeria (present-day Iraq) around 3500 B.C. [4]A _____*second*_____, more familiar form developed in Egypt a few hundred years later and came to be known as hieroglyphics. [5]The most durable form of sign writing blossomed in China about 2000 to 1500 B.C. [6]This method required learning thousands of different pictographs that represented various objects and actions.   *(Continues on next page)*

This passage is a combination of list and time order. Three early forms of sign writing are listed in a time sequence.

161

B. (6–9.) Fill in each blank with an appropriate transition from the box. Use each transition once.

> A. first   B. last of all   C. next
> D. second

¹To give first aid for severe external bleeding, one should ____*first*____ place direct pressure on the wound with a sterile gauze pad or any clean cloth, such as a washcloth, towel, or handkerchief. ²Press hard. ³Using a pad or cloth will help keep the wound free from germs and aid clotting. ⁴If you do not have a pad or cloth available, have the injured person apply pressure with his or her hand. ⁵_____*Second*_____, elevate the injured area above the level of the heart if you do not suspect a broken bone. ⁶_____*Next*_____, apply a pressure bandage to hold the gauze pads or cloth in place. ⁷If blood soaks through the bandage, add more pads and bandages to help absorb the blood. ⁸Do not remove any blood-soaked pads because doing so can interfere with the blood-clotting process. ⁹_____*Last of all*_____, if bleeding continues, call EMS personnel and see if you can apply pressure at a pressure point to slow the flow of blood.

__*B*__ 10. The pattern of organization of the above selection is
      A. list of items.
      B. time order.

> The passage describes the sequence of steps to take when giving first aid for severe external bleeding.

RELATIONSHIPS I: Mastery Test 3

A. Fill in each blank with an appropriate transition from the box. Use each transition once. Then, in the space provided, write the letter of the transition you have chosen.

A. also	B. another	C. during
D. furthermore	E. until	

___B___ 1. ¹Premarital sex does not always result from a desire for intimacy.

Lists two factors that can lead to premarital sex.

²_____Another_____ important factor is peer pressure. ³For young males, sexual experience is seen as a way to prove their manliness. ⁴For young females, especially ones with a poor self-image, sexual intimacy is regarded as a way to prove they are sexy and desirable.

___E___ 2. ¹The most extreme form of social control is capital punishment, that is, the execution of the criminal offender. ²_____Until_____ the

Time order pattern noting events in the eighteenth century (preceding the 1960s).

1960s, capital punishment was an integral part of the British criminal justice system. ³In the eighteenth century in particular, there were over two hundred crimes, ranging from high treason to petty thievery, for which people could be executed. ⁴These executions were held in full public view in the belief that the witnesses would be deterred from committing similar acts.

___A___ 3. ¹Up to a hundred years ago, people believed tomatoes to be poisonous. ²This is because the tomato belongs to a family of plants, the

List of reasons tomatoes were considered poisonous. Note that the words *Up to a hundred years ago* do not signal a time order pattern in this sentence.

Nightshade, which does have some poisonous members. ³People _____also_____ assumed the tomato to be poisonous because of the unpleasantly strong odor given off by the stem and leaves of the plant. ⁴The stem and leaves give off this odor because they are, in fact, toxic; but the fruit itself is not.

___D___ 4. ¹More than 9,000 pieces of man-made junk are now orbiting in space, mostly left over from exploded satellites. ²More space junk is being

List of facts about space junk.

added all the time. ³_____Furthermore_____, the number of pieces is increasing as they bump into one another and break into smaller bits.

Note: Items 3 and 4: Since *also* and *furthermore* are synonyms, students might reverse the order of these two answers. Either transition would be a correct choice for either item.

(Continues on next page)

_C_   5. [1]At the heart of the technological revolution was the microprocessor. [2]First introduced in 1970 by Intel, the microprocessor miniaturized the central processing unit of a computer, enabling small machines to perform calculations that previously only large machines could do. [3]_____*During*_____ the next decades, the power of these integrated circuits increased by a factor of seven thousand. [4]Computing chores that took a week in the early 1970s took only one minute by the year 2000, while the cost of storing one megabyte of information, or enough for a 320-page book, fell from more than $5,000 in 1975 to 17 cents in 2000. [5]The implications for business were enormous.

Time order pattern describing the evolution of the microprocessor over a thirty-year period.

B. (6–9.) Fill in each blank with an appropriate transition from the box. Use each transition once.

> A. first   B. last   C. next
> D. third

[1]If you mention the word *PROM* to people, they are going to think of a high-school rite of passage. [2]In fact, *PROM* is also the name of a proven study method. [3]The _____*first*_____ step in this system is to preview a reading assignment. [4]Note the title and read the first and last paragraphs; also look quickly at headings and subheads and anything in boldface or italic. [5]_____*Next*_____, read a selection straight through while marking off important ideas such as definitions, examples, and lists of items. [6]The _____*third*_____ step is to organize the material you've read by taking study notes on it. [7]Get all the important ideas down on paper in outline form, relating one idea to another as much as possible. [8]_____*Last*_____, memorize the study notes that you will need to remember for tests. [9]Do this by writing key words in the margins of your study outline and turning those words into questions. [10]For instance, the key words "three types of rocks" can be converted into the question "What are the three types of rocks?" [11]Recite the answers to these and other key questions until you can answer them without referring to your notes.

_B_   10. The pattern of organization of the above selection is
   A. list of items.
   B. time order.

This paragraph explains the sequence of steps in the PROM study method.

RELATIONSHIPS I: Mastery Test 4

A. (1–6.) Fill in each blank with an appropriate transition from the box. Use each transition once.

A. after	B. later	C. next
D. then	E. when	

¹_____*After*_____ a string of defeats which forced the Continental Army to retreat down through New Jersey, General George Washington was in despair. ²He managed to bring his troops across the Delaware River into Pennsylvania on December 11, 1776. ³The _____*next*_____ day, Congress, fearing a British attack, fled Philadelphia for Baltimore. ⁴But _____*then*_____ Washington broke the string of defeats on December 30–31, _____*when*_____ he recrossed the Delaware and surprised a British garrison at Trenton, New Jersey, taking 918 prisoners and killing 30 of the king's soldiers, while the American troops suffered only 5 casualties. ⁵Three days _____*later*_____, he won another victory at Princeton. ⁶The battles of Trenton and Princeton were among the most important of the war. ⁷They restored morale and allowed Washington to take his troops into winter camp—war in the 18th century was primarily a summer and fall activity, since the guns of the day fired poorly in cold weather—at Morristown, New Jersey. ⁸That meant the Continental Army would be around to fight again in 1777.

___*B*___ 6. The pattern of organization of the above selection is
   A. list of items.
   B. time order.

> The paragraph relates the sequence of historical events that enabled the Continental Army to fight again in 1777.

(Continues on next page)

B. (7–10.) Read the textbook passage below. Then answer the question and complete the outline that follows.   *Wording of answers may vary.*

> ¹Throughout history, political leaders have used lottery systems to benefit society in <u>several ways</u>. ²<u>One</u> function of lotteries was to fund military projects. ³Ancient Chinese warlord Cheung Leung made up a lottery system to pay for his army. ⁴The system he created is now known as the popular game Keno. ⁵American leader Benjamin Franklin used a lottery to buy the Continental Army a cannon during the Revolutionary War. ⁶Lotteries have <u>also</u> been used to pay for public works. ⁷China's Great Wall was funded in part by a lottery. ⁸The Romans used a lottery system approved by Augustus Caesar to pay for the construction of public buildings. ⁹Boston's Faneuil Hall was rebuilt with the money from a lottery organized by American revolutionary John Hancock. ¹⁰Many of today's American state lotteries fund public education. ¹¹Yet <u>another</u> use of lotteries has been to help the poor. ¹²Bruges, a Belgian town of the 15th century, created lotteries solely to help support the needy. ¹³The profits from today's New Zealand lotteries are also donated directly to charities and other nonprofit organizations.

   _A_   7. The pattern of organization of the above selection is

         A. list of items.   This paragraph lists the various ways that lotteries

         B. time order.   have been used to benefit society. Note the list words

                                                several ways.

    8–10. Complete the outline of the passage.

Main idea: Throughout history, political leaders have used lottery systems to benefit society in several ways.

    1. *Fund military projects*

    _____

    2. *Pay for public works*

    _____

    3. *Help support the needy*

    _____

                  The three major details are introduced by the addition transitions *One* (sentence 2), *also* (sentence 6) and *another* (sentence 11).

Note: In the paragraphs in Tests 4–6, list words and transitions that indicate each pattern of organization are underlined.

RELATIONSHIPS I: Mastery Test 5

A. (1–5.) Fill in each blank with an appropriate transition from the box. Use each transition once.

A. after	B. during	C. eventually
D. next	E. then	

[1]Franklin Roosevelt, the twentieth-century president most beloved by America's "common people," had been born into a world of old money and upper-class privilege. [2]The talented son of a politically prominent family, he seemed destined for political success. [3]_____*After*_____ graduating from Harvard College and Columbia Law School, he had married Eleanor Roosevelt, Theodore Roosevelt's niece and his own fifth cousin, once removed. [4]He served in the New York state legislature, was appointed Assistant Secretary of the Navy by Woodrow Wilson; and, at the age of thirty-eight, ran for vice-president in 1920 on the Democratic Party's losing ticket.

[5]_____*Then*_____, in 1921, Roosevelt was stricken with polio. [6]_____*During*_____ the next two years he was bedridden, fighting one of the most feared diseases of the first half of the twentieth century. [7]He _____*eventually*_____ lost the use of his legs, but gained, according to his wife Eleanor, a new strength of character that would serve him well as he reached out to depression-scarred America. [8]As Roosevelt explained it, "If you had spent two years in bed trying to wiggle your big toe, after that anything would seem easy." [9]In 1928 Roosevelt was sufficiently recovered to run for—and win—the governorship of New York. [10]The _____*next*_____ step in his remarkable political career was to accept the Democratic Party's presidential nomination in 1932.

___*B*___ 6. The pattern of organization of the above selection is
    A. list of items.   The passage details a sequence of important
    B. time order.   events in Franklin Roosevelt's life.

(Continues on next page)

167

B. (7–10.) Read the textbook passage below. Then answer the question and complete the outline that follows.   *Wording of answers may vary.*

> [1]One of a baby's major accomplishments <u>during</u> its first year of life is learning about **object permanence**, the understanding that something continues to exist even if you can't see it or touch it. [2]<u>In the first few months</u> of life, infants are very fickle. [3]"Out of sight, out of mind" seems to be their motto. [4]They will look intently at a little toy, but if you hide it behind a piece of paper, they will not look behind the paper or make an effort to get the toy. [5]<u>By about six months</u>, infants begin to grasp the idea that objects exist "out there"; a toy is a toy, and the cat is the cat, whether or not they can see the toy or the cat. [6]If a baby of this age drops a toy from her playpen, she will look for it; she also will look under a cloth for a toy that is partially hidden. [7]<u>By one year of age,</u> most babies have developed an awareness of the permanence of some objects. [8]That is when they love to play peek-a-boo.

_____B____ 7. The pattern of organization of the above selection is

        A. list of items.

        B. time order.

During (sentence 1), In the first few months (sentence 2), By about six months (sentence 5), and By one year of age (sentence 7) are time transitions used to signal the stages whereby a baby develops an awareness of object permanence.

8–10. Complete the map of the paragraph by writing in the missing supporting details.

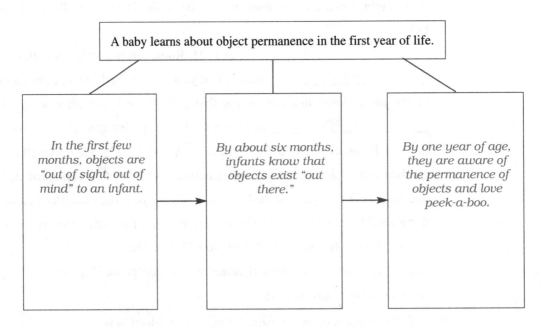

A baby learns about object permanence in the first year of life.

In the first few months, objects are "out of sight, out of mind" to an infant.

By about six months, infants know that objects exist "out there."

By one year of age, they are aware of the permanence of objects and love peek-a-boo.

See sentences 2, 5, and 7.

RELATIONSHIPS I: Mastery Test 6

A. (1–4.) Read the passage below, and then answer the question and complete the map that follows. *Wording of answers may vary.*

> [1]If parents decide to use punishment to control their children, its effectiveness can be increased in several ways. [2]The first involves consistency. [3]Punishment that is unpredictable is related to especially high rates of disobedience in children. [4]When parents permit children to act inappropriately on some occasions but scold them on others, children are confused about how to behave, and the unacceptable act persists. [5]Second, a warm relationship with children increases the effectiveness of an occasional punishment. [6]Children of involved and caring parents find the interruption in parental affection that accompanies punishment to be especially unpleasant. [7]As a result, they want to regain the warmth and approval of parents as quickly as possible. [8]Third, punishment works best when it is accompanied by an explanation. [9]Explanations increase the effectiveness of punishments because they help children recall the misdeed and relate it to expectations for future behavior.

_____A_____ 1. The pattern of organization of the above selection is

    A. list of items.

    B. time order.

                    The passage lists ways that the effectiveness of punishment can be increased. The list words in several ways are a clue.

2–4. Complete the map of the paragraph by writing in the missing supporting details.

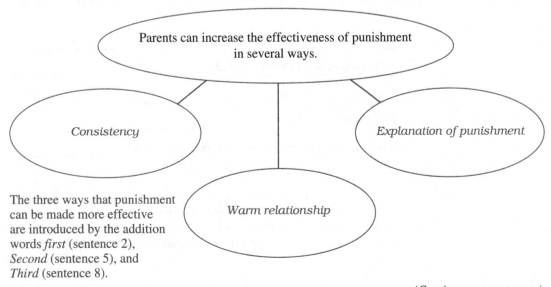

Parents can increase the effectiveness of punishment in several ways.

Consistency

Explanation of punishment

Warm relationship

The three ways that punishment can be made more effective are introduced by the addition words *first* (sentence 2), *Second* (sentence 5), and *Third* (sentence 8).

(Continues on next page)

169

B. (5–10.) Read the passage below, and then answer the question and complete the outline.   *Wording of answers may vary.*

> ¹Are you living with a person who verbally abuses you? ²If so, you owe it to yourself to change your situation. ³The way to succeed is to break the process into manageable steps. ⁴First and most important, you must believe that you are not to blame for the abuse. ⁵No doubt your abuser has convinced you that if only you would do A, B, or C differently, he or she would not "have" to become abusive. ⁶This is a lie. ⁷No one "has" to be abusive. ⁸Secondly, educate yourself about verbal abuse. ⁹Use books or the Internet to read about verbal abuse and how to deal with it. ¹⁰You'll find you are not alone, and that leads to the next step: Find a support group. ¹¹Identify people (friends, relatives, a teacher or minister or counselor) you can speak frankly to about your situation and who will give you help. ¹²With increased confidence, you are ready for the next step: Talk to your partner. ¹³As calmly and firmly as possible, state that you are a person who deserves respect and civil behavior, and that you will accept no less. ¹⁴Offer to go with your partner to a counselor who will help both of you learn new ways to communicate. ¹⁵If your partner does not respond, you must consider the final step: Leaving. ¹⁶You were not put here on earth to have your self-esteem destroyed by serving as someone else's verbal punching bag.

___B___   5. The pattern of organization of the above selection is
        A. list of items.   The passage describes a series of steps to follow,
        B. time order.   in order, in dealing with verbal abuse.

6–10. Complete the outline of the passage.

Main idea: To deal with verbal abuse, break the process into manageable steps.

1. *Believe you are not to blame for the abuse.*

2. *Educate yourself about verbal abuse.*

3. *Find a support group.*

4. *Talk to your partner.*

5. *If your partner does not respond, consider leaving.*

In sentence 4, the word *First* signals the first step.
The word *Secondly* in sentence 8 signals the second step.
In sentences 10 and 12, the signal words are *next step*.
The word *final* in sentence 15 signals the last step.

5

Relationships II

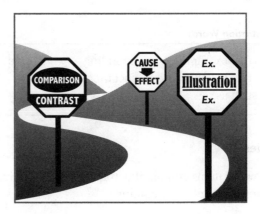

In Chapter 4, you learned how authors use transitions and patterns of organization to show relationships and make their ideas clear. You also learned about two common types of relationships:

- Relationships that involve **addition**
- Relationships that involve **time**

In this chapter you will learn about three other types of relationships:

- Relationships that involve **illustration**
- Relationships that involve **comparison and contrast**
- Relationships that involve **cause and effect**

As you will see, these relationships all involve transitional words and phrases, which are like signs on the road that guide travelers.

1 ILLUSTRATION

Words That Show Illustration

Put a check (✓) beside the item that is easier to understand:

___ Some common beliefs are really myths. Getting a chill will not give you a cold.

✓ Some common beliefs are really myths. For instance, getting a chill will not give you a cold.

The second item is easier to follow. The words *for instance* make it clear that the belief a chill will lead to a cold is a myth. *For instance* and other words and phrases like it are illustration words.

Illustration words indicate that an author will provide one or more *examples* to develop and clarify a given idea. Here are some common words that show illustration:

Illustration Words

(for) example	including	(as an) illustration	one
(for) instance	specifically	to illustrate	once
such as	to be specific		

Examples:

The following items contain illustration words. Notice how these words signal that one or more *examples* are coming.

- Although they are children's stories, famous fairy tales *such as* "Little Red Riding Hood" and "Snow White" are clearly filled with dark symbolic meanings.

- A number of famous historical figures, *including* Beethoven, Charles Dickens, and Winston Churchill, suffered from depression.

- Some of the world's languages are written right to left, or from the top of the page to the bottom. *For example,* Arabic, Hebrew, and Japanese are all written in something other than left-to-right form.

➤ *Practice 1*   *Answers may vary.*

Complete each item with a suitable illustration word or phrase from the box on the previous page. Try to use a variety of transitions.

> *Hint:* Make sure that each word or phrase that you choose fits smoothly into the flow of the sentence. Test each choice by reading the sentence aloud.

1. Body language often gives clues to a person's feelings about him or herself. Keeping one's arms crossed, _____*for example*_____, indicates a sense of low status or anxiety.

2. Technological advances _____*such as*_____ the Internet, cell phones, and fax machines have made working from home a practical reality for many people.

3. The definition of "deviant behavior" depends greatly on prevailing social norms. _____*For instance*_____, a man who wears women's clothing is considered deviant, while a woman wearing men's clothing is not.

4. Certain personal characteristics—_____*including*_____ a strong sense of competition, hostility, and impatience—have been linked to an increased chance of heart attack.

5. Some common phrases have meanings that are nearly forgotten. An _____*illustration*_____ is "mad as a hatter." The poisonous mercury that hat-makers used would cause them to lurch around, twitch, and otherwise act "mad."

Illustration words are common in all types of writing. One way they are used in textbooks is in the pattern of organization known as the definition and example pattern.

The Definition and Example Pattern

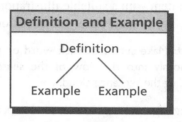

To get a sense of the definition and example pattern, try to arrange the following sentences in an order that makes sense. Put a *1* in front of the sentence that should come first, a *2* in front of the sentence that comes next, and a *3* in front of the sentence that should be last. The result will be a short paragraph. Then read the explanation that follows.

  2   For instance, anyone who has ever played a card game such as hearts is familiar with the heuristic to "Get rid of high cards first."

  1   Informal problems often call for a **heuristic**—a rule of thumb that suggests a course of action without guaranteeing an optimal solution.

  3   Another example is the situation in which a student tries to decide whether to take a particular course and follows the advice to "Ask friends how they liked the instructor."

You should have put a 1 in front of the second sentence, which presents the term *heuristic* and defines the term. That term is then supported by the example in the sentence beginning "For instance" and then the sentence that begins "Another example." As you can see, the definition and example pattern of organization includes just what its name suggests: a definition and one or more examples.

> *An Important Study Hint:* Good textbook authors want to help readers understand the important ideas and terms in a subject—whether it is psychology, sociology, business, biology, or any other field. Such authors often take time, then, to include key definitions. These ideas and terms are usually set off in *italic* or **boldface** print, and the definitions are signaled by such words as *is, are, is called, termed,* and *refers to.* Here are some definitions from a variety of textbooks:
>
> - **Sound bites** are short snippets of information aimed at dramatizing a news story rather than explaining its meaning in a substantive way.
>
> - A decline in attention that occurs because a stimulus has become familiar is called **habituation**.
>
> - **Tracking** refers to the smooth movements of the eye used to follow the track of a moving object.

- A unit of 1000 watts is called a **kilowatt** and is a commonly used measurement of electrical power.

- **Procedural liberties** are restraints on how the government is supposed to act; for example, citizens are guaranteed the due process of law.

- Physicists use the term **half-life** to describe the average time it takes for half of a batch of radioactive isotopes to undergo decay.

- **Gerrymandering** can be defined as the apportionment of voters in districts in such a way as to give unfair advantage to one racial or ethnic group or political party.

- Currently, the term **conservative** refers to those who generally support the social and economic status quo and are suspicious of efforts to introduce new economic arrangements.

- **Seismology**—the study and measurement of vibrations within the Earth—is dedicated to deducing our planet's inner structure.

  (**Note:** Sometimes a dash or dashes are used to signal a definition.)

If an author defines a term, you can assume that it is important enough to learn. So when reading a textbook, always do two things:

1) Underline key definitions.

2) Put an "Ex" in the margin next to a helpful example for each definition. When a definition is general and abstract, examples are often essential to make its meaning clear.

☑ Check Your Understanding

Identify the definition and example in the following paragraph.

[1]The <u>planning fallacy</u> refers to the fact that people consistently overestimate how quickly and easily they will achieve a goal and underestimate the amount of time or effort that will be required to reach that goal. [2]In a study that examined the planning fallacy, college students were asked to list an academic project that had to be completed within the next week and to estimate when they intended to begin the project, when they expected to complete the project, and how many hours they expected to put into it. [3]A week later, the students were asked if they had completed the project and

when. ⁴Although all the students had estimated that they would complete the project comfortably in the time indicated, one week later more than half the projects remained incomplete. ⁵Those that had been completed had typically taken, on average, nearly five days longer than had been estimated. ⁶So much for planning!

What term is being defined? _____ *Planning fallacy* _____

Which sentence contains the definition? _____ *1* _____

In which sentence does the example begin? _____ *2* _____

Explanation:

The term *planning fallacy* is defined in the first sentence, and the example begins in the second sentence and continues to the end.

➤ Practice 2

Each of the following passages includes a definition and one or more examples. Underline the term being defined. Then, in the spaces provided, write the number of the definition sentence and the number of the sentence where an example begins.

A.   ¹As children engage in routine daily activities, they construct scripts of these activities. ²Scripts represent the typical sequence of actions related to an event and guide future behaviors in similar settings. ³For instance, children who have been to a fast-food restaurant might have a script like this: Wait in line, tell the person behind the counter what you want, pay for the food, carry the tray of food to a table, open the packages and eat the food, gather the trash and throw it away before leaving. ⁴With this script in mind, children can act effectively in similar settings.

Term being defined: *scripts.* Transition: *For instance.* Example: Children in fast-food restaurants.

Definition __2__ *Example* __3__

B.   ¹All human beings are, to a large extent, the product of underline{enculturation}. ²This refers to the idea that our values, to a significant extent, are the result of the conditioning and shaping influences of our particular culture. ³For example, if I had grown up in India in the twentieth century, there is a good chance that I would be a Hindu and worship gods such as Shiva and Vishnu. ⁴If I had grown up in France in the 1400s, there is a good chance that I would have been taught to distrust and dislike the English. ⁵And if I had grown up in many parts of modern-day Africa, I might well view female circumcision as either something for the woman's own good or something worth little or no attention on my part.

Term being defined: *enculturation.* Transition: *For example.* Examples: Hinduism, distrust and dislike for English, female circumcision.

Definition __2__ *Example 1* __3__ *Example 2* __4__ *Example 3* __5__

2 COMPARISON AND CONTRAST

Words That Show Comparison

Put a check (✓) beside the item that is easier to understand:

_____ As a fish swims, it moves its tail, applying force against the water. The water, in turn, propels the fish forward. In a rocket motor, forces are exerted by hot gases that accelerate out the tail end, propelling the rocket forward.

__✓__ As a fish swims, it moves its tail, applying force against the water. The water, in turn, propels the fish forward. Similarly, in a rocket motor, forces are exerted by hot gases that accelerate out the tail end, propelling the rocket forward.

In the second item, the transition word *similarly* makes it clear that the author is comparing two forces. *Similarly* and words like it are comparison words.

Comparison words signal similarities. Authors use a comparison transition to show that a second idea is *like* the first one in some way. Here are some common words that show comparison:

Comparison Words

(just) as	both	in like fashion	in a similar fashion
(just) like	equal (ly)	in like manner	in a similar manner
alike	resemble	similar (ly)	(in) the same way
same	likewise	similarity	(in) common

Examples:

The sentences below contain comparison words. Notice how these words show that things are *alike* in some way.

- During the American Civil War, people in the North and the South were *equally* anguished by the bloody division of their country.

- Very young and very old people *resemble* one another in their dependence upon those around them.

- Car manufacturers often show beautiful women with their products, as if to suggest that owning the car will bring social rewards. *In the same way,* alcohol ads typically show people in fun or romantic settings.

➤ *Practice 3*

To the Instructor: Remind the students to use the hint on page 173 as they complete the following sentences.

Complete each sentence with a suitable comparison word or phrase from the box on the previous page. Try to use a variety of transitions.   *Answers may vary.*

1. The flu is particularly hazardous for babies, the elderly, and people in compromised health. ____*In the same way*____, pneumonia is a special danger for those three groups.

2. Many people now do all their banking online, ____*just as*____ they tend to do much of their shopping on the Internet.

3. ____*Both*____ Japanese and Korean cultures warn against smiling too much, believing that excessive smiling is silly and undignified.

4. The original computers were so large that they filled enormous rooms. ____*Just like*____ telephones, radios, and electronics of every kind, they are shrinking in size every year.

5. Lions, tigers, and other jungle cats are most active at night, when they do their hunting. The ____*same*____ trait can be seen in domesticated cats, who often spend the night prowling around their owners' houses.

Words That Show Contrast

Put a check (✓) beside the item that is easier to understand:

____ The movie was boring and pointless. It featured a talented cast and an award-winning screenwriter.

_✓_ The movie was boring and pointless even though it featured a talented cast and an award-winning screenwriter.

The first item is puzzling. What connection does the writer intend between the first and second sentences? The words *even though* in the second item make it clear that the writer is disappointed that the movie fell short despite its cast and screenwriter. *Even though* and words and phrases like it are contrast words.

Contrast words signal that an author is pointing out differences between subjects. A contrast word shows that two things *differ* in one or more ways. Contrast words also inform us that something is going to *differ from* what we might expect. Here are some common words that show contrast:

Contrast Words

but	instead (of)	even though	difference
yet	in contrast	as opposed to	different (ly)
however	on the other hand	in spite of	differ (from)
although	(on the) contrary	despite	unlike
nevertheless	converse (ly)	rather than	while
still	opposite		

Examples:

The sentences below contain contrast words. Notice how these words signal that one idea is *different from* another idea.

- In most Western cultures, it is considered normal to marry for love. *However,* in places where arranged marriages are the norm, it is assumed that love will follow marriage.

- *While* mammals have internal mechanisms that regulate body temperature, cold-blooded animals such as lizards must regulate their temperature by external means, such as basking on warm sunny rocks.

- Corporate executives urged employees to buy the company's stock *despite* the fact that they were selling it themselves.

➤ Practice 4   *Answers may vary.*

Complete each sentence with a suitable contrast word or phrase from the above box. Try to use a variety of transitions.

1. The comedian Robin Williams explains that his parents helped him become a cautious optimist. His mother would say "People are basically good" _____*while*_____ his father would be in the background saying, "There are still those who would throw you under a bus for a nickel."

2. A wise man explained that when he was young, he admired clever people. _____*However*_____, by the time he was old, he most admired kind people.

3. Many people believe that lava is the primary material ejected from a volcano, _____*but*_____ this is not always true. Explosive eruptions that eject huge quantities of gas, broken rock, and fine ash and dust occur just as frequently.

4. _____*Although*_____ parents who use physical punishment may think they are practicing good discipline, their children are likely to become violent and aggressive rather than well-behaved.

5. What makes one person seem warm and friendly, whereas another comes across as cold and aloof? One important ingredient appears to be having a positive outlook. People appear warm when they like things, praise them, and approve of them—in other words, when they have a positive attitude toward people and things. _On the other hand_ , people seem cold when they dislike things, disparage them, say they are awful, and are generally critical.

Comparison and contrast transitions often signal the comparison and/or contrast pattern of organization.

The Comparison and/or Contrast Pattern

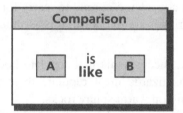
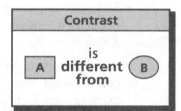

To get a sense of the comparison and/or contrast pattern, arrange the following group of sentences into an order that makes sense. Put a *1* in front of the sentence that should come first, a *2* in front of the sentence that comes next, and a *3* in front of the sentence that should be last. The result will be a short paragraph. Then read the explanation that follows.

___2___ However, gender differences remain in career choice and development.

___1___ Women's labor force participation is approaching that of men's, with 60 percent of adult women (versus 74 percent of men) in the labor force.

___3___ At present, married women still subordinate their career goals to their husbands', especially when children are involved.

You should have put a *1* in front of the second sentence, which is an introductory statement—that women's labor force participation is becoming comparable to that of men's. The main idea, that gender differences remain, is then presented in the sentence beginning with the contrast word *However*. And the sentence that starts with *At present* gives an example of a significant gender difference—that women will subordinate their career choices to their husbands'.

You will find authors using a **comparison** pattern to show how two things are alike and a **contrast** pattern to show how they are different. Sometimes an author will compare and contrast in the same paragraph, pointing out both similarities and differences between two things. Comparison or contrast transitions will signal what an author is doing.

☑ *Check Your Understanding*

In the following paragraph, the main idea is stated in the first sentence. As is often the case, the main idea suggests a paragraph's pattern of organization. Here the transition *different* is a hint that the paragraph may be organized as comparison or contrast (or both). Read the paragraph and answer the questions below. Then read the explanation that follows.

> ¹Men and women, of course, often have <u>different</u> concerns, so we might expect the content of their dreams to <u>differ</u>—and until recently, at least, that has been true. ²Typically, women have been more likely than men to dream about children, family members, familiar characters, friendly interactions, household objects, clothes, and indoor events. ³<u>In contrast</u>, men have been more likely than women to dream about strangers, weapons, violence, sexual activity, achievement, and outdoor events. ⁴<u>But</u> as the lives and concerns of the two sexes have become more <u>similar</u>, so have their dreams. ⁵In one recent study, the content of men's and women's dreams bore a close <u>resemblance</u>. ⁶Only two <u>differences</u> showed up: Men were more likely to dream about behaving aggressively, <u>while</u> women were more likely to dream about their anxieties.

1. Is this paragraph comparing, contrasting, or both? _____*Both*_____

2. What two things are being compared and/or contrasted? _____
   Men's and women's dreams

3. What are three of the comparison and/or contrast signal words used in the paragraph? ____*different, differ, In contrast, But, similar, resemblance,*____
   differences, while

Explanation:

This paragraph is both comparing and contrasting: how the traditional content of men's and women's dreams differs (contrasting), but how that content is now becoming similar (comparing). Two comparison transitions are used—*similar* and *resemblance*. Six contrast transitions are used—*different, differ, In contrast, but, differences,* and *while*.

➤ *Practice 5*   *Wording of answers may vary.*

The following passages use the pattern of comparison *or* the pattern of contrast. Read each passage and answer the questions that follow.

A.   ¹Abraham Lincoln and Frederick Douglass shared many <u>common</u> interests. ²<u>Both</u> loved music and literature and educated themselves (Douglass on the sly while a slave) by reading the <u>same</u> books: *Aesop's Fables,* the Bible, Shakespeare, and especially *The Columbian Orator,* a popular anthology of speeches for boys. ³<u>Both</u> were athletic, strong and tall: Douglass was about six feet tall; Lincoln, six feet, four inches, when the average height for men was five feet, seven inches. ⁴<u>Both</u> refrained from alcohol and tobacco at a time when many politicians "squirted their tobacco juice upon the carpet" and drank on the job. ⁵They were <u>equally</u> ambitious and had great faith in the moral and technological progress of their nation. ⁶And they were <u>alike</u> in calling slavery a sin. ⁷"If slavery is not wrong, nothing is wrong," Lincoln stated. ⁸For Douglass, slavery was not only a sin but also "piracy and murder."

Check (✓) the pattern which is used in this passage: There are five points of comparison: love of music and literature; athleticism and build; restrained habits; ambition and belief in progress; considering slavery a sin.

  ✓   Comparison

  ___ Contrast

What two things are being compared or contrasted?

  1. _____*Abraham Lincoln*_____   2. _____*Frederick Douglass*_____

B.   ¹**Personal distress** means our own emotional reactions to the plight of others—our feelings of shock, horror, alarm, concern, or helplessness. ²Personal distress occurs when people who witness an event are preoccupied with their own emotional reactions. ³<u>On the other hand</u>, **empathy** means feelings of sympathy and caring for others, in particular, sharing vicariously or indirectly in the suffering of others. ⁴Empathy occurs when the observer focuses on the needs and emotions of the victim. ⁵<u>While</u> personal distress leads us to feel anxious and apprehensive, empathy leads us to feel sympathetic and compassionate. ⁶Research suggests that the <u>different</u> emotions generated by personal distress and empathy may actually be accompanied by distinctive physiological reactions, including heart rate patterns and facial expressions.

Check (✓) the pattern which is used in this passage: Personal distress is being contrasted with empathy in terms of what they mean, when each occurs, and the emotions each generates. Note the terms are in **boldface** print.

  ___ Comparison

  ✓   Contrast

What two things are being compared or contrasted?

  1. _____*Personal distress*_____   2. _____*Empathy*_____

3 CAUSE AND EFFECT

Words That Show Cause and Effect

Put a check (✓) beside the item that is easier to understand:

_____ The best time to buy a car is near the end of the month. Car dealers often have a monthly quota of cars to sell.

__✓__ The best time to buy a car is near the end of the month because car dealers often have a monthly quota of cars to sell.

In the second item, the word *because* makes very clear just why the end of the month is the best time to buy a car. *Because* and words like it are cause and effect words.

Cause and effect words signal that the author is explaining *the reason* that something happened or *the result* of something happening. Here are some common words that show cause and effect:

Cause and Effect Words

therefore	so	owing to	because (of)
thus	(as a) result	effect	reason
(as a) consequence	results in	cause	explanation
consequently	leads (led) to	if…then	accordingly
due to	since	affect	depend(s) on

Examples:

The following examples contain cause and effect words. Notice how these words introduce a *reason* for something or the *results* of something.

- Young babies have weak necks and relatively heavy heads. *Consequently,* it is important to support the baby's head firmly when you hold him or her.

- Do not refrigerate potatoes. The *reason* is that a potato's starch will turn to sugar at low temperatures, making the vegetable taste odd.

- The student wanted to concentrate on studying for exams. *Therefore,* he locked his television in a closet.

➤ **Practice 6**

To the Instructor: Remind the students to use the hint on page 173 as they complete the following sentences.

Complete each sentence with a suitable cause and effect word or phrase from the above box. Try to use a variety of transitions.   *Answers may vary.*

1. A Greek philosopher observed that we should always try to be kind to each other _____ *because* _____ everyone we meet is fighting a great battle.

2. Contrary to some beliefs, tanning is not necessarily healthy. Prolonged exposure to the sun can _____*lead to*_____ problems such as sunburn, skin cancer, and early aging.

3. The gecko is a small lizard that can detach its tail. _____*As a result*_____, predators often end up holding the wriggling tail while the gecko escapes.

4. In medieval times, people believed that ringing church bells would dissipate lightning during thunderstorms. This unfortunate superstition _____*caused*_____ the deaths of over 100 bell ringers in a period when lightning struck 386 church steeples.

5. Meat requires special handling. It contains bacteria, and its moist, nutrient-rich environment favors microbial growth. Ground meat is especially susceptible _____*since*_____ it receives more handling than other kinds of meat and has more surface exposed to bacterial contamination.

Cause and effect transitions often signal the cause and effect pattern of organization.

The Cause and Effect Pattern

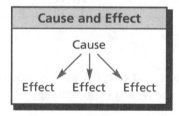
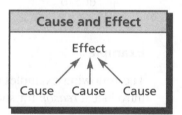

To get a sense of the cause and effect pattern, try to arrange the following sentences in an order that makes sense. Put a *1* in front of the sentence that should come first, a *2* in front of the sentence that comes next, and a *3* in front of the sentence that should be last. The result will be a short paragraph. Then read the explanation that follows.

___3___ Also, unemployment leads to an increased rate of attempted and completed suicides.

___2___ Not only can it cause economic distress; it can result in health problems and psychological difficulties as well.

___1___ Losing one's job is difficult at best and devastating at worst.

As the words *leads to, cause,* and *result in* suggest, this paragraph is organized in a cause and effect pattern. The paragraph begins with the general idea: "Losing one's job is difficult at best and devastating at worst." Next comes a detailed explanation of the results: "Not only can it cause economic distress; it can result in health problems and psychological difficulties as well. Also, unemployment leads to an increased rate of attempted and completed suicides."

Information in a **cause-effect pattern** addresses the questions "Why does a behavior or event happen?" and/or "What are the results of a behavior or event?" An author may then discuss causes, or effects, or both causes and effects.

Authors usually don't just tell what happened. They try to tell about events in a way that explains both *what* happened and *why.* A textbook section on the burning of the rain forests, for example, would be incomplete without a detailed account of all the consequences to the Earth of the destruction of these forests. Or if housing sales across the country go into a decline, journalists would not simply report the decrease in sales. They would also explore the reasons for and effects of that decline.

☑ Check Your Understanding

Read the paragraph below and see if you can answer the questions about cause and effect. Then read the explanation to see how you did.

[1]During the 1950s and 1960s, airports, bus terminals, and train stations often charged patrons to use the toilet. [2]People would have to pay a ten- to twenty-five-cent fee before they entered a stall. [3]Owners hoped that the fee would help pay for the cost of keeping the restrooms clean. [4]But for several reasons, pay toilets failed miserably. [5]For one thing, they angered patrons. [6]People accustomed to accessing a restroom for free became upset when they discovered they had to pay. [7]Many outraged bathroom-users vandalized the stalls and trashed the rooms in response, making cleanup even more expensive. [8]In addition, pay toilets caused more trouble than they were worth. [9]Employees had to be called in so often to fix broken locks that companies gradually realized the extra work wasn't worth a few more dollars. [10]A final explanation why pay toilets failed is that they triggered lawsuits from women's groups who claimed the toilets were unfair because females were forced to pay regardless while males could use the urinals for free. [11]Rather than spending money on high maintenance and lawsuits, companies opened the bathrooms for free use.

1. What is the single *effect* being discussed in the paragraph?

   The failure of pay toilets

2. What are the three *causes* discussed?

   A. *They angered patrons.*

   B. *They caused more trouble than they were worth.*

   C. *They triggered lawsuits from women's groups.*

3. What three cause and effect transitions are used in the paragraph?

reasons, caused, explanation

Explanation:

The paragraph's main idea is that "But for several reasons, pay toilets failed miserably." That point, or effect, is then supported by three causes: 1) angered patrons; 2) caused more trouble than they were worth; and 3) triggered lawsuits from women's groups. The cause and effect transitions used are *reasons, caused,* and *explanation.*

➤ **Practice 7**   *Wording of answers may vary.*

A. Read the paragraph below, looking for the one effect and the two causes. Then complete the outline that follows.

The major details are in sentence 3 (signaled by *explanation*) and sentence 7 (signaled by *reason*). Note that *since* and *cause* (sentence 6) and *because* (sentence 8) also reflect the cause-effect pattern.

¹Fainting was commonplace in Victorian England. ²Women were often seen falling into the arms of a nearby suitor if it was too warm outside, they became sad, or someone said something offensive. ³One explanation was the unusual dress of Victorian women. ⁴Females were expected to wear a corset underneath their clothes, and the corset was wrapped around their bodies and secured with ribbons. ⁵Made to make women's waists look smaller, corsets were often pulled so tight that internal organs became damaged and women could hardly breathe. ⁶Since their air supply and blood flow were limited, any physical activity could cause them to faint. ⁷The second reason women fell to the floor was cultural roles. ⁸Ladies pretended to faint because doing so was seen as delicate and feminine. ⁹Victorian women were expected to be weak and to rely on men to be the strong ones. ¹⁰The staging of fainting episodes helped them demonstrate they were fragile and ladylike.

Main idea *(the effect):* _____ *Victorian women often fainted.* _____

Major supporting details *(the causes):*

1. *Their tight undergarments cut off air supply and blood flow.*

2. *They knew that fainting made them seem delicate and feminine.*

B. Read the paragraph below, looking for the one cause and the three effects. Then complete the map that follows.

¹If our planet's sea levels were to rise, the result would be global problems. ²Rising sea levels would first cause problems by making a drastic change in existing coastlines. ³Specifically, a rise in sea levels of as little as 5 feet could move coastlines 150 feet inland, displacing coastal communities

and flooding low-lying cities all over the world. ⁴Next, rising sea levels would create threats to dikes and sea walls, making coastal areas more vulnerable to natural disasters. ⁵As seen in New Orleans after Hurricane Katrina, existing dikes and sea walls might be insufficient to defend against the increased storm surges, and disasters could become a yearly phenomenon. ⁶The most dangerous <u>effect</u> of a rise in sea levels would be an increase in global warming. ⁷<u>Since</u> liquid water absorbs more sunlight than frozen water does, a rise in sea level would eventually <u>cause</u> the oceans to warm, contributing to higher temperatures everywhere—and <u>causing</u> our polar ice caps to melt even faster. ⁸The problems created by a rising ocean could then quickly spiral out of control.

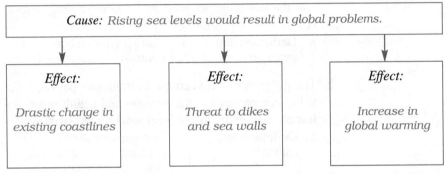

Cause: Rising sea levels would result in global problems.

Effect:

Drastic change in existing coastlines

Effect:

Threat to dikes and sea walls

Effect:

Increase in global warming

See sentences 2, 4, and 6.

A Note on Main Ideas and Patterns of Organization

As mentioned in Chapter 4, a paragraph's main idea often indicates its pattern of organization. For example, here's the main idea of the paragraph you just read:

If our planet's sea levels were to rise, the result would be global problems.

The word *result* indicates that this paragraph will be organized according to cause-and-effect order.

Paying close attention to the main idea can often give you a quick sense of a paragraph's pattern of organization and can be a helpful step in your understanding of the paragraph.

➤ *Practice 8*   Transitions that indicate each pattern of organization are underlined.

Most of the main ideas below have been taken from college textbooks. In the space provided, write the letter of the pattern of organization that each suggests.

___*B*___ 1. Contrary to popular stereotypes, being single is not always more difficult for women than for men.

  A. Definition and example   B. Comparison and/or contrast   C. Cause and effect

Contrasts the stereotype with the reality.

_____C_____ 2. The author of *The Paradox of Choice* argues that people in modern, affluent societies suffer depression and anxiety <u>because</u> they face an overabundance of choices in their personal lives.

    A. Definition and   B. Comparison and/or   C. Cause and effect
        example   contrast   *Cause:* too many choices;
                                      effect: depression and anxiety.

_____A_____ 3. What scientists call the "<u>terrestrial planets</u>" are the relatively small, rocky, high-density worlds: Mercury, Venus, Earth, Mars, and (although it isn't really a planet) Earth's moon.

    A. Definition and   B. Comparison and/or   C. Cause and effect
        example   contrast   Definition and example of
                                         terrestrial planets.

_____C_____ 4. The phenomenon of static electricity, including lightning, static cling, and the small sparks produced when walking across a wool rug on a cold winter day, is <u>caused</u> by electrical charges.

    A. Definition and   B. Comparison and/or   C. Cause and effect
        example   contrast   *Cause:* electrical charges; *effect:* the
                                       phenomenon of static electricity.

_____B_____ 5. The <u>differences</u> between the average pay packages for chief executives at big companies and the pension and health insurance givebacks being forced upon many lower-level workers are striking.

    A. Definition and   B. Comparison and/or   C. Cause and effect
        example   contrast   Contrasts pay packages for chief
                           executives with givebacks of low-level workers.

_____A_____ 6. Mass hysteria, a type of group behavior that involves a widely held and <u>contagious</u> anxiety, is <u>exemplified</u> by the witch-hunts of medieval times.

    A. Definition and   B. Comparison and/or   C. Cause and effect
        example   contrast   Definition and example of
                                         mass hysteria.

_____B_____ 7. Loneliness exists inside a person and cannot be detected simply by looking at the person, <u>while</u> aloneness is the objective state of being apart from other people.

    A. Definition and   B. Comparison and/or   C. Cause and effect
        example   contrast   Describes the differences between
                                    loneliness and aloneness.

_____C_____ 8. Researchers have identified several basic <u>causes</u> of frustration above and beyond daily hassles.

    A. Definition and   B. Comparison and/or   C. Cause and effect
        example   contrast   *Effect:* frustration; *causes*
            (other than daily hassles) are not named in the sentence.

    _A_   9. "Instrumental <u>aggression</u>" is aimed at gaining or damaging some object, <u>such as</u> when three-year-old Sarah pushes aside her playmate Lucetta in the sandbox and grabs Lucetta's bucket.

        A. Definition and   B. Comparison and/or   C. Cause and effect
           example   contrast   *Definition and example of*
                                                          instrumental aggression.

    _C_ 10. Declining support for the death penalty may be <u>due to</u> heightened awareness of cases in which innocent people have been sentenced to death and subsequently cleared, often by DNA evidence.

        A. Definition and   B. Comparison and/or   C. Cause and effect
           example   contrast   *Cause:* heightened awareness;
                                                     effect: declining support.

A Final Point

Keep in mind that a paragraph or passage may often be made up of more than one pattern of organization. For instance, consider the following passage:

    [1]The gestation period (length of pregnancy) of mammals <u>depends on</u> two factors. [2]The <u>first</u> is the mammal's size. [3]In general, smaller animals experience shorter pregnancies. [4]For example, a female rat gives birth only twenty-one days after becoming pregnant; a hamster's gestation period is only sixteen days; a horse, <u>however,</u> is pregnant for about forty-eight weeks. [5]The <u>second</u> factor that determines the gestation period is life span—longer-lived animals have longer pregnancies. [6]The gestation period of a lion, which can live up to twenty-eight years, is fifteen weeks. [7]Dolphins, which have lived as long as forty years, are pregnant for thirty-nine weeks. [8]You can see the relationship between gestation period and life span when you <u>compare</u> a possum to a cat. [9]<u>Although</u> the possum is slightly larger than a cat, it has a much shorter gestation period (thirteen days to the cat's sixty-two days). [10]<u>But</u> cats can live up to twenty years, while possums are elderly at 3.

The paragraph uses a cause-effect pattern: The length of pregnancy of mammals is caused by two factors. It also uses a list of items pattern (the two factors) as well as a bit of comparison and contrast.

CHAPTER REVIEW

In this chapter, you learned about three kinds of relationships that authors use to make their ideas clear:

- **Definitions and examples**

  — To help readers understand the important ideas and terms in a subject, textbook authors often take time to include key definitions (often setting them off in *italic* or **boldface**) and examples of those definitions. When reading a textbook, it is usually a good idea to mark off both definitions and examples. (Underline each definition, and put *Ex* in the margin next to each example.)

  — Transition words that signal the definition and example pattern include *for example, for instance, to illustrate,* and *such as.*

- **Comparison and/or contrast**

  — Authors often discuss how two things are alike or how they are different, or both.

  — Transition words that signal comparisons include *alike* and *similar.*

  — Transition words that signal contrasts include *but, however,* and *in contrast.*

- **Cause and effect**

  — Authors often discuss the reasons why something happens or the effects of something that has happened.

  — Transition words that signal causes include *reason* and *because.*

  — Transition words that signal effects include *therefore, consequently,* and *as a result.*

Note that pages 212–216 list and offer practice in all the transitions and patterns of organization you have studied in "Relationships I" and "Relationships II."

The next chapter—Chapter 6—will sharpen your ability to make inferences in reading.

On the Web: If you are using this book in class, you can visit our website for additional practice in understanding relationships that involve examples, comparison or contrast, and cause and effect. Go to **www.townsendpress.com** and click on "Online Exercises."

➤ Review Test 1

To review what you've learned in this chapter, answer each of the following questions by filling in the blank or writing the letter of the correct answer.

1. When authors present a term or idea, they often provide one or more
   _____examples_____ to help make that definition clear.

   See page 172.

_B_ 2. Words such as *likewise, just as*, and *similarly* are known as
   A. illustration words.
   B. comparison words.   See page 177.
   C. contrast words.

3. Words such as *but, however*, and *on the other hand* are known as
   _____contrast_____ words.   See pages 178–179.

_C_ 4. Words such as *therefore, as a result*, and *reason* are known as
   A. definition words.
   B. contrast words.   See page 183.
   C. cause and effect words.

_C_ 5. A cause and effect paragraph may include
   A. reasons.
   B. results.   See page 183.
   C. reasons and/or results.

➤ *Review Test 2*

The selection that follows is from the college textbook *A People and a Nation* (Houghton Mifflin), by Mary Beth Norton and others. Read it and then answer the relationships questions that follow. There are also questions on understanding vocabulary in context, finding main ideas, identifying supporting details, and recognizing implied main ideas.

Preview

The generation touched by the Great Depression never forgot its impact. Effects of the economic depression were felt in every corner of the country. Those effects, however, took different forms depending on one's occupation, race, gender, and geographical location. This reading provides a vivid description of hard times across America.

Words to Watch

bolstered (4): supported
marginal (5): very small in scale or importance
coerced (6): forced
affluent (10): well off

HOOVER AND HARD TIMES: 1929–1933

Mary Beth Norton and others

1 By the early 1930s, as the depression continued to deepen, tens of millions of Americans were desperately poor. In the cities, hungry men and women lined up at soup kitchens. People survived on potatoes, crackers, or dandelion greens; some scratched through garbage cans for bits of food. In West Virginia and Kentucky, hunger was so widespread— and resources so limited—that the American Friends Service Committee distributed food only to those who were at least 10 percent below the normal weight for their height. Reports of starvation and malnutrition spread. In November 1932, *The Nation* told its readers that one-sixth of the American population risked starvation over the coming winter. Social workers in New York reported there was "no food at all" in the homes of many of the city's black children. In Albany, New York, a ten-year-old girl died of starvation in her elementary school classroom.

2 Families, unable to pay rent, were evicted from houses and apartments. The new homeless poured into shantytowns, called "Hoovervilles" in ironic tribute to the formerly popular president, that had sprung up in most cities. Over a million men took to the road or the rails in desperate search for any sort of work.

Teenage boys and girls (the latter called "sisters of the road") also left destitute families to strike out on their own. With uncertain futures, many young couples delayed marriage. The average age at which people married rose by more than two years during the 1930s. Married people put off having children, and in 1933, the birth rate sank below replacement rates. (Contraceptive sales, with condoms costing at least $1 per dozen, did not fall during the depression.) More than 25 percent of women who were between the ages of twenty and thirty during the Great Depression never had children.

3   Farmers were hit especially hard by the economic crisis. The agricultural sector, which employed almost a quarter of American workers, had never shared in the good times of the 1920s. But as urbanites cut back on spending and foreign competitors dumped their own agricultural surpluses into the global market, prices for agricultural products hit rock bottom. Individual farmers tried to make up for lower prices by producing more, thus adding to the surplus and depressing prices even further. By 1932, a bushel of wheat that cost North Dakota farmers 77 cents to produce brought only 33 cents. Throughout the nation, cash-strapped farmers could not pay their property taxes or mortgages. Banks, facing their own ruin, refused to extend deadlines and foreclosed on the mortgages. In Mississippi, it was reported in 1932, on a single day in April approximately one-fourth of all the farmland in the state was being auctioned off to meet debts. By the middle of the decade, the ecological crisis of the Dust Bowl would drive thousands of farmers from their land.

4   Unlike farmers, America's industrial workers had seen a slow but steady rise in their standard of living during the 1920s, and their spending on consumer goods had bolstered° the nation's economic growth. In 1929, almost every urban American who wanted a job had one. But as Americans had less money to spend, sales of manufactured goods plunged and factories closed—more than 70,000 had gone out of business by 1933. As car sales dropped from 4.5 million in 1929 to 1 million in 1933, Ford laid off more than two-thirds of its workers in Detroit. All of the remaining workers at U.S. Steel, America's first billion-dollar corporation, were put on "short hours"; the huge steel company had no full-time workers in 1933. Almost a quarter of industrial workers were unemployed, and those who managed to hang onto a job saw the average wage fall by almost one-third.

5   For workers who had long been marginal°, discriminated against, or relegated to the lowest rungs of the employment ladder, the depression was a crushing blow. In the South, where employment opportunities for African Americans were already most limited, pressure for "Negro removal" grew. The jobs that most white men had considered below their dignity before the depression—street cleaners, bellhops, garbage collectors—seemed suddenly desirable as other jobs disappeared. African Americans living in the North did not fare much better. As industry cut production, African Americans were the first fired. An Urban League survey of 106 cities found black employment rates averaged 30 to 60 percent higher than rates for whites. By 1932, African American unemployment reached almost 50 percent.

6   Mexican Americans and Mexican nationals trying to make a living in the American Southwest also felt the twin

impacts of economic depression and racism. Concentrated in agricultural work, they saw their wages at California farms fall from a miserable 35 cents an hour in 1929 to a cruel 14 cents an hour by 1932. Throughout the Southwest, Anglo-Americans claimed that foreign workers were stealing their jobs. Campaigns against "foreigners" hurt not only Mexican immigrants but also American citizens of Hispanic background whose families had lived in the Southwest for centuries, long before the land belonged to the United States. In 1931, the Labor Department announced that the United States would deport illegal immigrants to free jobs for American citizens. This policy fell hardest on people of Mexican origin. Even those who had immigrated legally often lacked full documentation. Officials often ignored the fact that children born in the United States were U.S. citizens. The U.S. government officially deported 82,000 Mexicans between 1929 and 1935, but a much larger number—almost half a million people—repatriated to Mexico during the 1930s. Some left voluntarily, but many were coerced° or tricked into believing they had no choice.

7   Women of all classes and races shared status as marginalized workers. Even before the economic crisis, women were barred altogether from many jobs and paid at significantly lower rates than men. As the economy worsened, working women faced heightened discrimination. Most Americans already believed that men should be breadwinners and women homemakers. With widespread male unemployment, it was easy to believe that women took jobs from men. In fact, men laid off from U.S. Steel would not likely have been hired as elementary school teachers, secretaries, "sales girls,"

or maids. The job market was heavily segregated. Nonetheless, when a 1936 Gallup poll asked whether wives should work if their husbands had jobs, 82 percent of the respondents (including 75 percent of the women) answered no. Such beliefs translated into policy. Of 1500 urban school systems surveyed by the National Education Association in 1930 and 1931, 77 percent refused to hire married women as teachers, and 63 percent fired female teachers who married while employed.

8   The depression had a mixed impact on women workers. At first, women lost jobs more quickly than men. Women in low-wage manufacturing jobs were laid off before male employees, who were presumed to be supporting families. Hard times hit domestic workers especially hard, as middle-class families economized by dispensing with household help. Almost a quarter of women in domestic service—a high percentage of them African American—were unemployed by January 1931. And as jobs disappeared, women of color lost even these poorly paid positions to white women who were newly willing to do domestic labor. Despite discrimination and a poor economy, however, the number of women working outside the home rose during the 1930s. "Women's jobs," such as teaching, clerical work, and switchboard operators, were not hit so hard as "men's jobs" in heavy industry, and women—including married women who previously did not work for wages—increasingly sought employment to keep their families afloat during hard times. Still, by 1940 only 15.2 percent of married women worked outside the home.

9   Though unemployment rates climbed to 25 percent, most Americans did not lose their homes or their jobs during the depression. Professional and

white-collar workers did not fare as badly as industrial workers and farmers. Many middle-class families, however, while never hungry or homeless, "made do" with less. "Use it up, wear it out, make it do, or do without," the saying went, and middle-class women cut back on household expenses by canning food or making their own clothes; newspapers offered imaginative suggestions for cooking cheap cuts of meat ("Liver-burgers") or for using "extenders," cheap ingredients to make food go further ("Cracker-Stuffed Cabbage"). Though most families' incomes fell, the impact was cushioned by the falling cost of consumer goods, especially food. In early 1933, for example, a café in Omaha offered a ten-course meal, complete with a rose for ladies and a cigar for gentlemen, for sixty cents.

As housewives scrambled to make do, men who could no longer provide well for their families often blamed themselves for their "failures." But even for the relatively affluent°, the psychological impact of the depression was inescapable. The human toll of the depression was visible everywhere, and no one took economic security for granted anymore. Suffering was never equal, but all Americans had to contend with years of uncertainty and with fears about the future of their families and their nation.

10

Reading Comprehension Questions

Vocabulary in Context

_____C_____ 1. In the excerpt below, the word *destitute* (dĕs′tĭ-tōōt′) means
   A. abusive.
   B. reluctant.
   C. extremely poor.
   D. very large.

   People who are "in desperate search for any sort of work" are likely to be extremely poor.

   "Over a million men took to the road or the rails in desperate search for any sort of work. Teenage boys and girls (the latter called 'sisters of the road') also left destitute families to strike out on their own." (Paragraph 2)

_____D_____ 2. In the sentence below, the word *relegated* (rĕl′ĭ-gāt′ĭd) means
   A. lifted.
   B. transferred.
   C. attracted.
   D. assigned downward.

   The words *lowest rungs* indicate that the workers were assigned downward.

   "For workers who had long been marginal, discriminated against, or relegated to the lowest rungs of the employment ladder, the depression was a crushing blow." (Paragraph 5)

Central Point and Main Ideas

___B___ 3. Which sentence best expresses the implied central point of the selection?

A. Farmers were hit especially hard by the Great Depression.

B. Although some groups suffered more than others, the Great Depression forced virtually all Americans to contend with fear and uncertainty about the future.

C. During the Great Depression, many Americans were forced to "make do" with less.

D. Although minority groups and farmers were especially hard hit by the Great Depression, most Americans did not lose their homes or their jobs.   *Answer A covers only paragraph 3; answers C and D cover only paragraph 9.*

___A___ 4. The main idea of paragraph 3 is stated in the

A. first sentence.

B. second sentence.

C. third sentence.

D. final sentence.

Sentence 2 of the paragraph refers to the years before the depression. All the remaining sentences in paragraph 3 list details supporting the main idea that farmers were hit especially hard by the depression.

___C___ 5. The implied main idea of paragraphs 5–7 is that during the depression,

A. the U.S. government established a policy of deporting illegal immigrants to free jobs for American citizens.

B. most white Americans believed that women should not compete with men for jobs.

C. minority groups and women faced economic discrimination.

D. African Americans faced growing competition from whites for low-status jobs.   *Answer A covers only part of paragraph 6; answer B covers only part of paragraph 7; and answer D covers only part of paragraph 5.*

Supporting Details

___C___ 6. Large corporations such as Ford and U.S. Steel responded to the Great Depression by

A. investing in new and more efficient methods of production.

B. demanding that their female employees take extended leaves of absence.

C. laying off workers, reducing work hours, and lowering the wages of those still employed.

D. seeking loans from the federal government in order to keep from going bankrupt.   *See paragraph 4.*

___A___ 7. The prices for agricultural products fell during the depression because

    A. the supply of agricultural products far exceeded the demand for them.

    B. farmers weren't producing enough crops.

    C. the Dust Bowl, an ecological disaster, drove thousands from their land.

    D. bankers refused to extend credit to needy farmers.   See paragraph 3, the third and fourth sentences.

Transitions

___C___ 8. Which word in the following sentence indicates a cause and effect transition?

    A. *make*

    B. *more*   *Cause:* farmers producing more;

    C. *thus*   *effects:* greater surplus, depressed prices.

    D. *further*

    "Individual farmers tried to make up for lower prices by producing more, thus adding to the surplus and depressing prices even further." (Paragraph 3)

___A___ 9. The relationship of the second sentence below to the first sentence is one of

    A. contrast.   The second sentence contrasts the rise in number

    B. cause and effect.   of working women with the expected result of

    C. comparison.   discrimination and a poor economy

    D. illustration.   (fewer women with jobs).

    "And as jobs disappeared, women of color lost even these poorly paid positions to white women who were newly willing to do domestic labor. Despite discrimination and a poor economy, however, the number of women working outside the home rose during the 1930s." (Paragraph 8)

Patterns of Organization

___D___ 10. The pattern of organization in this selection is mainly one of

    A. definition and example.

    B. comparison.   *Cause:* the Great Depression; *effects:*

    C. contrast.   impact on various aspects of society.

    D. cause and effect.

Discussion Questions

1. This reading provides a great many facts about how the Great Depression affected various parts of the U.S. population. What did you learn from the reading that surprised you most?

2. The selection mentions that African Americans and people of Mexican origin were particularly hard hit during the depression, often facing discrimination as the competition for jobs became desperate. In your opinion, has the position of African Americans and Latinos improved since the depression, worsened, or stayed about the same? Explain your reasoning.

3. The authors spend most of their time describing the economic impact of the depression. In the final paragraph, however, they mention "the psychological impact of the depression." From what you have read here, what psychological effects would you infer the depression had on various groups?

4. The Great Depression led to economic hardship and social upheaval, yet somehow our system of government remained stable. How do you think Americans would respond today if we experienced a depression? For instance, how might the government respond if the unemployment rate reached 25 percent? How might the American public respond to widespread unemployment and reduction in wages?

Note: Writing assignments for this selection appear on page 563.

Check Your Performance			RELATIONSHIPS II
Activity	*Number Right*	*Points*	*Score*
Review Test 1 (5 items)	_____	× 6 =	_____
Review Test 2 (10 items)	_____	× 7 =	_____
		TOTAL SCORE =	_____%

Enter your total score into the **Reading Performance Chart: Review Tests** on the inside back cover.

RELATIONSHIPS II: Mastery Test 1

A. Fill in each blank with an appropriate transition from the box. Use each transition once. Then, in the space provided, write the letter of the transition you have chosen.

A. although	B. for example	C. reason
D. similarly	E. such as	

Hint: Make sure that each word or phrase that you choose fits smoothly into the flow of the sentence. Test each choice by reading the sentence aloud.

___*B*___ 1. [1]Repression involves keeping distressing thoughts and feelings buried in the subconscious. [2]___*For example*___, when you forget a dentist appointment or the name of someone you don't like, repression may be at work.

Definition and example of repression.

___*C*___ 2. [1]Aging is incredibly difficult for women. [2]They must compete with models on billboards who are 20 years old and perfect. [3]And they must also compete with not only younger women but also their younger selves. [4]It's the ___*reason*___ why there is so much plastic surgery and cosmetic dermatology.

Cause: competition with younger women; *effect:* a lot of plastic surgery.

___*D*___ 3. [1]When you stretch a thick, strong rubber band and release it, it snaps painfully back against your hand. [2]___*Similarly*___, an earthquake occurs when rock suddenly breaks along a more or less flat surface called a fault.

Compares snapping of a rubber band with an earthquake.

___*E*___ 4. [1]The "new politics" of today depends upon key operatives who charge hefty fees for their services—campaign consultants, pollsters, media producers, and fundraising specialists. [2]Over the years, some of these operatives, ___*such as*___ James Carville for the Democrats and Karl Rove for the Republicans, have developed almost legendary reputations.

Definition and examples of key operatives *in today's "new politics."*

___*A*___ 5. [1]Times have changed, and I know this because I have children, two of them, one born in the old days and one in modern times. [2]The older child grew up inhaling clouds of secondhand smoke, and the younger one lives in a house in which nobody ever thinks about smoking, ___*although*___ sometimes a guest has lurked in the backyard, like a convicted sex offender, and consumed a cigarette.

Contrasts a time in which smoking was acceptable with a time and place where it is not; also contrasts the backyard, where a guest goes to smoke, with a house in which no one ever smokes.

(Continues on next page)

199

B. Label each item with the letter of its main pattern of organization.

Here and in the tests that follow, transitions that indicate each pattern of organization are underlined.

A Definition and example	c Contrast
B Comparison	D Cause and effect

C 6. [1]In the typical fairy tale, a dashing young man and a beautiful young woman marry, have children, and live happily ever after. [2]<u>However</u>, that scenario does not match the realities of love and marriage in the 21st century. [3]Today, it is just as likely that the man and woman would first live together, then get married and have children, <u>but</u> end up getting divorced.   *Contrasts the fairy tale view of marriage with the reality of marriage in the 21st century.*

D 7. [1]The presence of others often <u>results in</u> making people work more efficiently. [2]An 1898 study showed that bicyclists rode faster when in a group than when alone. [3]The study also showed that children worked harder to pull in a fishing line when they were in a group than when they were alone.   *Cause: presence of others; effect: people work more efficiently.*

A 8. [1]One way that psychologists evaluate people is according to their tendency to "self-monitor." [2]<u>Self-monitoring</u> refers to the degree to which people attend to and control the impressions they make on others. [3]<u>For instance,</u> you are a high self-monitor if you are quick to adjust your tone of voice or what you say based on how you think others are responding.   *Defines and gives example of self-monitoring.*

D 9. [1]When people think of dangerous creatures, they usually think of Great White sharks, or perhaps grizzly bears, lions, or tigers. [2]But the creature that <u>causes</u> the most harm to humans, however indirectly, is the malaria-carrying Anopheles mosquito. [3]Mosquitoes which carry the deadly malaria parasite <u>cause</u> an estimated 2.7 million deaths per year. [4]Africa accounts for over 90% of reported cases of malaria. [5]Asia and South American have been hard hit, too, in part <u>due to</u> the malaria parasite's growing resistance to drugs. [6]Children are especially vulnerable to malaria. [7]In Africa, the disease kills one child in 20 before the age of five.   *Cause: malaria-carrying mosquitoes; effect: many deaths.*

B 10. [1]A human baby and a baby songbird are different in almost every imaginable way. [2]But the two share certain <u>similarities</u> when it comes to learning language—in the baby's case, speech, and in the bird's case, its particular song. [3]<u>Both</u> babies and songbirds learn their language from listening to their parents. [4]Babies and birds raised in isolation do not learn to communicate with sound. [5]<u>Both</u> go through a period of babbling. [6]A baby will string together words and phrases, such as "mama, ball, so big, peekaboo," in ways that make no sense. [7]Later, the baby will sort out those words to form thoughts and sentences. [8]<u>Similarly,</u> a baby songbird will sing tiny segments of its parents' song, but with those segments in the wrong order. [9]As it matures, it will learn to put the segments of song together in the right sequence.

Compares how human babies and baby songbirds learn language.

RELATIONSHIPS II: Mastery Test 2

A. Fill in each blank with an appropriate transition from the box. Use each transition once. Then, in the space provided, write the letter of the transition you have chosen.

A. effects	B. for instance	C. however
D. likewise	E. reasons	

Hint: Make sure that each word or phrase that you choose fits smoothly into the flow of the sentence. Test each choice by reading the sentence aloud.

___B___ 1. ¹The names of dog breeds often give a hint about what that dog was bred to do. ²_____*For instance*_____, the word *terrier* means "of the earth," suggesting that the dog likes to dig into the earth to hunt for burrowing animals.   *Terrier* illustrates the name of a dog that suggests what the dog was bred to do.

___C___ 2. ¹Cohabitation rates have increased dramatically over the past few decades. ²Most cohabiters are young adults who tend to be working couples. ³_____*However*_____, about 7 percent of cohabiters are retired adults of age 65 or more.   Contrasts the age of the majority of cohabitants with the age of the minority of cohabitants.

___E___ 3. ¹As people grow old, they often lose about an inch in height. ²There are two _____*reasons*_____. ³First, they have lost some fat and muscle tissue as they age. ⁴And second, the discs between their vertebrae have become slightly compressed.   Causes—lost fat and muscle, compressed discs; effect—loss of height.

___A___ 4. ¹The short- and longer-term consequences of childhood sexual abuse can be extremely damaging. ²Victims initially report fear, anxiety, depression, anger, and hostility. ³Long-term _____*effects*_____ may include depression, self-destructive behavior, feelings of isolation, poor self-esteem, and substance abuse.   *Cause:* childhood sexual abuse; *effects:* initial: fear, etc.; long-term: depression, etc.

___D___ 5. ¹Even in contemporary industrial societies where women have made great strides in the twentieth century, gender inequality and male privilege persist in marriage and family relationships. ²In America, it is still customary for the bride's family to pay for the wedding, and many wives continue to take their husbands' name. ³_____*Likewise*_____, many people believe that even when the husband's and wife's jobs are equal in terms of income and career advancement, the husband's job should take precedence.   Shows that the idea in sentence 2 is similar to the idea in sentence 3 because both demonstrate male privilege.

(Continues on next page)

B. Label each item with the letter of its main pattern of organization.

    A Definition and example   C Contrast
    B Comparison   D Cause and effect

___D___ 6. ¹In what is now considered a classic experiment, young children saw a film of an adult wildly hitting a five-foot-tall inflatable punching toy called a Bobo doll. ²As a result, when the children were given the opportunity to play with the Bobo doll themselves, most displayed the same kind of behavior, in some cases mimicking the aggressive behavior almost identically.

Cause: watching adult aggressive behavior; *effect:* child behaves aggressively.

___B___ 7. ¹A research team has managed to locate and complete testing on 44 rare pairs of identical twins separated early in life. ²The similarities in the twins' lives are uncanny. ³Identical twins Oskar Stohr and Jack Yufe were separated soon after birth. ⁴Oskar was sent to a Nazi-run school in Yugoslavia while Jack was raised in a Jewish home on a Caribbean island. ⁵When they were reunited for the first time in middle age, both showed up wearing similar mustaches, haircuts, shirts, and wire-rimmed glasses. ⁶A pair of previously separated female twins both arrived at the Minneapolis airport wearing seven rings on their fingers. ⁷One had a son named Richard Andrew, and the other had a son named Andrew Richard.

Compares the characteristics of two pairs of separated identical twins.

___A___ 8. ¹Self-handicapping is the tendency to sabotage one's performance to provide an excuse for possible failure. ²For example, when a big test is looming, self-handicappers put off studying until the last minute or go out drinking the night before the test. ³If, as is likely, they don't do well on the exam, they explain their poor performance by saying they didn't prepare. ⁴People use a variety of tactics for handicapping their performance: alcohol, drugs, procrastination, a bad mood, a distracting stimulus, anxiety, depression, and being overcommitted.

Defines and illustrates the term *self-handicapping.*

___D___ 9. ¹When animals such as bears and mice hibernate over the cold winter months, their heartbeats and breathing slow down dramatically, and their body temperatures fall. ²This drop into hibernation allows animals to reserve their energy during times that food is scarce. ³Consequently, they live through periods that would likely kill them if they were not hibernating.

Cause: hibernation; *effect:* survival.

___C___ 10. ¹Some significant gender differences exist in the display of need for power. ²Men with high power needs tend to show unusually high levels of aggression, drink heavily, act in a sexually exploitative manner, and participate more frequently in competitive sports. ³In contrast, women display their power needs with more restraint; this is congruent with traditional societal constraints on women's behavior. ⁴Women with high power needs are more apt than men are to channel those needs in a socially responsible manner, such as by showing concern for others or displaying highly nurturing behavior.

Contrasts the behavior of men and women with high power needs.

RELATIONSHIPS II: Mastery Test 3

Read each textbook paragraph below. Then answer the questions that follow.

A. ¹The individual acting in society is <u>like</u> an actor in a play. ²In the theater, the script sets the stage, defines the role that each actor will play, and dictates what actors say and do. ³<u>Similarly</u>, cultures present us with many preestablished social rules of behavior. ⁴For instance, when children enter school, they learn many rules of classroom behavior, such as sitting quietly in their seats or raising a hand to speak. ⁵In marriage, traditional roles prescribe that the husband should be the breadwinner and the wife should be in charge of childcare and housekeeping.

Compares an individual acting in society with an actor in a play.

___C___ 1. The main pattern of organization of the paragraph is
   A. definition and example.   C. comparison.
   B. cause and effect.   D. contrast.

2. One transition that signals the pattern of organization of this paragraph

   is _____*like* **or** *similarly*_____.

B. ¹Are you one of the millions of people who need a jolt from a caffeinated drink to do your job? ²If you are, you may be interested to know that drinks with caffeine in them first became widespread at the same time humanity was switching from farm to factory work. ³It seems that prior to the Industrial Revolution, the work schedule was basically a matter of following natural rhythms: sunrise, sunset, and the cycle of the seasons. ⁴The drink of choice was beer, which can interfere with completing tasks requiring coordinated movement. ⁵When the nature of work changed from relatively slow-paced farm work to one timed by clocks and aided by fast-paced machinery, humans had to adapt. ⁶Caffeinated beverages such as coffee, tea, and, later, colas helped people adjust to this new, faster-paced world. ⁷Imagine what the <u>consequences</u> would be if you drank beer while performing factory work. ⁸You might fall asleep, or worse! ⁹But legions of workers stayed wide awake and energetic <u>due</u> partly <u>to</u> the aid of caffeinated drinks.

Cause: change from farm work to factory work; effect: switch from beer to caffeinated beverages.

___B___ 3. The main pattern of organization of the paragraph is
   A. definition and example.   C. comparison.
   B. cause and effect.   D. contrast.

4. One transition that signals the pattern of organization of this paragraph

   is _____*consequences* **or** *due to*_____.

(Continues on next page)

C.   ¹A <u>social dilemma</u> exists when behavior that is advantageous for one party leads to disadvantageous outcomes for others. ²The classic <u>illustration</u> is to imagine yourself as a criminal and that you and your partner in crime have been taken to the police station on suspicion of having committed a crime. ³The police believe both of you are guilty, but they lack sufficient evidence to turn the case over to the district attorney for prosecution. ⁴The police officers place you and your partner in separate rooms, where each of you may confess or maintain your innocence. ⁵The police inform you that if both you and your partner remain silent, each of you will get off with three-year sentences. ⁶If both of you confess, you both will serve seven years. ⁷However, should you confess and implicate your partner while your coconspirator maintains his innocence, you will be released, but your partner will receive a fifteen-year prison term. ⁸The situation will be reversed should you maintain your innocence and your partner confesses.

Defines and illustrates the term social dilemma.

   A   5. The main pattern of organization of the paragraph is
- A. definition and example.
- B. cause and effect.
- C. comparison.
- D. contrast.

6. One transition that signals the pattern of organization of this paragraph

is   *illustration*   .

D.   ¹When adults in the United States meet for the first time, one of the first questions they ask each other is, "What do you do?" ²A person's occupation—doctor, lawyer, garbage collector, police officer, or mortician—affects how he or she is perceived by others and the nature of the interaction that will follow. ³<u>In the same way</u>, when college students meet, they often ask, "What's your major?" ⁴This is essentially the <u>same</u> question, in that it implies, "What occupation do you plan to enter after you graduate?"

Compares adults who ask each other's occupation with college students who ask each other's major.

   B   7. The main patterns of organization of the paragraph are cause and effect and
- A. definition and example.
- B. comparison.
- C. contrast.
- D. comparison and contrast.

8. One transition that signals the second pattern of organization of this

paragraph is   *In the same way* **or** *same*   .

RELATIONSHIPS II: Mastery Test 4

Read each textbook paragraph below. Then answer the questions that follow.

A.

This paragraph compares what's similar about Utah and Nevada (levels of income, education, urbanization, and medical care) and contrasts what's different (lifestyle and causes of death).

[1]The impact of values and lifestyle on health becomes apparent if we <u>contrast</u> Utah (home of the Mormons, who disapprove of alcohol, caffeine, tobacco, and extramarital sex) with the adjacent state of Nevada (home of a gambling industry that fosters a rather <u>different</u> lifestyle). [2]<u>Although</u> these two states have <u>similar</u> levels of income, education, urbanization, and medical care, Nevadans are more likely to die from cancer, strokes, heart attacks, lung disease, and AIDS. [3]They also are more likely to die in car wrecks, to be murdered, and to commit suicide.

_____D_____ 1. The main patterns of organization of the paragraph are cause and effect and
  A. definition and example.   C. contrast.
  B. comparison.   D. comparison and contrast.

2. One transition that signals the second pattern of organization of this paragraph is _____ *contrast* **or** *different* **or** *Although* **or** *similar* _____.

B.

Defines and illustrates the term *doublespeak.*

[1]*Doublespeak* is a term applied to the use of words that are evasive, ambiguous, or stilted for the purpose of deceiving or confusing the reader or listener. [2]The ethical use of doublespeak is highly questionable, but many organizational managers and politicians make use of it as a means, they hope, of softening the harsh blows of reality and to cover up bad news or mislead the public. [3]<u>For instance</u>, would you rather be "fired" from your job or be "downsized," "outsourced," or "offered a career-change opportunity"? [4]Would you prefer to be "laid off" or to be "transitioned" because the company you've been working for is being "reorganized" or "reengineered," or is engaging in "decruitment" (the opposite of recruitment)? [5]If you had participated in the Gulf War or the Iraqi War, would you have preferred to hear that your organization's "massive bombing attacks killed thousands of civilians" or that your "force packages" successfully "visited a site" and "degraded," "neutralized," or "sanitized" targets? [6]As you become "chronologically gifted" (i.e., old), maybe you will learn the meaning of these terms and phrases, but it seems new ones are constantly being developed.

_____A_____ 3. The main pattern of organization of the paragraph is
  A. definition and example.   C. comparison.
  B. cause and effect.   D. contrast.

4. One transition that signals the pattern of organization of this paragraph is _____ *For instance* _____.

(Continues on next page)

C.   [1]According to psychologists, boys gain independence from their mothers more easily than girls do. [2]In the first place, society expects boys to be more self-reliant. [3]As children, they have more physical freedom to explore their environment. [4]They are encouraged to compete, take risks, and achieve. [5]Girls, <u>on the other hand</u>, are kept closer to home. [6]They are taught to win approval from others. [7]Being obedient and passive keeps them dependent longer. [8]Secondly, boys don't have to change the sex of their first and primary love object. [9]They don't have to abandon Mother; they only have to find another female. [10]Girls, <u>however,</u> have to transfer their feelings from their mother to someone of the opposite sex. [11]Rebelling against Mother is essential to test and prove the girl's ability to break away.

Contrasts how easy it is for boys to gain independence from their mothers with how difficult it is for girls to do the same.

___C___ 5. The main patterns of organization of the paragraph are list of items and
      A. definition and example.   C. contrast.
      B. comparison.   D. comparison and contrast.

6. One transition that signals the second pattern of organization of this paragraph is _____ *on the other hand* **or** *however* _____.

D.   [1]Frogs may be cute little amphibians to some and a nuisance to others, but they actually play an important role in nature. [2]Known as environmental or bio-indicators, these creatures have the capability of revealing the environmental health of an area. [3]The <u>reason</u> for this is that frogs have permeable skin, which allows toxins or pollutants to move freely into their bodies, where the poisons can concentrate. [4]This sensitivity is heightened since frogs spend their life cycle both on land and in the water. [5]So if an area is abundant with frogs, chances are that the environment is healthy in terms of air and water quality. [6]If the frog population in an area is dwindling, it could be an early indicator that the environment is unhealthy, or that it is changing. [7]<u>Thus</u>, frogs provide an early warning signal that undesirable changes either have occurred or are looming.

This paragraph explains why frogs are important in nature.
Cause: their permeable skin; *effect:* absorption of toxins and poisons, which in turn reveals the environmental health of an area.

___B___ 7. The main pattern of organization of the paragraph is
      A. definition and example.   C. comparison.
      B. cause and effect.   D. contrast.

8. One transition that signals the pattern of organization of this paragraph is _____ *reason* **or** *Thus* _____.

RELATIONSHIPS II: Mastery Test 5

A. Read the textbook paragraph below. Then answer the question and complete the outline that follows.

> [1]Prior to the 1960s, almost everyone in America wore some type of hat. [2]But <u>due to</u> a number of lifestyle changes, few of today's Americans wear hats. [3]For one thing, America changed from an outdoor culture to an indoor culture. [4]When Americans used to spend so much time traveling and working outdoors, hats helped them keep the warmth in during the winter and the sun out during the summer. [5]<u>Since</u> most of today's Americans have heated homes and spend little time outside, there is no longer a need to wear hats for protection. [6]In addition, the widespread use of cars made wearing hats awkward. [7]While it used to be more popular to walk or take public transportation to a job site, the majority of today's workers drive their own cars. [8]The low ceiling in most cars makes it difficult to wear any sort of headgear, and few drivers want to keep putting their hats on and taking them off. [9]Last, <u>because</u> fewer people wear hats, wearing them has become socially unacceptable in many situations. [10]While it used to be considered proper to wear a hat, today's schools and offices often have dress codes that prohibit headgear.

_B_ 1. The main patterns of organization of the paragraph are list of items, contrast, and

    A. definition and example.

    B. cause and effect.

    C. comparison.

Causes—three changes in lifestyle; effect—fewer hats worn today.

2–5. Complete the outline of the paragraph by writing in the main idea and the three major supporting details. *Wording of answers may vary.*

In sentence 3, the words For one thing signal the first major supporting detail. The words In addition in sentence 6 signal the second major detail. In sentence 9, the word Last signals the third major detail.

Note the contrast pattern in each of the major supporting details. In each case, the lifestyle of the past is contrasted with today's.

Main idea: *Due to a number of lifestyle changes, few of today's Americans wear hats.*

1.   *Change from outdoor culture to indoor culture—hats are no longer needed for protection against heat or cold.*

2.   *Change from walking or taking public transportation to driving cars—low ceilings in cars make wearing hats awkward.*

3.   *Change in dress code—hats used to be considered proper but are no longer socially acceptable in many situations.*

(Continues on next page)

B. Read the textbook paragraph below. Then answer the question and complete the map that follows.   *Wording of answers may vary.*

¹Psychologists distinguish between two types of loneliness: emotional and social. ²Both types of loneliness can cause considerable distress, but they are not the same. ³Emotional loneliness occurs when an intimate attachment figure is absent. ⁴An example would be a child missing a parent; an adult, his or her spouse; or an individual missing an intimate friend. ⁵Or a widow might feel intense emotional loneliness after the death of her husband, but still have social ties to her friends and family. ⁶Social loneliness, on the other hand, occurs when a person is lacking a sense of being integrated into a community. ⁷A young couple moving to a new state might not feel emotional loneliness, as they have each other. ⁸But they are likely to experience social loneliness until they put down roots in their new community. ⁹It is quite possible to experience one type of loneliness without the other.

___A___ 6. The main organizational patterns of the paragraph are contrast and
       A. definition and example.   Defines and gives examples of *social* and
       B. cause and effect.   *emotional* loneliness. The passage also
       C. comparison.   contrasts the two terms, using the
                                transition *on the other hand.*

7–10. Complete the map of the paragraph by writing in the major and minor supporting details.

| Psychologists distinguish between two types of loneliness: emotional and social. |

| Emotional loneliness — feeling the absence of an intimate attachment figure | Social loneliness — lacking a sense of being integrated into a community |

| *Ex.* — Child missing parent; adult missing spouse; individual missing intimate friend; widow missing husband | *Ex.* — Young couple moving to a new state, before putting down roots in the community |

The first major supporting detail occurs in sentence 3. An example follows in sentence 4. The second major detail occurs in sentence 6, which contains the contrast transition *on the other hand.* An example follows in sentences 7–8.

RELATIONSHIPS II: Mastery Test 6

A. Read the textbook paragraph below. Then answer the question and complete the outline that follows.

> [1]An experiment with surgery patients shows how touching can have <u>different</u> meanings. [2]A nurse whose job it was to tell patients about their upcoming surgery purposely touched the patients twice, once briefly on the arm when she introduced herself, and then for a full minute on the arm during the instruction period. [3]When she left, she also shook the patient's hand. [4]The nurse's touches <u>affected</u> women and men <u>differently</u>. [5]For the women patients, the touching was soothing. [6]It lowered their blood pressure and anxiety both before the surgery and for more than an hour afterward. [7]The touching upset the men, <u>however</u>. [8]Their blood pressure and anxiety increased. [9]Experimenters have suggested that the men found it harder to acknowledge dependency and fear. [10]<u>Instead of</u> a comfort, the touch was a threatening reminder of their vulnerability.

___D___ 1. One organizational pattern of the paragraph is   *Contrasts women's*
(or B)   A. definition and example.   C. comparison.   *and men's reactions*
           B. cause and effect.   D. contrast.   *to touch.*

    2. A transition that signals this pattern of organization is _____.

              different **or** *differently* **or** *however* **or** *Instead of*

___B___ 3. A second organizational pattern of the paragraph is   *Cause:* touching;
(or D)   A. definition and example.   C. comparison.   *effect:* blood pressure
           B. cause and effect.   D. contrast.   *and anxiety go up or down.*

    4. A transition that signals this pattern of organization is _____.

                       affected

5–6. Complete the outline of the paragraph by writing in the two major supporting details.

Main idea: An experiment with surgery patients showed how touching can have different meanings.

1. *For women patients, touching was soothing—lowering blood pressure and anxiety .*

2. *For men, touching was upsetting—blood pressure and anxiety increased.*

(Continues on next page)

B. Read the textbook paragraph below. Then answer the question and complete the map that follows.

Wording of answers may vary.

Cause:
Union victory;
effects:
abolition of
slavery
(sentence 2);
new political
majority
(sentence 5);
and ability to
acquire free land
(sentence 8).
Note that the
effects are also
presented in a
list pattern.
Also (sentence 5)
and *Another*
(sentence 8)
signal this
pattern.

¹The triumph of the Union in the Civil War <u>led to</u> several fundamental changes in the nature of the American republic. ²No <u>consequence</u> of the Civil War was as basic as the abolition of slavery in the United States. ³The Emancipation Proclamation made it possible for many slaves to gain freedom. ⁴Once hundreds of thousands of blacks left their masters to flee to the Union lines, it was ridiculous to imagine a return to the old ways.

⁵The Civil War also created a new political majority. ⁶Since the founding of the republic, Southerners played a role in the national government out of proportion to their numbers. ⁷By seceding from the Union, the South opened the way for the northern Republican Party to take its place in the position of political power. ⁸Another momentous innovation of the Civil War years was the ability of citizens to acquire free land. ⁹Before the war, Southern fear of new free states in the territories paralyzed every attempt to liberalize the means by which the federal government disposed of its western lands. ¹⁰Without the influence of Southern congressmen, the Homestead Act was passed, providing every head of family with the opportunity to receive 160 acres of public land for free.

___B___ 7. The main pattern of organization of the paragraph is

    A. definition and example.   C. comparison.

    B. cause and effect.   D. contrast.

8–10. Complete the map of the paragraph by writing in the three major supporting details.

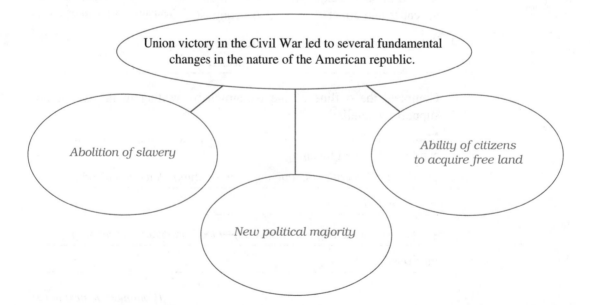

Union victory in the Civil War led to several fundamental changes in the nature of the American republic.

Abolition of slavery

New political majority

Ability of citizens to acquire free land

TO THE STUDENT

The pages that follow contain two mastery tests that offer additional practice in the skills covered in Chapters 4 and 5:

- Relationships that involve **addition**
- Relationships that involve **time**
- Relationships that involve **illustration**
- Relationships that involve **comparison and/or contrast**
- Relationships that involve **cause and effect**

For ease in reference, the lists of words that show these relationships have been reprinted on the next page.

Addition Words

one	to begin with	also	further
first (of all)	for one thing	in addition	furthermore
second (ly)	other	next	last (of all)
third (ly)	another	moreover	final (ly)

Time Words

before	immediately	when	until
previously	next	whenever	often
first (of all)	then	while	frequently
second (ly)	following	during	eventually
third (ly)	later	as (soon as)	final (ly)
now	after	by	last (of all)

Illustration Words

(for) example	including	(as an) illustration	one
(for) instance	specifically	to illustrate	once
such as	to be specific		

Comparison Words

(just) as	both	in like fashion	in a similar fashion
(just) like	equal (ly)	in like manner	in a similar manner
alike	resemble	similar (ly)	(in) the same way
same	likewise	similarity	(in) common

Contrast Words

but	instead (of)	even though	difference
yet	in contrast	as opposed to	different (ly)
however	on the other hand	in spite of	differ (from)
although	on the contrary	despite	unlike
nevertheless	converse (ly)	rather than	while
still	opposite		

Cause and Effect Words

therefore	so	owing to	because (of)
thus	(as a) result	effect	reason
(as a) consequence	results in	cause	explanation
consequently	leads (led) to	if ... then	accordingly
due to	since	affect	depend(s) on

RELATIONSHIPS I AND II: Mastery Test 1

A. Fill in each blank with an appropriate transition from the box. Use each transition once. Then, in the spaces provided, write the letter of the transition you have chosen.

A. conversely	B. due to	C. for example
D. later	E. other	

_____E_____ 1.

Lists the two basic strategies in the war on drugs.

[1]The war on drugs consists of two basic strategies. [2]One is punitive: using law enforcement to stop the supply of drugs and punish drug sellers and users. [3]The _____other_____ is supportive: using drug prevention (or education) and treatment to reduce the demand for drugs and help drug addicts.

_____D_____ 2.

Presents, in time order, a baby's changing nutritional needs during the first year of life.

[1]The nutritional needs of a baby change over the first year of life. [2]Most babies do best if they are fed a diet of only breast milk and/or formula for the first four to six months. [3]At that time, parents can begin to offer a single-grain cereal, such as rice cereal, with added iron. [4]_____Later_____, the baby should be offered no more than one new food every week, with the parent watching for signs of an allergic reaction to any food.

_____B_____ 3.

Cause: difference in American and Asian cultural beliefs; *effect:* Asian students' higher scores in math and science.

[1]It has long been noted that students in most Asian countries score higher in tests of math and science than do American students. [2]In all probability, this is _____due to_____ a basic difference in cultural beliefs. [3]North American parents and teachers emphasize innate ability—the idea that some people are just naturally "good at math." [4]Asian parents and teachers believe strongly that any student can do better by working harder.

_____C_____ 4.

Gives examples of varying rates of cancer in different ethnic and gender groups.

[1]Cancer seems to occur in different degrees in different ethnic and gender groups. [2]_____For example_____, African American men have the world's highest rate of prostate cancer. [3]Native American men are more likely than white American men to develop lung cancer or colorectal cancer. [4]And Vietnamese American and Hispanic American women have higher than average rates of cervical cancer.

_____A_____ 5.

Contrasts who is in charge in hospital and hospice care.

[1]When life's end is near, more and more people and their families are turning to some form of hospice care, rather than traditional hospitalization. [2]In a hospital, medical professionals are in charge, with the patient and family members often feeling pushed aside and somewhat bewildered by all that is going on. [3]_____Conversely_____, in a hospice setting, the patient and family are in charge. [4]They decide what medical treatments they will ask for or accept, and friends and family members are deeply involved in the dying person's care.

(Continues on next page)

B. Fill in each blank with an appropriate transition from the box. Use each transition once. Then, in the spaces provided, write the letter of the transition you have chosen.

A. after	B. for instance	C. for one thing
D. however	E. in contrast	

___D___ 6. [1]Researchers find that adults who call themselves "very religious" are less afraid of death than those who describe themselves as "less religious." [2]This would suggest that the more religious one is, the less afraid one is of death. [3]_____*However*_____, this pattern breaks down when people who describe themselves as "completely non-religious" are questioned. [4]They report themselves as equally unafraid of death as the "very religious."

Contrasts fear of death in religious and non-religious adults.

___A___ 7. [1]Early in childhood, children are likely to connect moral judgments with adult observation. [2]They feel guilty or ashamed only if a parent or teacher sees them violating a moral rule. [3]A 7-year-old candy thief, for instance, is unlikely to feel guilty unless he is caught in the act. [4]But _____*after*_____ the age of 10 or 11, that same child is likely to make behavioral choices based on how guilty, ashamed, or proud he thinks he will feel.

Uses time order to describe stages in the development of children's moral judgments.

___B___ 8. [1]When you notice "the man in the moon," you are demonstrating a phenomenon called pareidolia. [2]<u>Pareidolia</u> is the name psychologists give to people's tendency to mistake a vague, random stimulus for a recognizable image—most often a human face. [3]_____*For instance*_____, people often think they perceive faces in clouds, wallpaper designs, geologic formations, paint swirls, and other meaningless formations.

Defines and gives an example of *pareidolia*.

___E___ 9. [1]The usual standard for good vision in an adult is "20/20," meaning that subject can see something 20 feet away as well as the average person. [2]_____*In contrast*_____, a person with "20/100" vision has to be as close as 20 feet to see something that the ordinary person can see at 100 feet. [3]In other words, the higher the second number, the poorer the person's vision.

Contrasts 20/20 vision with 20/100 vision.

___C___ 10. [1]The sales of fur tumbled to an all-time low in the late 1980s, thanks largely to the efforts of groups like People for the Ethical Treatment of Animals (PETA). [2]But in recent years, fur has made a fashion comeback. [3]Why? [4]_____*For one thing*_____, designers have been incorporating fur into blended fabrics, making it less obvious that it is real fur. [5]For another, the anti-fur movement is simply less novel and chic than it was in years past.

Lists two reasons for fur's fashion comeback.

RELATIONSHIPS I AND II: Mastery Test 2

Read each selection and answer the questions that follow. Note that paragraphs D and E have **two** patterns of organization.

A. [1]The "psychological consequences" of product use are internal, personal outcomes, such as how a product makes you feel. [2]For instance, using Nexxus shampoo might make you feel more attractive; wearing Gap sportswear might make you feel more (or less) stylish; and eating an ice cream cone from Baskin-Robbins might make you feel happy. [3]Consumers may also think in terms of the "social consequences" of product use, which might include "My friends will like/respect/envy me if I buy an iPod; my mother will think I am a smart shopper if I buy this jacket on sale."

_C_ 1. The main pattern of organization of the selection is
A. comparison and/or contrast.
B. time order.
C. definition and example.

Defines *psychological consequences of product use* and gives an example. (Note that sentence 3 gives an example of a different term, *social consequences*.)

2. One transition that signals the pattern of organization of this paragraph is
_____ For instance **or** include _____.

B. [1]A growing body of evidence shows that living in a concentrated pocket of poverty intensifies all the ill effects of family poverty. [2]When the whole neighborhood is poor, parents have fewer other resources to rely on, and children have more violent adult models and fewer supportive ones. [3]Rates of child abuse rise, along with rates of aggression and delinquency in children. [4]When the whole neighborhood also lacks what sociologists call connectedness and stability—when the adults do not collaborate to monitor the children and do not provide practical or emotional support to one another—the results are still worse.

_C_ 3. The main pattern of organization of the selection is
A. time order.
B. definition and example.
C. cause and effect.

Cause: family poverty; *effects:* increases in child abuse, aggression and delinquency, etc.

4. One transition that signals the pattern of organization you selected is
_____ effects **or** results _____.

C. [1]Crispus Attucks was born in about 1723, the son of a slave and a Native American woman. [2]He is thought to have escaped from slavery in 1750. [3]After that he worked as a sailor and laborer in Boston. [4]Like many Colonial sailors, he hated the presence of the occupying British troops because they could force sailors to serve in the Royal Navy. [5]On March 5, 1770, a crowd gathered to protest the presence of the British. [6]Attucks spoke to the crowd, waving a club and urging other colonists to attack the British. [7]The British soldiers then opened fire, killing Attucks as well as four white men. [8]Attucks's death in the Boston Massacre was an important milestone along the road to the American Revolution.

(Continues on next page)

_A_   5. The main pattern of organization of the selection is
 A. time order.   Describes, in time order, the sequence of events
 B. contrast.   leading to the death of Crispus Attucks in the
 C. definition and example. Boston Massacre.

6. One transition that signals the pattern of organization you selected is
 in about 1723 **or** _in 1750_ **or** _After_ **or** _On March 5, 1770_ **or** _then_ .

D.   [1]According to a recent _Consumer Reports_ article, as much as 25 percent of Americans' expenditures on medical care are wasted on unnecessary treatments, procedures, tests, or hospitalization. [2]Several possible explanations can be suggested for this waste of time, money, and resources. [3]One possible explanation is the profit motive. [4]The more medical services provided, the greater the income for members of the medical-care industry. [5]Another possible reason is the desire of doctors and hospitals to avoid being sued by patients for undiagnosed or improperly treated sickness or injury. [6]Finally, because most U.S. patients do not pay directly for medical care, they probably are less interested in keeping costs down. [7]They may demand treatments that are not appropriate or necessary. [8]In any case, we clearly are not making the most efficient use of our medical-care resources.

_B_   7. The main patterns of organization of the selection are list of items and
 A. comparison and/or contrast.   Causes—profit motive, need to avoid
 B. cause and effect.   lawsuits, lack of patient interest in keeping
 C. definition and example.   costs down. Effect—time and money wasted
                                  on unnecessary medical treatments.

8. One transition that signals the pattern of organization you selected is
 explanations **or** _explanation_ **or** _reason_ **or** _because_ .

E.   [1]Epidemiology is the study of the origin and spread of disease in a given population. [2]Epidemiology emerged as an applied science in 1854, when the English physician John Snow discovered the source of one of London's periodic cholera epidemics. [3]Specifically, he had gone to the neighborhoods where the patients lived and asked them what they did every day, where they worked, what they ate and drank, and many other questions about their lives and activities. [4]Finally, after sifting through a huge pile of information, Snow hit upon the clue to the origin of the disease. [5]He found that they all had one thing in common: They had drunk water from a particular pump on Broad Street. [6]Snow simply shut off the pump and, with that simple act, stopped the epidemic in its tracks. [7]Not until many years later, with the discovery of germs, could anyone explain why shutting down the pump was effective. [8]Dr. Snow had removed the source of the cholera bacterium.

_A_   9. The main patterns of organization of the selection are time order and
 A. definition and example.
 B. comparison.   Defines and gives an example of
 C. contrast.   _epidemiology._

10. One transition that signals the pattern of organization you selected is
 Specifically .

6

Inferences

You have probably heard the expression "to read between the lines." When you "read between the lines," you pick up ideas that are not directly stated in what you are reading. These implied ideas are often important for a full understanding of what an author means. Discovering the ideas in writing that are not stated directly is called *making inferences,* or *drawing conclusions.*

Look at the cartoon below. What inferences can you make about it? Check (✓) the **two** inferences that are most logically based on the information suggested by the cartoon.

____ A. The dog requires more than one leash to keep it securely tied to the parking meter.

_✓_ B. The dog has eaten the other dogs tied up at the parking meter.

____ C. The dog is ordinarily a friendly dog.

_✓_ D. The dog is waiting for its owner to return.

Explanation:

A. *The dog requires more than one leash to keep it securely tied to the parking meter.*

The dog requires and has only one leash. The other leashes are in his mouth. You should not have checked this item.

B. *The dog has eaten the other dogs tied up at the parking meter.*

Three other leashes are in the mouth of this big, hostile-looking dog. You should have checked this item.

C. *The dog is ordinarily a friendly dog.*

It may or may not ordinarily be a friendly dog, but it doesn't look friendly here, and it obviously has not been friendly to other dogs. You should not have checked this item.

D. *The dog is waiting for its owner to return.*

It is a reasonable inference that the owner who tied up the dog will return—and will be in for a surprise!

INFERENCES IN READING

In reading, we make logical leaps from information stated directly to ideas that are not stated directly. As one scholar has said, inferences are "statements about the unknown made on the basis of the known." To make inferences, we use all the clues provided by the writer, our own experience, and logic.

You have already practiced making inferences in this book. Do you remember the following sentence on page 12 of the introductory chapter?

Marcella uses a lot of *hyperbole* to express herself: a restaurant is never just "good"—it's "the most fabulous food in the universe"; her boyfriend isn't just "good-looking"—he's "divine beyond belief."

That sentence does not tell the meaning of *hyperbole*, but the examples help us infer that *hyperbole* means "overstatement."

You also made inferences in the chapter on implied ideas. There you used the evidence in selections to figure out main ideas that were implied rather than stated directly. In this chapter, you will get a good deal of practice in making a variety of inferences about reading selections and other material.

Inferences in Short Passages

☑ *Check Your Understanding*

Read the following passage and then check (✓) the **two** inferences most logically based on the information provided.

> Mark Twain said: "When I was a boy of 14, my father was so ignorant I could hardly stand to have the old man around. But when I got to be 21, I was astonished at how much the old man had learned in seven years."

  ✓   A. Teenagers tend to think they know it all and that adults do not.

  ___   B. Even old people are capable of learning a great deal.

  ___   C. The older fathers get, the less foolish they become.

  ✓   D. As a young person matures, he learns to respect the knowledge of adults.

Explanation:

A. Experience tells us that teenagers often think they know more than their parents' generation. Twain's observation is a humorous statement of this truth. You should have checked this item.

B. Twain's age (14) when he thought his father was ignorant and the age (21) at which he is astonished at the "old man's" learning are clues that it is Twain who has changed, not his father. You should not have checked this item.

C. There is nothing in the statement to support the inference that Twain's father was actually foolish. Again, it is Twain's viewpoint that has changed, not his father. You should not have checked this item.

D. Experience tells us that when young people begin to face the same life challenges that adults face, they gain new respect for the knowledge adults possess. Clearly, as Twain reached manhood, he began to respect his father. You should have checked this item.

> ## Practice 1

Passage 1:
Answer A
is suggested
by "When
will people
understand." B is
suggested by
"scars upon our
souls." C and D
are wrong; the
passage suggests
that the words are heard and understood, but painful.

Passage 2:
Answer A is
suggested by
"my small . . .
world." C is
suggested
because one can
"walk through"
and be freed.
B and D are
wrong; Winfrey associates books with freedom, not accomplishments or success.

Passage 3:
A and B are
wrong; the
passage is humorous,
not regretful or
sad. C can be
inferred: Mencken
suggests that
politicians are
dishonest and lack common sense and decency. D is supported by "inaccurate to say I hate everything."

Passage 4:
Answer A is
wrong; the
passage says
devils "should
be fought" and
suggests they
can be defeated.
B can be inferred:
the devils "in
our hearts"
are our own
worst impulses.
C has no support.
D can be
inferred: we
improve ourselves by fighting the devils in our own hearts.

For each of the following passages, check (✓) the **two** inferences most logically based on the information provided.

1. "When will people understand that words can cut as sharply as any blade, and that those cuts leave scars upon our souls." —Unknown author

   ✓ A. People seldom reflect on how deeply their words can wound others.

   ✓ B. Emotional wounds can be just as painful as physical ones.

   ___ C. Sometimes we fail to listen to the words of others.

   ___ D. People do not always understand each other's words.

2. "I can't imagine I could have become the person I am now without books. How could I know there was another world beyond my small, isolated, feeling-abandoned world? Books became synonymous with freedom. They showed that you can open doors and walk through." —Oprah Winfrey

   ✓ A. The author of this statement probably had a difficult childhood.

   ___ B. Everyone who reads can accomplish great things.

   ✓ C. Books can open doors to new possibilities in one's life.

   ___ D. Reading can show people how to achieve success.

3. "It is inaccurate to say I hate everything. I am strongly in favor of common sense, common honesty, and common decency. This makes me forever ineligible for public office." —H.L. Mencken

   ___ A. The author regrets the fact that he will never be elected to office.

   ___ B. The author must be a very unhappy man.

   ✓ C. The author believes that many politicians are liars or crooks.

   ✓ D. The author has probably been accused of being overly critical.

4. "The only devils in this world are those running around in our own hearts, and that is where all our battles should be fought." —Mahatma Gandhi

   ___ A. Devils can defeat the best efforts of good people.

   ✓ B. People should try to overcome their own worst impulses.

   ___ C. There are no really evil people in the world.

   ✓ D. Rather than blame others, we should instead seek ways to improve ourselves.

5. "One reads books in order to gain the privilege of living more than one life. People who don't read are trapped in a mine shaft, even if they think the sun is shining. Most New Yorkers wouldn't travel to Minnesota if a bright star shone in the west and hosts of angels were handing out plane tickets, but they might read a book about Minnesota, and thereby form some interesting

Passage 5: Answer A is wrong: the passage suggests that reading lessens but does not eliminate loneliness. B is correct: the passage compares non-readers to people trapped in mineshafts. C is not supported. D can be inferred: Keillor speaks of New Yorkers who read about Minnesota and "thereby might form interesting and useful impressions."

and useful impression of us. This is the benefit of literacy. Life is lonely; it is less so if one reads." —Garrison Keillor

___ A. Reading is a sure antidote for loneliness.

✓ B. People who do not read do not realize how much they limit their view of the world.

___ C. The author considers Minnesotans to be superior to New Yorkers.

✓ D. Reading enables people to establish connections with people and places they might otherwise look down upon or fear.

Inferences in Paragraphs

☑ *Check Your Understanding*

Read the following textbook passage and then check (✓) the **three** inferences that can most logically be drawn from the information provided.

[1]Let's suppose that you have a ticket to fly to some exotic destination. [2]There will be 200 passengers plus crew on board your plane. [3]You are excited about your trip, but on the way to the airport, the radio program you are listening to is interrupted by an announcement that five U.S. jets will be hijacked that day. [4]All will crash—and all passengers and crew will die. [5]There is no doubt that five planes will go down, that 1,000 terrified passengers and crew will plunge to their deaths. [6]The reporter adds that the airlines have decided to stay open for business. [7]Do you still fly? [8]After all, the chances are good that *yours* will not be one of the five planes. [9]My best guess is that you turn around and go home, that U.S. airports will be eerily silent that day. [10]Nicotine—with its progressive emphysema and several types of cancer—kills about 400,000 Americans each year. [11]This is the equivalent of five fully loaded, 200-passenger jets with full crews crashing each and every day—leaving no survivors. [12]Who in their right mind would take the risk that *their* plane will not be among those that crashed? [13]Yet that is the risk that smokers take.

✓ A. The author implies that many Americans don't like to think about the harmful effects of smoking.

___ B. The author implies that chances are good that fewer Americans will smoke in the future.

✓ C. The author suggests that too many people risk their lives by smoking.

___ D. The author suggests that people would be willing to take their chances on a plane crash if the odds are in their favor.

___ E. This excerpt is probably from a business textbook.

✓ F. This excerpt is probably from a textbook that deals with social problems.

Explanation:

A. This is a logical inference. The author presents statistics showing the harmful effects of smoking. Life experience tells us that few people like to think about the negative consequences of their behavior.

B. This is not a logical inference. There is nothing in the passage to indicate that fewer Americans will smoke in the future.

C. This is a logical inference. The author presents statistical evidence that the nicotine in cigarettes kills about 400,000 Americans each year.

D. This is not a logical inference. The author says that airports would be inactive and silent on a day when five jets were to be hijacked.

E. This is not a logical inference. The focus of the passage is health, not business.

F. This is a logical inference. Clearly any behavior that kills 400,000 Americans each year is a social problem.

Guidelines for Making Inferences in Reading

The paragraphs that follow will give you practice in making careful inferences when you read. Here are three guidelines to that process:

1 **Never lose sight of the available information.** As much as possible, base your inferences on the facts. For instance, in the passage about the risks of smoking, we are told that most Americans would refuse to fly if they knew that jets were to be hijacked, but that many Americans continue to risk their lives despite the known dangers of smoking. On the basis of those facts, we would not conclude that fewer Americans will smoke in the future.

It's also important to note when a conclusion lacks support. For instance, the conclusion that the smoking passage is from a business textbook has no support in the passage, which focuses on the health costs of smoking rather than the economic costs.

2 **Use your background information and experience to help you in making inferences.** For instance, life experience tells us that people don't like to dwell on the negative consequences of their behavior. Therefore, you can conclude that American smokers don't like to think about the harmful effects of smoking.

The more you know about a subject, the better your inferences are likely to be. So keep in mind that if your background in an area is weak, your inferences may be shaky. If your car suddenly develops a tendency to stall, an auto mechanic's inferences about the cause are likely to be more helpful than your inferences.

3 **Consider the alternatives.** Don't simply accept the first inference that comes to mind. Instead, consider all of the facts of a case and all the possible explanations. For example, the mechanic analyzing why your car stalls may first think of and then eliminate several possibilities before coming to the right conclusion.

➤ **Practice 2**

Read the following passages, most of them from textbooks. Then, in the space provided, write the letter of the most logical answer to each question, based on the information given in the passage.

A. ¹If your roommate is washing the dishes and says acidly, "I hope you're enjoying your novel," the literal meaning of his words is quite clear, but you probably know very well that he is not expressing a concern about your reading pleasure. ²He is really saying, "I am furious that you are not helping to clean up after dinner." ³Other emotions can be expressed through tone of voice as well. ⁴When Mae West, a once famous film star and master of sexual innuendo, asked, "Why don't you come up and see me sometime?" her voice oozed sensuality. ⁵Similarly, if you receive a phone call from someone who has very good or very bad news, you will probably know how she feels before she has told you what happened. ⁶In the same way, we can literally hear the fear in a person's voice, as we do when we listen to a nervous student give an oral report.   Answer B is supported by sentence 3 and applies to all the examples in the passage. Answer A applies to only sentence 6.

_B_ 1. Which of the following would be a good title for this passage?   Answer
   A. Humans Can Sense Fear   C is incorrect because the passage
   B. It's Not What You Say; It's How You Say It   is about messages
   C. Getting Along with Others   expressed by tone of voice,
                                    not about how to get along.

_C_ 2. The author uses the example of Mae West in order to suggest that
   A. movie stars used to be far sexier than they are now.
   B. Mae West probably never experienced a moment of nervousness in her life.
   C. people are capable of conveying much meaning through voice quality.   See sentences 3–4. A person whose "voice oozed sensuality" is
                                    a good example of this point. Answers A and B are not supported.

_B_ 3. The author probably mentions the fear in a nervous student's voice because she feels
   A. that students are needlessly nervous about giving oral reports.
   B. it is an experience that many people are familiar with.
   C. that students should not be forced to give oral reports.

   Most people do feel nervous when they have to give oral reports, so this familiar situation would also be a strong example of the point. Answers A and C are not supported.

B. [1]When sociologists first examined children's picture books in the 1970s, they found that it was unusual for a girl to be the main character. [2]Almost all the books featured boys, men, and even male animals. [3]The girls, when pictured at all, were passive and doll-like, whereas the boys were active and adventuresome. [4]While the boys did things that required independence and self-confidence, most girls were shown trying to help their brothers and fathers. [5]Feminists protested these stereotypes and even formed their own companies to publish books that showed girls as leaders, as active and independent.

[6]The result of these efforts, along with the changed role of women in society, is that children's books now have about an equal number of boy and girl characters. [7]Girls are also now depicted in a variety of nontraditional activities. [8]Researchers find, however, that males are seldom depicted as caring for the children or doing grocery shopping, and they never are seen doing housework. [9]As gender roles continue to change, I assume that this, too, will change.

Item 1:
The girls were pictured as "passive and doll-like"; the depictions are "stereotypes." This suggests that the writer feels that more active role models were needed. A is incorrect because the passage describes how boys and girls are depicted, not what they are really like. B is not supported.

_____C_____ 4. We can infer that the author of this passage believes that

   A. in real life, boys tend to be more active and independent than girls.
   B. the feminist criticisms of children's books in the 1970s had little merit.
   C. girls should be given books that show them acting with self-confidence and a sense of independence.

Item 2:
Answer C can be inferred from the feminists' protest and their wish to show girls as active and independent and as leaders. Answers A and B are not supported.

_____C_____ 5. We can infer from the passage that feminists believe that

   A. male authors intentionally tried to harm young girls.
   B. girls should perform only nontraditional tasks.
   C. reading books can influence how girls think and act.

Item 3:
See sentence 9. Answer A is incorrect because the passage does not discuss what happens in real life. C is incorrect because the passage does not suggest the depiction is unrealistic; and the words *the changed role of women* (sentence 6) contradict this statement.

_____B_____ 6. We can conclude from this passage that

   A. in real life, males seldom care for children or do housework.
   B. children's books will continue to reflect changing gender roles.
   C. children's books now unrealistically depict girls engaged in nontraditional tasks.

C. [1]In 1887 the town of Salisbury, North Carolina, had done little to recover from the Civil War. [2]It was poor, dirty, and full of saloons. [3]Then a Tennessee preacher appeared in town, set up a big tent, and preached that Salisbury needed to go to work. [4]Idleness had brought corruption; working in a cotton mill was the most Christian act his audience could perform. [5]The result was the Salisbury Cotton Mills. [6]The evangelical appeal of the cotton mill crusade helped create a myth that cotton mills were built and run mainly to aid the lower classes. [7]The creation of mill towns helped to promote the image of mill owners as "fathers" to their employees. [8]The company built houses, stores, schools, and even churches for their workers.

Item 1:
Answer B
is supported
by paragraph 2.
A and C are
incorrect
because
sentences 9–15
contradict them
and sentences
6–7 describe these ideas as a "myth" and an "image."

⁹But in reality, many mill owners proved not to be such good fathers. ¹⁰Mill workers tended to be poor whites; often an entire family worked an average of twelve hours a day. ¹¹Wages were as low as fifty cents a day and were not usually paid in cash, but in "trade checks." ¹²The trade checks were accepted as rent for company houses or could be used to buy goods in company stores. ¹³So some mill workers never saw any cash. ¹⁴They merely turned their trade checks back over to the mill owners in return for supplies and housing. ¹⁵The result was high profits that caused the textile industry boom in the South.

Item 2:
Sentences 12–14
suggest that trade checks
kept workers depen-
dent on the mill
owners, since the
checks could
be used
only at company stores.
A is contradicted by
sentence 11. C is
incorrect because the checks were used for the financial gain and control of the owners.

___B___ 7. From the passage we can infer that most cotton mill owners
   A. were charitable "fathers" who wanted to improve the lives of those in the lower class.
   B. were businessmen who wanted to make as much money as possible.
   C. were religious men who wanted to help people overcome idleness.

___B___ 8. "Trade checks" were given in order to
   A. insure that workers would receive a fair wage.
   B. keep the workers dependent on the mill owners.
   C. make it convenient for workers to pay for rent and groceries.

Item 3:
See sentences 3–6;
it was a "myth" that
the cotton mills were
built and run mainly to aid the lower classes. B is contradicted by the second paragraph. C is not
supported.

___A___ 9. The author implies that religion
   A. was used to manipulate the lower class.
   B. helped the lower class gain power.
   C. was practiced differently in the upper and lower classes.

D. ¹A psychologist employed seven assistants and one genuine subject in an experiment in which they were asked to judge the length of a straight line that they were shown on a screen. ²The seven assistants, who were the first to speak and report what they saw, had been instructed to report unanimously an evidently incorrect length. ³The eighth member of the group, the only naïve subject in the lot, did not know that his companions had received such an instruction, and he was under the impression that what they reported was really what they saw. ⁴In one-third of the experiments, he reported the same incorrect length as they did. ⁵The pressure of the environment had influenced his own reaction and had distorted his vision. ⁶When one of the assistants, under the secret direction of the experimenter, started reporting the correct length, it relieved that pressure of the environment, and the perception of the uninformed subject improved accordingly.

___C___ 10. We can infer that this passage is probably from
   A. a biology textbook.
   B. a business textbook.
   C. a social science textbook.

A psychologist is conducting the experiment.
Psychology is a social science.

___A___ 11. This passage suggests that
    A. people tend to be influenced by the actions of others.
    B. people can be forced into saying just about anything.
    C. most people will change their minds when they see that they are in the minority.   See sentence 4. B is not supported; there is no discussion of the use of force. C is contradicted by sentence 6.

___B___ 12. The genuine subjects in the experiment can best be described as
    A. bright.
    B. pressured.   See sentence 5. Answers A and C are not supported.
    C. foolish.

E.   [1]World War I caught most people by surprise. [2]Lulled by a century of peace, many observers had come to regard armed conflict as an anachronism, a dead relic rendered unthinkable by human progress. [3]Convinced that the major powers had advanced too far morally and materially to fight, these optimists believed that nation-states would settle disputes through diplomacy. [4]By the early 1900s, peace societies abounded on both sides of the Atlantic, nurturing visions of a world without war, and the Hague Conferences of 1899 and 1907 seemed to bear out these hopes by codifying international law in order to establish procedures for the peaceful resolution of conflict. [5]World War I shattered these dreams, demonstrating that death and destruction had not yet been banished from human affairs.

___A___ 13. Even if we do not know their definitions, we can infer that the words *anachronism* and *relic* have to do with
    A. the past.
    B. the present.   If people have been "lulled by a century of peace," they would think armed conflict a thing of the past.
    C. the future.

___B___ 14. Just before World War I, people tended to believe that war
    A. would always be a necessary evil.
    B. was a human vice that could be overcome by decent people.
    C. was beneficial for nations seeking land and power.   Sentences 2–4 support answer B and contradict answer A. Answer C is not supported.

___A___ 15. The onset of World War I
    A. probably shattered the ideals of many thinkers of the time.
    B. may have grown out of disagreements between international peace societies.
    C. might never had occurred if there had been more laws in place.

    Sentence 5 says it "shattered . . . dreams" of a world without war. Answers B and C are not supported.

INFERENCES IN LITERATURE

Inference is very important in reading literature. While writers of factual material usually state directly much of what they mean, creative writers often provide verbal pictures that *show* what they mean. It is up to the reader to infer the point of what the creative writer has said. For instance, a nonfiction writer might write the following:

> It would be really hard to feel what others feel. It's better not to know.

Compare the above with the following lines on the same topic from George Eliot's *Middlemarch*, considered by many the greatest of English novels:

> If we had a keen vision and feeling of all ordinary human life, it would be like hearing the grass grow and the squirrel's heart beat, and we should die of that roar which lies on the other side of silence. As it is, we walk about well wadded with stupidity.

Eliot uses vivid images that help us infer a profound human truth—that behind the surface we often carry around a great deal of pain—a "roar . . . on the other side of silence." So as to not die from experiencing the pain of others, we protect and wad ourselves with ignorance and stupidity. To get the most out of literature, you must often infer the meanings behind the words.

A Note on Figures of Speech

Creative writers often use comparisons known as **figures of speech** to imply their meanings and give us a fresh and more informed way of looking at something. The two most common figures of speech are similes and metaphors.

Simile—a comparison introduced with *like, as,* or *as if.*

PEANUTS: © United Feature Syndicate, Inc.

In the cartoon, Snoopy writes about a pair of beautiful eyes that they are "like two supper dishes"! (The joke, of course, is that the comparison is hardly a flattering one.)

In the quotation from *Middlemarch*, George Eliot uses two similes. To see and feel all ordinary human life, she says would be "like hearing the grass grow and the squirrel's heart beat."

Here's another example. Instead of saying, "The morning after the party, my mouth felt awful," you could express the same idea vividly by saying, "The morning after the party, my mouth felt like a used ashtray." The simile shows just how nasty your mouth felt. It gives us more information than the line that simply tells us your mouth felt awful.

Here are some other similes:

- Abandoned houses lined the city street *like tombstones.*
- That too-thin teenage girl has arms *like matchsticks.*
- The look the hostess gave me was *as welcoming as a glass of ice water in my face.*
- The used car salesman attached himself to prospective customers *like Velcro.*
- My mind was becoming *as calm as the surface of a quiet mountain lake.*

Metaphor—an implied comparison, with *like, as,* or *as if* omitted.

The 23rd Psalm in the Bible is the source of some of the world's best-known metaphors, including "The Lord is my shepherd." The comparison suggests that God is like a shepherd who looks after his sheep.

Here are some other metaphors:

- The candidate waded into *a sea of people* to shake hands.
- The movie was *a bomb.*
- Her disapproval was *an ice pick to my heart.*
- The algebra problems were *a forest of tiny enemies*, jeering at me from the page.
- To people searching for information, the Internet is a vast *candy store* of facts.

➤ Practice 3

Use a check (✓) to identify each figure of speech as either a simile or a metaphor. Then, in the space provided, answer each inference question that follows.

___C___ 1. To Jennifer, the psychology course was a banquet of ideas.

    ___ simile   _✓_ metaphor   It is a comparison without *like* or *as.*
     You can infer that Jennifer   Just as a banquet can provide many
                                                    tasty foods, so the psychology
     A. finds her psychology course rather tedious.   course provides many
     B. likes to eat during her psychology course.   interesting ideas.
     C. finds her psychology course quite interesting.

___B___ 2. After I ate that meal, I felt as if I had swallowed a barbell.

     _✓_ simile   ___ metaphor   *As if* signals a simile.

You can infer that the meal was

A. sweet.

B. heavy.

C. spicy.

A barbell is heavy,
suggesting that the meal was heavy.

___A___ 3. When Don started to run track again after his knee operation, he felt like a bus on the racetrack at the Indy 500.

✓ simile   ___ metaphor

You can infer that Don

A. felt slow and awkward.

B. felt cheerful and optimistic.

C. knew he would never regain his old form.

Like signals a simile.
Both Don after his knee operation
and a bus on a racetrack
are comparatively slow and awkward.

___A___ 4. Tina says that her first boyfriend was an economy car, but her current one is a luxury sedan.

___ simile   ✓ metaphor

You can infer that Tina's current boyfriend

A. is a big improvement over her first one.

B. is an auto mechanic.

C. is a family man.

This metaphor implies that Tina's
first boyfriend was only
average (an economy car),
but her current boyfriend is
way above average,
perhaps rich (a luxury sedan).

___C___ 5. The CEO of the company gave a talk to his employees that was one part sugar and one part sandpaper.

___ simile   ✓ metaphor

You can infer that the CEO

A. was hard to understand.

B. led a company that sold both groceries and home products.

C. was both encouraging to and critical of his employees.

To speak in a sugary way
suggests encouragement.
Sandpaper suggests
harshness (criticism).

➤ **Practice 4**

The following is a true story written by sports columnist and Pulitzer Prize nominee Bill Lyon. In just under 900 words, Lyon describes a memorable event that happened before the start of a professional basketball game in Portland. Read the story and then decide what inferences can be made about it.

One Shining Moment

[1]There she stood at center court, this little girl with the big, big voice, poised for the moment of a lifetime, the house lights dimmed, 20,000 people waiting expectantly for her, 20,000 people ready to hear her sing . . .

. . . and the words wouldn't come.

[2]They lodged in her throat and couldn't be budged, no matter how mightily she strained. [3]It was the song she knew by heart, the one she had heard a million times, the one she had sung over and over and over, the very one that she had

rehearsed in a dressing room perfectly—every single run-through dead solid perfect—only minutes before, for heaven's sake. [4]But now the words all tumbled over each other, crazy-quilted in a jumbling, confusing mishmash:

rocket's last gleaming . . . twilight's red glare . . . flag's not there . . . oh, say can you see . . . yet wave . . .

[5]She wanted to disappear, of course. [6]She wanted the floor to open up and swallow her. [7]Or a spaceship to beam her up and carry her off. [8]Natalie Gilbert, a 13-year-old eighth grader, was living the nightmare each of us, in moments of morbid, fearful imagining, has conjured.

[9]And then, suddenly, silent as a shadow, he was there, standing beside her, his left arm protectively, comfortingly around her, and he was whispering the forgotten words and she began to nod her head—*yes, yes, I remember now*—and she began to mouth the words, and then he started to sing them, softly, and she joined in, hesitantly at first, but with a growing confidence, and soon they were a duet, and he was urging the crowd on with his right hand, and soon the duet had 20,000 backups, 20,000 people singing partly out of relief, partly out of compassion, partly out of pride, and rarely has the national anthem of the United States of America been rendered with such heartfelt gusto.

[10]It was a glorious, redemptive moment.

[11]Surely, you thought, sport has never been grander.

[12]In fact, it says here that, for all the acrobatic, aeronautic, pyrotechnic, cruise-o-matic moments that the NBA playoffs have presented to us thus far this spring, all pale in comparison to the night of April 25, in the Rose Garden in Portland, Oregon, shortly before the Trail Blazers met the Dallas Mavericks in the third game of their series.

[13]That is when Maurice Cheeks, once the quintessential point guard, selfless and without ego and pretense, for many meritorious seasons a Philadelphia 76er, and most recently the coach of the Blazers, came to the rescue of Natalie Gilbert.

[14]"I don't know why I did it," he said. [15]"It wasn't something I thought about. [16]It's one of those things you just do."

[17]Except, of course, no one else thought to do it.

[18]Everybody else did precisely what most of us would do in such a situation—study the ceiling, develop a sudden interest in our shoes, shift from side to side, paralyzed, frozen to the spot, embarrassed for the little girl, empathizing furiously, wishing desperately it would all end: *Please, let her remember the words. Please. Somebody do something.*

[19]Maurice Cheeks, himself a father, did what all fathers, and grandfathers, too, in moments of heroic reverie, dream they would do. [20]He tried to make the world go away.

[21]Seeing as how his team was one loss away from elimination, he might have been expected to have other things on his mind than a junior high school girl who had won a contest to sing "The Star-Spangled Banner" before tip-off of the most crucial game of the year.

22And yet, there he was, not sure how exactly, walking to center court. 23And once there, this thought stabbed him:

24"I wasn't sure whether I knew the words myself," he said, laughing.

25"I just didn't want her to be out there all alone."

26For those of us who chronicled Maurice Cheeks during his tenure in Philadelphia, what he did was totally in character. 27The man was never the self-absorbed prima donna so many have become. 28He played a spare, bare-bones, beautifully economical game, and wanted very much to disappear as soon as the game was over. 29He had no more a desire for the spotlight than he did for flamboyance on the court.

30The best point guards are sharers and protectors and soothers. 31The best of them understand how to get the ball to the right people in the right place at the right time. 32The best of them watch out for everybody else.

33Maurice Cheeks is still a point guard at heart.

34The Trail Blazers haven't given Portland much to be proud of. 35It is a dysfunctional team, full of head cases and temperamental malcontents. 36But in one impromptu moment, Maurice Cheeks gave everyone a reason to be proud.

37It has become a touchstone, this act of compassion. 38There isn't a TV network that hasn't played snippets of the coach coaching the little girl singing the anthem.

39There is a reason so many want to show it, to write of it, to celebrate it. 40Because it resonates so, because it strums one of our most emotional chords, because it reminds us of the stirring capabilities of the human spirit.

41"I guess," Maurice Cheeks said, a bit uncomfortable at the thought, "it has become a moment."

42Oh, yes. 43Yes, it has.

44One shining moment.

45Of grace.

Item A:
Not supported.
Item B: Yes.
See sentence 9.
Item C: Not supported; many young people are excellent performers.
Item D: Not supported; this might have been the first time.
Item E: Yes. In helping Natalie, Maurice Cheeks demonstrates a fatherly concern which links him to the world outside of basketball.
Item F: Not supported. **Item G:** Yes. See sentence 27. **Item H:** Yes. Maurice Cheeks is a professional coach. His actions demonstrate that he is unspoiled and compassionate.

Check (✓) the **five** inferences that can best be made about the story.

____ A. Natalie Gilbert will never sing in front of an audience again.

✓ B. The audience was inspired by the fact that Maurice Cheeks helped Natalie Gilbert sing the national anthem.

____ C. Young people should not be encouraged to perform in front of live audiences.

____ D. Natalie always got stage fright when she performed.

✓ E. Maurice Cheeks knows that there's more to life than basketball.

____ F. Natalie had never sung in public before.

✓ G. Professional athletes tend to be so self-involved that they are unable to relate to ordinary people.

✓ H. Not all professional athletes and coaches are spoiled and self-centered.

Item I: Yes. See   ✓   I. Bill Lyon thinks that professional sports needs more people like
sentences 34–36.   Maurice Cheeks.
Item J: Nothing
in the passage   ___   J. Maurice Cheeks is a professional singer as well as an athlete.
supports this inference.

INFERENCES IN TABLES AND GRAPHS

You have already tried your hand at making inferences about a picture—the
cartoon involving the dog at the beginning of this chapter. To understand many of
the cartoons in newspapers and magazines, you must use your inference skills.
Other "pictures" that require inferences are tables and graphs, which combine
words with visual representations. Authors of textbooks, professional and
newspaper articles, and other materials often organize large amounts of material
into tables and graphs. Very often, the graphs and tables are used to show
comparisons and changes that take place over time.

As with other reading material, to infer the ideas presented in tables and
graphs, you must consider all the information presented.

Steps in Reading a Table or Graph

To find and make sense of the information in a table or graph, follow a few steps.

1 Read the title. It will tell you what the table or graph is showing in general.

  • What is the title of the graph on the next page? _____
  _____*Stages of Sleep*_____

2 Check the source. At the bottom of a table or graph, you will usually find the
source of the information, an indication of the reliability of its material.

  • What is the source for the graph on the next page? _____
  _____*Dianne Hales,* An Invitation to Health, *11th edition*_____

3 Read any labels or captions at the top, the side, or underneath that tell
exactly what each column, line, bar, number, or other item represents. This
information includes such things as quantities, percentages, and years.

☑ *Check Your Understanding*

Study the graph below and then check (✓) the **three** inferences that are most logically based on the information in the graph. Then read the explanation that follows.

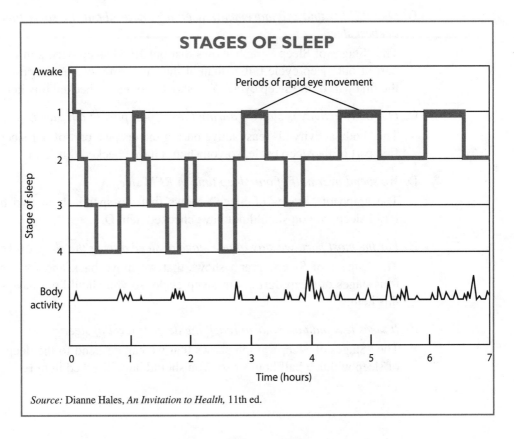

STAGES OF SLEEP

Periods of rapid eye movement

Source: Dianne Hales, *An Invitation to Health,* 11th ed.

  ✓   A. Our deepest sleep occurs early in the sleep cycle.

  ____   B. Our REM (rapid eye movement) sleep occurs at about the same time as our deepest sleep.

  ✓   C. Our body activity is slowest during the deepest part of our sleep.

  ____   D. We spend over half of our sleep time in REM sleep.

  ____   E. For the most part, we stay in one stage of sleep during the sleep cycle.

  ✓   F. It takes less than an hour to reach the deepest level of sleep.

Explanation:

A. *Our deepest sleep occurs early in the sleep cycle.*

The "Stages of Sleep" graph shows that we are in the deepest sleep in the first three hours or so of the sleep cycle. You should have checked item A.

B. *Our REM (rapid eye movement) sleep occurs at about the same time as our deepest sleep.*

The "Stages of Sleep" graph shows that our REM sleep occurs in the second part of our sleep cycle rather than at the same time of our deepest sleep, in the first part of the sleep cycle. You should not have checked this item.

C. *Our body activity is slowest during the deepest part of our sleep.*

The "body activity" is least active during the deepest part of our sleep, in the first part of the sleep cycle, so you should have checked this item.

D. *We spend over half of our sleep time in REM sleep.*

The graph of "Stages of Sleep" shows that we spend about two hours in REM sleep, so you should not have checked item D.

E. *For the most part, we stay in one stage of sleep during the sleep cycle.*

The "Stages of Sleep" graph shows that we move back and forth between four stages of sleep during our sleep cycle, so you should not have checked this item.

F. *It takes less than an hour to reach the deepest level of sleep.*

The "Stages of Sleep" graph shows that we can descend to the deepest level of sleep within a half hour or so. You should have checked item F.

➤ *Practice 5*

Read the table below, following the steps on page 232. Then check (✓) the **three** inferences that are most logically based on the table.

Who Gets What? Income Shares of American Households

The following table demonstrates how much of the nation's income is received by people within each quintile (or fifth) of the population.

INCOME QUINTILE	1960	1970	1980	1990	2002
Lowest fifth	4.9	5.5	5.1	4.6	3.5
Second fifth	11.8	12.0	11.6	10.8	8.8
Third fifth	17.6	17.4	17.5	16.6	14.8
Fourth fifth	23.6	23.5	24.3	23.8	23.3
Highest fifth	42.0	41.6	41.6	44.3	49.7

Source: U.S. Census Bureau, "Income in the United States," Table A-3, 2003

Item A: Yes, they received nearly 50% of the nation's income, making them America's richest people.

Item B: Yes. See the percentages under the column for 2002.

Item C: No, the poor got poorer. Their share of national income declined from 4.9% to 3.5%.

Item D: Yes. Although they had a slight dip in 1970 and 1980, overall their income has risen from 42.0% to 49.7%—a gain of 7.7%.

✓ A. The people in the highest fifth are the richest people in America.

✓ B. The people in the lowest fifth received just 3.5 percent of the nation's income in 2002, while the people in the highest fifth received 49.7 percent of the nation's income.

___ C. In the years between 1960 and 2002, the poor have not gotten richer or poorer but have stayed about the same.

✓ D. In the years between 1960 and 2002, the rich have been getting richer.

___ E. From 1980 to 2002, a period of great economic growth, both the poorest people and the richest people experienced a growth in income.

___ F. From 1980 to 2002, a period of great economic growth, both people in the middle income groups and the richest people experienced a growth in income.

Item E: No. Although the richest experienced a rise, the poorest had a decline from 5.1% to 3.5%.

Item F: No. The share of national income declined for people in the middle income groups, but rose for the richest people.

CHAPTER REVIEW

In this chapter, you learned the following:

- Many important ideas in reading are not stated directly, but must be inferred. To make inferences about implied ideas, use the information provided as well as your own experience and logic.

- Inferences are also a key part of reading literature and such visual materials as cartoons, tables, and graphs.

The next chapter—Chapter 7—will help make you aware of an author's purpose and tone.

On the Web: If you are using this book in class, you can visit our website for additional practice in making inferences. Go to **www.townsendpress.com** and click on "Online Exercises."

➤ Review Test 1

To review what you've learned in this chapter, answer each of the following questions by filling in the blank or writing the letter of the correct answer.

1. We make inferences by "reading between the lines" and picking up ideas that are not directly _____*stated*_____ in what we are reading.
   See page 217.

2. A reader must make _____*inferences*_____ when determining the meaning of words through context and when deciding on implied main ideas.
   See page 218.

___D___ 3. To make sound inferences, we must use
   A. all the information provided by the writer.
   B. our own experience.   See pages 218 and 222–223.
   C. logic.
   D. all of the above.

4. Creative writers often use comparisons to suggest what they mean. _____*Similes*_____ are direct comparisons introduced with *like* or *as* or *as if*, and metaphors are implied comparisons with *like* or *as* or *as if* omitted.
   See pages 227–228.

5. In textbooks we must often _____*infer*_____ the ideas presented
   in graphs and tables.

See page 232.

➤ *Review Test 2*

The essay below is followed by questions on inferences and also on the skills you
have practiced in previous chapters.

Preview

Why are women so very critical of the way they look? And why are men so very
. . . not? Humorist Dave Barry explores this difference between the sexes in a way
that ties together supermodels, lawn care, and a well-known plastic doll.

Words to Watch

bloat (4): swell
regimen (5): process
mutation (8): an organism resulting from a DNA change
bolster (9): make stronger

THE UGLY TRUTH ABOUT BEAUTY

Dave Barry

1   If you're a man, at some point a woman
will ask you how she looks.

2   "How do I look?" she'll ask.

3   You must be careful how you answer
this question. The best technique is to
form an honest yet sensitive opinion,
then collapse on the floor with some kind
of fatal seizure. Trust me, this is the
easiest way out. Because you will never
come up with the right answer.

4   The problem is that women generally do not think of their looks in the
same way that men do. Most men form
an opinion of how they look in the
seventh grade, and they stick to it for the
rest of their lives. Some men form the
opinion that they are irresistible stud
muffins, and they do not change this
opinion even when their faces sag and
their noses bloat° to the size of eggplants
and their eyebrows grow together to form
what appears to be a giant forehead-
dwelling tropical caterpillar.

5   Most men, I believe, think of themselves as average-looking. Men will think
this even if their faces cause heart failure
in cattle at a range of 300 yards. Being
average does not bother them; average is
fine, for men. This is why men never ask
anybody how they look. Their primary
form of beauty care is to shave
themselves, which is essentially the same

form of beauty care that they give to their lawns. If, at the end of his four-minute daily beauty regimen°, a man has managed to wipe most of the shaving cream out of his hair and is not bleeding too badly, he feels that he has done all he can, so he stops thinking about his appearance and devotes his mind to more critical issues, such as the Super Bowl.

6   Women do not look at themselves in this way. If I had to express, in three words, what I believe most women think about their appearance, those words would be: "not good enough." No matter how attractive a woman may appear to be to others, when she looks at herself in the mirror, she thinks: woof. She thinks that at any moment a municipal animal-control officer is going to throw a net over her and haul her off to the shelter.

7   Why do women have such low self-esteem? There are many complex psychological and societal reasons, by which I mean Barbie. Girls grow up playing with a doll proportioned such that, if it were human, it would be seven feet tall and weigh 81 pounds, of which 53 pounds would be bosoms. This is a difficult appearance standard to live up to, especially when you contrast it with the standard set for little boys by their dolls . . . excuse me, by their action figures. Most of the action figures that my son played with when he was little were hideous-looking. For example, he was very fond of an action figure (part of the He-Man series) called "Buzz-Off," who was part human, part flying insect. Buzz-Off was not a looker. But he was extremely self-confident. You could not imagine Buzz-Off saying to the other action figures: "Do you think these wings make my hips look big?"

8   But women grow up thinking they need to look like Barbie, which for most

women is impossible, although there is a multibillion-dollar beauty industry devoted to convincing women that they must try. I once saw an Oprah show wherein supermodel Cindy Crawford dispensed makeup tips to the studio audience. Cindy had all these middle-aged women applying beauty products to their faces; she stressed how important it was to apply them in a certain way, using the tips of their fingers. All the women dutifully did this, even though it was obvious to any sane observer that, no matter how carefully they applied these products, they would never look remotely like Cindy Crawford, who is some kind of genetic mutation°.

9   I'm not saying that men are superior. I'm just saying that you're not going to get a group of middle-aged men to sit in a room and apply cosmetics to themselves under the instruction of Brad Pitt, in hopes of looking more like him. Men would realize that this task was pointless and demeaning. They would find some way to bolster° their self-esteem that did not require looking like Brad Pitt. They would say to Brad: "Oh YEAH? Well, what do you know about LAWN CARE, pretty boy?"

10   Of course many women will argue that the reason they become obsessed with trying to look like Cindy Crawford is that men, being as shallow as a drop of spit, WANT women to look that way. To which I have two responses:

11   1. Hey, just because WE'RE idiots, that does not mean YOU have to be; and

12   2. Men don't even notice 97 percent of the beauty efforts you make anyway. Take fingernails. The average woman spends 5,000 hours per year worrying about her fingernails; I have never once, in more than 40 years of listening to men talk about women, heard a man say, "She

has a nice set of fingernails!" Many men would not notice if a woman had upward of four hands.

13   Anyway, to get back to my original point: If you're a man, and a woman asks you how she looks, you're in big trouble. Obviously, you can't say she looks bad. But you also can't say that she looks great, because she'll think you're lying, because she has spent countless hours, with the help of the multi-billion dollar beauty industry, obsessing about the differences between herself and Cindy Crawford. Also, she suspects that you're not qualified to judge anybody's appearance. This is because you have shaving cream in your hair.

Reading Comprehension Questions

Vocabulary in Context

   A   1. In the excerpt below, the word *demeaning* (dĭ-mēn′ĭng) means
- A. insulting.
- B. difficult.
- C. strange.
- D. disgusting.

The passage suggests that men have enough self-esteem to view efforts to improve their looks as insulting.

"I'm just saying that you're not going to get a group of middle-aged men to sit in a room and apply cosmetics to themselves under the instruction of Brad Pitt, in hopes of looking more like him. Men would realize that this task was pointless and demeaning." (Paragraph 9)

Central Point and Main Ideas

   C   2. Which sentence best expresses the implied central point of the selection?

Answer A covers only parts of paragraphs 7 and 8. Answer B does not address the contrasting attitudes of men and women toward appearance. Answer D covers only paragraphs 1–3 and 13.

- A. Women have been brought up to believe that they should look like real-life Barbie dolls, even though this is impossible.
- B. In our society, women tend to have lower self-esteem than men.
- C. Because of the way they have been brought up, most women spend far more time worrying about their appearance than men do.
- D. It is impossible for men to tell women the truth about how they look because women will not believe them.

   D   3. The implied main idea of paragraphs 8 and 9 is that

The two paragraphs contrast what men and women have been led to believe about their looks. Answers A and C cover only paragraph 8. Answer B is not supported.

- A. middle-aged women who try to look like Cindy Crawford are foolish.
- B. men have more important things to do than to compare themselves to Brad Pitt.
- C. the beauty industry convinces many women that they should try to look like Cindy Crawford, an impossible task.
- D. in contrast to women, men have not been led to believe that their looks are the most important thing about them.

Supporting Details

___B___ 4. The author's son played with an action figure who was
   A. attractive and self-confident.
   B. hideous-looking but self-confident.
   C. neither attractive nor self-confident.
   D. worried about the size of his hips.

   See paragraph 7.
   Buzz-Off is an example of a
   hideous-looking action figure
   who is nonetheless self-confident.

___D___ 5. One thing the author has never heard a man say is
   A. "I'm shallow as a drop of spit."
   B. "Honey, you look bad."
   C. "Honey, you look great."
   D. "She has a nice set of fingernails."

   See paragraph 12.

Transitions

___B___ 6. The relationship of the second sentence below to the first sentence is one of
   A. addition.
   B. cause and effect.
   C. time.
   D. comparison.

   Cause: Barbie; *effect:* low self-esteem.
   The word *reasons* signals
   a cause and effect relationship.

   "Why do women have such low self-esteem? There are many complex psychological <u>reasons</u>, by which I mean Barbie." (Paragraph 7)

Patterns of Organization

___C___ 7. The selection mainly
   A. defines and illustrates related terms.
   B. narrates a series of events in time order.
   C. compares and contrasts women's attitudes toward their physical appearance with men's.
   D. lists a variety of strategies that women and men can use to change their attitudes toward physical appearance.

   The first sentence in
   paragraph 4 suggests a comparison/contrast pattern of organization.

Inferences

___C___ 8. We can infer from paragraph 5 that the author believes that
   A. most men are ugly, not average-looking.
   B. most men are afraid to ask people how they really look.
   C. most men don't spend much time grooming themselves or thinking about the way they look.
   D. the Super Bowl is a critical issue.

   Answers A and B are unsupported.
   The humorous tone of the selection indicates that the Super Bowl
   is not really a critical issue. Therefore Answer D is incorrect.

___A___ 9. Based on paragraph 6, we can infer that the author believes that

Barry says that most women think their appearance is "not good enough." Answers B, C, and D are not supported. (D is not supported because the words *impossible* and *ever* make it too absolute.)

A. most women have an unrealistically negative view of their own appearance.

B. most women waste time in front of mirrors because they're spoiled and lazy.

C. many women become uncontrollably angry when they see themselves in a mirror.

D. it is impossible for a woman to ever be pleased with her appearance.

___A___ 10. We can conclude from the last two paragraphs that many women

Barry says that men don't notice 97% of the beauty efforts women make. Answers B, C, and D are not supported because the paragraphs do not discuss these issues.

A. overestimate the amount of attention men pay to women's appearances.

B. dislike men because they care so little about their own appearance.

C. are annoyed that the beauty industry forces them to spend countless hours worrying about their appearance.

D. believe that men with shaving cream in their hair are big trouble.

Discussion Questions

1. Although Barry's piece is written for laughs, he obviously has something serious to say about women and men and their feelings about their appearances. In non-humorous language, how would you rephrase his main points?

2. Think about the women you know. How much time would you say that they devote to clothing, hairstyles, and makeup? On the basis of your answer, do you agree with the author's view that women spend far too much time worrying about how they look? Why or why not?

3. Do you agree or disagree with the author's negative view of the role Barbie dolls play in shaping American girls' image of themselves? Once the girls have grown up, to what extent would you say that external forces, such as the media and the fashion industry, influence their feelings about their own appearances? Explain your reasoning.

4. Do you agree with Barry that men are generally satisfied with their own appearance? Why might their standards be so different from those of women?

Note: Writing assignments for this selection appear on page 563.

Check Your Performance   **INFERENCES**

Activity	Number Right	Points		Score
Review Test 1 (5 items)	_____	× 6	=	_____
Review Test 2 (10 items)	_____	× 7	=	_____
		TOTAL SCORE	=	_____%

Enter your total score into the **Reading Performance Chart: Review Tests** on the inside back cover.

INFERENCES: Mastery Test 1

For each item, put a check (✓) by the **two** inferences most logically based on the information provided.

Passage 1:
A—The author makes no reference to himself in the quotation.
B—Social and economic disadvantages are obstacles. For Washington, who was born a slave, over-coming obstacles defines success.
C—The statement ignores the idea of overcoming obstacles, since a millionaire's son would have few obstacles to overcome.
D—The author would not admire someone who had achieved success without overcoming obstacles.

1. "Success is to be measured not so much by the position that one has reached in life as by the obstacles which he has overcome." —Booker T. Washington

_____ A. The author considers himself to be a hero.

✓ B. People can achieve success even if they were born with few, if any, social and economic advantages.

_____ C. The author is telling us that we should naturally respect the son of a millionaire.

✓ D. The author does not necessarily admire all successful men.

2. "Our only hope will lie in the frail web of understanding of one person for the pain of another." —John Dos Passos

✓ A. If we don't learn to better understand each other, we may all be doomed.

_____ B. Some people are very skillful in hiding their personal pain from others.

Passage 2:
A—The words *Our only hope* and *frail web* suggest the possibility of doom. B—Nothing in the quotation suggests that pain is being hidden.
C—Contradicted by the idea that there can be a "web of understanding."
D—Empathy is another word for the understanding Dos Passos speaks of.

_____ C. It is impossible to comprehend the pain of others.

✓ D. Everyone needs empathy—the ability to walk in another's shoes.

3. "You must be the change you wish to see in the world." —Mahatma Gandhi

✓ A. People should lead by setting a good example for others to follow.

✓ B. Before you can make the world a better place, you must first conquer your own inner demons.

_____ C. Don't criticize others until you have first attained perfection.

_____ D. It's harder to change the world than it is to change yourself.

Passage 3:
A—If people see you change for the better, they will be more likely to make similar changes.
B—If you can't conquer your own demons, what *can* you conquer?
C—Gandhi does not suggest that perfection is attainable. D—Gandhi doesn't say which is more difficult.

4. "I have decided to stick with love. Hate is too great a burden to bear." —Martin Luther King, Jr.

✓ A. Martin Luther King, Jr., was tempted to hate his adversaries, but realized that harboring such an emotion would only hurt himself.

_____ B. Only very strong people can successfully carry the burden of hate.

_____ C. It takes a strong person to hate someone else.

✓ D. Hate is a waste of time and energy.

Passage 4: A—The words "I have decided" suggest that the author was tempted to hate, but decided against it. B—The author suggests that hate is a burden which cannot be successfully carried.
C—The author does not say one must be strong to hate, only that hatred is a great burden. D—We know that Martin Luther King, Jr. used his time and energy to work for constructive change.

(Continues on next page)

A—The metaphor of a heart as a "dark forest" suggests that people can never entirely know each other.

5. "The heart of another is a dark forest, always, no matter how close it has been to one's own." —Willa Cather

  ✓   A. People can never really completely know each other.

  ___   B. People who have been close friends often become enemies.

  ✓   C. Even the most intimate friends may keep secrets from one another.

  ___   D. Some people like to keep others in the dark in order to trick them.

B—There is no reference to enemies in the quotation.

C—Cather suggests that even those who are close friends, and who presumably would know what is in each other's heart, can keep secrets from one another. The words *a dark forest* support this idea.

D—There is no suggestion of trickery in the quotation.

INFERENCES: Mastery Test 2

A. (1–4.) Put a check (✓) by the **four** inferences that are most logically based on the details in the cartoon.

Part A: **Item A**— The problem is not with the remote; the problem is that the man is not pointing it at a TV.

Items B, C, and H—The cartoon implies that Americans are so used to looking at TV that they no longer recognize books, much less read them.

Item D—The man doesn't appear interested in reading books. His anger is directed at the remote, not the books.

Item E—The caption indicates that the man is an American.

Item F—The symbols in the thought bubble indicate that the man is cursing the remote.

Item G—The fact that the man has a remote suggests that he owns a TV set.

WHY AMERICANS DON'T READ...

___ A. Something is the matter with the man's remote control.

✓ B. The man thinks his bookshelf is a TV set.

✓ C. The man no longer recognizes books when he sees them.

___ D. The man is angry because he doesn't have a new book to read.

___ E. The man in the cartoon is not an American.

✓ F. The man believes that his remote control is not working properly.

___ G. The man does not own a TV set.

✓ H. The cartoonist believes that watching TV makes people less literate.

B. (5–10.) Read the passages below. Then check the **two** inferences that are most logically supported in each passage.

Part B—5–6: **Item A**—Referring to himself as Superman suggests that Ali is not a modest man.

Item B— The passage refers to Ali as a "boxing legend." Also, experience tells us that Ali is one of the world's most famous men.

Item C— The attendant's reply suggests that if Ali doesn't fasten his seat belt, he has to get off the plane—and also that Ali is not Superman.

Item D—We don't know how Ali responded.

5–6. [1]Shortly before takeoff, a flight attendant approached boxing legend Muhammad Ali and asked him to fasten his seat belt. [2]Ali gave her his famous smile and said, "Superman don't need no seat belt."

[3]"That may be," said the flight attendant. [4]"But Superman don't need no airplane, either."

___ A. Ali was a modest man.

✓ B. Ali assumed the flight attendant knew who he was.

✓ C. The flight attendant wasn't going to give a famous passenger special privileges.

___ D. Ali never did fasten his seat belt.

(Continues on next page)

245

7–8:   7–8. [1]Group A of college students was asked to chaperone delinquent juveniles on a
Item A—By first field trip to the zoo. [2]Only 32 percent said yes. [3]Group B of college students
asking for a two- was asked to commit to two years' service as volunteer counselors to delin-
year
commitment, quent children. [4]All said no. [5]But when that request was immediately followed
then making a up by a request to chaperone the zoo field trip, 56 percent of Group B said yes.
much more
modest request, ✓ A. It is good strategy to ask first for more than you really hope to receive.
people got a
better response. ___ B. College students in general do not feel any obligation to help others.

Item B— ___ C. The college students would probably have agreed to volunteer for
A 32% and a   two years with elderly people.
56% positive
response ✓ D. A promise to volunteer for two years is a big commitment.
indicates
that some 9–10. [1]Personal distress means our own emotional reactions to the plight of
college students others—our feelings of shock, horror, alarm, concern, or helplessness.
feel obligated [2]Personal distress occurs when people who witness an event are preoccupied
to help others.
with their own emotional reactions. [3]In contrast, empathy means feelings of
Item C— sympathy and caring for others, in particular, sharing vicariously or
The passage indirectly in the suffering of others. [4]Empathy occurs when the observer
does not mention focuses on the needs and emotions of the victim. [5]Personal distress leads us
elderly people. to feel anxious and apprehensive; empathy leads us to feel sympathetic and
Item D—See compassionate. [6]Research suggests that the distinctive emotions generated by
sentences 3–4. personal distress and empathy may actually be accompanied by distinctive
The fact that physiological reactions, including heart rate patterns and facial expressions.
none of the
students ✓ A. People who experience personal distress in response to the plight of
volunteered for   others are less likely to take constructive action than people who feel
two years implies   empathy.
that they felt it was a
big commitment. ___ B. People who experience personal distress in response to the plight of
                others will respond in roughly the same way as people who feel
9–10:   empathy.
Item A—See ___ C. The author suggests that feelings of personal distress are more
sentences   realistic than feelings of empathy.
2 and 5.
They are ✓ D. The author suggests that empathy is a more positive emotion than
"preoccupied"   personal distress.
with their own feelings.

Item B—The passage contradicts this by suggesting that people who feel personal distress will be less
likely than people who feel empathy to respond positively to the plight of others.

Item C—The passage does not discuss which reaction is more realistic.

Item D—See sentence 5. Sympathy and compassion are clearly more positive reactions than anxiety
and apprehension.

INFERENCES: Mastery Test 3

A. (1–4.) Put a check (✓) by the **four** inferences that are most logically based on the details in the cartoon.

Copyright 2003 by Randy Glasbergen. www.glasbergen.com

GLASBERGEN

"What fits your busy schedule better, exercising one hour a day or being dead 24 hours a day?"

Item A: The fact that the doctor is asking the patient what fits his busy schedule better, exercising or being dead, suggests that the patient has claimed he is too busy to exercise.

Item B: If the patient had an incurable illness, the doctor would not be recommending exercise.

Item C: We don't know if the patient will follow the doctor's advice. The expression on his face indicates that he is not happy to hear the advice.

✓ A. The patient has claimed he is too busy to exercise.

___ B. The patient has an incurable illness.

___ C. The patient will take the doctor's advice and begin exercising.

✓ D. The doctor believes the patient needs to exercise more.

___ E. The patient is angry at the doctor.

___ F. Currently, the patient exercises more than an hour a day.

✓ G. The doctor has just examined the patient.

✓ H. Exercise can help people live longer.

Item D: The doctor implies that unless the patient starts exercising an hour a day, he will soon die.

Item E: The patient looks surprised and dismayed, but not angry.

Item F: Experience tells us that doctors would not tell overweight patients to cut back on exercise.

Item G: The doctor is wearing a stethoscope and carrying a clipboard. The patient has stripped down to his undershirt and shorts. There is an examining table in the background.

Item H: Experience tells us that exercise can help us live longer. In the cartoon, the doctor is saying, in effect, that *not* exercising will result in death.

(Continues on next page)

B. (5–10.) Read the passage below from J.R. Moehringer's acclaimed memoir *The Tender Bar.* Then check the **six** statements after the passage which are most logically supported by the information given.

> [1]Mom said that "Grandpa is a real-life Scrooge, and not just with money." [2]Grandpa hoarded love, my mother said, as if he were afraid of one day running out. [3]He'd ignored her and her sister and brother while they were growing up, giving them no attention or affection whatsoever. [4]She described one family outing at the beach when she was five. [5]Seeing how sweetly the father of her cousin played with his children, my mother asked Grandpa to put her on his shoulders in the ocean. [6]He did, but then carried her past the waves, and when they were out far, when she could barely see the shore, she became frightened and pleaded with him to let her down. [7]So he threw her. [8]Down she went, plunging to the bottom, gulping seawater. [9]She fought her way to the surface, gasped for air, and saw Grandpa— laughing. [10]"You wanted to be let down," he told her, oblivious to her tears. [11]Staggering out of the surf, alone, my mother had a precocious epiphany: Her father was not a good man. [12]In that realization, she told me, came a release. [13]She felt independent. [14]I asked her what "independent" meant. [15]"Free," she said.

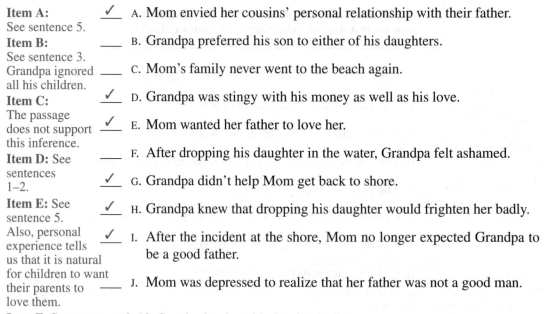

Item A:
See sentence 5.

✓ A. Mom envied her cousins' personal relationship with their father.

Item B:
See sentence 3.
Grandpa ignored all his children.

___ B. Grandpa preferred his son to either of his daughters.

Item C:
The passage does not support this inference.

___ C. Mom's family never went to the beach again.

✓ D. Grandpa was stingy with his money as well as his love.

Item D: See sentences 1–2.

✓ E. Mom wanted her father to love her.

Item E: See sentence 5.
Also, personal experience tells us that it is natural for children to want their parents to love them.

___ F. After dropping his daughter in the water, Grandpa felt ashamed.

✓ G. Grandpa didn't help Mom get back to shore.

✓ H. Grandpa knew that dropping his daughter would frighten her badly.

✓ I. After the incident at the shore, Mom no longer expected Grandpa to be a good father.

___ J. Mom was depressed to realize that her father was not a good man.

Item F: See sentences 9–10. Grandpa laughs at his daughter's distress.

Item G: See sentence 11.

Item H: See sentences 6–7.

Item I: See sentences 11–12.

Item J: See sentences 12–15. Mom was relieved to be free of false hopes concerning her father.

INFERENCES: Mastery Test 4

A. Identify the figure(s) of speech in each sentence as either a simile or a metaphor. Then answer each inference question that follows.

_B_ 1. In *The Divine Comedy,* Dante writes that at midlife he found himself "in a dark wood with no clear path through."

    A. simile   B. metaphor   This sentence omits the words *like, as,* or *as if,* which are found in similes.

_C_ 2. You can infer that Dante

    A. has been in this spot before.

    B. is hopeful despite doubts.

    C. is bewildered.

The words *dark wood* and *no clear path* indicate that Dante is bewildered, not hopeful. Nothing in the statement suggests that he has been in this spot before.

_A_ 3. A woman without a man is like a fish without a bicycle.

    A. simile   B. metaphor

This statement uses the word *like* to make a comparison.

_B_ 4. You can infer that a woman

    A. cannot function without a man.   A fish does not need a bicycle to swim,

    B. does not need a man to function.   just as a woman does not need a man to function.

    C. cannot ride a bicycle without a man.

_B_ 5. The accident at the chemical plant released a witch's brew into the atmosphere.   This statement does not use *like, as,* or *as if.*

    A. simile   B. metaphor

The chemicals are being compared to a witch's brew, suggesting

_C_ 6. You can infer that the chemical company   a harmful mixture. Answer A

    A. will quickly explain the cause of the accident. is not supported. Answer

    B. deliberately planned to get rid of some chemicals. B is contradicted

    C. released a mix of harmful chemicals into the atmosphere.   by the word *accident.*

B. (7–10.) Read the textbook passages below. Then check (✓) the **two** statements after the passage which are most logically supported by the information given.

7–8. [1]Two recent series of studies indicate that the adolescent's biological and cognitive maturation may play a role in unbalancing the family system during early adolescence. [2]Several researchers have demonstrated that family relationships change during puberty, with conflict between adolescents and their parents increasing—especially between adolescents and their mothers—and closeness between adolescents and their parents diminishing somewhat. [3]Although puberty seems to distance adolescents from their parents, it is not associated with familial "storm and stress." [4]The conflict is

(Continues on next page)

7–8:

Item A—See sentence 2.

Item B—The passage does not draw a distinction between girls and boys as to who bicker more with their mothers.

Item C—The passage states that conflicts between parents and adolescents increase during puberty (sentence 2), but that parents and children still love and respect one another (sentence 5). This suggests that adolescence is a normal but trying period.

Item D—No other period of life is discussed.

9–10:

Item A—Experience tells us that the new technologies eventually became available to the poor. Also, the words *and later for most others* (sentence 2) indicate the gap was not "unbridgeable."

Item B—See sentence 3.

Item C—The passage does not indicate that the poor were angry.

Item D—See sentences 4–6. Access to privacy increased in the late 19th and early 20th centuries.

more likely to take the form of bickering over day-to-day issues like household chores than outright fighting. ⁵Similarly, the diminished closeness is more likely to be manifested in increased privacy on the part of the adolescent and diminished physical affection between teenagers and parents, rather than any serious loss of love or respect between parents and children.

  ✓   A. Fathers may not notice much change in their relationships with their adolescent children.

  ___   B. During adolescence, girls are more likely than boys to bicker with their mothers.

  ✓   C. Adolescence is a normal but sometimes trying period.

  ___   D. Adolescence is the most difficult period of life.

9–10. ¹In the late 19th and early 20th centuries, new technologies led to momentous changes in home life. ²Advanced systems of central heating (furnaces), artificial lighting, and modern indoor plumbing resulted in a new kind of consumption, first for middle-class households and later for most others. ³Whereas formerly families bought coal or chopped wood for cooking and heating, made candles for light, and hauled water for bathing, they increasingly connected to outside pipes and wires for gas, electricity, and water. ⁴Moreover, these utilities helped create new attitudes about privacy. ⁵Middle-class bedrooms and bathrooms became comfortable private retreats. ⁶Even children could have their own bedrooms, complete with individualized decoration. ⁷Also, though not affordable for the poor, central heat and artificial light made it possible for the middle class to enjoy a steady, comfortable temperature and turn night into day, while indoor plumbing removed the unpleasant experiences of the outhouse.

  ___   A. In the late 19th and early 20th centuries, new technologies created unbridgeable gaps between the middle class and the poor.

  ✓   B. In the late 19th and early 20th centuries, new technologies helped reduce the amount of labor associated with housekeeping.

  ___   C. The poor were angry that they could not enjoy the new technologies available to the middle class.

  ✓   D. In the early 19th century, people didn't have as much access to privacy as they would later have.

INFERENCES: Mastery Test 5

A. (1–5.) Read the passage below. Then check the **five** statements after the passage which are most logically supported by the information given.

¹None of us escape the changes that the years bring. ²Lines deepen, jowls sag, chins seem to melt, eyelids droop. ³We may not greet these changes with joy, but until recent years, we learned to live with them. ⁴More than live with them, in fact; many of us learned to cherish the changes that time wrought on the faces of those we loved. ⁵A spouse's laugh lines or a parent's furrowed brow became dear to us, as visible signs of the person's evolving inner being. ⁶But that is changing. ⁷The increasing popularity of cosmetic surgery—ever more drastic and at ever-younger ages—is turning us into a nation of smooth-faced ciphers: personality-challenged masks with unlined brows and wide, surprised eyes. ⁸Instead of admiring their elders as models of graceful aging, youngsters today see their grandparents getting nipped and tucked in a never-ending—and unwinnable—battle against nature. ⁹Ordinary people are increasingly following the leads of youth-obsessed celebrities, who have been desperately fighting the anti-aging battle for decades. ¹⁰It is to the point where it is surprising to find some brave Hollywood soul who is willing to look his or her years. ¹¹When an icon like Robert Redford, long admired for allowing his handsome face to grow more craggy and weather-beaten, showed up in public with a shiny new facelift, many hearts sank. ¹²Who will stand up for the beauty that comes with age?

Item A: See sentences 5–7. Signs of "graceful aging" are contrasted with the "personality-challenged masks" of those who have had cosmetic surgery.

Item B: The passage states that cosmetic surgery is becoming increasingly popular at ever-younger ages, but does not suggest that the "very young" are being targeted by plastic surgeons.

Item C: The growing popularity of cosmetic surgery suggests that people prefer appearance to emotional maturity.

Item D: See sentences 8–9.

Item E: Not mentioned in the passage.

Item F: Although the writer is disappointed that Redford had a face-lift, she stops far short of calling him a coward.

Item G: See sentences 3–4. Experience tells us that most people are more concerned about their own appearance than someone else's.

Item H: Not supported.

Item I: See sentence 11.

Item J: See sentence 9. People are paying attention to what celebrities are doing, not to what young people are saying.

✓ A. Signs of aging give people's faces a beauty and dignity which surgically altered faces lack.

___ B. Plastic surgeons now mostly market themselves to the very young.

✓ C. People today celebrate appearance over emotional maturity.

✓ D. Our society has an unrealistic obsession with appearing youthful.

___ E. People no longer treat senior citizens with love and respect.

___ F. In sharp contrast to his on-screen image, Robert Redford is actually a coward.

✓ G. People often appreciate signs of aging in others' faces more than in their own.

___ H. Robert Redford has found it hard to get movie roles as he has grown older.

✓ I. The writer previously admired Robert Redford more than she does now.

___ J. Young people today often encourage their elders to get cosmetic surgery.

(Continues on next page)

B. (6–10.) Read the passage below from Frank McCourt's acclaimed memoir *Teacher Man*. Then check the **five** statements after the passage which are most logically supported by the information given.

[1]Phyllis wrote an account of how her family gathered the night Neil Armstrong landed on the moon, how they shuttled between the living room television and the bedroom where her father lay dying. [2]Back and forth. [3]Concerned with the father, not wanting to miss the moon landing. [4]Phyllis said she was with her father when her mother called to come and see Armstrong set foot on the moon. [5]She ran to the living room, everyone cheering and hugging till she felt this urgency, the old urgency, and ran to the bedroom to find her father dead. [6]She didn't scream, she didn't cry, and her problem was how to return to the happy people in the living room to tell them Dad was gone.

[7]She cried now, standing in front of the classroom. [8]She could have stepped back to her seat in the front row, and I hoped she would because I didn't know what to do. [9]I went to her. [10]I put my left arm around her. [11]But that wasn't enough. [12]I pulled her to me, embraced her with both arms, let her sob into my shoulder. [13]Faces around the room were wet with tears till someone called, Right on, Phyllis, and one or two clapped and the whole class clapped and cheered and Phyllis turned to smile at them with her wet face and when I led her to her seat she turned and touched my cheek and I thought, This isn't earthshaking, this touch on the cheek, but I'll never forget it: Phyllis, her dead father, Armstrong on the moon.

✓ A. McCourt was teaching a course that involved writing.

✓ B. Phyllis did not want to spoil her family's joy at the moon landing.

___ C. Phyllis's fellow students thought she should have told her family immediately that her dad was dead.

___ D. Phyllis regretted that she wasn't in the bedroom with her dad when he died, but knew that she wasn't really at fault.

___ E. Phyllis will continue to feel guilty about missing her dad's death.

___ F. Phyllis's family did not care about her father.

✓ G. The events we tend to remember aren't necessarily earthshaking.

___ H. McCourt should not have embraced a student.

___ I. McCourt was probably not a very effective teacher.

✓ J. To McCourt, Phyllis's story shows how life goes on in the midst of death.

Item A: Phyllis must be reading her paper aloud, as often happens in a writing course.

Item B: See sentence 6.

Item C: See sentence 13. Also, the passage does not suggest that Phyllis actually delayed telling her family that her dad was dead, merely that she thought a moment about how to tell them.

Item D: Phyllis's calm reaction to her father's death (sentence 6) suggests that she did not berate herself for missing it. It was natural for her to want to see the moon landing.

Item E: Phyllis's smile at her classmates' encouragement (sentence 13) suggests that she does not feel guilty.

Item F: See sentences 1–3.

Item G: See sentence 13.

Item H: See sentences 10–11 and 13. As Phyllis's and her classmates' reactions indicate, McCourt did exactly what was needed.

Item I: The passage suggests that McCourt's students were highly engaged in the classroom—a sign of an effective teacher.

Item J: See sentence 13.

INFERENCES: Mastery Test 6

A. Read the graph below. Then check the **five** statements that are most logically based on the graph.

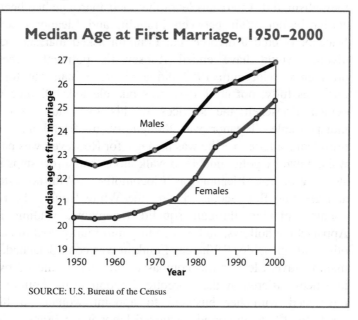

Median Age at First Marriage, 1950–2000

SOURCE: U.S. Bureau of the Census

Item A: No. For women, the rise begins in the mid-1960s.

Item B: Yes. The age has continuously increased for both men and women since 1965.

Item C: Yes. In 1960, the age for first marriage begins to rise for both women and men. This trend continues through 2000.

Item D: No. The rise was non-existent or slow until 1975.

Item E: Yes. The line representing males is always higher than the line representing females.

Item F: In 1950 they married at 20+ years; in 2000 the age was 25+ years.

Item G: No. The difference is only five years.

Item H: The fact that the age is rising suggests the opposite.

Item I: The fact that people are remaining single longer supports this inference.

Item J: No. In 1950, there was a difference of almost three years. After 50 years, a two-year difference is still present.

____ A. The median age for first marriage has been increasing gradually since the mid-1950s.

✓ B. The median age for first marriage has been increasing gradually since the mid-1960s.

✓ C. The median age for first marriage rose steadily from 1960 to 2000.

____ D. The median age for first marriage has risen with dramatic quickness over the years.

✓ E. In the period shown, men have always married at an older age than women.

✓ F. In the 1950s, women married at an age almost five years younger than they did fifty years later.

____ G. In the 1950s, women married at an age almost ten years younger than they did fifty years later.

____ H. Based on the graph, there is probably more pressure for young people to marry now than there was over fifty years ago.

✓ I. Based on the graph, remaining single has become a more acceptable lifestyle.

____ J. Based on the trends shown, women and men will probably marry at about the same age within the next decade.

(Continues on next page)

253

B. Read the following textbook passage. Then check the **five** statements after the passage which are most logically supported by the information given.

Item A: See sentence 2.

Item B: Sentence 2 contradicts this statement.

Item C: Since few were aware of it (sentence 2), Roosevelt's affair did not hurt his chance to become president.

Item D: See sentence 5. Experience tells us that divorce is common nowadays, and current attitudes reflect that fact.

Item E: See sentence 10.

Item F: See sentence 15. Eleanor Roosevelt's activism helped, not hurt, her husband's election chances.

Item G: See sentence 10.

Item H: See sentences 10–15. The fact that Eleanor Roosevelt is described as "remarkable" in sentence 1 suggests that most of what she did was untraditional.

Item I: Not supported.

Item J: See sentences 4 and 12–15.

[1]Not the least of President Franklin Roosevelt's assets was his remarkable wife, Eleanor. [2]Only much later, in the age of anything-goes journalism, did Americans learn that their marriage had been shattered years earlier by an affair between Franklin and Eleanor's personal secretary. [3]Eleanor offered a divorce, but Franklin asked that she stay with him. [4]A divorce would have ended Roosevelt's political career short of the presidency. [5]Not until 1952 did a divorced man run for the presidency, unsuccessfully; not until 1980 was one elected. [6]Divorce would also have denied Roosevelt the services of his one aide who may be called indispensable. [7]Eleanor was thought of by friend and foe alike as the president's alter ego. [8]She was his legs, for Roosevelt was paralyzed from the waist down by polio, unable to walk more than a few steps in heavy, painful steel leg braces. [9]Eleanor was a locomotive. [10]With no taste for serving tea and greeting Boy Scouts visiting the White House, she raced around the country, picking through squalid tenements, wading in the mud in Appalachian hollows, and descending into murky coal mines to see how the other half made do. [11]Whereas Franklin was cool, detached, calculating, and manipulative, Eleanor was compassionate, deeply moved by the misery and injustices suffered by the "forgotten" people at the bottom of society. [12]She interceded with her husband to appoint women to high government positions. [13]She supported organized labor when Franklin had to straddle a politically difficult decision. [14]She made the grievances of Americans her particular interest and persuaded her husband to name blacks to high government posts. [15]Much of the affection that came to Franklin in the form of votes was earned by "that woman in the White House."

✓   A. At the time, few Americans were aware of Franklin and Eleanor's marital problems.

___   B. The press during the Roosevelts' era reported extensively on Franklin's romantic adventures.

___   C. Franklin Roosevelt's affair hurt his chance to become president.

✓   D. Attitudes toward divorce have changed significantly since the days of Eleanor and Franklin Roosevelt.

✓   E. Eleanor Roosevelt believed in gaining firsthand information about the problems of people at the bottom of society.

___   F. Eleanor Roosevelt's activism harmed her husband's election chances.

✓   G. Eleanor Roosevelt was not very domestic, but she was very involved in national concerns.

___   H. Eleanor Roosevelt was in most ways a very traditional First Lady.

___   I. The author of this passage disapproved of Eleanor Roosevelt's activism.

✓   J. Eleanor Roosevelt's decision to stay with her husband, Franklin, affected the course of American history.

7

Purpose and Tone

Newspaper photos often have a purpose and tone. The purpose of the photo above, for example, is to inform us of the return of American soldiers killed in Iraq; the tone is one of solemnity, reverence, and respect. And behind what you read, there are often a purpose and tone as well. Consider that what you read has been written by a person with thoughts, feelings, and opinions. Whether this author is a sportswriter, a newspaper columnist, a novelist, or a friend sending you a letter, he or she works from a personal point of view. That point of view is reflected in (1) the purpose of a piece of writing as well as (2) its tone—the expression of the author's attitude and feeling. Both purpose and tone are discussed in this chapter.

PURPOSE

Authors write with a reason in mind, and you can better evaluate their ideas by determining what that reason is. The author's reason for writing is also called the **purpose** of a selection. Three common purposes are as follows:

- To **inform**—to give information about a subject. Authors with this purpose wish to provide facts that will explain or teach something to readers.

  For example, the main idea of an informative paragraph about bosses might be "Bosses have different styles of supervising." The author may then go on to describe an authoritarian boss whose word is law, contrasted with a more democratic boss who welcomes employees' input.

- To **persuade**—to convince the reader to agree with the author's point of view on a subject. Authors with this purpose may present facts, but their main goal is to argue or prove a point to readers.

  The main idea of a persuasive passage about bosses might read "Bosses should listen to their employees but take ultimate responsibility for making decisions." The author might then go on to support the point with details about problems that result from indecisive bosses.

  Note that words like *should*, *ought*, and *must* are often meant to convince us rather than to inform us.

- To **entertain**—to amuse and delight; to appeal to the reader's senses and imagination. Authors with this purpose entertain in various ways, through fiction as well as nonfiction.

  The main idea of a humorous paragraph about bosses might be "My boss is so dumb that he once returned a necktie because it was too tight."

While the cover and title of anything you read—books, articles, and so on—don't necessarily suggest the author's main purpose, often they do. Here are the covers of three books. See if you can guess the primary purpose of each of these books.

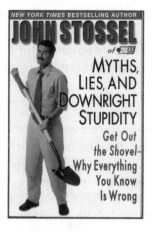

_A_ Primary purpose:
  A. to inform
  B. to persuade
  C. to entertain

_B_ Primary purpose:
  A. to inform
  B. to persuade
  C. to entertain

_C_ Primary purpose:
  A. to inform
  B. to persuade
  C. to entertain

As you probably concluded, the main purpose of the textbook is to inform; the main purpose of _Myths, Lies, and Downright Stupidity_ is to persuade (note the subtitle: "Get Out the Shovel—Why Everything You Know Is Wrong"); and the main purpose of the timeless story _The Hound of the Baskervilles,_ by Arthur Conan Doyle, is to entertain.

☑ *Check Your Understanding*

Read each of the three paragraphs below and decide whether the author's main purpose is to inform, to persuade, or to entertain. Write in your answers, and then read the explanation that follows.

1.   ¹The typical American gobbles three burgers and four orders of fries every week. ²Toss in the pizzas, the popcorn, the sugary breakfast cereals, the sodas, the snack cakes, candy bars, ice cream and everything else we eat in lieu of real food in this society, and your body is like an eighteen-wheeler roaring down a high-fat highway straight to obesity and an early grave. ³Fast food is bad food. ⁴It's loaded with bad stuff like fat and sugar and sodium. ⁵It's packed with chemicals that are in there to make it taste and smell and feel like it's real food. ⁶What it lacks is vitamins, minerals, fiber, all the stuff you really need.

   Purpose: _____ _Persuade_ _____

2.   ¹I don't know which is harder, taking my body to the doctor or my car to the garage. ²Both worry me. ³I'm always afraid they'll find something I didn't know about. ⁴The only advantage of taking my body to the doctor over taking my car to the garage is that the doctor never asks me to leave it overnight.

Purpose: _____ *Entertain* _____

3.   ¹Personal contact is necessary for common cold viruses to spread. ²The viruses must get into the nose, where they can infect the nasal membranes. ³Inhaling contaminated droplets produced when someone else coughs or sneezes may be one way to catch a cold. ⁴Cold viruses can remain infective even if they are outside the body for a few hours. ⁵Therefore, you can also catch a cold if you handle something that is contaminated with a cold virus—for example, the doorknob of a classroom or a restroom door—and then scratch your nose or rub your eyes with your contaminated fingers. ⁶The cold viruses can reach your nose when you rub your eyes because the virus can be passed down the tear ducts that go from the eyes into the nasal cavities.

Purpose: _____ *Inform* _____

Explanation:

In the first paragraph, the writer's purpose is to *persuade* readers that Americans should not indulge in fast food. The purpose of the second paragraph is to *entertain* with its playful and exaggerated details (clearly, the doctor is not going to ask the writer to leave his body overnight). The purpose of the third paragraph is to *inform* readers about how cold viruses spread.

Note: At times, writing may blend two or even three purposes. A persuasive article on the importance of avoiding junk foods, for example, might include a good many facts and even some comic touches. Remember in such cases to focus on the author's primary purpose. Ask yourself, "What is the author's main idea?"

➤ Practice 1

Label each item according to its main purpose: to inform (**I**), to persuade (**P**), or to entertain (**E**).

____I____   1. The average American carries $8,562 in credit-card debt.
                      An informative fact presented without emotion or humor.

____P____   2. High schools should require students to take a course in money management.   Persuasive clue: *should*.

____I____   3. The pigeon is one of the few birds that drinks by suction, rather than by tipping its head back to let gravity do the work.   Objective information.

_E_ 4. My doctor told me he had good news and bad news. I said, "Doc, only tell me the good news, all right?" He said, "All right. They're going to name a new disease after you." Humorous because, in delivering the good news, the doctor is also communicating the bad news.

_I_ 5. The writer Edgar Allan Poe married his first cousin, Virginia, when she was only 13. Straightforward information.

_P_ 6. The taboo against marriage between cousins is outdated and should be discarded. Persuasive clue: *should*.

_E_ 7. Cleaning the house is such a waste of time; a year later, you just have to do it again. The humor is in the length of time between cleanings.

_I_ 8. Lips often feel chapped and dry because they are protected only by a very thin layer of skin that contains no oil glands. A verifiable and informative fact.

_P_ 9. It would be better for students to attend small schools in their own neighborhoods, rather than being bused to large consolidated schools. Persuasive clue: *better*.

_E_ 10. My dog sleeps on the couch all day while I commute for an hour to a job I hate in order to make money to buy dog food. And I think that *he's* the dumb animal? The humor comes from the ease of the "dumb" dog's life compared with the stress that his owner goes through to feed him.

➤ Practice 2

In the space provided, indicate whether the primary purpose of each passage is to inform (**I**), to inform *and* persuade (**I+P**), or to entertain (**E**).

_I+P_ 1. ¹The Intrepid Fallen Heroes Fund provides assistance to our nation's military heroes—those who have been critically injured in the performance of duty—and their families. ²Double and triple amputations, severe head or body trauma, blindness, deafness, and partial or full paralysis are just some of the injuries our heroes have to endure today and for the rest of their lives. ³Many of our injured military personnel and veterans, who come from all branches of the armed forces, are treated at Brooke Army Medical Center in San Antonio, Texas. ⁴The American people, our military constituents, and allies around the world are united in heart for the care and rehabilitation of these men and women, who have sacrificed and are still suffering so much for the freedoms we enjoy today. ⁵Providing them with the best possible care is a small price to pay to say "thank you" for a job well done.

The author informs us of what the Intrepid Fallen Heroes Fund does and tries to persuade us to support it.

⁶This is why I would like to urge you to join this very special effort to help support those brave men and women by contributing to the Fund. ⁷100% of your donation goes directly to building this vitally-needed rehabilitation center. ⁸Browse our website at www.fallenheroesfund.org and join our effort in supporting our troops!

_____I_____ 2. ¹War is a state of widespread conflict between states, organizations, or relatively large groups of people, which is characterized by the use of lethal violence between combatants or upon civilians. ²Other terms for war, which often serve as euphemisms, include "armed conflict," "hostilities," and "police action." ³War is contrasted with peace, which is usually defined as the absence of war.

⁴A common perception of war is as a series of military campaigns between at least two opposing sides involving a dispute over sovereignty, territory, resources, religion or a host of other issues. ⁵A war to liberate an occupied country is sometimes characterized as a "war of liberation," while a war between internal elements of the same state may constitute a civil war.

The passage has no persuasive intent and is not funny. It simply defines war.

_____E_____ 3. ¹Only one ticket agent was on duty at the airline counter. ²As a result, a long line formed, filled with inconvenienced travelers. ³Suddenly, an irate passenger pushed his way to the front. ⁴He threw his ticket down and said, "I *have* to be on this flight, and it has to be *first class*."

⁵The agent replied, "Sir, I'll be happy to assist you, but I've got to help these folks first."

⁶The passenger was unimpressed. ⁷Loudly, he demanded, "Do you have any idea who I am?"

⁸Without hesitating, the gate agent smiled and grabbed the public address microphone. ⁹"May I have your attention, please?" she began, her voice sounding throughout the terminal. ¹⁰"We have a passenger here *who does not know who he is.* ¹¹If anyone can help him find his identity, please come to Gate D2."

The ticket agent is clearly making fun of the irate passenger.

TONE

A writer's **tone** reveals the attitude that he or she has toward a subject. Tone is expressed through the words and details the writer selects. Just as a speaker's voice can project a range of feelings, a writer's voice can project one or more tones, or feelings: anger, sympathy, hopefulness, sadness, respect, dislike, and so on. Understanding tone is, then, an important part of understanding what an author has written.

To appreciate the differences in tone that writers can employ, read the following statements by students of a demanding teacher.

She hates students, that's all there is to it. I can't wait until I'm out of her class. (*Tone:* Bitter, angry)

She's tough, but she's also really good. I've learned more from her than I've learned from any other teacher. (*Tone:* Fair, objective)

Yeah, I love her. Just like I love sleeping on a bed of nails or having bamboo slivers pushed under my fingernails. (*Tone:* Sarcastic)

I might as well just stop going to class now. I'm never going to understand the material. It's hopeless. (*Tone:* Pessimistic)

I think if I talk to her and explain what I'm having trouble with, she can help me sort it out. I'm going to figure out a way to deal with this. (*Tone:* Optimistic)

Words That Describe Tone

Below and on the next two pages are two lists of words commonly used to describe tone. With the exception of the words *matter-of-fact* and *objective*, the words reflect a feeling or judgment. The words in the first list are more familiar ones. Brief meanings are given in parentheses for the words in the second list. Refer to these meanings as needed to learn any words you don't know yet.

Some Words That Describe Tone

accepting	critical	joyous
admiring	cruel	loving
affectionate	curious	playful
alarmed	defensive	praising
amused	determined	regretful
angry	disapproving	respectful
apologetic	doubtful	self-critical
appreciative	encouraging	self-pitying
approving	excited	serious
ashamed	fearful	sorrowful
calming	forgiving	sympathetic
caring	frightened	threatening
cheerful	grateful	tragic
conceited	humorous	warm
concerned	insulting	worried

More Words That Describe Tone—With Their Meanings

ambivalent	(*uncertain about a choice*)
arrogant	(*full of self-importance; conceited*)
bewildered	(*confused; puzzled*)
bitter	(*angry; full of hate*)
compassionate	(*deeply sympathetic*)
cynical	(*distrustful and disbelieving*)
depressed	(*very sad or discouraged*)
despairing	(*giving up hope*)
detached	(*emotionally uninvolved*)
disbelieving	(*unbelieving*)
distressed	(*suffering sorrow, misery, or pain*)
hypocritical	(*false*)
impassioned	(*filled with strong feeling*)
indignant	(*angry about something wrong, unfair, or mean*)
instructive	(*teaching*)
ironic	(*contrary to what is expected or intended*)
lighthearted	(*happy and carefree*)
malicious	(*intending to do harm*)
matter-of-fact	(*sticking to facts; unemotional*)
mocking	(*making fun of and/or looking down upon something*)
nostalgic	(*longing for something or someone in the past*)
objective	(*not influenced by feelings or personal prejudices*)
optimistic	(*looking on the bright side of things*)
outraged	(*fiercely angered and shocked*)
pessimistic	(*looking on the gloomy, unfavorable side of things*)
pleading	(*begging*)
prideful	(*full of pride or exaggerated self-esteem*)
remorseful	(*guilty over a wrong one has done*)
revengeful	(*wanting to hurt someone in return for an injury*)
reverent	(*showing deep respect*)
sarcastic	(*sharp or wounding; ironic*)
scheming	(*tricky*)
scornful	(*looking down on someone or something*)
self-mocking	(*making fun of or looking down on oneself*)
sentimental	(*showing tender feelings; romantic; overly emotional*)
solemn	(*involved with serious concerns*)

(Continues on next page)

More Words That Describe Tone—With Their Meanings

straightforward	(*direct and honest*)
suggestive	(*tending to suggest an idea*)
superior	(*looking down on others*)
tolerant	(*respectful of other views and behavior; patient about problems*)
uncertain	(*doubting*)

☑ Check Your Understanding

Below are five statements expressing five reactions to Wal-Mart moving into a town. Five different tones are used:

A. accepting	B. cynical	C. indignant
D. threatening	E. worried	

Label each statement according to which of these five tones you think is present. Then read the explanation that follows.

_*E*_ 1. Wal-Mart may create an economic underclass in our town. Its employees aren't paid enough to live on, and they have very poor benefits.

_*A*_ 2. Wal-Mart is a fact of life. It's going to hurt some people, but at least we'll be able to buy a lot of things at lower prices.

_*D*_ 3. Wal-Mart had better not ever try to move into our town. They'll run into opposition like they've never seen before. We're not going to just lie down and let them take over.

_*B*_ 4. Our local government says Wal-Mart will benefit everyone. That's a joke. Wal-Mart is mainly going to benefit itself and our local politicians.

_*C*_ 5. Wal-Mart is run by a family of billionaire hypocrites who make huge profits by crushing little towns. They wave the flag about how great they are for America and then sell us stuff mostly made in China.

Explanation:

The first item has a *worried* tone, as the writer suggests that Wal-Mart's low wages and benefits may have a negative economic effect on the town. In the second item, the writer's statement that "Wal-Mart is a fact of life" indicates *acceptance*, as does her effort to balance the negative aspects of Wal-Mart with the benefit of lower prices. The tone of the third item is *threatening* because of the writer's clearly stated intention to help block Wal-Mart's move. In the fourth item, the writer clearly does not believe local government's claim that Wal-Mart will benefit everyone; her comment "That's a joke" gives the item a *cynical* tone. In the fifth item, the writer is *outraged* and *indignant* at what she perceives as the uncaring greed and hypocrisy of Wal-Mart.

A Note on Irony and Sarcasm

One commonly used tone is that of **irony**, which involves a contrast between expectations and reality. This contrast is often humorous. Both language and situations can be ironic.

Following are a few examples of **sarcasm**, an often biting form of verbal irony. Notice that the irony of each quotation lies in the contrast between what is said and what is actually meant.

- A telemarketer interrupts you in the middle of dinner. You say to him, "I'm so glad you've called. I hate eating dinner while it's still hot."

- A friend asks how you like your new boss. You reply, "He's great. It's refreshing working for someone who has half my IQ."

- You break up with your girlfriend, who becomes hysterical and slaps you. You say to yourself afterward, "I think she took that well."

- At a family reunion, an uncle becomes extremely drunk, starts insulting people, and then passes out. You remark, "I simply can't understand why people say he has a drinking problem."

- An instructor has an extremely cold, businesslike manner. You tell a classmate, "I really like the warmth and concern she shows her students."

As you can see, irony is a useful tone for humor and can be used to imply exactly the opposite of what is said or what is done.

Irony also refers to situations that involve a contrast between what is expected or intended and what actually happens. We could call it ironic, for example, if the arsonist responsible for a string of fires turned out to be a city firefighter, or if a bank were robbed by two guards that were hired to protect it. Here are a few more examples of this type of irony:

- While fastening his seat belt to keep himself safe, a man loses control of his car and crashes.

- A preacher who is fiercely critical of gays turns out to have a secret homosexual life.

- Ludwig van Beethoven, perhaps the greatest composer who ever lived, became totally deaf and could not hear his own music.

- Finally losing patience with her chronically unemployed husband, a woman files for divorce. The next week, the husband wins a multi-million-dollar lottery.

- Jerome Rodale, the father of the modern organic food movement, often bragged, "I'm going to live to be 100 unless I'm run down by a sugar-crazed taxi driver." Instead, he dropped dead at age 72 while appearing on a talk show.

The five examples above show that irony also describes meaningful situations that are contrary to what is intended or expected.

☑ Check Your Understanding

Explain the irony in the cartoon below.

Frank and Ernest

- The irony in the sign that a communication workshop will be "sometime tonight in a room upstairs" is that _____ *it communicates very poorly—*

_____ *it fails to communicate just when and where the workshop will be.*

Explanation:

The irony is that the sign advertising the communication workshop fails to communicate just when and where the workshop will be.

➤ *Practice 3*

A. Below are five statements expressing different attitudes about eating. Five different tones are used:

> A. ambivalent   B. detached   C. humorous
> D. impassioned   E. superior

For each statement, write the letter of the tone that you think is present. Use each tone once.

___B___ 1. Eating is just another chore. There should be a protein pill we could simply swallow every day and be done with it.   "Just another chore" and "be done with it" indicate that the writer is emotionally uninvolved.

___C___ 2. My husband's idea of a seven-course meal is a steak and a six-pack.
Clearly not a seven-course meal. A sign of a humorous attitude.

___D___ 3. Too many things we eat poison our bodies! People must cut out junk food and empty carbs and white flour and sugar. Eating wisely can make all the difference to our health.   The extreme language is a sign of an impassioned attitude.

___A___ 4. I love to eat, but I hate what food does to my body. After I eat something delicious, I think, "I didn't need that."   Shows indecisiveness about eating; loves eating, hates the results of food.

___E___ 5. I don't understand why people make such a big deal about food. Just eat when you're hungry and don't eat when you aren't. What's so hard about that?   "I don't understand why people . . ." and "What's so hard about that?" suggest the speaker is "above it all."

B. Following are five statements expressing different attitudes about exercise. Label each statement with the tone of voice that you think is present. Choose each tone from the following box, and use each tone only once.

> A. humorous   B. matter-of-fact   C. optimistic
> D. pessimistic   E. self-critical

___B___ 6. Exercise is just something that is part of my daily routine. I get up in the morning, exercise, shower and shave, eat something, and head off for school. It's all pretty automatic for me.   Grouping exercising with activities such as showering and shaving suggests a matter-of-fact attitude.

___D___ 7. What's the point of exercising and taking care of yourself? You're always hearing about people who live healthy lifestyles and just drop dead anyway.   "What's the point" and "just drop dead anyway" suggest a gloomy viewpoint.

___E___ 8. I know I ought to exercise more. I just always find an excuse not to. I guess I don't have much self-discipline.   "I don't have much self-discipline" is self-criticism.

___A___ 9. I hate exercise with all my heart. The only reason I do it is because it feels so good when I stop.   Doing something for the pleasure of stopping it suggests a humorous view.

___C___ 10. I've begun an exercise program that I know I can stick with. I think it's just a matter of weeks before I start seeing some really great results.

"I know I can stick with" and "seeing some really great results" suggest looking at the bright side of things.

➤ Practice 4

Each passage on the pages that follow illustrates one of the tones in the box below. In each space, put the letter of the one tone that best applies. Use each letter only once. Three tones will be left over.

Remember that the tone of a selection reflects the author's attitude. To find the tone of a paragraph, ask yourself what attitude is revealed by its words and phrases.

A. amused	B. appreciative	C. despairing	D. instructive
E. optimistic	F. outraged	G. sentimental	H. sympathetic

___B___ 1. ¹Some days I like to stop and think about all the small, wonderful things that grace my ordinary day-to-day existence. ²To begin with, I generally open my eyes to see the adoring face of my dog resting on the pillow beside me. ³No matter how sleep-rumpled, dragon-breathed, and swollen-eyed I am, he always greets with me a look that says, "Good morning, you beautiful thing!" ⁴Next, I swing my feet out of bed and into my soft, comfy sheepskin-lined slippers. ⁵Heaven! ⁶I wander sleepily into the bathroom, and there awaits something else I'm thankful for every day—unlimited hot water. ⁷As I splash it luxuriously over my face, I feel wakefulness, warmth and life beginning to return. ⁸From the bathroom I head to the kitchen, where I encounter the queen of all that is wondrous. ⁹I refer, of course, to coffee. ¹⁰The making of that first cup of the day—the measuring, the aroma, the sound of the dripping water, the anticipation, the taste—*ahhhhhh*. ¹¹Life is so good.

Phrases such as *wonderful things, thankful for, wondrous,* and *ahhhhhh. Life is so good* all indicate appreciation for the "wonderful things that grace" the writer's daily life.

___C___ 2. . . . Out, out, brief candle!
Life's but a walking shadow, a poor player
That struts and frets his hour upon the stage
And then is heard no more. It is a tale
Told by an idiot, full of sound and fury,
Signifying nothing.

(From Shakespeare's *Macbeth*)

The speaker despairingly communicates his negative view of life, comparing it to the shadow of a poor player (wandering actor) and a tale told by an idiot (meaningless). To feel that life signifies nothing is to despair.

Note: In these passages and in the tests that follow, words and phrases that indicate tone are underlined in red in this *Instructor's Edition*.

_H_   3. ¹While it's common to complain about work, being *without* work is <u>a terrible thing</u>. ²Work gives structure to our days and dignity to our lives. ³One of the first questions we ask new acquaintances is "What do you do?" meaning "What kind of *work* do you do?" ⁴Without work, we lack a very basic part of our identity. ⁵That's why <u>it is so sad to consider the plight of people in this country who are deprived of the comfort and stability of a steady job</u>. ⁶The reasons for their lack of employment are many. ⁷There may not be jobs available in their areas. ⁸Perhaps they cannot afford the transportation or childcare necessary to hold down a job. ⁹Often the jobs for which they are qualified do not pay a living wage. ¹⁰They may have grown up surrounded by beaten-down men and women who have taught them that holding a job is not possible. ¹¹In many cases they have attempted to find work, but the obstacles they had to climb over and their own self-doubt were too much to deal with. ¹²Slowly and steadily, <u>a sense of defeat overwhelmed and poisoned them</u>, leaving them without hope or direction. ¹³<u>In their place, it is doubtful that any one of us would do better</u>.

With phrases such as *a terrible thing, it is so sad, who are deprived*, etc., the writer shows pity and concern for those without work.

_D_   4. ¹In *The Catcher in the Rye,* Holden Caulfield yearns to protect children like his younger sister Phoebe. ²He tells Phoebe that when he hears the song about the catcher in the rye, he imagines children playing in a field, innocent and free. ³But somewhere in that field there is a cliff, and sooner or later, the children will come near the cliff. ⁴Holden wants to be there to catch them, to keep them from falling off the field. ⁵He believes that it is his calling to be the catcher, to be their protector. ⁶The rye field becomes a symbol for the freedom and purity of childhood. ⁷Holden wants to shield the children from the hidden cliff, which symbolizes the cruel realities of the adult world.

This passage instructs the reader about the meaning of *The Catcher in the Rye.* (Note that Holden may exhibit some sentimentalism about childhood, but the passage itself is instructive.)

_F_   5. ¹Can we talk about Hummers for a minute? ²By "hummers," I don't mean the graceful, light, tiny hummingbirds, which would be a pleasant topic of conversation. ³I mean <u>the grossly enormous, bloated, gas-guzzling monstrosities</u> that you see monopolizing two or three lanes of your local highway. ⁴You know—the ones that <u>look as if they should be delivering medical supplies to refugee camps</u> rather than ferrying suburban kids to soccer games. ⁵The ones that <u>sprawl</u> over two parking spaces instead of just one. ⁶The ones that <u>gulp</u> so much gas that driving them costs only slightly less than flying your own private jet. ⁷The ones whose owners exude a <u>bloated, aggressive attitude</u> to match that of their vehicles—<u>an attitude that says, "Hey, get out of my way, loser!</u> ⁸I'm driving a car that costs more than your house, so don't think I'm going to slow down just because you and your loser family are crossing the street in front of me! ⁹And don't think that I'll give a moment's thought to what my car and I are doing

The author's extremely negative manner of characterizing Hummers and their owners clearly conveys a sense of outrage.

to contribute to America's oil dependency or the destruction of the ozone layer, because you know what? [10]I can afford this <u>ridiculous display of wealth and bad taste</u>, and that's all I care about!"

CHAPTER REVIEW

In this chapter, you learned that part of reading critically is to do the following:

- Be aware of an author's **purpose**: the reason why he or she writes. Three common purposes are to inform, to persuade, and to entertain.

- Be aware of **tone**—the expression of the author's attitude and feeling about a subject. A writer's tone might be objective—the case in most textbook writing—or it might be lighthearted, sympathetic, angry, affectionate, respectful, or any of the other tones shown on pages 261–263.

  One important tone to recognize is **irony**: saying one thing but meaning the opposite.

The next chapter—Chapter 8—will explain another part of reading critically: recognizing an author's point and evaluating the support for that point.

On the Web: If you are using this book in class, you can visit our website for additional practice in identifying an author's purpose and tone. Go to **www.townsendpress.com** and click on "Online Exercises."

➤ *Review Test 1*

To review what you've learned in this chapter, answer each of the following questions by filling in the blank or writing the letter of the correct answer.

1. The main purpose of almost any textbook is to _____ *inform* _____ .

2. Typically the purpose of a news report is to _____ *inform* _____ , the purpose of an editorial is to _____ *persuade* _____ , and the purpose of a mystery novel or adventure story is to _____ *entertain* _____ .

Items 1 and 2: See pages 256–257.

__T__ 3. *True or false?* The purpose of some writing may be to persuade as well as to inform, or even to inform, persuade, *and* entertain.   See page 258.

4. The tone of a selection helps reveal the author's _____ *attitude* _____ toward and feeling about his or her subject.   See page 260.

5. A writer is using an ironic tone if he or she says one thing but means the _____ *opposite* _____ .   See page 264.

➤ *Review Test 2*

The selection that follows is from the college textbook *Social Problems* (Pearson Prentice-Hall) by James M. Henslin. Read it and then answer the questions on purpose and tone that follow. There are also questions on the skills you have practiced in previous chapters.

Preview

When you think "crime," what are the first images that pop into your head? Probably not ones of expensively dressed executives holding meetings in tastefully appointed offices. And yet as this essay makes clear, many of today's most damaging crimes have had their origins in just such settings.

Words to Watch

infamous (5): having an exceedingly bad reputation
malice (6): evil intent
brazen (8): bold

WHITE-COLLAR CRIME

James M. Henslin

1   When corporate scandals hit the news, we learn about top corporate executives who steal outrageous amounts of money. Occasionally, as with the bankruptcy of Enron, billions of dollars go unaccounted for. Sociologist Edwin Sutherland coined the term **white-collar crime** for crimes "committed by people of respectable and high social status in the course of their occupation."

2   No one knows for sure how much white-collar crime costs the nation, but estimates place the bill at about $600 billion a year. This is more than the cost of all street crime. Most white-collar crime never comes to the surface, but that which does can be enlightening. The most notorious example in recent years is the fraud at Enron, which cost stockholders more than $50 billion. Eleven thousand employees also suffered huge losses in their pensions. Bank robbers risk their lives for $10,000, but corporate executives manipulate computers and documents to make millions of illegal dollars for their corporations—or to rip off those same companies.

3   The two major types of white-collar crime are those committed by employees *on behalf of* a corporation and those committed *against* a corporation. In crimes committed *on behalf of* a corporation, employees break the law in order to benefit their company. Examples include car manufacturers knowingly selling dangerous automobiles, drug companies faking test data so they can keep their drugs on the market, and corporations engaging in price fixing and tax dodging.

4   It is not uncommon for corporations listed on the major stock exchanges to produce a criminogenic (crime-causing) culture. The corporate culture revolves around not only corporate profits but also personal achievement and recognition. Pressures to increase profits and to climb the corporate ladder, combined with the insulation of executives from the consequences of their decisions, often lead to an "ethical numbness" or insensitivity.

5   The corporate culture so dominates its members that even respectable people can end up calculating the cold-blooded deaths of others for profit. This is illustrated by the infamous° "Pinto case." The Pinto was a car manufactured by Ford in the 1970s. After three young women in Indiana burned to death when their Pinto burst into flames following a rear-end crash, the Ford Motor Company was charged with reckless homicide. No executives were charged, just Ford itself. It was alleged that Ford knew that in a rear-end collision the Pinto's gas tank could rupture, spew gas, and burn passengers to death. (Never mind how a corporation can know anything. The commonsense view is that it is the people in the corporation who know things, and they who make criminal decisions. Common sense and the legal system, however, often walk different paths.)

6   Disclosed at the trial was heartwrenching evidence that revealed the cold-blooded malice° of Ford's executives. Installing a simple piece of plastic would have corrected the problem, at a cost of just $11 per car. The Ford

executives faced a difficult decision—whether to pay the $11 or to sentence drivers and passengers to fiery deaths. Now, that is a really difficult choice—at least it was for these executives. The memo below shows their cost-benefit analysis—a comparison of what it would cost the company to make the change ("Costs") or to pay for the deaths ("Benefits," meaning the amount of benefits that would have to be paid). As you can see, the cost of installing the plastic was high ($137 million) compared to the amount of money that would have to be paid if they simply allowed people to die ($49.5 million). Their estimates turned out to be too low: Several hundred people burned to death, and many others were disfigured.

7   With the right lawyers and connections, people can get away with murder. Ford was acquitted. The company recalled its 1971–1976 Pintos for fuel tank modifications and launched a publicity campaign to maintain an image of a "good" company. Ford executives claimed that the internal memo was misunderstood. They said that it "related to a proposed federal safety standard, and

not to the design of the Pinto." Despite causing hundreds of deaths, no Ford executives were arrested or tried in court. They remained free, wealthy, and respected in their communities.

8   You might think that such a cold, brazen° act would never be repeated by a U.S. automobile company. Unfortunately, such an expectation would be wrong. In 1998, a thirteen-year-old boy was burned to death when the gas tank of an Oldsmobile Cutlass station wagon ruptured. When GM was sued, a memo was discovered in which GM calculated the cost to fix the problem at just $4.50 per vehicle. GM also calculated the cost of lawsuits and figured these would average just $2.40 per car. Able to save an estimated $2.10 per car, GM did not fix the problem.

9   The Pinto and Cutlass cases confirm that the powerful can and do manipulate our legal system. They can and do escape punishment for their crimes—including, in these instances, what I would call serial murder. Can you possibly imagine similar judicial results if poor people plotted to kill automobile executives?

Ford's Internal Memo on the Pinto: "Benefits and Costs Relating to Fuel Leakage Associated with the Static Rollover Test Portion of FMVSS 208"

BENEFITS.
Savings: 180 burn deaths, 180 serious burn injuries, 2,100 burned vehicles.
Unit cost: $200,000 per death, $67,000 per injury, $700 per vehicle.
Total benefit: $(180 \times \$200,000) + (180 \times \$67,000) + (2,100 \times \$700) = \$49.5$ million.

COSTS.
Sales: 11 million cars, 1.5 million light trucks.
Unit cost: $11 per car, $11 per truck.
Total cost: $(11,000,000 \times \$11) + (1,500,000 \times \$11) = \$137$ million.

Reading Comprehension Questions

Vocabulary in Context

__A__ 1. In the sentence below, the word *notorious* (nō-tôr′ē-əs) means

    A. known widely and usually unfavorably.

    B. amusing.   Many people know about the fraud at Enron and

    C. highly reliable.   have an unfavorable opinion of the company.

    D. viewed with respect.

    "The most notorious example in recent years is the fraud at Enron, which cost stockholders more than $50 billion." (Paragraph 2)

Central Point and Main Ideas

__C__ 2. Which sentence best expresses the central point of the selection?

Answer A is incorrect because the selection does not examine how often such people are rewarded.

    A. The corporate culture usually rewards people who are capable of calculating the cold-blooded deaths of others for profit.

    B. Automobile manufacturers such as Ford and GM are especially likely to engage in cold-blooded malice.

B is incorrect because the passage does not say car manufacturers are especially likely to act maliciously.

    C. Unlike street criminals, white-collar criminals seldom pay for their cold-blooded crimes, even though they cost the nation hundreds of billions a year.

D covers only paragraph 4.

    D. American corporations revolve around corporate profits, personal achievement, and recognition; but this leads to the insulation of executives.

__D__ 3. The implied main idea of paragraph 6 is that

    A. Ford executives couldn't afford to correct the problems associated with their cars without going bankrupt.

    B. Ford executives underestimated the number of people who would be burned to death in their cars.

    C. Ford executives failed to fix the problem associated with their cars because it was technologically difficult to do so.

    D. Ford executives were unwilling to make their cars safe because they believed that it would be cheaper to simply pay death benefits to the survivors of those burned to death in their cars.   Answer A is incorrect because there is no indication the correction would cause bankruptcy.

B covers only one detail of the paragraph.

C is contradicted by the second sentence of the paragraph.

Supporting Details

___B___ 4. The problem with the Ford Pinto was that it
  A. tended to roll over when going around sharp turns.
  B. had a gas tank that would rupture and burst into flames following rear-end collisions.
  C. often stalled out, resulting in rear-end collisions and multi-car pileups.
  D. had a defective braking system.   See paragraph 5.

Transitions

___D___ 5. The relationship between the second sentence below and the first sentence is one of
  A. addition.
  B. cause and effect.
  C. comparison.
  D. definition-example.

> The word *Examples* in the second sentence signals a definition-example relationship. The passage defines crimes "committed ... *on behalf of* a corporation."

"In crimes committed *on behalf of* a corporation, employees break the law in order to benefit their company. Examples include car manufacturers knowingly selling dangerous automobiles, drug companies faking test data so they can keep their drugs on the market, and corporations engaged in price fixing and tax dodging." (Paragraph 3)

___A___ 6. The relationship between the second sentence below and the first sentence is one of
  A. contrast.
  B. addition.
  C. cause and effect.
  D. comparison.

> The commonsense view is contrasted with the reality of the legal system. The word *however* in the second sentence signals a contrast relationship.

"The commonsense view is that it is the people in the corporation who know things, and they who make criminal decisions. Common sense and the legal system, however, often walk different paths." (Paragraph 5)

Patterns of Organization

Item 7:   _B_   7. In paragraphs 4–6, the author
Paragraphs 4–6 mainly
show that Ford's failure
to fix the Pinto led to
the deaths of several
hundred people. Answer
A is incorrect because
the passage describes
only how Ford dealt
with one problem.
C is
incorrect

A. lists ways in which the Ford Motor Company tried to hide the possible problems associated with their cars.

B. shows the consequences of corporate willingness to put profits over human life.

C. describes a series of events in the order in which they happened.

D. contrasts irresponsible corporations such as Ford with corporations that act in a responsible manner.

Inferences

because
the passage does not
describe events in
chronological order.
D is incorrect because
there is no mention of
corporations that
behave responsibly.

   _C_   8. We can infer from this selection that the author believes that some Ford and GM executives

A. were only doing as he would have done under similar circumstances.

B. were justified in saving their companies millions of dollars.

C. should have been put in jail as punishment for their crimes.

D. were no better or no worse than the majority of American citizens.

Item 8: See paragraphs 7–9. Note phrases such as *get away with murder, escape punishment,* and *serial murder.*

Purpose and Tone

Item 9:   _B_   9. The author's main purpose in writing this selection is to
Answer A is wrong;
there is nothing
entertaining about this
selection.
C is incorrect because
there is no mention of
safety ratings.
D is incorrect because
the passage uses only
Ford and
GM as examples.

A. entertain readers with outrageous but true stories about faulty American cars.

B. inform readers that seemingly respectable corporations have sometimes acted in cold-blooded, immoral ways.

C. warn people to carefully check out the safety rating of any car they are thinking of buying.

D. persuade readers never to buy Ford or GM cars.

   _D_ 10. The author's tone throughout this selection may be characterized as

A. depressed.

B. detached.

C. revengeful.

D. indignant.

Language such as "heart-wrenching evidence that revealed cold-blooded malice" (paragraph 6) and the conclusions reached in paragraph 9 clearly indicate that the author is indignant. Also, the sarcasm of statements like "Now, that is a really difficult choice" (paragraph 6) indicate the author is indignant.

Discussion Questions

1. The article mentions that none of the Ford executives who were responsible for the Pinto-related deaths were ever arrested and that, in fact, they remained respected members of their communities. Why do you think this happened? What factors might have led them to escape punishment and public censure?

2. If white-collar crime takes a greater economic toll than street crime, why do you think most people are so much more indignant and angry about street crime?

3. Do you agree that "The powerful can and do manipulate our legal system. They can and do escape punishment for their crimes"? Can you think of other examples that demonstrate this point?

4. What, if anything, can society do to ensure that white-collar criminals do not escape punishment for the crimes they commit?

Note: Writing assignments for this selection appear on page 564.

Note: Writing assignments for this selection appear on page 564.

Check Your Performance			PURPOSE AND TONE
Activity	*Number Right*	*Points*	*Score*
Review Test 1 (5 items)	_____	× 6 =	_____
Review Test 2 (10 items)	_____	× 7 =	_____
		TOTAL SCORE =	_____%

Enter your total score into the **Reading Performance Chart: Review Tests** on the inside back cover.

PURPOSE AND TONE: Mastery Test 1

A. In the space provided, indicate whether the primary purpose of each item is to inform (**I**), to persuade (**P**), or to entertain (**E**).

___*I*___ 1. Experts believe that between 3 and 5 percent of American children have some form of Attention Deficit Hyperactivity Disorder (ADHD).
Informative statement about ADHD. Clue: *Experts believe.*

___*I*___ 2. Studies show that boys are three times more likely to develop ADHD than girls. Objective information. Clue: *Studies show.*

___*P*___ 3. Parents and teachers are too quick to put children on medication for ADHD when the kids are actually just normal and high-spirited.
Persuasive clue: *too quick.*

___*E*___ 4. A mother was talking about her son, recently diagnosed with Attention Deficit Disorder. "I don't understand," she said. "We pay plenty of attention to him!" The humor lies in the mother's misunderstanding of
who is supposed to have an attention deficit.

___*P*___ 5. Parents of children with ADHD should experiment with modifying the children's diet rather than putting them on medication.
Persuasive clue: *should.*

B. Each of the following passages illustrates better than the others one of the five different tones identified in the box below. In the space provided, put the letter of the tone that best applies to each passage. Use each tone once.

A. admiring	B. alarmed	C. determined
D. reverent	E. sarcastic	

___*D*___ 6. Amazing grace! How sweet the sound
That saved a wretch like me!
I once was lost, but now am found;
Was blind, but now I see.

5 'Twas grace that taught my heart to fear,
And grace my fears relieved;
How precious did that grace appear
The hour I first believed!

Through many dangers, toils and snares,
10 I have already come;
'Tis grace hath brought me safe thus far,
And grace will lead me home.

The words are from a religious hymn entitled "Amazing Grace." Words like grace, precious, believed, and lead me home show reverence.

___*C*___ 7. [1]The experience I had writing my first college essay was unforgettable. [2]I received a C- for the essay. [3]Scrawled next to the grade was the comment "Not badly written, but ill-conceived." [4]I remember going to the instructor

(Continues on next page)

277

The passage illustrates the author's determination to do better on future writing assignments (see sentences 15–17). Even when the author is "confused and angry," he or she rereads the essay "several times" to figure out what the instructor meant.

after class, asking about his comment as well as the word *Log* that he had added in the margin at various spots. ⁵"What are all these logs you put in my paper?" I asked, trying to make a joke of it. ⁶He looked at me a little wonderingly. ⁷"Logic," he answered, "logic." ⁸He went on to explain that I had not thought out my paper clearly. ⁹There were actually two ideas rather than one in my thesis, one supporting paragraph had nothing to do with either idea, and so on. ¹⁰I've never forgotten his last words: ¹¹"If you don't think clearly," he said, "you won't write clearly."

¹²I was speechless, and I felt confused and angry. ¹³I didn't like being told that I didn't know how to think. ¹⁴I went back to my room and read over my paper several times. ¹⁵Eventually, I decided that my instructor was right. ¹⁶"No more logs," I said to myself. ¹⁷"I'm going to get these logs out of my papers."

___E___ 8.

Tom "Big Shot" Lewis's actions indicate that he is inconsiderate and does not have potential. Therefore, the author's tone is sarcastic.

¹Let me list some of the reasons I'm happy that my sister Sophie is marrying Tom "Big Shot" Lewis. ²First, Tom is a considerate human being. ³He realizes that doing conventional "nice" things, like remembering his girlfriend's birthday or giving her a Christmas present, would just distract her from the important things in life, like ironing his shirts. ⁴Secondly, he's got such potential. ⁵It's true that he's not working now; in fact, since we've known him he hasn't held a job for more than two months. ⁶But I'm sure any day now his plan to become a traveling disk jockey is going to materialize. ⁷Then he'll be able to pay Sophie back all the money she's lent him.

___A___ 9.

The underlined words reveal the author's admiration of Jackie Kennedy.

¹Jackie Kennedy knew how to live with grace. ²From her trademark sunglasses to her French-inspired outfits and feminine pumps, she always dressed with a style of her own. ³As the First Lady, she brought a youthful classiness to her role, the likes of which the White House had never before seen. ⁴Americans often remember her smiling and waving gently, as she stepped gracefully from airplane ramps and stage platforms. ⁵As a hostess, she never missed a beat. ⁶Using her charm and wit, she made guests feel right at home. ⁷Even when her husband, the president, was killed, Jackie faced the spotlight with graceful dignity. ⁸In the hearts of many, she will always be an unforgettable American icon.

___B___ 10.

The statistics given, along with the underlined words, are evidence that the writer is alarmed.

¹In the United States today there are 35 million geriatric patients—defined as over the age of 65. ²Of these, 4.5 million are older than 85, now characterized as the "old old." ³Yet the American Medical Directors Association, which credentials physicians in long-term care, has certified only 1,900 such doctors in the entire country; only 2 percent of physicians in training say they want to go into geriatric care. ⁴As we baby boomers go about our lives, frozen into our routines of work and family responsibilities, a vast inland sea of elders is building. ⁵By 2020 there will be an estimated 53 million Americans older than 65, 6.5 million of whom will be "old old." ⁶Many of you will be among them. ⁷How will America possibly cope with this flood of old folks, each with a unique set of medical and financial circumstances?

PURPOSE AND TONE: Mastery Test 2

A. In the space provided, indicate whether the primary purpose of each item is to inform (**I**), to persuade (**P**), or to entertain (**E**).

_____*I*_____ 1. With more than 400 billion cups consumed annually, coffee is the world's most popular beverage.   An informative statement about coffee.

_____*P*_____ 2. Instead of buying diamonds, people should save their money and buy gorgeous synthetic stones like cubic zirconia.   Persuasive clue: *should*.

_____*E*_____ 3. The bank says that I have no money left in my checking account, but that can't be true. I have plenty of checks left.   The humor lies in the writer's apparent failure to realize that money must be in the account for the checks to be worth anything.

_____*I*_____ 4. Albinism, the lack of color-producing pigment in the skin, hair, and eyes, can affect people of any race.   Defines *albinism* and presents a fact about it.

_____*P*_____ 5. Telemarketers should be required to immediately identify themselves as such when beginning a phone conversation.   Persuasive clue: *should*.

_____*E*_____ 6. [1]How do these celebrities stay so impossibly thin? [2]Simple: They have full-time personal trainers, who advise them on nutrition, give them pep talks, and shoot them with tranquilizer darts whenever they try to crawl, on hunger-weakened limbs, toward the packet of rice cakes that constitutes the entire food supply in their 37,000-square-foot mansions. [3]For most celebrities, the biggest meal of the day is toothpaste (they use reduced-fat Crest).   Exaggeration is used to point out the lengths to which celebrities will go to stay thin.

_____*P*_____ 7. [1]An Internet revolution is taking place right now. [2]We are in the infant stages of what promises to be one of the most important new developments in Internet history—and well positioned early investors have the potential to profit enormously. [3]BUT YOU MUST ACT NOW. [4]It's happened more times than you might believe. . . . [5]Sometimes just one smart decision—one strategic investment move—can earn you staggering profits. [6]The key? [7]Pinpointing the exact tipping point when a smart idea becomes a highly profitable investment vehicle. [8]For this new market, that time is now! [9]The key is information and timing, and now the world's leading growth stock guru (his investment gains have averaged up to 100% a year) is opening his exclusive advisory service to a few fortunate investors. [10]This is your opportunity to capitalize on his expertise.   The passage appears to give some information, but the real purpose is to persuade potential investors to become clients of a stock guru.

(Continues on next page)

B. Each of the following passages illustrates better than the others one of the five different tones identified in the box below. In the space provided, put the letter of the tone that best applies to each passage. Use each tone once. (Three tone choices will be left over.)

A. ambivalent	B. angry	C. defensive
D. ironic	E. regretful	F. suggestive

_____B_____ 8. ¹It has been rumored for years that some major league baseball stars were taking steroids to increase their ability to hit home runs. ²But not until early in 2005 did major league baseball finally require mandatory steroid testing and strict penalties for steroid use. ³Why did it take baseball bigwigs so long to clamp down on the illegal substances? ⁴The only answer can be sheer profit-driven hypocrisy.
⁵Players who "bulked up" with the aid of steroids tended to hit more home runs than they otherwise could have. ⁶More home runs generated greater fan excitement. ⁷Greater fan excitement meant higher ticket sales, and more money for owners and players alike. ⁸Who really cared that steroid use could lead to serious side effects? ⁹Who cared that old-time ballplayers were having their records broken by drug-injected Godzillas? ¹⁰Who cared that steroid use by pro ballplayers could set a bad example for the nation's youth? ¹¹Certainly not major league baseball, that is, until a spate of bad publicity forced its hand.

The author is angry at major-league baseball owners for taking a long time to clamp down on steroid use in order to make more money.

_____C_____ 9. ¹I am a hunter. ²Do you hate me already? ³Probably; most people seem to have made up their minds that hunting is a terrible thing, even if they don't know anything about it. ⁴And if hunting is a bad thing, then I must be a bad person for doing it. ⁵But I don't think I'm a bad person. ⁶I do not go hunting primarily for the kill. ⁷In fact, there have been many more times that I've come home empty-handed from a hunt than otherwise. ⁸The biggest reason that I go hunting is that I love being in the wilderness and in the company of my hunting buddies. ⁹But even if I do manage to bag a deer or a pheasant for my table, I don't feel guilty about it. ¹⁰Hunters kill a fraction of the wild animals that automobiles mow down on our highways every year. ¹¹The hunting licenses we buy help to fund state wildlife management programs. ¹²Responsible hunting helps to keep wildlife populations in check, rather than letting flocks and herds expand to the point that animals are starving and diseased.

The author suspects that many people hate him and defends himself by giving reasons why being a hunter does not make him a bad person.

_____F_____ 10. ¹Feeling a sense of privacy and comfort, I allow the sound of my own voice to soothe my mind and body, while I speak slowly and softly. ²My body is slowing down as though everything is moving in slow motion. ³With every word I say, I feel more relaxed and at peace. ⁴Moment by moment, my mind is becoming as clear as the surface of a calm and quiet mountain lake.
⁵As my mind clears, I use my imagination to relax more deeply while I read. ⁶I imagine that I am sitting on a comfortable chair on a beautiful beach as I read. ⁷With my peripheral vision I see the golden sand that surrounds me . . . and the waves as they crash on the shore. ⁸I hear the gentle and rhythmic sounds they make.

The author is trying to suggest a state of deep relaxation.

PURPOSE AND TONE: Mastery Test 3

A. In the space provided, indicate whether the primary purpose of each item is to inform (**I**), to persuade (**P**), or to entertain (**E**).

_____I_____ 1. When two complete thoughts are combined into one sentence by a joining word like *and, but,* or *so,* a comma is used before the joining word.
Information on punctuation.

_____P_____ 2. Any adult who is convicted of having molested a child should be sentenced to jail without parole for a minimum of twenty years.
Persuasive clue: *should.*

_____E_____ 3. I am famous for my backyard weed garden; my children tease me for having a "black thumb." The humor lies in the speaker's lack of gardening ability.

_____P_____ 4. [1]What's remarkable about us humans is that, unique among creatures, we know we are doomed. [2]Yet we stubbornly persist in defying the odds. [3]The same DNA that dictates the bell curve of our lives—growth, maturity, decline—also contains a gene for relentless self-improvement. [4]We insist, and must insist, on continuing to grow.
Persuasive clue: *must.*

_____E_____ 5. [1]I'm a very susceptible person, easily influenced, a natural-born follower with no sales resistance. [2]When I walk into a store, clerks wrestle one another trying to get to me first. [3]My wife won't let me watch infomercials because of all the junk I've ordered that's now piled up in the garage. [4]My medicine cabinet is filled with vitamins and baldness cures.
The writer is making fun of his own inability to resist a sales pitch.

_____P_____ 6. [1]When the next diet book comes out promising major weight loss with minor effort, there will be 200 million chubby Americans waiting to believe it. [2]Well, tough, but it's not true. [3]The dreary, persistent fact is that diets don't work; 95 percent of them fail, which is why setting weight loss as your goal is generally a bum idea. [4]The almost certain failure can infect your attitude toward fitness, while the yo-yoing up and down actually makes you gain weight. [5]So <u>don't diet</u>. [6]Our advice is, basically, <u>forget about it</u>. [7]Instead, <u>exercise six days a week and make it a rule of your life to quit eating crap</u>.

The writer is trying to convince us that exercising is a better weight-reduction strategy than dieting.

_____I_____ 7. [1]Abraham Maslow proposed that human motives are organized into a hierarchy of needs—a systematic arrangement of needs, according to priority, in which basic needs must be met before less basic needs are aroused. [2]This hierarchical arrangement is usually portrayed as a pyramid, with the needs toward the bottom of the pyramid, such as physiological or security needs, being the most basic. [3]Higher levels in the pyramid consist of progressively less basic needs. [4]When a person manages to satisfy a level of needs reasonably well (complete satisfaction is not necessary), this satisfaction activates needs at the next level.

The passage presents, without emotion or humor, straightforward facts about Maslow's hierarchy of needs.

(Continues on next page)

B. Each of the following passages illustrates better than the others one of the five different tones identified in the box below. In the space provided, put the letter of the tone that best applies to each passage. Use each tone once. (Three tone choices will be left over.)

A. admiring	B. disbelieving	C. fearful
D. indignant	E. optimistic	F. regretful

_F_ 8. [1]In the face of busy days, long work hours, and extended after-school activities, the American dinnertime has become <u>all but obsolete</u>. [2]The dinner hour <u>used to be a refuge</u>, a time when family members could enjoy each other's company over a warm, nutritious meal. [3]But distracted by other obligations, today's families have traded that valuable together time for things of less importance. [4]Husbands and wives have <u>lost that precious moment of sharing</u> after a hard day's work. [5]<u>Parents no longer have a built-in opportunity to give valuable counsel and encouragement</u> to their children. [6]Likewise, children have <u>lost a slot of guaranteed attention time</u> with their parents. [7]The slow transition to on-the-go fast food and TV dinners may not have been noticed by families adapting to the faster-paced world. [8]But the close bonds once formed over home-cooked meals will certainly be <u>missed</u>.

> The author regrets that the American dinnertime has become a thing of the past. The frequent use of words suggesting loss is a clue.

_D_ 9. [1]<u>It never ceases to astound me</u> that puppies are sold in pet stores. [2]And chances are that the <u>unfortunate</u> animals <u>imprisoned</u> in tiny cages have already been <u>mistreated</u> all their lives. [3]They are typically born at "puppy farms" whose only aim is to produce many sellable animals as quickly as possible, without regard for the animals' health. [4]Female dogs are kept pregnant constantly, quickly wearing out their health, and are killed when they lose the ability to reproduce. [5]Puppies born from such <u>exhausted, worn-out</u> mothers are kept in <u>filthy</u> crates until they are shipped out to a pet store for sale. [6]Not only are their lives <u>miserable</u>, but their health and temperaments are likely to be poor. [7]<u>There is no excuse for</u> puppy farms or the pet stores that help support them.

> The author is deeply angered at what he or she perceives as the cruel and wrongful treatment of puppies.

_C_ 10. [1]In the afternoon I fell asleep in the living room with the soft autumn sun coming through the window. [2]It was dusk when I awakened, and I could tell that it had gotten cooler. [3]As my eyes opened, they glanced out the window into a yard that was now <u>filled with dark shadows</u>. [4]Out of some instinct, I averted my eyes so they did not scan around the yard. [5]<u>I half felt I would see something moving out there, something I would not want to see</u>. [6]I quickly closed the miniblinds to the windows. [7]Then, as I fumbled to find the wall switch and turn on a light, I was suddenly aware of a <u>faint scratching sound</u>. [8]It was coming from the door to the basement, and I sensed that <u>someone was trying to break in</u>.

> The author is afraid of a break-in. Several details establish the sense of fear.

Name _____

Section _____ Date _____

SCORE: (Number correct) _____ × 10 = _____%

PURPOSE AND TONE: Mastery Test 4

A. In the space provided, indicate whether the primary purpose of each item is to inform (**I**), to persuade (**P**), or to entertain (**E**).

_____I_____ 1. On any given day, approximately 160,000 kids decide to skip school to avoid being bullied by their peers. A matter-of-fact statement.

_____P_____ 2. For every year he or she is in school, each student should be required to read at least ten books. Persuasive clue: *should*.

_____E_____ 3. In a successful marriage, a bride promises to obey her husband at all times, and the groom promises that his first words to his wife will always be "Yes, dear." An amusing comment on who really obeys whom in marriage.

_____P_____ 4. It would benefit students if high-school math departments offered courses in managing a bank account and basic investing as well as algebra and geometry. Persuasive clue: *would*.

_____E_____ 5. ¹To win an argument, one rule is to drink liquor. ²Suppose you are at a party and some hotshot intellectual is expounding on the economy of Peru, a subject you know nothing about. ³If you're drinking some health-fanatic drink like grapefruit juice, you'll hang back, afraid to display your ignorance, while the hotshot enthralls your date. ⁴But if you drink several large martinis, you'll discover you have *strong views* about the Peruvian economy. ⁵You'll be a *wealth* of information. ⁶You'll argue forcefully, offering great insights and even upsetting furniture. ⁷People will be impressed. ⁸Some may leave the room. The author is making fun of people who drink liquor and get into arguments.

The writer presents only facts about gun violence; he or she does not urge a course of action.
(An appropriate course of action might logically be *inferred*, but no such recommendation is *stated*.)

_____I_____ 6. ¹Guns are being used more widely than ever in our society and in other parts of the world. ²The fatality rate for gun injuries is 30 percent higher than the fatality rate for injuries of all causes (less than 1 percent). ³More than 60 percent of the homicides and 55 percent of the suicides committed each year in the United States involve the use of guns. ⁴Gun violence is a leading killer of teenagers and young men, especially African American men, and the use of semiautomatic assault weapons by individuals and gang members is common. ⁵Colleges and universities are not immune to gun violence. ⁶A recent study found that 4.3 percent of college students had a working firearm at college. ⁷Of these, nearly half stated that they had the gun for protection.

By describing how one can "find an existence that enables one to be kind," the author implies that this is what we should do.

_____P_____ 7. ¹When asked by his nephew what he ought to do in life, Henry James replied: "Three things in human life are important. ²The first is to be kind. ³The second is to be kind. ⁴And the third is to be kind." ⁵The key to those words is the repetition—the insistence that one find an existence that enables one to be kind. ⁶How to do so? ⁷By wading in, over and over, with that purpose in mind, with a willingness to sail on, tacking and tacking again, helped by those we aim to help, guided by our moral yearnings on behalf of

(Continues on next page)

others, on behalf of ourselves with others: a commitment to others that won't avoid squalls and periods of drift, a commitment that will become the heart of the journey itself.

B. Each of the following passages illustrates better than the others one of the five different tones identified in the box below. In the space provided, put the letter of the tone that best applies to each passage. Use each tone once. (Three tone choices will be left over.)

A. approving	B. bewildered	C. disapproving
D. malicious	E. objective	F. pessimistic

_____A_____ 8.

The writer's statement that the rejection of gender stereotyping has "benefited our society immensely" indicates an approving tone.

¹Androgyny, or the blending of both feminine and masculine qualities, is more clearly evident in our society now than ever before. ²Today it is quite common to see men involved in raising children (including changing diapers) and doing routine housework. ³On the other hand, it is also quite common to see women entering the workplace in jobs traditionally managed by men and participating in sports traditionally played by men. ⁴Men are not scoffed at when their eyes tear during a sad movie. ⁵Women are not laughed at when they choose to assert themselves. ⁶The rejection of many sexual stereotypes has probably benefited our society immensely by relieving people of the pressure to be 100 percent "womanly" or 100 percent "macho."

_____C_____ 9.

The writer's choice of examples of today's concept of freedom, combined with sentence 7, suggests his or her disapproval.

¹Freedom, in this culture, means that whatever makes you happy is okay. ²This is the freedom of a fourteen-year-old child. ³Freedom to eat a whole box of doughnuts in one sitting. ⁴Freedom to make a mess, to be loud and obnoxious, to blow things up, to inflict injury for the thrill of it, to conceive babies without care or thought for the consequences. ⁵Mostly, it is freedom from authority, particularly parental authority which, when it exists at all now, often functions at a level qualitatively no higher than a child's. ⁶Under this version of freedom, there is no legitimate claim for any authority to regulate human desires—not even the personal conscience—nor any appropriate scale of management, and all supposed authorities are viewed as corrupt, mendacious, and irrelevant. ⁷This view of freedom is not what Hamilton, Jefferson, Madison, and the other founders had in mind.

_____F_____ 10.

The writer predicts the many negative consequences of global warming and indicates that it is inevitable.

¹Human activities are to blame for a dramatic increase in global warming, and the effects are and will continue to be <u>disastrous</u>. ²The average global temperature has risen about 1 degree Fahrenheit since the late 19th century, and scientific models show that it will rise another 2.2 to 10 degrees Fahrenheit in the next decade. ³This will lead to an <u>increase in the frequency and intensity of extreme weather events such as floods, droughts, heat waves, and hurricanes</u>. ⁴<u>Crops will fail, glaciers will melt, sea levels will rise, and animal and plant species will be wiped out</u>. ⁵Political and business leaders who are in a position to work to counteract global warming are too invested in the status quo to take significant actions, so there is <u>little chance that this crisis will be averted</u>.

PURPOSE AND TONE: Mastery Test 5

Read the passages below. Then carefully consider the questions that follow, and, in the spaces provided, write the letters of the best responses.

Items 1–2:
The author entertains us with the vivid and amusing contrast between his temperature preference and his wife's. The tone is lighthearted.

A. ¹I wake up and bounce out of bed in a pleasant mood and then notice that I can see my breath. ²There is frost on the bathroom mirror and a thin sheet of ice in the toilet. ³So I trot downstairs and turn up the thermostat. ⁴I like the house to be cozy, as if we had a blazing fire in each room, but <u>I am married to Nanook of the North, who feels a person of character can put on a warm sweater and be comfortable at 58 degrees.</u>

⁵The furnace rumbles in the basement, and I make coffee and fetch the paper. ⁶<u>Then she appears in the kitchen in her woolens and says, "The thermostat was set at 85. ⁷Do we have elderly people coming for breakfast?"</u> ⁸I explain that I had found the thermostat set low. ⁹"Put on a sweater," she says.

___C___ 1. The primary purpose of this paragraph is to
   A. inform.   B. persuade.   C. entertain.

___B___ 2. The predominant tone of this paragraph can be described as
   A. scornful.   C. conceited.
   B. lighthearted.   D. revengeful.

Items 3–4:
The paragraph presents facts about Heifer International without persuading us to donate to it. The only anecdote concerns Don West's experience that led him to found the organization. Calling Heifer International a "remarkable organization" and mentioning its "unique feature" and that it is active in 115 countries indicates an admiring tone.

B. ¹During the Spanish Civil War in the late 1930s, Indiana farmer Dan West was serving as a volunteer relief worker. ²He grew frustrated with having to decide how to distribute limited food aid. ³Upon returning home, he founded the <u>remarkable organization</u> now known as Heifer International, whose aim is to provide permanent hunger relief by giving families their own livestock. ⁴Donors to Heifer International can purchase an entire animal or a "share" of a gift animal, which is then given to a family in need. ⁵A <u>unique feature of</u> Heifer International's program is that recipient families are required to pass at least one of their animal's female offspring along to a neighboring family. ⁶That family in turn passes on one of its animals, and so on. ⁷As of 2006, <u>Heifer International had distributed sheep, rabbits, honeybees, pigs, llamas, water buffalo, chicks, ducks, goats, geese and trees as well as heifers in 115 countries around the world.</u>

___A___ 3. The primary purpose of this paragraph is to
   A. inform readers about the existence and work of Heifer International.
   B. persuade readers to donate to Heifer International.
   C. entertain readers with anecdotes about relief ventures in other countries.

___C___ 4. The tone of this paragraph can be described as
   A. critical.   C. admiring.
   B. straightforward.   D. amusing.

(Continues on next page)

Items 5–6:
The passage informs us of the problem of identity theft. It defines identity theft, gives two reasons it is increasing, and names four signs that one might be a victim.

C. [1]"Identify theft" sounds like something out of a futuristic movie, but it's very much a problem in the here and now. [2]Identity theft is committed by a person who has gained access to your personal information and is passing himself off as you, usually to make purchases or conduct illegal activity. [3]With the increasing popularity of credit cards and, especially, the rising number of people making purchases over the Internet, identity theft is becoming much more common. [4]Signs that you have been a victim of identity theft include getting letters or phone calls saying you have been approved or turned down for credit you never applied for; seeing charges on your credit card statement for things you didn't buy; failing to receive your credit card statements in the mail; or receiving calls from collection agencies concerning accounts you never opened.

_A_ 5. The primary purpose of this paragraph is to
    A. inform.   B. persuade.   C. entertain.

_C_ 6. The predominant tone of this paragraph can be described as
    A. sympathetic.   C. instructive.
    B. cheerful.   D. detached.

Items 7–8:
The writer is disgusted that virtually nothing is required of potential parents. Words such as *awfully messed-up priorities* (sentence 5) and *ignorant and uninformed parents* (sentence 6) suggest the writer's disgust. By contrasting the lack of thought that goes into producing a baby with the thought given to adopting a pet, the writer further emphasizes this disgust.

D. [1]When you adopt a dog from the pound, you have to fill out an application and prove that you will be a suitable owner. [2]When you want to drive a car, you have to pass a driver's test and get a license. [3]When you want to become a citizen of this country, you must prove you know something about the history and government of the U.S. [4]But to become a parent—certainly the hardest and most important job anyone ever does, if it's done right—you don't have to do anything but produce a baby. [5]This state of affairs reflects some awfully messed-up priorities. [6]I am sick of seeing, almost every day, another tragic news story about a helpless infant battered, starved, or otherwise mistreated by ignorant and uninformed parents. [7]At the very minimum, middle-school and high-school students should be required to take classes in parenting and child care. [8]Beyond that, a pregnant couple should be required to show they have a plan to care for and raise their child. [9]Too many children are brought into this world with even less thought than is given to adopting a pet. [10]And once those children get here, they receive far less affection and caring than a dog or cat.

_B_ 7. The primary purpose of this paragraph is to
    A. inform.   B. persuade.   C. entertain.

_C_ 8. The main tone of this paragraph can be described as
    A. tolerant.   C. disgusted.
    B. apologetic.   D. depressed.

PURPOSE AND TONE: Mastery Test 6

Read the paragraphs below. Then carefully consider the questions that follow, and, in the spaces provided, write the letters of the best responses.

Items 1–2:
The writer conveys information in a way that appeals to the reader's senses and imagination. She feels a sense of joy that the mystery of language has been revealed to her and anticipates that other barriers will be swept away, as well.
The writer's choice of words further supports this tone.

A. ¹Someone was drawing water, and my teacher placed my hand under the spout. ²As the cool stream gushed over one hand, she spelled into the other the word *water*, first slowly, then rapidly. ³I stood still, my whole attention fixed upon the motion of her fingers. ⁴Suddenly I felt a misty consciousness as of something forgotten—a <u>thrill</u> of returning thought; and <u>somehow the mystery of language was revealed to me.</u> ⁵I knew that "w-a-t-e-r" meant the <u>wonderful</u> cool something that was flowing over my hand. ⁶The living word <u>awakened</u> my soul, gave it light, hope, joy, set it free! ⁷There were barriers still, it is true, but barriers that could in time be swept away.

—From *The Story of My Life,* by Helen Keller, a blind and deaf woman

_C_ 1. The primary purpose of this paragraph is to
   A. inform.   B. persuade.   C. inform and entertain.

_A_ 2. The tone of this paragraph can be described as
   A. optimistic and joyful.   C. matter-of-fact.
   B. lighthearted and sentimental.   D. warm but self-pitying.

Items 3–4:
Persuasive clue: *should* (used twice in sentence 9). The facts the writer presents in sentences 1–7 indicate his or her distress. The writer's choice of words (see underlined words) indicates his or her passion.

B. ¹In the Civil War, 365,000 Northern soldiers were killed, and 133,000 soldiers from the South died. ²In World War I, 116,000 American soldiers were killed. ³In World War II, 407,000 died; 54,000 died in Korea; 58,000 in Vietnam.

⁴More than a million Americans have died in our wars, each one much loved by someone. ⁵Twelve of my classmates died in World War II, but my memory of them comes at unexpected times—not on Memorial Day—and I would like to see the effort we now put into this one day redirected.

⁶There are men in every country on earth—mostly men—who spend full time <u>devising new ways for us to kill each other.</u> ⁷In the United States alone, <u>we spend seven times as much on war as on education.</u>

⁸<u>There's something wrong here.</u> ⁹On this Memorial Day, we <u>should</u> certainly honor those who have died in war, but we <u>should</u> dedicate this day not so much to their memory, but to the search for a way to end the idiocy of the wars that killed them.

_B_ 3. The primary purpose of this paragraph is to
   A. inform.   B. persuade.   C. entertain.

_A_ 4. The tone of this paragraph can be described as
   A. passionate and distressed.   C. detached and matter-of-fact.
   B. admiring and sentimental.   D. worried but optimistic.

(Continues on next page)

Items 5–6:
The paragraph, which is the beginning of the Declaration of Independence, argues for the right of citizens to throw off unjust government. The words *it is their duty* (sentence 5) suggest that this is something people must do. The language and sentence structure of the passage are dignified and purposeful.

C. [1]We hold these truths to be self-evident, that all men are created equal, that they are endowed by their Creator with certain unalienable rights, that among these are life, liberty and the pursuit of happiness. [2]That to secure these rights, governments are instituted among men, deriving their just powers from the consent of the governed. [3]That whenever any form of government becomes destructive of these ends, it is the right of the people to alter or to abolish it, and to institute new government, laying its foundations on such principles and organizing its powers in such form, as to them shall seem most likely to effect their safety and happiness. [4]Prudence, indeed, will dictate that governments long established should not be changed for light and transient causes; and accordingly all experience hath shown that mankind are more disposed to suffer, while evils are sufferable, than to right themselves by abolishing the forms to which they are accustomed. [5]But when a long train of abuses and usurpations, pursuing invariably the same object, evinces a design to reduce them under absolute despotism, it is their right, it is their duty, to throw off such government, and to provide new guards for their future security.

___B___ 5. The primary purpose of this paragraph is to
   A. inform.   B. persuade.   C. inform and entertain.

___A___ 6. The tone of this paragraph can be described as
   A. solemn and determined.   C. alarmed and pessimistic.
   B. bitter and indignant.   D. indignant and superior.

Items 7–8:
The writer of this passage is advising us of the correct attitude toward life. The imperatives *(Go, remember, be,* etc.) urge us to do these things. The underlined words suggest the optimistic and inspirational tone.

D. [1]Go placidly amid the noise and the haste, and remember what peace there may be in silence. [2]As far as possible, without surrender, be on good terms with all persons. [3]Speak your truth quietly and clearly; and listen to others, even to the dull and the ignorant; they too have their story. . . .

[4]Beyond a wholesome discipline, be gentle with yourself. [5]You are a child of the universe, no less than the trees and the stars; you have a right to be here. [6]And whether or not it is clear to you, no doubt the universe is unfolding as it should.

[7]Therefore, be at peace with God, whatever you conceive Him to be. [8]And whatever your labors and aspirations in the noisy confusion of life, keep peace in your soul. [9]With all its sham, drudgery and broken dreams, it is still a beautiful world. [10]Be cheerful. [11]Strive to be happy.

___B___ 7. The primary purpose of this paragraph is to
   A. inform.   B. persuade.   C. entertain.

___D___ 8. The predominant tone of this paragraph can be described as
   A. warm but self-pitying.   C. reflective and nostalgic.
   B. worried and sorrowful.   D. optimistic and inspirational.

8

Argument

Many of us enjoy a good argument. A good argument is not an emotional experience in which people allow their anger to get out of control, leaving them ready to start throwing things. Instead, it is a rational discussion in which each person advances and supports a point of view about some matter. We might argue with a friend, for example, about where to eat or what movie to see. We might argue about whether a boss or a parent or an instructor is acting in a fair or an unfair manner. We might argue about whether certain performers or sports stars deserve to get paid as much as they do.

In an argument, the two parties each present their supporting evidence. (In the playful cartoon above, the wife's supporting evidence is simply that the husband has no say about where they will go for Thanksgiving!) The goal is to determine who has the more solid evidence to support his or her point of view.

Argumentation is, then, a part of our everyday dealings with other people. It is also an important part of much of what we read. Authors often try to convince us of their opinions and interpretations. Very often the most important things we must do as critical readers are

1   Recognize the **point** the author is making.

2   Decide if the author's support is **relevant**.

3   Decide if the author's support is **adequate**.

This chapter will give you practice in doing the above, first in everyday arguments and then in textbook material.

THE BASICS OF ARGUMENT: POINT AND SUPPORT

A good argument is one in which a point is stated and then persuasively and logically supported. Here is a point:

> *Point:* **Evidence suggests that men are more romantic than women.**

You may well disagree with this, especially if you are a woman. "Why do you say that?" you might legitimately ask. "Give your reasons." Support is needed so you can decide for yourself whether a valid argument has been made. Suppose the point is followed by these three reasons:

1.   Studies indicate that men fall in love more easily than women, whereas women fall out of love more easily than men.

2.   In interviews, women are more likely than men to say they would marry someone they didn't love.

3.   Research shows that men hold more romantic beliefs such as "Love lasts forever" than women do.

Clearly, the details provide solid support for the point. They give you a basis for understanding and agreeing with the point. Of course, you may want to see the research. You may question just what is meant by the word "romantic." And based on your personal experience, you might decide to disagree. You could then try to provide evidence that supports your point of view.

Many issues in everyday life are the subject of argument. Is single life preferable to married life? Should abortions be banned? Should gay marriages be legalized? Should the death penalty exist? Should mercy killing be permitted? Should the United States have gotten involved in Iraq? Should handguns be banned? Should contraceptives be distributed in schools?

For all these and many other complex issues, there are no easy answers, and arguments about them are bound to persist. Typically, even when one of these issues goes in some form before the U.S. Supreme Court, where all the support is examined in great detail, the judges are often unable to reach a unanimous opinion.

Given the complexity of important issues, we must try our best to think as clearly as we can about them. We must decide what we individually think after close consideration of all the evidence available.

☑ Check Your Understanding

Let's look at another example:

Point: Hitting children at times is (*or* is not) a good way to discipline them.

What is your point of view? Is it OK for adults to hit children at times?

___ OK ___ Not OK

Circle in the list below the letters of the **three** reasons that you feel solidly support your point of view. And in the space underneath, feel free to add another reason or two that you feel support your point.

A. Hitting a child is the quickest and most effective way to let the child know that he or she has done wrong.

If "OK" is checked, these answers should be circled: A, C, E.

If "Not OK" is checked, these answers should be circled: B, D, F.

B. Hitting a child teaches him that bigger people are allowed to hurt smaller people. This can lead to the child becoming a bully to smaller children.

C. Disciplinary methods other than spanking, such as a "time out," withdrawing a privilege, or reasoning with the child, just drag out the punishment. It's better to just get it over with.

D. Children who are spanked learn that hitting is the appropriate response to anger. They are likely to become violent adults, to abuse their partners, and to hit and even abuse their own children.

E. It is a parent's job to teach a child to respect and obey those in authority. If a parent doesn't use firm discipline such as hitting, the child will grow up to be a misbehaving, disrespectful adult.

F. Even parents who intend to spank their child only gently can easily lose their temper and hit the child harder than they planned. Many cases of child abuse have begun with "only a spanking."

At your option, write here any other reason(s) you may have in support of your position: _____ *Answers will vary.* _____

_____

_____

Explanation

If you think it's **not** OK to hit kids, you would have chosen B, D, and F as your support. If you think it **is** OK, you would have chosen A, C, and E. The heart of the matter here is that you must determine, by careful and clear thinking, your own point of view about a given issue. Your aim is to construct a valid argument—one supported by what you feel are the most logical facts, examples, reasons, or other evidence.

The Point and Support of an Argument

In everyday life, of course, people don't simply say "Here is my point" and "Here is my support." Even so, the basic structure of point and support is just under the surface of most opinions, and to evaluate an opinion and argument, you need to examine the unspoken support.

The following activity will help sharpen your understanding of a point and its support. The activity may also deepen your sense of the complexity of many everyday issues.

➤ *Practice 1*

For each statement, choose your point of view by checking "I agree" or "I disagree." Then circle the letters of the three items that support your point of view. At your option, add, in the space provided under each item, additional support for your point of view.

> **Note** Be forewarned: People are passionate about many of the following issues. You will probably agree or disagree strongly with some of the evidence. The purpose here is not to endorse either side of a given issue, but rather to sharpen your sense of the point and support that is the backbone of any argument. A secondary purpose is to encourage civilized adult discussion of some important matters in our country today.

1. *Point:* **The death penalty should exist for certain crimes.**

If "I agree" is checked, these answers should be circled: A, C, D.

If "I disagree" is checked, these answers should be circled: B, E, F.

____ I agree   ____ I disagree

A. Certain crimes, such as the rape and murder of a child, are so heinous that there is no possibility of rehabilitation for the perpetrator. Such a person has given up his right to be treated as a human being and deserves nothing but death. Society should not have to put up with such individuals.

B. The death penalty does not deter anyone from committing a crime. It is absurd to believe that anyone thinks, "I am willing to risk life in prison, but not execution" before acting.

C. The death penalty acts as a strong deterrent to crime. It serves as a reminder that there are certain acts that society will not tolerate.

D. It is a misuse of taxpayers' money to keep killers alive on death row. The cost of providing prisoners with food, housing and medical care for decades is staggering. Our tax dollars can be put to far better use.

E. The death penalty is inconsistently and unfairly applied. Poor minority criminals without access to good legal representation are far more likely to be executed than more affluent white criminals.

F. The great majority of developed nations have rejected capital punishment as a remnant of a barbaric system of justice. The United States is alone among affluent Western nations in retaining it. By allowing capital punishment, the U.S. has aligned itself philosophically with such countries as Libya, Vietnam, Iran, and China and against countries that include Mexico, Canada, Italy, France, Australia, England, Norway, and Sweden.

Optional additional support for your point of view: _____ *Answers will vary.*

_____

_____

I agree:
A argues some crimes are so bad they require the death penalty. C argues it is a strong deterrent. D argues it wastes tax money to keep prisoners alive.

I disagree:
B argues it deters no one. E argues it is inconsistently and unfairly applied. F argues that most developed countries have rejected the death penalty.

Optional minority point of view: Is there one point for the other side that you have some sympathy for? If so, put its letter here: _____. (Some issues are so complex that you may, to some extent, have a divided point of view.)

2. **Point: Contraceptives should be distributed in high schools.**

____ I agree   ____ I disagree

If "I agree" is checked, these answers should be circled: C, D, F.

If "I disagree" is checked, these answers should be circled: A, B, E.

A. Distributing contraceptives in high school amounts to condoning teen sexual activity. High school students should be encouraged to postpone sexual activity until they are older, not given the message that it's OK to be sexually active.

B. Part of having good moral values is to "just say no" and to refrain from sex outside of marriage. Teenage virginity is a virtue that should be promoted, not discouraged. By making contraceptives available, schools will discourage chaste behavior.

C. Most people who would use a contraception-distribution program are sexually active already. The program would help prevent unwanted pregnancies that would happen otherwise.

D. Although sex education should ideally come from one's parents, many parents are not willing or able to do the job. The school is the logical next best source for education about and help with contraception.

I agree:
C argues it would help prevent unwanted pregnancies.
D argues schools must do what parents are unable or unwilling to do. F argues it is part of teaching responsible sexuality.

I disagree:
A argues it condones teenage sexual activity. B argues it discourages chaste behavior.
E argues contraceptives should be distributed by medical professionals.

E. There can be a lot of confusion and misunderstanding about how to use contraceptives properly, how effective they are, and whether they prevent the spread of STD's. Distributing them at school will just add to that confusion. Medical professionals, not high school personnel, should be the ones to provide people with contraceptives and education about using them properly.

F. Sex is a normal part of life, not something to be hidden away as if it were shameful. Responsible sexuality should be taught at school like any other life skill, and making contraceptives available should be part of that teaching.

Optional additional support for your point of view: _____Answers will vary._____

Optional minority point of view: Is there one point for the other side that you have some sympathy for? If so, put its letter here: _____. (Some issues are so complex that you may, to some extent, have a divided point of view.)

3. *Point:* **Abortion should be banned.**

If "I agree" is checked, these answers should be circled: A, C, E.

If "I disagree" is checked, these answers should be circled: B, D, F.

____ I agree   ____ I disagree

A. Abortion is murder. A fetus is a human being from the moment of conception. Just as it is illegal to kill a full-term baby, it should be illegal to kill an unborn baby.

B. Abortion is preferable to having women bear unwanted babies. Every day there are stories in the news about unwanted children being abused and neglected. There are already too many unwanted children in the world. Abortion is a practical solution to that problem.

C. Legal abortion encourages sexual immorality. People are less careful about using contraception if they have the option of abortion.

D. Abortion is a woman's civil right. Almost invariably, it is the woman who ends up bearing most of the responsibility for raising a child. It should be the woman's choice whether or not to bear a child.

E. Abortion cheapens the sanctity of life in all its forms. If abortion is legal, people will soon want to legalize the killing of the sick, the mentally retarded, the elderly, and other helpless individuals.

I agree:
A argues that abortion is murder.
C argues it encourages sexual immorality.
E argues it cheapens the sanctity of life and will lead to other legalized killings.

I disagree:
B argues that it is a practical solution to unwanted children.
D argues that it is a woman's right.
F argues that the moral decision should be up to the individual.

F. It is an individual decision whether or not abortion is morally right or wrong. If a person has religious scruples against abortion, she is free not to have an abortion. But someone else's religious beliefs should not be the basis for law.

Optional additional support for your point of view: _____*Answers will vary.*_____

_____

_____

Optional minority point of view: Is there one point for the other side that you have some sympathy for? If so, put its letter here: _____. (Some issues are so complex that you may, to some extent, have a divided point of view.)

4. *Point:* **Gay couples should be legally allowed to marry.**

If "I agree" is checked, these answers should be circled: C, D, E.

___ I agree   ___ I disagree

A. Throughout history, marriage has been defined as the union of a man and a woman. Centuries of tradition should not be tossed out in order to accommodate gay couples.

If "I disagree" is checked, these answers should be circled: A, B, F.

B. Many people consider homosexuality to be morally wrong. It is offensive to them to see the state and/or church recognize gay marriages.

C. Gay marriage would represent a strengthening of our society. Marriage of any type encourages "family values" such as commitment and monogamy.

I agree:
C argues it would strengthen society.
D argues it allows gay people to participate more fully in society.
E argues it would give gay couples appropriate legal and financial protections.

D. Gay people deserve to have their committed relationships recognized and honored as much as straight people. Being able to marry would allow gays to take a further step in "coming out" into full participation in society.

E. The legal and financial protection offered by marriage should be the right of gay couples as well as straight couples.

F. Gay marriage is unnecessary. Gays may be offered "civil unions" that offer some legal protection, but stop short of being called marriage.

I disagree:
A argues it would destroy centuries of tradition.
B argues it is offensive to many.
F argues it is unnecessary because the protections can be made available through civil unions.

Optional additional support for your point of view: _____*Answers will vary.*_____

_____

_____

Optional minority point of view: Is there one point for the other side that you have some sympathy for? If so, put its letter here: _____. (Some issues are so complex that you may, to some extent, have a divided point of view.)

5. *Point:* **Physicians should be allowed to assist in suicide.**

If "I agree" is checked, these answers should be circled: A, C, E.

If "I disagree" is checked, these answers should be circled: B, D, F.

___ I agree   ___ I disagree

A. Knowing they have the option of requesting physician-assisted suicide gives many terminally ill patients peace of mind. In fact, many people who have made arrangements for physician-assisted suicide end up not using the option. They still benefit from the knowledge that if their suffering becomes too intense, they can control when and how they die.

B. Life belongs to God. It should end only when God decides to end it. Any form of suicide is wrong.

C. Physician-assisted suicide relieves the patient's family of the heavy responsibility of deciding when to withdraw further care. A person can choose to die when she is ready, knowing that her family will not have to decide to "pull the plug" if she becomes unresponsive and unable to make her wishes known.

D. If physician-assisted suicide is legal, sick, elderly people will be pressured to make use of it. Instead of honoring and caring for our sick elders, we will become a society that wants to hurry them into death when they become infirm.

E. Physician-assisted suicide allows patients to opt out of suffering through a long, painful death. Enduring such a death is as agonizing for their loved ones as it is painful for the patients themselves.

F. The purpose of a physician is to heal the sick. It is a perversion of the physician's role to ask doctors to assist in suicide.

I agree:
A argues that it gives people peace of mind.
C argues that it relieves families of difficult responsibilities.
E argues that it prevents needless suffering.

I disagree:
B argues that any form of suicide is wrong.
D argues the elderly will be pressured to use it.
F argues that it perverts the doctor's role.

Optional additional support for your point of view: _____ *Answers will vary.* _____

Optional minority point of view: Is there one point for the other side that you have some sympathy for? If so, put its letter here: _____. (Some issues are so complex that you may, to some extent, have a divided point of view.)

RELEVANT SUPPORT

Once you identify the point and support of an argument, you need to decide if each piece of evidence is **relevant**—in other words, if it really applies to the point. The critical reader must ask, "Is this reason relevant support for the argument?"

In their desire to win an argument, people often bring up irrelevant support. For example, in asking you to vote for him, a political candidate might say, "I'll vote to lower your taxes." But your town or state might have such financial problems that lowering taxes would not be possible. You would then want to look closely at other reasons why you should or should not vote for this candidate.

An excellent way to develop skill in recognizing relevant support is to work on simple point-support outlines of arguments. By isolating the reasons of an argument, such outlines help you think about whether each reason is truly relevant. Paying close attention to the relevance of support will help you not only in your reading, but also in making and supporting points in your own writing.

☑ Check Your Understanding

Consider the following outline. The point is followed by six facts, only three of which are relevant support for the point. In the spaces, write the letters of the **three** relevant statements of support.

> *Point:* Despite their fearsome image, sharks have more to fear from humans than humans do from sharks.
>
> A. Some species of sharks are able to detect as little as one part per million of blood in seawater.
> B. Shark-fin soup is considered a great delicacy in the Far East, and hundreds of thousands of sharks have been slaughtered simply for their fins.
> C. Sharks can range in size from hand-sized pygmy sharks to plankton-eating whale sharks which grow to a maximum length of 49 feet.
> D. It's estimated that 100 million sharks, skates, and rays are caught and killed each year.
> E. Some populations of large sharks have fallen by as much as 90 percent due to accelerated fishing activities in recent decades.
> F. Large sharks such as great whites, tiger, and bull sharks have been known to attack people, perhaps mistaking them for seals.
>
> *Items that logically support the point:* ____*B*____   ____*D*____   ____*E*____

Explanation:

The three statements that support the idea that humans are dangerous to sharks are B, D, and E. The other three statements provide interesting facts about sharks but do not offer relevant support for the point in question. (You could not cite any of these interesting facts about sharks as support for the idea that sharks are dangerous. If you did so, you would be *changing the subject* by introducing irrelevant support.)

➤ *Practice 2*

Each point is followed by three statements that provide relevant support and three that do not. In the spaces, write the letters of the **three** relevant statements of support.

> *Hint*: To help you decide if a sentence is relevant, ask yourself, "Does this provide logical support for the point being argued?"

1. **Point:** E-waste, or waste from discarded computers and other electronic equipment, is currently the most rapidly growing waste problem in the world.

Answers C, D, and F do not support the point that E-waste is a growing problem. C offers a solution; D is a fact about software; F is a fact about computer support jobs.

    A. Amounts of electronic waste are increasing nearly three times more quickly than amounts of other municipal wastes.

    B. Discarded electronics equipment contains lead, mercury, cadmium, PCBs, dioxins, and other toxic substances.

    C. Some components in discarded computers can be successfully recycled.

    D. The United States is a world leader in the development of computer software programs.

    E. Environmental, health, and safety regulations make recycling E-waste unprofitable in the United States, so we have been shipping it around the world to countries with inadequate environmental protections.

    F. The United States has been increasingly outsourcing its computer support jobs to India and other developing nations.

Items that logically support the point: ___A___ ___B___ ___E___

2. **Point:** Childhood obesity has a number of causes.

    A. Overweight children are at risk for a number of health problems throughout their lives.

Answers A, C, and F do not concern causes of childhood obesity. A is a result; C is a fact about it; F describes a way to cope with the problem.

    B. The increasing popularity of computers, video games, and other electronic entertainment has caused children to become more sedentary.

    C. It is estimated that about 18 percent of American children are overweight.

    D. Many kids live in areas where they cannot safely go outside for physical exercise.

    E. Fatty fast food and high-calorie snacks make up a large portion of many children's diets.

    F. There are a growing number of "fat camps" aimed at helping youngsters lose weight during vacation.

Items that logically support the point: ___B___ ___D___ ___E___

Answers A, D, and E do not support the point that former prisoners often continue to commit crimes. A is about what prisoners suffer from; D is about who commits violent crimes; and E concerns the academic success of some prisoners.

3. **Point:** A major problem with prisons is that they fail to teach their clients to stay away from crime.

   A. A number of prisoners are suffering from mental illness, addiction, or both.
   B. Three out of every four prisoners have been in prison before.
   C. When prisoners convicted of violent crimes are released, in just three years half are back in prison.
   D. Far more men than women are imprisoned for violent crimes.
   E. Some prisoners earn their GEDs or higher degrees while in prison.
   F. More than seventy percent of those jailed for stealing cars, burglary, and robbery commit similar crimes after they are released.

   Items that logically support the point: ___B___   ___C___   ___F___

Answers B, C, and F do not provide examples of other foods which are high in vitamin C. B is about citrus fruit production; C is about the problem of not getting enough vitamin C; and F is about what vitamin C may do for people.

4. **Point:** Contrary to popular belief, citrus fruits are not the only foods which are high in vitamin C.

   A. Potatoes provide about 20 percent of all the vitamin C in the U.S. diet.
   B. Florida and California are two states which lead the nation in producing oranges and other citrus fruits.
   C. Sailors once got the disease known as scurvy on long ocean voyages because they were deprived of foods that were high in vitamin C.
   D. A single serving of broccoli, green pepper, or cauliflower provides nearly the entire recommended daily amount of vitamin C.
   E. Cantaloupes and strawberries are high in vitamin C.
   F. Evidence is inconclusive that taking large amounts of vitamin C can prevent colds.

   Items that logically support the point: ___A___   ___D___   ___E___

Answers A, B, and D do not explain how the Internet has provided expanded opportunities for people to meet and develop relationships. A is about the origins of the World Wide Web; B tells how Internet sexual predators are caught; and D explains how to protect children.

5. **Point:** The Internet, despite scare stories about online predators, has dramatically expanded opportunities for people to meet and develop relationships.

   A. In 1990, Swiss engineers created the World Wide Web by connecting a set of computers that all used the same communications program.
   B. Law enforcement officers sometimes pose as teenagers in Internet chat rooms in order to lure sexual predators out into the open.
   C. The Internet offers a wealth of new opportunities to interact for those normally separated because of geography, physical infirmity, or social anxiety.
   D. Parents should carefully monitor their children's use of the Internet and block sites that are inappropriate for minors to view.

E. Internet groups provide a safer way to communicate for people who have often been the target of hostility and discrimination in the past (for example, gays and transsexuals).

F. Internet groups for those with grave illnesses (cancer, diabetes, AIDS, multiple sclerosis, and so on) provide important information and support to their subscribers.

Items that logically support the point: _____C_____ _____E_____ _____F_____

ADEQUATE SUPPORT

A valid argument must include not only relevant support but also **adequate** support—substantial enough to prove the point. For example, it would not be valid to argue "Abortion is wrong" if one's only support was "My sister had an abortion and has regretted it ever since." Such an important issue would require more support than the attitude and experience of a single relative. Arguing a point that doesn't have adequate support is called "jumping to a conclusion" or "hasty generalization."

You will seldom see a textbook author jump to a conclusion; instead, the author's approach will be to present the existing data about a given subject and then to draw reasonable conclusions based upon that data. As always, the key to understanding will be to focus on what points the author is making and what support is being provided for those points.

☑ *Check Your Understanding*

In the argument below, four supporting reasons are given, followed by four possible conclusions. The evidence (that is, the supporting reasons) adequately supports only one of the points; it is insufficient to support the other three. Check (✓) the **one** point that you think is adequately supported.

Support:
- A happily married man or woman might attribute a spouse's distracted manner to stress at work.
- An unhappily married man or woman might attribute a distracted manner to a decline in affection.
- A happily married man or woman might attribute a spouse's unexpected gift to a desire to show love.
- An unhappily married man or woman might consider an unexpected gift as evidence of guilt about something.

Which **point** is adequately supported by all the evidence above?

____ A. Men or women who surprise their partners with gifts have probably been cheating on them.

✓ B. Happily and unhappily married spouses tend to interpret their partners' behaviors differently.

___ C. People who are happily married are often deluding themselves about reality.

___ D. Spouses should give one another gifts more often.

Explanation:

The correct answer is B. All of the supporting items back up the idea that one partner's interpretation of the other partner's behavior can be influenced by whether they are happy or unhappy in the marriage. None of the other three items, A, C, or D, is backed up by the items of support.

➤ Practice 3

In each group that follows, the support is from experiments, surveys, studies, and other evidence in textbooks. Check (✓) the **point** in each case that is adequately supported by the evidence.

Group 1

Support:

- Ads in magazines such as *Glamour, Ebony*, and *Esquire* are four times more likely to display women's buttocks, legs, stomach, shoulders, or back than to show men's.
- In television beer commercials, the camera shots are significantly more likely to focus on women's bodies than on men's bodies.
- In newspapers, a typical photograph of a man dedicates two-thirds of the space to his face, while the typical photograph of a woman dedicates only one-half of the space to her face.

_C_ 1. Which **point** is adequately supported by all the evidence above?
- A. The media are responsible for much of the gender inequality in our society.
- B. Exploitation of women is the single greatest problem in American society today.
- C. Media images tend to emphasize men's faces and women's bodies.
- D. Most news and entertainment media are controlled by men.

> Answers A and B do not work because the support items do not mention other causes of gender inequality or other social problems. Answer D is incorrect because the items say nothing about control of media.

Group 2

Support:

- Engaging in stimulating activities and hobbies can help older adults retain sharp mental abilities.
- Elderly people who remain socially active are by and large happier than those who do not.
- Volunteering to help others tends to increase elderly people's overall sense of life satisfaction.

____A____ 2. Which **point** is adequately supported by all the evidence above?

  A. There are steps people can take to make their elder years enjoyable.
  B. Growing old is a difficult and challenging process.
  C. A person who is not socially outgoing cannot have an enjoyable life.
  D. Helping other people is the single most effective way to increase one's life satisfaction.   Answer B does not work because the items are not about the difficulties of aging. C is incorrect because one still might get pleasure from volunteer work and from activities and hobbies. D is incorrect because no comparison is made with other ways of increasing satisfaction.

Group 3

Support:

- Neurotic individuals tend to appraise events as more stressful than other individuals and to become more distressed by problems.
- Neurotic people report more health problems and visit the doctor more often than other individuals, although their symptoms are often found to have no physical basis.
- Neurotic individuals often suffer from a range of anxieties that seem exaggerated to others.

____D____ 3. Which **point** is adequately supported by all the evidence above?

  A. Neurotic people are seriously mentally ill and need to be institutionalized.
  B. Neurotic disorders are very rare.
  C. It is impossible for neurotic people to make friends.
  D. Being neurotic produces a range of problems that make life difficult.   Answers A, B, and C are unsupported because nothing is said in the support about what should be done, about the frequency of disorders, or about making friends.

Group 4

Support:

- The Constitution requires that a U.S. president be at least 35 years old.
- As of 2006, every U.S. president has been a white male.
- The Constitution requires that a U.S. president be a natural-born U.S. citizen.

_C_ 4. Which **point** is adequately supported by all the evidence above?
- A. No one who is not a white male will ever be U.S. president.
- B. The U.S. Constitution's requirements for the presidency are unfair.
- C. There are both formal requirements and traditional expectations for becoming president of the United States.
- D. It is it past time for a woman and for someone of a minority race to be U.S. president.   Answers A, B, and D are unsupported because nothing is said about the future, about fairness, or about what should happen.

Group 5

Support:

- In ancient Rome, wealthy citizens who aspired to political office expanded their influence by donating extremely expensive entertainments to the rest of the population of the city on a regular basis.
- Julius Caesar owed much of his political success to the fact that he was better than his rivals at providing the people with elaborate outdoor entertainment.
- One of Julius Caesar's public shows included a gladiatorial contest, stage-plays for every quarter of Rome performed in several languages, chariot races, athletic competitions, and a mock naval battle.

_B_ 5. Which **point** is adequately supported by all the evidence above?
- A. Above all, ancient Romans enjoyed chariot races.
- B. In ancient Rome, politicians were the ones who provided elaborate outdoor entertainment to the masses.
- C. In ancient Rome, leaders wasted their time providing free entertainment to the masses.
- D. Julius Caesar's skill at organizing mass entertainment was more important than his skill as a general.   The support does not say which event was most enjoyable (A), that the entertainment was a waste of time (C), or anything about Julius Caesar's skills as a general (D).

A Note on Argument in Textbook Writing

In most textbook writing, argument takes the form of well-developed ideas or theories (in other words, points) that are supported with experiments, surveys, studies, expert testimony, reasons, examples, or other evidence. Textbook arguments generally have solid support, but recognizing the author's points and asking yourself whether the support is relevant and adequate will help you be an involved and critical reader.

CHAPTER REVIEW

In this chapter, you learned the following:

- A good argument is made up of a point, or a conclusion, and logical evidence to back it up.
- To critically read an argument, you must recognize the **point** the author is making.
- To think through an argument, you need to decide if each piece of evidence is **relevant**.
- To think through an argument, you also need to decide if the author's support is **adequate**.
- Textbook arguments generally have solid support, but recognizing the author's point and watching for relevant and adequate support will help you become a more involved and critical reader.

The next chapter—Chapter 9—will explain other aspects of being a critical reader: separating fact from opinion, detecting propaganda, and recognizing errors in reasoning.

On the Web: If you are using this book in class, you can visit our website for additional practice in evaluating arguments. Go to **www.townsendpress.com** and click on "Online Exercises."

➤ Review Test 1

To review what you've learned in this chapter, answer each of the following questions by filling in the blank.

1. A good argument advances a clear _____*point*_____ of some kind.

2. The second basic part of a good argument is solid _____*support*_____.

3. Many issues in everyday life are the subject of continuing argument because the issues are so _____*complex*_____ that there are no easy answers or solutions.
   Items 1 and 2: See page 290.
   Item 3: See pages 290–291.

4. Good thinkers have the ability to look at evidence and decide what logical point or _____*conclusion*_____ can be drawn from that evidence.

See page 300.

5. Good thinkers have the ability to decide whether there is a(n) _____*adequate*_____ amount of evidence to convincingly support a point.

See page 300.

➤ Review Test 2

The essay below is followed by questions on argument and also the skills covered in previous chapters.

Preview

It's hard to argue that we're winning the war on drugs. So why wage it at all? There are compelling arguments for legalizing narcotics. In this essay, an opponent of legalization considers and refutes those points.

Words to Watch

futile (1): useless
wretched (12): of poor quality; very bad
Pandora's box (13): a source of many unforeseen troubles

A VOTE AGAINST LEGALIZING DRUGS

Gail Rollins

1   Why not legalize drugs? A number of respected individuals have raised the question. They include conservative columnist William F. Buckley, Jr., Nobel Prize-winning economist Milton Friedman, Mayor Kurt Schmoke of Baltimore, U.S. Rep. Fortney Stark of California, former Seattle police chief Norm Stamper, and Boston University professor Jeffrey Miron, among others. The war on drugs has been lost, they say; it's time to stop wasting the enormous resources that American society has been pouring into a futile° battle and start addressing the issue of drug abuse as a massive public health problem, not a legal one.

2   The points they make sound persuasive on their surface. But upon examination, it's clear that they amount to a doomed social experiment that would lead to catastrophe.

3   Let us look in turn at their usual claims, beginning with *"Legalizing drugs would mean the end of drug-related crime."*

4   Presumably it's true that if all forms of narcotics were given blanket legalization, the role of drug lords, corrupt government officials, pushers and drug

gangs would be phased out of existence. However, it does not follow that addicted persons would be less driven to desperate measures to obtain their needed fix. Drugs would still not be free. Addicts would still find it difficult to hold down a job and earn enough to support their habit. The killings, robberies, muggings and prostitution in order to get cash to spend on narcotics would not cease. With the enormous growth in the number of addicts each year, the opposite would very likely be true.

5   *"The government could tax drug sales and regulate the purity of narcotics if they were sold legally."*

6   The advocates of legalization point out that two other addictive substances —alcohol and tobacco—are legal and subject to government regulation. True enough. But consider this: According to the *Journal of the American Medical Association,* alcohol and tobacco combined are responsible for about 520,000 deaths a year. In 2000, the death toll connected with illegal drug use (including not only overdoses but drug-related homicide, suicide, motor vehicle accident, HIV infection, hepatitis, etc.) was only 17,000. No one imagines that *fewer* people would use drugs if the substances were taxed and regulated. The death rates would soar, creating an unimaginable toll of human misery.

7   *"The war on drugs is simply too expensive and too ineffective. The country can't afford to continue spending money at this rate."*

8   Granted, the price tag attached to fighting drug abuse is phenomenal. It's estimated that the federal government is spending about $20.4 billion a year on direct drug-enforcement activities. Add to that the costs for the state and local battles, plus the uncounted billions spent on feeding and housing those imprisoned for drug-related crimes (more than half of all federal prisoners fall in this category), and you end up with some breathtaking sums.

9   But legalizing narcotics would have its own enormous economic toll, not to mention the spiritual cost. Addiction would claim a countless number of citizens. "People say only 10 percent of those who drink are the problem drinkers, so they assume that only 10 percent of the people who take drugs will become addicts," said Mitchell Rosenthal, president of Phoenix House, a New York City-based drug rehabilitation program. "But there is no reason to believe that if we made crack available in little crack shops that only 10 percent would be addicted; the number would probably be more like 75 percent."

10   Currently, drug abuse costs American industry billions per year through lost productivity. Federal estimates say that at least 10 percent of workers now use illegal drugs while on the job. Imagine how those figures would soar if the restraints were off currently law-abiding citizens. If we didn't risk arrest and disgrace, how many of us could resist trying some seductive-sounding drug "just once"—perhaps crack cocaine, thought to be the most addictive substance on the planet? And what would be the fate of addicts if narcotics were available legally? In the words of one Los Angeles musician, addicted to cocaine for three years: "I'd be dead . . . I'd just sit down with a big pile of the stuff and snort it until I dropped."

11   But perhaps the most disturbing aspect of the move to legalize narcotics is

the quiet current of racism that whispers, "Those people are going to kill themselves anyway. I'm not going to waste my tax dollars trying to save them." A voice murmuring through parts of middle-class America says, "What does it matter if drugs wipe out a generation—as long as it's a generation of poor black and Hispanic kids who will just drain our society of welfare dollars throughout their lives?"

12   Is this an exaggeration? If so, where is the compassion for "those people" and their agonizing problems? Where is the public outcry over our country's gutting of education and job-training programs—the only kind of "drug prevention" that effectively addresses the real cause of most drug abuse: poverty and despair? When the buying power of the minimum wage has fallen 33 percent since 1968, is it surprising that poor teenagers choose the lucrative jobs offered them by drug dealers over flipping hamburgers? Where was the public protest in 2006, when Congress slashed financial aid to college students by $12 billion, even as the cost of college continued to soar? In 2004, when the number of children living in poverty rose to its highest level in ten years, did more fortunate Americans rise up to offer a hand? Those who would legalize narcotics are willfully ignoring the reason the underprivileged turn to drugs in such massive numbers: because drugs offer the only available escape from their wretched° existence.

13   Legalizing narcotics would open a deadly Pandora's box°, unleashing an unimaginable host of evils in this country. It is a notion that must not be seriously entertained.

Reading Comprehension Questions

Vocabulary in Context

___B___ 1. In the sentence below, the word *lucrative* (loo′krə-tĭv) means

    A. highly skilled.

    B. profitable.

    C. creative.

    D. boring.

> What kind of jobs would be the opposite of poorly paying ones such as flipping burgers?

"When the buying power of the minimum wage has fallen 33 percent since 1968, is it surprising that poor teenagers choose the lucrative jobs offered them by drug dealers over flipping hamburgers?" (Paragraph 12)

Central Point and Main Ideas

___D___ 2. Which sentence best expresses the central point of the selection?

    A. Because many drugs are so highly addictive, the death toll would soar if drugs were legalized.

    B. Legalizing drugs would not lower crime rates because addicts would still find it difficult to hold down a job and earn enough to support their habit.

    C. People who argue that drugs should be legalized don't really care if drug abuse wipes out a generation of poor black and Hispanic kids.

    D. Legalizing drugs in America would do nothing to address the underlying social problems that lead to drug abuse; it would also result in more drug addicts and continuing crime.   Answer A covers only paragraph 6; answer B covers only paragraph 4; answer C covers only paragraph 11.

___A___ 3. Which sentence best expresses the main idea of paragraph 1?

    A. Some respected Americans have urged America to legalize drugs.

    B. Some conservatives, such as William F. Buckley, support the legalization of drugs.

    C. Some respected Americans feel that the war on drugs has been lost.

    D. Some respected Americans agree that drug abuse is more a health problem than a legal problem.   Answer B is too narrow. Answers C and D do not mention the question of legalizing drugs.

Supporting Details

___D___ 4. According to the president of a drug rehabilitation program in New York City, if crack was made available in little crack shops,

    A. the percentage of those who tried it and went on to become addicted would be about 10%.

    B. the percentage of crack addicts would be less than the percentage of people who are problem drinkers.

    C. the percentage of crack addicts would equal the number of people who are problem drinkers.

    D. the percentage of those who tried it and went on to become addicted would be about 75%.   See the last sentence in paragraph 9.

Transitions

___D___ 5. The relationship expressed below is one of

    A. illustration.

    B. addition.   *Cause:* drugs offer escape; *effect:* underprivileged turn to drugs in massive numbers. The words *reason* and *because* signal a cause and effect relationship.

    C. contrast.

    D. cause and effect.

"Those who would legalize narcotics are willfully ignoring the <u>reason</u> the underprivileged turn to drugs in such massive numbers: <u>because</u> drugs offer the only available escape from their wretched existence." (Paragraph 12)

Patterns of Organization

__B__ 6. The overall pattern of organization in paragraph 12 is one of
- A. contrast.
- B. list of items.
- C. comparison.
- D. time order.

The paragraph lists examples of issues that create the "wretched existence" that some people "are willfully ignoring."

Inferences

__A__ 7. The author suggests that
- A. Americans need to address the social causes of most drug abuse rather than legalize drugs.
- B. poor teenagers should be willing to flip burgers rather than deal drugs.
- C. people who seek to legalize drugs have the best interests of poor blacks and Hispanics in mind.
- D. education and job-training programs fail to address the real causes of drug abuse. See paragraph 12. Answer B is contradicted by paragraph 12, sentence 4. C is contradicted by paragraphs 11–12. D is contradicted by paragraph 12, sentence 3.

Purpose and Tone

__B__ 8. On the basis of the reading—including its last sentence—we might conclude that the author's intention is
- A. only to inform.
- B. both to inform and to persuade.
- C. to entertain and to persuade.

The writer cites evidence indicating that the legalization of drugs would not be a good thing and also tries to persuade us not to legalize them. In the last sentence, the words *must not* signal a persuasive purpose.

__D__ 9. The author's tone in this selection may be characterized as
- A. uncertain.
- B. sarcastic.
- C. detached.
- D. concerned.

Phrases such as *an unimaginable toll of human misery, where is the compassion, their agonizing problems,* and *wretched existence* all demonstrate that the writer is deeply concerned about the issue she addresses.

Argument

__C__ 10. Three of the items below are supporting details for an argument. Write the letter of the statement that represents the **point** of this argument.
- A. In 2006, Congress slashed financial aid to college students by $12 billion.
- B. In 2004, the number of children living in poverty rose to its highest level in ten years.
- C. America has failed to address issues of poverty and lack of opportunity which lead to drug abuse.
- D. The buying power of the minimum wage has fallen 33 percent since 1968.

Answers A, B, and D are examples of America's failure to do something about the problems of poverty and lack of opportunity.

Discussion Questions

1. Before reading this essay, did you agree that drugs should be legalized—or did you disagree? Did the essay change your opinion in any way? If so, which of the author's points did you find most convincing?

2. Do you think drug abuse prevention programs, of the sort offered in many elementary and middle schools, are effective? Why or why not? What could make them work better?

3. The author states that the underprivileged turn to drugs as an escape from their wretched lives. Yet drug abuse is a growing problem in middle-class and wealthy communities as well. Why do you think this is so?

4. Imagine that you have just been elected president of the United States after promising the voters that you will do something significant to address the nation's drug problem. What steps would you take?

Note: Writing assignments for this selection appear on page 564.

Check Your Performance   **ARGUMENT**

Activity	*Number Right*	*Points*	*Score*
Review Test 1 (5 items)	_____	× 6 =	_____
Review Test 2 (10 items)	_____	× 7 =	_____
		TOTAL SCORE =	_____ %

Enter your total score into the **Reading Performance Chart: Review Tests** on the inside back cover.

ARGUMENT: Mastery Test 1

A. In each group, one statement is the point of an argument, and the other statements are support for that point. In the space provided, write the letter of the point of each group.

___C___ 1. A. Debates over who could drive the car created serious conflicts between parents and teenagers.

B. The use of automobiles for Sunday outings was thought to have led to a decline in church attendance.

C. The first automobiles were a cause for alarm in many communities.

D. Autos were seen as giving young people too much freedom and privacy, serving as "portable bedrooms" that couples could take anywhere.   Answers A, B, and D give reasons why many communities were alarmed by the introduction of automobiles.

___D___ 2. A. During the 1920s, banks began offering the country's first home mortgages.

B. Retail sellers of everything from cars to irons in the 1920s allowed customers to pay in installments.

C. In the 1920s, about 60 percent of mortgages and 75 percent of all radios were purchased on the installment plan.

D. The use of installment credit became very popular with banks, retail sellers, and consumers during the 1920s.   Answers A, B, and C illustrate the widespread availability of installment credit during the 1920s.

___B___ 3. A. Most women today continue to work in a relatively small number of traditional "women's" jobs, and full-time female workers earn only 68 cents for every $1 paid to men.

Answers A, C, and D each

B. Despite all that has been achieved in terms of women's rights, many injustices still remain.

support the idea that many injustices to women still exist.

C. Today, the economic plight of women involved in the 50% of marriages that end in divorce is often grave.

D. Although female-headed families constitute only 15 percent of the U.S. population, they account for over 50% of the poor population.

___B___ 4. A. Printed newspapers are limited by the amount of news that can be printed in one edition, but online papers have no such limitations.

Answers A, C, and D list the advantages online newspapers have over traditional newspapers.

B. More and more people are reading online newspapers because they realize that online papers have certain advantages over traditional newspapers.

C. Online papers can be updated continuously, since they have no edition deadlines.

D. Online newspapers are interactive—e-mail addresses, bulletin boards, and chat rooms allow readers to provide quick feedback to the paper.

(Continues on next page)

B. Read the three items of support (the evidence) in the group below. Then, in the space provided, write the letter of the point that is adequately supported by that evidence.

> ### *Support:*
> - Eating chocolate releases serotonin in the human brain, resulting in feelings of pleasure.
> - Chocolate contains caffeine, a stimulant that restores alertness.
> - Dark chocolate contains antioxidants that have health benefits such as protecting blood vessels and promoting cardiac health.

_B_ 5. Which **point** is adequately supported by all the evidence above?
   A. Sweet treats are actually good for your health.
   B. Chocolate can have a significant impact on the human body.
   C. Dark chocolate is healthier than milk chocolate.
   D. Chocolate could be considered a drug.

> Each item gives an example of how chocolate affects the human body.
> Answer A is wrong because the items specifically refer to chocolate, not
> all sweet treats. Answer C relates only to the third supporting detail.
> Answer D is incorrect because the items do not say anything about
> whether or not chocolate is a drug.

ARGUMENT: Mastery Test 2

A. In each group, one statement is the point of an argument, and the other statements are support for that point. In the space provided, write the letter of the point of each group.

___A___ 1. A. Adult-structured sports promote healthy child development.
        B. Adult-structured sports teach children how to accept authority and prepare them for the realistic competition they will face as adults.
        C. Practices and games regularly scheduled by adults ensure that children get plenty of exercise.
        D. Adult-structured sports enable parents and children to create healthy bonds.   Answers B, C, and D provide examples of how adult-structured sports help children develop.

___D___ 2. A. Physicians never hold up cabbies, but many do cheat Medicare.
        B. Bookkeepers don't rob convenience stores, but they have been known to take money from their employers' accounts.
        C. Instead of mugging, pimping, and burglary, the privileged evade income tax, bribe public officials, and embezzle money.
        D. The more privileged social classes find alternatives to the street crime generally committed by the lower classes. Answers A, B, and C illustrate how the more privileged social classes break the law in ways that are different from those of the lower classes.

___C___ 3. A. Only 4 out of every 100,000 men in China die of heart disease each year, compared with 67 in the United States.
        B. Chinese people eating traditional foods consume three times the fiber of people eating the American way, take in about half the fat, and have blood cholesterol values about half of what they are in the United States.
        C. Despite consuming 20 percent more food energy each day than we do, Chinese who eat traditional Chinese foods have a far healthier diet than Americans.
        D. Chinese living in China also suffer much less cancer of the colon and rectum than do Chinese who have adopted a Western diet.

    Answers A, B, and D support the notion that the traditional Chinese diet is far healthier than the American diet.

(Continues on next page)

B. Read the three items of support (the evidence) in each group below. Then, in the space provided, write the letter of the point that is adequately supported by that evidence.

Item 4:

Answer A is incorrect because the experiment does not demonstrate that *any* crow can construct a simple tool. It does, however, indicate that *some* crows can (answer D). B is incorrect because crows are not compared to other birds. C is incorrect because nothing is said about researchers' preferences.

Support:

- Animal researchers tested two crows, Betty and Abel, to see whether they would choose a hooked wire or a straight wire to use for getting some food out of a tube.
- During one session Abel snatched the hooked wire away from Betty, leaving Betty with only the straight wire to use.
- When Betty realized the straight wire wouldn't work, she bent it into a hook with her beak.

_D_ 4. Which **point** is adequately supported by all the evidence above?
   A. A crow can construct a simple tool.
   B. Crows have proven themselves to be the smartest birds.
   C. Researchers prefer to work with crows because they are so intelligent.
   D. Research indicates that some crows can construct simple tools.

Support:

- In cancer, cells begin to reproduce in a rapid, disorganized fashion.
- As this cell reproduction lurches out of control, the teeming new cells clump together to form tumors.
- If this wild growth continues unabated, the spreading tumors cause tissue damage and begin to interfere with normal functioning in the affected areas.

_B_ 5. Which **point** is adequately supported by all the evidence above?
   A. There are a host of new ways that cancer can be treated.
   B. Cancer is a very serious disease because cancer cells tend to overwhelm the body.
   C. There are various types of cancers which attack different organs in the body.
   D. Some but not all tumors are cancerous.

   Item 5: Answers A, C, and D are incorrect because the support says nothing about treatments, types of cancers, or kinds of tumors.

ARGUMENT: Mastery Test 3

A. In each group, one statement is the point of an argument, and the other statements are support for that point. In the space provided, write the letter of the point of each group.

_____B_____ 1.
Answers A, C, and D give examples of ways in which American schools are failing to meet the needs of their male students.

A. Although boys in elementary school are developmentally two years behind girls in reading and writing, they are expected to learn the same material in the same way.

B. American schools are failing to meet the needs of their male students.

C. Males are 30% more likely to drop out of school than females.

D. Today's teachers tend to rely on teaching strategies that appeal to the females in their classes, but alienate their male students.

_____D_____ 2.
Answers A, B, and C provide examples of specific dietary restrictions of different religions.

A. During certain days of Lent, the period prior to Easter, many Christians refrain from eating meat.

B. Muslims fast from sunup to sundown during the holy month of Ramadan.

C. Dietary restrictions permit Orthodox Jews to eat beef, but not pork, fish but not shellfish, and they dictate special handling methods for permitted foods.

D. Throughout the world, many religions place restrictions on what kind of foods can be consumed and when they can be consumed.

B. Each point is followed by three statements that provide relevant support and three that do not. In the spaces, write the letters of the **three** relevant statements of support.

Answer B suggests that elephants in zoos don't have enough room to roam. Answers E and F give specific examples of ways that zoo living harms elephants. Answer A has nothing to do with choosing the best environment for captive elephants. Answers C and D support the notion that zoos are beneficial to elephants.

3–5. _Point:_ To better provide for their well-being, zoo elephants should be transferred to large nature preserves.

A. Adult elephants can consume from 300 to 600 pounds of food a day.

B. Elephants in the wild are accustomed to roaming up to thirty miles a day.

C. Zookeepers try to provide their captive elephants with the best possible veterinary care.

D. In zoos, elephants are fed balanced, highly nutritious diets.

E. Zoo elephants often suffer from degenerative joint problems and chronic foot infections which are the result of standing for long periods on concrete or other unnatural surfaces.

F. Small enclosures in zoos often cause behavioral problems in elephants, including repetitive swaying and head-bobbing, as well as increased aggression toward zookeepers and other elephants.

Items that logically support the point: ___B___   ___E___   ___F___

(Continues on next page)

315

6–8. **Point:** People react to stress at three levels: emotional, physiological, and behavioral.

    A. Because today's society is so fast-paced, people are subject to a great deal of stress.

    B. When you groan in reaction to a traffic report, you're experiencing an emotional response to stress.

    C. When your pulse quickens and your stomach knots up, you're exhibiting physiological responses to stress.

    D. Working in a hospital emergency room is certainly a highly stressful occupation.

    E. Research has demonstrated that some people are better at handling stress than others.

    F. When you shout insults at another driver, your verbal aggression is a behavioral response to the stress at hand.

Items that logically support the point: *B*   *C*   *F*

Answers B, C, and F illustrate how people react to stress on an emotional level, on a physiological level, and on a behavioral level. Answer A is incorrect because it is about a cause of stress; answer D is incorrect because it is about a stressful job; and answer E is incorrect because it is about differences in how well people handle stress.

ARGUMENT: Mastery Test 4

A. In the following group, one statement is the point of an argument, and the other statements are support for that point. In the space provided, write the letter of the point of this group.

___D___ 1. A. Children whose parents do not use alcohol tend to abstain or to drink only moderately.

Answers A, B, and C provide examples of how the family setting shapes attitudes and beliefs about drug and alcohol use.

B. A recent study suggests that children are more likely to abuse alcohol if their family tolerates deviance in general or encourages indulgent activities and pleasure-seeking.

C. Adolescents who have been physically assaulted or sexually abused in their homes are at an increased risk for drug abuse.

D. The family setting in which a child grows up helps shape his or her attitudes and beliefs about drug and alcohol use.

B. Read the three items of support (the evidence) in each group below. Then, in the space provided, write the letter of the point that is adequately supported by that evidence.

Support:

- The atmosphere on Mars is 95% carbon dioxide, with only small traces of oxygen.
- Liquid water, which is necessary to sustain life, does not exist on Mars.
- Dangerous dust storms frequent Mars, sometimes engulfing the entire planet.

___D___ 2. Which **point** is adequately supported by all the evidence above?

A. Mars is one of the most dangerous planets.

B. It is not known whether extraterrestrial beings exist on Mars.

C. Mars is a unique planet.

D. It would be impossible for humans to live on Mars.

All the evidence indicates that the characteristics of Mars make it unable to support human life (answer D). Answers A, B, and C are not supported. Answers A and C are incorrect because there is no comparison to other planets. Answer B is incorrect because extraterrestrial beings are not discussed.

(Continues on next page)

C. (3–5.) For the following statement, choose your point of view by checking "I agree" or "I disagree." Then circle the letters of the **three** items that logically support your point of view.

Point: Prostitution should be legalized.

If "I agree" is checked, these answers should be circled: A, D, E.

If "I disagree" is checked, these answers should be circled: B, C, F.

____ I agree   ____ I disagree

A. Prostitutes perform a service for society. They provide sex for people who otherwise cannot find sexual partners. They may even help marriages by reducing sexual demands on wives. There is no way to put an end to the "world's oldest profession."

B. Prostitution is immoral, and we should not legalize immoral activities. The foundation of society is the family, and we should take steps to strengthen the family, not tear it apart by approving sex as a commercial transaction outside the family.

C. The legalization of prostitution will not stop sexually transmitted diseases. For example, the HIV virus can be transmitted before the disease shows up in blood tests. Even though prostitutes are licensed, they will spread AIDS during this interval.

D. If prostitution is declared a legal occupation, the government can regulate it. If the government licenses prostitutes, it can collect taxes and require prostitutes to have regular medical checkups. Prostitutes can be required to display a dated and signed medical certificate stating that they are free of sexually transmitted diseases.

E. Prostitution stigmatizes and marginalizes women who want to work as prostitutes. It corrupts some police officers, who accept bribes to allow prostitutes to work. Some prostitution is run by organized crime, with women held in bondage. Legalization of prostitution will eliminate these problems.

F. Prostitution degrades women. To legalize prostitution is to give society's approval to their degradation. It also would affirm class oppression: Most prostitutes come from the working class and serve as objects to satisfy the sexual desires of men from more privileged classes.

I agree:
Answer A argues that prostitutes provide a valuable service to society.
Answer D argues that if prostitution is legalized, government can regulate it and make it safer.
Answer E argues that legalization of prostitution could eliminate problems such as stigmatization of prostitutes, corruption of some police officers, and the influence of organized crime in prostitution.

I disagree:
Answer B argues that prostitution is immoral.
Answer C argues that legalization of prostitution would not stop prostitutes from spreading sexually transmitted diseases.
Answer F argues that prostitution degrades women.

ARGUMENT: Mastery Test 5

A. In each group, one statement is the point of an argument, and the other statements are support for that point. In the space provided, write the letter of the point of each group.

_____B_____ 1. A. Charity work gives celebrities a chance to escape the strangeness of life in the spotlight and connect with "regular" people.

Answers A, C, and D detail the advantages for celebrities of doing charity work.

B. Modern-day celebrities have found it beneficial to engage in charitable work.

C. Charity work gives many celebrities a positive public image.

D. Domestic or international charity work allows celebrities to make a difference in the world without becoming involved in controversial political issues.

_____D_____ 2. A. The multicultural movement has led to ethnic revivals in many cities and the nation itself.

Answers A, B, and C provide examples of changes that multiculturalism has brought to American society.

B. The new appreciation of cultural diversity is reflected in efforts to bring the language, literature, and perspective of various ethnic groups into classrooms.

C. Multiculturalism has raised people's consciousness about the importance of gender, disability, sexual orientation, and other differences that were previously neglected.

D. Multiculturalism has brought fundamental changes to American education and American society as a whole.

B. (3–5.) The point below is followed by three statements that provide relevant support and three that do not. In the spaces, write the letters of the **three** relevant statements of support.

Answers B, D, and E provide reasons why owners should neuter their pets: less likely to bite; less likely to develop illness; eases the burden on shelters. Answer A states where neutering is practiced. Answer C discusses neutering fees. Answer F describes what people believe about neutering.

Point: Animal owners should neuter their pets.

A. Neutering is mainly practiced in first-world countries.

B. Neutering makes pets less likely to bite people.

C. Some animal shelters offer more reasonable rates for neutering than others.

D. Neutering pets makes them less likely to develop illnesses.

E. Having pets neutered helps ease the burden on crowded animal shelters.

F. Some people believe that neutering makes animals less protective of their owners.

Items that logically support the point: _____B_____   _____D_____   _____E_____

(Continues on next page)

C. (6–8.) For the following statement, choose your point of view by checking "I agree" or "I disagree." Then circle the letters of the **three** items that logically support your point of view.

Point: High-school students should be required to participate in the daily Pledge of Allegiance.

If "I agree" is checked, these answers should be circled: A, B, F.

If "I disagree" is checked, these answers should be circled: C, D, E.

____ I agree   ____ I disagree

A. Requiring students to pledge allegiance to the flag is an exercise in respect for authority. It reminds them that as they should show respect to the flag, they should also show respect to their teachers and other figures in authority.

B. Pledging allegiance to the flag is a constructive way of affirming our identity, as a group and as Americans.

C. To require students to pledge their allegiance is a violation of their civil liberties. In America, we are free to hold views that would interfere with our willingness to say the pledge.

D. The Pledge of Allegiance, with its phrase "one nation, under God," represents a violation of the separation of church and state. Students who are non-believers or who do not believe that God favors one country over another should not be asked to recite the pledge.

E. Requiring the recitation of the Pledge of Allegiance is a way to promote blind, simplistic nationalism. Such nationalism has no place in a democratic society.

F. Any person benefiting from living in the United States should be, at the minimum, willing to publicly declare his allegiance to the country.

I agree:
Answers A, B, and F argue that reciting the Pledge of Allegiance teaches respect, affirms our identity as Americans, and is the least an American can do in return for the benefit of living in the United States.

I disagree:
Answers C, D, and E argue that reciting the Pledge of Allegiance violates civil liberties, violates the separation of church and state, and promotes blind nationalism.

ARGUMENT: Mastery Test 6

A. In each group below, one statement is the point of an argument, and the other statements are support for that point. In the space provided, write the letter of the point of each group.

_____B_____ 1.

Answers A, C, and D support the idea that obesity is a pressing health problem in today's world.

A. Half of all American adults are overweight.

B. Obesity is one of the most pressing heath concerns in today's world.

C. At least 25% percent of all Americans under the age of 19 are overweight or obese.

D. Increases in obesity rates have occurred in both sexes, in all social classes and age groups, and in many other countries.

_____C_____ 2.

Answers A, B, and D illustrate the spiritual and legal differences between marriage and cohabitation.

A. In marriage, the assumption is permanence; in cohabitation, couples agree to remain together "as long as it works out."

B. For marriage, individuals make public vows that legally bind them as a couple; for cohabitation, they simply move in together.

C. The difference between cohabitation and marriage is spiritual and legal commitment.

D. Marriage requires a judge to authorize its termination; when a cohabiting relationship sours, the couple simply separates.

B. (3–5.) The point below is followed by three statements that provide relevant support and three that do not. In the spaces, write the letters of the **three** relevant statements of support.

Answers A, D, and F provide examples of popular movies that reflect our fears. Answer B discusses owners' fears of dropping attendance. Answer C is about advances in special effects. Answer E describes differences in men's and women's film preferences.

Point: Our society's taste in movies is sometimes influenced by what we fear.

A. The plots of some movies are based on out-of-control computers, such as the science-fiction classic, *2001: A Space Odyssey*, in which an evil computer named Hal attempts to sabotage a space mission to Jupiter.

B. Owners of movie theaters fear that the increasing popularity of in-home entertainment centers may cause a drop in theater attendance.

C. Great improvements in digital technology have enabled today's moviegoers to experience special effects unheard of a generation ago.

D. In the 1950s, movies such as *Godzilla* and *The Beast from 20,000 Fathoms* reflected our fear of the effects of radiation on living beings.

E. Generally, women tend to be more interested in movies that feature emotional relationships, whereas men tend to gravitate toward movies with plenty of action.

F. Movies about serial killers such as *The Silence of the Lambs* engage our concern about falling victim to people who appear normal but are secretly homicidal maniacs.

Items that logically support the point: _____A_____ _____D_____ _____F_____

(Continues on next page)

C. (6–8.) For the following statement, choose your point of view by checking "I agree" or "I disagree." Then circle the letters of the **three** items that logically support your point of view.

Point: **Affirmative action is a good idea.**

If "I agree" is checked, these answers should be circled: B, C, E.

If "I disagree" is checked, these answers should be circled: A, D, F.

___ I agree   ___ I disagree

A. Affirmative action stigmatizes the people that benefit from it. It suggests that they hold their jobs because of race rather than merit.

B. Affirmative action is good for everyone, because it leads to the development of a larger minority middle and upper class. This will result in more stable, self-sufficient minority communities that will act as full participants in society.

C. Affirmative action recognizes that merit alone has never been the basis for people to get ahead. People have always been hired or promoted because of factors such as whom they know (or are related to) or where they went to school. Affirmative action helps "level the playing field" by giving a hand to people not already tied into such influential networks.

D. Affirmative action is discrimination in reverse form. It makes a person's race more important than the individual's training or ability to perform a job.

E. White people have benefited from generations of preferential treatment, and have come to think that they have rightfully earned their place at the top of society. Affirmative action forces them to share benefits that they did not fairly earn.

F. By edging qualified non-minority people out of jobs, affirmative action forces them to pay for past inequalities that they had nothing to do with.

I agree:
Answer B argues that affirmative action helps build stable, self-sufficient minority communities.
Answer C argues that affirmative action helps "level the playing field."
Answer E argues that affirmative action forces whites to share benefits that they did not fairly earn.

I disagree:
Answer A argues that affirmative action stigmatizes those who benefit from it.
Answer D argues that affirmative action is reverse discrimination.
Answer F argues that affirmative action is unfair to qualified non-minority people.

9

Critical Reading

Skilled readers are those who can *recognize* an author's point and the support for that point. **Critical readers** are those who can *evaluate* an author's support for a point and determine whether that support is solid or not. In this book, you have already had practice in evaluating support—deciding when inferences are valid and when they are not (pages 218–235) and determining whether supporting evidence is relevant (pages 296–300) and adequate (pages 300–303). This chapter will extend your ability to read critically in three ways. It will explain and offer practice in each of the following:

- Separating fact from opinion
- Detecting propaganda
- Recognizing errors in reasoning

SEPARATING FACT FROM OPINION

Fact

A **fact** is information that can be proved true through objective evidence. This evidence may be physical proof or the spoken or written testimony of witnesses. Following are some facts—they can be checked for accuracy and thus proved true.

Fact: Abraham Lincoln, whose nickname was "Honest Abe," had no formal education or religion; he was president of the United States from 1861 to 1865 on a salary of $25,000 a year.

(You can look up in historical documents the above facts about Lincoln.)

Fact: At least four out of five adults will experience lower back pain at some point in their lives.

(Extensive medical research confirms that this statement is true.)

Fact: Quitting smoking now greatly reduces serious risks to your health.

(You can look this up in government reports by the U.S. Surgeon General; this fact also appears by law on many cigarette packs and ads.)

Opinion

An **opinion** is a belief, judgment, or conclusion that cannot be objectively proved true. As a result, it is open to question. Following are some opinions:

Opinion: With the exception only of George Washington, Abraham Lincoln was the greatest leader our country has ever had.

(Many people might agree with this statement, but others would not. There is no way to prove it definitively. *Greatest* is a **value word**, a word we use to express a value judgment. Value words are signals that an opinion is being expressed. By their very nature, these words represent opinions, not facts.)

Opinion: The best treatment for lower back pain is physical therapy.

(There is no consensus in the scientific community that this is true.)

Opinion: Smoking is the worst of America's drug addictions.

(Many people, such as those coping with alcoholism, might disagree.)

Points about Fact and Opinion

There are several points to keep in mind when considering fact and opinion.

1 Statements of fact may be found to be untrue.

For example, the United States went to war in Iraq because of the fact that Iraq had weapons of mass destruction. However, this widely accepted fact later proved to be untrue. The point is that facts can turn out to be errors, not facts. It is not unusual for evidence to show that a "fact" is not really true. It was once considered to be a fact that the world was flat, for example, but that "fact" also turned out to be an error.

2 **Value words** (ones that contain a judgment) often represent opinions. Here are examples of these words:

Value Words

best	great	beautiful
worst	terrible	bad
better	lovely	good
worse	disgusting	wonderful

Value words are generally subjective, not objective. While factual statements report on observed reality, subjective statements evaluate or interpret reality. For example, the observation that it is cloudy outside is objective. The statement that the weather is bad, however, is subjective, an evaluation of reality. (Some people—for example, farmers whose crops need water—consider rain to be good weather.)

3 The words *should* and *ought to* often signal opinions. Those words introduce what some people think should, or ought to, be done. Other people may disagree.

Adults who molest young children ought to be put to death.

Homosexuals should repent for their behavior.

4 Don't mistake widely held opinions for facts. Much information that sounds factual is really opinion. A real estate agent, for example, might say, "At the price listed, this rancher is a great buy." Buyers would be wise to wonder what the value word *great* means to the agent. Or an ad may claim that a particular automobile is "the most economical car on the road today," a statement that at first seems factual. But what is meant by *economical*? If the car offers the most miles per gallon but the worst record for expensive repairs, you might not agree that it's economical.

As we will see in later parts of this chapter, advertisers and politicians often try to manipulate us by presenting opinions as if they were facts. For instance, one politician may claim that another will be soft on terrorism or will waste our tax dollars. But accusations are often not facts. Clear-thinking citizens must aim to get below the surface of claims and charges and determine as much factual truth as possible.

5   Finally, remember that much of what we read and hear is a mixture of fact and opinion. Our job, then, is to draw upon existing fact and opinion and to arrive at an informed opinion. On our Supreme Court, for example, nine justices deliberate in order to deliver informed opinions about important issues of our time. But even these justices often disagree and deliver split decisions. The reality is that most of what matters in life is very complex and cannot be separated into simple fact and opinion. Our challenge always is to arrive at the best possible informed opinion, and even then there will be people who disagree with us.

Fact and Opinion in Reading

In general, textbook authors try to be as factual as possible. Most textbook material is based on scientific observation and study, and textbook authors do their best to present us with all the facts and objective informed opinion. On the other hand, many essays, editorials, political speeches, and advertisements may contain facts, but those facts are often carefully selected to back up the authors' opinions.

☑ Check Your Understanding

To sharpen your understanding of fact and opinion, read the following statements and decide whether each is fact or opinion. Put an **F** (for "fact") or an **O** (for "opinion") beside each statement. Put **F+O** beside the **one** statement that is a mixture of fact *and* opinion. Then read the explanation that follows.

> *Hint:* Remember that opinions are signaled by value words—words such as *great* or *hard* or *beautiful* or *terrible* that express a value judgment. Take care to note such words in your reading.

___*F*___ 1. There are so many guns in the United States that if you gave one to every adult, you would run out of adults before you'd run out of guns.

___*F*___ 2. In 1828, New York became the first state to restrict abortion; by 1900 it had been made illegal throughout the country.

___*O*___ 3. Legalized abortion is the main cause of sexual misbehavior in the United States.

_F_   4. Many people have nightmares in which they are falling and wake up right before they hit the ground.

_O_   5. If you have a nightmare in which you are plunging to the ground and you don't wake up before you hit the ground, you'll die.

_O_   6. It is a fact that overpopulation is the number one problem facing the world today.

_F_   7. About two hundred babies are born worldwide every minute.

_F_   8. The first animated feature film was *Snow White and the Seven Dwarfs*, released in 1937 by the Disney studio.

_O_   9. Today's computer-animated films are not as good as the old hand-drawn animated ones.

_F+O_ 10. The 1940 animated film *Fantasia*, which combined animation with classical music, is the most imaginative movie ever made.

Explanation:

1. This is a fact. Statistical records show that there are a greater number of guns in the country than there are adults.

2. These are facts that could be looked up in historical records.

3. This is an opinion. Some people would argue, for example, that sexual misbehavior existed before abortion became an option.

4. This is a fact that can be confirmed by checking medical research on nightmares.

5. This is obviously an opinion—and an old joke!

6. This is an opinion. Just saying that something is a fact doesn't make it so. Other people would say, for example, that global warming is the most immediate problem we face today.

7. This is a fact that can be confirmed by population and census records.

8. This is a fact that can be confirmed by checking film records.

9. This is an opinion. Many people might disagree.

10. The first part of the sentence is a fact that can be confirmed by checking movie records and watching the film. The second part is a opinion; other people might nominate some other film as the most imaginative one ever made.

Note: In the practices and tests that follow, value (judgment) words and opinions are underlined in red in this *Instructor's Edition.*

➤ *Practice 1*

Read the following statements and label each fact with an **F**, each opinion with an **O**, and the two statements of fact *and* opinion with an **F+O**.

___O___ 1. Young people today <u>should</u> spend more time reading and less time on their computers. *Should signals an opinion.*

___F___ 2. More than 70 percent of households containing children under age 19 own at least one personal computer. **Items 2 and 3:**
Each of these is a fact that can be confirmed by statistical research.

___F___ 3. Cotton is the world's most widely-used fabric.

___O___ 4. Clothes made of cotton are always <u>better</u> choices than other clothes. *Better is a value word.*

Item 5:
The first part is a fact which can be confirmed by surveying doctors who treat skin allergies. The second part is an opinion; other people might believe that respiratory or food allergies are worse.

___F+O___ 5. Cotton clothing is often recommended for people with skin allergies, which are the <u>most irritating</u> kind of allergies to have.

___F___ 6. A starfish eats by moving its stomach outside its body, then wrapping its stomach around its prey. *Can be confirmed by scientific research.*

___O___ 7. No sea creature is more <u>bizarre</u> and <u>interesting</u> than the starfish. Some people might find other sea creatures more interesting.

___F___ 8. In Las Vegas, there is one slot machine for every eight city residents. *Statistical research can confirm this.*

___O___ 9. Gambling is a <u>harmless diversion</u> that <u>should</u> be legal everywhere. Others may view gambling as a vice that should be illegal everywhere. Signal: *should.*

___F+O___ 10. Since the legalization of gambling in Nevada in 1931, Las Vegas has become a <u>hotbed of sin and corruption</u>. The first part can be confirmed by historical research. The second part is an opinion; others might find Las Vegas to be a center of harmless entertainment.

DETECTING PROPAGANDA

Advertisers, salespeople, and politicians are constantly promoting their points: "Buy our product," "Believe what I say," and "Vote for me." Often they lack adequate factual support for their points, so they appeal to our emotions by using propaganda techniques.

Part of being a critical reader is having the ability to recognize these propaganda techniques for the emotional fluff that they are. The critical reader strips away the fluff to determine whether there is solid support for the point in question. None of us wants to accept someone else's point as a result of emotional manipulation.

This section will introduce you to six common propaganda techniques:

- Bandwagon
- Testimonial
- Transfer
- Plain Folks
- Name Calling
- Glittering Generalities

While there are other propaganda techniques, the ones described below are among the most common. They all use emotional appeals to distract from the fact they are not providing solid evidence to support their points.

1 Bandwagon

Old-fashioned parades usually began with a large wagon carrying a brass band. Therefore, to "jump on the bandwagon" means to join a parade, or to do what many others are doing. The **bandwagon** technique tells us to buy a product or support a certain issue because, in effect, "everybody else is doing it."

An ad may claim that more and more people are getting their evening news from anchorperson Chet Miller. Or a political ad may feature people from all walks of life speaking out in support of a certain political candidate. The ads imply that if you don't jump on the bandwagon and get on the winning side, the parade will pass you by.

Here are two examples of ads that use the bandwagon appeal:

> An ad announces a sale giving us a chance to buy the most popular SUV in America today.

> In a soft drink ad, a crowd of young people follow a young woman on skates who is drinking a diet soda.

- Check (✓) the ad below that uses bandwagon appeal.

    _____ 1. A beautiful woman in a slinky red dress is shown driving the sponsor's car.

    ___✓___ 2. An ad for a weight-loss pill features an attractive couple who are "just two of the millions" who have decided to get their bodies back with the new diet formula.

    > The phrase *just two of the millions* alerts us to the bandwagon technique.

2 Testimonial

Famous athletes often appear as spokespersons for all sorts of products, from soft drinks to automobiles. Movie and TV stars make commercials endorsing products or political issues. The idea behind the **testimonial** approach is that the testimony of famous people influences the viewers that admire these people.

What consumers must remember is that famous people get paid to endorse products. In addition, these people are not necessarily experts about the products or the political issues or candidates they promote.

Here are two examples of real ads that have used the appeal of testimonials:

> A famous actor is shown coping with a swarm of photographers in order to get a bottle of his favorite beer.

> A popular TV talk show hostess appears in an ad that indicates she uses a certain credit card.

- Check (✓) the ad below that uses a testimonial.

_____ 1. Numerous people crowd around the department store door, waiting for the store to open.

___✓___ 2. A famous actress says that she loves to use a certain hair coloring.

> The words *famous actress* signal the use of the testimonial approach.

3 Transfer

The most common type of propaganda technique is **transfer,** in which products or candidates try to associate themselves with something that people admire or love. In the illustration on page 328, we see a political candidate saying "Vote for Me" and standing next to a beauty queen wrapped in a U.S.A. banner.

There are countless variations on this ad, where a beautiful and sexy woman and/or an American flag or some other symbol of the U.S.A. appears in the ad with a product or candidate or cause. The hope is that we will *transfer* the positive feelings we have towards a beautiful or sexy-looking person to the product being advertised, or that we will *transfer* the patriotism that we feel to a product or candidate. Over the years, advertisers have found that beauty and sex "sell" and that appeals to patriotism often succeed. In short, transfer often works.

Here are two examples of real ads that have used the appeal of transfer:

> An American flag is in the background of an ad for U.S. Savings Bonds.

> A tanned blonde in a bikini is stretched out on the beach, holding in her hand a certain suntan lotion.

- Check (✓) the ad below that uses transfer.

___✓___ 1. A beer company sponsors the Daytona 500 auto race with the line "America's Race and America's Beer."

_____ 2. A picture of a can of soda, beaded with frosty drops of moisture, bears the caption, "You know it's got to be good."

> The word *America's* signals the transfer technique.

4   Plain Folks

Some people distrust political candidates who are rich or well educated. They feel that these candidates, if elected, will not be able to understand the problems of the average working person. Therefore, candidates often use the **plain folks** technique, presenting themselves as ordinary, average citizens. They try to show they are just "plain folks" by referring in their speeches to hard times in their lives or by posing for photographs while wearing a hard hat or mingling with everyday people.

Similarly, the presidents of some companies appear in their own ads, trying to show that their giant corporations are just family businesses run by ordinary folks.

Here are two examples of real ads that have used the appeal of plain folks:

> Average-looking American kids are shown at home trying and enjoying a cereal.

> The president of a poultry company talks to us as if he's an everyday shopper looking for a quick, easy meal to make, just like us.

- Check (✓) the ad below that uses a plain-folks approach.

  _____ 1. A famous basketball player wears the sponsor's sneakers.

  __✓___ 2. The president of a car company is shown playing on the lawn with his young children. He says, "I'm head of this company, but I'm also a dad who is concerned about automobile safety."

  > The president is showing that he is a regular guy.

5   Name Calling

Name calling is the use of emotionally loaded language or negative comments to turn people against a product or political candidate or cause. An example of name calling would be a political candidate's labeling an opponent "soft," "radical," or "wimpy."

Here are two examples of name calling taken from real life:

> In the 1950s, during the early days of the "cold war" with the Soviet Union, an exaggerated concern about communism in this country brought charges of un-Americanism against many.

> During a taste test, consumers described the other leading brand of spaghetti sauce as "too salty" and "thin and tasteless."

- Check (✓) the ad below that uses name calling.

  __✓___ 1. A political ad implies that a candidate who does not support the war in Iraq is anti-American.

  _____ 2. A pastor describes how when his house burned down, his home insurance company responded quickly and helpfully.

  Suggesting someone is anti-American for such a reason is name calling.

6   Glittering Generalities

A **glittering generality** is an important-sounding but unspecific claim about some product, candidate, or cause. An example is saying that a certain television is "simply the best" or having a sign that reads "Sam Slick for Mayor: Integrity, Dedication, Care." A glittering generality uses fine and virtuous words but says nothing definite.

Here are two examples from real ads that use glittering generalities:

> A room deodorizer exclaims, "Experience the freshness!"

> A canned-food ad boasts of "nutrition that works."

- Check (✓) the ad below that uses a glittering generality.

  _✓_ 1. A car ad claims, "It just feels right."

  _____ 2. A movie star looks over her dark sunglasses and says, "Maybe you can't be a celebrity. But you can look like one in glasses like mine."   The car ad tells us nothing definite about the car.

➤ *Practice 2*

In the space provided, write the letter of the propaganda technique that applies to each item.

A. bandwagon	B. testimonial	C. transfer
D. plain folks	E. name calling	F. glittering generalities

  _B_ 1. A <u>Hall-of-Fame quarterback</u> claims that a certain drug relieves his acid reflux.   Signal words: *Hall-of-Fame quarterback.*

  _C_ 2. A <u>beautiful blonde</u> wearing an evening gown drapes herself against a high-priced brand of women's clothing.   Signal words: *beautiful blonde.*

  _A_ 3. "<u>Millions of satisfied users</u> can't be wrong," says the announcer of an ad for an anti-acid pill. Signal words: *Millions of satisfied users.*

  _D_ 4. In a TV ad, a wealthy politician appears, dressed in a flannel shirt and jeans, at a county fair.   The wealthy politician wants to look just like everybody else.

  _F_ 5. A realtor advertises that she "will always be there for you."   The ad says nothing definite.

  _E_ 6. "My opponent is forcing people out of their homes and businesses so that developers can reap huge profits," claims a candidate for mayor.   The candidate's remarks are extremely negative.

  C   7. A local auto dealership runs a newspaper ad featuring images of Abraham Lincoln and George Washington every President's Day.
> The auto dealership is manipulating feelings of patriotism to sell cars.

  A   8. A magazine ad for a family beach resort advises us to "See for yourself why <u>thousands of families</u> fall in love with Crestwood Beach each year."   Signal words: *thousands of families.*

  B   9. A famous golf star appears on the back of a cereal box and promotes it as part of a balanced diet.   Signal words: *famous golf star.*

  D 10. A woman whose name is on a line of frozen pizzas is shown in her own kitchen, wearing an apron, chopping tomatoes and onion for pizza sauce. She says, "Before it goes on my pizza, my sauce has to pass my personal test."   The celebrity is doing her own cooking.

RECOGNIZING ERRORS IN REASONING

So far in this chapter, you have gotten practice in separating fact from opinion and in spotting propaganda. In this section you will learn about some common errors in reasoning—also known as **fallacies**—that take the place of the real support needed in argument. As shown in the illustration, a valid point is based on a rock-like foundation of solid support; a fallacious point is based on a house of cards that offers no real support at all. Regrettably, these fallacies appear all too often in political arguments, often as the result of deliberate manipulation, other times as the result of careless thinking.

You've already learned about two common fallacies in Chapter 8, "Argument." One of those fallacies is sometimes called **changing the subject**. Attention is diverted from the issue at hand by presenting irrelevant support— evidence that actually has nothing to do with the argument. The second fallacy covered in Chapter 8 is sometimes called **hasty generalization**—in which a point is based on inadequate support. To be valid, a point must be based on an adequate amount of evidence. To draw a conclusion on the basis of insufficient evidence is to make a hasty generalization.

Below are six other common fallacies that will be explained in this section.

Three Fallacies That Ignore the Issue

- Circular Reasoning
- Personal Attack
- Straw Man

Three Fallacies That Oversimplify the Issue

- False Cause
- False Comparison
- Either-Or

In all of these fallacies, a point is argued, but no true support is offered for that point.

Fallacies That Ignore the Issue

Circular Reasoning

Part of a point cannot reasonably be used as evidence to support it. The fallacy of including such illogical evidence is called **circular reasoning** or **begging the question**. Here is a simple and obvious example of such reasoning: "Alan Gordon is a great manager because he is so wonderful at managing." The supporting reason ("he is so wonderful at managing") is really the same as the conclusion ("Alan Gordon is a great manager"). We still do not know *why* he is a great manager. No real reasons have been given—the statement has merely repeated itself.

Can you spot the circular reasoning in the following arguments?

1. The climate in California is perfect because it's just beautiful.
2. Hybrid cars are economical because they cost so little to run.

The point is that California's weather is perfect, and the support (it's just beautiful) is simply another way of restating the point. The second claim—that hybrid cars are economical—gets no real support; to say they cost so little to run is just to restate the point. The careful reader should say, "Give me supporting evidence, not a repetition."

- Check (✓) the item that contains an example of the circular reasoning fallacy.

    ___✓___ 1. Exercise is healthful because it improves your well-being.

    _____ 2. Exercise is healthful because it reduces blood pressure, high cholesterol, and body fat.   In effect, item 1 says that exercise is healthful because it improves your health. The two statements mean the same thing.

Personal Attack

This fallacy involves an unfair **personal attack** on an individual rather than on his or her position. Here's an example:

> That woman should not be on a church committee. She just got divorced for the second time.

A woman's divorce or divorces have nothing to do with her ability to contribute to a church committee. Personal attack ignores the issue under discussion and concentrates instead on the character of the opponent.

- Check (✓) the item that contains an example of the personal attack fallacy.

  _____ 1. Our school guidance counselor should be asked to resign. She cursed at a student last week.

  ___✓___ 2. Our school guidance counselor should be asked to resign. One of her sons is gay.   Whether her son is gay or not has nothing to do with the guidance counselor's ability to perform her job.

Straw Man

The **straw man** fallacy suggests that an opponent favors an obviously unpopular cause—when the opponent really doesn't support anything of the kind.

In everyday debates, rather than take on a real opponent, it's tempting to create a man (or woman) of straw and battle it instead. Here is an example:

> Senator Crosley supports a bill to limit the purchase of handguns. She wants to take guns out of the hands of law-abiding citizens and put them into the hands of criminals!

Senator Crosley does not, of course, want to put guns into the hands of criminals. But her opponent wants voters to think that she does and so misrepresents and falsifies her position.

- Check (✓) the item that contains an example of the straw man fallacy.

  ___✓___ 1. My neighbors are voting against the new school budget. They want our students to fall behind students in developing nations like India and China.

  _____ 2. My neighbors are voting against the new school budget. They oppose the salary increases for the superintendent and his staff.

  There may be valid reasons to vote against a new school budget. It is unlikely the neighbors would want the students to fall behind.

Fallacies That Oversimplify the Issue

False Cause

You have probably heard someone say as a joke, "I know it's going to rain today because I forgot to bring an umbrella." The idea that someone can make it rain by forgetting an umbrella is funny because the two events obviously have nothing to do with each other. However, with more complicated issues, it is easy to make the mistake known as the fallacy of **false cause**. The mistake is to assume that because event B *follows* event A, event B *was caused by* event A.

Consider this argument:

> My favorite TV show was moved to a different time slot this season. No wonder it's now getting canceled.

But there could be reasons other than the move to a new time slot for the program's getting canceled. Perhaps the show has less competent writers; perhaps a favorite actor has left the show; perhaps network executives want a different programming direction. In any case, it's easy but dangerous to assume that just because A *came before* B, A **caused** B.

- Check (✓) the item that contains an example of the fallacy of false cause.

    _✓_ 1. Many fast-food commercials on TV are hard to resist. That's why I've gained a lot of weight.

    _____ 2. Many fast-food commercials on TV are hard to resist. If I'm not careful, I'll eat too many burgers, shakes, and fries.

    > There could be reasons for weight gain besides the power of commercials.

False Comparison

When Shakespeare wrote, "Shall I compare thee to a summer day," he meant that both the woman he loved and a summer day were beautiful. In some ways—such as being a source of humidity or pollen, for example—his love did not resemble a summer day at all. Comparisons are often a good way to clarify a point. But because two things may not be alike in all respects, comparisons (sometimes called **analogies**) often make poor evidence for arguments.

In the error in reasoning known as **false comparison**, the assumption is that two things are more alike than they really are. For example, read the following argument:

When your brother was your age, he was already married and raising a family. So why aren't you married, Dean?

To judge whether or not this is a false comparison, consider how the two situations are alike and how they differ. They are similar in that both involve persons of the same age. But the situations are different in that Dean is an individual with choices and goals that are different from those of his brother. (For example, perhaps Dean wants to continue his education or focus on his career, or perhaps he has not met the right person yet.) The differences in this case are more important than the similarities, making it a false comparison.

- Check (✓) the item that contains an example of the fallacy of false comparison. (The other item contains an example of false cause.)

    <u> ✓ </u> 1. My dad takes an anti-depressant, so I don't see what's wrong with my smoking marijuana.

    <u>   </u> 2. My dad takes an anti-depressant, so I'm probably going to have a mood disorder some day.   The situations are very different. An anti-depressant is a doctor-prescribed medication. Generally speaking, marijuana is not.

Either-Or

It is often wrong to assume that there are only two sides to a question. Offering only two choices when more actually exist is an **either-or** fallacy. For example, the statement "You are either with us or against us" assumes that there is no middle ground. Or consider the following:

Women must decide whether they want to have a career or have children.

This argument fails to allow for other alternatives, such as working part-time or sharing child-rearing responsibilities with a partner. While some issues have only two sides (Will you take that job, or won't you?), most have several.

- Check (✓) the item that contains an example of the either-or fallacy. (The other item contains an example of false cause.)

    <u>   </u> 1. You're ignoring my cat. You must be angry with me about something.

    <u> ✓ </u> 2. You're ignoring my cat. You must hate animals.

    There could be many reasons (other than hating animals) that the person is ignoring the cat. For example, the person could be stressed about a situation at work or just focused on something else.

➤ *Practice 3*

A. In the space provided, write the letter of the fallacy contained in each argument. Choose from the three fallacies shown in the box below.

> **A** Circular reasoning *(a statement repeats itself rather than providing a real supporting reason to back up an argument)*
>
> **B** Personal attack *(ignores the issue under discussion and concentrates instead on the character of the opponent)*
>
> **C** Straw man *(an argument is made by claiming an opponent holds an extreme position and then opposing that extreme position)*

____A____ 1. The divorcing couple didn't get along well because they were so incompatible.   In effect, this says that the couple didn't get along well because they didn't get along well.

____B____ 2. Professor Johnson is up for tenure at the college, but he shouldn't get it. His ex-wife was arrested last week for shoplifting.   The professor's ex-wife has nothing to do with his teaching ability.

Item 3: The candidate is misrepresenting ____C____ 3. My opponent opposes the Medicare reform bill. Apparently she his opponent's position. It is unlikely that the opponent would want to see the elderly eat cat food. wants to see the elderly forced to eat cat food in order to pay for their prescription drugs.

____B____ 4. I will not tolerate my child going to a Sunday school class with a teacher who belongs to a motorcycle club.   Upstanding citizens sometimes belong to motorcycle clubs.

____C____ 5. The governor disapproves of armed militias patrolling our border with Mexico. Clearly he wants this nation to be overwhelmed by waves of illegal immigrants.   It is unlikely that the governor would want the nation to be overrun by illegal immigrants.

B. In the space provided, write the letter of the fallacy contained in each argument. Choose from the three fallacies shown in the box below.

> **A** False cause *(the argument assumes that the order of events alone shows cause and effect)*
>
> **B** False comparison *(the argument assumes that two things being compared are more alike than they really are)*
>
> **C** Either-or *(the argument assumes that there are only two sides to a question)*

____C____ 6. Are you going to become a vegetarian, or do you intend to eat like a normal person?   Vegetarianism is increasingly seen as "normal." In the view presented, either you are a vegetarian or you are normal.

____A____ 7. Ever since I switched schools, my grades have gone down. My new teachers are doing a poor job.   There could be other reasons for the student's declining grades.

Item 8:   _B_   8. When I was a girl, people didn't have to get their cats and dogs
The situation in the past   vaccinated for rabies, so I don't see why we have to shell out the
was very different from   money to do it.
the situation today. Due
to the increase in   _A_   9. Lisa went out with a guy who lied and said he was single when he
population   was actually married with two kids. She never should have dated
density of both   someone she met on the Internet.   The Internet is not the reason the
people and pets,   man lied. He probably would have lied no matter where she met him.
an outbreak
of rabies could   _B_   10. The crime rate would drop if we would do what some Middle
spread rapidly.   Eastern countries do and chop off the hands of convicted thieves.

Our society is radically different from Middle Eastern societies.

CHAPTER REVIEW

In this chapter, you learned that critical readers evaluate an author's support for a point and determine whether that support is solid or not. Critical reading includes the following three abilities:

- **Separating fact from opinion.** A **fact** is information that can be proved true through objective evidence. An **opinion** is a belief, judgment, or conclusion that cannot be proved objectively true. Much of what we read is a mixture of fact and opinion, and our job as readers is to arrive at at the best possible informed opinion. Textbooks and other effective writing provide informed opinion—opinion based upon factual information.

- **Detecting propaganda.** Advertisers, salespeople, and politicians often try to promote their points by appealing to our emotions rather than our powers of reason. To do so, they practice six common propaganda techniques: bandwagon, testimonial, transfer, plain folks, name calling, and glittering generalities.

- **Recognizing errors in reasoning.** Politicians and others are at times guilty of errors in reasoning—fallacies—that take the place of the real support needed in an argument. Such fallacies include circular reasoning, personal attack, straw man, false cause, false comparison, and either-or.

The final chapter in Part One—Chapter 10—will provide an overall approach to the skill of active reading.

On the Web: If you are using this book in class, you can visit our website for additional practice in critical reading. Go to **www.townsendpress.com** and click on "Online Exercises."

➤ Review Test 1

To review what you've learned in this chapter, answer each of the following questions by filling in the blank.

1. Value or judgment words such as *best, worst, great,* and *beautiful* often represent not facts but _____*opinions*_____.   See page 325.

2. Textbook authors work very hard to back up all of their opinions with _____*facts*_____.   See page 326.

3. **Propaganda techniques** (*bandwagon, transfer, testimonial, plain folks, name calling,* and *glittering generalities*) are emotional appeals used to distract us from the lack of relevant and adequate ___*support* (**or** *evidence*)___ for a given point.   See page 329.

4. In the most common propaganda technique, _____*transfer*_____, products or candidates try to associate themselves with appealing images such as beautiful people or symbols of America such as the flag.   See page 330.

5. **Fallacies** (*circular reasoning, personal attack, straw man, false cause, false comparison,* and *either-or*) are errors in reasoning also used to distract us from the lack of relevant and adequate ___*support* (**or** *evidence*)___ for a given point.   See pages 333–334.

➤ Review Test 2

The essay below is followed by questions on critical reading skills as well as on the skills you have practiced in previous chapters.

Preview

When it comes to radically altering your world view, nothing compares with parenthood. Issues that you previously shrugged off are suddenly of tremendous importance because they are going to affect your child. In this reading, newspaper columnist Steve Lopez describes how becoming the father of a baby girl gave him a new and troubling perspective on our sex-saturated society.

Words to Watch

tawdry (3): cheap
vapid (3): dull; meaningless
lurid (5): intended to shock
surreptitiously (17): secretly

A SCARY TIME TO RAISE A DAUGHTER

Steve Lopez

1   Three months ago, with my wife's contractions getting closer and closer, we flicked on the TV as a distraction before going to the hospital.

2   Bad idea.

3   No one expects a great deal of enlightenment from the tube these days. But as we switched from one tawdry° and vapid° reality or dating show to another, I wondered if we should have our heads examined for bringing a child into this world.

4   Especially a girl.

5   It's not just television that scares me. It's the Internet, pop music, radio, advertising. The most lurid° elements of each medium now dominate pop culture, and the incessant, pounding message, directed primarily at young people, is that it's all about sex.

6   Sure, some of us boomers had our flower child days of free love, but that was a social revolution, not a corporate-driven campaign.

7   Today, if you haven't just had it, you're a loser. If you don't expect to have it in the immediate future, try plastic surgery, because sex appeal—the one true standard of human achievement—is the only thing worth aspiring to.

8   Yes, I'll admit it: I'm frazzled about all of this because I have a baby girl. Each day, I feel a little more like Dan Quayle, who was once ridiculed for wagging a finger at television's Murphy Brown, an unwed mom.

9   Where's Dan Quayle when you need him?

10   At my daughter's first checkup, our pediatrician mentioned that he routinely has pregnant patients in their early teens. I shook my head and said it's no wonder, given what kids see on TV and the Internet.

11   Forget that, the doctor said. Go for a drive and take a look at some billboards. Belts are unbuckled. Bras are undone. Everyone is on the make.

12   While contemplating these horrors as a new dad, I got an e-mail one day from actress Susan Dey, who has volunteered at the Rape Treatment Center in Santa Monica for fifteen years.

13   Dey was America's grooviest teenager in a more innocent media era—she played Laurie on *The Partridge Family*. She told me she had gotten an unsolicited email directing her to a Web site with college girls having live sex. Dey checked it out and was horrified at what is essentially a

guide for frat boys on how to nail co-eds.

14   "A little alcohol will always loosen up the college chicks!" the site advises, complete with graphic results.

15   "These are the girls we see at the rape center," Dey said with disgust.

16   Gail Abarbanel, director of the center, said 50% of rape victims are 18 or younger, and the rapists are acquaintances 80% of the time.

17   "We see a lot of cases where raped women are incapacitated by drugs or alcohol, sometimes surreptitiously°," Abarbanel said. "We even have a few cases where victims have been tagged."

18   The rapist will use a felt-tip pen to mark his conquest, she said, just as a gangbanger leaves his tag on a wall.

19   When I asked Abarbanel what was going on, she said kids are saturated as never before with marketing and entertainment that's all about sex and violence. Subtlety and restraint are quaint, nostalgic notions, as is attentive parenting.

20   Another factor, I think, is that very little in the culture encourages independent thinking, and that makes peer pressure all the more powerful. "Look at what's happening with oral sex in the bathrooms of middle schools," Abarbanel said, telling me that, in workshops at local schools, they hear stories about how commonplace it's become.

21   I've got friends who told me they turn the radio off while taking their kids to school, because it's routine to hear shock jocks carrying on about oral sex. Next time I was in my car, I flipped through the FM dial and, in nothing flat, found that very thing on two stations.

22   A couple of weeks after we met, Dey called again to say I ought to have a look at the photos in the Abercrombie & Fitch store at the Grove in the Fairfax District. We met there Thursday and took a tour.

23   On both floors of the store, which markets to a young crowd, the walls were plastered with huge blowups of fresh-faced, great-looking teens who are either nude or nearly nude.

24   In one, a topless girl is playing the violin while in the clutches of a shirtless boy, and a carefully placed strand of hair is all that keeps her from being completely revealed.

25   In another, a naked girl is sandwiched by two boys, her breasts completely visible but for a bit of strategic air brushing. The three of them are holding a blanket over what appear to be nude lower bodies.

26   An odd advertising campaign, you'd have to say—all this nudity being used to sell clothes.

27   It's all about an image, a clerk explained.

28   Yeah, I gathered as much.

29   "The message is, you should be a sexual object," Dey said outside the store. "Like I've been saying, connect the dots."

30   She had been telling me the problem isn't the photos in the store, or billboards on the street, or TV shows, or movies, or the Internet. It's all of those things together.

31   "I taught my daughter to love her body, but that's not what this is about," Dey said. "A boy's not cool if he hasn't just done it. His whole manhood is at stake. I don't think we were ever targeted the way they're targeting this generation, and when does it stop?

32   "I would love it if parents said, 'No, I'm not putting my credit card down for this.' Can you imagine what would happen if parents said to Madison Avenue, 'I want my 13-year-old to be a 13-year-old'?"

Reading Comprehension Questions

Central Point and Main Ideas

__C__ 1. Which sentence best expresses the central point of the selection?

    A. The author is disgusted by the idea that our young people are exposed to negative messages.

    B. The author contrasts the free love social revolution of his day with the corporate-driven campaigns of today.

    C. The author is concerned that his baby daughter may eventually fall victim to the idea, promoted by our sex-saturated culture, that it's good to be a sex object.

    D. The author visits an Abercrombie & Fitch store with an actress and is shocked to see that it is plastered with nude images of young people.   Answer A does not mention that the message is sexual or Lopez's concern for the impact on young women. Answer B covers only paragraph 6. Answer D covers only paragraphs 22–27.

Supporting Details

__D__ 2. A startling fact that Lopez's pediatrician mentions is that

    A. he was once a flower child in the days of free love.

    B. he knows actress Susan Dey, once America's grooviest teenager.

    C. his own daughter was drugged and raped by a frat boy.

    D. he routinely has pregnant patients in their early teens.

    See paragraph 10.

Patterns of Organization

__C__ 3. Paragraphs 22–28 in large part

    A. contrast the clerk's attitude toward sex with that of the author.

    B. narrate a series of events in time order.

    C. provide illustrations of the use of sex to sell products.

    D. discuss the consequences of using sex to sell clothing to teenagers.

    The Abercrombie & Fitch photos use sex to sell clothing.

Inferences

__C__ 4. The last two paragraphs of the selection suggest that parents should

    A. relax and let their 13-year-olds do whatever they want.

    B. encourage their boys to prove their manhood by having sex.

    C. refuse to pay for products which tell teens that it's good to be a sex object.

    D. use cash instead of credit cards to make purchases.

    The paragraphs clearly suggest that parents refuse to use their credit cards to support companies which use sex to sell to teens. The paragraphs contradict answers A and B. Answer D is incorrect because the paragraphs suggest not to buy the products at all (not that it is all right to use cash to buy them).

Purpose and Tone

_A_ 5. In paragraph 7, the author's tone is
   A. sarcastic.
   B. ambivalent.
   C. detached.   The writer does not really believe that sex appeal
   D. solemn.   is the one true standard of human achievement.

Argument

_D_ 6. Three of the items below are supporting details for an argument. Write the letter of the statement that represents the point of these supporting details.
   A. Some Web sites encourage frat boys to use alcohol in order to get co-eds to have sex with them.
   B. The director of a rape treatment center says that 50% of rape victims are 18 or younger.
   C. A pediatrician says that he routinely has pregnant patients in their early teens.
   D. Girls and young women are often sexually victimized by males.

Answers A, B, and C are examples of the sexual victimization of girls and young women.

Critical Reading

_C_ 7. The sentence below is
   A. A fact.   The first part of the sentence is an opinion,
   B. an opinion.   with which some people might disagree. The
   C. both fact and opinion.   second part of the sentence is factual; it reports
       what the writer was thinking at the time.

   "But as we switched from one <u>tawdry</u> and <u>vapid</u> reality or dating show to another, I wondered if we should have our heads examined for bringing a child into this world." (Paragraph 3)

_D_ 8. The use of a pretty, topless girl to sell clothing is an example of the propaganda technique of
   A. testimonial.
   B. plain folks.   The image uses sex appeal and hopes it
   C. bandwagon.   will transfer to the product.
   D. transfer.

_C_ 9. When a store "plasters the walls with images of fresh-faced, great-looking teens who are either nude or semi-nude," it is using the propaganda technique of
   A. testimonial.
   B. plain folks.
   C. bandwagon.
   D. name calling.

Many images of teens together suggest a bandwagon approach.

_D_ 10. The statement "If you haven't just had [sex], you're a loser" is an example of the logical fallacy of
   A. circular reasoning.
   B. personal attack.
   C. straw man.
   D. either-or.

The statement assumes that there is no middle ground between two extremes.

Discussion Questions

1. Do you agree with Lopez that this is a particularly challenging time to raise a child? Which of his concerns do you share? Do you think his concerns are groundless or exaggerated?

2. How much effect do you believe that marketing campaigns such as Abercrombie & Fitch's have on young people and their views on sexuality? Do you agree with the author that such messages result in negative consequences for young people, especially girls—or do you disagree? Explain.

3. According to the selection, 50% of rape victims are 18 or younger, and the rapists are acquaintances 80% of the time. In your view, what changes can we make as a society to help ensure that fewer girls and young women fall victim to rape?

4. Why do you think Lopez is particularly concerned about raising a girl in today's society? How is the impact of a sexualized society different for boys than it is for girls?

Note: Writing assignments for this selection appear on page 565.

Check Your Performance   **CRITICAL READING**

Activity	Number Right	Points	Score
Review Test 1 (5 items)	_____	× 6 =	_____
Review Test 2 (10 items)	_____	× 7 =	_____
	TOTAL SCORE	=	_____%

Enter your total score into the **Reading Performance Chart: Review Tests** on the inside back cover.

CRITICAL READING: Mastery Test 1 (Fact and Opinion)

A. Identify facts with an **F**, opinions with an **O**, and the one combination of fact *and* opinion with an **F+O**.   *Note:* In Tests 1 and 2, words indicating opinions are underlined in red in this *Instructor's Edition*.

Items 2, 3, 5, 7, 8, and 10 all state scientific or statistical information that can be verified by research.

___O___ 1. Overpopulation is the number one problem facing the world today.

___F___ 2. The world population reached 6 billion in the year 2000, and it is projected to be 7 billion by the year 2013.

___F___ 3. Blood transfusions were dangerous before scientists identified the four different types of human blood, making it possible to match donors and patients according to blood type.

Item 12: It can be verified that heroin is illegal. Some people may feel that it should not be made available for any reason.

___O___ 4. The identification of blood types is the most important scientific discovery in recent history.

___F___ 5. The elephant's closest living relative is an African mammal called the hyrax, which is about the size of a large rabbit.

___O___ 6. The hunting of elephants is immoral and should be banned completely.

___F___ 7. Elephants can communicate by making sounds at a lower frequency than the human ear is able to detect.

___F___ 8. Although not commonly used during the time period, contact lenses were first manufactured in 1887.

___O___ 9. Most people are more attractive when they wear contact lenses instead of glasses.

___F___ 10. Heroin is derived from the opium poppy, *Papaver somniferum*, which means "the poppy that brings sleep."

___O___ 11. Addiction to heroin is not as bad as addiction to crack cocaine.

___F+O___ 12. In the United States, heroin is illegal for any purposes, although it should be available as a treatment for pain in those with terminal disease.

B. Following are eight short movie reviews. Identify a factual review with an **F**; identify a review that includes both facts about the movie *and* the reviewer's opinion with an **F+O**.

That it was the first "Rocky" film can be verified in film histories. The factual details of the plot can be verified by watching the film.

___F+O___ 13. **Rocky:** The first, and by far the best, of Sylvester Stallone's "Rocky" franchise. A Philadelphia punk gets a chance to fight the heavyweight champ in an exhibition match. Stallone is memorably awkward and lovable as Rocky Balboa, and Talia Shire shines as Adrian, the shy girl who believes in him. *(Continues on next page)*

_F_ 14. ***The Wizard of Oz:*** Winner of the 1939 Academy Awards for Best Original Score and Best Original Song ("Over the Rainbow"). Sixteen-year-old Judy Garland plays the young heroine Dorothy Gale, who is swept away from her home in Kansas to the magical Land of Oz.

_F_ 15. ***King Kong:*** Latest (2005) remake of the story about the big ape and the girl he loves. It's a big-budget production from Peter Jackson (of *The Lord of the Rings* fame). Naomi Watts and Jack Black star, with Kong embodied by actor Andy Serkis. At 187 minutes, this version is nearly twice as long as the 1933 original *King Kong* with Fay Wray.

_F+O_ 16. ***Night of the Living Dead:*** This 1968 low-budget horror <u>classic</u> <u>still has the power to shock</u>. <u>Groundbreaking</u> both for its gore and its <u>sly</u> comments on racism, *Night of the Living Dead* is a <u>must-see</u> for fans of the genre.

_F+O_ 17. ***Singin' in the Rain:*** <u>Everybody's favorite romantic musical comedy</u>. If the sight of Gene Kelly joyfully leaping onto a lamppost and splashing through puddles as he dances in the ecstasy of new love <u>doesn't bring a smile to your face, you are beyond hope.</u>

_F+O_ 18. ***Modern Times:*** Made in 1936, Charlie Chaplin's last silent film is a <u>brilliant</u> protest against the dehumanization of man in the Industrial Age. Playing his <u>famous</u> "Little Tramp" character, Chaplin is seen in a succession of <u>hilarious, sharply satirical</u> scenes as an assembly-line worker, a shipyard worker, a night watchman, and more.

_F_ 19. ***The Godfather:*** Winner of the 1972 Academy Awards for Best Actor (Marlon Brando), Best Picture, and Best Screenplay, *The Godfather* tells the story of the aging patriarch of a crime family (Brando) transferring control to his initially reluctant son (Al Pacino). Runs just under three hours.

_F+O_ 20. ***On the Waterfront:*** "I coulda been a contender!" This <u>strangled, heartbroken protest</u> from ex-boxer turned longshoreman Terry Malloy (Marlon Brando) <u>has entered the gallery of immortal movie lines</u>. After witnessing a murder ordered by his <u>corrupt</u> union boss, Terry <u>must</u> struggle with his conscience. <u>Stellar</u> performances by a range of Hollywood heavyweights that include Rod Steiger, Karl Malden, Lee J. Cobb, and Eva Marie Saint.

Item 16: That it was made in 1968 and was a low-budget film are verifiable facts.

Item 17: That the film is a romantic musical comedy and that Kelly does leap onto a lamppost and splash through puddles can be confirmed by viewing the film, by consulting a guide to movies, or by Googling *"Singin' in the Rain* Gene Kelly lamppost."

Item 18: That it was made in 1936 and was Chaplin's last silent film are verifiable facts.

Item 20: Who performed in the film and what Terry Malloy says and does can be confirmed by watching the film or by consulting a guide to movies.

CRITICAL READING: Mastery Test 2 (Fact and Opinion)

A. Identify facts with an **F**, opinions with an **O**, and the one combination of fact *and* opinion with an **F+O**.

Items 1, 3, 4, 7, 8, and 10 all state information that can be verified by research in appropriate sources.

Item 12: The description of what happens in greyhound racing is factual. Saying it is abuse is opinion; some people would say it is entertainment.

___F___ 1. Magicians can often tell when a hidden card comes up by seeing the pupils of the person who put it in the deck dilate in recognition.

___O___ 2. Magicians aren't as talented as people seem to think they are.

___F___ 3. At least ten magicians have died trying to perform a "bullet-catching" trick.

___F___ 4. Overall, human life expectancy is nearly twice as long as it was in 1840.

___O___ 5. Many people are obsessed with stretching out their lives as far as possible.

___O___ 6. Many people who suffer from depression are weak and self-pitying.

___F___ 7. Some 15 million people in the United States suffer from major depression.

___F___ 8. The percentage of people who regularly watch network news has declined in recent years.

___O___ 9. CNN is the most reliable source of news.

___F___ 10. Gutenberg invented the printing press in the 1450s, and the first book ever to be printed on it was the Bible.

___O___ 11. In a few short years, books will be obsolete because everyone will be able to access reading material online.

___F+O___ 12. In greyhound racing, which amounts to animal abuse, the dogs chase an artificial rabbit as they speed around the racetrack.

B. Following are eight short book reviews. Identify a factual review with an **F**; identify a review that includes both facts about the book *and* the reviewer's opinion with an **F+O**.

That the book is a first-person account of slave life is a fact. The underlined words signal opinion.

___F+O___ 13. ***Narrative of the Life of Frederick Douglass:*** This book is the most powerful first-person account of slave life ever written. Douglass, a man of fiery temperament and passionate intelligence, makes the reader feel every lash of the whip and suffer every barbarity he witnessed. Highly recommended.

(Continues on next page)

Items 14, ___F___ 14. ***The Scarlet Letter:*** Hester Prynne is a young woman living in colonial
15, 18, 19: Boston, then under the control of stern Puritans. When she becomes
All of these pregnant by an unknown lover, her punishment is to wear the letter A
details can be (for adultery) forever. Hester's refusal to name her partner in sin sets in
confirmed by motion a series of events that will change two men's lives forever.
reading the
book.
___F___ 15. ***Black Beauty:*** This first-person account of a horse's life tells of Black
Beauty's succession of homes and owners. Along the way he learns of
the lives and fortunes of other horses. Set in 19th century London, the
book was written as a protest against the maltreatment of animals.

Item 16: ___F+O___ 16. ***Pride and Prejudice:*** One of Jane Austen's most popular novels, the
The details of the book tells the story of the Bennet family, whose five daughters are
story are factual. destined for poverty unless they marry well. <u>Witty</u> Elizabeth Bennet,
The underlined the second oldest of the daughters, <u>takes such pleasure</u> in disliking rich,
words indicate proud Mr. Darcy that <u>the reader can only suspect</u> the two will end up
opinions. together. How this <u>unlikely</u> relationship progresses creates a <u>delightful</u>
reading experience.

Item 17: ___F+O___ 17. ***The Shame of the Nation:*** Although the racial segregation of
That school America's schools officially ended in 1954, author Jonathan Kozol
segregation ended makes it clear in this <u>devastating</u> book that schools serving black and
in 1954 and that Hispanic children are <u>woefully inadequate</u>, and <u>getting worse</u>. Kozol's
Kozol has written a <u>meticulous</u> research contradicts the <u>empty words</u> of those who claim
book critical of that all America's children have equal opportunity.
schools serving
black and
Hispanic ___F___ 18. ***The Grapes of Wrath:*** Winner of the Pulitzer Prize for Fiction in 1940,
children John Steinbeck's novel is the account of one Depression-era family, the
are facts. Joads, traveling from the ruins of their Oklahoma farm to what they
The underlined believe will be an Eden of opportunity in California. The Joads struggle
words indicate to maintain their hope in the face of the challenges of migrant life.
opinions.

___F___ 19. ***Year of Magical Thinking:*** Essayist Joan Didion and her husband,
novelist John Gregory Dunne, were just sitting down to dinner after
visiting their seriously ill daughter when Dunne collapsed and died.
This book is Didion's account of the next twelve months—adjusting to
her husband's absence while dealing with her daughter's critical illness.

Item 20: ___F+O___ 20. ***No Ordinary Time: Franklin and Eleanor Roosevelt:*** Historian Doris
The details can be Kearns Goodwin chronicles how the private lives of the White House
confirmed by occupants have a direct bearing on national policy as she simultane-
reading the book. ously explores the <u>often tumultuous</u> marriage of Franklin and Eleanor
The underlined Roosevelt in a time of international crisis. An <u>invaluable</u> contribution to
words signal our understanding of the Roosevelts and their era, this <u>page-turner</u>
opinions. <u>reads like a skillfully written novel</u>.

CRITICAL READING: Mastery Test 3 (Propaganda Techniques)

A. Each pair of items below illustrates a particular propaganda technique. On the line next to each item, write the letter of the main technique being used.

_C_ 1. • An aspirin company says that <u>millions</u> of Americans use its product.

       • A cell phone ad shows a <u>roomful</u> of concertgoers taking their phones out <u>in unison</u> and waving them in the air.

    A. Name calling   C. Bandwagon
    B. Testimonial   D. Plain folks

_B_ 2. • A milk advertisement shows photographs of <u>A-list celebrities</u> with milk mustaches.

       • A <u>famous singer</u> tells television viewers how she overcame her battle with acne by using a particular brand of skin care products.

    A. Name calling   C. Bandwagon
    B. Testimonial   D. Plain folks

_D_ 3. • A large chain store uses <u>pictures of actual employees</u> in its advertisements.

       • The president of the United States gives the press a tour of his ranch while <u>wearing jeans and playing with his dog</u>.

    A. Name calling   C. Bandwagon
    B. Testimonial   D. Plain folks

_C_ 4. • A <u>beautiful woman</u> in office attire is seen enjoying a juicy hamburger.

       • A <u>huge American flag</u> is used as a backdrop for a political speech.

    A. Testimonial   C. Transfer
    B. Name calling   D. Glittering generalities

_B_ 5. • American political leaders refer to a certain part of the world as the "<u>axis of evil</u>."

       • Anti-tobacco advertisers use the term "<u>Big Tobacco</u>" in campaigns to vilify tobacco companies and executives.

    A. Testimonial   C. Transfer
    B. Name calling   D. Glittering generalities

Note: In Tests 3 and 4, words indicating a particular propaganda technique are underlined in red in this *Instructor's Edition.*

(Continues on next page)

_D_   6. • An ad calls a car "an American revolution."

        • A cellular phone company ad proclaims, "Dream meets delivery. Promise meets performance."

        A. Testimonial   C. Transfer
        B. Name calling   D. Glittering generalities

B. Below are descriptions of four actual ads. On each line, write the letter of the main propaganda technique that applies to the ad.

        A Bandwagon   D Plain folks
        B Testimonial   E Name calling
        C Transfer   F Glittering generalities

_C_   7. An ad for a spicy fast-food premium chicken sandwich shows an attractive young woman on a motorcycle. She explains that when she needs her spice, she goes for this new flavor sandwich. "How can I not like it?" she says. "It's bold, spicy and hot. . . just like me."

_B_   8. TV personality Ellen DeGeneres appears in an ad which features a questionnaire she has filled out listing her card as American Express.

_F_   9. "Beyond shiny. Beyond beauty. Beyond healthy," reads an ad for a line of hair care products. Above the text, a woman stands next to an elevator. The elevator's top button, titled "Hair Heaven," has been pushed.

_A_   10. An ad for chocolate candy shows people giving the chocolates to each other as gifts. A woman hugs her friend after receiving a box of chocolates. A mother accepts a box of chocolates from her grown daughter with a smile. In the office, a boss gives a box of chocolates to each employee. A couple brings chocolates as a hostess gift. A young girl presents a box of chocolates to her teacher. In the last scene, all the people in the ad are shown simultaneously while the announcer says, "It's everyone's way to say thank you."

CRITICAL READING: Mastery Test 4 (Propaganda Techniques)

A. Each pair of items below illustrates a particular propaganda technique. On the line next to each item, write the letter of the main technique being used.

D   1. • A bank advertises "A Return to Better Banking."

     • "Beyond Precision," claims a car ad.

      A. Testimonial   C. Transfer

      B. Name calling   D. Glittering generalities

C   2. • An ad encouraging women to buy right-hand diamond rings reads: "Women of the world, raise your right hand."

     • A TV ad claims that more and more people in the region are getting their evening news from a certain anchor team.

      A. Name calling   C. Bandwagon

      B. Testimonial   D. Plain folks

C   3. • A very attractive middle-aged woman wearing a long, flowered dress walks with a cute little girl in a field of wildflowers to advertise a drug which claims to reverse bone loss.

     • Local retail stores display the American flag in their storefront windows.

      A. Testimonial   C. Transfer

      B. Name calling   D. Glittering generalities

A   4. • An Academy Award-winning actress encourages us to "discover the excitement" of her home state.

     • In a magazine ad, an Olympic gold medalist ice skater is shown giving her kitchen appliances a score of a perfect ten.

      A. Testimonial   C. Transfer

      B. Name calling   D. Glittering generalities

D   5. • A middle-aged woman in pajamas, bathrobe, and slippers is shown using a new brand of facial tissue.

     • In a TV commercial, a blue-collar employee of a large corporation tells how much he loves his job.

      A. Name calling   C. Bandwagon

      B. Testimonial   D. Plain folks

(Continues on next page)

_B_   6. • A politician refers to a candidate in the opposing party as a "<u>girly man</u>."

  • An ice cream maker says, "Our vanilla ice cream has four ingredients: Milk, cream, sugar, and vanilla" and that the ingredients in a competitor's vanilla ice cream read like "<u>a chemistry experiment.</u>"

A. Testimonial	C. Transfer
B. Name calling	D. Glittering generalities

B. Below are descriptions of four actual ads. On each line, write the letter of the main propaganda technique that applies to the ad.

A	Bandwagon	D	Plain folks
B	Testimonial	E	Name calling
C	Transfer	F	Glittering generalities

_F_   7. A diamond ad shows a picture of a woman with light emanating from her finger, where a ring would be. Below, the text reads: "A diamond is forever. Forever timeless. Forever unique. Forever a force of nature. <u>Forever all the things that make a woman … </u>"

_C_   8. A very pretty <u>teenage girl in a satiny top</u> stands under a <u>movie marquee</u> which reads *Escape from Toxic Town*. The text of the ad reads: "In a world where evil threatens your face, there's the detoxifying formula of Noxzema Triple Clean Blackhead Cleanser. A daily dose purifies your pores, helping to prevent blackheads and reduce breakouts. Doesn't your face deserve a <u>Hollywood ending?</u>"

_B_   9. Singer <u>Sheryl Crow</u> wears a milk moustache as she tells us, "To keep the crowd on their feet, I keep my body in tune. With milk. Studies suggest that the nutrients in milk can play an important role in weight loss. So if you're trying to lose weight or maintain a healthy weight, try drinking 24 ounces of low-fat or fat-free milk every twenty-four hours as part of your reduced-calorie diet … It's a change that'll do you good."

_D_ 10. A commercial shows an <u>average-looking young couple</u> looking unhappily at a bare spot beside their house. An announcer's voice says, "Home improvement projects got you down? Come into McGowan Hardware, and we'll solve your problems together!" We see the couple chatting with a <u>friendly-looking hardware employee</u>, then cheerfully working to build their own patio.

CRITICAL READING: Mastery Test 5 (Errors in Reasoning)

A. Each pair of items below illustrates a particular error in reasoning. On the line next to each item, write the letter of the logical fallacy contained in both items. Choose from the three fallacies shown in the box below.

> **A** Circular reasoning *(a statement repeats itself rather than providing a real supporting reason to back up an argument)*
>
> **B** Personal attack *(ignores the issue under discussion and concentrates instead on the character of the opponent)*
>
> **C** Straw man *(an argument is made by claiming an opponent holds an extreme position and then opposing that extreme position)*

___A___ 1. • Capital punishment is wrong because it is immoral. To say something is immoral is to say that it is wrong.
 • Sports cars will continue to be popular as long as people enjoy driving them. This is the same as saying that people like sports cars because they like them.

___B___ 2. • Our biology teacher believes in evolution. He must be one of those godless liberals. Many people who believe in evolution are religious.
 • That senator supports abortion. She has no right calling herself a Christian. Some Christians support abortion.

___B___ 3. • Mary McGee would make a terrible governor. She'd probably get irrational because she's middle-aged. Middle-aged women are not particularly irrational.
 • I suggest you think twice before taking a class with that instructor. He was seen coming out of a gay bar. The fact that the instructor may be gay is irrelevant to his teaching ability.

___A___ 4. • Scott can't seem to throw anything out because he is a pack rat. By definition, a pack rat is someone who doesn't throw anything out.
 • Coca-Cola is the world's best-selling soft drink for the simple fact that more people buy it than any other soda. Saying more people buy Coca-Cola is the same as saying it is the best-selling soft drink.

___C___ 5. • Our neighbors say they won't object if minorities buy the house across the street. Evidently it doesn't matter to them if the neighborhood goes downhill. The statement illogically assumes that the neighbors don't care about their neighborhood.
 • The president supports drilling for oil off the Gulf Coast of Florida. Apparently he doesn't care if a huge oil spill wrecks our tourism industry. The statement illogically assumes that the president is indifferent to a huge oil spill that would ruin tourism in Florida.

(Continues on next page)

B. In the space provided, write the letter of the fallacy contained in each pair of arguments. Choose from the three fallacies shown in the box below.

> **A** False cause *(the argument assumes that the order of events alone shows cause and effect)*
>
> **B** False comparison *(the argument assumes that two things being compared are more alike than they really are)*
>
> **C** Either-or *(the argument assumes that there are only two sides to a question)*

Item 6: ___A___ 6. • My cousin stole a car and wrecked it when he was 15. That's what
There may have been   happens to children of divorced parents.
other reasons why the
cousin became a car   • I woke up in the night feeling sick to my stomach. That restaurant
thief. Perhaps the   where I had dinner must have served spoiled food.
person who felt sick to his stomach had a stomach virus.

Item 7: ___B___ 7. • Adults are allowed to have wine or mixed drinks with their meals, so
There are many differ-   teenagers should have this privilege also.
ences between adults and
teenagers—including   • In nature, the male lion rules over the females, so I believe that men
maturity, experience, and should dominate women.
body chemistry—that make the comparison false. Similarly, there are many differences between humans
and lions.
        ___C___ 8. • In choosing a car, you need to decide whether to get a safe vehicle or
Item 8:   one that's fun to drive.
Some vehicles are both
safe and fun to drive. • If Sonya doesn't check want ads and send out at least several
There are other ways to   resumés every day, then she must not be serious about finding a job.
go about finding a job besides checking want ads and sending out resumes.

Item 9: ___A___ 9. • Ever since Ryan started listening to rap music, he's become rude and
Ryan may have become   disrespectful. That music should be banned.
rude and disruptive for
reasons that have   • TV shows these days are showing more and more skin. No wonder
nothing to do with   teenage behavior is so outrageous.
rap music. And outrageous teenage behavior may have many causes besides skin shown on TV.

        ___B___ 10. • I went to State University and did just fine, so I don't see why my
Item 10:   son needs to go to a fancy private college.
There are many
differences between   • Back in my day, when a person got old, his children took care of
the past and the present him. I don't see why my children want to put me in assisted living.
that make these comparisons invalid. For example, the private college might have innovative or
advanced programs that aren't available at State University. And if the adult children all work outside
the home, they might not have the resources to care for an elderly parent in their own homes.

CRITICAL READING: Mastery Test 6 (Errors in Reasoning)

A. Each pair of items below illustrates a particular error in reasoning. On the line next to each item, write the letter of the logical fallacy contained in both items. Choose from the three fallacies shown in the box below.

> A **Circular reasoning** (*a statement repeats itself rather than providing a real supporting reason to back up an argument*)
>
> B **Personal attack** (*ignores the issue under discussion and concentrates instead on the character of the opponent*)
>
> C **Straw man** (*an argument is made by claiming an opponent holds an extreme position and then opposing that extreme position*)

___C___ 1. • Our senators voted to reduce the nation's defense budget. Why do they want to weaken America?   The defense budget may contain waste.

   • The mayor is campaigning to legalize gambling in this city. He doesn't seem to mind if poor people blow all their food and rent money at the slots.   The mayor probably believes that legalized gambling will add to the city's tax base and attract tourists.

___B___ 2. • Linda Randolph is a recovering alcoholic and should never have been put into a management position.

   • That man should not be allowed to have a radio show. He was convicted of having a prescription drug addiction.   People who have recovered from substance abuse are capable of holding responsible jobs.

___C___ 3. • My opponent voted to raise the minimum wage to $7.00 an hour. He must want many small business owners to go bankrupt.

   • You want to get your eyebrow pierced? Next you'll want to stay out all night and experiment with heroin, too, and I won't allow you to start down that road.   It is unlikely that the opponent wants small business owners to go bankrupt or that piercing one's eyebrow will result in taking heroin.

___A___ 4. • My brother-in-law just lies around all day because he is so lazy.

   • Landscaping improves the appearance of a home since it is beautiful to look at.   By definition, someone who lies around all day is lazy. Similarly, landscaping that is beautiful to look at would improve a home's appearance.

___B___ 5. • Even if you're very sick, don't go to the ER at that hospital. Three people died there last week.   Very sick and injured people often die in hospitals, no matter what kind of care they receive.

   • That actress is such a conceited person that she is bound to spoil the new movie she is in.   Conceited people can be great performers.

(Continues on next page)

B. In the space provided, write the letter of the fallacy contained in each pair of arguments. Choose from the three fallacies shown in the box below.

> A False cause (*the argument assumes that the order of events alone shows cause and effect*)
>
> B False comparison (*the argument assumes that two things being compared are more alike than they really are*)
>
> C Either-or (*the argument assumes that there are only two sides to a question*)

Item 6:   _C_   6. • Renee switched to a low-fat diet but still got cancer. Low-fat diets are no healthier than high-fat diets.
Assumptions: either a low-fat diet prevents cancer, or it is worthless; either her boyfriend looks at other women, or he really loves her.
  • My boyfriend likes to look at other women when we go to the beach. That shows he doesn't really love me.

Item 7:   _A_   7. • Ever since I broke off with my boyfriend, my life has gone downhill. I need to forgive him and restart our relationship.
Breaking up with the boyfriend may not be the reason life went downhill; and life going downhill may not be a reason to restart the relationship.
  • Twelve months after the youth recreation center opened, the crime rate in our town had risen 15 percent. Clearly the center is attracting bad characters.
The crime rate may have risen for many reasons besides the opening of the center.

Item 8:   _B_   8. • Why should I have to take algebra? I'm not going to be a professional mathematician.
Algebra can be helpful in many occupations. The cost of college has risen considerably since the 1970s.
  • Nobody helped me pay for college back in the 1970s, and my kids shouldn't expect me to help them, either.

Item 9:   _A_   9. • This year the murder rate has increased in our city. The police commissioner should be replaced.
The police commissioner is not necessarily the cause of the increased crime rate. And the quarterback's failure to shave probably did not cause the team to win.
  • The day their quarterback didn't shave was the day his team broke a three-game losing streak. He's decided not to shave again until they lose.

Item 10:   _C_   10. • Why did you hire a teenage babysitter? Wouldn't you rather have someone who knows what she's doing?
Some teenage babysitters are highly competent. In a democracy, the president is not above criticism.
  • Do you support our president's policies, or are you un-American?

10

Active Reading and Study

Active readers are involved in what they are reading. They think and ask questions as they read, looking for the author's main points and the support for those points. After—or as—they read, they take notes and use an effective study method to help them master those notes. Active readers are the opposite of passive readers (such as the light-haired girl pictured in the *Peanuts* cartoon above), whose minds do not really pay attention to what they read.

So far in this book you have practiced a number of active reading skills that should help you become a more active reader. In this final chapter, you'll learn how to deepen your active reading by including writing and study.

Here in a nutshell is what you should do to read actively, whether an essay or a textbook chapter or any other material:

- Ask yourself, "What is the point?" and "What is the support for the point?"
- Pay close attention to titles and other headings, and also mark off definitions, examples, and enumerations.

For example, read the following classic essay by the philosopher Bertrand Russell. Have your pen in hand, and see if you can mark off the central point and number the supporting points. Then answer the questions that follow.

Three Passions

Bertrand Russell

¹Three passions, simple but overwhelmingly strong, have governed my life: the longing for love, the search for knowledge, and unbearable pity for the suffering of mankind. ²These passions, like great winds, have blown me hither and thither, in a wayward course, over a deep ocean of anguish, reaching to the very verge of despair.

(1)   ³I have sought love, first, because it brings ecstasy—ecstasy so great that I would often have sacrificed all the rest of life for a few hours of this joy. ⁴I have sought it, next, because it relieves loneliness—that terrible loneliness in which one shivering consciousness looks over the rim of the world into the cold unfathomable lifeless abyss. ⁵I have sought it, finally, because in the union of love I have seen, in a mystic miniature, the prefiguring vision of the heaven that saints and poets have imagined. ⁶This is what I sought, and though it might seem too good for human life, this is what—at last—I have found.

(2)   ⁷With equal passion I have sought knowledge. ⁸I have wished to understand the hearts of men. ⁹I have wished to know why the stars shine. ¹⁰And I have tried to apprehend the Pythagorean power by which number holds sway above the flux. ¹¹A little of this, but not much, I have achieved.

¹²Love and knowledge, so far as they were possible, led upward toward (3) the heavens. ¹³But always pity brought me back to earth. ¹⁴Echoes of cries of pain reverberate in my heart. ¹⁵Children in famine, victims tortured by oppressors, helpless old people a hated burden to their sons, and the whole world of loneliness, poverty, and pain make a mockery of what human life should be. ¹⁶I long to alleviate the evil, but I cannot, and I too suffer.

¹⁷This has been my life. ¹⁸I have found it worth living, and would gladly live it again if the chance were offered me.

- What is the author's **point**? Write your answer in the space below.

    Three passions have governed Bertrand Russell's life.

- What is the author's **support** for his point? Write your answer in the spaces below.

    1. *Love—because it brings joy and relieves loneliness*

    2. *Knowledge—to understand others and the universe*

    3. *Pity—because there is so much suffering and evil in the world*

Note: Throughout this chapter, main ideas of paragraphs and central points of passages are underlined in red in this *Instructor's Edition.*

Explanation:

The author's point might be expressed as "Three strong passions have governed my life." His support might be summarized as:

1. Love, which brings joy and relieves loneliness.
2. Knowledge, to help understand the hearts of others and the "why's" of the universe, such as why the stars shine.
3. Pity, because there is much suffering and evil in the world.

A passive reader would read the essay once and that would be it. An active reader reads the essay while at the same time asking the two basic questions, "What is the author's point, and how does he support his point?" (The active reader pays attention to the title "Three Passions" and notes that Russell makes a point about the title in his very first sentence.) The active reader then writes out the answers to the basic questions. ***The very act of writing helps an active reader study and master and remember the material.*** In a nutshell, the study method to use with your reading is to locate *and then write notes* on the point(s) and support(s) of a selection.

When notetaking, apply, as needed, all three of the writing techniques—outlining, mapping, and summarizing—that have been explained on pages 66–77.

☑ Check Your Understanding

Read the following selection (it's helpful to have your pen in hand to mark off material), and then write down its main point and support in the space provided.

Note that an enumeration and definitions are keys to important ideas here. You can easily mark off the items in the enumeration as 1, 2, and 3.

[1]Humanistic psychologist Carl Rogers believed that people are basically good and are endowed with tendencies to fulfill their potential. [2]Each of us is like an acorn, primed for growth and fulfillment, unless thwarted by an environment that inhibits growth. [3]Rogers theorized that a growth-promoting climate for people required three conditions. [4]The first of those conditions is genuineness. [5]According to Rogers, people nurture our growth by being genuine—by dropping false faces and being open with their own feelings. [6]The second condition, said Rogers, is by offering "unconditional positive regard"—an attitude of total acceptance toward another person. [7]We sometimes enjoy this gratifying experience in a good marriage, a close family, or an intimate friendship in which we no longer feel a need to explain ourselves and are free to be spontaneous without fear of losing another's esteem. [8]Finally, Rogers said that people nurture growth by being empathic—by nonjudgmentally reflecting our feelings and meanings. [9]"Rarely do we listen with real understanding, true empathy," he said. [10]"Yet listening, of this very special kind, is one of the most potent forces for change that I know."

Point: *According to Carl Rogers, a growth-promoting climate for people*

requires three conditions.

Support:

1. *Genuineness—dropping false faces and being open with one's feelings*

2. *Unconditional positive regard—total acceptance of another person*

3. *Being empathic—nonjudgmentally reflecting our feelings and meanings*

Explanation:

The third sentence expresses the main idea, or point, of the passage. (Note the list words *three conditions* that signal the main idea.) That point is then developed with three supporting details, clearly marked by the addition words *first, second*, and *Finally.*

> ### Practice 1
>   *Wording of answers may vary.*

Read the following short textbook passages from different disciplines (again, it's helpful to have your pen in hand and mark off material) and then write down their main points and support in the spaces provided.

1   Selection from a History Text

Note: An enumeration is a key to important ideas here.

¹The United States experienced falling birth rates in the nineteenth century. ②²Several factors explain this decline in birth rates. ³First, America was becoming an urban nation, and birth rates have historically been lower in cities than in rural areas. ⁴On farms, where young children worked at home or in the fields, each child born represented an addition to the family work force. ⁵In the wage-based urban economy, children could not contribute significantly to the family income for many years, and a new child ②represented another mouth to feed. ⁶Second, infant mortality fell as diet and medical care improved, and families did not have to bear many children to ③ensure that some would survive. ⁷Third, awareness that smaller families meant improved quality of life seems to have stimulated decisions to limit family size—either by abstaining from sex during the wife's fertile period or by using contraception and abortion. ⁸Families with six or eight children became rare; three or four became more usual. ⁹Birth control technology—diaphragms and condoms—had been utilized for centuries, but in this era new materials made devices more convenient and dependable.

Point: *Three factors explain why the United States experienced falling birth*

rates in the 19th century.

Support:

1. *America was becoming urban—birth rates are lower in cities.*

2. *Infant mortality fell—families did not have to bear as many children.*

3. *For a better quality of life, people decided to limit family size.*

2 Selection from a Communications Text

Note: Titles, an enumeration, and definitions and examples are keys to important ideas here.

Three Kinds of Noise

[1]Communications scholars define noise as anything that interferes with the delivery of the message. [2]A little noise might pass unnoticed, while too much noise might prevent the message from reaching its destination in the first place. [3]There are at least three different types of noise: semantic, mechanical, and environmental.

Semantic Noise

(1) [4]Semantic noise occurs when different people have different meanings for different words and phrases. [5]For example, if you ask a New Yorker for a "soda" and expect to receive something that has ice cream in it, you'll be disappointed. [6]The New Yorker will give you a bottle of what is called "pop" in the Midwest.

Mechanical Noise

(2) [7]Noise can also be mechanical. [8]This type of noise occurs when there is a problem with a machine that is being used to assist communication. [9]A TV set with a broken focus knob, a pen running out of ink, a static-filled radio, and a keyboard with a broken space bar are all examples of mechanical noise. [10]In addition, problems that are caused by people encoding messages to machines can also be thought of as a type of environmental noise. [11]Thus typographical and printing errors are examples of mechanical noise.

Environmental Noise

(3) [12]A third form of noise can be called environmental. [13]This type refers to sources of noise that are external to the communication process but that nonetheless interfere with it. [14]Some environmental noise might be out of the communicator's control—a noisy restaurant, for example, where the communicator is trying to hold a conversation. [15]Some environmental noise might be introduced by the source or the receiver; for example, you might try to talk to somebody who keeps drumming his or her fingers on the table. [16]A reporter not getting a story right because of a noisy room is an example of someone subjected to environmental noise.

Point: *There are at least three different types of noise.*

Support:

1. *Semantic—different people have different meanings for words and phrases*

   Example: *A "soda" in New York is called "pop" in the Midwest.*

2. *Mechanical—problem with a machine used to assist communication*

   Example: *A pen running out of ink; a static-filled radio*

3. *Environmental—noise that interferes with the communication process*

   Example: *A noisy restaurant; someone drumming fingers*

3 Selection from a Biology Text

Note: A title, definition, and examples are keys to important ideas here.

Elements

[1]If all matter could be reduced to its pure states, we would find that there are 92 naturally occurring kinds of matter (and a number that are synthetic). [2]These kinds of matter are the chemical elements.

① [3]A *chemical element* is a substance that cannot be separated into simpler substances through ordinary chemical means. [4]Each element has specific properties that make it different from other elements. [5]The properties of elements include their most common physical state (solid, liquid, or gas), color, odor, texture, boiling and freezing points, chemical reactivity, and others. [6]Elements can actually be broken down further, such as by bombarding them with high-energy particles, but then their properties would change and the products would no longer represent that element. [7]This is just another way of saying that the properties define the element.

② [8]Familiar elements include sulfur, phosphorus, oxygen, nitrogen, carbon, and hydrogen. [9]These six elements, often referred to by the acronym SPONCH, are important because they make up about 99% of living matter. [10]The SPONCH elements are not the only ones important to life. [11]The remaining elements are rare in organisms and of less interest to biologists.

Point: *Chemical element—one of 92 naturally occurring kinds of matter that cannot be separated chemically into similar substances*

Support: *1. Each element has specific properties that make it different from other elements: physical state, color, odor, texture, boiling/freezing points, etc.*

2. SPONCH—six familiar elements (sulfur, phosphorus, oxygen, nitrogen, carbon, and hydrogen) that make up 99% of living matter

A TEXTBOOK STUDY SYSTEM

You have now practiced, in a nutshell, a study system that really works:

1 Read the material, looking for the main points and supports.

Very often the clues to important ideas will be titles, enumerations, definitions, and examples. Note that it helps to have your pen in hand so you can mark off material as you read.

2 Take written notes on the main points and supports.

What has been done above with the short essay by Bertrand Russell and the three short textbook selections can be done with longer essays and textbook selections as well. As you read, look for (and mark off) important ideas and then take notes on those ideas. The very act of notetaking—of writing ideas out on paper—will help you study and master those ideas. *What many students do not realize is that taking notes on a subject can help in thinking about and understanding the subject. Writing is thinking.* Effective reading often means more than looking for important ideas; it means marking them off and writing them down as well.

A Detailed Study System

There are a variety of very similar "textbook study systems" that are just a larger-scale version of what you have done with the Russell essay and the short textbook selections. Two of these study systems, for example, are SQ3R (the letters stand for *Survey, Question, Read, Recite, Review*) and PRWR. Here is the PRWR system, which directs you to study what you read by taking four steps:

1 Preview the chapter to get an general overview and "a lay of the land" before you start reading. Note the title, which is probably a summary of what the whole chapter is about, and quickly read the first and last paragraphs of the chapter, which may introduce or summarize main ideas in the chapter.

2 Read and underline or otherwise mark what seem to be the important ideas in the chapter. In particular, look for and underline *definitions,* and set off *examples* of those definitions with an "Ex." Also look for *enumerations*—major lists of items, which may already be numbered 1, 2, 3, etc. or which you can number yourself.

3 Write (or type into your computer) study notes on the chapter. *Actual writing and notetaking is a key to successful learning.* In the very act of deciding what is important enough to write down and then writing it down, you begin to learn and master the material.

Organize your notes into a rough outline that shows relationships between ideas. Write main headings at the margin of your notes, and indent subheads about half an inch away from the margin. Print each term being defined and put an *Ex.* beside each example of a definition. Number items in any list, and be sure to include a heading that tells what each list is about.

4 **Recite** your study notes until you can say them to yourself without looking at them. It helps to put key words in the margin of your notes. For example, if you are studying the three kinds of noise, write the following in the margin:

> *3 kinds of noise*
> *1. Semantic*
> *2. Mechanical*
> *3. Environmental*

Then look at the first, "semantic," and see if you can recite what it means. After you can recite "semantic" and give an example without looking at it, go on to "mechanical." When you can recite it and give an example without looking at it, go back and test yourself on "semantic." ***Repeated self-testing is the key to effective learning.***

After you can recite the definitions and examples of "semantic" and "mechanical," go on and test yourself on "environmental." When you can recite it, go back and test yourself on all three. It is impossible to be passive in your study if you continue this strategy of repeated self-testing.

➤ *Practice 2*   *Wording of answers may vary.*

Read the following textbook selections from different disciplines and then write down their important ideas in the space provided. Taking notes on these selections will give you the practice you need to take notes on longer textbook selections.
Keep in mind the following:

1. Research has shown that tests are based primarily on material that an instructor presents in class. Never make the mistake of thinking that textbook notetaking will take the place of going to class regularly and taking good notes.

    Your textbook notes and study usually supplement what you are learning in class.

2. When taking notes on textbook material, don't lose sight of the forest for the trees. Here in a nutshell is what you should do to be an active reader and notetaker:

    • Ask yourself, "What is the point?" and "What is the support for the point?"

    • Pay close attention to (and write down) titles and other headings, and also mark definitions, examples, and enumerations.

1   Selection from a Health Text

Note: The answer to the question in the title is one of the important ideas in this selection.

Why Is Everyone So Angry?

¹According to the AAA Foundation for Traffic Safety, violent aggressive driving—which some dub "road rage"—has been rising by 7 percent per year. ²Sideline rage at amateur and professional sporting events has become so widespread that a Pennsylvania midget football game ended in a brawl involving more than one hundred coaches, players, parents, and fans.

³No one seems immune. ⁴Women fly off the handle just as often as men, although they're less likely to get physical. ⁵The young and the infamous, including several rappers and musicians sentenced to anger management classes for violent outbursts, may seem more volatile, but ordinary senior citizens have erupted into "line rage" and pushed ahead of others simply because they feel they've "waited long enough" in their lives.

⁶"Everyone everywhere seems to be hotter under the collar these days," observes Sybil Evans, a conflict resolution expert who singles out three primary culprits: time, technology, and tension. ⁷"Americans are working longer hours than anyone else in the world. ⁸The cell phones and pagers that were supposed to make our lives easier have put us on call 24-7-365. ⁹Since we're always running, we're tense and low on patience, and the less patience we have, the less we monitor what we say to people and how we treat them."

¹⁰For years, therapists encouraged people to "vent" their anger. ¹¹However, recent research shows that letting anger out only makes it worse. ¹²"Catharsis is worse than useless," says psychology professor Brad Bushman of Iowa State University, whose research has shown that letting anger out makes people more aggressive, not less. ¹³"Many people think of anger as the psychological equivalent of the steam in a pressure cooker that has to be released or it will explode. ¹⁴That's not true. ¹⁵People who react by hitting, kicking, screaming, and swearing aren't dealing with the underlying cause of their anger. ¹⁶They just feel more angry."

¹⁷Over time, temper tantrums sabotage physical health as well as psychological equanimity. ¹⁸By churning out stress hormones, chronic anger revs the body into a state of combat readiness, multiplying the risk for stroke and heart attack—even in healthy individuals. ¹⁹In one study by Duke University researchers, young women with "Jerry-Springer-type anger," who tended to slam doors, curse, and throw things in fury, had higher cholesterol levels than those who reacted more calmly.

Study notes:

Reason for anger: 1. Time—working longer hours

2. Technology—cell phones and pagers make us available 24/7

3. Tension—we're always running

Danger in venting anger: <u>Makes anger worse; doesn't deal with underlying</u>
<u>causes of anger</u>

Results of anger: <u>Sabotages physical as well as mental health—increased</u>
<u>risk of stroke and heart attack</u>

2   Selection from a Business Text

Note: An enumeration is the key to the important ideas here.

What Is Work?

[1]Most people know when they are working and when they are playing. [2]They often have difficulty explaining what the difference is, though. [3]Stop here and take a moment to see if you can differentiate between work and play. [4]Write a definition of work and play before proceeding.

[5]Some will say that the difference between work and play is that people get paid to work. [6]If payment is the criterion, then mowing one's lawn or dusting one's home can be considered play. [7]So payment cannot be the sole criterion for differentiating between work and play. [8]Some might argue that work is the performance of some task one does not like. [9]Then mowing and dusting would fit with going to work. [10]But many people, if not most, like their work or at least find it tolerable. [11]Therefore, liking or disliking a task is not a criterion for differentiating between work and play. [12]We might next try to examine the task itself, but a professional athlete's work is engaging in sports that nonprofessionals would classify as play. [13]How, then, can we differentiate between work and play?

[14]As shown in Table 1.1, <u>differentiating between work and play requires that three factors be examined</u>:

- the task's purpose
- the attitude of the person performing the task
- the reward or rewards received by the person performing the task

Table 1.1 Differentiating between Work and Play

	Work	**Play**
Task Purpose	Has a definite purpose	May or may not have a purpose
Personal Attitude	Task viewed as work	Task viewed as play
Task Reward	External and internal	Internal

[15]The difference between work and play is in the person and the person's reason for performing a task.

①   *Purpose.* [16]Work has a definite purpose. [17]Something is being accomplished when work is being performed. [18]Some resource, either material, financial, informational, or human, is being transformed. [19]Play, however, does not have to have a purpose. [20]Sometimes people engage in play for its own sake. [21]Other times play, like work, has an outcome, as when people grow gardens for recreation and also produce food.

②   *Attitude.* [22]The second criterion to be examined is the attitude of the person performing a task. [23]A task may be work if the person performing it believes it is work. [24]If the person performing a task thinks it is play, then to

Ex.   that person it is play. [25]To a professional athlete, playing baseball feels like work. [26]Therefore, part of the determination of whether a task is work or play resides in the individual.

③   *Reward.* [27]The final criterion for whether a task is work or play is whether an internal or an external reward is received for performing the task. [28]External rewards are given for work; internal rewards are received from play. [29]External rewards are given to the task performer from someone else,

Ex.   like an employer. [30]Money may be the most common external reward. [31]Others are promotions, praise, recognition, or status. [32]In contrast, internal rewards (for play) are received from the performance of the task. [33]Internal

Ex.   rewards include curiosity satisfaction, enjoyment, a sense of achievement, or the meeting of charitable, personal, or philanthropic goals.

Study notes:

Point: *Three factors help us differentiate between work and play.*

1. *Purpose: Work has a definite purpose (something being accomplished). Play does not have to have a definite purpose.*

2. *Attitude: A task may be work or play depending on the attitude of the person performing the task (example: professional baseball players).*

3. *Reward: External rewards are given for work (example: money); internal rewards are received for play (example: enjoyment).*

3   Selection from a Sociology Text

Note: An enumeration and examples are keys to important ideas.

(1) [1]Few aspects of social life affect the way people behave and think as much as social class does. [2]For one thing, it largely determines their life chances—the likelihood that individuals and groups will enjoy opportunities for living healthy and long lives. [3]Broadly considered, life chances have to do with people's level of living and their options for choice. [4]For example, social

Ex. class affects education. [5]The higher the social class of parents, the further their children go in school and the better they perform. [6]Long-term poverty experienced during childhood affects cognitive ability, and poverty experienced during adolescence affects cognitive achievement. [7]By 5 years of age, youngsters who have always lived in poverty have IQs on average 9 points lower than those who were never poor; this gap cannot be explained by differences in mothers' education, divorce rates, or race.

(2)   [8]Class also affects health and life expectancy. [9]As a doctor expressed in the *Journal of the American Medical Association*, "Lower socioeconomic status (SES) is probably the most powerful single contributor to premature morbidity and mortality, not only in the United States but worldwide." [10]Health is affected by income, education, and social class in all industrialized societies. [11]As with education, childhood poverty continues to affect health into adult-

Ex. hood. [12]Although health risk factors including obesity, smoking, and lack of exercise are more common among people of low socioeconomic classes, researchers also point to differences in exposure to occupational and environmental health hazards in explaining class differences in morbidity and mortality.

(3)   [13]Social class affects life chances in other ways. [14]During the Vietnam
Ex. War, some 80 percent of the 2.5 million men who served in Southeast Asia
Ex. came from working-class and impoverished backgrounds. [15]When the *Titanic* sank in 1912, passengers traveling in first class were more than twice as likely to survive as those traveling third class.

(4)   [16]Social class also affects people's style of life—the magnitude and
Ex. manner of their consumption of goods and services. [17]Convenience foods— TV dinners, potato chips, frozen pizza, and Hamburger Helper—are more frequently on the menus of lower-income than those of higher-income

Ex. households. [18]Lower-class families drink less vodka, Scotch, bourbon, and imported wine but consume more beer and blended whiskey. [19]Social class
Ex. even affects such things as the styles of furniture people buy and the programs they watch on television.

(5)   [20]Social class is associated with various patterns of behavior. [21]For
Ex. instance, voting increases with socioeconomic status in most Western
Ex. nations. [22]And people in the lower classes begin sexual activities at a younger age, but people in the upper classes are more tolerant of sexual variations and engage in a wider variety of sexual activities. [23]In sum, one's social class leaves few areas of life untouched.

Study notes:

Point: *Social class has a significant impact on how people behave and think and affects people in almost every area of life.*

1. *Determines life chances—people's level of living and options for choice*

   Ex.— *Higher class = more education (go farther; do better)*

2. *Affects health and life expectancy—lower-class people die sooner*

   Ex.— *Lower class = more obesity; more exposure to environmental hazards*

3. *Affects exposure to dangerous situations*

   Ex.— *Lower class = 80% of soldiers in Vietnam; most victims on* Titanic

4. *Affects people's style of life—consumption of goods and services*

   Ex.— *Lower class = more convenience foods and beer*

5. *Is associated with certain patterns of behavior*

   Ex.— *Higher classes are more likely to vote*

CHAPTER REVIEW

In this chapter, you learned what it takes to be an active as opposed to a passive reader:

- Active readers think and ask questions as they read. Active readers ask, "What is the point?" and "What is the support for the point?" Active readers also pay close attention to titles and other headings, as well as definitions, examples, and enumerations.

- Active readers often have a pen in hand as they read so they can mark off what seem to be the important ideas.

- Active readers often use a reading study system. In a nutshell, they *preview* a selection first; then they *read and mark off* what seem to be the important ideas; next, they *take written notes* on that material; and finally, they *recite their notes* until they can remember them.

On the Web: If you are using this book in class, you can visit our website for additional practice in active reading and study. Go to **www.townsendpress.com** and click on "Online Exercises."

➤ **Review Test 1**

To review what you've learned in this chapter, answer each of the following questions by filling in the blank.

1. In addition to asking "What is the point?" and "What is the support for the point?" active readers also notice titles, definitions, _____examples_____, and enumerations.
   See page 359.

2. When you read material, looking for main points and supports, it helps to have a pen in hand so you can _____mark_____ off material as you read.
   See pages 359–360.

3. When studying material, it is often not enough to just mentally note the points and supports. You should also _____write_____ them down.
   See pages 361 and 365.

4. Textbook study systems typically suggest that before you start reading an essay or chapter, you first _____preview_____ it to get an overall sense of the selection.
   See page 365.

5. To master important material and avoid passive study, you should _____recite_____ your study notes until you can say them to yourself without looking at them.
   See page 366.

➤ **Review Test 2**

Here is a chance to practice active reading on a selection from a college textbook, *Psychology Applied to Modern Life* (Wadsworth), by Wayne Weiten and Margaret A. Lloyd. Read it and mark off the central point and major supporting details, including enumerations, definitions, and examples. Then answer the questions on the skills you have practiced in previous chapters.

Preview

How do you behave with a job interviewer, as opposed to someone you're hoping to date? How would your manner differ if you were asking an instructor to extend a deadline on a project, rather than asking someone to pay a debt he or she owed you? As you read this selection, you will recognize some of the many ways you adapt your behavior depending on the situation.

Words to Watch

chauvinistic (2): convinced that one's own kind (gender, race, etc.) is superior
exemplary (6): worthy of imitation

IMPRESSION MANAGEMENT

Wayne Weiten and Margaret A. Lloyd

1 Interestingly, people think others notice and evaluate them more than is the actual case. This common tendency is aptly termed *the spotlight effect*. People also normally strive to make a positive impression on others to be liked, respected, hired, and so forth. **Impression management** refers to usually conscious efforts by people to influence how others think of them.

2 To see impression management in operation, let's look at a study of behavior in simulated job interviews. In this study, female job applicants were led to believe that the man who would interview them held either traditional, chauvinistic° views of women or just the opposite. The researchers found that applicants who expected a chauvinist presented themselves in a more traditionally feminine manner than subjects in the other condition. Their self-presentation efforts extended to both their appearance (they wore more makeup) and their communication style (they talked less and gave more traditional answers to a question about marriage and children). In a job interview, people are particularly attentive to making a good impression, but impression management also operates in everyday interactions, although individuals may be less aware of it. Let's look at some common impression management strategies.

Impression Management Strategies

3 One reason people engage in impression management is to claim a particular identity. Thus, you select a type of dress, hairstyle, and manner of speech to present a certain image of yourself. Tattoos and body piercings also create a specific image. A second motive for impression management is to gain liking and approval from others—by editing what you say about yourself and by using various nonverbal cues such as smiles, gestures, and eye contact. Because self-presentation is practiced so often, people usually do it automatically. At other times, however, impression management may be used intentionally—to get a job, a date, a promotion, and so forth. Some common self-presentation strategies include ingratiation, self-promotion, exemplification, intimidation, and supplication.

4 **Ingratiation.** Of all the self-presentation strategies, ingratiation is the most fundamental and most frequently used. Ingratiation is behaving in ways to make oneself likable to others. For instance, *giving compliments* is effective, as long as you are sincere (people dislike insincerity and can often detect it). *Doing favors for others* is also a common tactic, as long as your gestures aren't so spectacular they leave others feeling indebted. Other ingratiation tactics

include *expressing liking for others* and *going along with others* (to get others to like you, it helps to do the thing that they want to do).

5   **Self-promotion.** The motive behind self-promotion is earning respect. You do so by playing up your strong points so you will be perceived as competent. For instance, in a job interview, you might find ways to mention that you earned high honors at school and that you were president of the student body and a member of the soccer team. To keep from coming across as a braggart, you shouldn't go overboard with self-promotion. For this reason, false modesty often works well.

6   **Exemplification.** Because most people try to project an honest image, you have to demonstrate exemplary° behavior to claim special credit for integrity or character. Danger-fraught occupations such as those in the military or law enforcement provide obvious opportunities to exemplify moral virtue. A less dramatic, but still effective, strategy is to behave consistently according to high ethical standards—as long as you don't come across as self-righteous. Also, your words and deeds need to match unless you want to be labeled a hypocrite.

7   **Intimidation.** This strategy sends the message, "Don't mess with me." Intimidation usually works only in nonvoluntary relationships—for instance, when it's hard for workers to find another employer or for an economically dependent spouse to leave a relationship. Obvious intimidation tactics include threats and the withholding of valuable resources (salary increases, promotions, sex). A more subtle tactic is emotional intimidation—holding over a person's head the threat of an aggressive outburst if you don't get your way. The other self-presentation strategies work by creating a favorable impression; intimidation usually generates dislike. Nonetheless, it can work.

8   **Supplication.** This is usually the tactic of last resort. To get favors from others, individuals try to present themselves as weak and dependent—as in the song, "Ain't Too Proud to Beg." Students may plead or break into tears in an instructor's office in an attempt to get a grade changed. Because of the social norm to help those in need, supplications may work; however, unless the supplicator has something to offer the potential benefactor, it's not an effective strategy.

9   Individuals tailor their use of self-presentation strategies to match the situation. For instance, it's unlikely that you'd try intimidating your boss; you'd be more likely to ingratiate or promote yourself with her. Thus, to make a good impression, you must use the strategies skillfully.

Reading Comprehension Questions

Central Point and Main Ideas

___D___ 1. Which sentence best expresses the central point of the selection?

    A. Impression management is particularly noticeable in job interviews, but also operates in everyday interactions.

    B. Most people strive to make a positive impression on others.

    C. People often engage in impression management to gain approval from others.

    D. People use various impression management strategies to influence how others think of them.   Answer A covers only the next-to-last sentence of paragraph 2. Answer B is an introductory detail from paragraph 1. Answer C covers only the fourth sentence of paragraph 3.

Supporting Details

___A___ 2. According to the selection, the most frequently used self-presentation strategy is

    A. ingratiation.

    B. self-promotion.   See paragraph 4.

    C. exemplification.

    D. intimidation.

Transitions

___D___ 3. The relationship of the second sentence below to the first sentence is one of

    A. time.

    B. addition.   The second sentence gives an illustration of

    C. cause and effect.   the term defined in the first sentence.

    D. illustration.

> "Ingratiation is behaving in ways to make oneself likable to others. For example, *giving compliments* is effective, as long as you are sincere (people dislike insincerity and can often detect it)." (Paragraph 4)

Patterns of Organization

___B___ 4. The main patterns of organization of the selection are

    A. time order and contrast.

    B. list of items and cause and effect.

    C. time order and illustration.   After paragraphs 1–2 introduce the subject,

    D. contrast and illustration.   paragraph 3 lists the motives for engaging in impression management. Paragraphs 4–8 list and describe five specific strategies. Throughout the selection motives (causes) and effects are explained. Example from paragraph 5: *Cause:* desire to earn respect; *effect:* engage in self-promotion.

Inferences

___D___ 5. Based on this selection, we can infer that a religious leader would most likely use
    A. ingratiation.
    B. self-promotion.   People expect religious leaders to behave
    C. supplication.   according to high ethical standards.
    D. exemplification.

Purpose and Tone

___C___ 6. The author's tone can best be described as
    A. encouraging and optimistic.   This selection, from a college textbook,
    B. sarcastic and playful.   is intended to be instructive and
    C. instructive and straightforward.   straightforward. It explains and
    D. concerned and sympathetic.   clearly illustrates the strategies.

Argument

7. Label the point of the following argument with a P and the two statements of support with an S. Label with an X the one statement that is neither the point nor the support of the argument.

    ___S___ A. One obvious ingratiation tactic involves giving compliments.

    ___P___ B. People who engage in ingratiation employ a variety of tactics.

    ___S___ C. Expressing liking for others is another common ingratiation tactic.

    ___X___ D. Ingratiation is the most fundamental self-presentation strategy.
        Statements A and C provide examples of ingratiation tactics.
        Statement D does not support the point (in statement B)
        that people use a variety of tactics.

Critical Reading

___A___ 8. A political candidate who stands in front of a large American flag to remind voters that he is a decorated war veteran is using the impression management strategy of
    A. exemplification and the propaganda technique of transfer.
    B. intimidation and the propaganda technique of bandwagon.
    C. supplication and the propaganda technique of plain folks.
    D. ingratiation and the propaganda technique of testimonial.

    The candidate is attempting to exemplify moral virtue and patriotism.

___B___ 9. A student who supplicates her teacher by exclaiming, "If I don't pass this course, my life will be ruined!" is guilty of the fallacy of
A. circular reasoning.
B. either-or.
C. straw man.
D. false comparison.

The student fails to see a middle ground (such as making up the credit) between the two extremes.

___D___ 10. For reading, notetaking, and study, the key to important ideas in this selection are
A. titles and subtitles.
B. definitions and examples.
C. enumerations.
D. all of the above.

Titles and subtitles help focus on what each section is about. The strategies (paragraphs 4–8) give definitions and examples. Paragraph 3 enumerates motives.

Discussion Questions

1. Discuss a time when you (or someone you know) used one of the strategies mentioned in the selection to make an impression. What happened as a result? On the basis of this result, would you say the strategy worked? Why or why not?

2. In the first paragraph of the reading, the example is given of how job applicants might alter their behavior in response to what they believed to be true about the interviewer. To what extent do you think this alteration in behavior is a good strategy when job-seeking? What could be its downside?

3. The authors point out that choices in such things as dress, hairstyle, and manner of speech act as a sort of shorthand by which a person declares "I am a member of this group." What are some of the particular "identities" that you see people currently declaring in their fashion and language choices? What groups are they claiming membership in?

4. In your view, in which occupations is it particularly important to make a good impression? Why?

Note: Writing assignments for this selection appear on page 565.

A Final Activity

Now, using separate paper, take study notes on the selection you have just read, "Impression Management." An enumeration, definitions, and examples are keys to important ideas.

Sample study notes (wording of student notes may vary):

Impression management—usually conscious efforts by people to influence how others think of them

Example—In simulated job interviews, women who believed that the interviewer held traditional views of women behaved in a more traditionally feminine way.

Reasons to use impression management:
1. *To claim a particular lifestyle*
2. *To gain approval from others*
3. *To get a job, a date, a promotion, etc.*

Common self-presentation strategies:
1. *Ingratiation—behaving in ways to make oneself likable*
   Ex.—giving compliments, doing favors
2. *Self-promotion—playing up your strong points*
   Ex.—in a job interview, mentioning your school achievements
3. *Exemplification—demonstrating behavior worth imitating*
   Ex.—behaving consistently according to high ethical standards
4. *Intimidation—sending a "don't mess with me" message (usually works only in nonvoluntary relationships)*
   Ex.—threats, withholding of something valuable
5. *Supplication—presenting oneself as weak and dependent*
   Ex.—pleading or crying in an instructor's office

Check Your Performance	ACTIVE READING AND STUDY		
Activity	*Number Right*	*Points*	*Score*
Review Test 1 (5 items)	_____	× 6 =	_____
Review Test 2 (10 items)	_____	× 7 =	_____
	TOTAL SCORE	=	_____%

Enter your total score into the **Reading Performance Chart: Review Tests** on the inside back cover.

ACTIVE READING AND STUDY: Mastery Test 1

Complete the study notes that follow the selection below, taken from a psychology text.

Phobias

[1]A *phobia* is an intense, unrealistic fear. [2]In this case, the anxiety is focused so intensely on some object or situation that the individual is acutely uncomfortable around it and will often go to great pains to avoid it. [3]There are three types of phobias, as explained below.

(1)

Ex.   [4]*Specific phobia* is the least disruptive of the phobias. [5]Examples include intense fear of heights, dogs, blood, hypodermic injections, and closed spaces. [6]Individuals with a specific phobia generally have no other psychological problems, and their lives are disrupted only if the phobia creates a direct problem in daily living. [7]For example, a fear of elevators would be highly disruptive for a person who works in a skyscraper, but it probably would not be for a vegetable farmer.

(2)

     [8]Other forms of phobia, by their very nature, frequently cause problems for the individual. [9]The term *social phobia* is used to describe extreme anxiety about social interactions, particularly those with strangers and those

Ex.   in which the person might be evaluated negatively. [10]Job interviews, public speaking, and first dates are extremely uncomfortable for individuals with social phobias. [11]Persons with social phobias usually have unrealistically negative views of their social skills and attempt to avoid evaluation. [12]Because this kind of phobia hampers and limits social interactions, it can seriously disrupt the individual's social and occupational life.

(3)

     [13]*Agoraphobia* is the most impairing of all the phobias. [14]Literally meaning "fear of open spaces," agoraphobia involves an intense fear of leaving one's home or other familiar places. [15]In extreme cases, the agoraphobic individual is totally bound to his or her home, finding a trip to the mailbox an almost intolerable experience. [16]Other agoraphobic individuals are able to travel freely in their neighborhood but cannot venture beyond it. [17]A 30-year-old German man recounts his experience with agoraphobia in the following passage.

Ex.   [18]I start a little walk down the street about a hundred feet from the house. [19]I am compelled to rush back, in horror of being so far away . . . a hundred feet away . . . from home and security. [20]I have never walked or ridden, alone or with others, as a normal man, since that day. . . .

Note: In these tests, definitions and other important ideas are underlined in red in this *Instructor's Edition.*

(Continues on next page)

Note: You may put your study notes on this page, or your instructor may ask you to use separate paper.

Study notes: *Wording of answers may vary.*

Definition of phobia: *An intense, unrealistic fear* _____

Three types of phobias, with descriptions and examples:

1. ___*Specific*___ — ___*least disruptive*___ _____

   _____

   Ex. — *Fear of heights* _____

2. ___*Social*___ — ___*extreme anxiety about social interactions,*___

   especially with strangers and in which the person might be evaluated

   negatively _____

   Ex. — *Job interview* _____

3. ___*Agoraphobia*___ — *most impairing of all phobias; means "fear of*

   open spaces" and involves intense fear of leaving one's home or other

   familiar places _____

   Ex. — *Individual so totally bound to home that even trip to the mailbox is*

   intolerable _____

Note that there are ten answers here: a definition of *phobia* and three types of phobias, each requiring a name, a definition, and an example. Each answer is worth 10 points. The definition of *phobia* appears in sentence 1. The three types of phobias are introduced in sentences 4, 9, and 13–14, respectively.

ACTIVE READING AND STUDY: Mastery Test 2

Complete the study notes that follow the selection below, taken from a sociology text.

Owning Feelings and Opinions

Ex.
¹Owning feelings or opinions, or crediting yourself, means making "I" statements to identify yourself as the source of a particular idea or feeling. ²An "I" statement can be any statement that has a first-person pronoun such as *I, my, me,* or *mine*. ³"I" statements help the listener understand fully and accurately the nature of the message. ⁴For example, instead of saying "Advertising is the weakest department in the corporation" (an unsupported assertion), say "I believe advertising is the weakest department in the corporation." ⁵Likewise, instead of saying "Everybody thinks Collins is unfair in his criticism," say "It seems to me that Collins is unfair in his criticism." ⁶Both of these examples contrast a generalized or impersonal account with an "I" statement.

⁷Why do people use vague references to others rather than owning their ideas and feelings? ⁸There are two basic reasons.

(1)

Ex.
1. To strengthen the power of their statements. ⁹If listeners doubt the statement "Everybody thinks Collins is unfair in his criticism," they are bucking the collective evaluation of countless people. ¹⁰Of course, not everybody knows and agrees that Collins is unfair. ¹¹In this instance, the statement really means that one person holds the belief. ¹²But people often think that their feelings or beliefs will not carry much power, so they feel the need to cite unknown or universal sources for those feelings or beliefs.

(2)

Ex.
2. To escape responsibility. ¹³Similarly, people use collective statements such as "everybody agrees" and "anyone with any sense" to escape responsibility for their own feelings and thoughts. ¹⁴It seems far more difficult for a person to say "I don't like Herb" than it is to say "No one likes Herb."

¹⁵The problem with such generalized statements is that at best they are exaggerations and at worst they are deceitful and unethical. ¹⁶Being both accurate and honest with others requires taking responsibility for our own feelings and opinions. ¹⁷We all have a right to our reactions. ¹⁸If what you are saying is truly your opinion or an expression of how you really feel, let others know and be willing to take responsibility for it. ¹⁹Otherwise, you may alienate people who would have respected your opinions or feelings even if they didn't agree with them.

(Continues on next page)

Study notes: *Wording of answers may vary.*

Note: The first item—the definition of "owning feelings"—has been inserted for you.

Definition of "owning feelings":   *Making "I" statements to identify yourself as the source of a particular idea or feeling. The statement must have a first-person pronoun such as "I", "me," or "mine."*

    Ex. — *Instead of saying "Advertising is the weakest department in the corporation," say "I believe advertising is the weakest department in the corporation."*

Reasons (with examples) why people do not "own" feelings:

1. *To strengthen the power of their statements.*

    Ex. — *"Everybody thinks Collins is unfair" has more power than "I think Collins is unfair."*

2. *To escape responsibility.*

    Ex. — *It's far more difficult to say "I don't like Herb" than it is to say "No one likes Herb."*

> Note that there are five answers here: an example for a definition,
> an enumeration of two reasons, and examples of those reasons.
> Each answer is worth 20 points.
>
> The answers for the blanks appear in sentence 4, Item 1 in bold print,
> paragraph 3, Item 2 in bold print, and sentence 14, respectively.

ACTIVE READING AND STUDY: Mastery Test 3

Complete the study notes that follow the selection below, taken from a health text.

Why Men and Women Drink

[1]In recent years, researchers have been comparing and contrasting the reasons why men and women drink. [2]Undergraduate women and men are equally likely to drink for stress-related reasons; both perceive alcohol as a means of <u>tension relaxation</u>. [3]Both genders may engage in *compensatory drinking,* consuming alcohol to heighten their sense of masculinity or femininity. [4]Some psychologists theorize that men engage in *confirmatory drinking;* that is, they drink to reinforce the image of masculinity associated with alcohol consumption.

⑤Here are some <u>other reasons</u> why men, women, or both drink:

- **Inherited susceptibility.** [6]For both women and men, genetics accounts for 50 to 60 percent of a person's vulnerability to a serious drinking problem. [7]Female alcoholics are more likely than males to have a parent who abused drugs or alcohol, who had psychiatric problems, or who attempted suicide.

- **Childhood traumas.** [8]Female alcoholics often report that they were physically or sexually abused as children or suffered great distress because of poverty or a parent's death.

- **Depression.** [9]Women are more likely than men to be depressed prior to drinking and to suffer from both depression and a drinking problem at the same time. [10]Young men who drink, as well as those who drink heavily, have high levels of depression and distress.

- **Relationship issues.** [11]Single, separated, or divorced men and women drink more and more often than married ones.

- **Psychological factors.** [12]Both men and women may drink to compensate for feelings of inadequacy. [13]Women who tend to ruminate or mull over bad feelings may find that alcohol increases this tendency and makes them feel more distressed.

- **Employment.** [14]Women who work outside the home are less likely to become problem drinkers or alcoholics than those without paying jobs. [15]The one exception: women in occupations still dominated by men, such as engineering, science, law enforcement, and top corporate management.

- **Self-medication.** [16]More so than men, some women feel it's permissible to use alcohol as if it were a medicine. [17]As long as they're taking it for a reason, it seems acceptable to them, even if they're drifting into a drinking problem.

(Continues on next page)

383

Study notes: *Wording of answers may vary.*

Why both men and women drink:

1. Tension relaxation
_____

2. Compensatory drinking—alcohol to heighten sense of masculinity or
   femininity

One theory why men drink: Confirmatory drinking—to reinforce the image
   of masculinity associated with drinking.
_____

Other reasons for drinking:

1. Inherited susceptibility. Genetics, especially with females, accounts for 50
   to 60 percent of vulnerability to a serious drinking problem.

2. Childhood traumas—especially females abused as children or distressed
   because of poverty or parental death

3. Depression—especially women and young men
_____

4. Relationship issues. The single, separated, or divorced drink more than the
   married.

5. Psychological factors—to compensate for feelings of inadequacy
_____

6. Employment—especially women without paying jobs
_____

7. Self-medication—especially women who tell themselves alcohol is a
   medicine

Note that there are ten answers here: an initial enumeration
(two reasons both men and women drink), a definition, and
a second enumeration (seven other reasons for drinking).

Answers for the first three blanks appear in sentences
2, 3, and 4, respectively. Reasons for drinking correspond
to the bulleted boldface headings in the selection.

ACTIVE READING AND STUDY: Mastery Test 4

Complete the study notes that follow the selection below, taken from a political science text.

Who Wins Congressional Elections?

[1]Everyone in Congress is a politician, and politicians continually have their eyes on the next election. [2]The players in the congressional election game are the incumbents and the challengers.

[3]*Incumbents* are individuals who already hold office. [4]Sometime during each term, the incumbent must decide whether to run again or to retire voluntarily. [5]Most decide to run for reelection. [6]They enter their party's primary, almost always emerge victorious, and typically win in the November general election, too. [7]Indeed, the most important fact about congressional elections is this: *Incumbents usually win.*

[8]Thus, the key to ensuring an opponent's defeat is not having more money than the opponent, although that helps. [9]It is not being more photogenic, although that helps, too. [10]The best thing a candidate can have *Ex.* going for him or her is simply to be the incumbent. [11]Even in a year of great political upheaval such as 1994, in which the Republicans gained 8 seats in the Senate and 53 seats in the House, 92 percent of incumbent senators and 89 percent of incumbent representatives won their bids for reelection.

[12]Not only do more than 90 percent of the incumbents seeking reelection win, but most of them win with more than 60 percent of the vote. [13]Perhaps most astonishing is the fact that even when challengers' positions on the issues are closer to the voters' positions, incumbents still tend to win.

A Different Picture in the Senate

[14]The picture for the Senate is a little different. [15]Even though senators still have a good chance of beating back a challenge, the odds of reelection are often not as handsome as for House incumbents; senators typically win by narrower margins.

(1) [16]One reason for the greater competition in the Senate is that an entire state is almost always more diverse than a congressional district and thus provides a larger base for opposition to an incumbent. [17]At the same time, (2) senators have less personal contact with their constituencies, which on average are nearly ten times larger than those of members of the House of (3) Representatives. [18]Senators also receive more coverage in the media than representatives do and are more likely to be held accountable on (4) controversial issues. [19]Moreover, senators tend to draw more visible challengers, such as governors or members of the House, whom voters

(Continues on next page)

already know and who have substantial financial backing—a factor that lessens the advantages of incumbency. [20]Many of these challengers know that the Senate is a stepping stone to national prominence and sometimes even the presidency.

[21]Despite their success at reelection, incumbents often feel quite vulnerable. [22]As Thomas Mann put it, members of Congress perceive themselves as "unsafe at any margin." [23]Thus, they have been raising and spending more campaign funds, sending more mail to their constituents, visiting their states and districts more often, and staffing more local offices than ever before. [24]They realize that with the decline of partisan loyalty in the electorate, they bear more of the burden of obtaining votes.

Study notes: *Wording of answers may vary.*

Who wins congressional elections? *Usually incumbents (individuals who already hold office)—more than 90 percent of them, with 60 percent of the vote.*

Why is the picture different in the Senate?

1. *Entire state is more diverse than a congressional district, providing a larger base for opposition to an incumbent.*

2. *Senators have less personal contact with potential voters.*

3. *Senators receive more coverage in the media and are more likely to be held accountable on controversial issues.*

4. *Senators tend to draw more visible challengers, whom the voters know and who have more financial backing.*

Note that there are five answers here: an answer to the basic question in the title of the selection and an enumeration of four reasons why the picture is different in the Senate.

The answer for the first blank appears in sentences 3, 7, and 12.
The answers for the second through fifth blanks appear in sentences 16, 17, 18, and 19, respectively.

ACTIVE READING AND STUDY: Mastery Test 5

Complete the study notes that follow the selection below, taken from a biology text.

The Laws of Thermodynamics

[1]The laws of thermodynamics are time-honored principles that describe the behavior of energy. [2]These laws are based on certain observations about the behavior of matter and energy that are remarkably invariable from one instance to the next. [3]Such consistency leads to predictions. [4]What happens, for example, to objects raised above the ground and then released? [5]What happens to an object that is heated and then set aside, away from the heat? [6]Everyone can predict that the first object will fall to the ground and that the second will cool. [7]Such observations, made time and again, have eventually led to the formulation of laws of nature.

The First Law

(1) [8]The first law of thermodynamics states that *energy can neither be created nor destroyed, but it can be converted from one form to another.* [9]Understandably, the first law is also called the law of conservation of energy. [10]What the first law means is that the total amount of energy present in a system remains constant. [11]The concept refers to idealized conditions that exist only in what is called an "isolated system"—one in which matter and energy cannot enter and leave. [12]Such systems do not really exist (except perhaps as the universe itself) but are contrived as models by scientists who wish to test their ideas under hypothetical conditions that can be limited and controlled.

Energy Transitions: A Case History

Ex. [13]Energy changes occur in a variety of ways. [14]When you start your lawnmower engine, you can begin to appreciate the idea of energy conservation. [15]Consider that the gasoline in the lawnmower's tank is a veritable storehouse of chemical energy, locked away in the chemical bonds that hold the carbon and hydrogen of the gasoline molecules together. [16]As you pull the cord, a mix of gasoline vapor and air encounters an electrical discharge from the spark plug, and the engine starts. [17]Chemical energy in the fuel molecules becomes heat energy, and heat then expands the gases in the engine cylinder. [18]The next energy transformation is to mechanical energy, or energy of motion, which comes about when the expanding gases push against the piston. [19]The piston moves up and down, its connecting rod rotating the crankshaft, which spins the lawnmower blade. [20]At certain points in the piston's movement, valves open, and the expanding gases escape into

(Continues on next page)

the surroundings, their energy dissipating as heat. [21]The escaping gases—carbon dioxide and water vapor—are at a considerably lower energy level than gasoline, and the difference between the two energy levels is to be found in exhausted heat and the energy of motion. [22]The latter largely becomes heat as well, as the moving parts of the lawnmower encounter friction.

[23]What we see here is characteristic of energy as it changes form. [24]Energy transformations are accompanied by the formation of heat, and when such heat has dissipated, it is no longer capable of work, at least as far as that system (in this case, the lawnmower) is concerned. [25]The transition of systems with great energy to systems with low energy extends beyond lawnmowers; it is a tendency of the universe at large. [26]Physicists express this general observation in the *second law of thermodynamics*.

The Second Law

② [27]The second law of thermodynamics tells us that energy transitions are imperfect—that some energy is always lost, usually as heat, in each

Ex. transition. [28]Again, in the transitions from the chemical bond energy in gasoline to the mechanical energy in the spinning lawnmower blade, much of the original energy is lost as heat. [29]The energy is not lost from the system; it is just that such heat energy is normally not available to do useful work.

Study notes: *Wording of answers may vary.*

The Laws of Thermodynamics—   Time-honored principles that describe the

behavior of energy.

1. *The First Law—* Energy can neither be created nor destroyed, but it can be

   converted from one form to another.

   Ex. — In a lawnmower, chemical energy converts to heat energy and then

   to mechanical energy (energy of motion).

2. *The Second Law—* Energy transitions are imperfect—some energy is

   always lost, usually as heat, in each transition.

   Ex. — In the transition from chemical bond energy in gasoline to

   mechanical energy in a spinning lawnmower blade, much of the original

   energy is lost as heat, which is normally not available to do useful work.

Note that there are five answers here: three definitions and two examples that accompany definitions.

The answer to the first blank appears in sentence 1. The answers to the remaining blanks appear in sentences 8, 15–19, 27, and 28–29, respectively.

ACTIVE READING AND STUDY: Mastery Test 6

Complete the study notes that follow the selection below, taken from a business text.

Motivational Factors (Satisfiers)

[1]We've all probably seen organizations that function in rundown buildings, yet morale and productivity are high. [2]One researcher (Herzberg) contends that people's attitudes toward their jobs far outweigh the importance of working conditions or environment. [3]Herzberg has provided a list of motivational factors, or satisfiers, that can be said to motivate individuals and to produce job satisfaction.

(1)   [4]Achievement is important to many employees. [5]Is it to you? [6]Achievement means feeling that you've accomplished a goal; that is, you've finished something that you've started. [7]Some work situations provide this feeling; others, such as assembly-line work, often make feelings of achievement difficult. [8]This is especially true when cycle times (the time needed to

Ex.   complete one task) are as short as 6 seconds or less. [9]One former student working for a food company that prepared institutional meals had a job that repeated every 2 seconds. [10]His task was to place two slices of white bread on a tray as it passed by on a conveyor belt (later, others added meat, condiments, etc., to produce a sandwich). [11]Thirty times a minute the same task was performed, and he never saw the finished product. [12]Not much of a sense of achievement there.

(2)   [13]Many employees appreciate recognition. [14]It gives the employee a feeling of worth and self-esteem. [15]Don't you like to know how you stand in a work situation? [16]When you and other employees know how you are doing, even when the results aren't completely satisfactory, you at least know that your boss is concerned about you. [17]There's a tendency for managers to overlook the need for giving employees recognition and feedback on their performance. [18]Some managers think that it's unnecessary to say anything to an employee when a job has been done well. [19]"Charlie knows he does good work" is a far too typical managerial attitude. [20]Charlie, like most employees, might not be certain what his boss really thinks of his performance without some form of overt recognition.

(3)   [21]The job itself is a highly important motivating factor. [22]Have you ever thought about why some employees are chronically late? [23]In many cases, it's because they dread going to their 9-to-5 jobs. [24]They derive little satisfaction from their monotonous jobs and as a result would like to be able to say, as that defiant country song puts it, "Take this job and shove it!" [25]People who like their jobs tend to be far more motivated to avoid absenteeism and lateness.

(4)   [26]Growth and advancement opportunities also serve to motivate. [27]In a sense, these are like the old carrot and stick philosophy. [28]Don't you, like many

(Continues on next page)

389

employees, tend to move in directions that help you obtain the "carrot," for example, a promotion with more salary? [29]However, managers must keep in mind that if employees never get to "taste the carrot" but only feel the "stick," then their interest in carrots will tend to fade. [30]Motivational tools should never be used to manipulate people. [31]They should be used sincerely, with the employee's as well as the organization's interests in mind.

⑤   [32]Responsibility is another factor that motivates many employees. [33]Some people will forego taking sick leave when they don't feel well out of a sense of responsibility. [34]It provides a sense of accomplishment and fills an internal need to see things done right. [35]Even the behavior of some so-called troublemakers in organizations has been modified after they have been given added responsibilities.

⑥   [36]Herzberg believes that the ideal form of feedback is one that is inherent to the job. [37]In this situation, the person does not have to be told that he or she *Ex.* has done a good job; it is known automatically. [38]For example, when a radiographer examines an x-ray film she has just taken, she knows it if is good or if it needs to be repeated. [39]The feedback is immediate and inherent.

Study notes: *Wording of answers may vary.*

Central point: *One researcher (Herzberg) has provided a list of motivational*

factors, or satisfiers, that can be said to motivate individuals and produce

job satisfaction.

1. *Achievement—feeling that you've accomplished a goal (something that you've started).*

2. *Recognition—provides a feeling of worth and self-esteem.*

3. *The job itself—people who like their jobs tend to be far more motivated to avoid absenteeism and lateness.*

4. *Growth and advancement possibilities also motivate people—these are like the old carrot and stick philosophy.*

5. *Responsibility—provides a sense of accomplishment and fills an internal need to see things done right.*

6. *Feedback—ideal form is inherent to the job.*

Ex. — *Radiographer knows right away if an x-ray film she has taken is good.*

Note that there are eight answers here: the central point of the selection, an enumeration with six items (and descriptions of those items), and an example for the final item.

The central point of the selection is found in sentence 3. The answers for the next seven blanks are found in sentences 6; 13–14; 21 and 25; 26–27; 32; and 34, 36, and 38, respectively.

Part II

TEN READING SELECTIONS

INTRODUCTION TO THE READINGS

This part of the book is made up of ten reading selections that will help you practice the skills presented in Part One.

The first five readings are from a variety of college textbooks:

- From a communications text: "Personal Conflict Styles"
- From a health text: "Cardiovascular Disease Risk Factors"
- From a sociology text: "Collective Behavior"
- From a business text: "Types of Nonverbal Symbols"
- From a sociology text: "Sports: Illustrating the Three Perspectives"

Following each of the readings are reading comprehension and discussion questions and an activity titled "Active Reading and Study of a Textbook Selection." The activity will help demonstrate to you that the keys to important ideas in textbook reading are often titles and subtitles, enumerations, and definitions and examples. The activity will also serve to underscore a point already made: *the very act of taking notes helps you understand and master textbook material.*

The second five readings represent other kinds of writing you might expect to encounter in college courses:

- A historical document: "A Civil War Soldier's Letter to His Wife"
- A research-based essay: "Single-Sex Schools: An Old Idea Whose Time Has Come"
- An interpretative essay: "A King's Folly"
- An excerpt from a famous autobiography: "In My Day" from the Pulitzer-Prize-winning *Growing Up*
- A classic science essay: "The Spider and the Wasp"

Following each of the second group of readings are reading comprehension questions, an activity in either outlining or summarizing, and discussion questions.

Note: Writing assignments for each reading selection may be found in the Appendix, beginning on page 559.

1

Personal Conflict Styles
Ronald B. Adler,
Russell F. Proctor II,
and Neil Towne

Preview

Nobody gets through life without experiencing conflict. But when faced with conflict, our responses vary. This reading from *Looking Out/Looking In* (Thomson Wadsworth) provides descriptions of common responses to conflict, along with their pros and cons. The descriptions will help you not only identify your own personal style, but also evaluate its effectiveness.

Words to Watch

status quo (4): the existing condition
emblems (8): symbols
amiable (13): friendly

1 People can act in several ways when their needs aren't met. Each way has very different characteristics, as we can show by describing a common problem. At one time or another almost everyone has been bothered by the neighbor's barking dog. You know the story: Every passing car, distant siren, pedestrian, and falling leaf seems to set off a fit of barking that makes you unable to sleep, socialize, or study. In a description of the possible ways of handling this kind of situation, the differences between nonassertive, directly aggressive, passive-aggressive, indirect, and assertive behavior should become clear.

NONASSERTIVE BEHAVIOR

2   Nonassertion is the inability or unwillingness to express thoughts or feelings in a conflict. Sometimes nonassertion comes from a lack of confidence. At other times people lack the awareness or skill to use a more direct means of expression. Sometimes people know how to communicate in an assertive way but choose to behave nonassertively.

5   Faced with the annoyance of a barking dog next door, a nonassertive person might try to ignore the noise by closing the windows and turning up the radio. Other nonassertive responses would be to deny that the problem even exists or to hope that it would go away. None of these alternatives sounds very appealing. They probably would lead the nonassertive communicator to grow more and more angry at the neighbors, making

PEANUTS: © United Feature Syndicate, Inc.

3   Nonassertion is a surprisingly common way of dealing with conflicts. One study revealed that dating partners do not express roughly 40 percent of their relational grievances to one another. Another study examined the conflict level of spouses in "nondistressed" marriages. Over a five-day period, spouses reported that their partner engaged in an average of thirteen behaviors that were "displeasurable" to them but that they had only one confrontation during the same period.

4   Nonassertion can take a variety of forms. One is avoidance—either physical (steering clear of a friend after having an argument) or conversational (changing the topic, joking, or denying that a problem exists). People who avoid conflicts usually believe that it's easier to put up with the status quo° than to face the conflict head-on and try to solve it. Accommodation is another nonassertive response. Accommodators deal with conflict by giving in, putting the others' needs ahead of their own.

a friendly relationship difficult. Nonassertion also can lead to a loss of self-respect. It's hard to respect yourself when you can't cope with even an everyday irritation.

6   Nonassertion isn't always a bad idea. You might choose to keep quiet or give in if the risk of speaking up is too great: getting fired from a job you can't afford to lose, being humiliated in public, or even risking physical harm. You might also avoid a conflict if the relationship that it involves isn't worth the effort. Even in close relationships, though, nonassertion has its logic. If the issue is temporary or minor, you might let it pass. It might even make sense to keep your thoughts to yourself and give in if the issue is more important to the other person than it is to you. These reasons help explain why the communication of many happily married couples is characterized by "selectively ignoring" the other person's minor flaws. This doesn't mean that a key to successful relationships is avoiding all conflicts.

Instead, it means that it's smart to save energy for the truly important ones.

7 Like avoidance, accommodation can also be appropriate, especially in cases in which the other person's needs may be more important than yours. For instance, if a friend wants to have a serious talk and you feel playful, you'd most likely honor her request, particularly if the friend is facing some kind of crisis and wants your help. In most cases, however, accommodators fail to assert themselves either because they don't value themselves sufficiently or because they don't know how to ask for what they want.

DIRECT AGGRESSION

8 In contrast to nonassertion, direct aggression occurs when a communicator expresses a criticism or demand that threatens the face of the person at whom it is directed. Communication researcher Dominic Infante identified several types of direct aggression: character attacks, competence attacks, physical appearance attacks, maledictions (wishing the other ill fortune), and teasing, ridicule, threats, swearing, and nonverbal emblems°.

9 Direct aggression can have a severe impact on the target. Recipients can feel embarrassed, inadequate, humiliated, hopeless, desperate, or depressed. These results can lead to decreased effectiveness in personal relationships, on the job, and in families. There is a significant connection between verbal aggression and physical aggression, but even if the attacks never lead to blows, the psychological effects can be devastating. For example, siblings who were teased by a brother or sister report less satisfaction and trust than those whose relationships were relatively free

of this sort of aggression, and high school teams with aggressive coaches lose more games than those whose coaches are less aggressive.

Aggressive behavior can punish the 10 attacker as well as the victim. Men who view conversations as contests and partners as opponents are 60 percent more apt to die earlier than those who are less aggressive. Newly married couples whose disagreements are marked by sarcasm, interruptions, and criticism suffer a drop in the effectiveness of their immune systems.

You could handle the barking dog 11 problem with direct aggression by abusively confronting your neighbors, calling them names, and threatening to call the dogcatcher the next time you see their dog running loose. If your town has a leash law, you would be within your legal rights to do so, and thus you would gain your goal of bringing peace and quiet to the neighborhood. Unfortunately, your direct aggression would have other, less productive consequences. Your neighbors and you would probably cease to be on speaking terms, and you could expect a complaint from them the first time you violated even the most inconsequential of city ordinances. If you live in the neighborhood for any time at all, this state of hostilities isn't very appealing. This example shows why research confirms what common sense suggests: Unlike other conflict styles, direct aggression is judged incompetent by virtually everyone who encounters it.

To be fair, there are probably times 12 when direct aggression is the only realistic option. In abusive or life-threatening situations, for instance, it might be necessary to "fight fire with fire." There are also occasions in which all other methods have been exhausted and you decide to go for the "win" no matter what it costs. For instance, after repeated appeals to your neighbors, you might finally call the dogcatcher because you're more concerned with peace and quiet than with maintaining relations with neighbors who don't seem to care about your concerns. Later in this section we'll discuss how being assertive (rather than aggressive) can allow you to "win" without requiring someone else to "lose."

PASSIVE AGGRESSION

13 Passive aggression occurs when a communicator expresses hostility in an obscure or manipulative way—a behavior that might be termed "crazymaking." It occurs when people have feelings of resentment, anger, or rage that they are unable or unwilling to express directly. Instead of keeping these feelings to themselves, a crazymaker sends aggressive messages in subtle, indirect ways, thus maintaining a front of kindness. This amiable° facade eventually crumbles, however, leaving the crazymaker's victim confused and angry at having been fooled. The targets of the crazymaker can either react with aggressive behavior of their own or retreat to nurse their hurt feelings. In either case, passive aggression seldom has anything but harmful effects on a relationship.

14 You could respond to your neighbors and their barking dog in several crazymaking, passive-aggressive ways. One way would be to complain anonymously to the city pound and then, after the dog has been hauled away, express your sympathy. Or you could complain to everyone else in the neighborhood, hoping that their hostility would force the offending neighbors to quiet the dog or face being social outcasts.

15 There are a number of shortcomings to this sort of approach, each of which illustrates the risks of passive aggression. First, there is the chance that the crazymaking won't work: The neighbors might simply miss the point of your veiled attacks and continue to ignore the barking. On the other hand, they might get your message clearly, but either because of your lack of sincerity or out of sheer stubbornness, they might simply refuse to do anything about it. In either case, it's likely that in this and other instances, passive aggression won't satisfy your unmet need.

16 Even when passive aggression proves successful in the short run, a second shortcoming lies in its consequences over the longer term. You might manage to intimidate your neighbors into shutting up their dog, for instance, but in winning the battle you could lose what would become a war. As a means of revenge, they could wage their own campaign of crazymaking by such tactics as badmouthing your sloppy gardening to other neighbors or phoning in false complaints about your loud parties. It's obvious that feuds such as this one are counterproductive and outweigh the apparent advantages of passive aggression.

INDIRECT COMMUNICATION

17 The clearest communication is not necessarily the best approach. Indirect communication conveys a message in a roundabout manner, in order to save face for the recipient. Although indirect communication lacks the clarity of aggressive or assertive communication, it

involves more initiative than nonassertion. It also has none of the hostility of passive-aggressive crazymaking. The goal is to get what you want without arousing the hostility of the other person. Consider the case of the barking dog. One indirect approach would be to strike up a friendly conversation with the owners and ask if anything you are doing is too noisy for them, hoping they would get the hint.

18   Because it saves face for the other party, indirect communication is often kinder than blunt honesty. If your guests are staying too long, it's probably kinder to yawn and hint about your big day tomorrow than to bluntly ask them to leave. Likewise, if you're not interested in going out with someone who has asked you for a date, it may be more compassionate to claim that you're busy than to say, "I'm not interested in seeing you."

19   At other times we communicate indirectly in order to protect ourselves. You might, for example, test the waters by hinting instead of directly asking the boss for a raise or by letting your partner know indirectly that you could use some affection. At times like these, an indirect approach may get the message across while softening the blow of a negative response.

20   The advantages of self-protection and face-saving for others help explain why indirect communication is the most common way by which people make requests. The risk of an indirect message, of course, is that the other party will misunderstand you or fail to get the message at all. There are also times when an idea is so important that hinting lacks the necessary punch. When clarity and directness are your goals, an assertive approach is in order.

ASSERTION

Assertion occurs when a message 21 expresses the speaker's needs, thoughts, and feelings clearly and directly without judging or dictating to others. A complete assertive message includes a description of the other person's behavior, an interpretation, and statements of feelings, consequences, and intentions.

An assertive course of action in the 22 case of the barking dog would be to wait a few days to make sure that the noise is not just a fluke. If the barking continues, you could introduce yourself to your neighbors and explain your problem. You could tell them that although they might not notice it, the dog often plays in the street and keeps barking at passing cars. You could tell them why this behavior bothers you. It keeps you awake at night and makes it hard for you to do your work. You could point out that you don't want to be a grouch and call the pound. Rather than resort to that, you could tell them that you've come to see what kind of solution you can find that will satisfy both of you. This approach may not work, and you might then have to decide whether it is more important to avoid bad feelings or to have peace and quiet. But the chances for a happy ending are best with this assertive approach. And no matter what happens, you can keep your self-respect by behaving directly and honestly.

READING COMPREHENSION QUESTIONS

Vocabulary in Context

___D___ 1. In the sentence below, the word *ordinances* (ôr′dn-ən-sĭs) means
   A. organizations.
   B. licenses.   A person would be most likely to
   C. activities.   violate regulations.
   D. regulations.

   "Your neighbors and you would probably cease to be on speaking
   terms, and you could expect a complaint from them the first time
   you violated even the most inconsequential of city ordinances."
   (Paragraph 11)

___B___ 2. In the excerpt below, the word *facade* (fə-sŏd′) means
   A. determination.
   B. outward appearance.   "A front of kindness" is the same as an
   C. certainty.   "amiable facade."
   D. foundation.

   "Instead of keeping these feelings to themselves, a crazymaker
   sends aggressive messages in subtle, indirect ways, thus
   maintaining a front of kindness. This amiable facade eventually
   crumbles, however, leaving the crazymaker's victim confused and
   angry at having been fooled." (Paragraph 13)

Central Point and Main Ideas

___D___ 3. Which sentence best expresses the central point of the selection?
   A. At one time or another, almost everyone has been bothered by
      neighbors, but most likely handled the situation in different ways.
   B. When confronted with neighbors who have a barking dog, it is best
      to take an assertive approach.
   C. There are both benefits and drawbacks to using the indirect method
      to communicate your needs to others.
   D. When communicating one's needs in a conflict situation, there are
      clear differences between nonassertive, directly aggressive, passive-
      aggressive, indirect, and assertive behaviors.

   Answer A covers only paragraph 1.
   Answer B covers only paragraphs 21–22.
   Answer C covers only paragraph 20.

_____A_____ 4. The implied main idea of paragraph 5 is that faced with the annoyance of a barking dog next door,

Answer B covers only the first sentence, where it is stated, not implied. Answer C covers only the second sentence. Answer D covers only the fourth sentence.

    A. a nonassertive person might act in ways that are unsatisfactory.

    B. some nonassertive people try to ignore the noise by closing the windows and turning up the radio.

    C. another nonassertive response would be to deny that the problem even exists or to hope it will go away.

    D. the nonassertive communicator will grow more and more angry at the neighbors.

_____C_____ 5. The implied main idea of paragraph 11 is that

The focus of paragraph 11 is on the negative consequences of direct aggression. A covers only the first sentence. D covers only the second sentence. B fails to take the "less productive consequences" into account.

    A. one way to respond to the barking dog problem would be to abusively confront and threaten your neighbors.

    B. direct aggression can bring peace and quiet to a neighborhood.

    C. direct aggression would probably produce negative consequences.

    D. people who respond with direct aggression to a barking dog are acting within their legal rights.

_____A_____ 6. The implied main idea of paragraph 22 is that, in the case of the barking dog,

    A. an assertive approach should be thought out carefully in advance.

    B. an assertive approach often does not work.

    C. an assertive approach should always be a last resort.

    D. you might have to decide whether it is more important to avoid bad feelings or to have peace and quiet.

An explanation as lengthy and detailed as the one described in paragraph 22 would have to be carefully planned. Answers B and C are not supported. Answer D is too narrow; it covers only part of the third sentence from the end.

Supporting Details

_____C_____ 7. According to the selection, the communication of many happily married couples is characterized by

    A. avoiding all conflicts, both important and unimportant.

    B. indirectly suggesting that the other person correct his or her annoying behavior.

    C. selectively ignoring the other person's minor flaws.

    D. direct assertions which include a description of the other person's behavior, an interpretation, and statements of feelings, consequences, and intentions.

Sentence 7 in paragraph 6 supports answer C. Answer A is contradicted by the last sentence of paragraph 6. Nothing in the selection connects answer B or D with the idea of a happy marriage.

____D____ 8. According to the selection, newly married couples whose disagree-
ments are marked by sarcasm, interruptions, and criticism
  A. tend to suffer a loss of self-respect.
  B. tend to die earlier than other couples.   See the last sentence
  C. are guilty of crazymaking behavior.   in paragraph 10.
  D. suffer a drop in the effectiveness of their immune systems.

____D____ 9. One drawback of indirect communication is that
  A. it can lead to a loss of self-esteem.   See sentence 2
  B. it can cause people to seek revenge against you.   in paragraph 20.
  C. it can cause the other party to lose face.
  D. the other party may misunderstand you or fail to get the message at all.

Transitions

____C____ 10. The relationship of the second sentence below to the first sentence is
one of   The two sentences contrast two possible reactions that the
  A. comparison.   neighbors might have: they might fail to get your message;
  B. illustration.   or they might get the message, but refuse to do anything
      about it. *On the other hand* signals the contrast.
  C. contrast.   Note that within the second sentence,
  D. cause and effect.   there is a cause and effect relationship.

"The neighbors might simply miss the point of your veiled attacks
and continue to ignore the barking. <u>On the other hand</u>, they might
get your message clearly, but either because of your lack of
sincerity or out of sheer stubbornness, they might simply refuse to
do anything about it." (Paragraph 15)

Patterns of Organization

____A____ 11. The main pattern of organization of this selection is
  A. list of items.   The pattern is indicated by the central
  B. time order.   point—that people respond to conflict in
  C. comparison.   various ways. The selection then lists and
  D. contrast.   illustrates various behaviors.

Inferences

____B____ 12. On the basis of this selection, we can infer that people who lack self-
confidence are most likely to engage in   See sentence 2 in paragraph 2.
  A. direct aggression.   Also, since nonassertive behavior often takes
  B. nonassertive behavior.   the form of avoidance and accommodation
  C. indirect communication.   (paragraph 4), we can infer that those who
  D. assertion.   engage in it lack confidence.

_A_ 13. We can infer from this selection that people who communicate indirectly are

    A. sensitive to the feelings of others.

    B. expressing hostility to others.

    C. blunt to the point of rudeness.

    D. sneaky.

> See paragraphs 17–19. Words and phrases such as *to save face for the recipient, kinder, more compassionate,* and *face-saving for others* suggest this inference.

Purpose and Tone

_A_ 14. The authors' primary purpose in this selection is to

    A. inform.

    B. persuade.

    C. entertain.

> The selection explains various conflict styles.

_D_ 15. The tone of the selection is mainly

    A. scornful.

    B. sympathetic.

    C. humorous.

    D. objective.

> No words of scorn, sympathy, or humor are included; pros and cons of each personal conflict style are presented directly.

Argument

_B_ 16. Write the letter of the statement that is the point of the following argument. The other statements are support for that point.

    A. Targets of direct aggression can feel embarrassed, inadequate, humiliated, hopeless, or depressed.

    B. Direct aggression can lead to negative consequences for both the aggressor and the target.

    C. Aggressive people are more likely to die earlier than those who are less aggressive.

    D. People often react with hostility to those who use direct aggression against them.

> Statements A, C, and D describe specific negative consequences.

_D_ 17. Write the letter of the statement that is the point of the following argument. The other statements are support for that point.

    A. Nonassertion sometimes comes from a lack of confidence.

    B. Some people lack the awareness or skill to use a more direct means of expression.

    C. Some people behave nonassertively in certain situations in order to save their energy for more important conflicts.

    D. There are various reasons why some people behave nonassertively.

> Statements A, B, and C are three reasons why people behave nonassertively.

Critical Reading

<u>B</u> 18. The statement below is
   A. fact.   *Probably kinder* and *bluntly* are words
   B. opinion.   that express opinions.
   c. a mixture of fact and opinion.

      "If your guests are staying too long, it's <u>probably kinder</u> to yawn
      and hint about your big day tomorrow than to <u>bluntly</u> ask them to
      leave." (Paragraph 18)

<u>C</u> 19. The facts of the reading are probably based on
   A. the authors' observations of their own family members.
   B. stories clipped from local newspapers.
   c. a great deal of sociological research.
   D. oral histories of people who have lived in one neighborhood for a
      long time.   The breadth of information implies a broad-
                                      based foundation of sociological research.

<u>B</u> 20. A politician who uses the propaganda technique of name calling to
      attack his opponent probably has which of the following personal
      conflict styles?
   A. Nonassertive
   B. Direct aggressive   See paragraph 8.
   c. Passive-aggressive
   D. Assertive

ACTIVE READING AND STUDY
OF A TEXTBOOK SELECTION   *Wording of answers may vary.*

Complete the following study notes on the selection. Some items are already filled
in for you.

Note: Headings, enumerations, definitions, and examples are the keys to the
important ideas here.

Central point: *People respond in different ways when faced with a conflict*
          situation.

1. *Nonassertive behavior—the inability or unwillingness to express*
   thoughts or feelings in a conflict

   A surprisingly common way of dealing with conflicts

   Takes different forms:

a. _Avoidance—either physical (avoiding a friend after an argument) or conversational (changing the topic)_

b. _Accommodation—putting others' needs ahead of own_

   _Ex. ___ Close window and turn up radio to deal with barking dog._

2. _Direct aggression—a criticism or demand that threatens the face of the person at whom it is directed_

   Includes character and physical appearance attacks

   _Ex. ___ Could respond to barking dog by abusively confronting your neighbor_

   Can severely punish attacker and victim

3. _Passive aggression—expressing hostility in an obscure or manipulative way—"crazymaking"_

   _Ex. ___ Complain anonymously to the city pound and then express sympathy after dog hauled away._

4. _Indirect communication—convey a message in a roundabout manner in order to save face for the recipient_

   _Ex. ___ Strike up a friendly conversation with dog owners and ask if anything you're doing is too noisy for them._

5. _Assertion—expressing the speaker's needs, thoughts, and feelings clearly and directly without judging or dictating to others_

   _Ex. ___ Explain your problem about the dog to your neighbor to see if you can work together to find a solution._

Note that there are ten answers here: a central point, five major types of behavior, one type of nonassertive behavior, and three examples. Each answer is worth two points.

DISCUSSION QUESTIONS

1. How would you have handled the barking dog situation? In general, what would you say is your primary style of behavior in a conflict situation?

2. The authors state: "Over a five-day period, spouses reported that their partner engaged in an average of thirteen behaviors that were 'displeasurable' to them but that they had only one confrontation during the same period." Do you believe in the policy of letting most "displeasurable behaviors" go by without mentioning them? Or do you think it is better to immediately let a partner, family member, or colleague know when you are displeased about something? Explain your answer.

3. After reading this selection, do you feel that you might try to change your style of behavior in a conflict situation? If so, what style of behavior might you try now, and why?

● 4. It seems that every day we hear stories about people who resort to violence in response to conflict situations. Indeed, the United States has one of the highest murder rates in the world. In your view, why do so many Americans resort to an aggressive style of behavior in responding to conflicts?

Note: Writing assignments for this selection appear on page 566.

Check Your Performance   **PERSONAL CONFLICT STYLES**

Activity	Number Right	Points	Score
READING COMPREHENSION QUESTIONS			
Vocabulary in Context (2 items)	_____	× 4 =	_____
Central Point and Main Ideas (4 items)	_____	× 4 =	_____
Supporting Details (3 items)	_____	× 4 =	_____
Transitions (1 item)	_____	× 4 =	_____
Patterns of Organization (1 item)	_____	× 4 =	_____
Inferences (2 items)	_____	× 4 =	_____
Purpose and Tone (2 items)	_____	× 4 =	_____
Argument (2 items)	_____	× 4 =	_____
Critical Reading (3 items)	_____	× 4 =	_____
ACTIVE READING AND STUDY (10 items)	_____	× 2 =	_____
		TOTAL SCORE =	_____%

Enter your total score into the **Reading Performance Chart: Ten Reading Selections** on the inside back cover.

2

Cardiovascular Disease Risk Factors

Wayne A. Payne, Dale B. Hahn, and Ellen B. Mauer

Preview

Do you know if you are at increased risk for heart disease? There are steps you can take to protect yourself—but only once you've identified the factors that put you in danger. Being aware of your risks, as described in this selection from *Understanding Your Health* (McGraw-Hill), is a big step toward living a longer and healthier life.

Words to Watch

cardiovascular (1): of or relating to the heart or blood vessels
epidemiological (14): relating to the control of diseases
debilitating (20): making weak and infirm

1   As you know, the heart and blood vessels are among the most important structures in the human body. By protecting your cardiovascular° system, you lay the groundwork for a more exciting, productive, and energetic life. The best time to start protecting and improving your cardiovascular system is early in life, when lifestyle patterns are developed and reinforced. Of course, it is difficult to move backward through time, so the second-best time to start protecting your heart is today. Improvements in certain lifestyle activities can pay significant dividends as your life unfolds.

  The American Heart Association 2 encourages people to protect and enhance their heart health by examining the ten cardiovascular risk factors that are related to various forms of heart disease. A *cardiovascular risk factor* is an attribute that a person has or is exposed to that increases the likelihood that he or she will develop some form of heart disease. Three risk factors are those you will be unable to change. An additional six risk factors are those you can clearly change. One final risk factor is thought to be a contributing factor to heart disease. Let's look at these three groups of risk factors separately.

RISK FACTORS THAT CANNOT BE CHANGED

3   The three risk factors that you cannot change are increasing age, male gender, and heredity. Despite the fact that these risk factors cannot be changed, your knowledge that they might be an influence in your life should encourage you to make a more serious commitment to the risk factors you can change.

Increasing Age

4   Heart disease tends to develop gradually over the course of one's life. Although we may know of a person or two who experienced a heart attack in their twenties or thirties, most of the serious consequences of heart disease become evident as we age. For example, nearly 84 percent of people who die from heart disease are aged 65 and older.

Male Gender

5   Men have a greater risk of heart disease than do women prior to age 55. Yet when women move through menopause (typically in their fifties), their rates of heart disease become similar to men's rates. It is thought that women have a degree of protection from heart disease because of their natural production of the hormone estrogen during their fertile years.

Heredity

6   Obviously, you have no input in determining who your biological parents are. Like increasing age and male gender, this risk factor cannot be changed. By the luck of the draw, some people are born into families where heart disease has never been a serious problem, whereas others are born into families where heart disease is quite prevalent. In this latter case, children are said to have a genetic predisposition (tendency) to develop heart disease as they grow and develop throughout their lives. These people have every reason to be highly motivated to reduce the risk factors they can control.

7   Race is also a consideration related to heart disease. The prevalence of hypertension (high blood pressure) among African Americans is among the highest in the United States. More than one in every three African Americans has hypertension (two out of every three over age 65). Hypertension significantly increases the risk of heart disease, stroke, and kidney disease. Fortunately, as you will soon read, hypertension can be controlled through a variety of methods. It is especially important for African Americans to take advantage of every opportunity to have their blood pressure measured so that preventive measures can be started immediately if necessary.

RISK FACTORS THAT CAN BE CHANGED

8   Six cardiovascular risk factors are influenced, in large part, by our lifestyle choices. These risk factors are tobacco smoke, physical inactivity, high blood cholesterol level, high blood pressure, diabetes mellitus, and obesity and overweight. Healthful behavior changes

can help you protect and strengthen your cardiovascular system.

Tobacco Smoke

9 Approximately 46.5 million adults in the United States smoke cigarettes, and 28.5 percent of high school students are smokers. Smokers have a heart attack risk that is more than twice that of non-smokers. Smoking cigarettes is the major risk factor associated with sudden cardiac death. In fact, smokers have two to four times the risk of dying from sudden cardiac arrest than do nonsmokers. Smokers who experience a heart attack are more likely to die suddenly (within an hour) than are those who don't smoke.

10 Smoking also adversely affects non-smokers who are exposed to environmental tobacco smoke. Studies suggest that the risk of death caused by heart disease is increased about 30 percent in people exposed to secondhand smoke in the home. The risk of death caused by heart disease may even be higher in people exposed to environmental tobacco smoke in work settings (for example, bars, casinos, enclosed offices, some bowling alleys and restaurants), since higher levels of smoke may be present at work than at home. Because of the health threat to nonsmokers, restrictions on indoor smoking in public areas and business settings are increasing tremendously in every part of the country.

11 For years it was commonly believed that if you had smoked for many years, it was pointless to try to quit; the damage to one's health could never be reversed. However, the American Heart Association now indicates that by quitting smoking, regardless of how long or how much you have smoked, your risk of heart disease declines rapidly.

12 This news is exciting and should encourage people to quit smoking, regardless of how long they have smoked. Of course, if you have started to smoke, the healthy approach would be to quit now . . . before the nicotine controls your life and leads to heart disease or damages your lungs or leads to lung cancer.

Physical Inactivity

13 Lack of regular physical activity is a significant risk factor for heart disease. Regular aerobic exercise helps strengthen the heart muscle, maintain healthy blood vessels, and improve the ability of the vascular system to transfer blood and oxygen to all parts of the body. In addition, physical activity helps lower overall blood cholesterol levels for most people, encourages weight loss and retention of lean muscle mass, and allows people to moderate the stress in their lives.

14 With all the benefits that come with physical activity, it amazes health professionals that so many Americans refuse to become regularly active. The Center for Disease Control and Prevention reports that 60 percent or more of Americans do not achieve the recommended amount of physical activity each week and that 25 percent of Americans age 18 or older report no leisure-time physical activity. In terms of relative risk for developing cardio-vascular disease (CVD), physical inactivity is comparable to high blood pressure, high blood cholesterol, and cigarette smoking. Critical findings reported in the year 2000 from the highly respected Harvard Alumni Health Study support the contention that physical activity is closely associated with

decreased risk of coronary heart disease. After monitoring Harvard alumni for nearly twenty years in a variety of epidemiological° studies, researchers confirmed that sustained, vigorous physical activity produces the strongest reductions in CVD. Light and moderate physical activities such as golf, gardening, and walking are helpful in reducing CVD, but more vigorous activities (such as jogging, swimming, tennis, stair climbing, or aerobics) produce greater reductions in CVD. Additionally, Harvard researchers found that physical activity produces reductions in CVD whether the daily activity comes in one long session or in two shorter sessions of activity. The "bottom line" is this: to reduce your chances of experiencing CVD, you must engage in some form of regular, sustained physical activity.

15   If you are middle-aged or older and have been inactive, you should consult with a physician before starting an exercise program. Also, if you have any known health condition that could be aggravated by physical activity, check with a physician first.

High Blood Cholesterol Level

16   The third controllable risk factor for heart disease is high blood cholesterol level. Approximately 102 million American adults have a total cholesterol level of greater than 200 mg/dl (about 41 million have levels greater than 240 mg/dl). Generally speaking, the higher the blood cholesterol level, the greater the risk for heart disease. The table below shows ranges for cholesterol levels. When high blood cholesterol levels are combined with other important risk factors, the risk becomes much greater.

17   Fortunately, blood cholesterol levels are relatively easy to measure. Many campus health and wellness centers provide cholesterol screenings for employees and students. These screenings help identify people whose cholesterol levels (or profiles) may be dangerous. Medical professionals have linked people's diets to their cholesterol levels. People with high blood cholesterol levels are encouraged to consume a heart-healthy diet and to become physically active. In recent years, researchers have developed a variety of drugs that are very effective at lowering cholesterol levels.

High Blood Pressure

18   The fourth of the six cardiovascular risk factors that can be changed is high blood pressure, or hypertension. Approximately 58 million Americans have hypertension, one-third of whom have not been diagnosed. High blood pressure can seriously damage a person's heart and blood vessels. High blood pressure

Classification of Total Cholesterol Levels	
Total Cholesterol Level	**Classification**
< 200 mg/dl	Desirable blood cholesterol level
200–239 mg/dl	Borderline-high blood cholesterol level
> 240 mg/dl	High blood cholesterol level

causes the heart to work much harder, eventually causing the heart to enlarge and weaken. High blood pressure increases the risk of stroke, heart attack, congestive heart failure, and kidney disease.

19   When high blood pressure is seen with other risk factors, the risk for stroke or heart attack is increased tremendously. As you will soon see, this "silent killer" is easy to monitor and can be effectively controlled through a variety of approaches.

Diabetes Mellitus

20 Diabetes mellitus is a debilitating° chronic disease that has a significant effect on the human body. Approximately 17 million Americans have diabetes, one-third of whom have not been diagnosed. In addition to increasing the risk of developing kidney disease, blindness, and nerve damage, diabetes increases the likelihood of developing heart and blood vessel diseases. More than 65 percent of people with diabetes die of some type of heart or blood vessel disease. The cardiovascular damage is thought to occur due to the abnormal levels of cholesterol and blood fat found in individuals with diabetes. With weight management, exercise, dietary changes, and drug therapy, diabetes can be relatively well controlled in most people. Despite careful management of this disease, diabetic patients remain quite susceptible to eventual heart and blood vessel damage.

Obesity and Overweight

21 According to the 1999 National Health and Nutrition Survey, approximately 61 percent of American adults are overweight and 26 percent are obese. Even if they have no other risk factors, obese people are more likely than are nonobese people to develop heart disease and stroke. Obesity, particularly if of the abdominal form, places considerable strain on the heart, and it tends to worsen both blood pressure and blood cholesterol levels. Obese men and women can expect a greater risk of heart disease, diabetes, gallbladder disease, osteoarthritis, respiratory problems, and certain cancers. Maintaining body weight within a desirable range minimizes the chances of obesity ever happening. To accomplish this, you can elect to make a commitment to a reasonably sound diet and an active lifestyle.

ANOTHER RISK FACTOR THAT CONTRIBUTES TO HEART DISEASE

The American Heart Association 22 identifies one other risk factor that is associated with an increased risk of heart disease. This risk factor is one's individual response to stress.

Individual Response to Stress

Unresolved stress over a long period may 23 be a contributing factor to the development of heart disease. Certainly, people who are unable to cope with stressful life experiences are more likely to develop negative dependence behaviors (for example, smoking, underactivity, poor dietary practices), which can then lead to cardiovascular problems through changes in blood fat profiles, blood pressure, and heart workload.

READING COMPREHENSION QUESTIONS

Vocabulary in Context

___D___ 1. In the sentence below, the word *prevalent* (prĕ′və-lĕnt) means
   A. rare.
   B. cured.
   C. correct.
   D. common.

The sentence contrasts how rare heart disease is in some families with how common (or prevalent) it is in others.

> "By the luck of the draw, some people are born into families where heart disease has never been a serious problem, whereas others are born into families where heart disease is quite prevalent." (Paragraph 6)

___C___ 2. In the sentence below, the word *contention* (kən-tĕn′shən) means
   A. gathering.
   B. contest.
   C. argument.
   D. candidate.

Medical researchers generally gather evidence to support arguments.

> "Critical findings reported in the year 2000 from the highly respected Harvard Alumni Health Study support the contention that physical activity is closely associated with decreased risk of coronary heart disease." (Paragraph 14)

Central Point and Main Ideas

___C___ 3. Which sentence best expresses the central point of the selection?
   A. Even though some cardiovascular disease risk factors cannot be changed, it is still important to learn about them.
   B. There are three cardiovascular disease risk factors you cannot change and six you can.
   C. It is important for people to learn about cardiovascular disease risk factors that can and cannot be changed so they can better ensure their heart health.
   D. The best time to start improving your cardiovascular health is early in life, when lifestyle patterns are developed and reinforced.

Answer A covers only paragraph 3. Answer B covers only part of paragraph 2. Answer D covers only part of paragraph 1.

___A___ 4. The main idea of paragraph 10 is stated in its
   A. first sentence.
   B. second sentence.
   C. third sentence.
   D. fourth sentence.

Answers B and C give evidence to support the main idea that smoking also hurts nonsmokers. Answer D is a detail about one response to the problem.

_D_ 5. The implied main idea of paragraph 14 is that

    A. 60 percent of Americans don't achieve the recommended amount of physical activity each week.

    B. light and moderate physical activities are helpful in reducing CVD, but sustained, vigorous physical activity is better.

    C. it does not matter whether daily physical activity comes in one long session or in two shorter sessions.

    D. although the majority of Americans fail to get enough physical activity, it has been proven that regular, sustained physical activity lowers CVD.   Answer A is stated, not implied, and covers only part of sentence 2. Answer B covers only sentence 6. Answer C covers only sentence 7.

Supporting Details

_B_ 6. According to the selection, regular aerobic exercise does all of the following *except*

    A. help strengthen the heart muscle.

    B. eliminate the need to measure blood cholesterol levels.

    C. allow people to moderate the stress in their lives.

    D. improve the ability of the vascular system to transfer blood and oxygen to all parts of the body.   Answers A, C, and D are stated in paragraph 13, but answer B is not mentioned in the selection.

_C_ 7. The American Heart Association now indicates that

    A. if you have smoked for many years, it is pointless to try to quit.

    B. people are not adversely affected by secondhand smoke.

    C. people who quit smoking lower their risk of heart disease no matter how long they have smoked.

    D. the effects of quitting smoking after having smoked for many years are still unknown.   See sentence 2 in paragraph 11. Answers A, B, and D are contradicted in paragraphs 10–12.

Transitions

_B_ 8. The relationship of the second sentence below to the first sentence is one of

    A. cause and effect.

    B. comparison.   The comparison is between risk factors which cannot be changed.

    C. illustration.   The comparison transition is *Like*.

    D. addition.

"Obviously, you have no input in determining who your biological parents are. <u>Like</u> increasing age and male gender, the risk factor cannot be changed." (Paragraph 6)

Patterns of Organization

___B___ 9. The main pattern of organization in the selection is
- A. time order.
- B. list of items.
- C. definition and example.
- D. contrast.

The authors list and discuss cardiovascular disease risk factors.

Inferences

___C___ 10. On the basis of paragraph 7, we can infer that

See sentence 4 in paragraph 7. If African Americans have a prevalence of hypertension, and hypertension increases the risk of heart disease, stroke, and kidney disease, it is logical to conclude that African Americans have high rates of these conditions. A, B, and D are not suggested by the paragraph.

- A. African Americans are generally unaware of the connection between race and heart disease.
- B. people who are not African American seldom suffer from hypertension.
- C. African Americans also have high rates of heart disease, stroke, and kidney disease.
- D. very few African Americans currently get their blood pressure measured.

___A___ 11. On the basis of paragraphs 11–12, we can infer that for years

See the first sentence in paragraph 11. If people believed that the damage had already been done, they probably would not try to quit. Answers B, C, and D are not indicated in the passage.

- A. some smokers never tried to quit smoking because they thought it was pointless.
- B. most people had no idea that smoking could damage their health.
- C. the American Heart Association withheld important information from the American public.
- D. the number of people who smoked increased due to lack of information from the American Heart Association.

___D___ 12. The final paragraph of the reading suggests that
- A. people under stress usually have psychological problems.
- B. researchers are certain that unresolved stress leads to heart disease.
- C. stressful life experiences are far more likely to happen to people with heart disease.
- D. people who learn positive ways to cope with stress are at less risk of developing heart disease.

If unresolved stress may put one at risk, it is logical to infer that resolving stress would reduce the risk. Answer A is not suggested. Answer B is incorrect because the paragraph says only that there "may be" a connection, not that a connection is "certain." Answer C is incorrect because the paragraph suggests that stress leads to heart disease, not that heart disease leads to stress.

Purpose and Tone

_A_ 13. The purpose of this selection is
  A. both to inform and to persuade.
  B. both to persuade and to entertain.
  C. only to persuade.

> The authors explain cardiovascular disease risk factors so that readers can take steps to protect and enhance their heart health. (See the first sentence in paragraph 2.)

_C_ 14. The authors' tone can be described as
  A. ironic and ambivalent.
  B. sympathetic and lighthearted.
  C. concerned but encouraging.
  D. distressed but informal.

> The authors express concern over the fact that so many Americans engage in lifestyle activities which increase the risk of cardiovascular disease, but encourage us to take steps to alter our lifestyles and minimize our risks.

Argument

_B_ 15. Which item does **not** support the following point?

> The fact that 25% of Americans age 18 or older report no leisure-time physical activity has no bearing on the relationship between physical activity and a decreased risk of cardiovascular disease.

Point: Researchers have found that physical activity is closely associated with decreased risk of coronary heart disease.
  A. Light and moderate physical activities are helpful in reducing cardiovascular disease (CVD).
  B. Twenty-five percent of Americans age 18 or older report no leisure-time physical activity.
  C. Vigorous physical activity produces greater reductions in CVD than does light or moderate activity.
  D. Physical activity produces reductions in CVD whether the daily activity comes in one long session or in two shorter sessions.

16. Label the point of the following argument with a **P** and the two statements of support with an **S**. Label with an **X** the statement that is neither the point nor the support of the argument.
  _S_ A. High blood pressure causes the heart to work much harder, eventually causing the heart to enlarge and weaken.
  _S_ B. High blood pressure increases the risk of stroke, heart attack, congestive heart failure and kidney disease.
  _X_ C. High blood pressure is easy to monitor and can be controlled through a variety of measures.
  _P_ D. High blood pressure can have severe negative effects on health.

> Statement C is not about the negative effects of high blood pressure. Statements A and B describe some of the negative effects on health caused by high blood pressure.

Critical Reading

_A_ 17. The statement below is

A. fact.

B. opinion.

C. a mixture of fact and opinion.

A conclusion which has been supported by much clinical research.

"However, the American Heart Association now indicates that by quitting smoking, regardless of how long or how much you have smoked, your risk of heart disease declines rapidly." (Paragraph 11)

_B_ 18. The statement below is

A. fact.

B. opinion.

C. both fact and opinion.

Judgment words: *exciting* and *should*.

"This news is <u>exciting</u> and <u>should</u> encourage people to quit smoking, regardless of how long they have smoked." (Paragraph 12)

_C_ 19. A person who complains that he must choose between eating healthy foods or foods that taste good is committing the logical fallacy of

The person is assuming that there are no foods which are healthy *and* taste good.

A. straw man *(an argument is made by claiming an opponent holds an extreme position and then opposing that extreme position).*

B. false comparison *(the argument assumes that two things being compared are more alike than they really are).*

C. either-or *(the argument assumes that there are only two sides to a question).*

D. personal attack *(ignores the issue under discussion and concentrates instead on the character of the opponent).*

_B_ 20. A person who states that it's useless for him to adopt a healthy lifestyle, since his dad died at the age of 50, is committing the logical fallacy of

A. straw man *(an argument is made by claiming an opponent holds an extreme position and then opposing that extreme position).*

B. false comparison *(the argument assumes that two things being compared are more alike than they really are).*

C. either-or *(the argument assumes that there are only two sides to a question).*

D. false cause *(the argument assumes that the order of events alone shows cause and effect).*

The speaker's dad was most likely not well informed about healthy lifestyle choices, since what we know of them has expanded greatly in recent years. Therefore, the comparison isn't valid.

ACTIVE READING AND STUDY OF A TEXTBOOK SELECTION

Complete the following study notes on the selection. Some items and parts of items are already filled in for you.   *Wording of answers may vary.*

Note: Headings and enumerations are the keys to the important ideas here.

Central point: *To prevent heart disease, everyone should learn about the ten cardiovascular risk factors and eliminate as many of them as possible.*

1. *Risk Factors That Cannot Be Changed:*

    a. *Increasing Age   —nearly 84% of people who die from heart disease are aged 65 or over.*

    b. *Male Gender—men have greater risk of heart disease than do women prior to age 55.*

    c. *Heredity   —children may have genetic predisposition (tendency) to develop heart disease. Race is also a related consideration; prevalence of hypertension among African Americans is among the highest in the U.S.*

2. *Risk Factors That Can Be Changed:*

    a. *Tobacco Smoke   —About 46.5 million adults and about 28.5% of high school students smoke. Smokers have a heart attack risk more than twice that of nonsmokers.*

    Heart attack risk is about 30% greater for people exposed to secondhand smoke in the home.

    Good news—heart attack risk declines rapidly when a person stops smoking.

    b. *Physical Inactivity   —Regular aerobic exercise strengthens heart muscle, lowers blood cholesterol, moderates stress, and more.*

    60% of Americans are not physically active enough.

    Sustained, vigorous physical activity produces strong reduction in CVD.

c. *High Blood Cholesterol Level   —About 102 million American adults have a total cholesterol level of greater than 200 mg/dl. The higher the level, the greater the risk for heart disease. Drugs and diet can control.*

d. *High Blood Pressure — About 58 million Americans have hypertension, which can seriously damage a person's heart and blood vessels. It can be controlled.*

e. *Diabetes Mellitus —   A debilitating chronic disease; over 17 million Americans have diabetes, which can cause heart and blood vessel damage. It can be controlled.*

f. *Obesity and Overweight   —Over 60 % of American adults are overweight, and 26% are obese. More likely to develop heart disease and stroke.*

3. *Another Risk Factor Contributing to Heart Disease: Unresolved stress over a long period can contribute to heart disease.*

Note that there are ten answers here: one heading, seven risk factors (two that can't be changed, four that can, and one additional risk factor), and two sets of supporting details. Each answer is worth two points.

DISCUSSION QUESTIONS

1. Would you say that your risk of developing heart disease is low, medium, or high? Which of the cardiovascular risk factors mentioned in the selection do you possess? On the basis of what you have learned in this reading, is there anything you can do to decrease your risk of developing heart disease? Explain.

2. The selection lists the benefits that come with physical activity but states that health professionals are amazed that so many Americans refuse to become regularly active. In your view, why don't more Americans get the recommended amount of physical activity?

3. The selection mentions that people who are under stress are more likely to develop negative dependence behaviors—for example, smoking, under-activity, poor dietary practices—to deal with the stress. What are some positive ways that you know of that people use to cope with stress? Have you tried any of them? If so, have you found them to be effective? Why or why not?

4. The selection states that the best time to start protecting and improving one's cardiovascular system is early in life. We can't go back in time, but we can help to influence the younger generation. How can we encourage the younger generation to develop heart-healthy habits? What negative influences must we overcome to do so?

Note: Writing assignments for this selection appear on page 566.

Check Your Performance **CARDIOVASCULAR DISEASE**

Activity	Number Right	Points	Score
READING COMPREHENSION QUESTIONS			
Vocabulary in Context (2 items)	_____	× 4 =	_____
Central Point and Main Ideas (3 items)	_____	× 4 =	_____
Supporting Details (2 items)	_____	× 4 =	_____
Transitions (1 item)	_____	× 4 =	_____
Patterns of Organization (1 item)	_____	× 4 =	_____
Inferences (3 items)	_____	× 4 =	_____
Purpose and Tone (2 items)	_____	× 4 =	_____
Argument (2 items)	_____	× 4 =	_____
Critical Reading (4 items)	_____	× 4 =	_____
ACTIVE READING AND STUDY (10 items)	_____	× 2 =	_____
	TOTAL SCORE =		_____%

Enter your total score into the **Reading Performance Chart: Ten Reading Selections** on the inside back cover.

3

Collective Behavior
Michael Hughes and Carolyn J. Kroehler

Preview

You would probably agree with the statement that people act differently in public than they do in private. But as this reading makes evident, "public" takes many forms. Each of those forms has its unique effect on the individual's behavior.

Words to Watch

spontaneous (1): occurring seemingly without cause
folkway (8): traditional behavior or way of life of a community of people
dissemination (11): spread
psychogenic (11): originating in the mind
pathogenic (11): capable of causing disease
aggregation (14): gathering
volatile (14): likely to become violent

1 Rapid social change and the upheavals that result from it also make it more likely that people will engage in collective behaviors—ways of thinking, feeling, and acting that develop among a large number of people and that are relatively spontaneous° and unstructured. And collective behaviors can result in social change. From earliest recorded times, people have thrown themselves into a great many types of mass behavior, including social unrest, riots, manias, fads, panics, mass flights, lynchings, religious revivals, and rebellions. Consequently, no discussion of social change can neglect collective behavior.

VARIETIES OF COLLECTIVE BEHAVIOR

2 Collective behavior comes in a great many forms. To gain a better appreciation for the impact such behavior has on our lives, let us consider a number of

varieties of collective behavior at greater length.

Rumors

3   A rumor is a difficult-to-verify piece of information transmitted from person to person in relatively rapid fashion. We often think of rumors as providing false information, and in many cases this is true. But they also may be accurate or, at the very least, contain a kernel of truth. Rumors typically arise in situations in which people lack information or distrust the official sources of information. Rumors are both a form of collective behavior and an important element in most other forms of collective behavior.

4   Periods of anxiety and tension provide an environment in which rumors proliferate. After the September 11, 2001 terrorist attacks, rumors flew about a wide range of topics, including the sorts of biological and chemical weapons terrorists might unleash as well as the best antidotes to such weapons. Official information competed with rapidly circulating advice about sealing doors and windows with duct tape and laying in supplies of gas masks, food, water, and medicines.

5   Rumors tend to evolve and take on new details as people interact and talk, and with the Internet they can spread around the world in the time it takes to walk to your neighbor's house to gossip. The Internet also can be used to try to control rumors. A high-school student who is the subject of gossip may use a Web log—an online journal—to try to set the story straight or at least to provide readers with an alternate view of the story.

6   One type of rumor that is particularly common involves alleged contamination. In 2003 the Centers for Disease Control issued a list of currently circulating hoaxes and rumors that included e-mails about tainted cola products, poisonous perfume samples that arrive in the mail, underarm antiperspirants and deodorants that cause breast cancer, a child who died of a heroin overdose from a needle found on a playground, and online offers for antibiotics that protect users against bioterrorism.

Fashions and Fads

7   The uniformity of dress on college campuses is sometimes so extreme as to make it appear that students are required to wear certain uniforms. Black clunky-heeled platform shoes and black dresses are in for women one year; jeans, hiking boots, and flannel shirts another. Contemporary society is full of both fashions and fads. What is the difference?

8   A fashion is a folkway° that lasts for a short time and enjoys widespread acceptance within society. Fashion finds expression in styles of clothing, automobile design, and home architecture.

9   A fad is a folkway that lasts for a short time and enjoys acceptance among only a segment of the population. Fads often appear in amusements, new games, popular tunes, dance steps, health practices, movie idols, and slang. Adolescents are particularly prone toward fads; the fads provide a sense of identity and belonging with aspects of dress and gesture serving as signs of *in-group* or *out-group* status.

10   Some fads become all-consuming passions. Such fads are called crazes. Financial speculation has at times assumed craze proportions. In the famous Holland tulip mania in the 17th century, the value of tulip bulbs came to exceed their weight in gold; the bulbs were not planted, but bought and sold among speculators.

Mass Hysteria

11 Mass hysteria refers to the rapid dissemination° of behaviors involving contagious anxiety, usually associated with some mysterious force. For instance, medieval witch hunts rested on the belief that many social ills were caused by witches. Likewise, some "epidemics" of assembly-line illness—*mass psychogenic° illness*—derive from hysterical contagion. In recent years, episodes of mass psychogenic illness have occurred in U.S. plants packing frozen fish, punching computer cards, assembling electrical switches, sewing shoes, making dresses, and manufacturing lawn furniture. In most cases the workers complain of headache, nausea, dizziness, weakness, and breathing difficulty. However, health authorities, including physicians, industrial hygienists, and toxicologists, find no bacteria, virus, toxic material, or other pathogenic° agent to explain the symptoms. Mass psychogenic illness is usually a collective response to severe stress.

Panic

12 Panic involves irrational and uncoordinated but collective actions among people induced by the presence of an immediate, severe threat. For example, people commonly flee from a catastrophe such as a fire or flood. The behavior is collective because social interaction intensifies people's fright.

13 As with other forms of collective behavior, panics can be greatly amplified by modern information technologies. When the SARS (severe acute respiratory syndrome) epidemic spread from China to other countries in 2003, an "information epidemic" fueled a panic that affected the lives of millions of people. Although the total number of people who died from SARS worldwide was smaller than the number of people who die from choking on small objects every year in the United States, the panic about the disease resulted in economic losses in Asia of an estimated $30 billion. As Rothkopf explained the situation, "A few facts, mixed with fear, speculation and rumor, amplified and relayed swiftly worldwide by modern information technologies, affected national and international economies, politics, and even security in ways that are utterly disproportionate to the root realities." Rothkopf traces the cause of an information epidemic to mainstream media, specialist media, and Internet sites combined with "informal" media, including pagers, e-mail, faxes, cell phones, and text messaging, all of which may be transmitting rumor, interpretation, propaganda, or fact. Other information epidemics fueling panics and having significant economic consequences in recent years were associated with the sniper attacks in Washington, D.C.; the effect of the threat of another Gulf war on travel in that area; and the Enron company financial scandal.

Crowds

14 The crowd is one of the most familiar and at times spectacular forms of collective behavior. It is a temporary, relatively unorganized gathering of people in close physical proximity. Because a wide range of behavior is encompassed by the concept, sociologist Herbert Blumer distinguishes four basic types of crowds. The first, a casual crowd, is a collection of people who have little in common except that they may be viewing a common event, such as looking through a department store window, visiting a museum, or attending a movie. The second, a conventional

crowd, entails a number of people who have assembled for some specific purpose and who typically act in accordance with established norms, such as people attending a baseball game or a concert. The third, an expressive crowd, is an aggregation° of people who have gotten together for self-stimulation and personal gratification, such as occurs at a religious revival or a rock festival. And the fourth, an acting crowd, is an excited, volatile° collection of people who are engaged in rioting, looting, or other forms of aggressive behavior in which established norms carry little weight.

15   Although crowds differ from one another in many ways, they also share a number of characteristics:

1. *Suggestibility.* The behavior of crowd members is not guided by conventional norms. Individuals are usually more susceptible to images, directions, and propositions emanating from others.

2. *Deindividuation.* Deindividuation is a psychological state of diminished identity and self-awareness. People feel less inhibited in committing disapproved acts in a group.

3. *Invulnerability.* In crowd settings, individuals often acquire a sense that they are more powerful and invincible than they are in routine, everyday settings. Moreover, they feel that social control mechanisms are less likely to be applied to them as individuals, resulting in an increase in behavior not normally approved by society, such as aggression, risk taking, self-enhancement, stealing, vandalism, and the uttering of obscenities.

READING COMPREHENSION QUESTIONS

Vocabulary in Context

___C___ 1. In the excerpt below, the word *proliferate* (prə-lĭf′ə-rāt′) means
A. come into the open.
B. decrease.
C. increase.
D. educate.

> Context clue: If, after September 11, 2001, "rumors flew," what do these words suggest about the frequency of rumors?

"Periods of anxiety and tension provide an environment in which rumors proliferate. After the September 11, 2001 terrorist attacks, rumors flew about a wide range of topics . . ." (Paragraph 4)

___C___ 2. In the excerpt below, the words *emanating from* (ĕm′ə-nāt′ĭng frŭm) mean
A. turning from.
B. kept from.
C. coming from.
D. changing from.

> Individuals receive images, directions, and propositions that come from others.

"The behavior of crowd members is not guided by conventional norms. Individuals are usually more susceptible to images, directions, and propositions emanating from others." (Paragraph 15)

Central Point and Main Ideas

___B___ 3. Which sentence best expresses the central point of the selection?

Answer A covers only paragraphs 11–12. Answer C covers only paragraph 13. Answer D covers only paragraph 1.

A. Mass hysteria and panic are two collective behaviors which involve fear.

B. There are a number of varieties of collective behavior which have an impact on our lives.

C. New technologies such as pagers, e-mail, faxes, cell phones and text messaging tend to amplify speculation and rumor.

D. Mass behavior such as fads and panics are nothing new—in fact, they date from earliest recorded times.

___A___ 4. The main idea of paragraph 13 is expressed in its

A. first sentence.
B. second sentence.
C. third sentence.
D. fourth sentence.

Answers B, C, and D illustrate how modern information technologies amplify panics.

Supporting Details

___C___ 5. According to the selection, one type of rumor that is particularly common involves

A. terrorist attacks.
B. the SARS epidemic of 2003.
C. alleged contamination.
D. financial scandals such as Enron.

See the first sentence in paragraph 6.

___D___ 6. According to the selection, one example of mass hysteria would be

A. a high-school student who uses an online journal to try to set the story straight concerning gossip about himself.

B. the uniformity of dress on college campuses.

C. the response to the sniper attacks in Washington, D.C.

D. workers who complain of headaches, nausea, and breathing difficulties when no pathogenic agent can be found to explain their symptoms.

See paragraph 11. A is an example of a reaction to rumors. B is an example of fashion and fads. C is an example of panic.

Transitions

___D___ 7. The relationship of the second sentence below to the first sentence is one of

A. comparison.
B. illustration.
C. addition.
D. cause and effect.

Cause: From earliest recorded times, people have engaged in many collective behaviors.
Effect: Such behaviors should be discussed.
Cause and effect transition: *Consequently.*

"From earliest recorded times people have thrown themselves into a great many types of mass behavior, including social unrest, riots, manias, fads, panics, mass flights, lynchings, religious revivals, and rebellions. <u>Consequently</u>, no discussion of social change can neglect collective behavior." (Paragraph 1)

___B___ 8. What is the relationship of the second sentence below to the first?
A. Contrast
B. Comparison
C. Cause and effect
D. Addition

> The passage compares assembly-line illnesses with medieval witch hunts. Comparison transition: *Likewise*.

"For instance, medieval witch hunts rested on the belief that many social ills were caused by witches. <u>Likewise</u>, some 'epidemics' of assembly-line illness—mass psychogenic illness—derive from hysterical contagion." (Paragraph 11)

Patterns of Organization

___A___ 9. The main patterns of organization of this selection are list of items and
A. definition and example.
B. comparison.
C. contrast.
D. cause and effect.

> The selection defines and gives examples of various forms of collective behavior.

Inferences

___C___ 10. On the basis of paragraph 4, we can infer that after the terrorist attacks of September 11, 2001,
A. people were wrong to discuss what to do in response to the attacks.
B. official information about the attacks was not as accurate as information from other sources.
C. people were confused and uncertain as to how to react.
D. people were afraid to show any reaction.

Answers A, B, and D are unsupported. The passage details rumors about terrorist weapons and possible ways of responding to them—indications of confusion and uncertainty.

___B___ 11. On the basis of paragraph 11, we can infer that
A. health authorities don't look hard enough to uncover the causes of worker illnesses.
B. assembly-line workers sometimes find their work very stressful.
C. assembly-line workers tend to be mentally ill.
D. until now, assembly-line illnesses have been kept a secret from the general public.

See last sentence of paragraph. If mass psychogenic illness is usually a response to severe stress, then it is logical to conclude that assembly-line workers who experience these illnesses find their work very stressful. Answers A, C, and D are unsupported.

___C___ 12. On the basis of paragraph 13, we can infer that the SARS epidemic of 2003 was
A. one of the worst health disasters ever.
B. deliberately created by China.
C. exaggerated due to the availability of modern information technologies.
D. economically unimportant.

> See sentence 4 in paragraph 13. Answers A and D are contradicted by sentence 3. Answer B is not suggested.

Purpose and Tone

___B___ 13. The main purpose of this selection is to

The authors present
factual information
about the varieties of
collective behavior and
their impact on society
without seeking to
entertain or persuade.

A. entertain people with examples of outrageous rumors and fads.

B. inform people about the varieties of collective behavior and their impact on society.

C. persuade readers to avoid spreading rumors and getting caught up in unruly crowd behavior.

___B___ 14. The authors' tone when discussing crowds is largely

A. scornful.

B. instructive.

C. sarcastic.

D. worried.

The authors teach us about types of crowds and their characteristics.

Argument

15. Label the point of the following argument with a **P** and the two statements of support with an **S**. Label with an **X** the statement that is neither the point nor the support of the argument.

___S___ A. People feel less inhibited in committing disapproved acts when they are part of a group.

Statements A and C
are examples of the
"negative acts" referred
to in statement B.
Statement D is not an
example of negative
crowd behavior.

___P___ B. When people become part of a crowd, they sometimes commit negative acts.

___S___ C. In crowd settings, people sometimes engage in stealing, vandalism, and the uttering of obscenities because they feel invulnerable.

___X___ D. People attend crowded rock festivals and religious gatherings for purposes of self-stimulation and personal gratification.

16. Label the point of the following argument with a **P** and the two statements of support with an **S**. Label with an **X** the statement that is neither the point nor the support of the argument.

___P___ A. Mass hysteria involves people who believe their problems are the result of some mysterious force.

___S___ B. In medieval times, many people believed that social ills were caused by witches.

___X___ C. Health officials investigated cases of assembly-line illness.

___S___ D. In recent years, assembly-line workers believed that they were made ill as the result of packing frozen fish, punching computer cards, and manufacturing lawn furniture.

Statement C is not an example of mass hysteria. Statement B gives a medieval example. Statement D gives a recent example.

Critical Reading

___A___ 17. The paragraph below is made up of
   A. facts.
   B. opinions.
   C. facts and opinions.

The passage makes no judgments and contains no value words.

> "A fashion is a folkway that lasts for a short time and enjoys widespread acceptance within society. Fashion finds expression in styles of clothing, automobile design, and home architecture." (Paragraph 8)

___A___ 18. An advertisement which tells teens that they'll be part of the in-crowd if they wear a particular brand of sunglasses is using the propaganda technique of
   A. bandwagon.
   B. glittering generalities.
   C. plain folks.
   D. testimonial.

The words *part of the in-crowd* signal the bandwagon technique.

___B___ 19. Assembly-line illnesses illustrate the logical fallacy of
   A. either-or *(the argument assumes that there are only two sides to a question).*
   B. false cause *(the argument assumes that the order of events alone shows cause and effect).*
   C. false comparison *(the argument assumes that two things being compared are more alike than they really are).*
   D. straw man *(an argument is made by claiming an opponent holds an extreme position and then opposing that extreme position).*

Assembly-line workers who feel ill erroneously conclude that something in their work environment is making them sick.

___C___ 20. A mother says to her daughter: "I don't care if it's the current style. I didn't wear jeans and flip-flops to class, and neither should you." This statement is an illustration of the logical fallacy of
   A. either-or *(the argument assumes that there are only two sides to a question).*
   B. false cause *(the argument assumes that the order of events alone shows cause and effect).*
   C. false comparison *(the argument assumes that two things being compared are more alike than they really are).*
   D. straw man *(an argument is made by claiming an opponent holds an extreme position and then opposing that extreme position).*

Since fashion standards have changed since the mother's time, the comparison isn't valid.

ACTIVE READING AND STUDY OF A TEXTBOOK SELECTION

Complete the following study notes on the selection. Some items are already filled in for you. *Wording of answers may vary.*

Note: Headings, enumerations, definitions, and examples are the keys to the important ideas in this selection.

Central point: *Collective behaviors—ways of thinking, feeling, and acting that develop among a large number of people and that are relatively spontaneous and unstructured*

Varieties of Collective Behavior:

1. *Rumors—A rumor is a difficult-to-verify piece of information transmitted from person to person in relatively rapid fashion.*

   Ex. —After the 9-11-01 terrorist attacks, rumors flew about biological and chemical weapon attacks. On Internet, rumors spread very quickly.

2. *Fashions and Fads*

   Fashion—a folkway that lasts for a short time and enjoys widespread acceptance within society

   Ex. —Black dresses are "in" for women one year; jeans another.

   Fad—a folkway that lasts for a short time and enjoys acceptance among only a segment of the population

   Ex. —Dance or song

   Adolescents prone to fads; provide a sense of identity and are signs of in-group and out-group status.

   Craze—a fad that is an all-consuming passion

   Ex. —Famous tulip mania in Holland in 17th century

3. *Mass hysteria—refers to the rapid dissemination of behaviors involving contagious anxiety, usually associated with some mysterious force.*

   Ex. —Medieval witch hunts rested on belief that social ills were caused by witches.

Mass psychogenic illness—"epidemics" of assembly-line illness: workers making dresses, for example, complain of nausea, etc.

Usually a collective response to severe stress

4. *Panic—involves irrational and uncoordinated but collective actions among people induced by the presence of an immediate, severe threat.*

   Ex. —People commonly flee from a catastrophe such as flood.

   Another ex.—SARS epidemic in China became an information epidemic causing panic about the disease.

5. *Crowds—temporary, relatively unorganized gatherings of people in close physical proximity*

   Four basic types of crowds:

   a. *Casual crowd—a collection of people who have little in common except that they may be viewing a common event, such as a movie*

   b. *Conventional crowd—a number of people who have assembled for some specific purpose and who typically act in accordance with established norms, such as people attending a baseball game or a concert*

   c. *Expressive crowd—an aggregation of people who have gotten together for self-stimulation and personal gratification, such as occurs at a religious revival or a rock festival*

   d. *Acting crowd—an excited, volatile collection of people engaged in rioting, looting, or other forms of aggressive behavior in which established norms carry little weight*

   Shared characteristics of crowds:

   1. Suggestibility—susceptible to directions, etc.

   2. Deindividuation—people are less inhibited in committing disapproved acts in a group.

   3. Invulnerability—people acquire a sense they are powerful and invincible and may, for example, steal or vandalize as a result.

Note that there are ten answers here: a definition of collective behavior; three examples of collective behavior, with definitions; four types of crowds; and two examples of shared characteristics of crowds. Each answer is worth two points.

DISCUSSION QUESTIONS

1. We have all heard rumors (or seen them on the Internet) and perhaps have helped spread some. What rumors have you heard that later proved to be untrue? What rumors later turned out to be true? After reading this selection, do you have a better idea of which particular subjects or events are likely to give rise to rumors?

2. Reread the author's definitions of "fashion" and "fads" (paragraphs 7–10). What are some current examples of fashions? Of fads? To what extent would you say your own behavior is influenced by fashions or fads? Explain.

3. Have you ever been part of a group that became caught up in a panic or an example of mass hysteria? What was the situation? How did people behave? Were you aware of individuals who tried to either calm the situation or increase others' anxiety?

4. Have you ever personally been involved in some type of crowd behavior? If so, was the experience a positive one—or a negative one? Explain.

Note: Writing assignments for this selection appear on page 567.

Check Your Performance	COLLECTIVE BEHAVIOR		
Activity	*Number Right*	*Points*	*Score*
READING COMPREHENSION QUESTIONS			
Vocabulary in Context (2 items)	_____	× 4 =	_____
Central Point and Main Ideas (2 items)	_____	× 4 =	_____
Supporting Details (2 items)	_____	× 4 =	_____
Transitions (2 items)	_____	× 4 =	_____
Patterns of Organization (1 item)	_____	× 4 =	_____
Inferences (3 items)	_____	× 4 =	_____
Purpose and Tone (2 items)	_____	× 4 =	_____
Argument (2 items)	_____	× 4 =	_____
Critical Reading (4 items)	_____	× 4 =	_____
ACTIVE READING AND STUDY (10 items)	_____	× 2 =	_____
	TOTAL SCORE =		_____%

Enter your total score into the **Reading Performance Chart: Ten Reading Selections** on the inside back cover.

4

Types of Nonverbal Symbols
Michael Drafke

Preview

When we think of "communication," we initially think of language. But as this selection from *The Human Side of Organizations* (Pearson) makes clear, the words we use are only a part—possibly not even the most important part—of how we get our message across. In even the simplest social exchange, our nonverbal behavior does much of our talking for us.

Words to Watch

repertoire (7): types of behavior that a person habitually uses
in conjunction (9): together
rationale (11): set of reasons

1   To be in control of your communications and to always send the message that you want to send, you must first be aware of what type of nonverbal symbols exist. Once you are aware of the types of nonverbal communications that exist, you may focus on the ones that you use. Once you notice the ones you use, you can determine if they are appropriate or not. Here we will explore the following types of nonverbal communication:

- the eyes
- the face and head
- gestures
- touch

Although all of these are important, and they all combine to transmit our total message, some are used more extensively than others. In general, the hands, the face, and especially the eyes are the most expressive.

THE EYES

The eyes may be the single most important area for nonverbal communication.   2

People not only attend to the expressions made with the eyes but also to the amount of eye contact being made. Eye contact is the amount of time you look at another person's eyes, whether or not that person is looking back into your eyes. In general, Americans give more eye contact than they receive when they are listening. In other words, when two Americans are having a conversation, the listener looks at the speaker for a longer time than the speaker looks at the listener. The American speaker glances at the listener for brief periods and then breaks eye contact. The most common way to break eye contact in the United States is to look diagonally down and to the side. As one person speaks, then listens, then speaks, and then listens, the amount of eye contact given to the other person changes from less, to more, to less, to more again. Although the amount of eye contact varies with one's role, it is always of major importance to our communications.

3   Eye contact is important when speaking to individuals or when speaking to groups. Maintaining proper eye contact conveys a message of warmth and concern for the listener. When speaking to a group, give some eye contact to each person (or as many as possible) to show interest in the audience members. In business, making eye contact conveys trust and sincerity. Not making eye contact or making the wrong kind of eye contact can send the wrong message or an undesired one.

4   Eye contact for other than the accepted amount of time can vary from none, to too little, to too much. After reading this section, make a conscious effort to note the eye contact you give others, the eye contact they give you, and the circumstances under which eye contact is made. For example, if someone fails to make eye contact with you, try to determine why he or she did not. It may be that no one eye contact is the perfectly acceptable amount. For example, on the street or in close quarters (for example, in an elevator or while standing in line) or in other situations with strangers, no eye contact is often proper. On the street, anything more than a passing glance can have other meanings (as we shall see in a moment). A concerted effort not to make eye contact on the street can also mean that you do not want to acknowledge someone else's existence (like a beggar). When people you know or work with fail to make eye contact, it could be a signal that they believe they are superior, that they are arrogant, or that they hold you in contempt. Of course, sometimes it just means they are concentrating on a problem or some other thought.

5   Just as no eye contact is sometimes appropriate and other times not, so is a short amount of eye contact. In a room or hall, a short amount of eye contact, two to three seconds, is acceptable. Anything longer can be construed as staring or requires a "hello" or some type of nonverbal substitute. A small amount of eye contact can indicate a withdrawn individual. We may also give less eye contact when asked a question that is embarrassing or one that makes us uncomfortable. When confronted with an accusation, too little eye contact is likely to be perceived as an admission of guilt. However, in some cultures, looking down, and thus giving too little eye contact, is a sign of respect.

6   Giving too much eye contact, in other words, for longer than the accepted time given the situation, sends different messages depending on the circumstances. When speaking to a large group of people, you may give just about as much eye contact to a person as you wish. Otherwise, staring at someone is a

sign of recognition. It is acceptable for friends to look at each other for longer than the situationally acceptable time. If you do not know the person you are staring at, and you both seem to know it, then the message is that you want to know the person (in the case of two members of the opposite sex, or with two women); otherwise you will make that person feel uneasy (it's not polite to stare). Too much eye contact can also be threatening. This is especially true when a man stares at another man. In a work situation, long eye contact indicates anger or defensiveness. An angry subordinate may stare straight into the eyes of his or her boss when speaking, although normally the subordinate would look away. Prolonged eye contact with the boss can also be a challenge to the boss's authority (meaning you either dispute or reject the boss's authority over you). This demonstrates the importance of knowing the message different nonverbal communications send. You would not want to stare at your boss and send a message of anger unless you truly felt that way (and even then you might not want to). Also, as with other levels of eye contact, what is acceptable varies from country to country. Although too much eye contact might be threatening or rude in the United States, in Britain and in other cultures too little eye contact would be rude or impolite.

7   The eyes are extremely important for communication, but they are just one part of the repertoire°. The eyes and face combine to send stronger and more varied messages than either one could separately.

THE FACE AND HEAD

8   Research has identified a minimum of eight eyebrow and forehead positions, a minimum of eight eye and eyelid positions, and at least ten positions for the lower face. All of these are used not only in combination, but in rapid succession. Some of these facial/eye combinations will be described in order to increase your awareness of them.

9   Working in conjunction° with the eyes, the eyebrows are one of the most expressive areas of the face. Quickly raising both eyebrows, an "eyebrow flash," is another way of acknowledging someone. Raising the eyebrows and widening the eyes indicates surprise, astonishment, or even anger. Showing anger with the eyes and eyebrows can be accomplished by lowering the eyebrows and bringing them closer to the middle of the face. An alternative to this is the ability of some people to lower one eyebrow while simultaneously raising the other. More subtle movements and expressions are also possible, as when people squint ever so slightly to indicate interest in something, as if showing their mental focus through their eyes.

10   The mouth is also highly expressive. The most well known of all nonverbal cues involving the mouth is the smile. But the mouth is capable of much more, as most of us know. Tightening the mouth can indicate anger. Biting one side of the lower lip can show apprehension. Opening the mouth and leaving it open can indicate surprise. Turning up one corner of the mouth and tightening the cheek on the same side can be just as effective as saying "Oh, sure" to indicate disbelief. Note two things as you review these nonverbal cues. First, they are commonly used in conjunction with eye, eyebrow, and other gestures. Raising the eyebrows, widening the eyes, and opening the mouth combine to indicate surprise. For more expressiveness we might add movements of the entire head.

11   The most common head movements are nodding and shaking the head to say "Yes" and "No." Nodding the head can mean more than a simple "Yes." When Ray talks and Jeanette listens and nods her head, Jeanette is not only saying "Yes," but she is saying "Yes, I understand you." If Jeanette is now speaking and Ray is listening and nodding his head, then Ray is not only saying "Yes, I understand you"; he is also saying that he agrees. Nodding is so important that it can sometimes be used by you to get a positive reaction from someone who is hesitant to agree with your rationale° or your sales tactics. You cannot, however, just stand there bobbing your head up and down and hope for results. The nod must be used selectively and in conjunction with a persuasive argument; otherwise, you will look like one of those little dogs or figurines some people put in the back windows of their cars. Receiving a head nod is also important and can help you gauge the agreement, or lack thereof, of individuals and of groups. This is especially helpful when speaking to large groups where other, more subtle NVC (nonverbal communication) is not always available.

12   The head can be used to convey other messages besides "Yes," "No," and "I understand." Simply turning your head toward someone indicates the start of communications, whereas turning your head away can convey the end. Turning the head up and to one side can be a sign of haughtiness or indignation. Simply rotating the head to turn an ear to someone indicates an increased interest in hearing what that person has to say. Rotating the head with a slight frown indicates that you do not understand or do not agree with something. Tilting the head while your arms are crossed in front of your chest indicates that you are skeptical. Add a tightening of the mouth with one corner slightly raised, and you can convey displeasure with what the speaker is saying. Again, different areas can be used in combinations to transmit different messages. As with this last example, the hands and arms are often used in these combinations for added or more varied effects.

GESTURES

13   Adding hand and arm gestures to the NVC mix greatly increases our ability to communicate because hand gestures are almost as expressive as facial gestures. Making a fist indicates anger or tension. Wringing your hands shows nervousness. Hands clasped together in front of a person (with the fingers interlaced) can derail a forceful presentation because this gesture is seen as making an appeal or begging. Holding your fingertips together, kissing them, and immediately moving the hand away from the body in an arc is a sign of praise, especially for well-prepared food. Extending the fingers and then touching the index finger to the thumb is the O.K. or "Everything is all right" sign. Holding the hand up at elbow height with the fingers extended and together means "halt" or "stop." Holding the bridge of the nose with the thumb, index, and middle fingers indicates fatigue or a depressed reluctance at having to hear about or handle a situation. An index finger pointed at the temple and rotated indicates that you think someone odd or crazy. Sitting back with the fingers separated and the tips of the fingers of both hands touching demonstrates confidence or contemplation. Standing with your palms on your hips with the

thumb towards the back indicates confidence or aggressiveness. Poking a finger or object into someone's chest is also an aggressive signal. Hands clasped together behind the back indicates confidence and says, "I am in charge." Wagging the index finger back and forth is the same as saying "You were bad" or "You are wrong." Essentially it's an admonition or a sign of caution. Probably the most common hand gesture involving one person is waving hello or goodbye. Other hand gestures involve the arms or two people.

14   Many hand gestures made during a conversation involve the hands and the arms. Holding both hands out with the palms turned up at a 45-degree angle and shrugging the shoulders is telling someone that you don't know something. For example, Mary asks Don where Kassie is, and Don performs the gesture instead of saying "I don't know." Another hand-arm gesture, one that indicates a closed attitude, is crossing both arms in front of your chest. Raising one hand and arm almost level with one's head indicates that the person is strongly emphasizing a point. Raising both hands and arms over the head indicates victory. Other gestures involving the hands and arms are fairly common and well known, but some people use none. Not knowing what to do with their hands, they often put their hands in their pockets. This is not a positive gesture. Worse yet is to have your hands in your pockets and then jingle the coins or keys in them or to put your hands in your suit coat pockets.

15   Some hand and arm gestures involve two people, the most common of which is the handshake. A proper handshake in the United States is one in which the web at the base of your thumb is in contact with the web at the base of the other person's thumb. There should be a firm grip, the palms should not be sweaty, and the elbow is pumped about three to six times. Disinterest is shown when the handshake is weak and limp. When you offer your hand, your fingers should be extended and your hand should be held vertically. Offering the hand with the palm up is a sign of submissiveness, whereas offering the hand with the palm down is a sign of dominance. The handshake is only slightly different when it involves women—the elbow is pumped less often or not at all, but the hand is not released too quickly. For women, the hand is held for 2 to 3 seconds. If a man holds a woman's hand for much longer, it can be taken as a sign of sexual interest. Although the handshake is virtually required during introductions, it is also one of the few forms of touch that is uniformly accepted in business situations.

TOUCH

16   Strict rules govern acceptable ways to touch in organizations. Touch in general is seen as a sign of caring and concern. In business and organizations, touch is generally acceptable when it is to the upper back or to the arm. There are other concerns, though, than where the touch occurs. The length of the touch, the amount of pressure used, any movement while touching, the presence of others, the relationship between the people, and the gender of the person initiating the touch are variables that have subtle distinctions between acceptable and unacceptable.

17   If a man touches a woman and the touch lasts for too long (for more than a few seconds), the touch sends a sexual message. To be safe, a man must also use less pressure than a woman. Touching someone and then moving the hand or

rubbing the person sends a sexual message too strong for most business situations. Although a brief, light touch to the forearm is acceptable when others are present, almost any touch between a man and a woman can have a different or sexual undertone when the two are alone. Touching in hallways, in groups, in meetings, and in public, if done acceptably, can be an asset. Touching between genders in private is often too risky unless both are clear on the meaning. Longtime, close friends, and those leaving on long trips may hug, although this is more common with women than men. Another relationship between people that governs touch is rank. Here, people of higher rank can initiate acceptable touch with those of lower rank. In any of these cases, the safest course is to limit touch to handshakes and to the forearm, and only when others are present and it is appropriate and cannot be misinterpreted.

READING COMPREHENSION QUESTIONS

Vocabulary in Context

_D_ 1. In the sentence below, the word *concerted* (kən-sûr′tĭd) means
   A. careless.
   B. half-hearted.
   C. surprising.
   D. strong.

   If it's natural to look at people on the street, then what kind of effort would you have to make to avoid doing so?

   "A concerted effort not to make eye contact on the street can also mean that you do not want to acknowledge someone else's existence (like a beggar)." (Paragraph 4)

_D_ 2. In the excerpt below, the word *construed* (kən-stroōd′) means
   A. expected.
   B. challenged.
   C. welcomed.
   D. interpreted.

   If someone thinks eye contact is staring, what has he or she done to the eye contact?

   "In a room or hall, a short amount of eye contact, two to three seconds, is acceptable. Anything longer can be construed as staring or requires a 'hello' or some type of nonverbal substitute." (Paragraph 5)

_C_ 3. In the excerpt below, the word *admonition* (ăd′mŏ-nĭsh′ən) means
   A. surprise.
   B. connection.
   C. warning.
   D. gesture.

   Saying to someone, "You were bad" or "You were wrong" is the same as giving that person a warning. *A sign of caution* is a synonym clue.

   "Wagging the index finger back and forth is the same as saying 'You were bad' or 'You are wrong.' Essentially it's an admonition or a sign of caution." (Paragraph 13)

Central Point and Main Ideas

   D   4. Which point best expresses the central point of the selection?

The selection focuses on four kinds of nonverbal communication and the frequency of their use. Answer A covers only paragraph 7. B covers only the first sentence of paragraph 13. C is too narrow because the selection covers more than inappropriateness.

  A. The eyes are extremely important for communication, but they are only one of many methods of nonverbal communication that can be used in certain situations.

  B. It is important to know that hand gestures are almost as expressive as facial gestures.

  C. Many people are unaware that some of the nonverbal symbols they use to communicate are actually inappropriate in certain situations.

  D. There are four kinds of nonverbal communication, but some of them are used more frequently than others.

   A   5. The main idea of paragraph 6 is stated in its

  A. first sentence.
  B. second sentence.
  C. third sentence.
  D. last sentence.

Answers B and C describe different amounts of eye contact. Answer D gives an example of the idea presented in the next-to-last sentence.

   A   6. The main idea of paragraph 12 is stated in its

  A. first sentence.
  B. second sentence.
  C. third sentence.
  D. last sentence.

The second, third, and last sentences illustrate how the head can be used to convey other messages—an idea stated in the first sentence.

   A   7. The main idea of paragraph 13 is stated in its

  A. first sentence.
  B. second sentence.
  C. third sentence.
  D. last sentence.

Answers B and C illustrate types of hand gestures. Answer D gives a general description of other gestures.

   B   8. The implied main idea of the final two paragraphs of the selection is that

  A. in an organizational setting, a man must be careful when touching a woman.

  B. the rules governing acceptable touching in organizational settings depend on several different factors.

  C. touching, if done acceptably, can be an asset.

  D. rank is an important factor which governs touch in organizational settings.

Answers A, C, and D are too narrow because each covers only a part of paragraph 17.

Supporting Details

___C___ 9. According to the selection, prolonged eye contact in a work situation indicates
   A. confusion.
   B. an admission of guilt.   See sentence 8 in paragraph 6.
   C. anger or defensiveness.
   D. recognition.

___B___ 10. According to the selection, head movements are most commonly used to indicate
   A. surprise.
   B. "yes" or "no."   See the first sentence in paragraph 11.
   C. the start of communications.
   D. disagreement or displeasure.

___D___ 11. The selection states that in organizations, touch is generally seen as
   A. an indication of sexual interest.
   B. a way to communicate that one is of a higher rank than another.
   C. inappropriate.
   D. a sign of caring and concern.   See sentence 2 in paragraph 16.

Transitions

___D___ 12. The relationship between the two parts of the sentence below is one of
   A. illustration.
   B. cause and effect.
   C. time.
   D. comparison.

The sentence compares a short amount of eye contact to no eye contact. Comparison transition: *Just as.*

   "Just as no eye contact is sometimes appropriate and other times not, so is a short amount of eye contact." (Paragraph 5)

___B___ 13. The relationship of the second sentence below to the first is one of
   A. illustration.
   B. addition.
   C. time.
   D. cause and effect.

   "You would not want to stare at your boss and send a message of anger unless you truly felt that way (and even then you might not want to). Also, as with other levels of eye contact, what is acceptable varies from country to country." (Paragraph 6)

   Also signals that an additional detail is being presented.

Patterns of Organization

__C__ 14. The main pattern of organization of this selection is

    A. definition and example.

    B. comparison.   The selection lists types of nonverbal symbols.

    C. list of items.

    D. cause and effect.

Inferences

__B__ 15. We can conclude from this selection that

Answers A, C, and D are not indicated in the selection, which emphasizes that the appropriateness of many nonverbal symbols varies according to the situation.

    A. Americans tend to be less aware of the meaning of nonverbal symbols than people in other parts of the world.

    B. when communicating nonverbally, when and where you do something is often just as important as what you do.

    C. the same nonverbal symbols are appropriate for all situations.

    D. skill in communicating nonverbally cannot be taught—it is something you must be born with.

__B__ 16. We can infer from the selection that people who constantly nod in agreement at whatever others say risk being seen as

    A. arrogant and aggressive.   See paragraph 11, sentence 7. The

    B. weak-willed and dependent.   comparison with bobble-head figurines

    C. depressed and reluctant.   suggests that people who constantly nod

    D. guilty.   are weak-willed and dependent.

Purpose and Tone

__A__ 17. The main purpose of this selection is to

    A. inform people of the various types of nonverbal communication and how to use them successfully.

See paragraph 1, which states the purpose of the selection.

    B. entertain people with stories about how some people use nonverbal communication in inappropriate ways.

    C. persuade people that they need to learn to communicate nonverbally far more effectively than they have done before.

__C__ 18. From the tone of the last two paragraphs, we can infer that the author

    A. is critical of the need for strict rules governing acceptable ways to touch in organizations.

    B. is amused by the rules governing acceptable touch in organizations.

    C. accepts the need for strict rules governing acceptable ways to touch in organizations.

    D. rejects the strict rules which govern acceptable touch in organizations.

There is nothing critical, amused, or rejecting about the tone of the last two paragraphs. The author presents the rules in an objective fashion.

Argument

19. Label the point of the following argument with a **P** and the two statements of support with an **S**. Label with an **X** the statement that is neither the point nor the support of the argument.

   _S_ A. Sometimes people don't make eye contact because they are concentrating on a problem or some other thought.

   _P_ B. When people you know or work with fail to make eye contact, it could mean several different things.

   _S_ C. When a person fails to make eye contact with you, it could be a signal that he considers himself superior to you.

   _X_ D. It is interesting to note the eye contact you give to others, the eye contact they give to you, and the circumstances under which eye contact is made.   Answer D does not illustrate a possible meaning of failure to make eye contact. Answers A and C give specific examples of possible meanings.

Critical Reading

  _A_ 20. The statement below is

    A. fact.

    B. opinion.

    C. both fact and opinion.

"In general, the hands, the face, and especially the eyes are the most expressive." (Paragraph 1)   A fact which has been confirmed by research.

ACTIVE READING AND STUDY OF A TEXTBOOK SELECTION

Take brief notes on the selection, writing down two or three important ideas under each of the four subheadings.   *Answers may vary.*

Note: The overall central point, headings, and an enumeration and major details are keys to the important ideas in this selection. The very act of deciding which details to pick out and write down will help you get a sense of all of them.

Central point: *We communicate nonverbally in a number of ways.*

1. The Eyes

— Single most important area for nonverbal communication; people pay attention not only to eye expressions but also to amount of eye contact.

— Eye contact conveys message of warmth and concern for the listener and trust and sincerity in business situations.

— Beware of giving too much eye contact (as to boss or member of opposite sex or someone on the street); it may seem impolite or threatening.

2. The Face and Head

— The eyebrows along with eyes are one of most expressive areas of the face. Quickly raising both eyebrows is a way to acknowledge someone.

— The mouth is highly expressive, with the most well known nonverbal clue being the smile. Tightening the mouth can mean anger; biting one side can mean fear; opening it can mean surprise.

— The most common head movements are nodding and shaking the head to say "Yes" and "No." Use the nod selectively. Many other messages in head movements. Ex.—turning the head away can mean the end of a communication.

3. Gestures

— Hand gestures are almost as expressive as facial gestures. Most common hand gesture is waving hello or goodbye.

— Many hand and arm gestures. Ex.—crossing arms in front of chest expresses a closed attitude.

— Handshake should be firm with elbow pumped about three to six times.

4. Touch

— Strict rules govern acceptable ways to touch in an organization. Touch in general is seen as a sign of caring and concern. In business it is generally acceptable when it is to the upper back or to the arm.

— A touch that lasts too long can have sexual overtones. Another relationship that governs touch is rank, with people of higher rank able to initiate touch with those of lower rank.

Ten answers are required: the central point, two major details (the eyes; the face and head), and seven important supporting ideas: two for eyes, two for face/head, two for gestures, one for touch. Each answer is worth two points. (*Note:* Students' notes will definitely vary. In general, any answer that represents an important idea should receive credit.)

DISCUSSION QUESTIONS

1. What are some of the ways that you (or people you know) communicate nonverbally? What are the messages that you (or they) tend most often to convey? Have these nonverbal messages ever been misunderstood? Explain.

2. What differences does the author note between men's and women's nonverbal communication? What other differences have you noticed? In your opinion, what factors account for these differences?

3. Every culture has its own vocabulary of gestures. The author mentions a few common American gestures, such as indicating "OK!" by making a circle with the thumb and first finger. What are some gestures not mentioned here that you are familiar with, and what do they mean? Are they common to a group of friends, an age group, a nationality, a family, or another kind of group?

4. Now that you have read this selection, are there any forms of nonverbal communication that you would like to be able to use more effectively? In what ways might you benefit if you improved your command of nonverbal communication?

Note: Writing assignments for this selection appear on page 567.

Check Your Performance   **TYPES OF NONVERBAL SYMBOLS**

Activity	Number Right	Points	Score
READING COMPREHENSION QUESTIONS			
Vocabulary in Context (3 items)	_____	× 4 =	_____
Central Point and Main Ideas (5 items)	_____	× 4 =	_____
Supporting Details (3 items)	_____	× 4 =	_____
Transitions (2 items)	_____	× 4 =	_____
Patterns of Organization (1 item)	_____	× 4 =	_____
Inferences (2 items)	_____	× 4 =	_____
Purpose and Tone (2 items)	_____	× 4 =	_____
Argument (1 item)	_____	× 4 =	_____
Critical Reading (1 item)	_____	× 4 =	_____
ACTIVE READING AND STUDY (10 items)	_____	× 2 =	_____
		TOTAL SCORE =	_____%

Enter your total score into the **Reading Performance Chart: Ten Reading Selections** on the inside back cover.

5

Sports: Illustrating the Three Perspectives
Alex Thio

Preview

You think a sporting event is simply a couple of individuals or teams challenging each other? Think again. As this selection from *Sociology: A Brief Introduction* (Allyn and Bacon) makes clear, there is far more going on beneath the surface of a game than immediately meets the eye.

Words to Watch

coercion (chart on next page): force
aesthetic (5): related to beauty
homogeneity (6): being of the same type

1   The influence of sports reaches far and wide. Sports are particularly popular in the leisure-oriented American society. Most of us have had some experience with athletics as participants or spectators. Schools, from elementary to college, provide many sports opportunities. Many newspapers carry more news about sports than about politics, the economy, crime, or practically any other event. Radio and television newscasts rarely go on the air without a sports report. Football, basketball, baseball, and other games are often broadcast in their entirety, preempting regular programming. Sports exert so much influence on our lives that our everyday speech is full of sports imagery: "struck out," "touch base," "ballpark figure," "game plan," "teamwork," "cheap shot," "go all the way," and so on.

2   What, then, is the nature of this powerful aspect of our lives? From the three sociological perspectives, we can

see that sports are beneficial to society in some ways, harmful in other ways, and, like any other social interaction, governed by individuals' definitions of each other's actions.

importance of hard work, playing by the rules, and working as a team player, characteristics that help ensure success in a career and other aspects of life.

Major Perspectives In Sociology		
Perspective	**Focus**	**Insights**
Functionalist	Social order or stability	Society consists of interdependent groups pursuing common goals. Social order is maintained through social consensus, whereby people agree to cooperate in order to contribute to social order.
Conflict (including Feminist theory)	Social conflict or change	Society is made up of conflicting groups, such as women and men, each pursuing their own interests. Social order is maintained through coercion°, whereby social order is imposed by the powerful over the weak, such as how patriarchy is imposed by men on women.
Symbolic interactionist	Interaction between individuals	Society is composed of individuals interpreting each other's behavior. Social order is maintained through constant negotiations between individuals trying to understand each other's actions and reactions.

SPORTS AS BENEFICIAL TO SOCIETY

3 According to the functionalist perspective, sports contribute to the welfare of society by performing at least three major functions.

4 First, sports are conducive to success in other areas of life. Being competitive, sports inspire athletes to do their utmost to win, thereby helping them to develop such qualities as skill and ability, diligence and self-discipline, mental alertness, and physical fitness. These qualities can ensure success in the larger society. In the words of General Douglas MacArthur: "Upon the fields of friendly strife are sown the seeds that, upon other fields, on other days, will bear the fruits of victory." By watching athletes perform, spectators also learn the

5 Second, sports enhance health and happiness. Participants can enjoy a healthy, long life. The health benefit is more than physical. It is also psychological. Runners and joggers, for example, often find that their activity releases tension and anger as well as relieves anxiety and depression. Moreover, many people derive much pleasure from looking on their participation as a form of beauty, an artistic expression, or a way of having a good time with friends. Similarly, sports improve the quality of life for the spectators. Fans can escape their humdrum daily routines or find pleasure in filling their leisure time, as many Americans do when watching baseball, long known as the national pastime. They can savor the aesthetic° pleasure of

watching the excellence, beauty, and creativity in an athlete's performance. The fans can therefore attain greater happiness, life satisfaction, or psychological well-being.

6   Third, sports contribute to social order and stability by serving as an integrating force for society as a whole. Sports are, in effect, a social mechanism for uniting potentially disunited members of society. Through their common interest in a famous athlete or team, people of diverse racial, social, and cultural backgrounds can feel a sense of homogeneity°, community, or intimacy that they can acquire in no other way. Athletes, too, can identify with their fans, their community, and their country.

SPORTS AS HARMFUL TO SOCIETY

7   According to the conflict perspective, sports harm society by serving the interests of the relatively powerful over those of the powerless in at least two ways.

8   First, sports tend to act as an opiate, numbing the masses' sense of dissatisfaction with capitalist society. Involvement in sports as spectators tends to distract low-paid or unemployed workers from their tedious and dehumanizing jobs or frustrating joblessness. At the same time, sports tend to promote what Marx called "false consciousness," attitudes that support the established society rather than question it. The mostly working-class "soccer hooligans" in Great Britain are a good example. After their team loses in international soccer games, they often show "an exaggerated, embarrassing patriotism, a violent nationalism," by attacking foreigners. To divert their citizens'

attention from their miserable lives, governments of many poor countries also seize any opportunity that arises to whip up the masses into a frenzy of patriotic support for their teams. Such a nationalistic frenzy can be carried to extremes, as it was in 1969 when Honduras and El Salvador went to war against each other after a World Cup soccer match. All this serves to maintain the capitalist system by which the rich and powerful exploit the masses.

9   Second, sports reinforce social, gender, and racial inequalities in society. With regard to social inequality, the overemphasis on competition and winning has caused the loss of something all participants can enjoy equally— namely, the original elements of play and fun in sporting activities. This has turned many people into "couch potatoes," who spend more time watching than playing sports. Sports, then, have become big business, with powerful owners of professional teams exploiting the public and government. Aside from making enormous sums of money from the fans, team owners receive many tax breaks while enjoying the enviable position of being the only self-regulated (in effect, unregulated) monopoly in the nation. Team owners have further professionalized and bureaucratized sports. This, in turn, has led to an elitist system in which a very tiny group of owners and players become tycoons and superstars, while a huge number of potential players are transformed into mere spectators.

10   It is true that over the last two decades, sports participation among women has risen sharply, thanks to the women's liberation movement and the 1972 law that prohibits sex discrimination in school sports. Nevertheless, in most colleges and universities, more funds

continue to be spent on men's sports, especially football and basketball, than on women's athletic programs. Because of gender bias, men are even more likely than women to get top management and coaching jobs in women's programs. The sports arena is still considered a "man's world" in which women's leadership skills are devalued. Even the skills of superb women athletes are discounted by the media, which often describe female athletes as "pretty," "slim," "attractive," "gracious," and "lovely," as opposed to male athletes who are "brilliant," "cool," "courageous," "great," and "tough." In glorifying masculinity, sports further encourage male athletes to commit rape, sexual harassment, and physical abuse.

11   On the surface, the large number of remarkably successful African American athletes in basketball and football today may cast doubt on the existence of racial inequality in sports. But African Americans do suffer from racism in some ways, as indicated by the virtual absence of blacks in top positions as owners, managers, and coaches of professional teams.

12   Far more significantly, however, sports may help perpetuate the relatively high rate of poverty among African Americans. Traditionally, severe, widespread job discrimination has caused many poor African American youths to work extremely hard to develop athletic skills in order to make it in college and professional sports, which explains why most of the best athletes in the country are African American. Today, the enormous attention given by the white-dominated media to African American superstars further encourages many poor African American youths to give their all to athletics. But this intense concentration on sports has diverted attention

from academic work. This is tragic because, given the same hard work, it is far easier to become a professional in business, government, education, or any other field. The chances of becoming a professional athlete are extremely small. Only 1 or 2 percent of high school players with college athletic scholarships will end up in professional sports, while nearly 100 percent of their nonathlete peers with scholarships for academic achievement will become professionals in other, nonathletic fields. Understandably, the late black tennis star Arthur Ashe urged African American youths to spend two hours in the library for every hour spent on the athletic field.

SPORTS AS SYMBOLIC INTERACTION

While the functionalist and conflict 13 perspectives focus on the larger societal issues of sports that affect most people, symbolic interactionism homes in on the smaller, immediate issue of how athletes—or other individuals involved in a sport, such as coaches and fans—behave. According to this third perspective, if we define a situation as real, it is real in its consequences. Thus, if athletes define a game as one that they will win, they will likely win it. This may explain why Tiger Woods is currently the world's greatest golfer. After watching many golfers being interviewed on TV, hockey legend Wayne Gretzky had this observation: "Most golfers can't believe they won. Tiger sounds like he expected to win or can't believe he didn't." Let's take a closer look at how definition influences performance.

Great coaches know that they can get 14 their athletes to perform well by drumming certain ideas into their heads.

Foremost is the idea that the players are winners, so that they will think only of winning and never about the possibility of losing. Chances are high that they indeed will win because the image of themselves as winners will force them to concentrate only on the moves that ensure winning. This is basically the technique Jack Nicklaus, perhaps the greatest golfer of the past several decades, used to enhance his performance. Before every shot, he formed a mental picture in which he saw three things: (1) the target area the ball would land in, (2) the flight path of the ball to the target area, and (3) himself using the appropriate swing for that particular shot. In short, if athletes define themselves as winners, they are more likely to win. By the same token, if athletes define themselves as losers, they will very likely lose.

15   Whatever the content of self-definition, it does not necessarily come from within the person. It is more likely to originate from social interaction. Children under age 10, for example, often evaluate how good or bad they are at a sport based on what their significant others (parents, teachers, or coaches) say to them. Thus, children describe themselves in ways such as "I know I am a good runner because my mom says I am" and "I don't think that I'm a very good soccer player because my coach is always yelling at me."

16   Indeed, how others see us when they interact with us can shape how we define ourselves. But just as we often define our self-definition from our social environment, others also develop their image of us from their environment. In interacting with an African American athlete, for example, a coach tends to stereotype the athlete as naturally gifted in sports. This stereotype, part of the popular belief about African Americans in U.S. society, has a significant impact on the coach's interaction with the African American athlete. Most commonly, the coach will impose a higher standard of performance on an African American athlete than on a white athlete. And the African American athlete will be forced to work harder to achieve that high standard, which may partly explain why African American athletes usually outshine their white peers on the same team. Similarly, gender bias in the larger society has often led parents and teachers to discourage young women from playing basketball, soccer, and other so-called male sports, defining women who want to compete in these games as unfeminine. As a result, many women have responded by avoiding these sports and choosing the so-called female sports, such as aerobic dancing, swimming, gymnastics, and tennis. The popular definition of some sports as masculine and others as feminine can also influence the spectators. Masculine sports, for example, are more likely to cause fan violence than are feminine sports, such as gymnastics and swimming.

READING COMPREHENSION QUESTIONS

Vocabulary in Context

_D_   1. In the excerpt below, the words *are conducive* (kən-do͞o′sĭv) *to* mean

    A. are unrelated to.
    B. are harmful to.
    C. are critical to.
    D. contribute to.

> If sports "contribute to" the welfare of society, and the second sentence contains one of the ways they do so, then they must contribute to success. The words *contribute to* are a synonym clue.

"According to the functionalist perspective, sports contribute to the welfare of society, performing at least three major functions. First, sports are conducive to success in other areas of life." (Paragraphs 3–4)

_A_   2. In the sentence below, the word *opiate* (ō′pē-ĭt) means

    A. drug.
    B. reward.
    C. exhibition.
    D. punishment.

> Context clue: What would something that numbs a sense probably act like?

"First, sports tend to act as an opiate, numbing the masses' sense of dissatisfaction with capitalist society." (Paragraph 8)

_C_   3. In the excerpt below, the word *enhance* (ĕn-hăns′) means

    A. evaluate.
    B. report.
    C. improve.
    D. remember.

> Since Jack Nicklaus was a great golfer, what would any technique he chose likely do to his performance?

"Foremost is the idea that the players are winners, so that they will think only of winning and never about the possibility of losing. . . . This is basically the technique Jack Nicklaus, perhaps the greatest golfer of the past several decades, used to enhance his performance." (Paragraph 14)

Central Point and Main Ideas

_C_   4. Which sentence best expresses the central point of the selection?

See paragraph 2. Answer A covers only paragraphs 7–12. Answer B is incorrect because the relative benefits and negative effects are not evaluated. Answer D is incorrect because it does not include the three sociological perspectives.

    A. Overall, sports exert a harmful influence upon society because they reinforce social, gender, and racial inequalities.
    B. The benefits of participating in and watching sports far outweigh the negative effects that sports have on society.
    C. Sports are beneficial to society in some ways and harmful in other ways, and are governed by individuals' definitions of each other's actions.
    D. Sports improve the quality of life for some while harming others.

_D_ 5. The sentence that makes up paragraph 3 expresses the main idea of
  A. paragraph 4.
  B. paragraph 5.
  C. paragraph 6.
  D. paragraphs 4, 5, and 6.

> Paragraphs 4, 5, and 6 present and explain the three major functions of sports— the main idea stated in paragraph 3.

_B_ 6. Which of the following sentences expresses the main idea of paragraph 10?
  A. Even though more women are playing sports these days, colleges and universities continue to spend more money on men's athletics.
  B. Although women's participation in sports has risen in the past two decades, women in sports are still discriminated against and devalued.
  C. The sports arena is still considered a man's world.
  D. Even in women's sports, men are more likely than women to get top management and coaching jobs.

> Answer A covers only sentence 2. Answer C covers only sentence 4. Answer D covers only sentence 3.

Supporting Details

_B_ 7. The author states that it is tragic for
  A. African American youths to become involved in professional sports.
  B. African American youths to divert their attention from academic work to sports.
  C. young women to avoid basketball, soccer, and other so-called male sports.
  D. fans to behave violently as a result of sports.

> See sentences 3–5 in paragraph 12.

Transitions

_D_ 8. The relationship of the second sentence below to the first sentence is one of
  A. time.
  B. addition.
  C. cause and effect.
  D. contrast.

> "It is true that over the last two decades, sports participation among women has risen sharply, thanks to the women's liberation movement and the 1972 law that prohibits sex discrimination in school sports. <u>Nevertheless</u>, in most colleges and universities, more funds continue to be spent on men's sports, especially football and basketball, than on women's athletic programs." (Paragraph 10)

> The contrast is between rising sports participation among women and the fact that more funds continue to be spent on men's sports. Contrast transition: *Nevertheless*.

___B___ 9. The relationship of the second sentence below to the first sentence is
one of
    A. illustration.
    B. cause and effect.
    C. contrast.
    D. addition.

> *Cause:* How we think about situations influences those situations.
> *Effect:* If athletes believe they will win, then it is likely that they will win.
> Cause and effect transition: *Thus.*

"According to this third perspective, if we define a situation as real, it is real in its consequences. Thus, if athletes define a game as one that they will win, they will likely win it." (Paragraph 13)

Patterns of Organization

___C___ 10. The pattern of organization of paragraph 1 is
    A. time order.
    B. cause and effect.
    C. list of items.
    D. comparison.

> Paragraph 1 lists ways that sports influence society.

___B___ 11. The main pattern of organization of paragraphs 4–6 is
    A. time order.
    B. list of items.
    C. comparison.
    D. contrast.

> Paragraphs 4–6 list and explain three ways that sports benefit individuals and society.

Inferences

___D___ 12. On the basis of paragraph 4, we can infer that
    A. people who don't play sports won't become successful in life.
    B. watching athletes perform is usually a waste of time.
    C. anyone who plays sports will be successful in life.
    D. competitiveness can be seen as a positive social value.

> Paragraph 4 suggests that competition leads athletes to develop positive qualities which make it likely that they will make positive contributions to society.

Purpose and Tone

___C___ 13. The author's main purpose is to
    A. persuade readers to spend more time on academic pursuits and less time on athletics.
    B. entertain readers with the achievements of great athletes like Tiger Woods and Jack Nicklaus.
    C. inform readers of different sociological perspectives on the role of sports in our society.

> See paragraph 2.

___A___ 14. The general tone of the reading is
    A. objective and straightforward.
    B. light-hearted and comforting.
    C. mocking and prideful.
    D. pessimistic and angry.

> The author presents, in a straightforward manner, three sociological perspectives on sports.

Argument

15. Label the point of the following argument with a **P** and the three statements of support with an **S**.

___S___ A. There are large numbers of successful African American athletes in basketball and football.

___S___ B. The attention paid by the media to African American superstars influences African American youths to pay more attention to sports than academics.

___P___ C. Participating in sports can both help and harm African American youth.

___S___ D. The chances of anyone becoming a professional athlete are extremely small.

Statement A describes a way sports participation can help young African Americans. Statements B and D describe ways sports can harm them.

Critical Reading

___C___ 16. The statement below is

A. a fact.

B. an opinion.

C. both fact and opinion.

The first part of the statement is a verifiable fact. The second part is an opinion (value word: *best*). Other people give different reasons for why many excellent athletes are African American.

"Traditionally, severe, widespread job discrimination has caused many poor African American youths to work extremely hard to develop athletic skills in order to make it in college and professional sports, which explains why most of the best athletes in the country are African American." (Paragraph 12)

___B___ 17. A government which encourages its citizens to demonstrate their patriotism by joining a mass rally in support of its national soccer team is using the propaganda technique of

A. testimonial.

B. bandwagon.

C. glittering generalities.

D. name calling.

The words *joining a mass rally* signal the propaganda technique of bandwagon.

___C___ 18. An automotive company which employs a golf superstar to sell a particular brand of car is using the propaganda technique of

A. plain folks.

B. transfer.

C. testimonial.

D. glittering generalities.

The propaganda technique of testimonial uses famous people such as golf superstars to sell goods and services.

_____A_____ 19. Someone who states that African Americans are better athletes because they do better in sports is illustrating the logical fallacy of

Doing better in sports is the same as being a good athlete.

A. circular reasoning (*a statement repeats itself rather than providing a real supporting reason to back up an argument*).

B. straw man (*an argument is made by claiming an opponent holds an extreme position and then opposing that extreme position*).

C. false cause (*the argument assumes that the order of events alone shows cause and effect*).

D. false comparison (*the argument assumes that two things being compared are more alike than they really are*).

_____C_____ 20. Someone who votes for a political candidate based solely on the candidate's previous success as an athlete is guilty of the fallacy of

The skills needed to be a successful athlete are different from the skills needed to be a successful politician; therefore, the comparison isn't valid.

A. straw man (*an argument is made by claiming an opponent holds an extreme position and then opposing that extreme position*).

B. false cause (*the argument assumes that the order of events alone shows cause and effect*).

C. false comparison (*the argument assumes that two things being compared are more alike than they really are*).

D. circular reasoning (*a statement repeats itself rather than providing a real supporting reason to back up an argument*).

ACTIVE READING AND STUDY OF A TEXTBOOK SELECTION

Complete the following study notes on the selection. Some items and parts of items are already filled in for you.   *Wording of answers may vary.*

Note: Headings, enumerations, definitions, and examples are keys to the important ideas in this selection.

Central point: Three sociological perspectives can help us understand the

significance of sports in our lives.

1. Sports as Beneficial to Society

— Functionalist perspective: Society consists of interdependent groups cooperating

to pursue common goals.

— According to this perspective, sports perform three major functions:

a. Conducive to success in other areas of life.

Ex.—athletes or spectators learn the importance of hard work, playing by

the rules, and teamwork.

b. Enhance health and happiness.

Ex.—physical and emotional benefits for runners. Improved quality of life for spectators.

c. Contribute to social order and stability by serving as an integrating force for society as a whole.

Can bring together people of diverse racial, social, and cultural backgrounds.

2. Sports as Harmful to Society

— Conflict perspective: Society is made up of conflicting groups, such as men and women, each pursuing their own interests.

— According to this perspective, sports harm society by serving the interests of the powerful over the powerless in two ways:

a. Act as an opiate, numbing the masses' sense of dissatisfaction with capitalist society.

Ex.—involvement in sports as spectators distracts low-paid workers from their undesirable jobs.

b. Reinforce social, gender, and racial inequalities in society.

Ex.—people have turned into "couch potatoes" who spend more time watching than playing sports. Sports are big business for benefit of a tiny group of owners and players who become tycoons and superstars.

— Women's programs have expanded, but sports are still a "man's world."

— A few African Americans have benefited, but most sports offer a false hope that perpetuates the high rate of poverty among blacks.

3. Sports as Symbolic Interaction

— Symbolic interactionist perspective: Society is composed of individuals interpreting each other's behavior and constantly negotiating with each other.

— According to this perspective, sports help us understand how we behave.

Ex.—Coaches instill the idea of winning into their players. Players see themselves as winners, so they win.

Ex.—Coaches see African Americans as superior athletes (stereotyping), so they expect more of these athletes, who then outperform white teammates.

Stereotyping also discourages women from participating in "male" sports.

Ten answers are needed: three major details (the three perspectives), five minor details (three ways sports benefit society; two ways they are harmful), and definitions of two perspectives.

DISCUSSION QUESTIONS

1. As the selection makes clear, the influence of sports in our society reaches far and wide. How have sports influenced your life? Would you say that this influence has been positive, negative, or both? Explain.

2. In the selection, the author presents examples of how the positive self-image of certain athletes seems to improve their performance. Looking back on your life so far, do you believe that the image you have (or had) of yourself has ever influenced your behavior? Explain.

3. Do you agree that gender bias is still a factor in sports? What evidence do you have to support your opinion?

4. As is mentioned in the reading, African American athletes dominate much of the sports world. The author mentions a potentially negative consequence— that African American youngsters may focus on the unrealistic goal of becoming a sports star. Without discouraging them completely, what might parents, teachers, and community leaders do to encourage these young people to consider other, more realistic options?

Note: Writing assignments for this selection appear on page 568.

Check Your Performance   SPORTS

Activity	Number Right	Points	Score
READING COMPREHENSION QUESTIONS			
Vocabulary in Context (3 items)	_____	× 4 =	_____
Central Point and Main Ideas (3 items)	_____	× 4 =	_____
Supporting Details (1 item)	_____	× 4 =	_____
Transitions (2 items)	_____	× 4 =	_____
Patterns of Organization (2 items)	_____	× 4 =	_____
Inferences (1 item)	_____	× 4 =	_____
Purpose and Tone (2 items)	_____	× 4 =	_____
Argument (1 item)	_____	× 4 =	_____
Critical Reading (5 items)	_____	× 4 =	_____
ACTIVE READING AND STUDY (10 items)	_____	× 2 =	_____
		TOTAL SCORE =	_____ %

Enter your total score into the **Reading Performance Chart: Ten Reading Selections** on the inside back cover.

6

A Civil War Soldier's Letter to His Wife
Sullivan Ballou

Preview

When the American Civil War began in 1861, citizens on both sides of the conflict were driven by equally passionate convictions. One young volunteer was Sullivan Ballou, a 32-year-old lawyer who joined the Union army shortly after war was declared. On July 14, 1861, he wrote the following letter to his wife, Sarah, as he awaited orders in a camp just outside of Washington, D.C. His letter has achieved fame as both a personal expression of love and a heartfelt statement of one young soldier's devotion to his country. One week after writing the letter, Ballou was killed at the Battle of Bull Run.

Words to Watch

impelled (4): forced
communing (7): sharing my thoughts
wafted (10): passing gently through the air
buffet (11): strike against
frolics (14): playful actions

1   July 14th, 1861

2   Washington, D.C.

3   My very dear Sarah:

4   The indications are very strong that we shall move in a few days—perhaps tomorrow. Lest I should not be able to write you again, I feel impelled° to write lines that may fall under your eye when I shall be no more.

5   Our movement may be one of a few days' duration and full of pleasure—and it may be one of severe conflict and death to me. Not my will, but thine, O God, be done. If it is necessary that I should fall on the battlefield for my

country, I am ready. I have no misgivings about, or lack of confidence in, the cause in which I am engaged, and my courage does not halt or falter. I know how strongly American civilization now leans upon the triumph of the government, and how great a debt we owe to those who went before us through the blood and suffering of the Revolution. And I am willing—perfectly willing—to lay down all my joys in this life, to help maintain this government, and to pay that debt.

6   But, my dear wife, when I know that with my own joys I lay down nearly all of yours, and replace them in this life with cares and sorrows—when, after having eaten for long years the bitter fruit of orphanage myself, I must offer it as their only sustenance to my dear little children—is it weak or dishonorable, while the banner of my purpose floats calmly and proudly in the breeze, that my unbounded love for you, my darling wife and children, should struggle in fierce, though useless, contest with my love of country?

7   I cannot describe to you my feelings on this calm summer night, when two thousand men are sleeping around me, many of them enjoying the last, perhaps, before that of death—and I, suspicious that Death is creeping behind me with his fatal dart, am communing° with God, my country, and thee.

8   I have sought most closely and diligently, and often in my breast, for a wrong motive in thus hazarding the happiness of those I loved, and I could not find one. A pure love of my country and . . . "the name of honor that I love more than I fear death" have called upon me, and I have obeyed.

9   Sarah, my love for you is deathless; it seems to bind me to you with mighty cables that nothing but Omnipotence could break; and yet my love of country comes over me like a strong wind and bears me irresistibly on with all these chains to the battlefield.

10   The memories of the blissful moments I have spent with you come creeping over me, and I feel most gratified to God and to you that I have enjoyed them so long. And hard it is for me to give them up and burn to ashes the hopes of future years, when God willing, we might still have lived and loved together and seen our sons grow up to honorable manhood around us. I have, I know, but few and small claims upon Divine Providence, but something whispers to me—perhaps it is the wafted° prayer of my little Edgar—that I shall return to my loved ones unharmed. If I do not, my dear Sarah, never forget how much I love you, and when my last breath escapes me on the battlefield, it will whisper your name.

11   Forgive my many faults, and the many pains I have caused you. How thoughtless and foolish I have oftentimes been! How gladly would I wash out with my tears every little spot upon your happiness, and struggle with all the misfortune of this world, to shield you and my children from harm. But I cannot. I must watch you from the spirit land and hover near you, while you buffet° the storms with your precious little freight, and wait with sad patience till we meet to part no more.

12   But, O Sarah! If the dead can come back to this earth and flit unseen around those they loved, I shall always be near you; in the garish day and in the darkest night—amidst your happiest scenes and gloomiest hours—always, always; and if there be a soft breeze upon your cheek, it

shall be my breath; or if the cool air fans your throbbing temple, it shall be my spirit passing by.

13   Sarah, do not mourn me dead; think I am gone and wait for thee, for we shall meet again.

14   As for my little boys, they will grow as I have done, and never know a father's love and care. Little Willie is too young to remember me long, and my blue-eyed Edgar will keep my frolics° with him among the dimmest memories of his childhood. Sarah, I have unlimited confidence in your maternal care and your development of their characters. Tell my two mothers I call God's blessing upon them. O Sarah, I wait for you there! Come to me, and lead thither my children.

Sullivan

READING COMPREHENSION QUESTIONS

Vocabulary in Context

___B___ 1. In the excerpt below, the word *sustenance* (sŭs′tə-nəns) means
    A. hope for the future.
    B. nourishment.
    C. happy memories.
    D. concern for someone's welfare.

> Something that is eaten provides nourishment.

> "But, my dear wife, when I know that with my own joys I lay down nearly all of yours, and replace them in this life with cares and sorrows—when, after having eaten for long years the bitter fruit of orphanage myself, I must offer it as their only sustenance to my dear little children . . ." (Paragraph 6)

___B___ 2. In the excerpt below, the word *hazarding* (hăz′ərd-ĭng) means
    A. guessing.
    B. risking.
    C. enjoying.
    D. insuring.

> Ballou's wartime enlistment meant risking the happiness of his wife and children.

> "I have sought most closely and diligently, and often in my breast, for a wrong motive in thus hazarding the happiness of those I loved, and I could not find one." (Paragraph 8)

Answer A covers only one detail from paragraph 5. B covers only one detail from paragraph 6. C covers only a detail from paragraphs 13–14. D is supported throughout with ideas such as finding no "wrong motive" for his choice and "a pure love of my country" (paragraph 8).

Central Point and Main Ideas

_____D_____ 3. Which sentence best expresses the central point of the selection?

    A. The author is willing to suffer as much as other Americans suffered during the Revolution.

    B. The author realizes that if he is killed in battle, his wife and sons will suffer greatly.

    C. The author fully expects to see his wife and sons in eternal life.

    D. The author is willing to sacrifice his life and the happiness of his family to fight for a cause that he believes is just.

_____C_____ 4. The implied main idea of paragraph 14 is that the author

    A. knows that his sons will probably only have dim memories of him.

    B. regrets that his sons will never know a father's love and care.

    C. has confidence that even if he dies in battle, his wife will raise his sons properly so that they all can meet in Heaven.

    D. knows that his wife will need the help of others in raising the couple's two sons should he die in battle.

Answer A covers only sentence 2. Answer B covers only sentence 1. Answer D is contradicted by sentence 3.

Supporting Details

_____C_____ 5. The author believes that he and others owe a great debt to

    A. Divine Providence.

    B. the two thousand men who are sleeping around him.

    C. those who bled and suffered during the Revolution.

    D. President Lincoln.

See sentence 5 in paragraph 5.

_____B_____ 6. The author regrets that his two sons, like him, may

    A. have bitter memories of their father.

    B. never know a father's love and care.

    C. have a weak, unsupportive mother.

    D. be killed in battle.

See the first sentence of paragraph 14.

Transitions

_____D_____ 7. The relationship between the two sentences below is one of

    A. addition.

    B. cause and effect.

    C. comparison.

    D. contrast.

The author contrasts his desire to struggle for his family's happiness and shield them from harm with the realization that he cannot. Contrast transition: _But_.

"How gladly would I wash out with my tears every little spot upon your happiness, and struggle with all the misfortunes of this world, to shield you and my children from harm. **But** I cannot." (Paragraph 11)

Patterns of Organization

___B___   8. Paragraph 5 compares

Ballou is willing to
suffer and die for his
country just as
Americans did during
the Revolution.

A. American civilization as it is now with the way it used to be.

B. the author's willingness to die for his country with the sacrifices of those who suffered and died before him.

C. the author's own desires with those of his wife and children.

D. the author's debts with those who came before him.

___C___   9. This selection mainly

The focus
of the selection is upon
the personal sacrifices
involved in the author's
fight to preserve his
country. Answers A, B,
and D are not support-
ed because, except for a passing reference to the Revolution, there is no mention of those topics.

A. lists reasons why the author believes that the Union cause is just.

B. presents a series of historical events in time order.

C. contrasts the author's love of his country with the personal sacrifices involved in fighting to preserve his country.

D. compares his wife's support for the cause with his own.

Inferences

___B___ 10. In paragraph 6, the author wants his wife to know that

Answers A, C, and D
are not supported.
Ballou states that
in laying down his
joys, he also lays
down nearly all of his
family's joys—an expression of regret.

A. he considers himself weak and dishonorable.

B. he regrets that his commitment to the Union cause may hurt his family.

C. he is as proud and calm as the banner which flies nearby.

D. his love of country is useless.

___C___ 11. The phrase "and I, suspicious that Death is creeping behind me with his

The author is a soldier
in time of war;
therefore, it is logical
to infer that he
suspects that he may
soon die in battle.

fatal dart" suggests that the author

A. feels he will be struck with a dart.

B. believes that one of his own men will be responsible for his death.

C. suspects that he might not have long to live.

D. is naturally very suspicious.

___A___ 12. The "chains" that the author mentions in paragraph 9 refer to

We can infer that the
"chains" are another
word for the "cables"
which bind the author
to his wife.

A. the ties of love that connect him to his wife.

B. the way that slaves were routinely treated in the Confederacy.

C. the love that the author feels for his country.

D. his unwillingness to go to the battlefield.

___D___ 13. In paragraph 14, the author concludes that

A. he was raised by two women.

B. his sons will remember him forever.

C. his sons will have bitter memories of him for leaving them fatherless.

D. due to his wife's influence, his sons will turn out well.

See the third sentence of paragraph 14.
All the other answers are unsupported.

Ballou **B** 14. On the basis of paragraphs 11 through 14, we can infer that the author
refers to reunion after A. believes that his family might be better off without him.
death in paragraphs 13
and 14. Note phrases B. believes that he and his family will be reunited after death.
such as *I . . . wait for* C. believes that the dead are powerless to help the living.
thee, we shall meet
again, and *Come to me.* D. knows that his children will always remember him.

D 15. A reasonable conclusion we can draw from the reading is that

Answers A, B, and C A. the author is bitter about being forced to choose between his family
are unsupported. The focus and his country.
of the reading is the
author's belief that B. the author knows that his wife and children can never understand
duty to his country must his reasons for fighting.
outweigh his and his C. few men actually shared the author's belief in the Union cause.
family's personal
happiness. Note refer- D. the author believes that his duty to his country must outweigh his
ences such as the "fierce, personal happiness and that of his family.
though useless, contest" between his love for his wife (paragraph 6) and his love for his country and

Purpose and Tone that his love of his country "bears me irresistibly on" (paragraph 9).

A 16. The main purpose of this selection is to

The author neither A. inform Ballou's wife both of his love for her and his need to fight
tries to persuade his for a cause which he believes is just.
wife to change her
mind nor tells B. persuade his wife to change her mind about her support for the
amusing stories. Union cause.

C. entertain his wife with amusing stories of life in an army camp.

D 17. The tone of this selection can be described as

A. nostalgic and bitter.

B. affectionate and instructive. The author reveals his love for his wife
in language that is profoundly serious.
C. uncertain and worried.

D. loving and serious.

Argument

18. Label the point of the following argument with a **P** and the three
statements of support with an **S**.

S A. In paragraph 6, Ballou speaks of his "unbounded love" for his
wife.

S B. Toward the end of the letter, Ballou tells his wife that if the
dead can come back to this earth, he will always be near her.

P C. In this letter, Ballou seeks to reassure his wife of his profound
love for her.

S D. In paragraph 10, Ballou tells his wife that when his last breath
escapes him on the battlefield, it will whisper her name.

Answers A, B, and D are examples of
ways Ballou tries to reassure his wife.

Critical Reading

___A___ 19. The sentence below is one of

    A. fact.

    B. opinion.

> It is a fact that Ballou feels impelled to write to his wife, in case he should be killed and not be able to communicate with her again.

> "Lest I should not be able to write you again, I feel impelled to write lines that may fall under your eye when I shall be no more." (Paragraph 4)

___B___ 20. A housing development near the site of a major Civil War battlefield is called "Liberty Acres." What propaganda technique did the developer use in naming this development?

    A. testimonial.

    B. transfer.

    C. plain folks.

    D. bandwagon.

> The developer seeks to transfer the patriotic feelings aroused by the nearby battlefield to his housing project.

SUMMARIZING

Add the ideas needed to complete the following summary of "A Civil War Soldier's Letter to His Wife."   *Wording of answers may vary.*

Ballou begins his letter by telling his wife that the Union Army will probably move soon. Fearing that he may not be able to write to her again, he says that he is willing to lay down his life for a cause that he feels is just, but struggles with the thought that in laying down his own joys, he must also

See paragraph 6. _____*lay down nearly all of hers*_____ and leave for his children only

See paragraph 6. the _____*bitter fruit of orphanage*_____.

He goes on to say that even though his love for his wife is deathless, his

See paragraph 9. love of country bears him on *irresistibly* **or** *to the battlefield*. He tells his wife that should he die in battle, his last thoughts will be of her. He urges her to forgive him his faults and wishes that he could make her happy and shield

See paragraph 11, sentence 5. her and his children from harm. Unable to do that, he will instead ___*watch*___ _____*them from the spirit land*_____ and wait with sad patience until they meet again.

See paragraph 14, sentence 3. He concludes by telling her that he has unlimited ___*confidence*___ in her maternal care and ability to develop their sons' characters. He waits for her and expects her to lead his children to him.

DISCUSSION QUESTIONS

1. What does Sullivan Ballou's letter reveal about his character and principles? Does he deserve to be called a hero? Why or why not?

2. Do you agree with Sullivan Ballou's decision to fight for what he believed in, even though it meant risking the happiness and security of his wife and children? Why or why not?

3. The letter makes clear that author Sullivan Ballou believed he was carrying out a tradition of sacrifice in the defense of liberty that others had begun during the American Revolution. Do you believe that the recent wars in which America has been engaged continue this tradition—or depart from it? Explain.

4. Under what circumstances, if any, would you be willing to sacrifice your life for a cause?

Note: Writing assignments for this selection appear on page 568.

Check Your Performance	A CIVIL WAR SOLDIER'S LETTER		
Activity	*Number Right*	*Points*	*Score*
READING COMPREHENSION QUESTIONS			
Vocabulary in Context (2 items)	_____	× 4 =	_____
Central Point and Main Ideas (2 items)	_____	× 4 =	_____
Supporting Details (2 items)	_____	× 4 =	_____
Transitions (1 item)	_____	× 4 =	_____
Patterns of Organization (2 items)	_____	× 4 =	_____
Inferences (6 items)	_____	× 4 =	_____
Purpose and Tone (2 items)	_____	× 4 =	_____
Argument (1 item)	_____	× 4 =	_____
Critical Reading (2 items)	_____	× 4 =	_____
SUMMARIZING (5 items)	_____	× 4 =	_____
		TOTAL SCORE =	_____ %

Enter your total score into the **Reading Performance Chart: Ten Reading Selections** on the inside back cover.

7

Single-Sex Schools: An Old Idea Whose Time Has Come
Diane Urbina

Preview

> What happens when girls and boys are educated separately? According to many researchers, the results include better grades, stronger self-confidence, and more fulfilling careers. This essay argues that single-sex schools should be an option available to all students, not just those attending private schools.

Words to Watch

> *quaint* (1): charmingly old-fashioned
> *ensuing* (6): following
> *guffawing* (9): laughing coarsely
> *preening* (9): grooming oneself
> *alluring* (11): fascinating
> *demeaning* (11): insulting

1 In 1972, single-sex public schools were made illegal by Title IX, the federal law that prohibits sex discrimination in education. Since that time, boys' and girls' schools (and men's and women's colleges) have been limited to private schools whose high tuition fees are paid by students and their parents. The result is that single-sex education has become available to only a small percentage of students, and primarily those from well-off families. For most people, single-sex schools are thought of as something antique: a quaint° remnant of the distant past. And that's a shame. For there is increasingly persuasive evidence that single-sex education offers students— particularly girls—advantages that they cannot get in co-ed settings.

2 It has been demonstrated time and

time again that students who attend single-sex schools perform better academically. In the biggest study of its kind, researchers in Australia measured the academic performance of 270,000 students over a period of 20 years. The boys and girls who attended single-sex schools performed between 15 and 22 percentage points higher on standardized tests than students attending co-ed schools. A separate study in Britain looked at 979 elementary schools and 2954 high schools. Its results showed that the highest-achieving students were girls in single-sex schools, followed by girls in co-ed schools. Next came boys in single-sex schools. The lowest-achieving group was made up of boys in co-ed schools. Another study showed that girls who attend all-girl high schools are six times more likely to major in math or science in college.

3   Why would students perform better when in school with only those of their own gender? Researchers, teachers, and the students themselves have offered a variety of explanations. Some of the most convincing arguments have come from David Sadker and the late Myra Sadker, social scientists who spent twenty years looking at gender bias in education. They are the authors of *Failing at Fairness: How Our Schools Cheat Girls.* Although as the title suggests, the Sadkers' findings focus on how girls are short-changed by co-educational schools, they suggest that boys as well are better served by single-sex schools.

4   The advantages of single-gender schools are entangled and difficult to separate. A clearly defined one, however, is that girls and boys literally learn differently. This is not the same as the erroneous idea that boys and girls are "by nature" better suited to different fields of study (and, later, careers). That belief is a loaded one that has been used as a weapon against granting equal opportunities in education and employment. And the fact is *not* that boys are "just better" at math and science, while girls are "just better" at English and foreign languages.

5   Why, then, do standardized tests seem to show that boys have the edge in some fields and girls in others? There are several factors at play here. First, boys mature more slowly. According to Dr. Leonard Sax, author of *Why Gender Matters,* the part of the brain that governs language in a typical five-year-old boy is two or three years less developed than that of a typical five-year old girl. An average 14-year-old boy is even further behind—four or five years.

6   Eventually the boy's language ability catches up with the girl's, but it's easy to see that in those ensuing° years a lot of problems can occur in the classroom. Girls, typically, learn to read earlier and more easily. Boys are pushed to learn to read at an age when many of them are unprepared to do so, and later, to keep up with their female classmates. The results are ones almost everyone has observed: lots of boys who dislike reading and think they're no good at it, and lots of people who take it for granted that girls are "just better" at reading, writing, and other language skills.

7   And what about the girls? Again, according to Sax and other researchers, while girls' brains are on the fast track to develop their language centers, they are on a less hurried schedule to develop the areas that govern spatial relationships and geometry. These areas in boys' brains mature more quickly. The result? Girls who are thrown together with boys in school quickly conclude that they're "dumb at math and science."

8   In single-sex schools, the classroom curriculum could be designed with girls' and boys' learning differences in mind. In reading class, boys would be expected to keep pace with other boys, not with girls who seem impossibly more advanced. They could concentrate on reading material of particular interest to boys of their ages, rather than the stories and literature that are often selected by (mostly female) teachers for their (mostly female) enthusiastic readers. Girls could be introduced to math and science concepts in ways that particularly appeal to them. Girls are typically less interested in pure math at an early age, but they often enjoy learning the practical, problem-solving aspects of math. Teachers who understood and could appeal to the boys' or girls' learning style would have a far better chance of reaching more students than those who are trying to do "one size fits all" teaching.

9   Another great advantage of single-sex schools is that they take into account a very basic fact of life: Boys and girls act differently in each other's presence. Anyone who has observed a group of quietly talking boys turn into posturing, shoving, guffawing° loudmouths when girls come into view, or a group of sensible girls start giggling, shrieking, and preening° when boys approach, recognizes the truth of this statement.

10   There's nothing wrong with this flirting, attention-getting behavior. It's as old as the Neanderthals, and nothing is going to keep people from flirting with those whom they find attractive. The problem is that this perfectly normal social behavior creates at least two serious obstacles to learning. The first is simple: Flirting takes up a lot of time and energy that could be better used in the classroom. It's terribly difficult to concentrate on the difference between *ser* and *estar* in Spanish class when you're trying to figure out how to accidentally bump into the hunk in the second row after class. And boys and girls being boys and girls, such social plotting often becomes the focus of the school day. Both genders burn up the phone lines at night, not comparing notes on classes, but on who said what to whom and if anyone has a date for Saturday night.

11   The second, and a related, problem is that the presence of the opposite sex often influences students to act, well, stupid. Think again about the first point raised in this paper—the misconception that girls are naturally "good" at reading but "bad" at math, with the opposite being true for boys. If students believe that, then that "badness" becomes a sexual characteristic, just as a girl's curvy figure or a boy's deep voice is. A girl may think she seems "girlier," more feminine, more attractive, if she makes a point of being clueless in math class. A boy may think he's more macho, more alluring° to girls, if he loudly proclaims that he hates to read. As a result, students may deliberately flaunt their weaknesses in order to impress the opposite sex. In general, mixed classes tend to encourage such potentially harmful gender differences. In the presence of guys, many girls give in to the stereotype that says girls are "nice," quiet, passive, and non-athletic. Around girls, guys feel compelled to be "jocks," noisy, disruptive, and overbearing. In a single-sex school, none of this behavior would be necessary. Students could concentrate on learning, rather than competing with each other for the attention of a cute guy or girl, or demeaning° him- or herself in order to catch someone's eye. They could

develop their individual talents without the constant concern about what effect they were having on the cute girl or guy in the next seat.

12   A final reason that single-sex schools are advantageous concerns the behavior of teachers. As the Sadkers were compiling their 20 years of research, they took many hours of videotape of classrooms in action. When they played those tapes back, many of the teachers were surprised—and horrified—by what they saw. A few examples:

- Boys were eight times more likely to call out in class without raising their hands. In general, teachers accepted their behavior.

- Teachers were twice as likely to pick out boys in the class as role models.

- When boys raised their hands, they were five times more likely to be called on than girls.

- Teachers memorized boys' names more quickly than the names of girls.

- When a boy gave a wrong answer, teachers would spend time praising him, encouraging him, and trying to lead him to the right answer. When a girl gave a wrong answer, teachers generally just moved on to another student.

No one assumes that the teachers 13 involved "liked" boys better than girls. Rather, it is apparent than teachers as well as students are very much influenced by gender stereotypes. Because girls are (in general) less disruptive and demanding in a mixed-class setting, they receive less attention and affirmation. In general, the Sadkers concluded, girls in co-ed settings become the "audience," rather than the "players."

But in single-sex schools, girls and 14 guys can play *all* the roles—scientist, writer, musician, basketball player, artist, math whiz, track star. Without the presence of voices (spoken and unspoken) saying "Boys don't do that" or "Girls aren't good at that," they can develop their own gifts and talents, irrespective of gender. Without the constant pressure to impress the opposite sex, boys and girls can channel their energies into becoming the best people they can be, rather than forcing themselves into stereotypical molds. Single-sex schools could be the very best thing to happen to many students. It's time to bring these schools back.

READING COMPREHENSION QUESTIONS

Vocabulary in Context

___C___ 1. In the excerpt below, the word *flaunt* (flônt) means

A. hide.

B. investigate.

C. show off.

D. ignore.

Context clues: *makes a point* and *loudly proclaims*. Students who do these things are probably showing off.

"A girl may think she seems 'girlier' . . . if she makes a point of being clueless in math class. A boy may think he's more macho, more alluring to girls, if he loudly proclaims that he hates to read. As a result, students may deliberately flaunt their weaknesses in order to impress the opposite sex." (Paragraph 11)

Central Point and Main Ideas

___C___ 2. Which sentence best expresses the central point of the selection?

Answer A covers only paragraph 8. Answer B covers only paragraphs 9–11. Answer D covers only paragraph 2.

   A. In contrast to co-educational schools, single-sex schools can design the curriculum with girls' and boys' learning differences in mind.
   B. When boys and girls attend the same school, they tend to distract each other from academic pursuits.
   C. Single-sex schools would benefit both girls and boys because girls and boys learn differently and their behavior gets worse when they attend the same schools.
   D. Many studies have concluded that girls learn best in single-sex schools.

___A___ 3. The main idea of paragraph 2 is expressed in its
   A. first sentence.
   B. second sentence.
   C. third sentence.   Answers B, C, and D describe studies
   D. fourth sentence.   that support the main idea.

___B___ 4. The implied main idea of paragraph 4 is that

See sentences 2–3. Answer A is incorrect because the paragraph focuses on single-sex schools, not discrimination. Answers C and D are stated details in the paragraph.

   A. boys and girls shouldn't be discriminated against because they learn differently.
   B. one clearly defined advantage of single-sex schools is that, although boys and girls are not naturally better suited to different fields of study, they do learn differently.
   C. in the past, some people used the belief that boys and girls are better at different fields of study to justify unequal opportunities in education and employment.
   D. it's not true that boys are better at math and girls are better at English and foreign languages.

___B___ 5. The implied main idea of paragraph 10 is that
   A. flirting is a behavior as old as the Neanderthals.
   B. in mixed classes, boys and girls spend so much time flirting and in social plotting that they are distracted from their learning.
   C. social plotting often becomes the focus of the school day.
   D. rather than compare notes on classes, students often talk about who said what to whom or if anybody has a date for Saturday night.

   See sentences 3–6. Answers A, C, and D are stated
                               details in the paragraph.

Supporting Details

___D___ 6. According to the selection, girls who attend all-girl high schools are
   A. often very good at languages.
   B. likely to believe that they are stupid at science and math.
   C. likely to wish they were enrolled in mixed-class schools.
   D. six times more likely to major in math or science in college.

                               See the last sentence in paragraph 2.

_C_   7. According to the selection, a very basic fact of life is that
  A. girls are better at reading than boys are.
  B. boys do better in math and science than girls do.
  C. boys and girls act differently in each other's presence.   See the
  D. there is nothing wrong with flirting.   first sentence in paragraph 9.

_B_   8. According to the selection, girls receive less attention from teachers because
  A. teachers don't want to be seen as favoring girls.
  B. girls are less disruptive and demanding in mixed-class settings.
  C. teachers, who are mostly female, like boys better than girls.
  D. girls almost always have a better grasp of subject matter than boys do.   See sentence 3 in paragraph 13.

Transitions

_A_   9. The relationship expressed in the sentences below is one of
  A. cause and effect.   *Cause:* Girls believe that it is feminine and
  B. contrast.   attractive to be poor at math, and boys think it is
  C. addition.   macho to hate to read. *Effect:* Students deliberately
  D. illustration.   flaunt their weaknesses to impress the opposite sex.
        Transition: *As a result.*

  "A girl may think she seems 'girlier,' more feminine, more attractive, if she makes a point of being clueless in math class. A boy may think he's more macho, more alluring to girls if he loudly proclaims that he hates to read. As a result, students may deliberately flaunt their weaknesses in order to impress the opposite sex." (Paragraph 11)

Patterns of Organization

_D_ 10. The pattern of organization in paragraph 2 is
  A. time order.
  B. definition and example.   The author lists evidence which supports
  C. contrast.   the point that students in single-sex schools
  D. list of items.   perform better academically.

_B_ 11. Paragraph 12
  A. contrasts boys' behavior with that of girls.
  B. lists examples which show that teachers focus more attention on boys than girls in mixed classrooms.
  C. provides reasons why boys outperform girls in mixed classrooms.
  D. compares girls' behavior with that of boys in mixed classrooms.
        The bulleted items are the list of examples.

___D___ 12. This selection mainly
- A. presents, in time order, a sequence of events that occurred after Title IX prohibited sex discrimination in education.
- B. compares boys' classroom behavior with that of girls.
- C. contrasts how teachers react to boys with how they react to girls.
- D. gives reasons why single-sex classrooms would benefit boys and girls more than mixed classrooms.   Answer A is incorrect because Title IX is only an introductory detail. Answer B covers only paragraphs 9–11. Answer C covers only paragraph 12.

Inferences

___D___ 13. On the basis of paragraphs 5–6, we can infer that

See paragraph 6. Since boys develop language skills later than girls, it is logical to infer that they would benefit from not being pushed into reading.

- A. boys never catch up to girls in terms of language skills.
- B. very few boys like to read.
- C. because boys are pushed to read at an age when many of them are unprepared to do so, they never develop a lifelong reading habit.
- D. boys would benefit if they were not pushed into reading as early as they are.

___C___ 14. We can infer from paragraph 11 that many girls believe that boys

See sentences 4 and 8. Girls feel that it is "feminine" to be bad at math, quiet, passive, and non-athletic, and that boys will be "turned off" if they behave otherwise.

- A. really like to read.
- B. are clueless in math class.
- C. are turned off by assertive and athletic girls and those who are good in math.
- D. are turned off by quiet, passive, and non-athletic girls.

___A___ 15. We can infer from paragraph 13 that
- A. if girls were more disruptive and demanding in class, they might get more attention from teachers.
- B. teachers don't really like boys.
- C. teachers don't really like girls.
- D. girls who are disruptive and demanding in class are generally well-liked.   If boys get more attention from teachers because they are disruptive and demanding, we can conclude that girls who exhibit these characteristics would also get more attention.

Purpose and Tone

___C___ 16. The main purpose of this reading is to
- A. entertain readers with anecdotes about the foolish behavior of today's students.
- B. inform readers of ways in which American schools are short-changing the nation's youth.
- C. persuade readers to support the idea of single-sex public schools.

In paragraph 1, the author says it is "a shame" that more single-sex schools are not available. See also the title and the last two sentences of the reading. The author urges us to bring back same-sex schools.

Argument

17. Label the point of the following argument with a **P** and the two statements of support with an **S**. Label with an **X** the statement that is neither the point nor the support of the argument.

Answers A and C are examples of the point that in mixed classrooms, teachers generally pay more attention to boys than girls. Answer D does not support that point.

   _S__ A. When boys raise their hands, they are five times more likely to be called on than girls.

   _P__ B. In mixed classrooms, teachers generally pay more attention to boys than to girls.

   _S__ C. Teachers are twice as likely to pick out boys in the class as role models.

   _X__ D. Girls generally develop language skills earlier than boys do.

Critical Reading

_A_ 18. Paragraph 2 is made up of
   A. facts.
   B. opinions.
   C. both facts and opinions.

The paragraph reports verifiable research data.

_B_ 19. The sentence below is
   A. fact.
   B. opinion.
   C. both fact and opinion.

Value word: *best.*

"Single-sex schools could be the very best thing to happen to many students." (Paragraph 14)

_C_ 20. Girls who believe that they must make a choice between being attractive and being good at math are committing the fallacy of
   A. false cause *(the argument assumes that the order of events alone shows cause and effect).*
   B. circular reasoning *(a statement repeats itself rather than providing a real supporting reason to back up an argument).*
   C. either-or *(the argument assumes that there are only two sides to a question).*
   D. false comparison *(the argument assumes that two things being compared are more alike than they really are).*

Isn't it possible to be attractive *and* good in math?

OUTLINING

Complete the following outline of paragraphs 8–13 of the selection by filling in the four missing minor details.   *Wording of answers may vary.*

Central point: Single-sex classrooms have advantages over mixed classrooms.

1. Classroom curriculum could reflect girls' and boys' learning differences.
   a. Boys would be expected to keep pace in reading with other boys, not girls who develop reading skills earlier.
   b. Boys could read materials of particular interest to them.
   c. *Girls could be introduced to math and science concepts in ways that particularly appeal to them.*

See paragraph 8.

2. Single-sex schools would eliminate flirting between the sexes.
   a. *Flirting takes up a lot of time and energy that could be better used in the classroom.*

See paragraph 10.

   b. Social plotting that becomes the focus of the school day would also be curbed.

3. Boys and girls wouldn't feel the need to display "stupid" behaviors.
   a. *Girls wouldn't have to make a point of being clueless in math.*

See paragraph 11.

   b. Boys wouldn't proclaim that they hate reading.
   c. Girls would not be pressured to be nice, quiet, and nonathletic.
   d. *Boys would not feel compelled to be "jocks," noisy, disruptive, and overbearing.*

See paragraph 11.

4. Teachers would not shortchange girls.
   a. In mixed classrooms teachers devote much more attention to boys because boys are more disruptive and demanding.
   b. In single-sex classrooms, both boys and girls would get the attention they need.

DISCUSSION QUESTIONS

1. Which kind of school did you attend, a single-sex school or a co-ed school? Do your own school experiences reflect the observations made by the author concerning mixed and single-sex classrooms? For example, did you have the impression that boys were "just better" at certain skills, and girls were better at others? What might have given you this impression?

2. Do you agree with the conclusion of the selection—that single-sex schools are preferable to co-ed schools? Why or why not?

3. In your experience, do teachers treat boys and girls differently in the classroom? Have you seen any examples of the kinds of teacher behavior described in this selection? Explain.

4. The selection mentions the advantages of single-sex schooling. Can you think of any *negative* consequences of single-sex schooling? If so, what are they?

Note: Writing assignments for this selection appear on page 569.

Check Your Performance   **SINGLE-SEX SCHOOLS**

Activity	Number Right	Points	Score
READING COMPREHENSION QUESTIONS			
Vocabulary in Context (1 item)	_____	× 4 =	_____
Central Point and Main Ideas (4 items)	_____	× 4 =	_____
Supporting Details (3 items)	_____	× 4 =	_____
Transitions (1 item)	_____	× 4 =	_____
Patterns of Organization (3 items)	_____	× 4 =	_____
Inferences (3 items)	_____	× 4 =	_____
Purpose and Tone (1 item)	_____	× 4 =	_____
Argument (1 item)	_____	× 4 =	_____
Critical Reading (3 items)	_____	× 4 =	_____
OUTLINING (4 items)	_____	× 5 =	_____
	TOTAL SCORE =		_____%

Enter your total score into the **Reading Performance Chart: Ten Reading Selections** on the inside back cover.

8

A King's Folly
Beth Johnson and John Langan

Preview

"Once upon a time there was a king . . ."

How many fairy tales have begun like this? But what follows is no fairy tale. It is a story of passion and madness; of pride, vanity, and the darkest recesses of the human soul. It speaks of selfless love, of bottomless sorrow, and of truths recognized too late. It is a story for the ages.

Words to Watch

folly (title; 8): a lack of good sense
grizzled (8): gray-haired
flaws (17): pieces
wanton (22): cruel

1   Once upon a time there was a king. As a young man, he was bold and powerful, maybe even wise. But as he grew older, something terrible happened to him. He was surrounded by so many flattering, boot-licking men and women that he fell in love with himself and lost the ability to see clearly the world and people around him.

2   His downfall begins when the old king decides to retire. He calls his court together to hear his plan: he will divide the kingdom between his three daughters, then take turns living with them. But instead of simply dividing the land into thirds, the king makes the worst possible decision. He will divide the kingdom on the basis of how much his daughters claim to love him. "Which of you shall we say does love us most?" he asks. Then the vain old man sits back, waiting to hear his daughters' flattery.

3   His two oldest daughters, Goneril and Regan, are happy to play his game. They are cold and selfish, and they will say anything in order to enrich themselves. They take turns gushing over their father, claiming that they love him beyond their eyesight, their freedom, their very lives.

4   The king enjoys all this very much. He then turns to his youngest daughter, Cordelia. He loves this gentle young woman most of all, and he is sure she will win the contest for the best part of his kingdom. But her sisters' hypocrisy sickens her, and she refuses to speak.

5   The old king is embarrassed by her silence. He insists that she say something. She sadly explains that while she loves him as a daughter should, she cannot compete with her sisters' flowery words. Her father accuses her of being hard-hearted. "So young, and so untender?" he asks.

6   "So young, my lord, and true," she answers.

7   His pride wounded, the old man reacts like a spoiled child and flies into a fury. He announces that he will divide his kingdom into two, not three, parts. His older daughters will each have half the power in the land, while his youngest will be banished from the kingdom. Heartbroken, Cordelia leaves with her fiancé, the king of a neighboring country.

8   Meanwhile, the members of the court stand by silently—except for one. This is Kent, the king's only truly loyal friend. Kent is a grizzled° old warrior who will not be intimidated by the king's nonsense. He does not care if he is rude as he shouts at the king, his master, "What would thou do, old man?" He tells the king the truth: that he is a fool for putting his faith in empty words and rejecting his loyal daughter. In response,

the angry king compounds his folly° by banishing Kent from the land as well.

9   Utterly failing to see things as they truly are, the king has driven away the two people who truly love him. His foolish actions will have terrible consequences. Immediately, his two older daughters begin plotting against him. The old king goes to stay with Goneril, his oldest daughter. But instead of treating him with respect, Goneril makes it clear that he is unwelcome. She complains about the large group of knights that travel with him, and she encourages her own servants to neglect the old man. She takes a special dislike to her father's jester, or "fool," because he dares to criticize her. In riddles and jokes, the Fool tells the king that he was stupid to give his evil daughters so much power over him.

10   "Do thou call me a fool, boy?" the king asks.

11   The Fool agrees. "All thy other titles thou has given away; that thou was born with." He jokes that the king has made his daughters his mother; that he has handed them a rod and dropped his trousers to be whipped.

12   Goneril enters in time to hear the Fool criticizing her. She complains bitterly that the Fool and the king's knights are disrupting the peace of her court. She adds that the king himself is to blame for all of this by being too tolerant of their bad behavior. She darkly suggests that something will have to be done to discipline all of them.

13   The truth is beginning to dawn on the old king. Throughout his life, he has taken for granted being treated with courtesy and respect, even fear. But now he is seen merely as a powerless old man—a nuisance. He senses that Goneril's love was only for his wealth

and power, not for him. His whole identity seems to be in question as he begins to see his own monumental folly. If he is not a powerful king or respected father, who is he? He asks, "Who is it that can tell me who I am?"

14 Ignoring her father's distress, Goneril coolly orders that he get rid of half his knights, keeping only fifty. Enraged, the king announces that he will leave her castle and go stay with Regan, who he still assumes will love and care for him. He storms out, shouting the famous line, "How sharper than a serpent's tooth it is to have a thankless child!"

15 Goneril alerts Regan that their father is coming. When the king arrives and begins telling her how badly Goneril has treated him, Regan cruelly cuts him off, saying that her father should return to Goneril and ask her forgiveness.

16 Then Goneril arrives, and she and her father continue to quarrel. The king announces that he will never see her again. Instead, he and his hundred knights will stay permanently with Regan. But the two sisters team up to mock their father to his face, saying that he really has no need of more than ten, or five—or even one knight. And Regan adds that she will never take him in until he has apologized to Goneril.

17 Faced with his two sneering daughters, and having driven away in his blindness the one child who truly loved him, the king's world falls apart. Angry and humiliated, the powerless old man announces that he will go anywhere rather than stay with either of his daughters. He tries to make a blustery final speech to them, but he stumbles pathetically over his own words as he fights back his tears:

"Let not women's weapons, water-
    drops,

Stain my man's cheeks! No, you
    unnatural hags,
I will have such revenges on you both
That all the world shall—I will do
    such things—
What they are, yet I know not, but
    they shall be
The terrors of the earth. You think
    I'll weep;
No, I'll not weep.
I have full cause of weeping, but this
    heart
Shall break into a hundred thousand
    flaws°
Before I'll weep. O Fool! I shall go
    mad."

He staggers out into the night, 18 accompanied by his loyal old friend Kent (who has returned in disguise so he can be with his master) and the Fool. A fierce storm is building, but rather than let anyone go after the old man, Goneril and Regan are content to see the doors shut and their father left outside.

The king stumbles alone through the 19 howling wind and rain, and in his pain and suffering the very world seems to split open. He shouts in defiance at the weather, telling the storm that it cannot hurt him as his own daughters have. He is in a rage as well at himself for his own monstrous lack of judgment and vision. He strips off his clothes in the face of the driving wind and rain, asking, "Is man no more than this?"—no more than "a poor, bare, forked animal."

Eventually the Fool and Kent find 20 him and beg him to go with them to a nearby shack. But the king will not move. He does not care if he lives or dies; he is half-mad with guilt over how he has treated Cordelia. Meanwhile, an old friend of the king, the Earl of Gloucester, is hosting Regan and her husband at his castle. Gloucester is aware of the king's plight but has been told by his evil guests not to interfere. Gloucester leaves his castle in secret and finds the king, finally persuading him to take shelter.

21   Gloucester, too, has been a selfish father who has raised a treacherous child, and that son, Edmund, chooses this moment to strike at his father. Edmund rushes to tell Regan and her husband that his father has disobeyed them in order to help the old king. When Gloucester returns home, Regan shows the truly vicious side of her character. Accusing him of treason, she and her husband tie Gloucester to a chair and rip out his eyes, then throw him, too, out into the night. More than ever with this violent act, a sense of evil and darkness in humankind pervades the story.

22   Gloucester is eventually found by his older, loyal son, Edgar—a child that Gloucester in his foolishness and vanity has rejected, just as the king rejected his daughter Cordelia. To Edgar, Gloucester expresses his despair over the cruelty of fate, saying:

> "As flies to wanton° boys, are we to the gods;
> They kill us for their sport."

23   Everything now is falling into chaos. Although Regan and Goneril have succeeded in getting rid of their father, there is trouble brewing for them. Both feel a lustful love and desire for evil Edmund, and each wants to get rid of the other. News has come that Cordelia and an army are coming to try to rescue the old king. Then Goneril's husband, Albany, disgusted by her behavior, turns against his wife, telling her that she and Regan are "tigers, not daughters."

24   Cordelia and her army arrive, and she and her father are finally reunited. The old man is sleeping, and his doctor warns her that he is quite insane. Cordelia waits for him to awaken, tenderly kissing him and stroking his hair. When he wakes, there is a touching scene as he struggles to understand what is happening. He first believes that he is dead and Cordelia is an angel, and says to her:

> "You do me wrong to take me out of the grave;
> Thou are a soul in bliss; but I am bound
> Upon a wheel of fire, that mine own tears
> Do scald like molten lead."

When he realizes Cordelia is with him, he falls on his knees before her:

> "You must bear with me.
> Pray you now, forget and forgive: I am old and foolish."

25   But their reunion is brief. Regan's and Goneril's armies arrive, under the command of evil Edmund, and Cordelia and the old king are taken prisoner. The old man takes the news well, believing that at least he and his beloved daughter will be imprisoned together. He tries to cheer Cordelia, and hoping against hope, he imagines they can find safety in each other from all the horror around them:

> "Come, let's away to prison;
> We two alone will sing like birds in the cage.
> When thou dost ask me blessing, I'll kneel down,
> And ask of thee forgiveness: so we'll live,
> And pray, and sing, and tell old tales, and laugh."

26   But Edmund does not intend for them to live; he has ordered that they both be murdered in prison. Goneril's husband Albany arrives, hoping to take custody of the king and Cordelia, but Edmund, Regan, and Goneril all defy him.

27   Regan is sick; it becomes clear that Goneril has poisoned her to keep Edmund for herself. Edmund's brother Edgar arrives, and denounces Edmund for betraying their father. The two men fight, and Edmund falls, mortally wounded. With his last breath, he confesses that he has ordered the deaths of the king and Cordelia. Regan dies, and Goneril, seeing that Edmund is dying, commits suicide.

28   Goneril's husband, Albany, orders that the old king and Cordelia be released, but it is too late. The king staggers in, crazed with grief, holding dead Cordelia in his arms. He cries out:

"No, no, no life!

Why should a dog, a horse, a rat, have life,
And thou no breath at all? Thou'll come no more,
Never, never, never, never, never!"

29   Unable to bear his grief and guilt at the loss of Cordelia, the very essence of goodness and love, the king falls dead.

30   Surrounded by the bodies of the dead, Albany announces that Edgar and faithful Kent will become rulers of the land. But Kent says no, that he will soon join his king in death. Edgar is left to mourn the tragedies that have brought him to power.

31   And so, dark with folly and heartbreak and almost boundless evil, but illuminated by touches of loyalty, love, and forgiveness, the story ends. It is *King Lear*, the greatest of Shakespeare's tragedies, and for many the supreme masterwork in all of literature.

READING COMPREHENSION QUESTIONS

Vocabulary in Context

___C___ 1. In the excerpt below, the word *intimidated* (ĭn-tĭm′ĭ-dāt′ĭd) means

A. amused.
B. fooled.   If someone is a "grizzled old warrior" who doesn't care
C. frightened.   if he is rude to the king, he is not likely to be frightened.
D. annoyed.

Kent is a grizzled old warrior who will not be intimidated by the king's nonsense. He does not care if he is rude as he shouts at the king, his master, "What would thou do, old man?" (Paragraph 8)

___B___ 2. In the sentence below, the word *pervades* (pər-vādz′) means

A. reveals.
B. spreads throughout.   The sentence implies that "this violent act" is
C. disproves.   one of many; therefore, a sense of evil and
D. speeds up.   darkness spreads throughout the story.

"More than ever with this violent act, a sense of evil and darkness in humankind pervades the story." (Paragraph 21)

Central Point and Main Ideas

_D_ 3. Which sentence best expresses a central point of the selection?
   A. It is a common tragedy for children to disrespect their parents.
   B. When people grow old, they lose their common sense.
   C. It's impossible to predict the misfortune which lies in store for some people.
   D. Powerful people who believe the words of flatterers invite disaster upon themselves and others.   See paragraph 1. The focus of the story
                                                                 is on the folly of believing flatterers.

_B_ 4. The main idea of paragraphs 9–13 is that
   A. Goneril behaves disrespectfully to her father, the old king.
   B. because of Goneril's disrespect, the old king realizes that he has made a great mistake in giving her power over him.
   C. the Fool points out that the king has given his daughters the power to punish him as a mother would her son.
   D. Goneril believes that her father's knights and the Fool are disrupting the peace of her court.   Answers A, C, and D are details which
                                                                 support the main idea. Answer A is in

_C_ 5. The main idea of paragraph 16 is that   paragraph 9, C in 11, and D in 12.
   A. Goneril and her father continue to quarrel.
   B. the old king decides that he and his knights will stay with Regan.
   C. Goneril and Regan team up to humiliate their father.
   D. the two sisters believe that their father has no need of knights.
                                                       Answers A, B, and D are all supporting
_C_ 6. The main idea of paragraph 21 is that   details from the paragraph.
   A. Gloucester, like the old king, has raised a treacherous child.
   B. Regan is a truly vicious woman who severely punishes those she suspects of treason.
   C. as a result of his son Edmund's treachery, Gloucester is viciously attacked by Regan and her husband.
   D. Regan and her husband punish the selfish Gloucester for committing treason.   Answer A is a detail from the paragraph. Answer
                                                     B is too broad because we see Regan react only to
Supporting Details   Gloucester's "treachery." Answer D is unstated.

_D_ 7. The old king divides his kingdom on the basis of
   A. whom he loves most of all.
   B. his loyal friend's advice.   See paragraph 2.
   C. which of his three daughters demonstrates the most wisdom.
   D. which of his three daughters claims to love him the most.

_D_ 8. The person who orders the death of Cordelia is
   A. Goneril.
   B. Regan.   See paragraph 26. *Them* refers to the
   C. Edgar.   king and Cordelia.
   D. Edmund.

Transitions

___D___ 9. The transition words in the sentence below signal time order and

    A. cause and effect.

    B. contrast.

    C. illustration.

    D. comparison.

> The sentence compares Gloucester's rejection of Edgar with the king's rejection of Cordelia. Comparison transition: *just as.* (Time transition: *eventually.*)

"Gloucester is <u>eventually</u> found by his older, loyal son, Edgar—a child that Gloucester in his foolishness and vanity has rejected, <u>just as</u> the king rejected his daughter Cordelia." (Paragraph 22)

Patterns of Organization

___B___ 10. The selection mainly

    A. contrasts the kindness of Cordelia with the wickedness of her sisters.

    B. presents the consequences, in time order, of an old king's foolish decision.

    C. defines and provides examples of the word *hypocrisy*.

    D. lists different ways in which kings can make fools of themselves.

> Answers A and C are too narrow. Answer D is not supported.

Inferences

___B___ 11. We can conclude from paragraphs 4–6 that

    A. Cordelia does not love her father because he is foolish and vain.

    B. Cordelia is aware of her father's shortcomings, but loves him anyway.

    C. Cordelia does not truly understand what her father expects her to say.

    D. unlike her sisters, Cordelia is not good with words.

> Answers A, C, and D are not supported. The fact that Cordelia, a "gentle young woman," is sickened by her sisters' hypocrisy suggests that she is aware of her father's shortcomings, but loves him anyway.

___D___ 12. We can infer from paragraphs 9–11 that the Fool

    A. fears Goneril.

    B. believes that the king's daughters are right to punish their foolish father.

    C. will soon be banished by his master, the king.

    D. has better judgment with regard to Goneril and Regan than the old king does.

> Answer A is contradicted by the fact that he "dares to criticize her." Answers B and C are not supported. The Fool accurately describes the king's situation with regard to his daughters.

___D___ 13. Paragraph 24 suggests that

    A. Cordelia has forgiven her father for banishing her.

    B. the old king recognizes that he was unjust to Cordelia.

    C. the old king believes that he is in Hell.

    D. all of the above.

> Sentence 3 supports answer A; sentence 6 supports answer B; and sentence 5 supports answer C.

___D___ 14. We can conclude from the selection that
- A. once a person becomes rich and powerful, he should trust no one.
- B. it is better not to have wealth and power because they can make a person foolish.
- C. the worst thing in the world is to be poor.
- D. even the rich and powerful can lack common sense.   Answers A, B, and C are not supported. The old king could have trusted Cordelia and Kent; not all wealthy and powerful people become foolish; to be betrayed by one's children is surely worse than being poor.

Purpose and Tone

King Lear is a spellbinding story which teaches us about the dangers of flattery and persuades us that the simple virtues of love and honesty are superior to wealth and power.

___D___ 15. The authors' main purpose is to
- A. inform readers of what happens when a king trusts the empty words of flatterers.
- B. persuade readers that the simple virtues of love and honesty are superior to wealth and power.
- C. entertain readers by telling them a spellbinding story.
- D. all of the above.

___A___ 16. The Fool's tone in paragraph 11 is
- A. mocking and critical.
- B. amused and affectionate.
- C. light-hearted and joyous.
- D. bitter and pessimistic.

The Fool makes fun of the old king for making his daughters his mothers—a strong criticism.

___C___ 17. From the tone of paragraph 31, we can conclude that the authors' attitude toward Shakespeare is
- A. detached and ironic.
- B. matter-of-fact and objective.
- C. admiring and respectful.
- D. nostalgic and sentimental.

The words *greatest* and *supreme masterwork in all of literature* suggest an admiring and respectful tone.

Argument

___C___ 18. Three of the items below are supporting details for an argument. Write the letter of the statement that represents the point of these supporting details.
- A. Cordelia refuses to flatter her father, the old king, but simply tells him that she loves him as a daughter should.
- B. Cordelia and her army try to rescue her father.
- C. Throughout the story, Cordelia treats her father with loving respect.
- D. While Cordelia waits for her father to awaken, she tenderly kisses him and strokes his hair.

Answers A, B, and D support the point made in answer C— that Cordelia treats her father with love and respect.

Critical Reading

  _B_ 19. The statement that *King Lear* is "the greatest of Shakespeare's tragedies, and for many the supreme masterwork in all of literature," is
  A. fact.
  B. opinion.

> Judgment words that signal an opinion: *greatest* and *supreme masterwork.*

  _B_ 20. When the old king accuses his daughter Cordelia of being "untender" because she does not flatter him, he is committing the logical fallacy of
  A. personal attack *(ignores the issue under discussion and concentrates instead on the character of the opponent).*
  B. either-or *(the argument assumes that there are only two sides to a question).*
  C. false cause *(the argument assumes that the order of events alone shows cause and effect).*
  D. circular reasoning *(a statement repeats itself rather than providing a real supporting reason to back up an argument).*

> The old king, trapped in his either-or thinking, fails to see that refusal to flatter a person can be a sign of love (tenderness).

SUMMARIZING

Add the ideas needed to complete the following summary of "A King's Folly."

Wording of answers may vary.

Once upon a time, an old king foolishly decides to divide his kingdom

See paragraph 2. on the basis of _____*how much his daughters claim to love him*_____.

His two oldest daughters, Goneril and Regan, flatter him shamelessly, but his youngest daughter, Cordelia, who is sickened by her sisters' hypocrisy, refuses to speak. When she finally replies that she loves her father _____

See paragraph 5. _____*as a daughter should*_____, the old king becomes enraged and announces that he will divide his kingdom between Goneril and Regan and will banish Cordelia. The old king also banishes the only one of his friends, Kent, who has the courage to criticize the king's decision.

Later, when the king goes to stay with Goneril, she makes it clear that he is unwelcome. As the king's Fool makes fun of his master, saying he has made his daughters his mother, Goneril orders the king to get rid of half of his knights. Enraged, the king announces that he will _____*leave her castle*

See paragraph 14. _____*and go to stay with Regan*_____. However, Regan mocks him to his face and refuses to take him in unless he apologizes to Goneril. His identity shattered, the old king staggers out into the night, accompanied by

Kent, who has returned in disguise, and the Fool. A storm howls as the king

rages at the weather and himself for his own lack of _____

See paragraph 19._____*judgment and vision*_____.

    Meanwhile, an old friend of the king's, the Earl of Gloucester, is

hosting Regan and her husband at his castle. Although he has been warned

See paragraph 20. not to interfere, Gloucester leaves his castle in secret and _____*finds the king*_____

_____*and persuades him to take shelter.*_____. When Gloucester returns home, his

evil son, Edmund, betrays him to Regan and her husband, who _____

See paragraph 21._____*tie him to a chair*_____, rip out his eyes, and throw him out into the

night. Gloucester is eventually found by his older, loyal son, Edgar.

See paragraph 23. Meanwhile, Regan and Goneril become jealous of each other because they

each _____*feel love and desire for Edmund*_____. News arrives that Cordelia and

an army are coming to try to rescue the old king as Goneril's husband,

Albany, sickened by his wife's cruelty, turns against her. Cordelia and her

army arrive, and she and her father are reunited. But their reunion is brief, as

Regan and Goneril's armies arrive under the command of Edmund, who

takes Cordelia and the old king prisoner. Albany arrives, intending to free

Cordelia and the king, but Edmund, Regan, and Goneril defy him. Goneril

poisons Regan to keep Edmund for herself. Soon Edgar arrives and

See paragraph 27. fights and kills Edmund, who, with his last breath, confesses that

_____*he has ordered the deaths of the king and Cordelia*_____.

See paragraph 28. Regan dies, and Goneril commits suicide upon Edmund's death. Albany

orders that the old king and Cordelia be released, but it is too late. The old

king enters, carrying _____*the dead Cordelia*_____.

See paragraph 30. Unable to bear his grief and guilt at the loss of Cordelia, the king falls dead,

and Edgar _____*becomes the ruler*_____. So ends

Shakespeare's great tragedy, *King Lear*.

DISCUSSION QUESTIONS

1. Why do you think Lear sets up such a test for his daughters in order to divide his kingdom?

2. Does the old king deserve what he gets from Regan and Cordelia? Why or why not?

3. Which character, in your opinion, is the most evil figure in the story? Which character, after Cordelia, most embodies good in humankind?

4. After they have gotten what they wanted from him, Goneril and Regan both regard their elderly father as a nuisance and treat him with extreme disrespect. Based upon your experience, is a disrespectful attitude toward the elderly common or uncommon in today's society? Explain.

Note: Writing assignments for this selection appear on page 569.

Check Your Performance   **A KING'S FOLLY**

Activity	Number Right	Points	Score
READING COMPREHENSION QUESTIONS			
Vocabulary in Context (2 items)	_____	× 4 =	_____
Central Point and Main Ideas (4 items)	_____	× 4 =	_____
Supporting Details (2 items)	_____	× 4 =	_____
Transitions (1 item)	_____	× 4 =	_____
Patterns of Organization (1 item)	_____	× 4 =	_____
Inferences (4 items)	_____	× 4 =	_____
Purpose and Tone (3 items)	_____	× 4 =	_____
Argument (1 item)	_____	× 4 =	_____
Critical Reading (2 items)	_____	× 4 =	_____
SUMMARIZING (10 items)	_____	× 2 =	_____
		TOTAL SCORE =	_____ %

Enter your total score into the **Reading Performance Chart: Ten Reading Selections** on the inside back cover.

9

In My Day
Russell Baker

Preview

To see a parent becoming old and infirm is painful. It is a particularly awkward transition when the parent has been tough-minded and opinionated, as was Russell Baker's mother in her younger years. In this poignant essay from his autobiography *Growing Up*, Baker reflects on the difficulty of negotiating the shifting terrain as one's parent becomes a child.

Words to Watch

debris (15): scattered remains of something broken
drugstore cowboy (15): someone who is all talk and no action
libertine (15): an immoral person
banal (41): uninteresting and trivial
wrest (44): to pull forcibly
interrogators (49): questioners
exemplary (50): serving as a desirable model

1   At the age of eighty my mother had her last bad fall, and after that her mind wandered free through time. Some days she went to weddings and funerals that had taken place half a century earlier. On others she presided over family dinners cooked on Sunday afternoons for children who were now gray with age. Through all this she lay in bed but moved across time, traveling among the dead decades with a speed and ease beyond the gift of physical science.

2   "Where's Russell?" she asked one day when I came to visit at the nursing home.

3   "I'm Russell," I said.

4   She gazed at this improbably overgrown figure out of an inconceivable future and promptly dismissed it.

5   "Russell's only this big," she said,

holding her hand, palm down, two feet from the floor. That day she was a young country wife with chickens in the backyard and a view of hazy blue Virginia mountains behind the apple orchard, and I was a stranger old enough to be her father.

6   Early one morning she phoned me in New York. "Are you coming to my funeral today?" she asked.

7   It was an awkward question with which to be awakened. "What are you talking about, for God's sake?" was the best reply I could manage.

8   "I'm being buried today," she declared briskly, as though announcing an important social event.

9   "I'll phone you back," I said and hung up, and when I did phone back she was all right, although she wasn't all right, of course, and we all knew she wasn't.

10   She had always been a small woman—short, light-boned, delicately structured—but now, under the white hospital sheet, she was becoming tiny. I thought of a doll with huge, fierce eyes. There had always been a fierceness in her. It showed in that angry, challenging thrust of the chin when she issued an opinion, and a great one she had always been for issuing opinions.

11   "I tell people exactly what's on my mind," she has been fond of boasting. "I tell them what I think, whether they like it or not." Often they had not liked it. She could be sarcastic to people in whom she detected evidence of the ignoramus or the fool.

12   "It's not always good policy to tell people exactly what's on your mind," I used to caution her.

13   "If they don't like it, that's too bad," was her customary reply, "because that's the way I am."

14   And so she was. A formidable woman. Determined to speak her mind, determined to have her way, determined to bend those who opposed her. In that time when I had known her best, my mother had hurled herself at life with chin thrust forward, eyes blazing, and an energy that made her seem always on the run.

15   She ran after squawking chickens, an axe in her hand, determined on a beheading that would put dinner in the pot. She ran when she made the beds, ran when she set the table. One Thanksgiving she burned herself badly when, running up from the cellar oven with the ceremonial turkey, she tripped on the stairs and tumbled back down, ending at the bottom in the debris° of giblets, hot gravy and battered turkey. Life was combat, and victory was not to the lazy, the timid, the slugabed, the drugstore cowboy°, the libertine°, the mushmouth afraid to tell people exactly what was on his mind whether people liked it or not. She ran.

16   But now the running was over. For a time I could not accept the inevitable. As I sat by her bed, my impulse was to argue her back to reality. On my first visit to the hospital in Baltimore, she asked who I was.

17   "Russell," I said.

18   "Russell's way out west," she advised me.

19   "No, I'm right here."

20   "Guess where I came from today?" was her response.

21   "Where?"

22   "All the way from New Jersey."

23   "When?"

24   "Tonight."

25   "No. You've been in the hospital for three days," I insisted.

26   "I suggest the thing to do is calm down a little bit," she replied. "Go over to the house and shut the door."

27   Now she was years deep into the past, living in the neighborhood where she had settled forty years earlier, and she had just been talking with Mrs. Hoffman, a neighbor across the street.

28   "It's like Mrs. Hoffman said today: The children always wander back to where they come from," she remarked.

29   "Mrs. Hoffman has been dead for fifteen years."

30   "Russ got married today," she replied.

31   "I got married in 1950," I said, which was the fact.

32   "The house is unlocked," she said.

33   So it went until a doctor came by to give one of those oral quizzes that medical men apply in such cases. She failed catastrophically, giving wrong answers or none at all to "What day is this?" "Do you know where you are?" "How old are you?" and so on. Then, a surprise.

34   "When is your birthday?" he asked.

35   "November 5, 1897," she said. Correct. Absolutely correct.

36   "How do you remember that?" the doctor asked.

37   "Because I was born on Guy Fawkes Day," she said.

38   "Guy Fawkes?" asked the doctor. "Who is Guy Fawkes?"

39   She replied with a rhyme I had heard her recite time and again over the years when the subject of her birth date arose:

> *"Please to remember the Fifth of November,*
> *Gunpowder treason and plot.*
> *I see no reason why gunpowder treason*
> *Should ever be forgot."*

Then she glared at this young doctor, so ill informed about Guy Fawkes's failed scheme to blow King James off his throne with barrels of gunpowder in 1605. She had been a schoolteacher, after all, and knew how to glare at a dolt. "You may know a lot about medicine, but you obviously don't know any history," she said. Having told him exactly what was on her mind, she left us again.

40   The doctors diagnosed a hopeless senility. Not unusual, they said. "Hardening of the arteries" was the explanation for laymen. I thought it was more complicated than that. For ten years or more the ferocity with which she had once attacked life had been turning to a rage against the weakness, the boredom, and the absence of love that too much age had brought her. Now, after the last bad fall, she seemed to have broken chains that imprisoned her in a life she had come to hate and to return to a time inhabited by people who loved her, a time in which she was needed. Gradually I understood. It was the first time in years I had seen her happy.

41   She had written a letter three years earlier which explained more than "hardening of the arteries." I had gone down from New York to Baltimore, where she lived, for one of my infrequent visits and, afterwards, had written her with some banal° advice to look for the silver lining, to count her blessings instead of burdening others with her miseries. I suppose what it really amounted to was a threat that if she was not more cheerful during my visits I would not come to see her very often. Sons are capable of such letters. This one was written out of a childish faith in the external strength of parents, a naïve belief that age and wear could be overcome by an effort of will, that all she needed was a good pep talk to recharge a flagging spirit. It was such a foolish, innocent idea, but one thinks of parents differently from other people. Other people can become frail and break, but not parents.

42   She wrote back in an unusually cheery vein intended to demonstrate, I suppose, that she was mending her ways. She was never a woman to apologize, but for one moment with a pen in her hand she came very close. Referring to my visit, she wrote: "If I seemed unhappy to you at times—" Here she drew back, reconsidered, and said something quite different:

43   "If I seemed unhappy to you at times, I am, but there's really nothing anyone can do about it, because I'm just so very tired and lonely that I'll just go to sleep and forget it." She was then seventy-eight.

44   Now, three years later, after the last bad fall, she had managed to forget the fatigue and loneliness and, in these free-wheeling excursions back through time, to recapture happiness. I soon stopped trying to wrest° her back to what I considered the real world and tried to travel along with her on those fantastic swoops into the past. One day, when I arrived at her bedside, she was radiant.

45   "Feeling good today," I said.

46   "Why shouldn't I feel good?" she asked. "Papa's going to take me up to Baltimore on the boat today."

47   At that moment she was a young girl standing on a wharf at Merry Point, Virginia, waiting for the Chesapeake Bay steamer with her father, who had been dead sixty-one years. William Howard Taft was in the White House, Europe still drowsed in the dusk of the great century of peace, America was a young country, and the future stretched before it in beams of crystal sunlight. "The greatest country on God's green earth," her father might have said, if I had been able to step into my mother's time machine and join him on the wharf with the satchels packed for Baltimore.

48   I could imagine her there quite clearly. She was wearing a blue dress with big puffy sleeves and long black stockings. There was a ribbon in her hair and a big bow tied on the side of her head. There had been a childhood photograph in her bedroom which showed all this, although the colors, of course, had been added years later by a restorer who tinted the picture.

49   About her father, my grandfather, I could only guess, and indeed, about the girl on the wharf with the bow in her hair, I was merely sentimentalizing. Of my mother's childhood and her people, of their time and place, I knew very little. A world had lived and died, and though it was part of my blood and bone I knew little more about it than I knew of the world of the pharaohs. It was useless now to ask for help from my mother. The orbits of her mind rarely touched present interrogators° for more than a moment.

50   Sitting at her bedside, forever out of touch with her, I wondered about my own children, and their children, and children in general, and about the disconnections between children and parents that prevent them from knowing each other. Children rarely want to know who their parents were before they were parents, and when age finally stirs their curiosity, there is no parent left to tell them. If a parent does lift the curtain a bit, it is often only to stun the young with some exemplary° tale of how much harder life was in the old days.

51   I had been guilty of this when my children were small in the early 1960s and living the affluent life. It galled me that their childhoods should be, as I thought, so easy when my own had been, as I thought, so hard. I had developed the habit, when they complained about the steak being overcooked or the television being cut off, of lecturing them on the

harshness of life in my day.

52   "In my day all we got for dinner was macaroni and cheese, and we were glad to get it."

53   "In my day we didn't have any television."

54   "In my day . . ."

55   "In my day . . ."

56   At dinner one evening, a son had offended me with an inadequate report card, and as I leaned back and cleared my throat to lecture, he gazed at me with an expression of unutterable resignation and said, "Tell me how it was in your day, Dad."

57   I was angry with him for that, but angrier with myself for having become one of those ancient bores whose highly selective memories of the past become transparently dishonest even to small children. I tried to break the habit, but must have failed. A few years later my son was referring to me when I was out of earshot as "the old-timer." Between us there was a dispute about time. He looked upon the time that had been my future in a disturbing way. My future was his past, and being young, he was indifferent to the past.

58   As I hovered over my mother's bed listening for muffled signals from her childhood, I realized that this same dispute had existed between her and me. When she was young, with life ahead of her, I had been her future and resented it. Instinctively, I wanted to break free, cease being a creature defined by her time, consign her future to the past, and create my own. Well, I had finally done that, and then with my own children I had seen my exciting future become their boring past.

59   These hopeless end-of-the-line visits with my mother made me wish I had not thrown off my own past so carelessly. We all come from the past, and children ought to know what it was that went into their making, to know that life is a braided cord of humanity stretching up from some time long gone, and that it cannot be defined by the span of a single journey from diaper to shroud.

READING COMPREHENSION QUESTIONS

Vocabulary in Context

___A___ 1. In the excerpt below, the word *dolt* (dōlt) means

A. stupid person.

B. spot on the wall.

C. genius.

D. son.

What kind of person, according to the author's mother, would be ill-informed and not know any history?

"Then she glared at this young doctor, so ill informed about Guy Fawkes's failed scheme to blow King James off his throne with barrels of gunpowder in 1605. She had been a schoolteacher, after all, and knew how to glare at a dolt. 'You may know a lot about medicine, but you obviously don't know any history,' she said." (Paragraph 39)

_B_ 2. In the sentence below, the word *flagging* (flăg′ĭng) means
   A. terrible.
   B. weakening.
   C. challenging.   What kind of spirit would need recharging?
   D. definite.

> "This one was written out of a childish faith in the external strength of parents, a naïve belief that age and wear could be overcome by an effort of will, that all she needed was a good pep talk to recharge a flagging spirit." (Paragraph 41)

_C_ 3. In the excerpt below, the word *galled* (gôld) means
   A. puzzled.
   B. amused.   The author is annoyed that his children's childhood
   C. annoyed.   seems to be so much easier than his own.
   D. threatened.

> "If a parent does lift the curtain a bit, it is often only to stun the young with some exemplary tale of how much harder life was in the old days.
>
> "I had been guilty of this when my children were small in the early 1960s and living the affluent life. It galled me that their childhood should be, as I thought, so easy when my own had been, as I thought, so hard." (Paragraphs 50–51)

Central Point and Main Ideas

_D_ 4. Which sentence best expresses the central point of the selection?
   A. The author and his mother had many differences of opinion due to her forceful personality and his desire to escape her influence.
   B. The author is sad to see his mother become senile due to hardening of the arteries, even though she is happier that way.
   C. Children are not usually interested in their parents' past history until they get older themselves.
   D. When his mother becomes senile, the author regrets that he never learned much about her early life and suggests that young people should try to learn more about their parents' past.

Answer A does not include how the author feels now. Answer B covers only paragraph 40. Answer C covers only paragraphs 50–59.

_A_ 5. The main idea of paragraphs 11–15 is that the author's mother
   A. had once been strong-willed, active, and outspoken.
   B. was sometimes sarcastic to people who she felt were stupid or foolish.
   C. once burned herself badly when she fell down the stairs on Thanksgiving while carrying the roast turkey.
   D. looked down on people who disagreed with her.

Answer B covers only paragraph 11. Answer C covers only parts of paragraph 15. Answer D is not supported.

_C_ 6. Which of the following sentences best expresses the main idea of paragraph 40?

A. The doctors diagnosed the author's mother as being hopelessly senile.

Answers A, B, and D do not address the fact that the author's mother became happy due to her senility.

B. After her last bad fall, the author's mother became hopelessly senile.

C. The author's mother's senility made her happy because it allowed her to return mentally to a time when she had been loved and needed.

D. Before becoming senile, the author's mother had spent ten years in a rage because of her old age.

_B_ 7. The main idea of paragraphs 50–57 is that

A. the author is annoyed that his children have easy lives while his was hard.

B. both parents and children are responsible for the disconnections between them.

C. generally speaking, children who grew up in the 1960s had it easy.

D. most parents tend to bore their children with stories of how much harder life was in the old days.   Answer A is a detail in paragraph 51.
Answers C and D are not supported. (*Note:* If answer D stated that *some* parents tend to bore their children, then it would be supported.)

Supporting Details

_C_ 8. At first when his mother became senile, the author tried to "wrest her back to the real world," but soon

A. gave up visiting her entirely.   See paragraph 44.

B. paid little attention to what she said.

C. tried to travel along with her on her visits into the past.

D. challenged her on her recall of key dates and events.

_D_ 9. The author's mother remembers her own birthday because

A. her son, Russell, got married on the same date in 1950.

B. it was the same date that she began teaching school.

C. her son, Russell, often reminded her of that date.

D. she was born on Guy Fawkes Day, the subject of a rhyme she knew by heart.   See paragraphs 37–39.

_A_ 10. The selection uses all of the patterns of organization below **except**

A. definition and example.

B. cause and effect.

C. time order.

D. comparison and contrast.

Example of cause and effect: In paragraph 43, the author's mother explains the reason for her unhappiness.
Example of time order: Paragraph 44 begins with the time transition *Now, three years later.*
Example of comparison-contrast: In paragraph 10, the author contrasts what his mother once looked like with what she looks like now; contrast transition: *But.*

Inferences

_B_ 11. On the basis of paragraph 40, we can infer that the author

Since he realizes that his mother's senility is making her happy, the author begins to view it in a positive manner. Answers A, C, and D are not supported.

- A. believed that the doctors had misdiagnosed his mother's condition.
- B. began to view his mother's senility in a positive manner.
- C. could not understand his mother's desire to be loved and needed.
- D. believed that his mother would gradually come to her senses.

_D_ 12. On the basis of paragraph 41, we can infer that the author

The author uses the words *banal, childish, naïve,* and *foolish* to refer to the advice that he once gave his mother. This suggests that he now regrets giving the advice.

- A. knew that all his mother really needed was a good pep talk.
- B. visited his mother less often after he wrote telling her to look for the silver lining.
- C. always thought his mother was foolish and innocent.
- D. regrets the naïve advice he once gave his mother.

_A_ 13. On the basis of the selection, we can conclude that the author

- A. regrets that he did not learn more about his mother's youth when she was still in her right mind.

See the first sentence of paragraph 59. The other answers are unsupported.

- B. fears that he may become senile like his mother.
- C. recognizes that young people have very little to gain from learning about their parents' youth.
- D. believes that he is closer to his children than his mother was to him.

_B_ 14. The last two paragraphs of the reading suggest that

- A. it is hopeless to try to revisit the past.

See the last sentence of the selection: "We all come from the past . . ."

- B. a person's life is always connected to the lives of those who came before.
- C. it is hard to predict what will happen in the course of a single life.
- D. the course of most people's lives goes from exciting to boring.

_C_ 15. From the details Baker selects to describe his mother, we can conclude that his description of her is

- A. overly sentimental.
- B. without insight.
- C. realistic.
- D. totally unsympathetic.

The author presents both positive and negative aspects of his mother's personality, suggesting that his description of her is realistic.

Purpose and Tone

_D_ 16. The author's purpose is to

- A. inform us of his struggles to understand the differences in outlook which separate parents and children.
- B. entertain us with colorful stories about his mother, complete with dialog.
- C. persuade us that the past should not be taken lightly.
- D. all of the above.

The selection is informative, but also entertaining and persuasive. In the last paragraph, the words *ought to* signal a persuasive intent.

<u>D</u> 17. The general tone of the reading is
    A. self-pitying and tragic.
    B. ironic and detached.
    C. bitter and bewildered.
    D. remorseful and loving.

> The author regrets that he was in such a hurry to throw off his past that he never learned much about his mother, whom he loved, and also that he responds to his children in a transparently dishonest way.

Argument

<u>D</u> 18. One of the following statements is the point of an argument. The other statements are support for that point. Write the letter of the point of the argument.
    A. The author realized that he never really learned much about his mother's youth.
    B. His mother became senile and failed to recognize him.
    C. The author often lectured his children about how much harder his childhood was than theirs, but his lectures annoyed them.
    D. The author of the selection felt disconnected from both his mother and his children.

> Statements A, B, and C are examples of the disconnections the author felt from both his mother and his children.

Critical Reading

<u>A</u> 19. The statement below is
    A. a fact.
    B. an opinion.
    C. both fact and opinion.

> Two observations which can be confirmed by others.

"At the age of eighty my mother had her last bad fall, and after that her mind wandered free through time." (Paragraph 1)

<u>D</u> 20. When Russell Baker responds to his children's complaints by telling them how much harder life was in his day, he is committing the fallacy of
    A. straw man (*an argument is made by claiming an opponent holds an extreme position and then opposing that extreme position*).
    B. either-or (*the argument assumes that there are only two sides to a question*).
    C. false cause (*the argument assumes that the order of events alone shows cause and effect*).
    D. false comparison (*the argument assumes that two things being compared are more alike than they really are*).

> Quite possibly Baker's children face problems with which he never had to contend; therefore, the comparison is invalid.

SUMMARIZING

Wording of answers may vary.

Add the ideas needed to complete the following summary of "In My Day."

The author, Russell Baker, writes about his eighty-year-old mother who has become senile after her last bad fall. Confined to a hospital and then a nursing home, the old woman disturbs him by doing such things as _____

See paragraphs 2–5.

failing to recognize him and *calling him on the*

See paragraphs 6–8.

phone to tell him that she is being buried that day. .

While visiting his mother at a hospital in Baltimore, Baker recalls what a formidable and opinionated woman she once had been. In response to her flights of senility, Baker tries to bring her back to reality. The doctors come in, question her, and diagnose her as hopelessly senile when she fails their oral quiz. Shortly afterward, Baker comes to realize that his mother's senility

See paragraph 40.

has enabled her to *break free from a lonely and boring old age and to return mentally to a time when she was loved and needed* .

He then recalls the "naïve" letters he wrote her three years earlier in which

See paragraph 41.

he tried to *give her a pep talk to boost her spirits* , not realizing then that *parents, like other people, can "become frail and break."* .

Now, three years later, Baker has stopped trying to force his mother to recognize reality and attempts to travel mentally back through time with her as she imagines that she is a young girl again. Sitting at her bedside,

See paragraph 49.

however, Baker realizes that he actually *knows very little about his mother's childhood and her people* . He reflects on the disconnections

See paragraphs 50–51.

which separate parents and children. His own children, he realizes, are bored when he *lectures them about the hardships he endured growing up* ,

See paragraph 57.

recollections which he admits are *selective and therefore dishonest* .

See paragraph 58.

He further regrets that he did not learn more about his mother's youth when she *was still able to answer his questions* .

See paragraph 58.

Although children instinctively want to *break free from their parents and create their own pasts* , Baker reminds us that "we all come from the past" and that we "ought to know" that "[life] cannot be defined by the span of a single journey from diaper to shroud."

DISCUSSION QUESTIONS

1. How would you describe the author's mother, first as a young woman and then as an elderly one? Do you see any similarities between the young Mrs. Baker and the eighty-year-old Mrs. Baker? Between the eighty-year-old Mrs. Baker and her son Russell?

2. When her mind began to wander, Baker at first tried to bring his mother back to the present. Later, however, he played along with her "trips through time." Do you think he was right to stop correcting her mistakes? Why or why not?

3. Baker writes that "one thinks of parents differently from other people. Other people can become frail and break, but not parents." Why do you think people hold their parents to higher standards than they do other people, and find it harder to forgive their parents when they fall short?

4. Baker now regrets not knowing more of his family history. Once he became curious about his mother's past, she was no longer able to tell him about it. What can you—and other parents and children—do to overcome the "disconnections" between generations so that the family's past history can be preserved for the future?

Note: Writing assignments for this selection appear on page 570.

Check Your Performance			**IN MY DAY**
Activity	*Number Right*	*Points*	*Score*
READING COMPREHENSION QUESTIONS			
Vocabulary in Context (3 items)	_____	× 4 =	_____
Central Point and Main Ideas (4 items)	_____	× 4 =	_____
Supporting Details (3 items)	_____	× 4 =	_____
Inferences (5 items)	_____	× 4 =	_____
Purpose and Tone (2 items)	_____	× 4 =	_____
Argument (1 item)	_____	× 4 =	_____
Critical Reading (2 items)	_____	× 4 =	_____
SUMMARIZING (10 items)	_____	× 2 =	_____
		TOTAL SCORE =	_____%

Enter your total score into the **Reading Performance Chart: Ten Reading Selections** on the inside back cover.

10

The Spider and the Wasp
Alexander Petrunkevitch

Preview

The tarantula and the digger wasp are creatures linked by destiny. So that baby wasps may live, the tarantula must die. Such cruelties of nature are not uncommon. But what is surprising is the passive way in which the tarantula submits to its fate. In this essay from *Scientific American* magazine, noted naturalist Alexander Petrunkevitch analyzes the spider's cooperation in its own demise.

Words to Watch

progeny (1): offspring
crass (1): crude; not refined
tactile (8): related to the sense of touch
pungent (9): sharp-smelling
gargantuan (9): huge
chitinous (9): concerning the material that makes up an insect's exoskeleton
discriminating (10): selective
girth (11): middle
protruding (12): sticking out
olfactory (14): related to the sense of smell
simulating (15): pretending
initiative (16): power to act before others do
chasm (16): a deep opening in the earth's surface

1   In the feeding and safeguarding of their progeny°, insects and spiders exhibit some interesting analogies to reasoning and some crass° examples of blind instinct. The case I propose to describe here is that of the tarantula spiders and their arch-enemy, the digger wasps of the genus *Pepsis*. It is a classic example of

what looks like intelligence pitted against instinct—a strange situation in which the victim, though fully able to defend itself, submits unwittingly to its destruction.

2   Most tarantulas live in the tropics, but several species occur in the temperate zone, and a few are common in the southern United States. Some varieties are large and have powerful fangs with which they can inflict a deep wound. These formidable-looking spiders do not, however, attack man; you can hold one in your hand, if you are gentle, without being bitten. Their bite is dangerous only to insects and small mammals such as mice; for a man it is no worse than a hornet's sting.

3   Tarantulas customarily live in deep cylindrical burrows, from which they emerge at dusk and into which they retire at dawn. Mature males wander about after dark in search of females and occasionally stray into houses. After mating, the male dies in a few weeks, but a female lives much longer and can mate several years in succession. In a Paris museum is a tropical specimen which is said to have been living in captivity for twenty-five years.

4   A fertilized female tarantula lays from 200 to 400 eggs at a time; thus it is possible for a single tarantula to produce several thousand young. She takes no care of them beyond weaving a cocoon of silk to enclose the eggs. After they hatch, the young walk away, find convenient places in which to dig their burrows, and spend the rest of their lives in solitude. Tarantulas feed mostly on insects and millipedes. Once their appetite is appeased, they digest the food for several days before eating again. Their sight is poor, being limited to sensing a change in the intensity of light and to the perception of moving objects.

They apparently have little or no sense of hearing, for a hungry tarantula will pay no attention to a loudly chirping cricket placed in its cage unless the insect happens to touch one of its legs.

5   But all spiders, and especially hairy ones, have an extremely delicate sense of touch. Laboratory experiments prove that tarantulas can distinguish three types of touch: pressure against the body wall, stroking of the body hair, and riffling of certain very fine hairs on the legs called trichobothria. Pressure against the body, by a finger or the end of a pencil, causes the tarantula to move off slowly for a short distance. The touch excites no defensive response unless the approach is from above where the spider can see the motion, in which case it rises on its hind legs, lifts its front legs, opens its fangs, and holds this threatening posture as long as the object continues to move. When the motion stops, the spider drops back to the ground, remains quiet for a few seconds, and then moves slowly away.

6   The entire body of a tarantula, especially its legs, is thickly clothed with hair. Some of it is short and woolly, some long and stiff. Touching this body hair produces one of two distinct reactions. When the spider is hungry, it responds with an immediate and swift attack. At the touch of a cricket's antennae, the tarantula seizes the insect so swiftly that a motion picture taken at the rate of 64 frames per second shows only the result and not the process of capture. But when the spider is not hungry, the stimulation of its hairs merely causes it to shake the touched limb. An insect can walk under its hairy belly unharmed.

7   The trichobothria, very fine hairs growing from disklike membranes on the legs, were once thought to be the spider's hearing organs, but we now know that

they have nothing to do with sound. They are sensitive only to air movement. A light breeze makes them vibrate slowly without disturbing the common hair. When one blows gently on the trichobothria, the tarantula reacts with a quick jerk of its four front legs. If the front and hind legs are stimulated at the same time, the spider makes a sudden jump. This reaction is quite independent of the state of its appetite.

8   These three tactile° responses—to pressure on the body wall, to moving of the common hair, and to flexing of the trichobothria—are so different from one another that there is no possibility of confusing them. They serve the tarantula adequately for most of its needs and enable it to avoid most annoyances and dangers. But they fail the spider completely when it meets its deadly enemy, the digger wasp *Pepsis*.

9   These solitary wasps are beautiful and formidable creatures. Most species are either a deep shiny blue all over, or deep blue with rusty wings. The largest have a wing span of about four inches. They live on nectar. When excited, they give off a pungent° odor—a warning that they are ready to attack. The sting is much worse than that of a bee or common wasp, and the pain and swelling last longer. In the adult stage the wasp lives only a few months. The female produces but a few eggs, one at a time at intervals of two or three days. For each egg the mother must provide one adult tarantula, alive but paralyzed. The tarantula must be of the correct species to nourish the larva. The mother wasp attaches the egg to the paralyzed spider's abdomen. Upon hatching from the egg, the larva is many hundreds of times smaller than its living but helpless victim. It eats no other food and drinks no water. By the time it has finished its single gargantuan° meal and become ready for wasphood, nothing remains of the tarantula but its indigestible chitinous° skeleton.

10   The mother wasp goes tarantula-hunting when the egg in her ovary is almost ready to be laid. Flying low over the ground late on a sunny afternoon, the wasp looks for its victim or for the mouth of a tarantula burrow, a round hole edged by a bit of silk. The sex of the spider makes no difference, but the mother is highly discriminating° as to species. Each species of *Pepsis* requires a certain species of tarantula, and the wasp will not attack the wrong species. In a cage with a tarantula which is not its normal prey, the wasp avoids the spider, and is usually killed by it in the night.

11   Yet when a wasp finds the correct species, it is the other way around. To identify the species, the wasp apparently must explore the spider with her antennae. The tarantula shows an amazing tolerance to this exploration. The wasp crawls under it and walks over it without evoking any hostile response. The molestation is so great and so persistent that the tarantula often rises on all eight legs, as if it were on stilts. It may stand this way for several minutes. Meanwhile the wasp, having satisfied itself that the victim is of the right species, moves off a few inches to dig the spider's grave. Working vigorously with legs and jaws, it excavates a hole eight to ten inches deep with a diameter slightly larger than the spider's girth°. Now and again the wasp pops out of the hole to make sure that the spider is still there.

12   When the grave is finished, the wasp returns to the tarantula to complete her ghastly enterprise. First she feels it all over once more with her antennae. Then

her behavior becomes more aggressive. She bends her abdomen, protruding° her sting, and searches for the soft membrane at the point where the spider's leg joins its body—the only spot where she can penetrate the horny skeleton. From time to time, as the exasperated spider slowly shifts ground, the wasp turns on her back and slides along with the aid of her wings, trying to get under the tarantula for a shot at the vital spot. During all this maneuvering, which can last for several minutes, the tarantula makes no move to save itself. Finally the wasp corners it against some obstruction and grasps one of its legs in her powerful jaws. Now at last the harassed spider tries a desperate but vain defense. The two contestants roll over and over on the ground. It is a terrifying sight, and the outcome is always the same. The wasp finally manages to thrust her sting into the soft spot and holds it there for a few seconds while she pumps in the poison. Almost immediately the tarantula falls paralyzed on its back. Its legs stop twitching; its heart stops beating. Yet it is not dead, as is shown by the fact that if taken from the wasp it can be restored to some sensitivity by being kept in a moist chamber for several months.

13   After paralyzing the tarantula, the wasp cleans herself by dragging her body along the ground and rubbing her feet, sucks the drop of blood oozing from the wound in the spider's abdomen, then grabs a leg of the flabby, helpless animal in her jaws and drags it down to the bottom of the grave. She stays there for many minutes, sometimes for several hours, and what she does all that time in the dark we do not know. Eventually she lays her egg and attaches it to the side of the spider's abdomen with a sticky secretion. Then she emerges, fills the

grave with soil carried bit by bit in her jaws, and finally tramples the ground all around to hide any trace of the grave from prowlers. Then she flies away, leaving her descendant safely started in life.

In all this the behavior of the wasp 14 evidently is qualitatively different from that of the spider. The wasp acts like an intelligent animal. This is not to say that instinct plays no part or that she reasons as man does. But her actions are to the point; they are not automatic and can be modified to fit the situation. We do not know for certain how she identifies the tarantula—probably it is by some olfactory° or chemo-tactile sense—but she does it purposefully and does not blindly tackle a wrong species.

On the other hand, the tarantula's 15 behavior shows only confusion. Evidently the wasp's pawing gives it no pleasure, for it tries to move away. That the wasp is not simulating° sexual stimulation is certain, because male and female tarantulas react in the same way to its advances. That the spider is not anesthetized by some odorless secretion is easily shown by blowing lightly at the tarantula and making it jump suddenly. What, then, makes the tarantula behave as stupidly as it does?

No clear, simple answer is available. 16 Possibly the stimulation by the wasp's antennae is masked by a heavier pressure on the spider's body, so that it reacts as when prodded by a pencil. But the explanation may be much more complex. Initiative° in attack is not in the nature of tarantulas; most species fight only when cornered so that escape is impossible. Their inherited patterns of behavior apparently prompt them to avoid problems rather than attack them. For example, spiders always weave their webs in three dimensions, and when a spider finds that there is insufficient space to attach certain threads in the third dimension, it leaves the place and seeks another, instead of finishing the web in a single plane. This urge to escape seems to arise under all circumstances, in all phases of life and to take the place of reasoning. For a spider to change the pattern of its web is as impossible as for an inexperienced man to build a bridge across a chasm° obstructing his way.

17   In a way the instinctive urge to escape is not only easier but often more efficient than reasoning. The tarantula does exactly what is most efficient in all cases except in an encounter with a ruthless and determined attacker dependent for the existence of her own species on killing as many tarantulas as she can lay eggs. Perhaps in this case the spider follows its usual pattern of trying to escape, instead of seizing and killing the wasp, because it is not aware of its danger. In any case, the survival of the tarantula species as a whole is protected by the fact that the spider is much more fertile than the wasp.

READING COMPREHENSION QUESTIONS

Vocabulary in Context

___B___ 1. In the excerpt below, the word *formidable* (fôr′mĭ-də-bəl) means
    A. delicate.
    B. inspiring fear or dread.
    C. nervous.
    D. genuine.

> Something which is large and has powerful fangs would be capable of inspiring fear or dread.

"Some varieties are large and have powerful fangs with which they can inflict a deep wound. These formidable-looking spiders do not, however, attack man . . ." (Paragraph 2)

___A___ 2. In the excerpt below, the word *appeased* (ə-pēzd′) means
    A. satisfied.
    B. aroused.
    C. affected.
    D. changed.

> After a tarantula eats, its appetite is satisfied.

"Tarantulas feed mostly on insects and millipedes. Once their appetite is appeased, they digest the food for several days before eating again." (Paragraph 4)

____D____ 3. In the excerpt below, the word *evoking* (ĭ-vōk′ĭng) means

    A. using.

    B. challenging.

    C. hiding.

    D. bringing out.

> Since the tarantula "shows an amazing tolerance," the wasp's actions must fail to bring out any hostile response.

"To identify the species, the wasp apparently must explore the spider with her antennae. The tarantula shows an amazing tolerance to this exploration. The wasp crawls under it and walks over it without evoking any hostile response." (Paragraph 11)

Central Point and Main Ideas

____D____ 4. Which sentence best expresses the central point of the selection?

    A. Tarantulas are among the stupidest creatures in the natural world.

    B. The female digger wasp will go to great lengths to ensure that her offspring survive.

    C. Even though a digger wasp can disable and kill a tarantula, tarantulas will survive as a species because they are more fertile than wasps.

    D. In the conflict between digger wasps and tarantulas, the seemingly intelligent wasps win out over the tarantulas who act instinctively.

Answer A is not indicated in the selection. Answer B covers only paragraphs 10–13. Answer C covers only paragraph 17.

____C____ 5. Which of the following expresses the main idea of paragraphs 5–7?

    A. Spiders, particularly hairy ones such as the tarantula, have an extremely delicate sense of touch.

    B. Tarantulas have hair on their bodies as well as on their legs.

    C. The way that the tarantula responds to touch is dependent partly on whether it is hungry and partly on where it is touched.

    D. A hungry tarantula will attack and kill an insect that touches it, but a tarantula that is not hungry will merely shake the touched limb.

Answer A is a detail from paragraph 5. Answers B and D cover only parts of paragraph 6.

____B____ 6. Which sentence best expresses the main idea of paragraph 9?

    A. The solitary wasps are extremely beautiful but live only a few months.

    B. The wasps are beautiful but deadly to tarantulas, which they paralyze in order to feed their young.

    C. The sting of these wasps is much worse than that of a bee or common wasp.

    D. All that the wasp larva needs to survive is a disabled tarantula.

Answers A, C, and D are too narrow, each covering only one detail of the paragraph.

Supporting Details

__D__ 7. A female tarantula's care of its young consists of
    A. providing them with dead insects to feed on.
    B. hiding them in a below-ground nest.
    C. hovering nearby to defend them from predators.
    D. enclosing them, as eggs, in a silk cocoon.

See the second sentence in paragraph 4.

__A__ 8. Immediately after the digger wasp has satisfied itself that its victim is of the right species, it
    A. digs the tarantula's grave.
    B. stings the tarantula in the space where its leg joins its body.
    C. lays eggs.
    D. grasps one of the tarantula's legs in its powerful jaws.

See sentence 7 in paragraph 11.

Transitions

__C__ 9. The relationship of the second sentence below to the first sentence is one of
    A. cause and effect.
    B. addition.
    C. contrast.
    D. illustration.

The passage contrasts the behavior of the tarantula when it is hungry with its behavior when it isn't hungry. Contrast transition: *But*.

"At the touch of a cricket's antennae, the tarantula seizes the insect so swiftly that a motion picture taken at the rate of 64 frames per second shows only the result and not the process of capture. <u>But</u> when the spider is not hungry, the stimulation of its hairs merely causes it to shake the touched limb." (Paragraph 6)

Patterns of Organization

__A__ 10. The main pattern of organization of paragraphs 12–13 is
    A. time order.
    B. list of items.
    C. definition and example.
    D. comparison.

The paragraphs detail, in time order, how the wasp paralyzes and buries the tarantula in order to feed its young. Time transitions include *When, First, Finally,* and *After*.

__C__ 11. The main pattern of organization of paragraphs 14–15 is
    A. cause and effect.
    B. list of items.
    C. contrast.
    D. time order.

Paragraphs 14–15 contrast the wasp's intelligent-seeming behavior with the confused behavior of the tarantula. The contrast transition *On the other hand* links the two paragraphs.

Inferences

The author ___C___ 12. On the basis of paragraphs 14 and 15, we can infer that the author
states that "the wasp   A. is disgusted by the wasp's behavior.
acts like an intelligent B. fully understands the behavior of the tarantula.
animal," but the
tarantula behaves   C. is impressed by the behavior of the wasp but not by the behavior of
"stupidly." This suggests   the tarantula.
that he is impressed   D. is disgusted by the behavior of both the wasp and the tarantula.
by the wasp's behavior, but not by the tarantula's.

___A___ 13. We might conclude from the reading that
  A. animals that can modify their behavior to fit certain circumstances
     have an advantage over animals that cannot.
  B. creatures that cannot reason quickly die out.
  C. in a laboratory setting, tarantulas could probably be trained to attack
     digger wasps.
  D. the author has made documentary films on the behavior of
     tarantulas and wasps.   Answers B, C, and D are not indicated in the
                selection. The fact that the tarantula cannot modify its behavior
                causes it to fall victim to the wasp. See paragraphs 14–15.

Purpose and Tone

___A___ 14. The author's main purpose is to
  A. inform readers about a classic example of intelligence pitted against
     instinct in the animal kingdom.

In paragraph 1, the
author clearly states   B. persuade readers that all creatures, even insects and spiders, have a
his intent to inform   right to exist.
readers.
  C. entertain us with fascinating yet gory examples of the behavior of
     wasps and tarantulas.

___B___ 15. In describing the death struggle between the wasp and the tarantula, the
     author's tone is one of
  A. horror.
  B. detachment.   The author, a naturalist, is not emotionally
  C. admiration.   connected to the death struggle in any way.
  D. amusement.

___C___ 16. The general tone of the reading is
  A. sentimental.
  B. critical.   Overall, the author reports what he and
  C. instructive.   others have observed without being
  D. sympathetic.   sentimental, critical, or sympathetic.

Argument

_C_ 17. Write the letter of the statement that is the point of the following argument. The other statements are support for that point.

   A. The digger wasp pumps poison into the tarantula, which quickly paralyzes it.

   B. The tarantula seems helpless to defend itself against the digger wasp's attack.

   C. Although it is smaller than a tarantula, a digger wasp is the tarantula's worst enemy.

   D. The larva of the digger wasp feeds on the paralyzed tarantula until it is dead.   Answers A, B, and D support the point stated in answer C—that a digger wasp is the tarantula's worst enemy.

Critical Reading

_A_ 18. The reading is

   A. mainly fact.

   B. all opinion.

   C. about half fact and half opinion.

The selection is based upon the observations of scientists.

_B_ 19. The facts of the reading are probably based on

   A. the author's personal observations.

   B. a great deal of scientific research, including the author's.

   C. one or two cases where digger wasps have been observed to disable tarantulas.

   D. popular accounts of human encounters with tarantulas and wasps.

The breadth of the information suggests that it was based upon a great deal of scientific research, including that of the naturalist author. Also, in paragraph 5, the author refers to "laboratory experiments."

_C_ 20. People who argue that it's okay for them to engage in ruthless and selfish behavior on the basis of examples from the animal kingdom are illustrating the fallacy of

   A. either-or *(the argument assumes that there are only two sides to a question).*

   B. false cause *(the argument assumes that the order of events alone shows cause and effect).*

   C. false comparison *(the argument assumes that two things being compared are more alike than they really are).*

   D. straw man *(an argument is made by claiming an opponent holds an extreme position and then opposing that extreme position).*

There are enormous differences between the animal kingdom and human societies; therefore, the argument is invalid.

OUTLINING

Complete the outline of paragraphs 10–13 by filling in the missing major and minor details.   *Wording of answers may vary.*

Central point: The mother wasp finds and paralyzes an adult tarantula so that her offspring can feed on it.

1. _____ *Before the attack* _____

   a. When her egg is almost ready to be laid, she locates a tarantula burrow.
   b. To identify the correct species of tarantula, the wasp explores the tarantula with her antennae.
   c. *After the wasp is satisfied that the tarantula is the correct species, she digs the spider's grave.*

2. During the attack

   a. The wasp protrudes her sting.
   b. *She corners the tarantula and grasps one of its legs in her jaws.*

   _____

   c. The tarantula unsuccessfully tries to get away.
   d. The wasp pumps in poison at the spot where the spider's leg joins its body.
   e. The tarantula becomes paralyzed.

3. After the attack

   a. The wasp cleans herself and sucks some blood from the tarantula's wound.
   b. *The wasp drags the tarantula down to the bottom of the grave.*

   _____

   c. She lays her egg and attaches it to the tarantula.
   d. She fills in the grave with soil.
   e. She flies away, leaving her descendant to hatch and feed on the tarantula.

Item 1: The headings for 2 and 3 indicate the outline is organized around the sequence of events in the process of killing the tarantula.
Item 1c: See paragraph 11, sentences 7–8.
Item 2b: See paragraph 12, sentence 7.
Item 3b: See paragraph 13, sentence 1.

DISCUSSION QUESTIONS

1. Many people are frightened or disgusted by spiders and wasps. Yet this writer obviously finds both to be beautiful and fascinating creatures. What details about the wasp and the tarantula surprised or interested you most? What similarities to humans do these two species possess? Finally, what conclusions, if any, can we draw about human behavior on the basis of the interactions between the "intelligent" digger wasps and the "instinctual" tarantulas?

2. To us, the behavior of the tarantula with the digger wasp seems suicidal. Yet common sense tells us that the tarantula does not want to die in order to provide food for the wasp's offspring. What alternative explanations might there be for the tarantula's behavior?

3. Books, articles, and television shows about animal behavior are often very popular, with adults as well as children. How would you explain the fascination that animal behavior holds for people?

4. The tarantula, as a creature of instinct, can't choose whether to fight or flee, but people can. Think of a time when you were faced with a threatening situation. Did you choose to flee—or to fight? What factors in the situation helped you make your decision?

Note: Writing assignments for this selection appear on page 570.

Check Your Performance   THE SPIDER AND THE WASP

Activity	Number Right	Points	Score
READING COMPREHENSION QUESTIONS			
Vocabulary in Context (3 items)	_____	× 4 =	_____
Central Point and Main Ideas (3 items)	_____	× 4 =	_____
Supporting Details (2 items)	_____	× 4 =	_____
Transitions (1 item)	_____	× 4 =	_____
Patterns of Organization (2 items)	_____	× 4 =	_____
Inferences (2 items)	_____	× 4 =	_____
Purpose and Tone (3 items)	_____	× 4 =	_____
Argument (1 item)	_____	× 4 =	_____
Critical Reading (3 items)	_____	× 4 =	_____
OUTLINING (4 items)	_____	× 5 =	_____
	TOTAL SCORE =		_____%

Enter your total score into the **Reading Performance Chart: Ten Reading Selections** on the inside back cover.

Part III

COMBINED-SKILLS TESTS

Following are twenty tests that cover many of the skills taught in Part I and reinforced in Part II of this book. Each test consists of a short reading passage followed by questions on any of the following: vocabulary in context, central points and main ideas, supporting details, relationships, inferences, purpose and tone, argument, and critical reading.

Notes:

1. In the comments on test questions, the term "too narrow" describes an item that is only a detail within the selection. "Too broad" describes an item that covers a great deal more than is in the selection.

2. Because these combined-skills tests are on facing pages—**specifically so that students can see the full text and the questions on a single spread without having to flip back and forth**—you might not want to ask students to remove them from the book. One option instead would be to pass out copies of the model answer sheet that is on the next page. Or you could ask students to use a piece of notebook paper as their answer sheet.

SAMPLE ANSWER SHEET

Use the form below as a model answer sheet for the twenty combined-skills tests on the following pages.

Name _____

Section _____ Date _____

SCORE: (Number correct) _____ × 12.5 = _____%

COMBINED SKILLS: Test ____

1. _____

2. _____

3. _____

4. _____

5. _____

6. _____

7. _____

8. _____

COMBINED SKILLS: Test 1

Read the passage below. Then write the letter of the best answer to each question that follows.

[1]Animal researchers are rethinking their belief that play fights between animals are practice for the real thing. [2]A key piece of evidence that play fighting isn't about learning how to win is the fact that all animals both win and lose their play fights. [3]No young animal ever wins all his play fights; if he did, nobody would play with him. [4]When a juvenile animal is bigger, stronger, older, and more dominant than the other animal he is play fighting with, the bigger animal will roll over on his back and lose on purpose a certain amount of the time. [5]That's called *self-handicapping*, and all animals do it, maybe because if they didn't do it, their smaller friends would stop playing with them. [6]This is also called *role reversal*, because the winner and the loser reverse roles.

[7]Role reversal is such a basic part of roughhouse play that animals do it when they play games like tug-of-war, too. [8]A friend told me a story about her mixed-breed dog, when he was a year old and fully grown, playing with the four-month-old Labrador puppy next door. [9]The two dogs liked to play tug-of-war with a rope toy my friend had out on her terrace, but of course my friend's dog was so huge compared to the puppy that it was no contest. [10]If he used all his strength, he'd end up just whipping the puppy around the terrace like a Frisbee.

[11]But that's not what happened. [12]Pretty soon my friend noticed that the puppy was "winning" some of the tugs. [13]First my friend's mutt would pull the puppy across the terrace; then the puppy would pull him back a bit. [14]My friend said her dog was "keeping the puppy in the game," and I'm sure she's right.

[15]Some animal researchers say that the fact that all animals self-handicap might mean that the purpose of play fighting isn't to teach animals how to win, but to teach them how to win and lose. [16]All animals probably need to know both the dominant and the subordinate role, because no animal starts out on top, and no animal who lives to old age ends up on top, either. [17]Even a male who is going to end up as the alpha starts out young and vulnerable. [18]He has to know how to exhibit proper subordinate behaviors.

___B___ 1. In sentence 18, the word *subordinate* means
    A. bossy.
    B. lower in rank.
    C. harmful.
    D. playful.

> If dominant animals are on top, where are *subordinate* animals?

Note: Throughout the twenty combined-skills tests, transitions indicating the primary pattern of organization of each passage are underlined.

___C___ 2. According to some researchers, the fact that animals self-handicap might mean
    A. that they are imitating human behavior.
    B. that no animal starts out on top.   See sentence 15.
    C. that they need to learn both winning and losing behaviors.
    D. that they need to learn dominant behavior.

___C___ 3. What is the relationship of paragraphs 2 and 3 to paragraph 1?
    A. Time order
    B. List of items   The story about how the mixed-breed dog
    C. Illustration   played with a puppy illustrates role reversal.
    D. Cause and effect

___D___ 4. We can infer that the author's attitude toward dogs is
    A. amused and carefree.   The author's detailed description of dogs at
    B. superior but tolerant.   play indicates an understanding and approving
    C. detached and critical.   attitude. Her presentation of the results of
    D. understanding and approving.   animal research suggests that her attitude is not
                                              carefree; nor is it superior or critical.

Answer B is contra-
dicted by
sentence   ___A___ 5. We can reasonably conclude from this selection that
4, which explains that A. animal behavior is more complex than researchers previously
sometimes animals   thought.
"lose on purpose."   B. dogs dislike losing and will do anything to avoid it.
Answer C is not
supported. Answer D   C. dogs behave differently with each other when they know they are
is contradicted by   being watched.
sentence 16, which   D. once an animal is dominant, he stays that way for life.
suggests that animals lose their dominance once they become old.

___B___ 6. The tone of this passage is best described as
    A. dull and scientific.   The author presents facts about role
    B. informal yet informative.   reversal in animals in mostly informal
    C. preachy.   language. The story told to her by a friend
    D. sarcastic.   highlights the author's informal tone.

___C___ 7. Which is the most appropriate title for this selection?
    A. Myths about Animals   Answers A, B, and D do not
    B. Two Dogs at Play   address the topic of role reversal
    C. Animal Role Reversal during Play   among animals, which is clearly
    D. A Kind-Hearted Big Dog   the focus of the passage.

___C___ 8. Which statement best expresses the central point of the selection?
Answer A covers   A. A grown dog will occasionally let a puppy win at tug-of-war to
only sentences 11–14.   "keep him in the game."
Answer B covers
only sentence 1.   B. Some animal researchers no longer believe that play fights between
Answer D is too broad   animals are practice for the real thing.
because the selection C. Animals practice role reversal while play fighting because they need
focuses on role   to know both the dominant and subordinate roles.
reversal and what
dogs learn from it.   D. It can be entertaining and informative to watch two dogs at play.

COMBINED SKILLS: Test 2

Read the passage below. Then write the letter of the best answer to each question that follows.

¹While previous generations of American students have had to sit through tests, never have the tests been given so frequently, and never have they played such a prominent role in schooling. ²Exams used to be administered mostly to decide where to place kids or what kind of help they needed; only recently have scores been published in the newspaper and used as the primary criteria for judging children, teachers, and schools—indeed, as the basis for flunking students or denying them a diploma, deciding where money should be spent, and so on. ³Tests have lately become a mechanism by which public officials can impose their will on schools, and they are doing so with a vengeance.

⁴This situation is also unusual from an international perspective. ⁵"Few countries today give these formal examinations to students before the age of sixteen or so," two scholars report. ⁶In the U.S., we subject children as young as *six* to standardized exams, <u>despite</u> the fact that almost all experts in early childhood education condemn this practice. ⁷And it isn't easy to find other countries that give multiple-choice tests to students of any age.

⁸In short, our children are tested to an extent that is unprecedented in our history and unparalleled anywhere else in the world. ⁹Rather than seeing this as odd, or something that needs to be defended, many of us have come to take it for granted. ¹⁰The result is that most of today's discourse about education has been reduced to a crude series of monosyllables: "Test scores are too low. Make them go up."

_____B_____ 1. In sentence 10, the word *discourse* means
- A. warning.
- B. discussion.
- C. curriculum.
- D. agreement.

> The monosyllabic quotation is an example of the level of discussion today.

_____C_____ 2. Paragraph 2
- A. provides reasons why American students take so many standardized tests.
- B. compares former and current American attitudes toward standardized testing.
- C. contrasts American testing of students with practices in other countries.
- D. lists examples of current standardized tests.

> The paragraph contrasts American testing practices with testing practices in other countries. Contrast transition: *despite* (sentence 6).

___D___ 3. According to the selection, public officials use standardized tests to
A. decide where to place kids or what kind of help they need.
B. humiliate failing students.
C. decide where to enroll their own children.
D. recklessly impose their will on schools.

See sentence 3.

___B___ 4. The passage suggests that administering standardized tests to children as young as six
A. is helpful in determining whether a particular student should be promoted.
B. is not beneficial to the children involved.
C. is crucial to judging their academic ability.
D. is seldom done in America.

See sentence 6.

___A___ 5. We can infer that the author of this passage believes that standardized tests in America

Sentence 2 suggests that it is a mistake to make standardized tests the "primary criteria" for judging children, teachers, and schools.

A. detract from more important aspects of education.
B. should play a larger part in judging children, teachers, and schools.
C. have drawbacks, but are the most accurate method of judging the quality of education.
D. are entirely without value and should be eliminated.

___B___ 6. The author's tone with regard to standardized testing as used today in America can best be described as
A. sorrowful.
B. disapproving.
C. bewildered.
D. matter-of-fact.

Some excerpts that highlight the author's tone: "they are doing so with a vengeance" (sentence 3), "we subject children as young as *six* to standardized tests, despite the fact that almost all experts…condemn this practice" (sentence 6), "today's discourse about education has been reduced to a crude series of monosyllables" (sentence 10).

___A___ 7. Sentence 6 is a statement of
A. fact.
B. opinion.
C. fact and opinion.

The information has been documented by researchers.

___A___ 8. Which of the following statements best expresses the central point of the selection?
A. American schoolchildren are subjected to far too many standardized tests.
B. American public officials are overly concerned about standardized test scores.
C. Children in other countries generally take far fewer standardized tests than do American children.
D. Scores on standardized tests have been declining for decades.

Answer B covers only sentences 2–3. Answer C covers only sentence 5. Answer D is not supported.

COMBINED SKILLS: Test 3

Read the passage below. Then write the letter of the best answer to each question that follows.

¹Some psychologists are interested in resilience: the ability to "bounce back," recovering one's self-confidence, good spirits, and hopeful attitude, after extreme or prolonged stress. ²In particular, psychologists want to understand why some children who grow up in adverse circumstances (such as extreme poverty, dangerous neighborhoods, abusive parents, and/or exposure to drugs and alcohol) become well-adjusted adults, whereas others remain troubled—and frequently get into trouble—throughout their lives.

³One team of researchers identified 240 high-risk children in Hawaii who had experienced stress at birth, poverty, and family conflict, and followed their development for 40 years. ⁴Two-thirds of the children became involved in crime, but one-third became confident, competent, caring adults. ⁵The resilient members of this sample tended to be affectionate and outgoing from birth, which attracted other people to them. ⁶They had interests and talents (intellectual, artistic, athletic) that helped them make friends, develop a sense of purpose, and gain self-esteem. ⁷Equally important, they had warm, supportive relationships with at least one adult other than their parents who viewed them as special and important. ⁸Compared to their troubled peers—and to a control group of children who grew up in secure environments—the resilient children grew into adults with the highest percentage of stable marriages and lowest proportions of unemployment, divorce, and serious health problems. ⁹<u>Another</u> study of adolescents whose parents suffer from depression found that the most resilient teenagers had a strong relationship with an outside adult and a hobby at which they excelled, both of which gave them a sense of value. ¹⁰Taken together, these studies suggest that two ways to foster resilience in high-risk children are mentor programs (such as Big Brother/Sister, which teams an adult volunteer with a needy child) and after-school programs that offer a range of activities.

___D___ 1. In sentence 2, the word *adverse* means
  A. financially needy.
  B. desirable.
  C. highly unusual.
  D. unfavorable.

Example clues: extreme poverty, dangerous neighborhoods, abusive parents, and/or exposure to drugs and alcohol.

___B___ 2. Which of the following is **not** mentioned in this passage as a characteristic of resilient children?
  A. They tend to be outgoing and affectionate from birth.
  B. They tend to mentor younger children.
  C. They have special interests and talents.
  D. They receive encouragement from at least one adult other than their parents.

Answer A is mentioned in sentence 5; answer C is mentioned in sentence 6; answer D is mentioned in sentence 7.

Each ___B___ 3. Sentences 5–7 mainly
sentence lists a reason: A. contrast resilient with non-resilient children.
child is affectionate
and outgoing (5); has   B. list reasons why some high-risk children become confident, caring
interests and talents   adults.
(6); has supportive   C. provide steps in the process of conducting a psychological survey.
relationships (7).
                            D. narrate some typical events in the lives of high-risk children.

___C___ 4. The relationship of sentence 9 to sentence 8 is one of

A. illustration.
B. comparison.   Sentence 9 lists a second study. Addition transition:
C. addition.   *Another*. (Note that *Compared to* signals a
D. time.   comparison only within sentence 8.)

___B___ 5. This passage suggests that a root cause of crime is   Sentences 5, 6, 7,

A. poverty.   and 9 suggest that despite growing up under
                                                      adverse circumstances (poverty, dangerous
B. a lack of self-worth.   neighborhoods, abuse, exposure to
C. exposure to drugs and alcohol.   drugs/alcohol), resilient teenagers had
D. living in a dangerous neighborhood.   a sense of self-esteem which
                                     prevented them from becoming involved in crime.

___B___ 6. The author of this selection would probably agree with which of the
Sentence 10 suggests   following statements?
that mentoring
programs effectively   A. Children who grow up under adverse conditions naturally become
foster resilience in high-   criminals.
risk children. Therefore, B. People should be encouraged to mentor high-risk youth.
it is logical to conclude C. The ability to "bounce back" is determined at birth.
that people should be   D. There is little that society can do to support high-risk youth.
encouraged to become mentors.

___D___ 7. The author's tone can be described as

A. pessimistic and blaming.   The author cites research results which
B. indignant and self-righteous.   give the passage a serious tone, but
C. sentimental and pitying.   concludes with ways that people can help
D. serious and caring.   high-risk children (evidence of caring).

___A___ 8. Which is the most appropriate title for this selection?

A. Resilience and How to Foster It
B. The Troubled Environment of Today's Youth
C. Resilience: Something You're Born With
D. The Criminal Tendencies of High-Risk Youth

Answer B is too broad because the passage focuses on the role of
resilience in combating the troubled environment. Answer C is not
supported. Answer D does not address the topic of resilience.

COMBINED SKILLS: Test 4

Read the passage below. Then write the letter of the best answer to each question that follows.

¹Mention the word "parasite" and most people react by thinking "yuck." ²A parasite is by definition an organism that grows, feeds, and is sheltered by a "host" organism, to which it contributes nothing in return. ³In fact, some parasites go beyond "contributing nothing": they actually drive their hosts to suicidal behavior for the benefit of the parasite. ⁴For example, ants are sometimes invaded by tiny parasites called liver flukes. ⁵The flukes burrow into the ants' brains. ⁶In response, the ants do something that is quite insane. ⁷They spend the rest of their lives climbing to the tops of blades of grass. ⁸They climb, they fall, they climb again. ⁹This mad behavior actually makes complete sense, from the parasite's point of view. ¹⁰In order to complete its life cycle, the liver fluke needs to get into the digestive system of a cow or a sheep. ¹¹The quickest way to accomplish this is to place itself at the top of a blade of grass and wait for a grazing animal to come along. ¹²Therefore, what amounts to suicide for the ant insures that the fluke survives and reproduces. ¹³A similar example is seen in the three-spined stickleback, a kind of freshwater fish. ¹⁴The stickleback is frequently invaded by a tiny parasite that needs to end up in the belly of a bird in order to complete its life cycle. ¹⁵When the parasite infects the stickleback, it causes several changes in the fish. ¹⁶It turns it a lighter color, causes it to swim on the surface of the water, and darkens its eyes. ¹⁷All these changes make the fish more visible to a bird that happens to be flying over. ¹⁸The dark eyes even indicate to the bird in which direction the fish is swimming, thereby letting the bird know which way to dive in order to scoop the fish up. ¹⁹The fish dies, but the parasite lives on.

_B_   1. According to this selection, ants with liver flukes in their brains
    A. are more likely to be eaten by birds.
    B. repeatedly climb to the tops of blades of grass.
    C. turn a lighter color.   See sentences 6–8.
    D. attach themselves to cows and sheep.

_C_   2. Both liver flukes and the parasites in sticklebacks cause their hosts' death by
    A. draining off so many nutrients that the hosts die of starvation.
    B. driving the hosts so crazy that the hosts deliberately commit suicide.
    C. making it more likely that their hosts will be eaten by another animal.
    D. exposing them to disease-causing agents.

        Sentences 5–11 explain how liver flukes cause ants to be eaten by cows and sheep. Sentences 14–18 explain how parasites cause stickleback fish to be eaten by birds.

_____T_____ 3. TRUE OR FALSE? Both the liver fluke and the tiny parasites in stickle-backs complete their life cycles in the digestive systems of other animals. See sentences 10 and 14.

_____A_____ 4. The main pattern of organization used in the selection is
  A. definition and example.
  B. list of items.
  C. time order.
  D. contrast.

The passage defines the word *parasite* and provides examples of two parasites which drive their hosts to suicidal behavior. (Note that within each example, there is a cause and effect pattern.)

Nothing in the passage indicates that the author finds the behavior of parasites disgusting or vicious, nor the death of their hosts tragic. Rather, the author, in a straightforward manner, explains that the behavior of their hosts ensures the parasites' survival.

_____D_____ 5. The author of this passage would probably agree with which of the following statements?
  A. The behavior of some parasites is extremely disgusting.
  B. It is tragic that some animals must die so that others can live.
  C. Parasites are vicious animals.
  D. In nature, there are rational reasons for even the strangest behavior.

_____D_____ 6. You may reasonably infer from the examples in the passage that

Answers A, B, and C are unsupported. Sentences 4 and 14 suggest that there is nothing that ants and sticklebacks can do to resist being invaded by parasites.

  A. liver flukes are more intelligent than ants.
  B. the hosts of parasites want to die rather than endure any more torture.
  C. the hosts' life cycles remain intact thanks to the parasites.
  D. the hosts are powerless to resist the parasites' influence.

_____B_____ 7. Which title best summarizes the selection?
  A. The Life Cycle of the Liver Fluke
  B. Tiny but Powerful Parasites
  C. A Stickleback's Worst Enemy
  D. Avoiding Harmful Parasites

Answer A ignores the parasite that invades the stickleback. Answer C ignores the liver fluke. Answer D is not stated in the passage.

_____C_____ 8. The main idea of this passage is found in its
  A. first sentence.
  B. second sentence.
  C. third sentence.
  D. fourth sentence.

Answers A and B introduce the main idea, contained in the third sentence. Answer D supports the main idea.

COMBINED SKILLS: Test 5

Read the passage below. Then write the letter of the best answer to each question that follows.

¹Clearly, no society can shift from an economy based on manual labor to one based on knowledge unless its people are educated—illiterates cannot process written information. ²The vast transformation of work in industrial societies was based in part on vast changes in educational systems and practices.

³In 1647, only twenty-seven years after they had landed at Plymouth Rock, the Puritans of the Massachusetts Colony enacted a law embodying the very radical idea that all children should attend school—at the time almost no children went to school anywhere in the world. ⁴The Massachusetts School Law required that in any township having fifty households, one person must be appointed to teach the children to read and write, and the teacher's wages were to be paid either by the parents or the inhabitants in general. ⁵Furthermore, in any township having a hundred or more households, a school must be established, "the master thereof being able to instruct youth so far as they may be fitted for the university." ⁶Any community that failed to provide these educational services was to be fined "till they shall perform this order." ⁷As word spread that Massachusetts had passed a compulsory school law, it often was taken as further evidence that the Puritans were crazy.

⁸From these rustic beginnings, the ideal of public schools for all children became part of American culture—as settlers moved west, they took the "one-room schoolhouse" with them. ⁹Nevertheless, even 150 years ago, in most of the world, including Europe, most children were not schooled. ¹⁰Education was reserved for an elite few. ¹¹That America—still largely a frontier—was able to contribute so many important inventions to the Industrial Revolution during the nineteenth century is now seen as a result of its educational efforts. ¹²Moreover, as the Industrial Revolution spread, policies of mass education spread with it.

_____B_____ 1. In sentence 8, the word *rustic* means
   A. relating to city life.
   B. simple.
   C. routine.
   D. complicated.

   The Puritans designed a simple system for educating all children.

_____D_____ 2. This selection is mainly about
   A. the Massachusetts School Law enacted by the Puritans.
   B. the vast transformation of work in industrial societies.
   C. American contributions to the Industrial Revolution.
   D. educational practices and policies in early America.

   Answer A covers only sentences 3–6. Answer B is mentioned only in sentence 2. Answer C, although mentioned in sentence 11, ignores the idea of education in early America.

_____D_____ 3. According to this passage, the Massachusetts School Law of 1647
   A. was crazy.
   B. was a failure.   See sentence 3.
   C. affected only an elite few.
   D. created a new system of public education.

_____C_____ 4. The relationship of sentence 9 to sentence 8 is one of
   A. cause and effect.
   B. illustration.   The passage contrasts the American belief in
   C. contrast.   compulsory education with attitudes in other parts
   D. addition.   of the world. Contrast transition: *Nevertheless*.

_____D_____ 5. This passage suggests that as settlers moved west, they
See sentence 8. Logic   A. packed up their schoolhouses and took them with them.
suggests that the   B. concluded that education was a luxury they could not afford.
settlers did not literally
transport entire school- C. wanted their children to be educated, but didn't know how to go
houses, but instead took   about it.
the ideal of education   D. found ways to ensure that their children received an education.
with them.

_____B_____ 6. The author's tone is
   A. compassionate.   The author presents facts about how
   B. straightforward.   policies and practices of mass education
   C. approving.   spread with the Industrial Revolution.
   D. disapproving.

_____B_____ 7. Which statement can you reasonably infer from the passage?
Sentences 2 and 11   A. Small schools do a better job of educating than large schools do.
support answer B.   B. Education played a significant role in the Industrial Revolution.
Answers A, C, and D   C. Educational reform is needed to improve America's current
are not addressed in   economy.
the passage.   D. The Puritans were poor at school planning.

_____D_____ 8. Which statement best expresses the central point of this passage?
   A. A knowledge-based economy demands educated workers.
   B. The Massachusetts Colony was the first to require children to attend
       school.
   C. The Puritans were widely regarded to be offbeat in their practices.
   D. The idea that all children should be educated started with the
       Puritans of Massachusetts and spread with the Industrial Revolution.

Answer A covers only the introductory material
in sentence 1. Answer B covers only sentence 3.
Answer C covers only sentence 7.

COMBINED SKILLS: Test 6

Read the passage below. Then write the letter of the best answer to each question that follows.

¹Two automotive titans—Henry Ford and Alfred Sloan—symbolized the profound transformations that took place in American industry during the 1910s and 1920s. ²In 1913, the 50-year-old Ford revolutionized American manufacturing by introducing the automated assembly line. ³By using conveyor belts to bring automobile parts to workers, he reduced the assembly time for a Ford car from 12½ hours in 1912 to just 1½ hours in 1914. ⁴Declining production costs allowed Ford to cut prices—six times between 1921 and 1925, reducing a new Ford's cost to just $290. ⁵This was less than three months' wages for an average American worker, and it made cars affordable for the average family. ⁶To lower employee turnover and raise productivity, Ford also introduced a minimum daily wage of $5 in 1914—twice what most workers earned—and shortened the workday from nine hours to eight. ⁷Twelve years later, Ford reduced his workweek from six days to five. ⁸Ford demonstrated the logic of mass production: expanded production allows manufacturers to reduce costs and <u>therefore</u> increase the number of products sold, and higher wages allow workers to buy more products.

⁹Alfred Sloan, the president of General Motors from 1923 to 1941, built his company into the world's largest automaker not by refining the production process <u>but</u> by adopting new approaches to advertising and marketing. ¹⁰Sloan summed up his philosophy with these blunt words: "The primary object of the corporation was to make money, not just to make cars." ¹¹<u>Unlike</u> Ford, a farmer's son who wanted to produce an inexpensive, functional vehicle with few frills, Sloan was convinced that Americans were willing to pay extra for luxury and prestige. ¹²He advertised his cars as symbols of wealth and status, and in 1927 introduced the yearly model change, to convince motorists to trade in old models for newer ones with flashier styling. ¹³He also developed a series of divisions that were differentiated by status, price, and level of luxury, with Chevrolets less expensive than Buicks or Cadillacs. ¹⁴To make his cars affordable, he set up the nation's first national consumer credit agency in 1919.

¹⁵If Henry Ford demonstrated the efficacy of mass production, Sloan revealed the importance of merchandising in a modern consumer society.

_____B_____ 1. In sentence 15, the word *efficacy* means

    A. expansion.

    B. effectiveness.

    C. flexibility.

    D. drawbacks.

See sentences 3–8. Ford cut production time, made cars more affordable, and improved the workers' lives. These facts show that mass production was effective.

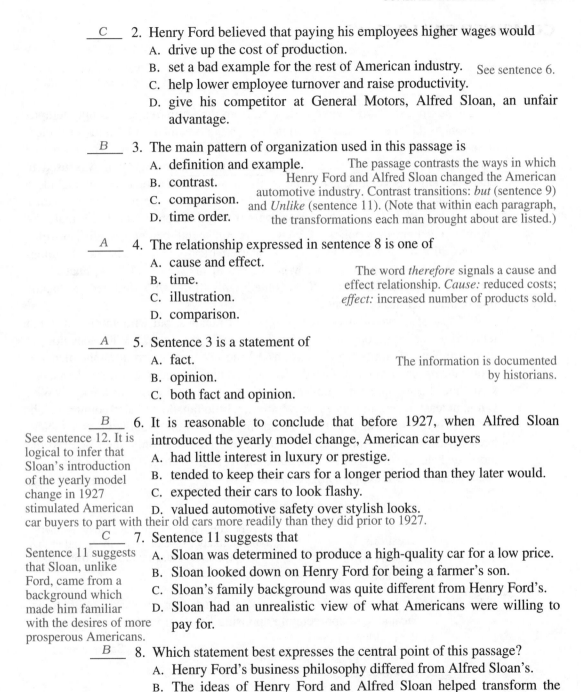

___C___ 2. Henry Ford believed that paying his employees higher wages would
A. drive up the cost of production.
B. set a bad example for the rest of American industry.   See sentence 6.
C. help lower employee turnover and raise productivity.
D. give his competitor at General Motors, Alfred Sloan, an unfair advantage.

___B___ 3. The main pattern of organization used in this passage is
A. definition and example.   The passage contrasts the ways in which
B. contrast.   Henry Ford and Alfred Sloan changed the American
C. comparison.   automotive industry. Contrast transitions: *but* (sentence 9)
D. time order.   and *Unlike* (sentence 11). (Note that within each paragraph, the transformations each man brought about are listed.)

___A___ 4. The relationship expressed in sentence 8 is one of
A. cause and effect.
B. time.   The word *therefore* signals a cause and effect relationship. *Cause:* reduced costs;
C. illustration.   *effect:* increased number of products sold.
D. comparison.

___A___ 5. Sentence 3 is a statement of
A. fact.   The information is documented
B. opinion.   by historians.
C. both fact and opinion.

___B___ 6. It is reasonable to conclude that before 1927, when Alfred Sloan
See sentence 12. It is   introduced the yearly model change, American car buyers
logical to infer that
Sloan's introduction   A. had little interest in luxury or prestige.
of the yearly model   B. tended to keep their cars for a longer period than they later would.
change in 1927   C. expected their cars to look flashy.
stimulated American   D. valued automotive safety over stylish looks.
car buyers to part with their old cars more readily than they did prior to 1927.

___C___ 7. Sentence 11 suggests that
Sentence 11 suggests   A. Sloan was determined to produce a high-quality car for a low price.
that Sloan, unlike
Ford, came from a   B. Sloan looked down on Henry Ford for being a farmer's son.
background which   C. Sloan's family background was quite different from Henry Ford's.
made him familiar   D. Sloan had an unrealistic view of what Americans were willing to
with the desires of more   pay for.
prosperous Americans.

___B___ 8. Which statement best expresses the central point of this passage?
A. Henry Ford's business philosophy differed from Alfred Sloan's.
B. The ideas of Henry Ford and Alfred Sloan helped transform the American manufacturing industry.
C. Chevrolets, Buicks, and Cadillacs have undergone many changes since the days of Henry Ford and Alfred Sloan.
D. Manufacturing in the early 1900s utilized mass production techniques in revolutionary ways.   Answer A does not include how the men transformed manufacturing. Answer C is not mentioned. Answer D covers only paragraph 1.

COMBINED SKILLS: Test 7

Read the passage below. Then write the letter of the best answer to each question that follows.

¹The English word *fanatic* is derived from the Latin *fanum*, meaning temple. ²It refers to the kind of madmen often seen in the precincts of temples in ancient times, the kind presumed to be possessed by deities or demons. ³The term first came into English usage during the seventeenth century, when it was used to describe religious zealots. ⁴Soon after, its meaning was broadened to include a political and social context. ⁵We have come to associate the term *fanatic* with a person who acts as if his or her views were inspired, a person utterly incapable of appreciating opposing points of view. ⁶The nineteenth-century English novelist George Eliot put it precisely: "I call a man fanatical when . . . he . . . becomes unjust and unsympathetic to men who are out of his own track." ⁷A fanatic may hear but is unable to listen. ⁸Confronted with those who disagree, a fanatic immediately vilifies opponents.

⁹Most of us would avoid the company of fanatics, but who among us is not tempted to caricature opponents instead of listening to them? ¹⁰Who does not put certain topics off limits for discussion? ¹¹Who does not grasp at euphemisms to avoid facing inconvenient facts? ¹²Who has not, in George Eliot's language, sometimes been "unjust and unsympathetic to those on a different track"? ¹³Who is not, at least in certain very sensitive areas, a little fanatical? ¹⁴The counterweight to fanaticism is open discussion. ¹⁵The difficult issues that trouble us as a society have at least two sides, and we lose as a society if we hear only one side. ¹⁶At the individual level, the answer to fanaticism is listening. ¹⁷Readers must be encouraged to listen to opposing points of view.

___A___ 1. In sentence 8, the word *vilifies* means
   A. speaks ill of.
   B. questions.
   C. reasons with.
   D. befriends.

A person who is "unjust and unsympathetic" would be likely to speak ill of others, rather than question, reason with, or befriend them.

___C___ 2. According to the selection, in ancient times fanatics were thought to be
   A. incapable of appreciating opposing points of view.
   B. the builders of temples.
   C. possessed by gods or demons.
   D. religious zealots.

See sentences 1–2.

_B_ 3. The relationship of sentence 4 to sentence 3 is one of
- A. addition.
- B. time.
- C. illustration.
- D. cause and effect.

The sentences describe the evolution of the term over time. The words *Soon after* signal a time transition.

_C_ 4. The main patterns of organization in paragraph 1 are definition-example and
- A. comparison.
- B. cause and effect.
- C. time order.
- D. contrast.

Paragraph 1 traces the evolution of the meaning of the word *fanatic* over time.

_A_ 5. The passage suggests that

See sentences 15–17, which urge us to listen to opposing points of view. Answers B, C, and D are unsupported.

- A. it is difficult but necessary to listen to opposing viewpoints.
- B. fanaticism has declined in modern times.
- C. the English novelist George Eliot was a fanatic.
- D. fanaticism serves a useful purpose.

_C_ 6. The purpose of this selection is to
- A. inform.
- B. persuade.
- C. both inform and persuade.
- D. entertain.

The passage informs us about the history of the word *fanatic* and tries to persuade us not to be fanatical with the words "Readers must be encouraged to listen to opposing points of view" (sentence 17).

_D_ 7. The author's tone is
- A. detached.
- B. threatening.
- C. pessimistic.
- D. concerned.

Sentence 15 highlights the author's concern.

_C_ 8. Which is the most appropriate title for this selection?
- A. A Brief History of Fanaticism
- B. We Are All Fanatics
- C. Fanaticism: Its Causes and Cure
- D. Difficult Issues Facing Society

Answer A covers only paragraph 1. Answer B covers only sentences 9–13. Answer D is not discussed.

COMBINED SKILLS: Test 8

Read the passage below. Then write the letter of the best answer to each question that follows.

¹Research reveals that males and females exhibit both similarities and differences in what they look for in a marital partner. ²Many characteristics, such as emotional stability, dependability, and pleasant disposition, are rated highly by both sexes. ³However, a few crucial differences between men's and women's priorities have been found, and these differences appear to be nearly universal across cultures. ⁴Women tend to place a higher value than men on potential partners' socioeconomic status, intelligence, ambition, and financial prospects. ⁵In contrast, men consistently show more interest than women in a potential partner's youthfulness and physical attractiveness.

⁶Most theorists explain these gender disparities in terms of evolutionary concepts. ⁷According to evolutionary theories, all organisms, including humans, are motivated to enhance their chances of passing on their genes to subsequent generations. ⁸Human females supposedly accomplish this end not by seeking larger or stronger partners, as in the animal kingdom, but by seeking male partners who possess or are likely to acquire more material resources that can then be invested in children. ⁹Men, on the other hand, are assumed to maximize their reproductive outlook by seeking female partners with good breeding potential. ¹⁰Thus, men are thought to look for youth, attractiveness, good health, and other characteristics presumed to be associated with higher fertility. ¹¹These evolutionary analyses of gender differences in mating are speculative, and there are alternative explanations, but they fit with the evidence quite well.

_B_ 1. In sentence 11, the word *speculative* means
- A. interesting.
- B. unproven.
- C. helpful.
- D. surprising.

If there are alternative explanations, this explanation must be unproven.

_D_ 2. According to the selection, men and women place an equally high value on
- A. socioeconomic status.
- B. physical attractiveness.
- C. youth.
- D. a pleasant disposition.

See sentence 2.

_T_ 3. TRUE OR FALSE? A key concept of evolution is that all organisms are driven to try to pass on their genes to later generations.

See sentence 7.

_B_   4. The relationship of sentence 3 to sentence 2 is one of
    A. list of items.
    B. contrast.
    C. cause and effect.
    D. addition.

> The sentences contrast the difference between priorities agreed upon and priorities men and women disagree about. Contrast transition: *However.*

_C_   5. The main patterns of organization of this selection are comparison-contrast and
    A. time order.
    B. list of items.
    C. cause and effect.
    D. definition and example.

> Cause and effect transition: *Thus* (sentence 10).
> *Cause:* Men want to pass on their genes to subsequent generations. *Effect:* They seek fertile women.

_A_   6. You can reasonably conclude from this passage that women
    A. are more likely to marry older, more financially stable men.
    B. often seek mates who are young, healthy, and attractive.
    C. don't care about a potential partner's emotional stability or dependability.
    D. prefer to marry men who are already supporting another woman's children.

> See sentence 4.

_A_   7. The main purpose of this selection is to
    A. inform readers about what men and women look for in a mate and why.
    B. entertain readers by highlighting differences between the sexes.
    C. persuade readers to be more selective when choosing a mate.

> The author presents facts and theories without attempting to entertain or persuade.

_A_   8. Which statement best expresses the central point of the passage?
    A. Males and females exhibit similarities and differences in what they look for in a mate.
    B. Evolutionary theories explain reasons for women's preferences when selecting a reproductive partner.
    C. There are differences in the way men and women seek potential partners.
    D. Human mating rituals are complex and resemble what happens in the animal kingdom.

> Answer B omits information on men's preferences.
> Answer C is incorrect because the focus of the passage is on similarities and differences in what men and women look for in potential mates, not in how they go about obtaining a mate.
> Answer D is contradicted by sentence 8.

COMBINED SKILLS: Test 9

Read the passage below. Then write the letter of the best answer to each question that follows.

¹One common sales trick, the foot-in-the-door technique, relies on getting the potential customer to grant an initial small request, which prepares the customer psychologically to grant a subsequent larger request. ²To my chagrin, I was outwitted—once—by a clever gang of driveway sealers who used this technique on me. ³One day while I was raking leaves in front of my house, these men pulled up in their truck and asked if they could have a drink of water. ⁴I, of course, said yes; how could I say no to a request like that? ⁵Then they got out of the truck and one said, "Oh, if you have some lemonade or soda, that would even be better; we'd really appreciate that." ⁶Well, all right, I did have some lemonade. ⁷As I brought it to them, one of the men pointed to the cracks in my driveway and commented that they had just enough sealing material and time to do my driveway that afternoon, and they could give me a special deal. ⁸Normally, I would never have agreed to a bargain like that on the spot; but I found myself unable to say no. ⁹I ended up paying far more than I should have, and they did a very poor job. ¹⁰I had been taken in by what I now see clearly was a novel twist on the foot-in-the-door sales technique.

¹¹The basis of the foot-in-the-door technique is that people are more likely to agree to a large request if they have already agreed to a small one. ¹²The driveway sealers got me twice on that: Their request for water primed me to agree to their request for lemonade, and their request for lemonade primed me to agree to their deal about sealing my driveway. ¹³One researcher has argued that the foot-in-the-door technique works largely through the principle of cognitive dissonance. ¹⁴Having agreed, apparently of my own free will, to give the men lemonade, I must have justified that action to myself by thinking, *These are a pretty good bunch of guys*, and that thought was dissonant with any temptation I might have had a few moments later, when they proposed the driveway deal, to think, *These people may be cheating me*. ¹⁵So I pushed the latter thought out of my mind before it fully registered.

   _D_   1. In sentence 2, the word *chagrin* means
      A. delight.
      B. horror.   When you realize that you have been
      C. confusion.   outwitted, what emotion do you feel?
      D. embarrassment.

   _C_   2. The author states that he found himself unable to say no to the driveway sealers because
      A. his driveway was in very poor condition, and he badly needed the work done.   See sentence 14. Answers A, B,
      B. he was afraid of angering them.   and D are unsupported.

C. he had convinced himself that they were good people.

D. the price they offered him was extremely low.

_____A_____ 3. Paragraph 1 mainly

Sentence 1 defines the foot-in-the-door technique. The rest of paragraph 1 gives an example of it based upon the author's own experience.

A. defines and gives an example of the foot-in-the-door technique.

B. contrasts the author's generous behavior with the trickiness of the workmen.

C. explains why the driveway sealing job turned out poorly.

D. compares an honest selling technique with a dishonest one.

_____C_____ 4. You can infer from this passage that

In sentence 2, the author specifies that he was outwitted only once. Also, sentence 8 says that the author would normally never agree to such a bargain.

A. agreeing to a small request inevitably leads to a larger request.

B. driveway sealers are among the most dishonest salespeople.

C. the author did not fall a second time for the foot-in-the-door technique.

D. the author called the police to complain about the driveway sealers.

(Answer A is incorrect because of the word *inevitably*.)

_____D_____ 5. The passage suggests that the author

A. has a background in psychology.

B. has learned from his experience with the driveway sealers.

C. is a nice person.

D. all of the above.

The author's familiarity with psychological research indicates a background in psychology. Sentence 2 indicates that the author learned from the experience. Giving lemonade to complete strangers indicates that the author is a nice person.

_____D_____ 6. The tone of this passage is

A. lighthearted and humorous.

B. bitter and vengeful.

C. sad and resentful.

D. instructive and casual.

There is nothing bitter, vengeful, sad, or resentful in the author's tone. The story about the driveway sealers is not intended to be lighthearted and humorous, but to illustrate the instructional point being made.

_____B_____ 7. Which statement best expresses the central point of the passage?

Answer A covers only sentence 1. Answer D covers only sentence 8. Answer C is too broad because only one sales technique is discussed.

A. Many tradespeople use the foot-in-the-door technique to cheat unwitting customers.

B. The foot-in-the-door technique is a common sales strategy in which the customer agrees to a small request and then cannot refuse a larger one.

C. Many people are victimized by clever sales techniques.

D. Do not trust tradespeople who offer you special deals.

_____C_____ 8. What is the most appropriate title for this selection?

A. Outwitted!

B. An Embarrassing Experience

C. Beware the Foot-in-the-Door Technique

D. Sneaky Sales Tricks

Answers A and B ignore the analysis of paragraph 2. Answer D is too broad because the passage discusses only one sales trick.

COMBINED SKILLS: Test 10

Read the passage below. Then write the letter of the best answer to each question that follows.

[1]Until recently, most researchers believed the human brain followed a fairly predictable developmental arc. [2]It started out open and versatile, gained shape and intellectual muscle as it matured, and reached its peak of power and nimbleness by age 40. [3]After that, the brain began a slow decline, clouding up little by little until, by age 60 or 70, it had lost much of its ability to retain new information and was fumbling with what it had. [4]But that was all right because late-life crankiness had by then made us largely resistant to new ideas anyway.

[5]That, as it turns out, is hooey. [6]More and more, neurologists and psychologists are coming to the conclusion that the brain at midlife—a period increasingly defined as the years from 35 to 65 and even beyond—is a much more elastic, much more supple thing than anyone ever realized.

[7]Far from slowly powering down, the brain as it ages begins bringing new cognitive systems on line and cross-indexing existing ones in ways it never did before. [8]You may not pack so much raw data into memory as you could when you were cramming for college finals, and your short-term memory may not be what it was, but you manage information and parse meanings that were entirely beyond you when you were younger. [9]What's more, your temperament changes to suit those new skills, growing more comfortable with ambiguity and less susceptible to frustration or irritation. [10]Although inflexibility, confusion and even later-life dementia are very real problems, for many people the aging process not only does not batter the brain; it actually makes it better.

[11]"In midlife," says UCLA neurologist George Bartzokis, "you're beginning to maximize the ability to use the entirety of the information in your brain on an everyday, ongoing, second-to-second basis. [12]Biologically, that's what wisdom is."

___B___ 1. In sentence 8, the word *parse* means
   A. reject.
   B. figure out.
   C. emphasize.
   D. review.

> If the meanings were "beyond you when you were younger," and your brain is now working better, what can you do to them now?

___C___ 2. According to this passage, as people age, they
   A. grow more susceptible to frustration and irritation.
   B. gain in short-term memory.
   C. grow more skilled at managing information.
   D. pack more raw data into their memory.

> Sentence 8 supports answer C and contradicts answers B and D. Answer A is contradicted by sentence 9.

_A_ 3. This selection primarily

    A. contrasts what researchers used to believe about the brain as it ages with what they believe now.

    B. defines the term "developmental arc."   See sentences 5–6.

    C. lists the biological effects of aging on the brain.

    D. explains why some people become confused and develop dementia in later life while others do not.

_D_ 4. The main organizational pattern of paragraph 1 is

    A. cause and effect.   The paragraph describes the sequence of events in

    B. definition and example.   the developmental arc. Time order words: *Until*

    C. comparison.   *recently* (sentence 1); *After that* and *until, by age*

    D. time order.   *60 or 70* (sentence 3); and *by then* (sentence 4).

_B_ 5. This passage suggests that

See sentences 11–12.   A. old people have a difficult time absorbing new ideas.

Answer A is not

supported. Answer C   B. wisdom is closely associated with maturity.

is incorrect because of   C. later-life dementia is inevitable.

the word *inevitable.*   D. the brain begins powering down during midlife.

Answer D is contradicted by sentence 7.

_C_ 6. The author's attitude towards aging seems to be one of

    A. fear.

    B. distaste.   The author presents evidence which indicates that

        the brain actually improves with age—suggesting

    C. respect.   a respectful attitude toward aging.

    D. worry.

_B_ 7. The writer uses a tone that is

    A. dry and scholarly.   An excerpt which highlights the author's

    B. optimistic.   optimistic tone: "for many people the aging

    C. bitterly critical.   process not only does not batter the brain; it

    D. undecided.   actually makes it better" (sentence 10).

_A_ 8. Which statement best expresses the central point of the passage?

    A. In contrast to what researchers previously believed, current research indicates that the brain actually improves as it ages.

    B. People at midlife lose short-term memory but gain the ability to manage information.

    C. Inflexibility, confusion, and late-life dementia are serious problems of old age.

    D. As people enter midlife, they often become less susceptible to frustration or irritation.

    Statement C is a detail mentioned in sentence 10.

    Statements B and D, details which support the main idea,

    are mentioned in sentences 8 and 9, respectively.

COMBINED SKILLS: Test 11

Read the passage below. Then write the letter of the best answer to each question that follows.

¹Suppose that you and three other individuals apply for a part-time job in the parks and recreation department, and you are selected for the position. ²How do you explain your success? ³Chances are, you tell yourself that you were hired because you were the most qualified for the job. ⁴<u>But</u> how do the other people interpret their negative outcome? ⁵Do they tell themselves that you got the job because you were the most able? ⁶Unlikely! ⁷<u>Instead</u>, they probably attribute their loss to "bad luck" or to not having had time to prepare for the interview. ⁸These <u>different</u> explanations for success and failure reflect the *self-serving bias*, or the tendency to attribute one's successes to personal factors and one's failures to situational factors.

⁹Research indicates that people are likely to take credit for their successes and to disavow their failures. ¹⁰To illustrate: In an experiment, two strangers jointly took a test. ¹¹They then received bogus success or failure feedback about their test performance and were asked to assign responsibility for the test results. ¹²Successful participants claimed credit, but those who failed blamed their partners. ¹³Still, people don't always rush to take credit. ¹⁴In another experiment in the just-cited study, participants were actual friends. ¹⁵In this case, participants shared responsibility for both successful and unsuccessful outcomes. ¹⁶Thus, friendship places limits on the self-serving bias.

¹⁷Although the self-serving bias has been documented in a variety of cultures, it seems to be prevalent in individualistic Western societies, where the emphasis on competition and high self-esteem motivates people to try to impress others as well as themselves. ¹⁸In contrast, Japanese subjects exhibit a *self-effacing bias* in explaining successes, as they tend to attribute their successes to the help they receive from others or to the ease of the task, while downplaying the importance of their ability. ¹⁹When they fail, Japanese subjects are more self-critical than subjects from individualistic cultures. ²⁰They are more likely to accept responsibility for their failures and to use their setbacks as an impetus for self-improvement. ²¹Studies have also failed to find the Western self-serving bias in Nepalese and Chinese samples.

___B___ 1. In sentence 9, the word *disavow* means
    A. believe in.
    B. deny responsibility for.
    C. doubt the truth of.
    D. promise to correct.

See sentences 10–12, which give an example. Note the antonym clue in sentence 9: *take credit for*.

___C___ 2. According to the passage, people in Western societies tend to attribute their failures to
   A. the negative influence of friends.
   B. personal shortcomings.   See sentence 8.
   C. situational factors.
   D. bias on the parts of others.

___B___ 3. In contrast to people in Western societies, the Japanese tend to attribute their successes to
   A. high self-esteem.
   B. the help they receive from others or the ease of the task.
   C. a strong desire for self-improvement.   See sentence 18.
   D. their own superior skills.

___D___ 4. The main pattern of organization used in paragraph 1 is
   A. time order.
   B. list of items.   The paragraph contrasts explanations for success with
   C. comparison.   explanations for failure. Contrast words: *But* (sentence
   D. contrast.   4), *Instead* (sentence 7), *different* (sentence 8).

___D___ 5. The relationship of sentence 16 to sentence 15 is one of
   A. time.
   B. addition.   *Cause:* friendship limits self-serving bias.
   C. definition and example.   *Effect:* friends share responsibility for success
   D. cause and effect.   and failure. Cause and effect transition: *Thus*.

___D___ 6. You could reasonably conclude from the passage that
See sentences 19–21,   A. Japanese society places responsibility for success or failure on the
which indicate the   group, rather than on the individual.
absence of the self-
serving bias in other   B. Western societies place little value upon friendship.
Asian countries   C. the lower one's self-esteem, the more likely one is to blame
besides Japan (and by   situational factors for one's failure.
inference, the presence D. self-effacement is valued in Asian societies generally.
of a self-effacing bias).

___A___ 7. Sentence 19 is a statement of
   A. fact.   See sentence 17. The information
   B. opinion.   is documented by researchers.
   C. both fact and opinion.

___A___ 8. Which statement best expresses the central point of the selection?
Answer B is incorrect— A. Whereas Westerners generally exhibit a self-serving bias, the Japanese
most Westerners, but not   and other Eastern cultures tend to exhibit a self-effacing bias.
most people from   B. Most people take credit for success but not for failure.
Eastern cultures, take
credit for success but C. The Japanese take more responsibility for failure than Westerners do.
not for failure.   D. Researchers have uncovered some interesting facts with regard to
Answer C covers only   people's attitudes toward success and failure.
sentences 18–20. Answer D is too broad because the passage focuses on self-
serving bias and self-effacing bias, not just on "some interesting facts" in general.

COMBINED SKILLS: Test 12

Read the passage below. Then write the letter of the best answer to each question that follows.

[1]Sociologists have discovered a number of causal factors in child abuse. [2]One is the *intergenerational transmission of violence:* Parents are likely to abuse their children if they have learned in childhood that it is all right to use violence in dealing with child-rearing problems. [3]This learning may come from *the experience of being abused as children.*

[4]Indeed, research has shown that child-abusing parents are more likely than nonabusing parents to have been abused themselves as children. [5]More specifically, about 30 percent of child abusers have been abused themselves, while only 3 or 4 percent of nonabusers had the same experience in the past. [6]But this should not be taken to mean that receiving early abuse inevitably leads to later abuse-giving because, contrary to popular belief, the *majority* (about 70 percent) of child-abuse victims do *not* grow up to become abusers. [7]A history of the abuser being abused is only one of the causal influences on child abuse, and not its only cause. [8]The other learned influence—the legitimacy of using violence to deal with problems—also comes from *having observed as children how parents and other significant adults use violence* to express anger, to react to stress, or to deal with marital problems. [9]This explains why researchers often find that child abusers are more likely than nonabusers to have been raised in homes with a great deal of marital conflict and violence.

[10]Another contributing factor to child abuse is the acceptance of the very popular view that physical punishment is a proper way of disciplining children. [11]Nearly half of all U.S. parents resort to physical punishment in an attempt to correct a child's misbehavior. [12]But there is a tendency for physical punishment (say, spanking or slapping) to spill over into child abuse (punching or kicking). [13]As a researcher has found, parents who approve of physical punishment are four times more likely to abuse their children than are parents who disapprove of such physical discipline. [14]Because of the social acceptance of physical punishment, child abusers tend to see their abusive behavior as good and proper. [15]This can be illustrated by the case of a father who had severely beaten his two boys, one five years old and the other only eighteen months old. [16]In the hospital where the boys were brought in for treatment of multiple bruises, lacerations, and fractures, the father said to the examining physician, "Children have to be taught respect for authority and be taught obedience. [17]I would rather have my children grow up afraid of me and respecting me than loving me and spoiled."

_____B_____ 1. In sentence 8, the word *legitimacy* means
   A. primary method.
   B. acceptability.
   C. dislike.
   D. sincerity.

If children often see parents and other significant adults using violence to deal with problems, how would they then view violent behavior?

_____D_____ 2. According to the selection, parents who approve of physical punishment
   A. almost always abuse their children.
   B. are 30 percent more likely to abuse their children than are other parents.
   C. rarely abuse their children.   See sentence 13.
   D. are four times more likely to abuse their children than are other parents.

_____B_____ 3. How many main causes of child abuse are mentioned in paragraph 2?
   A. One
   B. Two   See sentences 4 and 8, which explain
   C. Three   two main causes of child abuse.
   D. Four

_____D_____ 4. In general, this selection

See sentences 4, 8, and 10. The selection presents three major factors which cause parents to abuse their children.

   A. contrasts parents who abuse their children with parents who do not.
   B. defines the term *child abuse* and gives examples of it.
   C. illustrates the long-term effects of child abuse.
   D. lists the factors which cause parents to abuse their children.

_____A_____ 5. This selection is mostly based on
   A. fact.   The passage presents facts,
   B. opinion.   examples, and explanations.
   C. a mixture of fact and opinion.

_____D_____ 6. The tone of the third paragraph can be described as
   A. enthusiastic.
   B. tolerant.   The author presents the information and the
   C. ambivalent.   example in a straightforward and serious way.
   D. serious.

_____C_____ 7. Which of the following titles would be most suitable for this passage?
   A. The Case Against Physical Discipline   Answer A covers only
   B. An Abusive Father   paragraph 3. Answer B covers only sentences
   C. The Roots of Child Abuse   15–17. Answer D is incorrect because the
       author does not attempt to persuade us
   D. Let's Stamp Out Child Abuse   that child abuse can be stamped out.

_____C_____ 8. Which statement best expresses the central point of the passage?
   A. Many Americans wrongly believe that physical punishment is a good way to discipline children.

Answer A covers only paragraph 3. Answer B covers only sentence 6. Answer D is implied, but not supported.

   B. Contrary to popular belief, the majority of child abuse victims do not grow up to abuse their own children.
   C. The root causes of child abuse include being abused as a child, observing adults react to stressful situations with violence, and believing in physical punishment as a form of discipline.
   D. There are better ways to discipline children than physical punishment.

COMBINED SKILLS: Test 13

Read the passage below. Then write the letter of the best answer to each question that follows.

¹Italian Renaissance noblewoman Lucrezia Borgia (1480–1519) remains infamous today for using the poison arsenic to dispose of her personal and political enemies. ²Recent research, however, has cast doubt on whether Lucrezia actually poisoned anyone, arguing instead that her family's political enemies in Rome ruined her reputation. ³But whether or not Lucrezia Borgia actually used poison, few historians will dispute that the weapon was a great equalizer. ⁴Murder required administering a poison in repeated or large doses, tasks that women could conveniently perform <u>since</u> they were trusted with the preparation of food and the administration of medicines. ⁵As a group, women had plenty of <u>reasons</u> to commit murder, too—lack of economic opportunity, limited property rights, and difficulty in escaping the marriage bond. ⁶In his recent book *Elements of Murder: A History of Poison*, John Emsley describes multiple cases of women who killed to gain political power, get rid of husbands, collect insurance, cover up swindling and theft during domestic employment, and receive inheritances. ⁷In France, arsenic came to be called *poudre de succession*, "inheritance powder." ⁸One noblewoman, a true experimentalist, tested what dosages of arsenic would cause illness and death by sending gifts of food containing the substance to patients at a local hospital. ⁹She then poisoned her father to inherit his wealth and knocked off her two brothers so she would not have to share it.

¹⁰The favored poisons of the late 19th century were also an appealing instrument of murder, at least for the villain, <u>because</u> their effects on the body were gruesome. ¹¹Mercury, arsenic, antimony, lead, and thallium—some of the most common poisons—induced repeated vomiting and diarrhea and turned the body into wasting, stench-ridden flesh. ¹²Furthermore, the advantage to the murderer was that symptoms of poison closely resembled those of common diseases. ¹³Victims were usually consigned to their graves as dead of natural causes rather than objects of foul play.

¹⁴Poisoning was also relatively easy to get away with for centuries <u>because</u> possession of the murder weapon was by no means a clear indicator of guilt. ¹⁵Would-be poisoners could easily obtain the necessary materials from the shops of apothecaries or chemists, under the guise of using them in small doses for a cosmetic or medical purpose. ¹⁶In ancient times, stibnite powder, an antimony compound, was used as mascara. ¹⁷In the 19th century, a popular arsenic-based medication was used to treat syphilis, epilepsy, and skin disorders. ¹⁸During the 19th century, however, improved methods of chemical analysis increased the risk that a poisoner would be caught. ¹⁹The expert testimony of academic chemists, based on post-mortem detections of poisons in corpses, <u>led to</u> convictions.

___B___ 1. In sentence 19, the word *post-mortem* means
   A. before death.
   B. after death.
   C. causing death.
   D. preventing death.

When are corpses examined? (Note that the prefix *post* means *after*.)

___D___ 2. According to the author, poison in times past was
   A. usually traced in the dead victim's body.
   B. inconvenient to obtain at times.
   C. commonly given to hospital patients.
   D. administered in food and medicine.

See sentence 4.

___D___ 3. The relationship of sentences 8 and 9 to sentence 7 is one of
   A. list of items.
   B. time order.
   C. cause-effect.
   D. illustration.

Sentences 8 and 9 illustrate how one noblewoman used poison to inherit her father's wealth.

___B___ 4. The main pattern of organization used in this passage is
   A. time order.
   B. cause and effect.
   C. comparison.
   D. contrast.

Paragraph 1 explains what caused women in particular to use poison. Paragraph 2 explains why poisoning was popular in the 19th century. Paragraph 3 gives reasons why poisoning, until recently, was relatively easy to get away with. Cause and effect transitions: *since* (sentence 4), *reasons* (5), *because* (10), *because* (14), and *led to* (19).

Paragraph 2 explains that poison was an appealing murder weapon because its effects were gruesome and its symptoms resembled those of common diseases.

___A___ 5. Paragraphs 2 and 3 mainly
   A. list reasons why poison was an appealing murder instrument.
   B. contrast 19th century methods of murder with earlier methods.
   C. compare the effects on the body of various types of poison.
   D. all of the above.

Paragraph 3 explains that possessing poison "was by no means a clear indicator of guilt" (sentence 14).

___D___ 6. The tone of this selection is
   A. shocked.
   B. apologetic.
   C. concerned.
   D. objective.

The author presents facts about poisoners and poisons without expressing shock, apology, or concern.

See sentences 10–11. Answer B is contradicted by sentences 6–7. Answer C is contradicted by sentence 14. D is not supported.

___A___ 7. The author suggests that poisoners
   A. often enjoyed seeing their victims suffer.
   B. typically killed people they did not know well.
   C. were generally caught and convicted of their crimes.
   D. were mentally ill.

___C___ 8. Which title is most appropriate for the selection?
   A. Famous Poisoners
   B. Evil Women Throughout History
   C. Poison: A Popular Murder Weapon
   D. The Decline of Poison as a Murder Weapon

Answer A is not supported—the passage mentions only one famous poisoner (Lucrezia Borgia). Answer B is wrong because the focus of the selection is poison and poisoners, not evil women. Answer D covers only sentences 18–19.

COMBINED SKILLS: Test 14

Read the passage below. Then write the letter of the best answer to each question that follows.

¹In today's society, having a baby is nearly always associated with doctors and hospitals. ²But in the early days of America's independence, babies were born at home, and mother and baby were cared for by a midwife. ³Why, then, did doctors begin delivering babies? ⁴And what does this tell us about theories of social inequality?

⁵Martha Ballard was a midwife from 1785 to 1812. ⁶During that time, she delivered 816 babies and treated a wide variety of illnesses. ⁷According to historian Laurel Thatcher Ulrich, who used Ballard's diary to write her Pulitzer-Prize-winning *A Midwife's Tale*, the midwife's extensive knowledge was gained not through attendance at a medical school but on the job, working with other women and by herself to care for others in her community. ⁸Ballard's personal competitor was a young physician named Benjamin Page, who charged $6 to deliver a baby while she charged $2.

⁹Page was clearly less experienced and less capable than Ballard at delivering babies. ¹⁰For example, he misused the newly popular drug laudanum, a form of opium, putting one laboring woman into a stupor that stopped her labor completely. ¹¹In Ballard's opinion, Page was the cause of more than one infant's death. ¹²Furthermore, records indicate that deaths of mothers and babies increased rather than decreased when physicians began routinely attending births in the 19th century. ¹³Why, then, would people employ young, inexperienced physicians such as Page? ¹⁴Ulrich explains Page's appeal: "Ben Page had certain advantages: a gentlemanly bearing, a successfully completed apprenticeship, and credit with certain younger members of the educated elite. ¹⁵At this time, from the late 1700s to the 1840s, women who wished to start a career in midwifery did not have the option of going to medical school and making the kind of social connections with the elite that male physicians could."

¹⁶The case of Martha Ballard and Benjamin Page provides a clear example of the constraints that operate in the labor market. ¹⁷The change from a reliance on midwifery to employment of physicians occurred not <u>because</u> physicians were better than midwives at what they did, but <u>because</u> they were men and as such were already connected to other powerful institutions, including law, education, business, and politics. ¹⁸Young physicians such as Benjamin Page were employed—and paid higher rates—to do something they weren't very good at. ¹⁹Though midwives were as competent as or more competent than any physician at prenatal care and delivering babies, men had more power and were able to drive the women out of their traditional role.

_____C_____ 1. In sentence 16, the word *constraints* means

    A. opportunities.   C. restrictions.

    B. descriptions.   D. time limits.

Why couldn't Martha Ballard and other women go to medical school and make social connections among the elite? (Sentence 15)

_____C_____ 2. According to medical records,

    A. Benjamin Page was responsible for more infant deaths than Martha Ballard.

    B. the use of drugs during labor was the primary cause of infant deaths.

    C. death rates increased when physicians started delivering babies.

    D. more infant and mother deaths occurred during the late 1700s than any other time period.   See sentence 12.

_____B_____ 3. According to the passage, women in Martha Ballard's day

    A. seldom cared for mothers and babies.

    B. did not have the option of attending medical school.

    C. could have gone to medical school, but preferred on-the-job training.

    D. often used laudanum to aid laboring women.   See sentence 15.

_____C_____ 4. Which of the following is *not* a reason why people chose Benjamin Page to deliver their babies?

Answers A, B, and D are expressed in sentence 14. Answer C is contradicted by sentence 8.

    A. He had a gentlemanly bearing.

    B. He had successfully completed an apprenticeship.

    C. He charged less than a midwife for performing the same services.

    D. He knew other members of the young social elite.

_____D_____ 5. This selection's main pattern of organization is

The selection mainly gives reasons why male physicians, rather than midwives, began delivering babies. Cause and effect transition: *because* (sentence 17).

    A. comparison.   C. illustration.

    B. time order.   D. cause-effect.

_____D_____ 6. The relationship of sentence 10 to sentence 9 is one of

    A. addition.   C. contrast.

    B. definition and example.   D. illustration.

Sentence 10 illustrates how Page was less capable. Illustration transition: *For example.*

_____B_____ 7. The passage suggests that

Sentences 9 and 13 suggest that young physicians such as Page did not receive enough supervised training (experience) to prepare them to capably perform prenatal care and deliver babies.

    A. women are naturally much better at delivering babies than men are.

    B. medical schools in Page's time did not adequately prepare physicians to perform prenatal care and deliver babies.

    C. pregnant women preferred that midwives deliver their babies, but their husbands preferred male physicians.

    D. it would eventually become illegal to practice midwifery in the United States.

_____D_____ 8. Which statement best expresses the central point of this selection?

The focus of the selection is on reasons for men's dominance in the labor market, using Martha Ballard's competition with Benjamin Page as an example.

    A. Whether to employ a doctor or midwife to deliver a baby remains an important decision for women.

    B. Midwives traditionally have been more competent at delivering babies than physicians.

    C. Martha Ballard and Benjamin Page were competitors in the labor market in the late 1700s.

    D. The cases of Martha Ballard and Benjamin Page illustrate the truth that historically, men's dominance in the labor market has relied more on power and connections than on competence.

COMBINED SKILLS: Test 15

Read the passage below. Then write the letter of the best answer to each question that follows.

[1]In 1998, Karla Faye Tucker, age 38, was executed in Texas for murdering two people with a pickax 15 years earlier. [2]She was the first woman put to death by the state since the Civil War and the second woman in the United States officially killed since 1976, the year when the U.S. Supreme Court reinstated the death penalty. [3]Most Americans believe that the death penalty is an effective deterrent to murder. [4]Many sociologists, however, have for a long time found otherwise, given the following forms of evidence.

[5]First, the homicide rates in states that have retained the death penalty law are generally much higher than in states that have abolished it. [6]Southern states which still practice the death penalty generally have higher murder rates than the states in other regions, which have mostly abolished capital punishment. [7]This suggests that the death penalty does not appear to deter murder.

[8]Secondly, within the same states, murder rates generally did not go up after the death penalty was abolished. [9]Moreover, the restoration of capital punishment in states that had abolished it earlier did not lead to a significant decrease in homicides.

[10]A third piece of evidence came from comparing the number of homicides shortly before and shortly after executions of convicted murderers that had been widely publicized. [11]If the death penalty has a deterrent effect, the execution should so scare potential criminals that they would refrain from killing, and the number of homicides in the area should decline. [12]This may sound logical, but reality contradicts it. [13]In Philadelphia during the 1930s, for example, the number of homicides remained about the same in the period from 60 days before to 60 days after a widely publicized execution of five murderers. [14]This finding, among others, suggests that the death penalty apparently does not prevent potential killers from killing even when the state shows people that it means business.

[15]Why doesn't the death penalty seem to deter murder? [16]One reason is that murder is a crime of passion, most often carried out under the overwhelming pressure of volcanic emotion, namely, uncontrollable rage. [17]People in such a condition cannot stop and think about the death penalty. [18]Another reason is that the causal forces of murder, such as severe poverty and child abuse, are simply too powerful to be neutralized by the threat of capital punishment.

_B_   1. In sentence 3, the word *deterrent* means   If homicide rates in death-
    A. cure.   C. stimulus.   penalty states are much
    B. something that prevents.   D. excuse.   higher than in states *without*
                                   the death penalty, then what is the death penalty *not* being?

_B_   2. This selection mainly

Sentence 4 indicates a   A. narrates the history of the death penalty in America.
list of evidence will   B. lists evidence that the death penalty does not prevent murder.
follow. Paragraphs 2, 3, and 4 then list the evidence.

      C. contrasts murder rates in several Southern states with murder rates in several Northern states.

      D. compares the effectiveness of the death penalty to the effectiveness of life in prison.

_A_ 3. The relationship of sentence 9 to sentence 8 is one of

      A. addition.

      B. illustration.   Sentences 8 and 9 present two pieces of

      C. time.   evidence. Addition transition: *Moreover*.

      D. cause and effect.

_D_ 4. According to the passage, the homicide rates in states that have retained the death penalty are

      A. significantly lower than in states which have abolished the death penalty.

See sentence 5.

      B. slightly higher than in states which have abolished the death penalty.

      C. about the same as in states which have abolished the death penalty.

      D. generally much higher than in states that have abolished the death penalty.

_B_ 5. The selection suggests that

      A. if the United States abolished the death penalty, the murder rate would rise.

See sentences 3–4.

      B. it is a mistake to believe that the death penalty prevents murder.

      C. if the United States abolished the death penalty, the murder rate would decline.

      D. Karla Faye Tucker was wrongly convicted.

_A_ 6. On the basis of paragraph 5, we can infer that

      A. people who grow up in impoverished, abusive circumstances are more likely to commit murder than those who do not.

See sentence 18.

      B. people who commit murder usually coolly plan their crimes.

      C. there is nothing society can do to stop poverty and child abuse.

      D. people who commit murder have made a conscious decision to risk being executed.

_A_ 7. Sentence 2 is a statement of

      A. fact.   This information can be confirmed by

      B. opinion.   researching records of executions.

      C. both fact and opinion.

_B_ 8. Which title is most suitable for this passage?

      A. Let's Abolish the Death Penalty

      B. The Death Penalty: No Deterrent to Murder

      C. Women on Death Row   While the focus of the selection is the lack of

      D. Murder: A Crime of Passion   deterrent value in the death penalty,

the author stops short of advocating that it be abolished. Therefore, answer A is incorrect.

    Answer C covers only sentences 1–2. Answer D covers only sentence 16.

COMBINED SKILLS: Test 16

Read the passage below. Then write the letter of the best answer to each question that follows.

¹Today it is commonly assumed that the roots of violence in American society lie in our frontier heritage of violence and lawlessness. ²A popular vision of the frontier has grown up and been disseminated by dime novels, pulp newspapers, and television and movie Westerns. ³This vision is of a lawless land populated by violent men: outlaws, stagecoach robbers, gunslingers, vigilantes, claim jumpers, cattle rustlers, horse thieves, Indian fighters, border ruffians, and mule skinners. ⁴Most popular accounts of Western banditry, <u>however,</u> appear to be grossly exaggerated and romanticized. ⁵According to legend, Bat Masterson killed 30 men in gunfights. ⁶Actually he killed only three. ⁷Billy the Kid, who supposedly killed 21 men in his 21 years of life, also apparently killed only three.

⁸Legend holds that Kansas's brawling cattle towns witnessed a killing every night. ⁹<u>But</u> in fact, the towns of Abilene, Caldwell, Dodge City, Ellsworth, and Wichita recorded a grand total of 45 homicides during a 15-year span. ¹⁰That worked out to 1.5 murders per cattle traveling season, never exceeding five in one year. ¹¹In Deadwood, South Dakota—infamous for being the town where Wild Bill Hickok was shot in the back while playing poker in 1876—only four homicides (and no lynchings) took place in the town's most violent year. ¹²And even in Tombstone, Arizona, the site of the famous shoot-out at the O.K. Corral (where Marshal Virgil Earp, his brothers Wyatt and Morgan, and gambler Doc Holliday hurled the Clanton brothers "into eternity in the duration of a moment"), only five men were killed during the city's deadliest year.

¹³<u>Despite</u> the omnipresence of rifles, knives, and revolvers and the prevalence of saloons, gambling houses, and bordellos, crimes such as rape, robbery, and burglary were relatively rare. ¹⁴One miner wrote, "We could go to sleep in our cabins with our bag of gold dust under our pillows, minus locks, bolts, or bars, and feel a sense of absolute security."

___D___ 1. In sentence 13, the word *omnipresence* means
   A. scarcity.
   B. illegality.
   C. reputation.
   D. existence everywhere.

What would be the opposite of something that is "relatively rare"?

___C___ 2. According to popular legend, Kansas's cattle towns
   A. were not nearly as violent as other towns.
   B. were centers of rape, robbery, and burglary.
   C. witnessed a killing every night.
   D. were places of absolute security.

See sentence 8.

____D____ 3. Wild Bill Hickok
   A. actually killed only three men in gunfights, not 30.
   B. hurled the Clanton brothers "into eternity in the duration of a moment."

   C. was a gold miner.

   See sentence 11.

   D. was shot in the back while playing poker.

____A____ 4. This selection mainly

The selection contrasts the legends about violence on the frontier with the reality of the situation. Contrast transitions: *however* (sentence 4), *But* (9), and *Despite* (13).

   A. contrasts the mythology of the American frontier with the reality.
   B. describes in chronological order important gun battles of the American West.
   C. explores the effects of a lawless frontier culture.
   D. compares the early American West to the present-day American West.

____A____ 5. This passage suggests that

See sentences 1 and 4. According to the passage, life on the frontier was not all that violent— therefore, the roots of violence in American society do not lie in our frontier heritage.

   A. the roots of violence in American society do not lie in our frontier heritage.
   B. most Americans have little interest in the history of their country.
   C. most Americans have never believed the popular mythology of a violent West.
   D. the American West is less violent today than it was in frontier times.

____B____ 6. You can infer from this passage that
   A. most citizens of the frontier West did not own guns.
   B. the Clanton brothers were outlaws.   The fact that Marshal Virgil Earp
   C. gold miners were frequently the victims of crime.   and others shot the
   D. liquor was illegal in many Western towns.   Clanton brothers indicates
                                  that the Clanton brothers were probably outlaws.

____A____ 7. The primary purpose of this passage is to

The passage presents evidence suggesting that the level of violence in the frontier West was greatly exaggerated, but does not persuade or entertain.

   A. inform readers about the actual degree of violence in the frontier West.
   B. persuade readers that Billy the Kid and Bat Masterson do not deserve their reputations as killers.
   C. entertain readers with colorful stories about the old West.

____D____ 8. The central point of this passage is found in
   A. sentence 1.
   B. sentence 2.   Sentences 1–3 introduce the topic of frontier violence.
   C. sentence 3.   Sentence 4 expresses the main idea—that the reality of
   D. sentence 4.   the old West was far different from popular accounts.

COMBINED SKILLS: Test 17

Read the passage below. Then write the letter of the best answer to each question that follows.

[1]In James Thurber's classic short story, "The Secret Life of Walter Mitty," the meek, painfully shy central character spends much of his time weaving elaborate fantasies in which he stars as a bold, dashing adventurer. [2]Few people live in their imaginations to the extent Walter Mitty does, but everyone has daydreams: apparently effortless, spontaneous shifts in attention away from the here and now into a private world of make-believe.

[3]The urge to daydream seems to come in waves, surging about every 90 minutes and peaking between noon and 2 p.m. [4]According to some estimates, the average person spends almost half his or her waking hours fantasizing, though this varies from person to person and situation to situation. [5]Typically, we daydream when we would rather be somewhere else or be doing something else, so daydreaming is a momentary escape.

[6]Are daydreams random paths your mind travels? [7]Not at all. [8]Studies show that most daydreams are variations on a central theme: thoughts and images of unfulfilled goals and wishes, accompanied by emotions arising from an appraisal of where we are now compared to where we want to be. [9]Some people imagine pleasant, playful, entertaining scenarios, uncomplicated by guilt or worry. [10]By contrast, people who are extremely achievement-oriented tend to experience recurring themes of frustration, guilt, fear of failure, and hostility, reflecting the self-doubt and competitive envy that accompanies great ambition. [11]While most daydreaming is quite normal, it is considered maladaptive when it involves extensive fantasizing, replacing human interaction and interfering with vocational or academic success.

[12]Does daydreaming serve any useful function? [13]Some psychologists view daydreaming as nothing more than a retreat from the real world, especially when that world is not meeting our needs. [14]Other psychologists stress the positive value of daydreaming and fantasy. [15]Daydreams may provide a refreshing break from a stressful day and serve to remind us of neglected personal needs. [16]Freudian theorists tend to view daydreams as a harmless way of working through hostile feelings or satisfying guilty desires. [17]Cognitive psychologists emphasize that daydreaming can build problem-solving and interpersonal skills, as well as encourage creativity. [18]Moreover, daydreaming helps people endure difficult situations. [19]Prisoners of war have used fantasies to survive torture and deprivation. [20]Daydreaming and fantasy, then, may provide welcome relief from unpleasant reality and reduce internal tension and external aggression.

_____C_____ 1. In sentence 11, the word *maladaptive* means
    A. long and boring.
    B. filled with errors.
    C. not promoting healthy development.
    D. overly complicated.

What is the opposite of quite normal?

_C_   2. According to the passage,

   A. daydreaming is relatively rare.

   B. people generally daydream for two hours a day.   See sentence 8.

   C. daydreams usually contain a central theme.

   D. daydreams are random paths the mind travels.

_A_   3. For the most part, sentences 15–19

Sentence 20   A. provide examples of the usefulness of daydreaming.
summarizes what the
details in sentence   B. contrast the views of Freudian theorists with the views of others.
15–19 suggest—that
daydreaming can be   C. compare dated views of daydreaming with modern views.
useful.   D. explain the biological causes of daydreaming.

_A_   4. The main pattern of organization used in the final paragraph is

   A. list of items.

   B. definition and example.   The final paragraph lists reasons why
                                           daydreaming can have value.
   C. illustration.

   D. comparison.

Answers   _A_   5. The author's main purpose is to
B and C are not
supported. The passage   A. inform readers about daydreaming.
neither persuades   B. persuade readers that too much daydreaming can have negative
us of the negative   effects.
effects of daydreaming   C. entertain readers with examples of Walter Mitty's elaborate
nor entertains us with   fantasies.
examples of Walter Mitty's fantasies.

_A_   6. Sentences 4 and 5 are statements of

   A. fact.

   B. opinion.   They present evidence gathered
                           from psychological studies.
   C. both fact and opinion.

_D_   7. Which is the most appropriate title for this selection?

   A. Those Ridiculous Daydreamers   The passage gives no indication that
   B. The Dangers of Daydreaming   daydreaming is ridiculous, dangerous,
   C. Strange Daydreams   or strange. It does suggest a number of
   D. The Functions of Daydreaming   possible functions of daydreaming.

_D_   8. Which of the following statements best expresses the central point of
the selection?

Answer A covers only
sentences 6–8.   A. Daydreams are not random fantasies, but are usually variations on a
Answer B covers only   central theme.
sentences 9–10.
Answer C covers only   B. Whereas some people daydream about pleasant situations, other
sentences 1–2.   people's daydreams involve frustration, guilt, and hostility.
These details support
the central point,   C. James Thurber's creation, Walter Mitty, represents the daydreamer
expressed in answer   in all of us.
D.
                         D. Daydreams are a normal imaginative outlet and can serve a useful
purpose.

COMBINED SKILLS: Test 18

Read the passage below. Then write the letter of the best answer to each question that follows.

¹How many computers have you or your family gone through in the past ten years? ²How about televisions? ³Cell phones? ⁴Stereos? ⁵If you're like many Americans, you buy a new computer or other piece of electronic equipment as soon as new technology makes the one you own seem out of date. ⁶What do you do with your old electronic equipment when you buy something new? ⁷E-waste, or electronic waste, is currently the most rapidly growing waste problem in the world, with amounts of E-waste increasing nearly three times more quickly than amounts of other municipal wastes. ⁸And E-waste is toxic waste: computers and other electronic equipment contain lead, mercury, cadmium, barium, chromium, beryllium, PCBs, dioxins, and other pollutants. ⁹Consumers and business users have to pay recyclers to take E-waste off their hands.

¹⁰Recycling materials from electronic equipment is time-consuming and unprofitable—at least in industrialized nations. ¹¹So Americans ship it to other countries where the lack of environmental, health, and safety regulations make recycling E-waste profitable—and dangerous. ¹²For example, in Guiyu, China, about 100,000 men, women, and children are employed in taking computers apart—mostly by hand, and extracting copper from wiring, gold from capacitors, and other valuable products. ¹³Employees work with no protection for their hands, eyes, skin, and respiratory systems. ¹⁴Plastics are burned in the open air, acids are poured into canals and rivers, and lead-laden monitor glass and other components are dumped where heavy metals can leach into groundwater.

¹⁵Global inequality is at the root of E-waste exportation. ¹⁶In the wealthy industrialized United States, protected by multiple layers of regulations, wastes are generated and exported. ¹⁷In developing nations with few or no environmental and health regulations, on the other hand, poor people are willing and eager to work for $1.50 a day to handle toxic materials. ¹⁸As the authors of *Exporting Harm: The High-Tech Trashing of Asia* point out: "E-waste exports to Asia are motivated by brute global economics. . . . ¹⁹A free trade in hazardous wastes leaves the poorer people of the world with an untenable choice between poverty and poison—a choice that nobody should have to make."

_____D_____ 1. In sentence 19, the word *untenable* means

    A. not capable of being understood.

    B. worthy of being envied.

    C. unpredictable.

    D. unthinkable.

> What kind of choice is "a choice that nobody should have to make"?

_____C_____ 2. According to the selection, the number of people in Guiyu, China, who are employed in taking computers apart is

A. 1,000.
B. 10,000.
C. 100,000.
D. 1,000,000.

See sentence 12.

_____C_____ 3. Which of the following statements best expresses the main idea of paragraph 1?

Answer A covers only sentence 5. Answer B covers only sentence 7. Answer D covers only sentence 9. These are details which support the implied main idea, expressed in answer C.

A. Most Americans buy new electronic equipment when new technology makes the equipment they own seem out of date.
B. Electronic waste is increasing three times faster than other municipal wastes.
C. Electronic waste, which is toxic, is the most rapidly growing waste problem in the world.
D. Consumers and businesses pay recyclers to remove E-waste.

Cause: recycling waste is unprofitable;

_____C_____ 4. The relationship of sentence 11 to sentence 10 is one of *effect:* America

A. contrast.
B. illustration.
C. cause and effect.
D. addition.

ships E-waste elsewhere. Cause and effect transition: *So.*

_____D_____ 5. The relationship between sentences 16 and 17 is one of

A. definition and example.
B. addition.
C. time order.
D. contrast.

Sentences 16 and 17 contrast environ-mental regulations in the United States with the lack of environmental regulations in developing nations. Contrast transition: *on the other hand.*

_____A_____ 6. The selection suggests that

A. it is unfair to expect people in developing nations to recycle our dangerous E-waste without adequate safeguards.

See sentence 19, which argues that no one should have to choose between poverty and poison.

B. poor people in developing nations should be grateful for the opportunity to earn money recycling E-waste.
C. people in developing countries don't really care if their air and water is contaminated by E-waste.
D. There is nothing anyone can do about the problem of E-waste.

_____A_____ 7. The tone of this selection is

A. concerned and critical.
B. detached and instructive.
C. scornful and sarcastic.
D. straightforward and tolerant.

The author is concerned about and critical of recyclers working without protection (sentence 13), pollutants being released (14), motivation of "brute global economics" (18), and poor people having to choose between poverty and poison (19).

_____D_____ 8. The most appropriate title for this selection would be

A. The Roots of Global Inequality
B. America's Trash Is Asia's Cash
C. Industry in Asia
D. The Problems of E-Waste

Answers A and C are not supported. Answer B is too broad because it does not focus on E-waste and the problems the waste generates.

COMBINED SKILLS: Test 19

Read the passage below. Then write the letter of the best answer to each question that follows.

[1]Researcher Mary Koss drew heavy criticism when she published her findings that more than a quarter of all college women have experienced an act that met the legal definition of rape. [2]Her estimate was 10 to 15 times higher than comparable rates reported by the Bureau of Justice in statistics from their National Crime Victimization Survey (NCVS). [3]Why are the numbers so different?

[4]In cases of rape it seems that how the data are gathered is critical. [5]The NCVS questions used to determine these rates do not actually ask a woman if she has ever been raped. [6]Rape itself is never mentioned: it is up to the person being questioned to volunteer the information.

[7]An obvious way to get more information is to ask people directly whether they have been raped. [8]A national survey that asked this question of both men and women found that 9.2 percent of women and less than 1.0 percent of men had ever been raped in their lifetimes. [9]Both numbers are significantly higher than those that appear in the National Crime Survey.

[10]Even higher rates are obtained when the question is asked in a different way. [11]When respondents were asked if anyone had ever forced them to do something sexual, 22 percent women and 4 percent of men responded yes. [12]A study that Bonnie Fisher and her colleagues conducted of nearly 5,000 women attending U.S. colleges and universities also found that what is asked makes a big difference. [13]This study included a comparison component that used methods similar to those used in the NCVS. [14]The main study, which used extremely detailed questions about "unwanted sexual experiences," found rates of rape and attempted rape that were 11 and 6 times higher, respectively, than the rates found by the comparison study. [15]These rates are in line with those reported by Mary Koss for college women and by others for the general population. [16]The Fisher survey responses showed that 1.7 percent of the college women had experienced a rape and 1.1 percent an attempted rape during an average period of about seven months. [17]Projected over the five years that most students now spend getting an undergraduate degree, one-fifth to one-quarter of all college women would experience a rape or attempted rape.

[18]How many rapes we believe occur seems to depend primarily on how victims are asked about their experiences. [19]Fisher and her colleagues concluded, "The use of graphically worded screen questions . . . likely prompted more women who had experienced a sexual victimization to report this fact to the interviewer."

_____ C _____ 1. In sentence 13, the word *component* means
- A. viewpoint.
- B. conflict.
- C. part of a whole.
- D. recommendation.

See sentence 14, which suggests that the comparison component was only one section of Fisher's survey. The words *main study* are an antonym-like clue.

_____D_____ 2. According to the selection, the National Crime Victimization Survey
   A. was highly accurate.
   B. encouraged women to volunteer information by using extremely detailed questions.
   See sentences 5–6.
   C. disregarded the legal definition of rape.
   D. never actually asked women if they had been raped.

_____D_____ 3. According to the Fisher survey, the percentage of college women who would experience rape or attempted rape during their college careers is
   A. 1.7%.   C. 9.2%.   See sentence 17.
   B. 2.8%.   D. 20 to 25%.

This fact can be verified by analyz-   _____A_____ 4. Sentence 12 is a statement of
ing and comparing the   A. fact.   C. both fact and opinion.
results of several ways   B. opinion.
of gathering data.

_____C_____ 5. We can conclude from this selection that

Answers A, B, and D   A. the legal definition of rape needs to be changed.
are unsupported.
Fisher's study indica-   B. college women often invent stories of attempted rape.
ted that many victims   C. victims of rape or attempted rape are often reluctant to volunteer
of rape will not mention   information about their experience.
being raped unless   D. the incidence of rape is increasing in America.
directly prompted to do so. Therefore, answer C is correct.

_____D_____ 6. You can infer from this passage that
   A. rape occurs on college campuses more often than anywhere else.
   B. many of the subjects who talked to Mary Koss were not really raped.
   C. the authors of the NCVS deliberately designed their questions so as to make their rape findings artificially low.
   D. many women who are sexually victimized do not report the incident to the police. If women will not volunteer, in a survey such as the NCVS, the information that they have been raped, it is logical to infer that they will

_____A_____ 7. Which title would best summarize this passage?   not report incidences of rape to the police.
   A. Rape Data Depends Upon Questioning
   B. Rape on College Campuses
   C. Researcher Is Criticized for Methods Used   The focus of the passage is on the questions used to gather rape data.
   D. Men, Too, Are Sometimes Rape Victims

_____B_____ 8. Which statement best expresses the central point of the passage?
   A. The National Crime Victimization Survey results conflict with other reports and therefore may not be accurate.
   B. The reliability of data on rape depends on how and what victims are asked.
   C. Mary Koss and Bonnie Fisher conducted research on sexual victimization.
   D. Rape is a difficult subject for many people to talk about.

Answers A, C, and D are too narrow. Each covers only one aspect of the passage.

COMBINED SKILLS: Test 20

Read the passage below. Then write the letter of the best answer to each question that follows.

¹Before a German submarine launched two torpedoes at the U.S. destroyer *Greer*, heading for Iceland on September 4, 1941, the American ship had stalked the submarine for hours. ²Twice the *Greer* signaled the German submarine's location to British patrol bombers, one of which dropped depth charges on the submarine. ³After the torpedo attack, which missed its mark, the *Greer* also released depth charges. ⁴<u>But</u> when President Roosevelt described the encounter in a dramatic radio "Fireside Chat" on September 11, he declared that the German submarine, without warning, had fired the first shot, and he protested German "piracy" as a violation of the principle of freedom of the seas.

⁵Roosevelt did not tell the American people the full truth about the events of September 4, and what he did tell was misleading. ⁶The incident had little to do with freedom of the seas—which related to neutral merchant ships, not to U.S. warships operating in a war zone. ⁷Roosevelt's words amounted to a call to arms, <u>yet</u> he never asked Congress for a declaration of war against Germany. ⁸The president believed that he had to deceive the public in order to move hesitant Americans toward noble positions that they would ultimately see as necessary. ⁹Public opinion polls soon demonstrated that the practice worked, as most Americans approved the shoot-on-sight policy Roosevelt announced as a consequence of the *Greer* incident.

¹⁰Several years later, in his book *The Man in the Street* (1948), Thomas Bailey defended Roosevelt. ¹¹The historian argued that "because the masses are notoriously short-sighted, and generally cannot see danger until it is at their throats, our statesmen are forced to deceive them into an awareness of their own long-term interests." ¹²Roosevelt's critics, <u>on the other hand,</u> even those who agreed with him that Nazi Germany had to be stopped, have seen in his methods a danger to the democratic process, which cannot work in an environment of dishonesty and a usurping of congressional powers.

¹³Following Roosevelt, presidents have found it easier to exaggerate, distort, withhold, or even lie about the facts of foreign relations in order to shape a public opinion favorable to their policies. ¹⁴One result: the growth of the "imperial presidency"—the president's grabbing of power from Congress, and use of questionable means to reach his objectives. ¹⁵The practice of deception—for an end the president calls noble—was one of Roosevelt's legacies for a people and a nation.

Item 1:
What could a president do to Congress's powers that would be "a danger to the democratic process"? (See sentence 14. *Grabbing of power* is a synonym clue.)

_____D_____ 1. In sentence 12, the word *usurping* means
  A. criticizing.   C. influencing.
  B. supporting.   D. seizing without legal authority.

_____C_____ 2. An immediate consequence of the *Greer* incident was that
  A. the U.S. declared war on Germany.   See sentence 9.
  B. Germany declared war on the United States.
  C. Roosevelt announced a shoot-on-sight policy against Germany.
  D. Congress demanded that Roosevelt tell the truth about what had happened.

___C___ 3. According to the passage, President Roosevelt

See sentences 2–4. In reality, the *Greer* aided the British patrol bombers, who dropped depth charges on the German submarine.

    A. denied that the *Greer* had encountered a German submarine.

    B. told the American people that the *Greer* had stalked the German submarine for hours.

    C. misled the American people when he told them that the German submarine had fired the first shot.

    D. realized that it was impossible to deceive the American people.

___C___ 4. According to the selection, one long-term consequence of President Roosevelt's handling of the *Greer* incident was

    A. that the American public demanded greater congressional oversight of foreign policy.

    B. that many Americans learned to mistrust much of what future presidents told them.

    C. the growth of the "imperial presidency."

See sentence 14.

    D. diplomatic relations between the U.S. and Germany were permanently damaged.

___A___ 5. In this selection, the author mainly

Words which signal a contrast pattern of organization: *But* (sentence 4), *yet* (sentence 7), *on the other hand* (sentence 12).

    A. contrasts what really happened in the encounter between the *Greer* and the German submarine with what Roosevelt told the American people.

    B. lists reasons why our leaders are forced, at times, to deceive us.

    C. uses time order to provide a history of presidential deceptions since World War II.

    D. compares recent presidential deceptions with Roosevelt's deception concerning the *Greer* incident.

___B___ 6. We can infer that the U.S. destroyer *Greer* stalked the German submarine for hours because it

    A. realized the German submarine was close to the American coast.

    B. wanted to provoke a German attack.

    C. feared the submarine would attack the British patrol bombers.

Item 7: Excerpts that highlight the author's critical tone: "Roosevelt did not tell the American people the full truth… and what he did tell was misleading" (sentence 5); "Following Roosevelt, presidents have found it easier to exaggerate, distort, withhold, or even lie…" (13); "The practice of deception…was one of Roosevelt's legacies" (15).

    D. believed that the submarine was about to launch a torpedo against an American passenger liner.

Item 6: The *Greer* wanted to provoke a German attack so that Roosevelt could more easily sway American public opinion against Nazi Germany.

___B___ 7. The author's tone in this passage can best be described as

    A. admiring.   C. bitter.

    B. critical.   D. remorseful.

___A___ 8. Which sentence best expresses the central point of this selection?

    A. Roosevelt's deception concerning the *Greer* incident, however well-intentioned, had disturbing long-term consequences for the democratic process.

    B. It is impossible for presidents to rally support for important causes without occasionally resorting to deception.

    C. If Roosevelt had not deceived the American public with regard to the *Greer* incident, we never would have won the war with Germany.

    D. Although Roosevelt is remembered as a great president, he does not deserve his reputation.

See sentence 15. Answers B, C, and D are unsupported.

APPENDIXES

APPENDIXES

Pronunciation Guide

Each word in Chapter 3 of the Introduction, "Notes on Vocabulary in Context," is followed by information in parentheses that shows you how to pronounce the word. (There are also pronunciations for the vocabulary items that follow the readings in Parts I and II.) The guide below and on the next page explains how to use that information.

Long Vowel Sounds

ā	pay
ē	she
ī	hi
ō	go
o͞o	cool
yo͞o	use

Short Vowel Sounds

ă	hat
ĕ	ten
ĭ	sit
ŏ	lot
o͝o	look
ŭ	up
yo͝o	cure

Other Vowel Sounds

â	care
ä	card
îr	here
ô	all
oi	oil
ou	out
ûr	fur
ə	ago, item, easily, gallop, circus

Consonant Sounds

b	big
d	do
f	fall
g	dog
h	he

Consonant Sounds

j	jump
k	kiss
l	let
m	meet
n	no
p	put
r	red
s	sell
t	top
v	have
w	way
y	yes
z	zero
ch	church
sh	dish
th	then
th	thick
zh	usual

Note that each pronunciation symbol on the previous page is paired with a common word that shows the sound of the symbol. For example, the symbol ā has the sound of the *a* in the common word *pay*. The symbol ă has the sound of the *a* in the common word *hat*. The symbol ə, which looks like an upside-down *e* and is known as the schwa, has the unaccented sound in the common word *ago*. It sounds like the "uh" a speaker often says when hesitating.

Accent marks are small black marks that tell you which syllable to emphasize as you say a word. A bold accent mark (′) shows which syllable should be stressed. A lighter accent mark (′) in some words indicates a secondary stress. Syllables without an accent mark are unstressed.

Limited Answer Key

An important note: To strengthen your reading skills, you must do more than simply find out which of your answers are right and which are wrong. You also need to figure out (with the help of this book, the teacher, or other students) *why* you missed the questions you did. By using each of your wrong answers as a learning opportunity, you will strengthen your understanding of the skills. You will also prepare yourself for the review and mastery tests in Part I, the reading comprehension questions in Part II, and the combined-skills tests in Part III, for which answers are not given here.

ANSWERS TO THE PRACTICES IN PART I

1 Main Ideas

Practice 1

1. S	6. S
S	P
S	S
P	S
2. S	7. S
S	P
S	S
P	S
3. S	8. S
P	S
S	P
S	S
4. S	9. S
S	P
P	S
S	S
5. S	10. S
S	S
P	P
S	S

Practice 2 *(Wording of topics may vary)*

1. *Topic:* Halloween
   Main idea: Sentence 2

2. *Topic:* The American criminal justice system
   Main idea: Sentence 1

3. *Topic:* The ability to empathize
   Main idea: Sentence 1

4. *Topic:* Drive-in movies
   Main idea: Sentence 1

Practice 3

1. 3
2. 1
3. 8
4. 7

2   Supporting Details

Practice 1 *(Wording of answers may vary)*

A. *Main idea:* Animals communicate in their own ways.

   1. Nonverbal sounds
   2. Chemical signals
   3. Touch
   4. Visual signals

B. *Main idea:* Human diseases can be classified into a number of basic types.

   2. Hereditary
      Minor detail: Sickle-cell anemia
   3. Degenerative
      Minor detail: Arthritis
   4. Hormonal
      Minor detail: Diabetes
   5. Environmental
      Minor detail: Allergies and lead poisoning
   6. Deficiency
      Minor detail: Scurvy and pellagra

Practice 2 *(Wording of answers may vary)*

A. Photography was a serious business. Smiling would have taken too long. People didn't want to show their teeth.

B. *Major detail*: Debt

   Major detail: Crime

   Major detail: War and conquest
      Minor detail: Romans enslaved Greeks

Practice 3

   1. Passage A: C
   2. Passage B: B

3   Implied Main Ideas

Practice 1

Paragraph 1	Paragraph 3
1. B	1. C
2. A	2. A

Paragraph 2
1. B
2. B

Practice 2

1. D	3. C
2. C	

Practice 3 *(Wording of answers may vary.)*

A. *Topic:* Schools and colleges
   Implied main idea: Schools and colleges serve a number of functions in our society.

B. *Topic:* Body temperature
   Implied main idea: Several factors affect body temperatures in humans.

C. *Topic:* Ethanol **or** Ethanol's advantages
   Implied main idea: There are several advantages to using ethanol as an alternative fuel.

Practice 4

1. A	3. D
2. C	

4   Relationships I

Practice 1 *(Answers may vary.)*

1. also	4. In addition
2. moreover	5. Another
3. second	

Practice 2 *(Answers may vary.)*

1. after	4. Before
2. When	5. until
3. By	

Practice 3 *(Wording of answers may vary.)*

A. Main idea: There are three important lists people should make before going to the doctor.
1. All the medications they are taking
2. The symptoms they are experiencing
3. Any specific questions they have

B. Main idea: . . . a variety of techniques for tattoo removal.
1. Dermabrasion
2. Cryosurgery
3. Laser removal

Practice 4 *(Wording of answers may vary.)*

Main idea: *A furious Hitler quickly went on the attack against Britain.*
1. Used submarines against British shipping
2. Sent air force to destroy Britain's military defenses
3. Bombed civilian targets in London

Practice 5 *(Wording of answers may vary.)*

Main idea: To write effectively, practice four rules of thumb.
1. Decide what point you want to make.
2. Provide sufficient support for that point.
3. Organize your support.
4. Write clear, error-free sentences.

Practice 6

1. B	6. B
2. A	7. B
3. A	8. A
4. B	9. A
5. A	10. B

5 Relationships II

Practice 1 *(Answers may vary.)*

1. for example	4. including
2. such as	5. illustration
3. For instance	

Practice 2

A. *Scripts*; definition—sentence 2; example —sentence 3
B. *Enculturation*; definition—sentence 2; example 1—sentence 3; example 2—sentence 4; example 3—sentence 5

Practice 3 *(Answers may vary.)*
1. In the same way
2. just as
3. Both
4. Just like
5. same

Practice 4 *(Answers may vary.)*

1. while	4. Although
2. However	5. On the other hand
3. but	

Practice 5

A. Comparison: Abraham Lincoln and Frederick Douglass
B. Contrast: personal distress and empathy

Practice 6 *(Answers may vary.)*

1. because	4. caused
2. lead to	5. since
3. As a result	

Practice 7

A. *Main idea (effect):* Victorian women often fainted.
   Major supporting details (causes):
   1. Their tight undergarments cut off air supply and blood flow.
   2. They knew that fainting made them seem delicate and feminine.

B. *Main idea (cause):* Rising sea levels would result in global problems.
   Major supporting details (effects):
   1. Drastic change in existing coastlines
   2. Threat to dikes and sea walls
   3. Increase in global warming

Practice 8

1. B	6. A
2. C	7. B
3. A	8. C
4. C	9. A
5. B	10. C

6 Inferences

Practice 1

1. A, B
2. A, C
3. C, D
4. B, D
5. B, D

Practice 2

A. 1. B
   2. C
   3. B

B. 4. C
   5. C
   6. B

C. 7. B
   8. B
   9. A

D. 10. C
   11. A
   12. B

E. 13. A
   14. B
   15. A

Practice 3

1. Metaphor, C
2. Simile, B
3. Simile, A
4. Metaphor, A
5. Metaphor, C

Practice 4

B, E, G, H, I

Practice 5

A, B, D

7 Purpose and Tone

Practice 1

1. I
2. P
3. I
4. E
5. I
6. P
7. E
8. I
9. P
10. E

Practice 2

1. I+P
2. I
3. E

Practice 3

A. 1. B
   2. C
   3. D
   4. A
   5. E

B. 6. B
   7. D
   8. E
   9. A
   10. C

Practice 4

1. B
2. C
3. H
4. D
5. F

8 Argument

Practice 1

1. I agree: A, C, D
   I disagree: B, E, F

2. I agree: C, D, F
   I disagree: A, B, E

3. I agree: A, C, E
   I disagree: B, D, F

4. I agree: C, D, E
   I disagree: A, B, F

5. I agree: A, C, E
   I disagree: B, D, F

Practice 2

1. A, B, E
2. B, D, E
3. B, C, F
4. A, D, E
5. C, E, F

Practice 3

1. C
2. A
3. D
4. C
5. B

9 Critical Reading

Practice 1

1.	O	6.	F
2.	F	7.	O
3.	F	8.	F
4.	O	9.	O
5.	F+O	10.	F+O

Detecting Propaganda

1. Bandwagon: Ad 2
2. Testimonial: Ad 2
3. Transfer: Ad 1
4. Plain folks: Ad 2
5. Name calling: Ad 1
6. Glittering generalities: Ad 1

Practice 2

1.	B	6.	E
2.	C	7.	C
3.	A	8.	A
4.	D	9.	B
5.	F	10.	D

Recognizing Errors in Reasoning

1. Circular reasoning: item 1
2. Personal attack: item 2
3. Straw man: item 1
4. False cause: item 1
5. False comparison: item 1
6. Either-or: item 2

Practice 3

A. 1.	A	B. 6.	C
2.	B	7.	A
3.	C	8.	B
4.	B	9.	A
5.	C	10.	B

10 Active Reading and Study

Practice 1 *(Wording of answers may vary.)*

1. Selection from a History Text

   Point: Three factors explain why the United States experienced falling birth rates in the 19th century.

   Support:
   1. America was becoming urban—birth rates are historically lower in cities.
   2. Infant mortality fell—families did not have to bear as many children.
   3. For a better quality of life, people decided to limit family size.

2. Selection from a Communications Text

   Point: There are at least three different types of noise.

   Support:
   1. Semantic—different people have different meanings for words and phrases
      Example: A "soda" in New York is called "pop" in the Midwest.
   2. Mechanical—problem with a machine used to assist communication
      Example: A pen running out of ink; a static-filled radio
   3. Environmental—noise that interferes with the communication process
      Example: A noisy restaurant; someone drumming fingers

3. Selection from a Biology Text

   Point: Chemical element—one of 92 naturally occurring kinds of matter that cannot be separated chemically into similar substances

   Support:
   1. Each element has specific properties that make it different from other elements: physical state, color, odor, texture, boiling/freezing points, etc.
   2. SPONCH—six familiar elements (sulfur, phosphorus, oxygen, nitrogen, carbon, and hydrogen) that make up 99% of living matter

Practice 2 *(Wording of answers may vary.)*

1. Selection from a Health Text

   Reason for anger:
   1. Time—working longer hours
   2. Technology—cell phones and pagers make us available 24/7
   3. Tension—we're always running

   Danger in venting anger: Makes anger worse; doesn't deal with underlying causes of anger

   Results of anger: Sabotages physical as well as mental health—increased risk of stroke and heart attack

2. Selection from a Business Text

   Point: Three factors help us differentiate between work and play.
   1. Purpose: Work has a definite purpose (something being accomplished). Play does not have to have a definite purpose.
   2. Attitude: A task may be work or play depending on the attitude of the person performing the task (example: professional baseball players).
   3. Reward: External rewards are given for work (example: money); internal rewards are received for play (example: enjoyment).

3. Selection from a Sociology Text

   Point: Social class has a significant impact on how people behave and think and affects people in almost every area of life.
   1. Determines life chances—people's level of living and options for choice
      Ex.—Higher class = more education (go farther; do better)
   2. Affects health and life expectancy—lower-class people die sooner
      Ex.—Lower class = more obesity; more exposure to environmental hazards
   3. Affects exposure to dangerous situations
      Ex.—Lower class = 80% of soldiers in Vietnam; most victims on *Titanic*
   4. Affects people's style of life—consumption of goods and services
      Ex.—Lower class = more convenience foods and beer
   5. Is associated with certain patterns of behavior
      Ex.—Higher classes are more likely to vote

Writing Assignments

To the Instructor: Before assigning any of the following topics, you might want to go over with your students the guidelines that appear below and on the next page.

A BRIEF GUIDE TO EFFECTIVE WRITING

Here in a nutshell is what you need to do to write effectively.

Step 1: Explore Your Topic through Informal Writing

To begin with, explore the topic that you want to write about or that you have been assigned to write about. You can examine your topic through **informal writing**, which usually means one of three things.

First, you can **freewrite** about your topic for at least ten minutes. In other words, for ten minutes write whatever comes into your head about your subject. Write without stopping and without worrying at all about spelling or grammar or the like. Simply get down on paper all the information about the topic that occurs to you.

A second thing you can do is to **make a list of ideas and details** that could go into your paper. Simply pile these items up, one after another, like a shopping list, without worrying about putting them in any special order. Try to accumulate as many details as you can think of.

A third way to explore your topic is to **write down a series of questions and answers** about it. Your questions can start with words like *what, why, how, when*, and *where*.

Getting your thoughts and ideas down on paper will help you think more about your topic. With some raw material to look at, you are now in a better position to decide on just how to proceed.

Step 2: Plan Your Paper with an Informal Outline

After exploring your topic, plan your paper using an informal outline. Do two things:

- **Decide on and write out the point of your paper.** It is often a good idea to begin your paragraph with this point, which is known as the topic sentence. If you are writing an essay of several paragraphs, you will probably want to include your main point somewhere in your first paragraph. In a paper of several paragraphs, the main point is called the central point, or thesis.

- **List the supporting reasons, examples, or other details that back up your point.** In many cases, you should have at least two or three items of support.

Step 3: Use Transitions

Once your outline is worked out, you will have a clear "road map" for writing your paper. As you write the early drafts of your paper, use **transitions** to introduce each of the separate supporting items (reasons, examples, or other details) you present to back up your point. For instance, you might introduce your first supporting item with the transitional words *first of all*. You might begin your second supporting item with words such as *another reason* or *another example*. And you might indicate your final supporting detail with such words as *last of all* or *a final reason*.

Step 4: Edit and Proofread Your Paper

After you have a solid draft, edit and proofread the paper. Ask yourself several questions to evaluate your paper:

1 Is the paper **unified**? Does all the material in the paper truly support the main point?

2 Is the paper **well supported**? Is there plenty of specific evidence to back up the main point?

3 Is the paper **clearly organized**? Does the material proceed in a way that makes sense? Do transitions help connect ideas?

4 Is the paper **well written**? When the paper is read aloud, do the sentences flow smoothly and clearly? Has the paper been checked carefully for grammar, punctuation, and spelling mistakes?

WRITING ASSIGNMENTS FOR THE TWENTY READINGS

Note: The discussion questions accompanying the twenty readings can also make good topics for writing. Some of the writing assignments here are based on them.

Getting a Good Night's Sleep

1. Write a paragraph in which you explain three common reasons why people might not get enough sleep. Provide some detail that makes it clear why those reasons take precedence over sleeping for many people.

2. What changes would you have to make in your own routine in order to consistently get eight hours of sleep a night? Write a paragraph in which you explain those changes.

3. This essay explains how Americans would benefit from getting more regular sleep. Write an essay about another change in lifestyle that you believe Americans would benefit from. In your essay, describe three ways that you believe people's lives would be improved if they would follow your recommendation.

Drug-Altered Consciousness

1. "The use of mood-altering substances is morally wrong." Write a paragraph in which you explain why you agree or disagree with that statement.

2. This reading selection contains a number of interesting facts that are not common knowledge. What did you learn that surprised you? Write a paragraph in which you contrast what you knew previously about mood-altering substances with what you learned here. Your topic sentence could be something like this: "Before I read this selection, I had some inaccurate ideas about alcohol use."

3. Why do people use psychoactive substances? Write an essay in which you identify and explain several possible reasons. Add your thoughts on the possible benefits and drawbacks of each substance.

"Extra Large," Please

1. The author suggests that childhood obesity affects more than just a child and his or her family—it is a problem that society should be addressing. Do you agree? Write a paragraph explaining why you think childhood obesity should be regarded as a social problem. Alternatively, write a paragraph explaining why it should be seen as a private, individual issue.

2. Write a paragraph about the environment you lived in as a child and what opportunities for physical exercise were available.

3. What can parents do to encourage their children to eat well and get more exercise? Write an essay in which you suggest several ideas and how parents might put them into practice.

Skills of Effective Face-to-Face Conversationalists

1. Write a paragraph about an acquaintance that you think of as a good conversationalist. In the paragraph, describe two or three things about this person's conversational style that you think are particularly effective.

2. In a paragraph, explain what you think are your strongest point *and* your weakest point as a conversationalist. Give examples of each.

3. Along with *good* conversationalists, there are *poor* ones. Write an essay in which you describe three types of bad conversationalists. Use specific examples so your reader can understand why the type of person is boring, annoying, or otherwise difficult to talk to.

Hoover and Hard Times

1. What piece of information in this reading surprised or interested you the most? Write a paragraph that answers that question and explains your response.

2. Write a paragraph explaining how, in your opinion, current attitudes about women in the workforce compare with or contrast to the attitudes that existed during the Depression.

3. Write an essay in which you describe how racism *or* sexism seems to have been a factor in how people fared during the Depression. In your opinion, is racism or sexism still as great a factor in people's economic success today? Why or why not?

The Ugly Truth About Beauty

1. While many people are, like Barry, critical of the influence of Barbie dolls, the dolls are still extremely popular. Write a paragraph in which you explain why you would or would not encourage your own young daughter to "play Barbies."

2. The selection focuses on women's insecurity about their appearance. What kind of insecurities do you think are especially common among men? Write a paragraph in which you describe one such common male insecurity.

3. Looks are certainly part of why we find another person attractive, but they're not the only part. Write an essay in which you name three *non*-physical qualities that are important to you in a potential romantic partner. Explain why each of them matters to you.

White-Collar Crime

1. Which do you think is ultimately more damaging to society, street crime or white-collar crime? Write a paragraph defending your position.

2. Do you think the Ford auto executives deserve the author's harsh criticism? Or are you more sympathetic to the executives than he is? Write a paragraph in which you explain why you think the author is overly harsh *or* is justified in his position.

3. The author refers to what he calls the "ethical numbness" that results from the pressures to achieve "not only corporate profits but also personal achievement and recognition." Write an essay in which you give several real-life examples of what you consider "ethical numbness." These examples may be taken from the headlines or your personal observations.

A Vote Against Legalizing Drugs

1. Select one point that the author makes that you strongly agree *or* disagree with. Write a paragraph in which you explain why you feel strongly about that particular argument.

2. In your opinion, what is the single most significant reason that people use drugs? Write a paragraph in which you explain why you chose that reason.

3. If you had the power, what is one dramatic change you would impose on American society? Would you outlaw TV? Make college mandatory? Raise the drinking age to 25? Dismantle the military? Write an essay in which you explain the change you would make. Give several reasons to support your choice.

A Scary Time to Raise a Daughter

1. Write a paragraph in which you defend one of the following topic sentences: "Steve Lopez is right in saying that young teens today are strongly pressured to have sex" *or* "Steve Lopez is exaggerating the pressure on young teens to have sex."

2. Imagine you had a friend, a boy or girl in his or her early teens, who confided in you that he or she was feeling "out of it" and "like a loser" because he or she was a virgin. Your friend was thinking about getting it "over with" by taking the next sexual opportunity that came along and wanted to know what you thought about that plan. Write a paragraph explaining how you would respond.

3. Some people believe that being sexually active defines them as adults. But there are far more meaningful measures of maturity. Write an essay in which you name three characteristics that you believe define a true adult. Describe how those characteristics are demonstrated in an adult's life.

Impression Management

1. The authors write, "One reason people engage in impression management is to claim a particular identity. Thus, you select a type of dress, hairstyle, and manner of speech to present a certain image of yourself." Think of a person you know whose outward appearance seems to make a definite statement about his or her identity. In a paragraph, describe the person's appearance, and explain what identity he or she seems to be claiming.

2. What advice would you give to someone going into a job interview? Write a paragraph in which you explain how you think he or she should behave in order to maximize the chances of being hired.

3. The authors mention five "self-presentation strategies." Write an essay in which you describe three real-life situations in which you have utilized one of these strategies.

*10 Selections in the Back *

Personal Conflict Styles

1. "Crazy-making" is a very good description of passive-aggressive behavior. Write a paragraph about a time you've been subjected to someone's passive aggression, what the person did, and how you responded.

2. Of the approaches to handling personal conflict described in this reading, which best describes your own style? Are you satisfied with your own approach, or would you like to learn to get better at one of the others described here? Write a paragraph in which you answer both questions.

3. The selection describes five approaches to handling personal conflict: non-assertive behavior, direct aggression, passive aggression, indirect communication, and assertion. Write an essay in which you describe how a person might deal with the same situation three different ways—that is, using three of those techniques.

Cardiovascular Disease Risk Factors

1. What is a health problem that seems to run in your family? Write a paragraph about this problem: whom it currently affects, what effect it has on this person, and whether you are concerned that you will be affected.

2. Do you smoke? Have you smoked in the past? Are you a militant non-smoker? Write a paragraph in which you describe your personal relationship (or non-relationship) with cigarettes.

3. Write an essay in which you analyze your own risk of developing heart disease, based upon what you have learned in this reading. Name some of the risk factors that you possess; how serious you believe they are; and what, if anything, you are planning to do about them.

Collective Behavior

1. The Internet is a tremendous source of information, but as the reading points out, some of that information is not true. When you read an alarming story on the Internet or receive an e-mail passing on some warning, how do you determine whether or not to believe the information? Write a paragraph discussing this question.

2. Think of an example you have observed of a person acting differently in a crowd than when he or she was not in a crowd. In a paragraph, describe how the person's behavior altered. Provide a possible explanation for why his or her behavior changed.

3. What are some fads that have come and gone during your lifetime? Write an essay describing three of them. You might, for example, write about items that were popular to collect, ways of dancing, items of clothing, or a game or toy that "everybody" wanted.

Types of Nonverbal Symbols

1. Think of a person you have met who seemed socially awkward, in ways that revealed themselves nonverbally. Write a paragraph that analyzes that person's unspoken communication.

2. What are some gestures that are a common part of your nonspoken communication? Write a paragraph describing them in detail and explaining what they express. Imagine that you are writing for a visitor from another planet who knows nothing about human gestures.

3. Write an essay that compares and contrasts the nonverbal behavior of two people you know. Choose people who have very different styles: perhaps a very dominant man and a quiet, passive man; an outgoing, athletic girl and a socially withdrawn girl, etc.

Sports: Illustrating the Three Perspectives

1. Write a paragraph about a recreational activity that has been important in your life. Describe when and how you engage in the activity, and what it is about it that you enjoy.

2. What role did sports play in the high school you attended? Were athletes treated differently from other students? Write a paragraph describing the attitude toward sports at your school.

3. Overall, do you think that sports are beneficial to society—or *not* beneficial (or even harmful) to society? Write an essay that provides two or three reasons to support your opinion.

A Civil War Soldier's Letter to His Wife

1. Choose the one single adjective that you think best describes Sullivan Ballou's letter. Write a paragraph explaining your choice.

2. We do not know how Sarah Ballou responded to her husband's letter. Write an essay in which you compare and contrast two different ways she may have felt when she received it.

3. Do you believe dying for your country can be a noble act? Or are the people who, like Sullivan Ballou, believe that they are giving their lives for a good cause only fooling themselves? Write a paragraph or an essay in which you explore the question.

Single-Sex Schools: An Old Idea Whose Time Has Come

1. Write a paragraph in which you explain why you would *or* would not consider sending your child to a single-sex school. If the gender of the child would affect your decision, explain why.

2. While this reading concentrates on the advantages of same-sex schooling, there are downsides. In your opinion, what would be the greatest drawback of single-sex schooling? Write a paragraph discussing it.

3. Establishing same-sex schools would be just one way of attempting to improve the public school system. Write an essay in which you propose at least two other significant changes that you'd like to see adopted in public schools. Explain why you think these changes would be beneficial to students.

A King's Folly

1. Judging from this summary of *King Lear*, who would you say was the king's truest friend? Write a paragraph explaining your choice.

2. "Actions speak louder than words" is a saying that certainly applies to *King Lear.* Write a paragraph about a time in your life when you saw this proverb in action. It could be about a time when an acquaintance did something that was not in keeping with his or her words. Alternatively, your paragraph could be about when an acquaintance said little, but performed a meaningful action.

3. The story of King Lear has parallels to stories of modern celebrities who "have it all," then experience a series of very public losses—for example, scandalous divorces, lawsuits, episodes of substance abuse and rehabilitation, and feuds with former friends. Why do you think that celebrities seem more prone to such problems than ordinary people? Write an essay in which you discuss several possible explanations.

In My Day

1. Baker describes his mother vividly, calling her, among other things, "formidable," "fierce," and "sarcastic." Think of an older person of your acquaintance, and write a paragraph describing his or her character.

2. What is one wise or helpful lesson that an older person has imparted to you? Write a paragraph about this lesson and the person who taught it to you.

3. If you had a time machine, which aspects of your own family would you like to learn more about? Write an essay about three times and places where you would go and what you would try to learn there.

The Spider and the Wasp

1. The dictionary defines *instinct* as "an inborn pattern of behavior that is characteristic of a species." Write a paragraph in which you provide several examples of human instincts—behaviors that we seem to be born with, rather than learn.

2. Write a paragraph about a time when you were confronted in an aggressive way, either physically or verbally. How did you feel—physically *and* mentally—and what did you do?

3. Petrunkevitch describes the appearance, habits, and behaviors of the spider and the wasp in extremely fine detail, giving even readers who have never seen the creatures a very good idea of how they look and act. Write an essay in which you provide an equally detailed description of another animal—even one as common as a cat or dog or squirrel. Observe the animal closely and record your observations, so that your essay could make even someone who had never seen such an animal imagine it vividly.

Acknowledgments

Adler, Ronald B., Russell F. Proctor II, and Neil Towne, "Personal Conflict Styles." From *Looking Out, Looking In*, 11th edition, copyright © 2005. Reprinted by permission of Wadsworth, a division of Thomson Learning: www.thomsonrights.com. Fax 800-730-2215.

Baker, Russell, "In My Day." From *Growing Up* by Russell Baker. Copyright © 1982 by Russell Baker. Reprinted by permission of Don Congdon Associates, Inc.

Baldwin, Mike. Cartoons on pages 63 and 97. Copyright © by Mike Baldwin. Reprinted by permission of www.cartoonstock.com.

Barry, Dave, "The Ugly Truth About Beauty." From the *Miami Herald*, February 1, 1998. Copyright © 1998 by Dave Barry. Reprinted by permission of the author.

Davies, Alice M., "'Extra Large,' Please." Used with the permission of Alice M. Davies.

Drafke, Michael W. Selections on pages 368–369 and 389–390 and "Types of Nonverbal Symbols." From *The Human Side of Organizations*, 9th edition, copyright © 2006. Reprinted by permission of Pearson Education, Inc., Upper Saddle River, NJ.

Draughon, Dennis. Cartoon on page 245. Copyright © 2003 by *The Scranton Times/Shamrock Communications*. Reprinted by permission of the artist.

Edwards, George C., Martin P. Wattenberg, and Robert L. Lineberry. Selection on page 385. From *Government in America: People, Politics, and Policy*. Copyright © 2006 by Pearson Education. Reprinted by permission.

Glasbergen, Randy. Cartoon on page 247. Copyright © 2003 by Randy Glasbergen. Reprinted with permission of the artist.

Grandin, Temple, and Catherine Johnson. Selection on page 508. Adapted from *Animals in Translation: Using the Mysteries of Autism to Decode Animal Behavior*. Copyright © 2005 by Simon & Schuster, Inc.

Gray, Peter. Selection on page 524. From *Psychology*, 4th edition, copyright © 1991, 1994, 1999, and 2004 by Worth Publishers. Used with permission.

Hales, Dianne. Selections on pages 367 and 383. From *An Invitation to Health*, 11th edition. Copyright © 2005. Reprinted with permission of Wadsworth, a division of Thomson Learning: www.thomsonrights.com. Fax 800-730-2215.

Henslin, James M., "White-Collar Crime" and selections on pages 221 and 318. Used with the permission of James M. Henslin.

Hughes, Michael, et al. Selection on page 370 and "Collective Behavior." From *Sociology: The Core*, 7th edition, copyright © 2005. Reprinted with permission of The McGraw-Hill Companies.

Lahey, Benjamin B. Selection on page 379. From *Essentials of Psychology: An Introduction*, copyright © 2002. Reprinted with permission of The McGraw-Hill Companies.

Lopez, Steve. "A Scary Time to Raise a Daughter." From the *Los Angeles Times*, October 26, 2003. Copyright © 2003 by the *Los Angeles Times*. Reprinted with permission.

Lyon, Bill. Selection on pages 229–231. From the *Philadelphia Inquirer*, April 29, 2003. Used with the permission of Bill Lyon.

Martin, James Kirby et al. Selection on page 518. From *America and Its Peoples*, Volume 2, 5th edition, copyright © 2004 by James Kirby Martin, Randy Roberts, Steven Mintz, Linda O. McMurry, and James H. Jones. Reprinted by permission of Pearson Education, Inc.

McCourt, Frank. Selection on page 252. Reprinted with the permission of Scribner, an imprint of Simon & Schuster Adult Publishing Group, from *Teacher Man* by Frank McCourt. Copyright © 2005 by Green Peril Group. All rights reserved.

Moehringer, J. R. Selection on page 248. From *The Tender Bar*. Copyright © 2005 by J. R. Moehringer. Reprinted by permission of Hyperion. All rights reserved.

Morris, Charles G., and Albert A. Maisto. Selections on pages 522 and 540. From *Psychology: An Introduction*, 12th edition, copyright © 2005. Reprinted by permission of Pearson Education, Inc., Upper Saddle River, NJ.

Morris, Charles G., and Albert A. Maisto. Selection on page 512 and "Drug-Altered Consciousness." From *Understanding Psychology*, 7th edition, copyright © 2006. Reprinted by permission of Pearson Education, Inc., Upper Saddle River, NJ.

Norton, Mary Beth, et al. Selections on pages 110–111, 514, and 546 and "Hoover and Hard Times." From *A People and a Nation: A History of the United States*, 7th edition. Copyright © 2005 by Houghton Mifflin Company. Used with permission.

Payne, Wayne A., Dale B. Hahn, and Ellen B. Mauer, "Cardiovascular Disease Risk Factors." From *Understanding Your Health*, 9th edition, copyright © 2006. Reprinted with permission of The McGraw-Hill Companies.

Petrunkevitch, Alexander, "The Spider and the Wasp." From *Scientific American*, August 1952. Reprinted with permission. Copyright © 1952 by Scientific American, Inc. All rights reserved.

Photograph on page 255. From a collection of photographs of caskets at Dover Air Force Base publicly released by the United States Air Force.

Rollins, Gail, "A Vote Against Legalizing Drugs." Used with the permission of Gail Rollins.

Rooney, Andy. Excerpt on page 287. From *60 Minutes,* CBS, May 30, 2004.

Russell, Bertrand. Excerpted from *The Three Passions* by Bertrand Russell. Reprinted by permission of Taylor & Francis Books, Ltd. and The Bertrand Russell Peace Foundation.

Song, Sora, "Getting a Good Night's Sleep." *Time* Magazine, January 16, 2006. Copyright © 2006 Time Inc. Reprinted by permission.

Stark, Rodney. Selection on page 516. From *Sociology, 9th edition.* Copyright © 2004. Reprinted by permission of Wadsworth, a division of Thomson Learning: www.thomsonrights.com. Fax 800-730-2215.

Thio, Alex. Selection on page 530. From *Deviant Behavior*, 7th edition. Published by Allyn and Bacon, Boston, MA. Copyright © 2004 by Pearson Education. Reprinted by permission of the publisher.

Thio, Alex. Selection on page 536 and "Sports: Illustrating the Three Perspectives." From *Sociology: A Brief Introduction*, 6th edition. Published by Allyn and Bacon, Boston, MA. Copyright © 2005 by Pearson Education. Reprinted by permission of the publisher.

Urbina, Diane, "Single-Sex Schools: An Old Idea Whose Time Has Come." Used with the permission of Diane Urbina.

Verderber, Rudolph F., and Kathleen S. Verderber. Selection on page 381 and "Skills of Effective Face-to-Face Conversationalists." From *Communicate!*, 10th edition, by Verderber/Verderber. Copyright © 2002. Reprinted with permission of Wadsworth, a division of Thomson Learning: www.thomsonrights.com. Fax 800-730-2215.

Wallace, Robert A., Gerald P. Sanders, and Robert J. Ferl. Selections on pages 364 and 387–388. From *Biology: The Science of Life*, 4th edition, copyright © 1996 by HarperCollins Publishers Inc. Reprinted by permission of Addison Wesley Longman Publishers Inc.

Weiten, Wayne, and Margaret A. Lloyd. Selection on page 528 and "Impression Management." From *Psychology Applied to Modern Life, Adjustment in the 21st Century*, 8th edition, by Weiten/Lloyd. 2006. Reprinted with permission of Wadsworth, a division of Thomson Learning: www.thomsonrights.com. Fax 800-730-2215.

Wise, Gary, and Lance Aldrich. Cartoon on page 289. From "Real Life Adventures," copyright © 2005 by Universal Press Syndicate. Reprinted with permission.

Index